Koji Koyamada   Shinsuke Tamura
Osamu Ono (Eds.)

Systems Modeling and Simulation

Theory and Applications,
Asia Simulation Conference 2006

 Springer

Editors

Koji Koyamada
Professor
Center for The Promotion of Excellence in Higher Education
Kyoto University
Yoshida-nihonmatsu-cho, Sakyo-ku, Kyoto-shi 606-8501, Japan
E-mail: koyamada@mbox.kudpc.kyoto-u.ac.jp

Shinsuke Tamura
Professor
Faculty of Engineering
Fukui University
3-9-1 Bunkyo, Fukui City, Fukui Prefecture 910-8507, Japan
E-mail: tamura@fuis.fuis.fukui-u.ac.jp

Osamu Ono
Professor
Department of Electrical and Electronic Engineering
Meiji University
1-1-1 Higashimita, Tama-ku, Kawasaki-shi, Kanagawa 214-8571, Japan
E-mail: ono@isc.meiji.ac.jp

Library of Congress Control Number: 2006935982

ACM Computing Classification (1998): G.1, I.3, I.6, J.0

ISBN   4-431-49021-3 Springer Tokyo Berlin Heidelberg New York
ISBN   978-4-431-49021-0 Springer Tokyo Berlin Heidelberg New York

Springer is a part of Springer Science+Business Media
springer.com
© Springer 2007

Typesetting: Camera-ready by the editors and authors

SPIN: 11926207

Printed on acid-free paper

Preface

The Asia Simulation Conference 2006 (JSST 2006) was aimed at exploring challenges in methodologies for modeling, control and computation in simulation, and their applications in social, economic, and financial fields as well as established scientific and engineering solutions. The conference was held in Tokyo from October 30 to November 1, 2006, and included keynote speeches presented by technology and industry leaders, technical sessions, organized sessions, poster sessions, and vendor exhibits. It was the seventh annual international conference on system simulation and scientific computing, which is organized by the Japan Society for Simulation Technology (JSST), the Chinese Association for System Simulation (CASS), and the Korea Society for Simulation (KSS).

For the conference, all submitted papers were refereed by the international technical program committee, each paper receiving at least two independent reviews. After careful reviews by the committee, 65 papers from 143 submissions were selected for oral presentation. This volume includes the keynote speakers' papers along with the papers presented at the oral sessions and the organized sessions. As a result, we are publishing 87 papers for the conference in this volume.

In addition to the scientific tracts presented, the conference featured keynote presentations by five invited speakers. We are grateful to them for accepting our invitation and for their presentations. We also would like to express our gratitude to all contributors, reviewers, technical program committee members, and organizing committee members who made the conference very successful. Special thanks are due to Professor Shinsuke Tamura and Professor Osamu Ono, the Organizing Committee co-chairs of JSST 2006 for their hard work on the various aspects of conference organization.

Finally, we would like to acknowledge partial financial support for the conference from corporations related to simulation technologies. We also would like to acknowledge the publication support from Springer.

October 2006

Toshiharu Kagawa, General Chair

Conference Officials

General Chairperson

Toshiharu Kagawa (JSST)

International Steering Committee

Chair: Sadao Takaba (JSST)
Bohu. Li (CASS)
Tag Gon Kim (KSS)
Borut Zupancic (EUROSIM)
Robert Beauwens (IMACS)
Tony Jakeman (MSSANZ)
Francois Cellier (SCS)
Hiroshi Takeda (JSCES)
Hideo Tanaka (JSIAM)
Masataka Tanaka (JSCOME)
Masao Ikeda (SICE)
Yoiti Suzuki (ASJ)
Voratas Kachitvichyanukul (Thailand)
Myoung Ho Kim (Korea)
Alex Lehmann (Germany)
Michael McALeer (Australia)
Hikaru Samukawa (JSST)
Genki Yagawa (JSST)

Local Organizing Committee

Co-Chairs: Shinsuke Tamura (University of Fukui), Osamu Ono (Meiji University)
Shun. Dohi (NEC)
Yoshikazu Fukuyama (Fuji Electric Device Technology)
Hiroshi Hasegawa (Shibaura Institute of Technology)
Takayasu Kawamura (Meidensha)
Mitsunori Makino (Chuo University)
Tanroku Miyoshi (Kobe University)
Toshiro Sasaki (Hitachi)
Ken Yamazaki (Nihon University)
Ichie Watanabe (Seikei University)

Table of Contents

Keynotes

Oral Sessions

Computational Fluid Dynamics

Computational Engineering - I

Complex Systems - I

Simulation Platform

Computational Engineering - II

Complex Systems - II

Systems Design - I

Logistics and Manufacturing Systems

Transportation Systems - I

Parameter Estimation

Systems Design - II

Engineering Applications

Transportation Systems - II

High Level Architecture

Grid Computing

Visual Simulation

Organized Sessions

Hardware Acceleration Techniques

Surgical Simulation

VIZGRID

Simulations on Convergence of Computer Networks - I

Intelligent Signal Processing for Multimedia Systems

Simulations on Convergence of Computer Networks - II

Collaborative Visualization: Topological Approaches to Parameter Tweaking for Informative Volume Rendering

Issei FUJISHIRO *, Shigeo TAKAHASHI **, Yuriko TAKESHIMA *

* Institute of Fluid Science, Tohoku University
2-1-1 Katahira, Aoba-Ku, Sendai 980-8577, Japan
(E-mail: fuji@vis.ifs.tohoku.ac.jp)
** Graduate School of Frontier Science, The University of Tokyo
5-1-5 Kashiwanoha, Kashiwa, Chiba 277-8561, Japan

ABSTRACT

Data crisis ubiquitously arises in solving complex scientific problems. It has motivated us to develop a *Collaborative Visualization Environment* (*CVE*), which provides the users with the "serendipity" with the aid of effective data-centric tweaking of visualization-related parameters. To this end, we have proposed the concept of *Volume Data Mining* (*VDM*), which takes full advantage of knowledge in the field of differential topology to allow the users to explore the global structures and local features of target 4D volumes. In this paper, the effectiveness of our current CVE framework with several VDM tools is illustrated with applications to practical scientific simulation datasets.

KEY WORDS: Volume visualization, Volume rendering, Isosurfacing, Transfer function design

INTRODUCTION

Rapid increase in the performance of computing facilities has made it possible to analyze the correlations among model parameters in complex scientific problems. A huge number of simulation runs produce a multi-dimensional array of large-scale time-series (4D) volume datasets. For example, consider a mundane case where each run of a physical simulation code has 10^4 time-steps of regular-grid volumes consisting of 256^3 voxels with 8bit values. Even if we sample just eight values for each of the four related parameters, the entire data storage for the parameter study sizes up to 8 PB.

This kind of current situation, which is referred to as *data crisis* (or *information big bang* [1]), motivates us to urgently develop a *Collaborative Visualization Environment* (*CVE*), where the users are promised to possess a certain type of "serendipity" with the aid of effective *data-centric* tweaking of visualization-related parameters. As an initial attempt for establishing a promising CVE, we have proposed the concept of *Volume Data Mining* (*VDM*) [2], which takes full advantage of knowledge in the field of *differential topology* to allow the users to explore the global structures and local features of target 4D volumes.

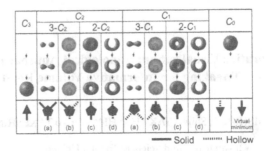

Figure 1: Classified connectivity at critical points and corresponding VST notations

VST

Our VDM relies heavily on the topological volume abstraction scheme, called *Volume Skeleton Tree (VST)*, which represents the topological skeleton of a given snapshot volume [3]. More specifically, VST is a kind of *level-set graph* which consists of volumetric *critical points* and their global connectivity to trace the topological transitions, such as appearance, disappearance, splitting, and merging, of an isosurface according to the change of its scalar field value. VST is a 3D extension of the *Reeb Graph*, which has been imported into the computer graphics community to delineate the topographic configuration of digital elevation data [4].

The behavior of an isosurface around a critical point can be classified as shown in Figure 1 [3]. The bottom row of the figure shows their corresponding graph representations, where the node represents a critical point and its incident link transitions of a single-connected component of an isosurface. Combining these components together allows us to form a VST, whose example can be found in Figure 2(a).

We have developed an efficient and robust method to extract adequate VSTs even from complex and/or noisy volume datasets using adaptive tetrahedralization and graph reduction [5].

VDM TOOLS

At present, we have the following seven topological VDM tools.

1) *Critical Point Histogram* [6]: Informative semi-translucent isosurfaces can be generated within a field interval containing a relatively large number of critical field values. These isosurfaces can be distinguished from each other by using an ingenious color transfer function with varying hue angle velocity.

2) *Critical/Representative Isosurface Extractor* [7]: A critical isosurface passing through more than one critical point and a representative isosurface with the intermediate value of a topologically-equivalent field interval play significant roles in visualizing the topological transitions and skeletal overview of a given volume dataset, respectively.

3) *Isosurface Embedding Finder* [7]: Rigorous analysis of VST can detect the embedding of isosurface components, and leading to a sophisticated spatially-dependent opacity transfer function to reveal the nested inner structures of a volume.

4) *Multi-Dimensional Transfer Function Designer* [8]: The local and global features of a given volume can be rendered using multi-dimensional transfer functions which involve as their domains, derived attributes such as the inclusion level, topological dis-

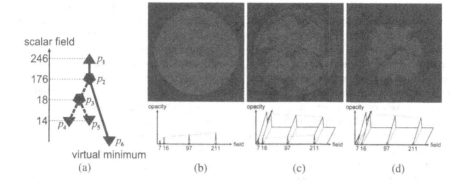

Figure 2: Visualizing simulated implosion in laser fusion. (a) The corresponding VST; (b) topologically-accentuated 1D opacity TF; (c) 2D opacity TF depending also on the inclusion level; and (d) 2D opacity TF that visualizes inner structures only. Data courtesy of Hitoshi Sakagami (Hyogo Prefectural University).

tance, and genus of isosurface components, as well as the distribution of critical points.

5) *Interval Volume Decomposer* [9]: An ordered traversal of VST allows us to look inside a volume by peeling outer topologically-equivalent sub-volumes from inner ones semi-automatically.

6) *Optimal Cross-Section Generator* [10]: Informative cross-sections which pass through critical volume features can be automatically generated.

7) *Optimal Viewpoint Locator* [11]: Optimal viewpoint allowing us to volume render a target volume without minimal occlusion of critical features can be automatically located.

Let us take herein an example to illustrate the effectiveness of a topological multidimensional transfer function. Figure 2 visualizes a snapshot volume for 3D fuel density distribution excerpted from a time-varying dataset simulating the process of implosion in laser fusion [8], where small bubble-spike structures evolve around a contact surface between a fuel ball (inner) and pusher (outer) during the stagnation phase.

The fuel-pusher contact surface can be identified with an isosurface extracted by observing the rapid gradients of the fuel density field, whereas the extracted isosurface has two nested connected components, and the contact surface of our interest is occluded by the other outer component residing in the pusher domain, which is a phantom surface induced by the action-reaction effect.

Figure 2(a) shows the VST for the implosion dataset, where the skeletal structure of the complex fuel density distribution has been extracted with an intentional control of VST simplification. A glance at the VST around the field interval $[14, 176]$ finds a nested structure where connected isosurface components corresponding to the three links $\overline{P_2P_3}$, $\overline{P_3P_4}$, and $\overline{P_3P_5}$ are included by another connected isosurface component corresponding to the link $\overline{P_2P_6}$ (note that the node P_2 is categorized as the case 3-C_1(b) in Figure 1). A volume-rendered image is shown with the topologically-accentuated 1D opacity TF in Figure 2(b), from which we can see that after the scalar field itself has been topologically-accentuated, we still suffer from a problem that the inner isosurface components of interest for the observer are indeed occluded by the outer spherical isosurface component. Contrary to this, as shown in Figure 2(c), if we devise the 2D opacity TF which depends on the inclusion level as well to assign a lower opacity value to voxels on the outer isosurface component than to voxels on the inner ones, we can observe the optically-deeper bubble-spike structures more clearly than in Figure 2(b). Furthermore, by assigning zero opacity to the outermost isosurface, we can "visually" segment the inner isosurface component, as shown in Figure 2(d).

T-MAP

So far, we have attempted to integrate the above-mentioned VDM tools into a single time-varying VDM framework, called *Topological Map (T-Map)*, as outlined in Figure 3 [12]. An abstract space, called *Topological Index Space (T-IS)*, serializes the VST's index quantities of snapshot volumes along the time axis. Color-coding of the T-IS, followed by tracking individual critical points using the 2D *expanded* T-IS allows the users to intuitively find candidates for *critical timing*, exactly when the volumetric topology structure varies dynamically. Such information can be utilized for the design of proper temporal transfer functions for producing informative volume-rendered animation of short time sequences containing the critical timings. By repeating *computational steering* based on the acquired knowledge, T-Map allows the users to "drill-down" the target phenomena.

Indeed, in Figure 3, a 4D volume dataset for simulated intermediate-energy collision of a proton and a hydrogen atom [2] is analyzed. By combining the visual analysis of the T-IS and knowledge from quantum physics, we can detect the critical timing just after

the collision occurs, and then take advantage of a topologically-accentuated transfer function to yield the comprehensible illustration of 3D distorted electron cloud, which captures an interesting arm-shaped electron density flux connecting the two topological spheres around the hydrogen nuclei. This easy-to-miss phenomenon has not been obtained from animations which commonly use the same transfer functions over the entire time interval.

Further potentials of T-Map to directly address the data crisis issues include:

1) *Abstract Parameter Study* [12]: By visual exploration of T-ISs and Expanded T-ISs, we can perform effective parameter study involving a bunch of simulated datasets.

2) *Selective Data Migration* [12]: The objective 4D volume dataset stored in tape libraries is examined entirely using VSTs in an offline manner to make the corresponding T-IS and expanded T-IS in advance. Then the user is allowed to investigate those spaces to visually identify partial temporal regions of interest containing major critical timings, and the corresponding portion of the dataset is migrated selectively into the disk space of a computing environment for further visual exploration.

CONCLUSION

In this paper, our initial work towards establishing a Collaborative Visualization Environment has been overviewed. Our on-going work includes further evaluation of the present schemes and framework with data-intensive applications encompassing fluid science to medical science. Developing an easy-to-use software platform is another challenging issue for popularizing the work.

This work has been partially supported by the Japan Society for Promotion of Science under Grant-in-Aid for Scientific Research (B) 18300026.

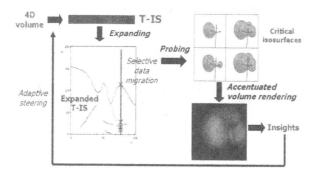

Figure 3: T-Map : A Framework for time-varying volume data mining

REFERENCES

1. Johnson, C., Moorhead, R., Munzner, T., Pfister, H., Rheingans, P., and Yoo, T. S., editors, NIH/NSF Visualization Research Challenges January 2006, IEEE Computer Society Press, 2006. [http://tab.computer.org/vgtc/vrc/index.html].

2. Fujishiro, I., Azuma, T., Takeshima, Y., and Takahashi, S., Volume Data Mining Using 3D Field Topology Analysis, Computer Graphics and Applications, 2000, **20**-5, pp. 46–51.

3. Takahashi, S., Takeshima, Y., and Fujishiro, I., Topological Volume Skeletonization and Its Application to Transfer Function Design, Graphical Models, 2004, **66**-1, pp. 24–49.

4. Takahashi, S., Ikeda, T., Shinagawa, Y., Kunii, T. L., and Ueda, M., Algorithms for Extracting Correct Critical Points and Constructing Topological Graphs from Discrete Geographical Elevation Data, Computer Graphics Forum, 1995, **14**-3, pp. C–181–192.

5. Takahashi, S., Nielson, G. M., Takeshima, Y., and Fujishiro, I., Topological Volume Skeletonization Using Adaptive Tetrahedralization, Proceedings of Geometric Modeling and Processing 2004, 2004, pp. 227–236.

6. Takesihma, Y., Terasaka, H., Takahashi, S., and Fujishiro, I., Applying Volume-Topology-Based Control of Visualization Parameters to Fluid Data, CD-ROM Proceedings of Fourth Pacific Symposium on Flow Visualization and Image Processing, 2003.

7. Takahashi, S., Takeshima, Y., Fujishiro, I., and Nielson, G. M., Emphasizing Isosurface Embeddings in Direct Volume Rendering, Scientific Visualization: The Visual Extraction of Knowledge from Data, Springer-Verlag, 2005, pp. 185–206.

8. Takeshima, Y., Takahashi, S., Fujishiro, I., and Nielson, G. M., Introducing Topological Attributes for Objective-Based Visualization of Simulated Datasets, Proceedings of Volume Graphics 2005, 2005, pp. 137–145, 236.

9. Takahashi, S., Fujishiro, I., and Takeshima, Y., Interval Volume Decomposer: A Topological Approach to Volume Traversal, Proceedings of Visualization and Data Analysis 2005, 2005, **5669**, pp. 95–102.

10. Mori, Y., Takahashi, S., Igarashi, T., Takeshima, Y., and Fujishiro, I., Automatic Cross-Sectioning Based on Topological Volume Skeletonization, Smart Graphics: Fifth International Symposium, SG 2005, Frauenwörth Cloister, Germany, August 22-24, 2005. Proceedings, 2005, pp. 175–184.

11. Takahashi, S., Fujishiro, I., , Takeshima, Y., and Nishita, T., A Feature-Driven Approach to Locating Optimal Viewpoints for Volume Visualization, Proceedings of IEEE Visualization 2005, 2005, pp. 495–502.

12. Fujishiro, I., Otsuka, R., Takeshima, Y., and Takahashi, S., T-Map: A Topological Approach to Visual Exploration of Time-Varying Volume Data, Proceedings of ISHPC2005, Springer Lecture Notes in Computer Science, 2005. (To appear).

A NEW ASPECT on PIV FOR GAS-LIQUID TWO-PHASE FLOW ANALYSIS

Fujio YAMAMOTO*

Graduate School of Engineering, University of Fukui
3-9-1 Bunkyo, Fukui-shi, 910-8507, Japan
(E-Mail:yamamoto@fv.mech.fuku-u.ac.jp)

ABSTRACT

Many types of algorithms for PIV and PTV have been developed from simple cross-correlation method to binary image cross-correlation method, Delaunay tessellation method, velocity gradient tensor method, and recursive cross-correlation method, etc. In parallel, useful post-processing schemes for PIV/PTV such as ellipsoidal equation method and inverse analysis method were proposed so that detailed flow structure could be evaluated. Most algorithms have been verified with the aid of numerical simulation techniques based on the fundamental equation of Navier-Stokes, equations of continuity. Recently some new PIV-CFD hybrid systems have been proposed. This paper concerns with such a history of the research and future possibilities for further advance in the PIV/PTV and the new hybrid systems which are applied to gas-liquid two-phase flow analysis

KEYWORDS: Flow visualization, PIV, PTV, PIV-CFD hybrid system, Gas-liquid two-phase flow

1. INTRODUCTION

PIV/PTV (Particle Image Velocimetry/Particle Tracking Velocimetry) techniques have been developing quickly in a few decades as an epoch-making measurement tool for 2D or 3D simultaneous whole flow field in the last two decades. The very fast progress has been supported by the remarkable progresses in the performance of the soft ware programs of imaging analysis and the imaging hard ware systems. For example, the ratio of pixel number to memory size and that of frame rate of CCD type video camera to data transferring rate from camera to personal computer are subjected to so-called silicon cycle law in evolution of computer whose speed-up pace is expressed by 4 times per three years. The standardization and general use of many types of imaging systems have been progressing due to the user-friendly applicability of internet and the quick development in large scale recording media which are represented by DVD/HDV. The imaging techniques have been employed to produce a lot of fruitful new results in wide fields of researches and industries. At the initial stage of PIV/PTV development, the techniques were applied to measure slow flows of single phase of liquid, but at present days they are occupying an important position as an essential measurement tool for the experimental fluid mechanics including the new fields such as multi-phase flows and micro-flows, because they are much more useful for simultaneous measurement of flow velocities in 2D or 3D space than the other one-point measurement techniques, such as LDV (Laser Doppler Velocimeter), HWA (Hot Wire Anemometer), Pitot tube, etc. Additional requirements for PIV/PTV have been expanded to the directions of higher accuracy measurement in spatio-temporal dimensions, more precise analysis of flow structure with complex deformation due to shear, rotation and dilatation, and more correct prediction of the next-time step flows. In order to satisfy the requirement recently some new proposals of PIV-CFD (Computational Fluid Dynamics) hybrid systems have been proposed. In this paper the author summarizes the history of the progresses in PIV/PTV algorithms which they have been developed in his lab since 1988 and describes their application of PIV/PTV in gas-liquid two-phase flows. He also tries to introduce the new research field of PIV-CFD hybrid systems

2. PROGRESSES IN ALOGORITHMS

2.1 From direct cross-correlation method to binary image cross-correlation method

In order to identify the tracer particle image distribution pattern in the 8-bit digital image data the brightness distribution cross- correlation method [1] was firstly developed as PIV (Particle Image Velocimetry) based on a similarity law for pattern recognition. When the particle number density is low and each particle image is recognized separately, a binary image cross-correlation method [2] as PTV (Particle Tracking Velocimetry) is very powerful because it can track each particle motion and analyze the velocity field for the particle center position. Another strong point of the binary image cross-correlation method is that the computation time can be reduced to the order of one tenth to one hundredth in comparison with that for the brightness distribution cross-correlation method because the value of cross-correlation for the former can be calculated at much faster speed using logical product summation in comparison with algebraic summation for the latter. We can also calculate each center position of particle in binary image with higher spatial resolution and then can obtain the velocities at particle positions with high accuracy. We proposed a technique for replacing real particle images with imaginary particle images have bigger size than the real size and as a result the image

analysis performance could be improved with great robustness for deformable flow field [3].

2.2 PTV based on triangular Delauney tessellation (DT Method)

Automatic triangular element construction techniques based on DT (Delauney tessellation) are used in the fields of FEM (Finite Element Method) and CG (Computer Graphics) as every knows. For the case of low particle number density, DT connects three center points of randomly scattered particle images which forms a triangle with the smallest deformation. When particles move at a short time interval, the element triangles formed by DT make some deformation. The cross-correlation is evaluated based on the overlapped area of two triangles with a common gravitation point after some translation at the interval, and then velocities are computed from the translation for the case of maximum cross-correlation value. This DT-PTV technique can decrease the computational load to the extent of one hundredth of other PTV techniques and then real time measurement are possibly realized [4]. See Figure 1.

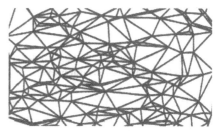

Figure 1 Triangular element by Delaunay tessellation [4]

2.3 PTV based on least square method for Velocity gradient tensor (VGT method)

Conventional PIV/PTV is still said to be not sufficient to measure boundary layer flows and turbulent flows. The reason is that the pattern identification is calculated based only on translation motion at a short interval with neglecting other deformation of fluid motion consisting of dilatation, shear and rotation.

VGT method evaluates the similarity of particle distribution pattern using least square method in the dimensions of velocity gradient tensor and then can measure the velocities more correctly when it is applied to deformable fluid flows. It is shown that even when a product value of velocity gradient times interval reaches 0.5, particle identification by the VGT method can be performed more correctly than the other techniques than by other PTV techniques. It can be applied with stronger robustness to a fluid motion with velocity gradient five times higher than for the case the maximal gradient when other PTV methods can be employed [5]. See Figure 2.

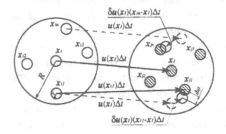

Figure 2 Robust pairing of particle cluster by VGT-PTV [5]

2.4 Image separation of bubbles and particles, and Gas-liquid two-phase flow measurement

Since bubble velocity and liquid velocity are different in gas-liquid two-phase flows, it is necessary to separate the images of bubbles from those particles which are put into liquid. Most image separation techniques are based on the differences in size and brightness of bubbles and particles. After the image separation is performed, velocities of each phase flow can be computed by application of PTV techniques to the images of each phase. Figure 3 shows the measurement results of rising bubble velocities and liquid velocities in a vessel, and the inverse energy cascade flow structures is discussed with this figure [6].

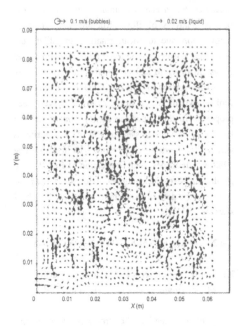

Figure 3 Velocity map of bubbles and particles in a bubbly plume flow [6]

We measured a gas-liquid two-phase flow in a horizontal channel to analyze the drag reduction mechanism under the wall shear flow [7]. The original image of objects (particles and bubbles), edge detected image of objects by image enhancement and bubble image without particles after image separation are shown in Figure 4 (a). After the image separation technique is applied, velocity profiles of each phase are calculated and they are shown in Figure 4 (b). We analyzed the shear stress components and Reynolds stress with the image measurement and discussed the drag reduction mechanism in comparison with the case of single phase flow. In this research we have introduced the new three terms of shear stresses which consists of time averaged values of velocity fluctuation components u' and v' as well as projection void fraction for the 2D bubbly flows.

Nowadays a CCD type of high speed video camera, as we used in the experiment of micro-bubble channel low, has world-widely been recognized as an essential tool. Consequently micro-PIV systems using a high speed video camera also have been progressing quickly in the fields of micro-fluid mechanics for medical use and fluid flow analysis in electronic devices, etc.

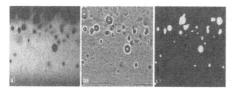

(a) from left: Original image, Image of objects detected by image enhancement, Bubble only image after separation

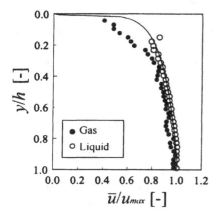

(b) Velocity profiles of each phase by VGT-PTV (h=5mm: half height of the channel, y: vertical coordinate, y=0:surface of upper wall, u: flow velocity)

Figure 4   Gas-liquid two-phase turbulent flows in a horizontal channel   [7]

Figure 5 shows the relative velocity vectors of bubbles. We discussed the bubble-bubble interaction in a still water vessel, Velocities are measured by 3D-PTV, which tracks three-dimensional motion of each bubble and they are rearranged and shown in a form of relative velocity map around a target bubble [8]. As a result, it is confirmed that bubbles are each other attracted in the horizontal direction but excluded in the vertical direction.

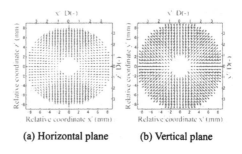

(a) Horizontal plane   (b) Vertical plane

Figure 5 Relative velocity vectors for bubble-bubble interaction in a vessel by 3-D PTV [8]

2.5 Recursive cross-correlation PIV applied in order of wave lengths for images

The recursive cross-correlation PIV presents velocity vector maps with very high spatial resolution after the values of cross-correlation are computed repeatedly step by step from coarse window of images with longer wave lengths to fine window with shorter ones. We applied this method to multi-phase flows, and successfully could obtain multiple velocity fields which express multiple structures of multi-phase flow consisting of translation velocity vectors of void waves, group vectors of bubble clusters and individual bubble velocity vectors [9]. Such a concept of multiple velocity vector fields is expected to be applied to construction and discussion of the spatial average model in LES, and will contribute to support the development of CFD for turbulent flows, multi-phase flows, reaction flows, and etc. See Figure 6.

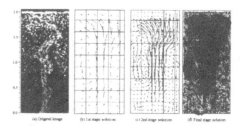

Figure 6 Recursive cross-correlation PIV and the measurement results for a bubble plume [9]

Moreover using the equation of translation motion of bubbles and particles in gas-liquid two-phase flows, it was shown that the velocity vectors of continuous phase (liquid) can be calculated inversely from the PTV velocity data of the dispersed phase flow [10]. We also are trying to newly apply the PIV-CFD hybrid systems for controlling bubbly flows based on the stochastic estimation method and POD method.

3. SUMMARY

The progresses in analytical algorithms for PIV/PTV have contributed to speed-up of data processing, automatic measurement, user friendly application and high accuracy in space and time. Since a great progress in imaging hard ware systems also can be expected, it may be possible that more and more numerical approaches such as PIV-CFD hybrid systems just as described in this paper will be proposed in future with a mutual assistance of their strong points . Although the conventional PIV/'TV techniques measure and analyze only flow velocities in multi-phase systems and turbulent flows, novel PIV-CFD hybrid techniques are challenging to possibly extract the elemental flow properties such as pressure, temperature etc in their internal structures. The new PIV-CFD hybrid systems also will be expectable to elucidate the spatio-temporal flow structures with higher accuracy than before and to lead to possible prediction of the next time step flow structures, which will be more useful for flow control.

REFRENCES

[1] Handbook of Particle Image Velocimetry, ed. by the Visualization Society of Japan, 2005, Morikita Shuppan, pp.68-82.

[2] Uemura, T., Yamamoto, F. and Koukawa, M., Binary Image Cross-correlation Method, J. of Flow Visualization, Japan, 1990, Vol.10-38. pp.196-201.

[3] Uemura,T., Yamamoto,F., Ohmi,K. A High Speed Algorithm of Image Analysis for Real Time Measurement of Two-dimensional Velocity Distribution, ASME FED-Vol. 85, 1989, Book No.H00554-1989, pp.129-133.

[4] Song,X., Yamamoto,F.,I guchi,M., Murai,Y., A New Tracking Algorithm of PIV and Removal of Spurious Vectors using Delaunay Tessellation, Exp. in Fluids, 1999, 26, 371-380.

[5] Ihsikawa,M. ,Murai,Y., Wada,A., Iguchi,M., Okamoto,K., Yamamoto,F., A Novel Algorithm for Particle Tracking Velocimetry using the Velocity Gradient Tensor, Exp. in Fluids, 2000, 29, 519-531.

[6] Murai,Y., Song,X., Takagi,T., Ishikawa,M., Yamamoto,F.,Ohta,J., Inverse Energy Cascade Structure of Turbulence in a Bubble Flow (PIV Measurement and Results), JSME Int., (B), 2000, 43, 188-196.

[7] Murai,Y., Oishi,Y., Takeda,Y. Yamamot,F., Turbulent Shear Stress Profiles in a Bubbly Channel Flow Assessed by Particle Tracking Velocimetry, Exp. in Fluids, 2006, DOI 1,1007/s00348-006-0142-9, pp.1-10.

[8] Murai,Y., Qu,J., Yamamoto,F., Three-Dimensional Interaction of Bubbles at Intermediate Reynolds Numbers, Multiphase Science and Technology, 2005,17, 1-23.

[9] Cheng,W., Murai,Y., Sasaki,T., Yamamoto,F., Bubble Velocity Measurement with Recursive Cross Correlation PIV Technique, Flow Measurement & Instrumentation, 2005, 16, 35-46.

[10] Cheng.W., Murai.Y., Yamamoto,F., Estimation of the Liquid Velocity Field in Two-phase Flows Using Inverse Analysis and Particle Tracking Velocimetry, Flow Measurement and Instrumentation, 2005, 16, 303-308.

Computational Material Diagnostics Based on Limited Boundary Measurements: An Inversion Method for Identification of Elastoplastic Properties from Indentation Tests

Alemdar HASANOGLU HASANOV

Applied Mathematical Sciences Research Center and Department of Mathematics
Kocaeli University, Ataturk Bulvarı
Umuttepe Campus, Izmit, Kocaeli, 41300 Turkey

(E-mail: ahasanov@kou.edu.tr)

ABSTRACT

Mathematical and computational framework of computational material diagnostics method based on limited indentation tests is proposed. An inversion method aims to determine elastoplastic properties from an indentation loading curve. Mathematical model, based on deformation theory, leads to quasi-static elastoplastic contact problem, given by the the monotonically increasing values $\alpha_i > 0$ of the indentation depth. The identification problem is formulated as an inverse problem of determining the stress-strain curve $\sigma_i = \sigma_i(e_i)$ from an experimentally given indentation curve $P = P(\alpha)$. The inversion method is based on the parametrization of the stress-strain curve, according to the discrete values of the indentation depth, and uses only *a priori* information as monotonicity of the unknown function $\sigma_i = \sigma_i(e_i)$. It is shown that the ill-conditionedness of the identification problems depends on the state discretization parameter Δe_i. An algorithm of optimal selection of state discretization parameters is proposed as a new regularization scheme. Remeshing algorithm presented here allows to find the unknown contact zone on each step of indentation with high accuracy. Numerical parametric studies are performed for different materials with various elastic and plastic properties. The obtained results show high predictive capability of the proposed computational model. The presented numerical results permit also to construct relationships between various parameters chracterizing material behaviour under spherical indentation.

KEY WORDS: Indentation Measurements, Elastoplastic Inverse Problem, State Discretization Parameter

INTRODUCTION

The idea of relating the measurable and non-measurable properties of deformable materials based on mathematical models, dates back to the works of Ishlinski [7] and Tabor [12]. Ishlinski, by using the method of characteristics for hyperbolic equations, has found a relationship between the Brinell hardness $\bar{H}_B = P/(2\pi R\alpha)$, and the yield stress $\sigma_0 = 0.383\bar{H}_B$, for a spherically symmetric indentation hardness test (here and below $P > 0$ is the measured loading force, $R > 0$ is the radius of a spherical indenter and $\alpha > 0$ is the indentation depth). However, in this model curvature of a contactable surface was ignored, and the problem was considered for a perfectly plastic materials. Later technological advances and the need to find experimentally non-measurable material properties by using measurable one on a small scale, led to an increasing interest in the development of new methods.

These methods may be divided into two groups. The first group contains various plasticity theories and models, which can adequately describe spherical indentation testing. Comparing all the plasticity models used for the spherical indentation Budiansky [1], and Fleck and Hutchinson [2] have concluded that *the deformation theory version of J_2 theory is used rather than the flow theory version not only because it is easier to implement numerically, but also because it gives essentially identical predictions to the flow theory, when stressing is nearly proportional (simple loading)*. In the second group various analytical and numerical methods have been developed to extract elastoplastic properties of deformable materials from a measured spherical indentation loading curve (see, [8-9, 11, 13] and references therein).

Within the framework of the J_2-deformation theory of plasticity, the mathematical theory of inverse problems related to determination of elastoplastic properties from an indentation loading curve has been formulated by the author [3-4]. The analysis given in [6] shows how the inverse problem becomes an ill-conditioned one, by increasing the value $\alpha > 0$ of the indentation depth, depending on the state discretization parameter of the stress-strain curve. Following to this analysis a regularization algorithm, *an optimal selection of the indentation parameters $\alpha_i > 0$*, was proposed for indentation problems [4, 6]. In this study, an inversion method to extract the elastoplastic properties of engineering materials from the measured spherical indentation (loading) curve $P = P(\alpha)$ is proposed.

THE MATHEMATICAL MODEL

Let the rigid spherical indenter is loaded with a normal force P, into an axially symmetric homogeneous body (sample) occupying the domain $\Omega \times [0, 2\pi]$, in the negative y-axis direction, as shown in Fig.1. The uniaxial quasi-static indentation process is simulated by monotonically increasing the value $\alpha > 0$ of the penetration depth. It is assumed that the penetration process is carried out without unloading, moment and friction. Then, because of symmetricity, for a given penetration depth $\alpha \in (0, \alpha^*)$ the axisymmetric indentation can be modeled by the following contact problem, in the cylindrical coordinates $(r, z) := (x, y)$.

Find the displacement field $u(x, y) = (u_1(x, y), u_2(x, y))$ *from the solution of the unilateral problem*

$$\begin{cases} -\dfrac{\partial}{\partial x}(x\sigma_{11}(u)) - \dfrac{\partial}{\partial y}(x\sigma_{12}(u)) + \sigma_{33}(u) = F_1(x, y), \\ -\dfrac{\partial}{\partial x}(x\sigma_{12}(u)) - \dfrac{\partial}{\partial y}(x\sigma_{22}(u)) + \sigma_{33}(u) = F_2(x, y), \quad (1) \\ (x, y) \in \Omega \subset R^2; \end{cases}$$

$$\begin{cases} u_2(x, l_y) \le -\alpha + \varphi(x), \\ \sigma_{22}(u) \le 0, \ [u_2(x, y) + \alpha - \varphi(x)]\sigma_{22}(u) = 0, \quad (2) \\ \sigma_{12}(u) = 0, \quad (x, y) \in \Gamma_0; \end{cases}$$

$$\begin{cases} \sigma_{11}(u) = 0, \sigma_{12}(u) = 0, \quad (x, y) \in \Gamma_\sigma; \\ u_1(0, y) = 0, \sigma_{12}(u) = 0, \quad (x, y) \in \Gamma_1, \quad (3) \\ \sigma_{12}(u) = 0, u_2(x, 0) = 0, \quad (x, y) \in \Gamma_u, \end{cases}$$

Here,

$\partial\Omega = \overline{\Gamma_0} \cup \overline{\Gamma_\sigma} \cup \overline{\Gamma_1} \cup \Gamma_u, \ \overline{\Gamma_0} \cap \overline{\Gamma_u} = \emptyset,$

$meas \ \Gamma_u \ne 0,$

$\Omega = \{(x, y) \in R^2 : 0 < x < l_x, 0 < y < l_y\},$

$l_x, l_y > 0, \ \Gamma_\sigma = \{(l_x, y) : 0 < y < l_y\},$

$\Gamma_0 = \{(x, l_y) : 0 \le x \le l_x\},$

$\Gamma_1 = \{(0, y) : 0 \le y \le l_y\},$

$\Gamma_u = \{(x, 0) : 0 \le x \le l_x\},$

and $\varphi(x) = \sqrt{R^2 - x^2}$ is

the surface of the spherical indenter, with the radius R (Fig 1).

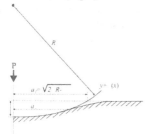

Fig.1 Geometry of rigid spherical indentation

Here the deformation theory version of J_2 theory [10] is used, and it is assumed that the stress-strain relationship is given as follows (Fig. 2):

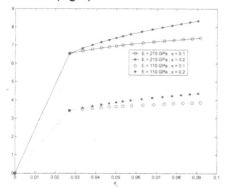

Fig.2 Stress-strain curves for different engineering materials

$$\sigma_i(e_i) = 3G[1 - g(e_i^2)]e_i, \quad e_i \in (0, e_i^*), \quad (4)$$

where

$$e_i(u) = (2/3)\left\{ \sum_{i,j=1,3} [\varepsilon_{ii}(u) - \varepsilon_{jj}(u)]^2 + 3\varepsilon_{12}^2(u) \right\}^{1/2}$$

is the strain intensity. The function $\sigma_i = \sigma_i(e_i)$ is assumed to be a monotone increasing concave one. The function $g = g(\xi), \xi = e_i^2$ called the plasticity function. Note that for power hardening materials the stress-strain relation is given by the Ramberg-Osgood curve $\sigma_i = \sigma_0(e_i/e_0)^\kappa$,

with the plasticity function $g(\xi) = 1 - (\xi/\xi_0)^{0.5(\kappa-1)}, \kappa \in [0,1]$. Here $\kappa \in [0,1]$ is a strain hardening exponent. The cases $g(\xi) = 0$ and $g(\xi) = 1 - \sqrt{\xi_0/\xi}$ in [8] correspond to pure elastic ($\kappa = 1$) and perfectly plastic ($\kappa = 0$) materials, respectively.

In conventional physical model of spherical indentation [2, 11], the friction between the indenter and the indented material has a negligible effect on the indentation curve and for this reason the contact on the common surface between the indenter and the sample can be assumed frictionless. Since an indentation test is non-destructive one (shallow indentation) and can be applied both to small samples or to fabricated machine and structural elements, the above physical model is used for large class of pure and alloyed engineering materials [1-2, 9, 11-13]. Note also that in the considered model we use only the loading of the part indentation curve, since the Ramberg- Osgood type of materials are considered. This, in particular, means that the resudial penetration depth $\alpha \in (0, \alpha_K)$ and loading force P should be used as a given data in the considered inverse problem. The unloading solution can be generated numerically from the solution corresponding to pure elastic case.

The inverse problem consists of identifying the stress-strain curve $\sigma_i = \sigma_i(e_i)$, from the measured spherical indentation loading curve $P = P(\alpha)$, $\alpha \in (0, \alpha_K)$, obtained from the quasi-static indentation process.

ANALYSIS OF THE IDENTIFICATION PROBLEM AND COMPUTATIONAL RESULTS

The identification/inverse problem of determining the stress-strain curve (4) from the measured spherical indentation loading curve $P = P(\alpha)$ is a complicated nonlinear process, which deals with elastoplastic material behaviour. The direct (contact) problem (1)-(3) is nonlinear not only due to the presence of the plasticity function $g(e_i^2(u))$, but also, in the sense that for each value $\alpha > 0$ of the penetration depth, the contact zone

$$\Gamma_c(\alpha) = \{(x, l_y) \in \Gamma_0 : u_2(x, l_y) = -\alpha + \varphi(x),$$
$$x \in (0, a_c(\alpha))\}, \quad a_c(\alpha) := \partial \Gamma_c(\alpha),$$

is unknown, and needs to be also determined [4]. Evidently, no analytical solution for indentation response is available. In addition to all difficulties, the inverse problem arising here is an ill-conditioned one. To show this, the following computational experiment has been realized for two types (rigid and soft) of materials ($E_1 = 210GPa$; $E_2 = 110GPa$) with different power hardening parameters $(\kappa_1 = 0.1; \kappa_2 = 0.2)$. The stress-strain curves of these materials are plotted in Fig. 2 (in all cases $e_0 = 0.027$). The corresponding theoretical values of the indentation loading curves $P = P(\alpha)$, $\alpha \in (0, \alpha_K)$, has been obtained from the numerical solution of contact problem (1) to (3). The results, plotted in Fig. 3, show that the inverse problem is most sensitive when the tested materials obey the same linear hardening behaviour, but different hardening parameters. Thus, for the first type of materials (with $E_1 = 210GPa$, and $\kappa_1 = 0.1, \kappa_2 = 0.2$) the maximum relative difference in the value of the loading force is $\Delta_P^{(1)} = \max_\alpha |(P(\alpha; E_1, \kappa_1) - P(\alpha; E_1, \kappa_2))$ $/ P(\alpha); E_1, \kappa_1)$ is $\Delta_P^{(1)} = 1.57 \times 10^{-2}$, while maximum relative difference

$\Delta_\sigma^{(1)} = \max_\alpha |(\sigma_i[E_1, \kappa_1] - \sigma_i[E_1, \kappa_2]) / \sigma_i[E_1, \kappa_1]|$ in the stress-strain curves is $\Delta_\sigma^{(1)} = 1.3 \times 10^{-1}$. The same results have been obtained for the second type of materials (with $E_2 = 110GPa$, $\kappa_1 = 0.1$ and $\kappa_2 = 0.2$: $\Delta_P^{(2)} = 1.56 \times 10^{-2}$, while $\Delta_P^{(2)} = 1.3 \times 10^{-1}$.

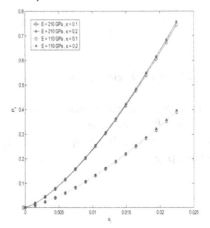

Fig3 The indentation curves corresponding to the data in Fig. 2.

These results show that the indentation curves corresponding to different power hardening materials, with the same elasticity E modulus and different power hardening parameters $\kappa_1 \neq \kappa_2$, may not be distinguishable. The inverse problem is most sensitive for this materials: small perturbations in the right hand side $P(\alpha)$ leads to essential deviations in the values of the function $\sigma_i = \sigma_i(e_i)$.

The discrete inverse problem is formulated by the parameterization of the curve (4), according to steps of indentation. Such a parameterization naturally leads to the piecewise-linear approximation of the stress-strain curve. For the pure elastic deformation case one need to find E_0 and e_0, and for further plastic states, and the angles β_k (slopes of the piecewise linear curve).

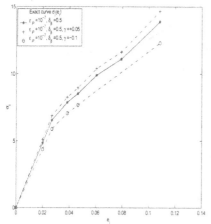

Fig4 Indentation of the stress-strain curve: $E = 210GPa$, $e_0 = 0.027$

Figure 4 shows the reconstruction of the stress-strain curves from noise free and noisy data. In the case of the noisy data, an accuracy of the reconstructed curve for the first to fourth plastic states is about $\varepsilon_\sigma = 1\%$ and $\varepsilon_\sigma = 6\%$ for the fifth plastic state. For the noisy data P_k^γ accuracy of the reconstruction decreases, in particular in the beginning plastic states.

For the noise factors $\gamma = 0.5; -0.1$ the relative errors rise up to $\varepsilon_\sigma = 12\%$ and $\varepsilon_\sigma = 7\%$, for the first and second materials, respectively. For the stabilization of the identification algorithm an influence of the relaxation parameter δ_β used. Thus, in the case of the large relaxation parameter $\delta_\beta^{(1)} = 0.5$ the following optimal selection of state discretization parameters were obtained: $e_1^{(1)} = 0.038$, $e_2^{(1)} = 0.043$, $e_3^{(1)} = 0.06$. The obtained results show that the presented inversion algorithm is also feasible in the presence of a noise factor $\gamma = 5 \div 10\%$.

Acknowledgement The work is a part of the computational material diagnostics system (CMD-system) project of the Applied Mathematical Sciences Research Center of Kocaeli University. The author acknowledges the support of TUBITAK

REFERENCES

1. Budiansky, B., A reassessment of deformation theories of plasticity, *Journal of Applied Mechanics*, 1959, **26**, pp.259-264.
2. Fleck, N.A. and Hutchinson, J.W., A reformulation of strain gradient plasticity. *Journal of the Mechanics and Physics of Solids*, 2001, **49**, pp.2245-2271.
3. Hasanov, A., An inverse problem for an elastoplastic medium, *SIAM Journal on Applied Mathematics*, 1995, **55**, pp.1736-1752.
4. Hasanov, A. and Seyidmamedov, Z., Determination of unknown elastoplastic properties in Signorini problem, *International Journal Non-Linear Mechanics*, 1998, **33**, pp.979-991.
5. Hasanov, A., Qualitative behaviour of solutions of unilateral elliptic problems with perturbing the unknown boundary. I. The Theory. *Applied Mathematics and Computation*, 2000, **109**, pp.249-260.
6. Hasanov, A., An inversion method for identification of elastoplastic properties for engineering materials from limited spherical indentation measurements, *Inverse Problems in Science and Engineering*, 2006 (to appear).
7. Ishlinski, A., An axisymmetric plasticity problem and Brinell number. *Journal of Applied Mathematics and Mechanics*, 1944, **8**, pp.204-224.
8. Johnson, K.L., The correlation of indentation experiments. *Journal Mechanics and Physics of Solids*, 1970, **18**, pp.115-126.
9. Johnson, K.L., *Contact Mechanics*, 1985, Cambridge Universiry Press, Cambridge.
10. Kachanov, L.M., *Fundamentals of the Theory of Plasticity*, 1974, Mir, Moscow.
11. Swadener, J.G., George, E.P. and Pharr, G.M., The correlation of the indentation size effect measured with indenters of various shapes. *Journal of the Mechanics and Physics of Solids*, 2002, **50**, pp.681-694.
12. Tabor, D., *Hardness of Metals*, 1951, Clarendon Press, Oxford.
13. Wei, Y. and Hutchinson, J.W., Hardness trends in micron scale indentation. *Journal of the Mechanics and Physics of Solids*, 2003, **51**, pp.2037-2056.

HLA Based ASP Platform and Its Federation Integration for Collaborative VPD on INTERNET

XIAO Tianyuan*, ZHANG Lingxuan*, FAN Wenhui*, LIANG Ce*, LIN Yu *

* The National CIMS Engineering Research Center
Automation Department of Tsinghua University
Beijing, 100084, China
(E-mail: xty-dau@tsinghua.edu.cn)

ABSTRACT

In this paper, the research progress of HLA based collaborative simulation platform in integrated virtual product development is discussed at first, then the RMF based collaborative simulation platform is presented, to overcome the shortcoming of single federation architecture. Considering the requirement of e-manufacturing, the ASP based collaborative simulation platform and its federation integration are introduced, including its architecture FIA, its integration specification FEI, and related critical techniques. Finally, two application examples of realized federation integration system are presented

KEY WORDS: RMF, ASP platform, collaborative VPD, FIA, FEI

NOMENCLATURE

HLA: High Level Architecture
RMF: Resource Management Federation
VPD: Virtual Product Development
ASP: Application Server Provider
FIA: Federation Integrated Architecture
FEI: Federation Executive Infrastructure

1. INTRODUCTION

Collaborative simulation has become the important feature of the modern simulation. HLA has become one of industrial standards, IEEE 1516; it means that the application areas of HLA have been extended from military to industry, typically, such as collaborative simulation of supply chain system, intelligent traffic system, large scale Markov chain, especially, integrated virtual product development, and so on.

In this paper, the research progress of HLA based collaborative simulation platform in integrated virtual product development is discussed at first, then the RMF based collaborative simulation platform is presented, to overcome the shortcoming of single federation architecture. Considering the requirement of e-manufacturing, the ASP based collaborative simulation platform and its federation integration are introduced, including its architecture FIA, its integration specification FEI, and related critical techniques. Finally, two application examples of realized federation integration system are presented in e-manufacturing.

2. THE RESEARCH PROGRESS OF HLA BASED COLLABORATIVE SIMULATION PLATFORM

16

As well defined collaborative simulation architecture, HLA can satisfy the requirement of collaborative VPD in some degree. Its OMT provides sufficient ability to describe and manage the models and other computing resources on the platform, its RTI separates data communication from simulation execution control, providing unified interface for interoperation among models and simulation tools under distributed environment.

2.1 RESEARCH PROGRESS

There are a lot of researches on collaborative simulation platform in VPD for recent years. For example, Hironori Hibino[1] and etc from Japan developed the distributed simulation system using HLA, to evaluate a very large manufacturing system by synchronizing several different simulators. A manufacturing adapter to connect manufacturing system simulators with HLA using a plug-in style is proposed. This is a single federation framework platform, that is, only one simulation federation is executed and the FOM and SOM can not be changed during platform running. In this case, the resource manager, as the federate of the federation, is responsible for the management of federates. This kind of platform suits the application of VPD that no confliction of shared resources exists.

One of characteristics for VPD is that several teams share distributed resources, including product models, CAD tools, CAE tools, simulation tools, and so on, and it is often necessary to create multi federations for deferent teams, while some resources are shared. It is important that ensuring no confliction of shared resources to occur.

Another typical collaborative simulation platform for VPD is COSIM, which is developed by Bohu Li[2], from China. COSIM is a kind platform of supporting multi federation framework. It can support collaborative multidiscipline simulation for complex product. COSIM consists of several groups of simulation components, which are integrated through the simulation framework; it separates the modeling and simulation of complex product from supported executive environment.

In this kind platform of supporting multi federation, the simulation resources are managed with model base on Web server. Users complete the configuration of simulation project in term of interaction with web server through local browser, and then web serer triggers simulation federation. In general, the structure of the platform is complex, and is un-full-HLA solution.

2.2 RMF BASED PLATFORM

All of these platforms based on current HLA, either single federation framework, or multi federation framework, have some limitation as following:

1) Inconvenient to construct multi federations

Under single federation architecture, once some resources are used by certain federation, they can not be used for another, otherwise, the confliction will occur, unless renaming them. It is inconvenient to construct multi federations; even HLA provides ability to support multi-federations.

2) No ability to start simulation model for HLA itself

HLA based federation corresponds one simulation execution. It means that simulation project is created when, and only when the federation has been constructed. Although the RTI supports the communication among all federates during runtime, but it has not ability to start execution of any simulation model.

Accounting above limitation, this paper presents the Resource Management Federation (RMF) based collaborative simulation platform. It means that the platform is consists of several nodes, which are defined a RMF. Every node is the federate of RMF, its OMT describes and manages local resources, including models, tools, and others. During the runtime of the platform, RMF always exists, and maintains resources through interaction mechanism of HLA federation, all simulation application federations is created under RMF control, so that the OMT can be dynamically built under HLA management.

The logical structure is divided into three layers, as shown in Fig 2.1. The lowest layer is RTI, which is the same as normal. RMF locates on RTI. It is general HLA federation, having itself FOM, OMT, and SOM. It is distinguished from the simulation federation in that its FOM describes the classes of resources existing in platform inside, its SOM describes the classes of resources interested by the federate (corresponding to the Order operation), and the classes of local resources owned the federate (corresponding to the Publish operation), in a word, RMF is responsible for the management of all federation resource, rather than simulation execution.

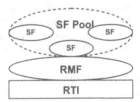

Fig. 2.1 the platform framework based on RMF

The RMF program is running respectively on every node of the collaborative simulation platform. It manages the simulation resource on itself node, and interacts with each other nodes, having following functions

- Recognizing the effective resources of bounded platform, and renewing them;
- Searching simulation resources based on interesting of users;
- Renting the simulation resources from another node owning the resource

according to the user's needs, and renting local resources to other node,
- Creating the OMT related to simulation project, including FOM and SOM,;
- Creating simulation federation;
- Monitoring the execution of all simulation federation, and treating the tasks arising from terminating a simulation federation.

The top layer is called as SFP (Simulation Federation Pool), which consists of simulation federations in active state. Each SF corresponds to one simulation project, which is created with simulation models entering the simulation project, distributed at related nodes.

The SF is created and executed under the control of RFM. So in this platform, two kinds of federations, one is RMF, another is SF. RMF specifies all of resources within the platform, and is responsible for dynamically creating SF and executing SF. SF is general federation as defined by HLA, but all of SF created during runtime of RMF become SF pool, which is the multi federation framework.

3. THE ASP BASED COLLABORATIVE PLATFORM [3],[4]

According to the definition of ASP given by the Industrial Association, a provider who provides the service focused on application, who sells or rent the application in a one-to-multiple sharing mode through centralized management data center (other than in client) and network (Fig. 3.1). In this paper, the ASP based collaborative VPD platform is mainly discussed.

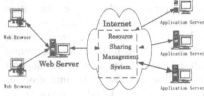

Fig. 3.1 ASP architecture

18

The functions of the platform are shown as in Fig. 3.2[5]. The collaborative platform is based on the Software Tool Resource Center and the Data Resource Center, and provides the functions of resources sharing and collaborative operation that can support the cooperative product development. The platform is composed of three functional levels with common resource centers. The functional levels are the management level, cooperation level and task implementation (service) level.

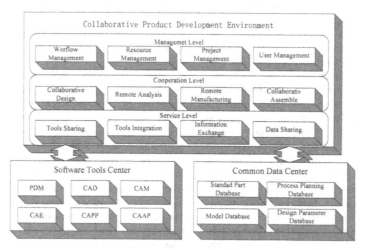

Fig3.2. the Framework of Cooperative Product Development Platform

The Management level is the top layer, which provides user management, project management, and workflow management related to the cooperative product development. The cooperation level is the middle layer, which provides specific capability under the Internet-based manufacturing environment, including the cooperative design, the remote simulation analysis, the cooperative virtual assemble and so on. The Service level is the bottom layer, which provides the service, including remotely sharing tool resources and data resources, information exchange tools integration and etc. The Software Tool Resource Center provides software tools, such as CAD, CAM, CAE, CAPP, PDM and computer aided assembling software based on HLA. The Common Data Resource Center provides standard part library, craftwork library, product model library, design parameter library and etc.

Auto-adaptive PNG format of image compression and extraction, local updating PNG format and cubic spline interpolation compression and transmission of image are adopted. Only 2M bandwidth can implement the Real-Time Synchronization in interactive collaborative designing.

From the view point of software realization, the platform can be divided into four layers: web explorer, web server, LAN control agent, and application server. It is developed with JAVA based on J2EE, so it can running on many kinds of operation systems, such as windows 2000/2003, Windows XP, UNIX, and Linux. It poses no additional demand to client except web explorer.

4. FEDERATION INTEGRATION OF ASP PLATFORMS

As networked manufacturing is progressed [6], more and more ASP based platforms have been created. Because of the absence of common integration standard, it is difficult for the platforms to interconnect, intercommunicate and interoperate with each other. As a result, it is difficult to collaborate among multi platforms, because of the difficulty of sharing distributed resources (public resources and professional resources). Also, the platform providers want to expand services, but individual platform is not able to include all kinds of service resources, generating an urgent need to integrate all these platforms.

Research and application of technology for networked manufacturing service platform integration has been carried out. It aims at constructing the infrastructure which support many kinds of services of multi-platform and multi-field, so that each platform can run in the form of integration as well as independently, and can enter federation and exit from federation freely, no influence to each others exist.

The Federation Integration Architecture (FIA) for Networked Manufacturing has been specified, referring to HLA and GLOBUS.[7] FIA is not a realization of system but a standard of integrated Architecture, which can implement the interconnection, intercommunication and, more importantly, interoperation among different platforms. Federation is a distributed system, consisting of many federates which can affect each other, and each federate is a concrete ASP manufacturing platform or an application, which is a member of a federation executive.

Federation Executive Infrastructure (FEI) is the software realization of services specified by FIA interface specification. Federation executive is a virtual world that, via a specific federate and related systems, is established by federation management according to federates' demand in order to implement the interactive actions. Its 6 Main management functions are the federation management, resource management, search management, charging management and security management. The example of integrating two ASP platforms is shown in Fig. 4.1.

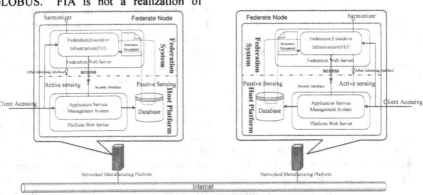

Fig 4.1 the Example of FEI Realization

The Key Techniques of realizing federation integration based on FEI include

- Dynamic resource information transmission technology based on data filtering scheme, using the idea of declaration management and data distribution management, based on matching scheme.

- Service dispatching technology for Distributed Shared Resources, with classifying and transforming shared resources based on taxology, keeping the balance between the dispatching results and response time of services.

- Mixed search technology across platforms based on configuration files mode and broadcast search mode.
- Security and accreditation technologies of federation Integration Platform, transforming the address of user id into uniform id, to avoid clients information to be obtained by other platforms
- Technologies of detection and data synchronization of shared dynamic resource.
- Integrated charging management that federation members establish and obey reciprocal agreement, referring to WTO mode.

5. TYPICAL APPLICATIONS

The ASP based collaborative design platforms, and their federation integration system, have been applied in more than 200 enterprises. Two typical Demonstration Applications are described as follows.

5.1 NETWORKED COLLABORATIVE VIRTUAL DEVELOPMENT [8]

C-Arm system is a set of robot arms named for the shape of its primary part and is widely used in medical X-Ray angiographic system. High safety and manipulation adaptability are especially required by medical product, but the great size, multi-freedom and randomness of the arm motion bring difficulty to design these aims, so collision prevention without excessive motion contour lose is the primary problem of motion control design.

Fig. 5.1 shows sketch map of the research object, the heart angiographic system. As marked out, the object contains many movable parts and 8 freedoms in all, so without right constrains to the motions, many collisions would occur during operation.

C-Arm system kinetic collision analysis and optimization have been carried out collaboratively under ADAMS (for simulating the mechanical part model) and MATLAB (for electrical/electronic part model) based on ASP platform. The practical product has been developed based on the digital prototype. It is proved that the collaborative design and development are more efficient, lower cost, less manpower and material resources consuming and more faithful compared with physical experimentation.

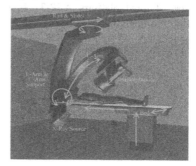

Fig. 5.1 Sketch map of Researched Object

5.2 APPLICATION EXAMPLE OF FEDERAL INTEGRATION SYSTEM

Various networked manufacturing service platforms have been gradually built up in Beijing according to different application patterns, such as park, industry, incubation base, big enterprises, etc; each platform has integrated a lot of superior resources with distinct features, such as different information resource libraries, various software tools, and so on. These platforms provide services on information, technology and application respectively, oriented towards all kinds of small and medium enterprises.

The federal integration among several ASP platforms has been realized, which means the realization of loose coupling integration and service sharing the resources across platforms. The ASP platforms have been "interconnected, inter-communicated and inter-operated". This federal service platform system, in the form of plug-in, is deployed in the same hardware server as the original service platform, and shares the same database with it. The only requirement for the client is to install IE6, and there is no need to add new equipment for HW environment.

For example, User1, who is the user on ASP-3 platform, wants to find cooperated partner to develop some product. He can found User2, who is the user of ASP-2 platform, through enterprise resource database of local platform ASP-3. When they are in cooperated design, they can use the cooperative design platform, CAD and simulation tools, and video meeting system on the platform ASP-1, as well as the metal resource database on ASP-2 platform (see Fig. 5.2). Under the federal integration system, they needn't to change their working environment to build up application federation to carry out their cooperative design and development.

Any of the federated platforms exits the federation due to what kind of reasons (server malfunction, network interrupted, abnormal shutdown, etc.), it would not affect other platforms' capability of keeping up with the created federation.

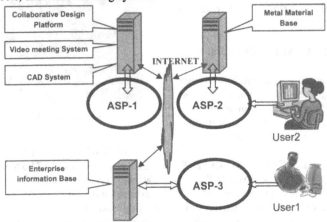

Figure 5.2 Application example of federate integration

6. CONCLUSION

In this paper, the research progress of HLA based collaborative simulation platform in integrated virtual product development is discussed. The Resource Management Federation based collaborative simulation platform overcomes the shortcoming of single federation architecture. ASP based collaborative simulation platform and its federation integration are introduced, including its architecture FIA, its integration specification FEI. The ASP platform based on federation integration makes the collaborative design and development more easy and effective.

REFERENCES

1. Hironori Hibino, Yoshiro Fukuda, Yoshiyuki Yura, Keiji Mituyuki, Manufacturing Adapter of Distributed Simulation Systems Using HLA, Proceedings of the 2002 Winter Simulation Conference, 1099~1107, (2002)
2. Bohu Li and etc., The Research on supported environment techniques for complex product collaboration manufacturing, Computer Integrated Manufacturing System----CIMS, Vol. 9, No. 8, Agu., 2003 (in Chinese)
3. Thomas, Jeroen, and Willcocks Leslie. Exploring ASP as sourcing strategy: theoretical perspectives, propositions for practice. Journal of Strategic Information Systems. 2002, 11(2): 153-177
4. Arulazi Dhesiaseelan, Venkatavaradan Ragunathan, Web Services Container Reference

Architecture (WSCRA), in: Michael Ley et al, Proc. of the IEEE Int. Conf. on Web Services (ICWS'04), San Diego, USA, IEEE Computer Society, pp. 806-805

5. WANG Yunli, XIAO Tianyuan, YANG Nan, et al. Research and implementation of collaborative product development platform [J]. Computer Integrated Manufacturing Systems. 2002, 8(8): 640-644.(in Chinese)

6. Vijay Machiraju, Akhil Sahai, Aad van Moorsel, in: Amit P. Sheth, et al, web service management network: an overlay network for federate service management. Integrated Network Management, 2003. IFIP/IEEE 8th Int. Symp. on, Colorado, USA, IEEE Computer Society, pp. 351-364, 2003

7. I. Foster, C. Kesselman, J. Nick, and S. Tuecke, Grid Services for Distributed System Integration, Computer, 35(6):37-46, Jun 2002

8. Gu Yue, Xiao Tianyuan, and Zhao Yinyan, Interference Analysis for C-Arm Angiographic System under Simulation Environment [C], Asian Simulation Conf./the 5th Conf. on System Simulation and Scientific Computing, 2002, 795-800.

The Simulation for Solute Transport in Soil using CIP Method

T. KIKUCHI*, K. NOBORIO**, K. KATAMACHI* and Y. ABE*

* Faculty of Software and Information Science
Iwate Prefectural University
Sugo 152-52, Takizawa-mura, Iwate,020-0193 Japan
(E-mail:g236c001@edu.soft.iwate-pu.ac.jp)
**Department of Agricalture
Meiji University
Higashi-mita 1-1-1, Tama-ku, Kawasaki-shi, Kanagawa,214-8571 Japan

ABSTRACT

Numerical methods for solute transport in soil are shown in the present paper.

The solute transport model is expressed by the Convective-Dispersion Equation (CDE). The property of this equation changes from parabolic to hyperbolic and vice versa depending on time and location. In the case of large advection, most numerical methods cause numerical oscillation or large damping. Numerical methods that provide sufficient accuracy for this problem are required. We simulate solute transport using four numerical methods including the Cubic-Interpolated Pseudo-Particle/ Propagation (CIP) method. And the accuracies of those numerical solutions are evaluated based on the maximal errors and the sum squared errors in four cases: large dispersion, large advection, Gaussian hill and triangle hill. As a result, the CIP method is found to have better overall accuracy.

KEY WORD: CIP method, Solute transport, Eulerian-Lagrangian method

NOMENCLATURE

C : Solute concentration [mol kg^{-1}]

D : Coefficient of dispersion [m^{2}s^{-1}]

v : Average bulk velocity [m s^{-1}]

P_e : Peclet number

C_u : Courant number

1. INTRODUCTION

The models of the mass transport in soil have been developed lately. Those are expressed by CDE (Convective-Dispersion Equation). The property of this equation changes from parabolic to hyperbolic and vice versa with time and location. In the case of large advection, most numerical methods cause numerical oscillation or large damping. Numerical method which gives sufficient accuracy in this problem, are required. To solve this, some methods have been proposed. Srivastava and Yeh used one-step backward particle tracking [1]. Zhang et al. used modified single-step reverse particle tracking [2]. Simunek and van Genuchten used upstream weighted formulation in the code SWMS_2D [3].

CIP (Cubic-Interpolated Psedo Particle / propagation) method was proposed by Takewaki et al. [4]. This is an Eulerian-Lagrangian scheme, which is the same concept as one-step backward particle tracking. In this method, a profile between two grid points is interpolated by cubic polynomial. And value and its spatial derivative of the profile are advected. CIP method seems to be effective for getting sufficient accuracy in this problem.

We simulated for the cases of solute transport in soil by using CIP and conventional methods, i.e. upwind scheme, two-step Lax-Wendroff scheme and Crank-Nicolson scheme. The accuracies of those numerical solutions are evaluated by using the sum squared error and the maximal value of errors at each grid points.

2. The Model of Solute Transport and Numerical Method

The one dimensional solute transport model without delay is described as:

$$\frac{\partial C}{\partial t} + \frac{\partial}{\partial x}\left(-D\frac{\partial C}{\partial x} + vC\right) = 0 \quad (1)$$

2.1. CIP method

Equation (1) can be rewritten as

$$\frac{\partial C}{\partial t} + v\frac{\partial C}{\partial x} = G$$

$$G \equiv D\frac{\partial^2 C}{\partial x^2}$$

This equation is then split into non-advection and advection phases, as below.

$$\frac{\partial C}{\partial t} = G \quad (2)$$

$$\frac{\partial C}{\partial t} + v\frac{\partial C}{\partial x} = 0 \quad (3)$$

Non Advection Phase Let C_i^n be $C(t_n, x_i)$. Equation (2) can be solved by the conventional numerical method, and $\tilde{C}$ is its solution.

For example, $\tilde{C}$ is expressed as

$$\tilde{C}_i = C_i^n \exp\left[\frac{G_i^n}{C_i^n}\Delta t\right] \quad (4)$$

$$G_i^n = D\frac{C_{i+1}^n - 2C_i^n + C_{i-1}^n}{\Delta x^2} \quad (5)$$

, and the spatial derivative $\tilde{C}'$ of $\tilde{C}$ is expressed as

$$\tilde{C}'_i = C_i'^n + \frac{\Delta t D}{\Delta x^2}\left(C_{i+1}'^n - 2C_i'^n + C_{i-1}'^n\right) \quad (6)$$

Advection Phase The solution of Equation (3) is obtained as follows:

$$C(t_{n+1}, x_i) = C(t_n, x_i - v\Delta t)$$

where i_m is the next grid in the upstream direction of i.

$$i_m = \begin{cases} i-1 & v > 0 \\ i+1 & v \le 0 \end{cases}$$

We assume that the profile F of C between x_i and x_{i_m} can be expressed by a cubic polynomial.

$$F(\xi) = a\xi^3 + b\xi^2 + c\xi + d$$

$$F'(\xi) = \frac{1}{\Delta x}\left(3a\xi^2 + 2b\xi + c\right)$$

$$\xi = \frac{|x - x_i|}{\Delta x}$$

where $F' = \frac{d}{dx}F$. Each coefficient is determined from the following conditions:

$$F(0) = \tilde{C}_i \quad F(1) = \tilde{C}_{i_m}$$

$$F'(0) = \tilde{C}'_i \quad F'(1) = \tilde{C}'_{i_m}$$

Finally, C^{n+1} and C'^{n+1} are obtained by Equations (7) and (8).

$$C_i^{n+1} = F\left(\frac{|v|\Delta t}{\Delta x}\right) \quad (7)$$

$$C_i'^{n+1} = F'\left(\frac{|v|\Delta t}{\Delta x}\right) \quad (8)$$

2.2. Other Methods

For the evaluation, three conventional methods are used.

2.2.1 Upwind scheme

Applying the forward difference formula for the time derivative and backward difference formula for the spatial derivative, we obtain the following:

$$C_i^{n+1} = C_i^n - \frac{\Delta t}{\Delta x^2} \left[-D \left(C_{i+1}^n - 2C_i^n + C_{i-1}^n \right) \right.$$
$$\left. + v\Delta x \left(C_i^n - C_{i-1}^n \right) \right] \qquad (9)$$

if $v > 0$.

2.2.2 Two-step Lax-Wendroff scheme

The centered difference is applied to the derivatives of both time and space. Equations (10) and (11) are formulations of Equation (1) using the two-step Lax-Wendroff scheme.

$$C_{i+\frac{1}{2}}^{n+\frac{1}{2}} = \frac{1}{2} \left(C_{i+1}^n + C_{i-1}^n \right)$$
$$- \frac{\Delta t v}{2 \Delta x} \left(C_{i+1}^n - C_{i-1}^n \right) \qquad (10)$$

$$C_i^{n+1} = C_i^n + \frac{\Delta t}{\Delta x^2} \left[D \left(C_{i+1}^n - 2C_i^n + C_{i-1}^n \right) \right.$$
$$\left. - v\Delta x \left(C_{i+\frac{1}{2}}^{n+\frac{1}{2}} - C_{i-\frac{1}{2}}^{n+\frac{1}{2}} \right) \right] \qquad (11)$$

2.2.3 Crank-Nicolson scheme

Moreover, in this scheme, the centered difference is applied to the derivatives of both time and space. However, the spatial derivative is evaluated at the average of the nth and $(n+1)$-th time levels. Equation (12) is the formulation of Equation (1) using the Crank-Nicolson scheme.

$$C_i^{n+1} - C_i^n + \frac{\Delta t}{2 \Delta x^2} \left[\Delta x v \left(C_{i+1}^{n+\frac{1}{2}} - C_{i-1}^{n+\frac{1}{2}} \right) \right.$$
$$\left. - 2D \left(C_{i+1}^{n+\frac{1}{2}} - 2C_i^{n+\frac{1}{2}} + C_{i-1}^{n+\frac{1}{2}} \right) \right] = 0 \quad (12)$$

$$C^{n+\frac{1}{2}} = \frac{1}{2} \left(C^{n+1} + C^n \right)$$

3. RESULTS OF SIMULATION

The solute transports in four cases are simulated by using various method. Their numerical solutions are compared with analytic solution introduced by van Genuchten and Wierenga [5]

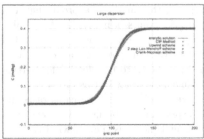

Figure 1 The case of large dispersion

Table 1 Maximal error and sum squared error in the case of large dispersion

	CIP	Upwind	2 step Lax-Wendroff	Crank-Nicolson
Maximal error	3.98E-3	1.56E-2	4.21E-3	6.46E-3
Ratio to CIP's error	1	3.92	1.06	1.62
Sum squared error	3.98E-4	8.90E-3	4.66E-4	9.07E-4
Ratio to CIP's error	1	22.36	1.17	2.28

3.1. The case of large dispersion and large advection

Firstly, the cases of large dispersion and large advection are simulated. Let initial and boundary condition be

$$t < 0 \quad x \geq 0 \quad C_i = 0.01 \quad [\text{mol kg}^{-1}]$$
$$t > 0 \quad x = 0 \quad C_i = 0.4 \quad [\text{mol kg}^{-1}]$$

in both cases.

In the case of large dispersion, let P_e and C_u be $P_e = v\Delta x/D = 1$, $C_u = v\Delta t/\Delta x = 0.2$. The numerical solutions using each method and analytic solution are shown in figure 1 after 500 steps. And maximal error, sum squared error and each ratio to the CIP's error are shown in Table 1. The errors of both the CIP method and the two-step Lax-Wendroff scheme are smaller than those of the other schemes. In addition, the CIP method has marginally less error than the two-step Lax-Wendroff scheme.

In the case of large advection, let P_e

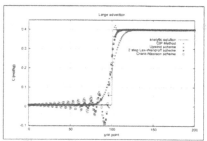

Figure 2 The case of large advection

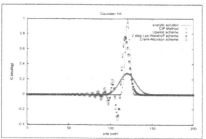

Figure 3 The case of Gaussian hill

Table 2 Maximal error and
sum squared error in the case of large dispersion

	CIP	Upwind	2 step Lax-Wendroff	Crank-Nicolson
Maximal error	1.44E-1	1.88E-1	2.52E-1	2.58E-1
Ratio to CIP's error	1	1.30	1.75	1.79
Sum squared error	4.36E-2	3.17E-1	2.10E-1	2.52E-1
Ratio to CIP's error	1	7.27	4.81	5.78

Table 3 Maximal error and
sum squared error in the case of Gaussian hill

	CIP	Upwind	2 step Lax-Wendroff	Crank-Nicolson
Maximal error	5.38E-2	7.17E-1	4.69E-1	4.95E-1
Ratio to CIP's error	1	13.32	8.71	9.20
Sum squared error	1.28E-2	2.40E+0	1.55E+0	1.89E+0
Ratio to CIP's error	1	187.50	121.09	147.66

and C_u be $P_e = \infty$, $C_u = 0.2$. Figure 2 shows the numerical solutions and analytic solution after 500 step. The two-step Lax-Wendroff and the Crank-Nicolson scheme cause numerical oscillation. The upwind scheme can not maintain the wave profile even though it does not cause oscillation. In contrast, the CIP method has no oscillation, and furthermore it maintains the wave profile. Table 2 shows the corresponding maximal errors and sum squared error. Both of the maximal error and the sum squared error of the CIP method are lower than those of the other methods.

3.2. The cases of Gaussian hill and triangle hill

Next, the following two problems using by Yeh [6] are solved. Initial and boundary condition are given by

$$C(x, 0) = C_0(x)$$

$$C(x, t) \rightarrow 0 \text{ as } |x| \rightarrow \infty$$

in which $C_0(x)$ is given by

$$C_0(x) = \exp\left[-\frac{(x - x_0)^2}{2\sigma_0^2}\right]$$

for a gaussian hill and

$$C_0(x) = \begin{cases} 1 - |x - x_0|/l_0 & |x - x_0| < l_0 \\ 0 & \text{otherwise} \end{cases}$$

for a triangle hill. In both cases , let P_e and C_u be $P_e = \infty$, $C_u = 0.2$. The numerical solutions and analytic solution for a gaussian hill and a triangle hill are shown in figure 3 and figure 4.

Figure 3 shows that the methods without CIP cause large damping. And the two-step Lax-Wendroff and the Crank-Nicolson scheme cause numerical oscillation.

Figure 4 shows the two-step Lax-Wendroff and the Crank-Nicolson scheme cause numerical oscillation near the rising point of the hill. The upwind scheme causes large damping. Table 3 and table 4

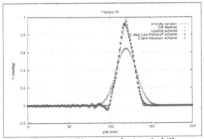

Figure 4 The case of triangle hill

Table 4 Maximal error and
sum squared error in the case of triangle hill

	CIP	Upwind	2 step Lax-Wendroff	Crank-Nicolson
Maximal error	3.80E-2	3.53E-1	9.45E-2	9.92E-2
Ratio to CIP's error	1	9.28	2.49	2.61
Sum squared error	3.56E-3	1.07E+0	7.46E-2	9.49E-2
Ratio to CIP's error	1	300.56	20.96	26.66

show the each corresponding maximal error and sum squared error. Also in these two cases, the error of the CIP method is the smallest among these four methods.

4. CONCLUSION

The present paper compares the numerical solutions of one-dimensional solute transport in soil obtained by four methods, i.e., the CIP method, the upwind scheme, the two-step Lax-Wendroff scheme, and the Crank-Nicolson scheme. Those accuracies are evaluated based on maximal error and sum squared error for four cases: large dispersion, large advection, Gaussian hill and triangle hill.

In the case of large dispersion, the CIP method and the two-step Lax-Wendroff scheme have lower errors than the other schemes. In addition, the CIP method has a marginally lower error than the two-step Lax-Wendroff scheme. In the cases of large advection, Gaussian hill and tri-

angle hill, all of the methods except for the CIP method cause numerical oscillation or large damping. Furthermore, the CIP method maintains the wave profile. In addition, the superiority of CIP is confirmed with respect to both the maximal error and the sum squared error. Based on these results, the CIP method is found to be useful for all cases.

References

[1] Srivastava, R., and T.-C. Jim Yeh , A three-dimensional numerical model for water flow and transport of chemically reactive solute through porous media under variably saturated condition, Advances in Water Resources, 1992, 15, pp.275-287.

[2] Zhang, R., K. Huang, and M. T. van Genuchten , An Efficient Eulerian-Lagrangian Method for Solving Solute Transport Problem in Steady and Transient Flow Fields, Water Resources Research,1993, 29-12, pp.4131-4138.

[3] Simunek, J., T. Vogel, and M. T. van Genuchten , The SWMS_2D Code for Simulating Water Flow and Solute Transport in Two-Dimensional Variably Saturated Media, U. S. Salinity Laboratory Agricultural Research Service U. S. Department of Agriculture Riverside, California, Research Report, 1994, 132.

[4] Takewaki, H., A. Nishiguchi, and T. Yabe , The Cubic-Interpolated Psedo-Particle(CIP) Method for Solving Hyperbolic-Type Equation, J. Comp. Physics, 1985, 61, pp.261-268.

[5] van Genuchten, M. T., and P. Wierenga , Solute dispersion coefficient and retardation factor, In A. Klute ed. Methods of Soil Analysis. American Society of Agronomy, Madison, 1986, pp.1025-1053.

[6] Yeh, G.T., A Lagrangian-Eulerian Method With Zoomable Hidden Fine-Mesh Approach to Solving Advection-Dispersion Equations, Water Resources Research, 1990, 26-6, pp.1133-1144.

Development of High Performance Simulator
for Tsunami

Ryosuke AKOH[1], Satoshi II[2] and Feng XIAO[3]

* Department of Energy Science, Tokyo Institute of Technology
4259 Nagatsuda, Midori-ku, Yokohama, 226-8502 Japan
(E-mail: [1]d06akou@es.titech.ac.jp, [2]d06ii@es.titech.ac.jp, [3]xiao@es.titech.ac.jp)

ABSTRACT

Most of the existing numerical models for the simulation of Tsunami are based on the 2D shallow water equations. However, for many situations, it is necessary to use the 3D model in addition to the shallow water models to evaluate the damage in the coast region with a reliable accuracy. So, we propose the multi-scale warning system for Tsunami by coupling the 2D shallow water model and the 3D Navier-Stokes model that solves explicitly the free water surface to cover the physical phenomena that have diverse scales in both time and space. As a part of such a system, we, in this paper, present the essential numerics of the models based on the CIP/MM FVM (CIP/Multi-Moment Finite Volume Method) and some simulation results with the real geographical data for the 2D large-scale cases.

KEY WORDS: Tsunami, Multi-scale, CIP/Multi-Moment Finite Volume Method, Shallow water equations

NOMENCLATURE

A : Jacobian matrix of flux function
c : speed of the gravity wave ($= \sqrt{gh}$)
F : fluxes
H : total height
h : water depth
g : gravitational acceleration
L : matrix of the left eigenvectors of A
U : conservative variables
u : velocity
W : primitive variables
z : bottom topography
Λ : diagonalized matrix of A

INTRODUCTION

Numerical simulation plays an essential role in the prevention and mitigation of the natural disasters caused by Tsunami and other violent oceanic waves, especially in providing warning forecasts immediately after the occurrence of an earthquake and in the assessment of the damage from a possible Tsunami. There are some widely used Tsunami models [1,2,3] based on 2D shallow water equations.

However, it is still demanding to build more accurate numerical models that can provide not only numerical solutions with high accuracy to the 2D shallow water based systems but also the details of the direct water impact evaluated by 3D simulations of water fronts.

Toward the establishment of a reliable multi-scale Tsunami simulating and warning system, numerical models for different scales have been being developed based on the framework of CIP/MM FVM (Constrained Interpolation Profile / Multi-Moment Finite Volume Method) [4] in our group. For the large-scale waves, we use 2D models based on the shallow water equations to predict the arrival time and the wave height of the Tsunami, which have been widely adopted in the existing models. For the small-scale waves, we use a 3D model based on the Navier-Stokes equations for the direct simulations of multi-phase fluids with free moving boundaries, to evaluate the impact of the water waves on the coastal structures. These component models are then coupled to cover the physical phenomena that have diverse scales in both time and space.

As one part of such a system, we, in the present study, propose the formulation for the shallow water wave model by applying the CIP/MM FVM with the theory of characteristics. The numerical scheme exactly preserves the balance between fluxes and the source terms.

THE NUMERICAL MODEL

In this section the essential aspects of CIP/MM FVM are briefly illustrated. More detailed description can be found in the references.

The underlying idea of a CIP/MM FVM is to utilize more than one type of moments of a physical field as the model variables. Different from the conventional finite volume method, the moments in a CIP/MM FVM are defined as the volume integrated averages (VIA) over a control volume, the surface integrated averages (SIA) over a plane segment or the point value (PV) at any specified point.

Different moments are temporally updated by different ways in CIP/MM FVM. For example, the conserved moment VIA is computed by a flux-based formulation, while the PV or the SIA, which needs not be exactly conserved, can be updated in time by a semi-Lagrangian method or an Euler method of non-conservative form. Thus, CIP/MM FVM provides a more flexible framework for building numerical models. In this paper, we use the third-order

Runge-Kutta method [5] to compute the time integrations

1D SHALLOW WATER MODEL

Here, we describe the formulation for 1D shallow water equations

Formulation without the source term

Without the source term, the 1D shallow water equations read as

$$\frac{\partial U}{\partial t} + \frac{\partial F}{\partial x} = 0, U = \begin{bmatrix} h \\ hu \end{bmatrix}, F = \begin{bmatrix} hu \\ hu^2 + 1/2gh^2 \end{bmatrix} \quad (1)$$

(1) can be recast in its non-conservative form as

$$\frac{\partial W}{\partial t} + A \frac{\partial W}{\partial x} = 0, W = \begin{bmatrix} h \\ u \end{bmatrix}, A = \begin{bmatrix} u & h \\ g & u \end{bmatrix}. \quad (2)$$

Owing to the hyperbolicity, the characteristic form of the shallow water equations can be derived as

$$L \frac{\partial W}{\partial t} + AL \frac{\partial W}{\partial x} = 0,$$
$$L = -\frac{1}{2ch} \begin{bmatrix} -c & -c \\ -h & h \end{bmatrix}, A = \begin{bmatrix} u+c & 0 \\ 0 & u-c \end{bmatrix}. \quad (3)$$

The following set of equations in terms of the characteristic variables (or the Riemann invariants) is derived from (3),

$$\begin{cases} \frac{g}{c}dh + du = 0, \text{on } C_1(X_0) : \frac{dx}{dt'} = u+c \\ \frac{g}{c}dh - du = 0, \text{on } C_2(X_0) : \frac{dx}{dt'} = u-c \end{cases} \quad (4)$$

Eq.(4) means that the solution at X_0 is determined from two curves along characteristics C_1 and C_2. If the variables at the upstream departure points of C_m are denoted by $h^{(m)}$ and $u^{(m)}$, then the primitive variables at X_0 can be found by the relations below,

$$\begin{cases} h^* = \frac{1}{2}\left\{ h^{(1)} + h^{(2)} + \frac{c}{g}\left(u^{(1)} - u^{(2)} \right) \right\} \\ u^* = \frac{1}{2}\left\{ u^{(1)} + u^{(2)} - \frac{g}{c}\left(h^{(1)} - h^{(2)} \right) \right\} \end{cases} \quad (5)$$

Then, once $h^{(m)}$ and $u^{(m)}$ are computed by the semi-Lagrangian solutions or the Euler method, PV of the conservative variables at all cell boundaries can be directly found. In this paper, we use the third-order TVD Runge-Kutta method to obtain the upwind point.

Concerning the updating of the cell-integrated average values of the conservative variables, we consider the following finite volume formulation in flux-form,

$$\frac{\partial^V U_i}{\partial t} = -\frac{1}{\Delta x_i}\{F_{i+1/2}(h,u) - F_{i-1/2}(h,u)\} \quad (6)$$

It is obvious that (6) exactly guarantees the conservation of $^V U$. In this paper, the numerical fluxes at each cell boundary are approximated with the point values sampled at different sub-steps of the third-order Runge-Kutta method.

Formulation with the source term

The 1D shallow water equations with a geometrical source term due to the bottom topography read as

$$\frac{\partial U}{\partial t} + \frac{\partial F}{\partial x} = S, S = \begin{bmatrix} 0 \\ -gh\frac{\partial z}{\partial x} \end{bmatrix} \quad (7)$$

If a numerical scheme does not preserve the fundamental balance,

$$\frac{\partial}{\partial x}\left(\frac{1}{2}gh^2\right) = -gh\frac{\partial z}{\partial x}, \quad (8)$$

between the source term and the flux gradient at the discrete level, it may result in spurious oscillations.

In this paper, we construct the well balanced formulation for VIA to decompose the integral of the source term into a sum of two parts [6] as follows,

$$-gh\frac{\partial z}{\partial x} = -g(h+z)\frac{\partial z}{\partial x} + \frac{1}{2}g\frac{\partial(z^2)}{\partial x}, \quad (9)$$

and then compute each of them in a way consistent with the corresponding flux terms.

Concerning the formulation for the PV, if we apply the discretization method to both

h and z respectively, the steady state will be collapsed. Thus, in order to satisfy the numerical balance, we apply the discritization method not to z but to the total height $H = h + z$, just like the surface gradient method (SGM)[7].

2D MODEL

The 2D models can be constructed either by a dimensional splitting where the 1D solver described above is implemented sequentially or by a fully 2D formulation where the VIA moments are computed through a finite volume formulation and the PV moments through a local Riemann solver. We have developed 2D models on both structured grids and unstructured grids [8] with well-balanced source terms.

NUMERICAL RESULTS

In this section, we present numerical results of several test problems for the 1-dimensional and 2-dimensional shallow water equations.

Test.1: 1D dam-break flow

In the first numerical test, the one-dimensional dam-break is solved in a domain of $[0,200]$. The mesh number is 201 and the time step is 0.1 [s]. The initial conditions are

$$h_0(x) = \begin{cases} 1.0[m] & 0.0 \le x \le 100.0, \\ 0.1[m] & 100.0 \le x \le 200.0, \end{cases} \quad (10)$$
$$u_0(x) = 0.0[m/s]$$

After the instantaneous collapse of the dam, the numerical solution is computed until 20.0 [s].

Comparisons of the exact solutions with the simulated water depths h, and the velocity u are presented in Fig.1. It shows that the present formulation captures accurately the shock with correct speed within few mesh points. The rarefaction part is also accurately simulated.

Figure 1 Numerical results of water depth (left) and velocity (right) at 20.0 [s].

Test.2: 1D Perturbation of a lake at rest

The purpose of the second problem is to test the present formulation for source term in the case of a small perturbation of a lake at rest with variable bottom topography. The bottom topography is given by

$$z(x) = \begin{cases} 0.25(1.0 + \cos(10.0\pi(x - 0.5))) & \text{if } 1.4 \le x \le 1.6, \\ 0.0 & \text{otherwise,} \end{cases} \quad (11)$$

where $x \in [0,2]$. The initial conditions are

$$H_0(x) = \begin{cases} 1.001\,[\text{m}] & \text{if } 1.4 \le x \le 1.6, \\ 1.0\,[\text{m}] & \text{otherwise,} \end{cases} \quad (12)$$
$$u_0(x) = 0.0\,[\text{m/s}]$$

The results at 0.2 [s] are shown in Fig.2. From these results that do not have spurious numerical oscillations, we know that the present formulation for source term preserves exactly the balance between the source term and flux gradient.

Figure 2 Numerical results of total height (left) and momentum (right) at 0.2 [s].

Test.3: A small perturbation of a steady-state lake in 2D

The third numerical test is widely used to evaluate numerical schemes for shallow water equations with source terms of bottom topography in 2D. The computational domain is $[0,2] \times [0,1]$, and the

bottom topography is given by,

$$z(x) = 0.8 \exp\{-5.0(x - 0.9)^2 - 50.0(y - 0.5)^2\} \quad (13)$$

The initial condition is given as follows,

$$H_0(x,y) = \begin{cases} 1.01\,[\text{m}] & \text{if } 0.05 \le x \le 0.15, \\ 1.0\,[\text{m}] & \text{otherwise,} \end{cases}$$
$$u_0(x,y) = 0.0\,[\text{m/s}], \quad (14)$$
$$v_0(x,y) = 0.0\,[\text{m/s}],$$

Fig.3 show 30 uniformly spaced contour lines of the surface level H at 0.12, 0.36, 0.6 [s]. The results obtained with the rectangular grid appear on the left side, while on the right we find the numerical solution obtained with the unstructured triangular grid.

The results indicate that numerical models can resolve the small-scale features of the flow very well.

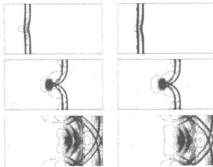

Figure 3 Numerical results of total height with rectangular grid (left) and triangular grid (right).

EXPERIMENT WITH REAL GEOGRAPHICAL DATA

As the preliminary test for real case, we computed the simulations with complex coastal-line and bottom topography based on the real geographical-data in Hokkaido region of Japan (Fig.4) [9] and in PhiPhi island region of Thiland (Fig.5).

From these results, it is observed the overall behavior of the surface waves has been captured with reasonable accuracy. We will further validate and improve the present models and make them more reliable for real cases.

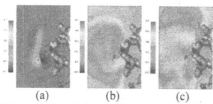

(a)   (b)   (c)

Figure 4 Simulation of Tsunami caused by the Hokkaido-nansei-oki earthquake, Japan 1993.

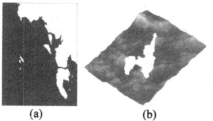

(a)   (b)

Figure 5 Simulation of Tsunami around PhiPhi island, Thailand.

CONCLUSIONS

Making use of some state-of-the-art numerical formulations, we have constructed an accurate and robust numerical model for simulating the propagation of Tsunami based on the shallow water equations. The numerical models have been validated by some idealized and "real-case" numerical experiments. The numerical results are quite promising.

Further validations and applications of the present model are still needed. The coupling with the 3D Navier-Stokes model for free interface flows (Fig.6), which have been separately developed in our group, will be carried out to build an integrated system for evaluating various waves of different scales.

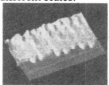 

Figure 6 Simulations of Tsunami with 3D Navier-Stocks model.

REFERENCES

1. F. Imamura. (1995), "Tsunami Numerical Simulation with the staggered Leap-frog scheme (Numerical code of TUNAMI-N1 and N2)," School of Civil Engineering, Asian Inst. Tech. and Disaster Control Res. Cntr., Tohoku Univ.
2. C. Thaicharoen, S. Weesakul, A. D. Gupta. (2005), "TSUNAMI PROPAGATION TO THAILAND A CASE STUDY: PHI PHI ISLAND," MTERM International Conference, 06-10.
3. V. V. Titov, F. I. Gonzalez. (1997), "IMPLEMENATATION AND TESTING OF THE METHOD OF SPLITTING TSUNAMI (MOST) MODEL," NOAA Technical Memorandum ERL PMEL-112.
4. F. Xiao. (2005), "CIP/Multi-Moment Finite Volume Method", J. Japan Soc. Comput. Engrg. Science, Vol.10, 1243-1248. (in Japanese)
5. C. W. Shu, (1988) "Total variation diminishing time discretizations", SIAM J. Sci. Statist. Comput., 9, 1073.
6. Y. Xing, C.-W. Shu. (2006), "High order well-balanced finite volume WENO schemes and discontinuous Galerkin methods for a class of hyperbolic systems with source terms", J. Comput. Phys., 214, 567.
7. J. G. Zhou, D. M. Causon, C. G. Mingham, D. M. Ingram. (2001), "The Surface Gradient Method for the Treatment of Source Terms in the Shallow-Water Equations," J. Comput. Phys., 168, 1.
8. S. Ii, M. Shimuta, F. Xiao. (2005), "A 4th-order and single-cell-based advection scheme on unstructured grids using multi-moments", Comput. Phys. Comm., 173, 17.
9. T. Ohmachi, H. Tsukiyama, H. Matsumoto. (2001), "Simulation of Tsunami Induced by Dynamic Displacement of Seabed due to Seismic Faulting," Bulletin of the Seismological Society of America, 91, 6, pp. 1898.

Monitoring of Unsteady Flow in a Pipeline with Integrating Measurement and Simulation

Kenji KAWASHIMA *, Shintaro INOUE**, Tatsuya FUNAKI* and Toshiharu KAGAWA*

* Precision and Intelligence Laboratory
Tokyo Institute of Technology
4259 R2-46 Midori-ku, Nagatsuta, Yokohama, 226-8503 Japan
(E-mail: kkawashi@pi.titech.ac.jp)
** Toyota Motor Corporation
(Former graduate school student of Tokyo Institute of Technology)

ABSTRACT

Measurement-integrated simulation (MI-simulation) is a numerical simulation in which experimental results are fed back to the simulation. Even if a rough grid is used, the calculation results become closer to those of the experiments. Therefore, the simulation is considered to be suitable for monitoring the state of a pipeline since the calculation time can be significantly shortened. MI-simulation has been applied to airflows passing an orifice plate in a pipeline. In this paper, the feedback values and the control methods of the simulation are investigated under unsteady oscillatory flow conditions. The accuracy and calculation time are compared when either the flow velocities or the pressures are fed back to the simulation. A P and PI controller are applied to obtain the feedback values. It is demonstrated that the calculation time could be considerably reduced over a general simulation for both velocity and pressure feedback, and especially with a P controller.

KEY WORDS: Flow measurement, Monitoring, Measurement-integrated simulation, unsteady flow

INTRODUCTION

Visualizing the state of plant or engine pipelines is very important to ensure safe operation and to diagnose faults. It is impossible, however, to monitor all pipeline states solely through experimental measurements. In addition, visualization through simulation is not always practical because a model must simulate an unsteady flow in a pipe over a long calculation time in order to obtain a good result, especially for turbulent conditions.

Measurement-integrated simulation (MI-simulation) is a numerical simulation in which experimental results are fed back to the simulation [1]. Even if coarse grids are employed, the calculated results are closer to those of the experiments. Therefore, this type of simulation is considered to be suitable for monitoring the state of pipelines since it is expected to reduce the calculation time.

A monitoring system for unsteady flow in pipelines using the simulation has been proposed. It has already been applied to airflows passing an orifice plate in a pipeline [2].

In this paper, the calculation time and accuracy of the proposed simulation are investigated when the feedback values are either the flow velocities or pressures. Moreover, a P and a PI controller are applied to obtain the feedback values and the results are compared to determine the overall effectiveness of the system.

MEASUREMENT INTEGRATED SIMULATION

Monitoring System

A diagram of the MI-integrated simulation applied to flow monitoring in a pipeline is shown in Figure 1. The velocity or pressure results are fed back into the calculation to compensate the accuracy of the simulation. Therefore, the calculation results became even closer to the experimental results, even though coarse grid was used and the compressibility and temperature change of the fluid was ignored.

Figure 2 shows the experimental setup of the tested pipeline with an orifice plate. The pipeline used in the experiment had a length of 2.5 m and a diameter of 10 mm. The orifice plate was installed 1.5 m from the inlet of the pipeline.

Figure 3 shows the measured velocities and pressures that are fed back to the simulation. The feedback positions of velocities A to F and pressures G to N are shown in Table 1. The positions were selected based upon the flow profile.

In this study, unsteady oscillatory flows are produced by an unsteady flow generator [3]. The flow velocities and pressures were measured in advance using hot-wire anemometers and semi-conductive type pressure sensors, respectively.

Table 1 Feedback positions

Feedback point	x [m]	r [mm]
A	1.5	2.5
B	1.55	2.5
C	1.55	7.5
D	1.6	2.5
E	1.6	7.5
F	1.6	12.5
G	1.525	25.0
H	1.575	25.0
I	1.625	25.0
J	1.675	25.0
K	1.725	25.0
L	1.775	25.0
M	1.825	25.0
N	1.475	25.0

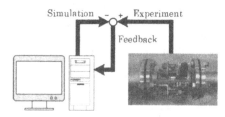

Figure 1. Diagram of MI-simulation

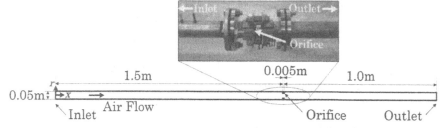

Figure 2. Tested pipeline with an orifice plate

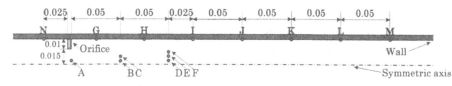

Figure 3. Measured points in the pipeline

35

Calculation procedure

The governing equations for the flow in the pipeline considered in this simulation are the continuity and Navier-Stokes equations given as

$$\frac{\partial u}{\partial x} + \frac{1}{r}\frac{\partial (rv)}{\partial r} = 0 \qquad (1)$$

$$\frac{\partial u}{\partial t} + u\frac{\partial u}{\partial x} + v\frac{\partial u}{\partial r} = -\frac{1}{\rho}\frac{\partial P}{\partial x} + \nu\left\{\frac{\partial^2 u}{\partial x^2} + \frac{1}{r}\frac{\partial}{\partial r}\left(r\frac{\partial u}{\partial r}\right)\right\} + f \qquad (2)$$

$$\frac{\partial v}{\partial t} + u\frac{\partial v}{\partial x} + v\frac{\partial v}{\partial r} = -\frac{1}{\rho}\frac{\partial P}{\partial r} + \nu\frac{\partial^2 v}{\partial x^2} + \nu\frac{\partial}{\partial r}\left\{\frac{1}{r}\frac{\partial}{\partial r}(rv)\right\} \qquad (3).$$

Here, u, v, P, ρ, ν and f are the velocity in the x-direction, velocity in the y-direction, pressure, viscosity, kinetic viscosity and the feedback artificial body force, respectively. The compressibility and temperature change of the fluid are ignored.

When the flow velocities are fed back, f is given as

$$f = u_{mean} \times \left\{K_p \times (u_e - u_s) + K_I \int_0^{t_{max}} (u_e - u_s)dn\right\} \qquad (4).$$

The next equation is applied for the pressure feedback.

$$f = K_p \times (P_e - P_s) + K_I \int_0^{t_{max}} (P_e - P_s)dn \qquad (5).$$

Here, u_{meas}, K_p and K_I are the measured velocity, the proportional gain and the integral gain, respectively. Subscripts e and s indicate the flow velocity or the pressure of measured values and the calculated values, respectively. Thus, measurement of the real flow is supplied to the numerical simulation to compensate for the difference between the real flow and the computation. It is clear from Equations (4) and (5) that a PI controller is used. If $K_I = 0$, the controller becomes a P controller.

The pipeline is divided into 5 and 50 meshes in the radial and lateral directions, respectively. Therefore, there are only 250 total meshes, which is relatively small compared with those utilized in a general simulation employing a commercially available software package.

The governing equations are discretized using the finite volume method on the staggered grid system and are solved with an algorithm using the SIMPLE method [4]. A flow chart of the calculation is shown in Figure 4. At first, the inlet flow and the outlet pressure are given as initial values. Second, the estimated pressure field $P*$ is given. In this research, the outlet pressure and $P*$ is assumed to be atmospheric pressure. Then, the estimated flow velocities $u*$ and $v*$ are calculated from Equations (1), (2) and (3), respectively. If the measured values are included in the control volumes at this time, f is calculated from either Equation (4) or (5), otherwise f is given as zero. Repeatable calculations are achieved to obtain converged solutions using the TDMA (TriDiagonal-Matrix Algorithm) method [4].

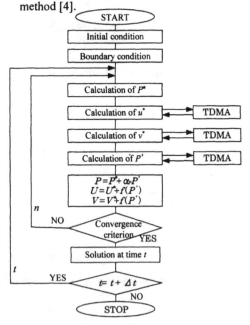

Figure 4. Flow chart

36

Table 2 Calculation conditions

Δx [m]	0.05
Δr [m]	0.005
Δt [s]	0.001
ρ [kg/m^3]	1.205
ν [m^2/s]	15.12×10^{-6}

Next, the compensation values for pressures P' are calculated and then the pressures and flow velocities are revised to their new values. At this point, the results are judged to determine whether the convergence criterion is satisfied. If it is satisfied, the calculation moves to the next time step. If it is not, the same procedure is repeated, as shown in Figure 4.

Table 2 shows the calculation conditions used in this research. Oscillatory unsteady airflows are introduced to the pipeline. The calculation time and the accuracy of the proposed simulation are investigated when the flow velocities or the pressures are fed back to the calculation.

SIMULATION RESULTS

Flow velocity feedback

At first, the flow velocities were measured and fed back with the P or PI controller. Figure 5 shows the results at a frequency of 1 Hz at position E. The inlet flow rate was given as a sinusoidal oscillatory flow whose average flow rate was 8.3×10^{-3} m^3/s and amplitude was 1.6×10^{-3} m^3/s. Therefore, the flow is satisfies the turbulent condition. The gains are determined by trial and error.

The upper figure shows the time dependent flow velocity curves in the x-direction and the lower figure shows the pressure curves. The solid lines indicate the measured values and the dotted lines represent the calculated results. It is obvious that the calculated velocity curves agree well with those of the experiment using either the P or the PI controller. The pressure curve shows some discrepancy when the PI controller is used.

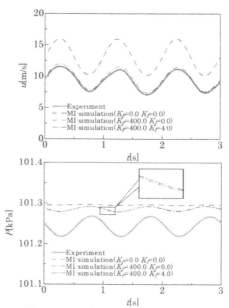

Figure 5. Calculation results at point E with velocity feedback

This difference, however, is less than 0.1 Pa, which is considered to be acceptable for monitoring the state of the pipeline.

Pressure feedback

Figure 6 shows the results when the pressures were fed back to the simulation. The conditions were same as those in Figure 5.

Both the flow velocity and pressure exhibit some difference when the P controller is used. The pressure curve coincides well with the experiment with the PI controller, although a small difference could be seen in the velocity profile.

Figure 7 shows the pressure distributions at the downstream side of the orifice plate. The upper, middle and lower figures display the result without the feedback, with the feedback and the result when a software package (Software Cradle, SCRYU/Tetra ver.5) utilizing three-dimensional calculations was used, respectively. The effectiveness of the feedback is obvious when the upper and the middle figures are compared.

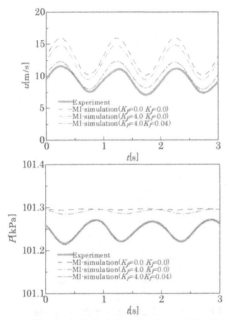

Figure 6. Calculation results at point E
with pressure feedback

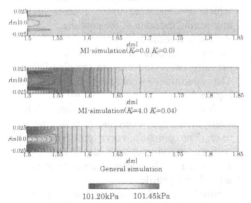

101.20kPa   101.45kPa

Figure 7. Pressure distributions

Table 3 Comparison of calculation time

	P controller	PI controller
Velocity feedback	0.46 hours	0.88 hours
Pressure feedback	0.56 hours	3.75 hours
General Simulation	24 hours	

When the results in the middle and lower figures are compared, there is a small difference. However, the proposed method can accurately represent the tendency of the pressure field well on the whole.

Calculation time

The calculation time for three cycles of the frequency is compared. The computer used in the simulations had a 3.2 GHz CPU with 1024 MB memory. The results are summarized in Table 3. It is clear that the velocity feedback with the P controller can significantly reduce the calculation time.

CONCLUSION

Measurement integrated simulation has been applied to unsteady oscillatory airflows passing an orifice plate in a pipeline. The feedback values and control methods for the simulation were investigated. The flow velocities or pressures were measured and fed back to the simulation. Then, either a P or a PI controller was applied to obtain the feedback artificial body forces. It was demonstrated that the calculation time was significantly reduced compared to a general simulation for both velocity and pressure feedback, and especially when the velocities were fed back using a P controller.

REFERENCES

1. T. Hayase, K. Nisugi and A. Shirai : Numerical realization for analysis of real flows by integrating computation and measurement, Int. J. for Numerical Methods in Fluids, Vol. 47, pp. 543/559 (2005).

2. S. Inoue, K. Kawashima, T. Funaki, T. Kagawa : Monitoring of unsteady flow field using measurement-integrated simulation, Trans. SICE, Vol. No. pp. (2006)(in Japanese).

3. K. Kawashima and T. Kagawa : Unsteady flow generator for gases using isothermal chamber, Measurement (IMEKO), 33-4, pp. 333/340 (2003).

4. Patankar SV : Numerical Heat Transfer and Fluid Flow, Hemisphere : Washington, DC, New York (1980).

CFD Simulation on LNG Storage Tank to Improve Safety and Reduce Cost

Kazuo KOYAMA

Engineering Section, Energy Production Department
Tokyo Gas Co., Ltd.
1-5-20, Kaigan, Minato-ku, Tokyo, 105-8527 Japan
(E-mail: kz_koyam@tokyo-gas.co.jp)

ABSTRACT

When a storage tank containing LNG (Liquefied Natural Gas) is further filled with different-density LNG, stratification may occur. It occasionally results in rollover accompanied by a sudden release of large amounts of BOG (Boil off Gas), which causes rapid tank-pressure rise and sometimes damage to the tank. In this paper, we study on tank filling procedures with different-density LNG by using CFD (Computational Fluid Dynamics) simulation, in order to improve safety and reduce LNG storage costs. The calculated results of a developed numerical model agree well with the measured data. A case study on the filling of a small tank indicates that the initial density difference, the initial LNG depth and the filling rate affect the final density difference, that is the density difference at the end of the filling that will directly be related to stratification.

KEY WORDS: LNG, Stratification, Rollover, CFD, CFX

NOMENCLATURE

A : Section area of LNG tank [m^2]

C_h : Hashemi constant [kg/m^{2}K$^{4/3}$s]

C_p : Specific heat capacity at constant pressure [J/kgK]

g : Gravity vector [m/s^2]

h : Enthalpy [J/kg]

k_h : Correction coefficient of C$_h$ [-]

m : Boil-off rate [kg/s]

N_p : Total number of phases [-]

p : Pressure [Pa]

p_0 : Vapor pressure in LNG tank [Pa]

Q : Interphase heat transfer [W/m^3]

r_α : Volume fraction of phase α [-]

S : Heat source [W/m^3]

$\mathbf{S}_M$: Momentum source [kg/m^{2}s^2]

S_{MS} : Mass source [kg/m^{3}s]

T : Temperature [K]

T_b : Boiling point of LNG at the surface

T_S : Bulk liquid temperature [K]   [K]↑

U : Vector of velocity [m/s]

λ : Thermal conductivity [W/mK]

λ_r : Latent heat of boil-off of LNG [J/kg]

μ : Viscosity [Pa·s]

ρ : Density [kg/m^3]

α : Subscript, refers to phase α

INTRODUCTION

LNG (Liquefied Natural Gas) storage tank is the essential facility of LNG receiving terminals in city gas industries. The density difference is a key issue to be considered whether or not LNG can safely be stored in LNG tanks. When a storage tank containing LNG is further filled with different-density LNG, stratification[1] may occur. It occasionally results in rollover[1] accompanied by a sudden release of large amounts of BOG (Boil off Gas), which causes rapid tank-pressure rise and sometimes damage to the tank. Since the rollover incident at LaSpezia LNG terminal in 1971, this phenomenon has been intensively investigated by experiments[2] and modeling for decades. However, there are few studies on tank filling procedures based on CFD (Computational Fluid Dynamics). Today, with an increase in the amount of LNG imports, especially by spot trading, it's becoming harder to store different-origin LNG in separate tanks. That's why a review of criteria for safely receiving of different-density LNG is strongly needed, which makes LNG terminal operations safer and more flexible, as well as reducing huge LNG storage costs. In this paper, we study on tank filling procedures with different-density LNG by using CFD simulation, with the assistance of CFX, a general purpose CFD software for heat transfer and fluid flow analysis by ANSYS Inc.

WHAT'S TANK FILLING OPERATION?

Figure 1 shows typical filling facilities of LNG storage tank. A tank commonly has two types of filling nozzles, top and bottom. Choice of filling point depends on whether the cargo LNG is more or less dense than the LNG already in the tank (the heel).

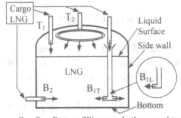

B_{1L}, B_{1T}: Bottom filling nozzle (In-ground tank)
B_2: Bottom filling nozzle (Above-ground tank)
T_1: Top filling nozzle
T_2: Top filling nozzle (Ring type)

Figure 1 Filling facilities of LNG tank

Basically, bottom filling of lighter LNG and top filling of heavier LNG are recommended. It's known that main factors that affect stratification are the choice of nozzle, the initial density difference, the depth of the heel and the filling rate.

MATHEMATICAL MODEL

We have an interest in the mixing behavior of two kinds of different-density LNG in a vertical cylindrical tank. To develop a numerical model of this liquid-liquid system, Eulerian-Eulerian Homogeneous Multiphase option of CFX is used. In this option, with the exception of volume fraction, a common flow field is shared by all fluids as well as other relevant fields such as temperature and turbulence.

Equations
Governing equations are as follows.
Continuity equation:

$$\frac{\partial}{\partial t}(r_\alpha \rho_\alpha) + \nabla \bullet (r_\alpha \rho_\alpha \mathbf{U}) = S_{MS\alpha} \quad (1)$$

where $\sum_{\alpha=1}^{N_L} r_\alpha = 1$ $\qquad$ (2)

N_P =2, for the cargo LNG and the heel.
No interphase mass transfer is assumed.
Momentum equation:

$$\frac{\partial}{\partial t}(\rho \mathbf{U}) + \nabla \bullet (\rho \mathbf{U} \otimes \mathbf{U} - \mu(\nabla \mathbf{U} + (\nabla \mathbf{U})^T)) = \mathbf{S}_M - \nabla p \quad (3)$$

where $\rho = \sum_{\alpha=1}^{N_P} r_\alpha \rho_\alpha$ $\qquad$ (4)

$$\mu = \sum_{\alpha=1}^{N_P} r_\alpha \mu_\alpha \qquad (5)$$

Newtonian fluid is assumed. As the interphase transfer terms have all cancelled out, Eq.(3) is essentially a single phase transport equation, with variable density and viscosity.
Thermal energy equation:

$$\frac{\partial}{\partial t}(r_\alpha \rho_\alpha h_\alpha) + \nabla \bullet (r_\alpha(\rho_\alpha \mathbf{U} h_\alpha - \lambda_\alpha \nabla T)) = Q_\alpha + S_\alpha \quad (6)$$

Compression work is neglected.

Turbulence model

Standard $k - \varepsilon$ turbulence model is used. In this model, μ in Eq.(3) is written by $\mu = \mu_l + \mu_t$, while λ_a in Eq.(6) by $\lambda_a = \lambda_{la} + \lambda_{ta}$, where subscript l refers to laminar, t to turbulent. μ_t is determined by $k - \varepsilon$ model, while λ_{ta} is given by $\lambda_{ta} = \mu_t C_{pa} / P_{rta}$, where P_{rta} is Turbulent Prandtl number.

Buoyancy

Buoyancy caused by the density difference is essential in this model. For buoyancy calculations, a source term is added to the momentum equations as follows:

$$S_M = (\rho - \rho_{ref})\mathbf{g} \tag{7}$$

where ρ_{ref} is the reference density.

Physical properties

Most LNG is composed of CH_4, C_2H_6, C_3H_8, C_4H_{10}, C_5H_{12} and N_2. On condition that p_0 is constant, each LNG is assumed as a pure substance of which all physical properties are constant, except for ρ_a (Eq.(8)), λ_r (Eq.(9)) and T_b (Eq.(10)).

$$\rho_a = a_a T + b_a \tag{8}$$
$$\lambda_r = c T_b + d \tag{9}$$
$$T_b = e r_a + f \tag{10}$$

where a_a, b_a, c, d, e and f are constant.

Boundary conditions

The liquid surface is assumed to be free-slip wall, while bottom and side-wall are no-slip. As liquid becomes deeper while filling, Moving Boundary option of CFX is used at the surface. The heat fluxes through tank walls, even in well insulated, cause convection and boil-off of the LNG. In this study, both the input heat fluxes and the removed latent heat caused by boil-off are taken into accounted, while the removed vapor mass is neglected. To estimate the rate of boil-off, Hashemi model[3] is used.

Hashemi model:

The boil-off rate m is given by

$$m = k_h C_h A (T_s - T_b)^{4/3} \tag{11}$$

Therefore, the heat flux through the surface caused by boil-off is $m\lambda_r / A$ $[W/m^2]$.

Calculation scheme

For transient term calculations, Second Order Backward Euler option of CFX is used, while for advection term, High Resolution option is used.

EVALUATION OF THE MODEL

In order to evaluate the numerical model for the validity, a test simulation is performed on the condition written below.

Simulation conditions

Tank dimensions:

Capacity: 200,000 $[m^3]$. Diameter: 72 [m]

Operation:

Bottom filling of lighter LNG using nozzle type B_{1L} (See Figure 1). No pumping out.

3-D Mesh statistics:

Element types: Tetra, Wedge, Pyramid
Number of nodes: 62,286
Number of elements: 152,795

Other conditions:

Physical properties and filling conditions are given in Table 1 and 2. Where, ρ_0 , T_0, H and H_0 stand for the initial density, the initial temperature, the height of the LNG

Table 1 Physical properties

Property	Cargo LNG	Heel LNG
ρ [kg/m³] $= aT + b + \rho_0$	a=-1.286 b=109.39	a=-1.147 b=131.38
μ_l [10^{-4}Pa·s]	1.2	1.5
λ_l [W/mK]	0.2	0.2
Cp [kJ/kgK]	3.4	3.0
T_0 [K]	113.85	114.55

Table 2 Filling conditions

Density difference $(\rho - \rho_0)/\rho_0$	0.08
Initial depth H/H_0	0.26
Filling rate [10^3t/h]	11
Time for filling [h]	4.4

and the maximum height of the LNG.

Results

The density contour (Figure 2) shows that the lighter LNG fed by the bottom nozzle reaches the free surface driven by buoyancy, then spreads along the surface, forming a slow convective flow in the tank.

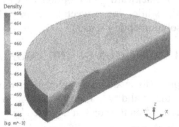

Figure 2 Density contour (30 min)

Comparison with measured data

Comparison of the calculated density profiles with the measured data by the actual filling operation is shown in Figure 3. They agree very well, except for the first half an hour or so. The difference would be caused by the inconsistency between simulation and actual condition such as the filling rate fluctuations in the beginning of the filling. So, it is concluded this modeling is good.

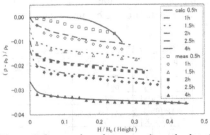

Figure 3 Comparison between the calculated density profile and the measured data

CASE STUDY

To review the main factors which affect stratification, a case study is conducted on the filling of a small tank, installed in a satellite LNG terminal. Five cases of simulation are performed as follows.

Simulation conditions
Tank dimensions:
Capacity: 650 [t]. Diameter: 13 [m].
Operation:
Bottom filling of lighter LNG using nozzle type B_2(Figure 1), with 4[t/h] pumping out.
3-D Mesh statistics:
Element types: Tetra, Wedge, Pyramid
Number of nodes: 56,791
Number of elements: 178,180
Other conditions:
Physical properties and filling conditions are given in Table 3 and 4.

Table 3 Physical properties

Property	LNG-A	LNG-B	Heel LNG
ρ [kg/m³] =aT+b	a=-1.24 b=586.49	a=-1.33 b=573.35	a=-1.24 b=614.42
μ_l [10⁻⁴Pa·s]	1.33	1.22	1.61
λ_t [W/mK]	0.21	0.21	0.21
Cp [kJ/kgK]	3.18	3.44	2.92
T_0 [K]	113.55	112.65	114.69

Table 4 Filling conditions

Case No.	1	2	3	4	5
Filled LNG & Density	A	B	A	A	A
difference $\Delta\rho/\rho_0\times100$	5.7	10.4	5.7	5.7	5.7
Initial depth [m]	5	5	8	5	5
Filling rate [t/min]	0.6	0.6	0.6	0.2	0.6
Time for filling [min]	35	35	35	35	75

Results and discussion

The volume fraction contour (Figure 4) and the transient volume fraction profiles at the tank center (Figure 5) indicate that buoyancy-driven flow governs the mixing, and the profile becomes nearly stable soon after the filling. Figure 6 shows the transient density difference of each case. Here, let FDD be the final density difference, that is to say the density difference at the end of the filling operation that will directly be related to stratification. Case 1 is the bench mark to be compared with others. The

figure indicates,
(1) Larger initial density difference leads to larger FDD.
(2) Deeper heel leads to less FDD.
(3) Lower filling rate leads to less FDD.
(4) Longer filling leads to larger FDD.
(5) After the filling, the density difference either remains nearly stable or slowly decreases.

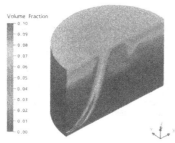

Figure 4 Volume fraction contour of lighter LNG (Case 3, 10 min)

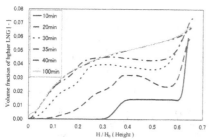

Figure 5 Transient volume fraction profiles at the tank center (Case 3)

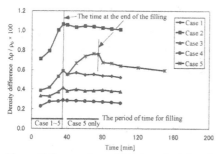

Figure 6 Comparison of the transient density difference of each case at the tank center

These results demonstrate that FDD depends on the initial density difference, the initial depth of the heel and the filling rate. If stratification occurs, the profiles of both volume fraction and density appear to be like step functions. So in practice, it is necessary to predict whether the existing profiles are likely to lead to stratification or not, with heat input to the LNG, even if they don't look like steps at present.

CONCLUSIONS

Tank filling procedures with different-density LNG are studied by CFD simulation. A numerical model is developed, and verified by the measured data. A case study on the filling of a small tank indicates that the final density difference (FDD) depends on the initial density difference, the initial depth of the heel and the filling rate. It is concluded that this CFD simulation method is effective in establishing safety guidelines to avoid stratification in cooperation with LNG terminal operation engineers, which makes storage management safer and more flexible. However, further studies are required regarding another types of filling procedures such as heavier LNG filling, not mentioned in this paper. And for those studies, gas-liquid multiphase model may be required. For one thing, BOG above the free surface of the LNG will affect the mixing behavior.

REFERENCES

1. N. Baker, M. Creed, Stratification and Rollover in Liquefied Natural Gas Storage Tanks, Institution of Chemical Engineers Symposium Series, 1995, pp.621-634.
2. A. Kamiya, M. Tashita, Y. Sugawara, An Experimental Study on LNG Rollover Phenomenon, The National Heat Transfer Conference, American Society of Mechanical Engineers, August 1985.
3. H. T. Hashemi and H. R. Wesson, Cut LNG storage costs, Hydrocarbon Processing, August 1971, pp.246-249.

A New BEM Analysis of 2-D Acoustic Fields for Avoiding Fictitious Eigenfrequency Problem

Youri ARAI*, Masataka TANAKA* and Toshiro MATSUMOTO**

*Department of Mechanical Systems Engineering, Shinshu University, Nagano, 380-8553 Japan
(E-mail: youri@artist.shinshu-u.ac.jp)

**Department of Mechanical Science and Engineering, Nagoya University Nagoya, 464-8603 Japan

ABSTRACT

This paper deals with a new boundary element analysis of acoustic fields governed by Helmholtz equation for avoiding the fictitious eigenfrequency problem. It is well known that the solution of external acoustic field by a boundary integral equation without any care is violated when the frequency coincides with a proper one of the internal domain surrounded by external area of interest. This paper proposes a new boundary intergal formulation and its implementation to circumvent the fictitious eigenfrequency problem. In the proposed methodology, two systems of boundary integral equations can be used: One equation is the combined boundary integral equation proposed by Burton - Miller, and the other is the normal derivative of boundary integral equation, multiplied by the same coupling parameter as in the Burton - Miller expression. The proposed approach is implemented, and its effectiveness is demonstrated by comparing the numerical results with those obtained by Burton - Miller approach.

KEYWORDS: Computational Mechanics, Boundary Element Method, Acoustics, Helmhotz Equation, Fictitious Eigenfrequency

INTRODUCTION

In solving an external or internal problem containing the sub-domain by means of boundary integral equation, the numerical solutions are violated at eigenfrequencies of the sub-domain[1][2][3]. It is important to avoid this problem and get an accurate numerical solution. There are some investigations to avoid this problem, e.g. by locating some external points to sub-domain[4], by employing a combined integral equation[5], by using Green's function of a multiply connected domain, etc.

This paper proposes a new boundary element analysis of acoustic fields for avoiding the fictitious eigenfrequency problem. The formulation is limited to 2-D problems, but its extention to 3-D problems is straightforward and will be reprorted in another paper[6]. This approach uses two boundary integral equations depending on the location of the source point when a quadratic boundary element is used for discretization. The effectiveness and validity of the proposed method is demonstrated through numerical computation of some simple examples.

THEORY

As mentioned before, the proposed method uses two kinds of boundary integral equations depending on the location of the source point. One is the combined boundary integral equation by Burton - Miller[5], and the other is normal derivative boundary integral equation multiplied by the same coupling parameter as above. If the combined boundary integral equation is applied to all the nodal points, the fun-

damental solutions which relate two boundary integral equations, that is, the usual boundary integral equation and its normal derivative expression must always be evaluated at all nodal points. The computation of coefficient matrices for the final system of equations is more troublesome than in the proposed method.

In this section, the two boundary integral equations have been derived, and a new technique is proposed to obtain the numerical solution for avoiding the fictitious eigenfrequency problem.

Ordinary Boundary Integral Equation (OBIE)

Under the assumption of time-harmonic vibration with an infinitesimal amplitude, the acoustic fields are governed by the Helmholtz equation[7]:

$$\nabla^2 p(x) + k^2 p(x) + f(x) = 0 \qquad (1)$$

where p is sound pressure, k the wavenumber and f the source term. A boundary integral formulation of the above Helmholtz equation (1) yields after the uniform potential condition is considered, the following boundary integral equation[1]:

$$\int_\Gamma \{q^*(x,y) - Q^*(x,y)\} p(x) \, d\Gamma(x)$$
$$+ \int_\Gamma Q^*(x,y) \{p(x) - p(y)\} \, d\Gamma(x)$$
$$= -i\omega\rho \int_\Gamma p^*(x,y) \, v(x) d\Gamma(x) + I p^*(x^s, y)$$

$$(2)$$

44

where I is the intensity of point sound source, $p^*(x,y)$ the fundamental solution for Helmholtz equation, $q^*(x,y)$ its normal derivative and $Q^*(x,y)$ the normal derivative of fundamental solution for Laplace equation.

Normal Derivative Boundary Integral Equation (NDBIE)

The normal derivative boundary integral equation (NDBIE) is the gradient of Eq. (2) with respect to $n(y)$. Differentiation of Eq. (2) with respect to the coordinates of the source point y and taking into account the uniform gradient condition[8], we obtain

$$\int_\Gamma \left\{\tilde{q}^*(x,y) - \tilde{Q}^*(x,y)\right\} p(x)\, d\Gamma(x)$$

$$+ \int_\Gamma \tilde{Q}^*(x,y)\left\{p(x) - p(y)\right.$$

$$\left. - r_m(x,y)\, p_{,m}(y)\right\} d\Gamma(x)$$

$$= -i\omega\rho \int_\Gamma \left\{\tilde{p}^*(x,y) - \tilde{u}^*(x,y)\right\} v(x) d\Gamma(x)$$

$$- i\omega\rho \int_\Gamma \tilde{u}^*(x,y)\left\{v(x) - n_m(x)\, p_{,m}(y)\right\} d\Gamma(x)$$

$$+ I\tilde{p}^*(x^s, y) \tag{3}$$

where $\tilde{(\,)} = \partial()/\partial n(y)$.

Both Eq. (2) and (3) will fail to yield a unique solution, if the frequency coincides with any eigenfrequency of sub-domains. This is because the integral equations do not satisfy the condition of $p = 0$ in sub-domain.

Burton - Miller proposed a combined boundary integral equation, and proved that the combined boundary integral equation always has the trivial solution $p = 0$ in sub-domain unless the complex coupling parameter α which combines two boundary integral equations does not become Im $(\alpha) \neq 0$. The new method proposed in the present paper, however, does not employ the combined boundary integral equation at all the nodal points. If the source point is located on the middle point of boundary element with quadratic interpolationfunctions, the combined integral equation is used, while if the source point is located on the extreme nodes of the element, Eq. (3) multiplyed with the same coupling parameter as above is used, and vice versa.

Uniqueness of the solution by the proposed method

The proposed method of solution uses either of the two boundary integral equations in the following:

$$-\frac{1}{2}\left\{p(y) + \alpha q(y)\right\}$$

$$+ \int_\Gamma \left\{q^*(x,y) + \alpha \tilde{q}^*(x,y)\right\} p(x)\, d\Gamma(x)$$

$$- \int_\Gamma \left\{p^*(x,y) + \alpha \tilde{p}^*(x,y)\right\} q(x)\, d\Gamma(x) = 0 \tag{4}$$

$$-\frac{1}{2}\alpha q(y) + \alpha \int_\Gamma \tilde{q}^*(x,y)\, p(x)\, d\Gamma(x)$$

$$-\alpha \int_\Gamma \tilde{p}^*(x,y)\, q(x)\, d\Gamma(x) = 0 \tag{5}$$

where α is the complex coupling parameter.

To avoid the fictitious eigenfrequency problem, we now consider the external problem as shown in Fig. 1, and denote an infinite space domain by Ω and its sub-domain by $\bar{\Omega}$. It is now assumed that Eq. (4) is used if the source point y lies on Γ_1, and Eq. (5) is employed if the source point lies on Γ_2.

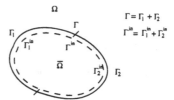

Figure 1   External problem

If the source point y lies in sub-domain $\bar{\Omega}$, Eq. (4) and (5) become

$$\int_\Gamma \left\{q^*(x,y) + \alpha\tilde{q}^*(x,y)\right\} p(x)\, d\Gamma(x)$$

$$= \int_\Gamma \left\{p^*(x,y) + \alpha\tilde{p}^*(x,y)\right\} q(x)\, d\Gamma(x),$$

$$y \text{ in } \bar{\Omega} \tag{6}$$

$$\alpha \int_\Gamma \tilde{q}^*(x,y)\, p(x)\, d\Gamma(x)$$

$$= \alpha \int_\Gamma \tilde{p}^*(x,y)\, q(x)\, d\Gamma(x), \quad y \text{ in } \bar{\Omega} \tag{7}$$

Eq. (6) and (7) would exhibit nonuniqueness, if the left-hand sides of the two equations became identically zero for some $p \neq 0$. To confirm that the proposed method avoids the fictitious eigenfrequency problem, the following two equations should have the trivial solution of $p = 0$.

$$\int_\Gamma \left\{q^*(x,y) + \alpha\tilde{q}^*(x,y)\right\} p(x)\, d\Gamma(x) = 0,$$

$$y \text{ in } \bar{\Omega} \tag{8}$$

$$\alpha \int_\Gamma \tilde{q}^*(x,y)\, p(x)\, d\Gamma(x) = 0 , \quad y \text{ in } \bar{\Omega} \tag{9}$$

45

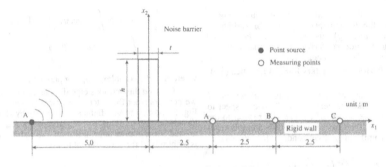

Figure 2 Analysis model

Introducing the potential theorem, a double-layer potential $W(y)$ is defined as

$$W(y) = \int_\Gamma q^*(x,y)\, p(x)\, d\Gamma(x), \quad y \in \Omega, \bar{\Omega}, \Gamma \tag{10}$$

and using this potential, Eq. (8) and (9) become

$$W(y) + \alpha \frac{\partial W(y)}{\partial n_y} = 0, \quad y \text{ in } \bar{\Omega} \tag{11}$$

$$\alpha \frac{\partial W(y)}{\partial n_y} = 0, \quad y \text{ in } \bar{\Omega} \tag{12}$$

A simply connected boundary Γ^{in} is defined inside the real boundary Γ (see Fig. 1), and the source point y lies on Γ^{in}. Then, Green's second identity can be applied to W and its complex conjugate $\bar{W}$, that is,

$$\int_{\Gamma_1^{in}} \left\{ \frac{\partial W(y)}{\partial n_y} \bar{W}(y) - W(y) \frac{\partial \bar{W}(y)}{\partial n_y} \right\} d\Gamma(y)$$
$$+ \int_{\Gamma_2^{in}} \left\{ \frac{\partial W(y)}{\partial n_y} \bar{W}(y) - W(y) \frac{\partial \bar{W}(y)}{\partial n_y} \right\} d\Gamma(y)$$
$$= 0 \tag{13}$$

If the complex coupling parameter is $|\alpha| \neq 0$, then $\partial W(y)/\partial n_y = \partial \bar{W}(y)/\partial n_y = 0$ on Γ_2 from Eq. (12). By considering the relationship with W and $\partial W/\partial n_y$ from Eq. (11), and writing α explicitly in real and imaginary components, Eq. (13) finally becomes

$$2i\mathrm{Im}(\alpha) \int_{\Gamma_1^{in}} \left| \frac{\partial W(y)}{\partial n_y} \right|^2 d\Gamma(y) = 0 \tag{14}$$

Eq. (14) yields $\partial W/\partial n_y = 0$, unless the imaginary part of the coupling parameter $\mathrm{Im}(\alpha)$ is not zero. Due to the definition of W, p from Eq. (11) has the trivial solution (i.e. zero). It may be concluded, therfore, that the proposed method avoids the fictitious eigenfrequency problem.

NUMERICAL ANALYSIS

To demonstrate the versatility of the proposed method for avoiding the fictitious eigenfrequency problem, we now consider a two-dimensional model shown in Fig. 2 in which a point sound source is located at point A. It is assumed that the infinite horizontal plane and the noise barrier are subject to the rigid condition in which the particle velocity $v = 0$. Furthermore, it is assumed that the intensity of point sound source A is $(2.0, 0.0)$ [Pa], the sound speed $C_0 = 340$ [m/s], and mass density 1.2 [kg/m^3]. It is noted that symmetry with respect to x_1 axis (the infinite horizontal plane) is taken into account, whereas symmetry with respect to x_2 axis is not considered. Thickness of noise barrier is given $t = 0.34$ [m] and height $h = 3.0$ [m]. The values of frequency have been taken from 1 [Hz] to 2 [kHz] with an interval 0.5 [Hz]. Three evaluation points of sound pressure are located on the horizontal ground as shown in Fig. 2. The surface of noise barrier is discreted by means of the quadratic element with length 0.02 [m] uniformly, and the total number of elements is 317. Sound pressure is calculated at each measuring point, and an average value is taken, then finally transformed to the Sound Pressure Level (SPL). The complex coupling parameter is defined as i/k (k is the wavenumber) from the literature [9].

Fig. 3 shows the numerical results obtained by applying OBIE. Numerical results indicate that if there is no care about the fictitious eigenfrequency problem, then the results are violated at several frequencies as shown in Fig. 3. Figures 4 and 5 show the numerical results obtained by using the Burton - Miller boundary integral equation for all the nodes and those by the proposed method, respectively. It can be seen that both the methods can avoid the fictitious eigenfrequency problem and always provide accurate results.

46

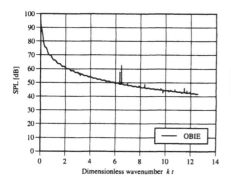

Figure 3   Numerical results obtained by OBIE

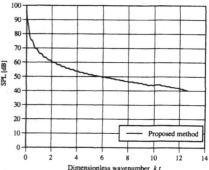

Figure 5   Numerical results obtained by proposed method

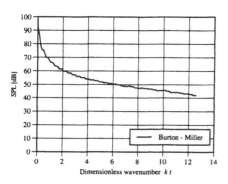

Figure 4   Numerical results obtained by Burton - Miller equation used at all the nodes

CONCLUSION

The new boundary element method for the solution of acoustic problems governed by Helmholtz equation has been proposed, and its implementation has been presented. The proposed method can always give accurate solutions circumventing the fictitious eigenfrequency problem similarly to Burton - Miller approach. The proposed method can calculate the system matrix easier than the Burton - Miller approach when it is used at all the nodal points. The proposed method is effective for the numerical solution of the acoustic problems with higher frequency and complicated domain shape, because accurate analysis of such acoustic fields requires a larger number of elements and nodal points.

References

[1] Tanaka, M. et al., *Boundary Element Method*, Baifukan, (1991).

[2] Kobayashi, S. et al., *Wave Analysis and Boundary Element Method*, Kyoto University Press Online, (2000).

[3] Chen, I. A. et al., Analytical Study and Numerical Experiments for Radiation and Scattering Problems Using the CHIE Method, *Journal of Sound and Vibration*, Vol.248, pp.809–828, (2001).

[4] Schenck, H. A., Improved Integral Formulation for Acoustic Radiation Problems, *Journal of the Acoustical Society of Americal*, Vol.44, pp.41-58, (1968).

[5] Burton, A. J. & Miller, G. F., The Application of Integral Equation Methods to the Numerical Solution of Some Exterior Boundary-Value Problems, *Journal of Proceedings of the Royal Society of London, Series A*, Vol.322, pp.201–210, (1971).

[6] Arai, Y. et al., A New Boundary Element Analysis of 3-D Acoustic Fields Avoiding the Fictitious Eigenfrequency Problem, *Transactions of the Japan Society of Mechanical Engineers, Series C* (submitted)

[7] Itimiya, R., *Acoustic Engineering of Mechanics*, Corona Publishing Co.,Ltd., (1992).

[8] Arai, M. et al., Highly Accurate Analysis by Boundary Element Method Based on Uniform Gradient Condition (Application for Formulation of Classical Potential Problem), *Transactions of the Japan Society of Mechanical Engineers, Series A*, Vol.61, No.581, pp.161–168, (1995).

[9] Cunfare, K. A. & Koopmann, G., A Boundary Element Analysis for Acoustic Radiation Valid for All Wavenumbers, *Journal of the Acoustical Society of America*, Vol.85, No.1, pp.39–48, (1989).

Theoretical Study of Resonant Tunneling Characteristics in Rectanglar Single Barrier Strctures with Outer Wells

Hiroaki Yamamoto, Masamichi Horita, and Hiromichi Nezu

Dept. of Information Science, University of Fukui

Fukui 910-8507, JAPAN

(E-mail:yamamoto@i1nws1.fuis.fukui-u.ac.jp)

ABSTRACT

It is found out that the resonant tunneling occurs in a rectangular single-barrier structure with asymmetrical outer wells : Usually, some tunneling probability below unity transmission exists in a single-barrier structure. Analytical expressions of the tunneling transmission coefficient and the resonance condition have been derived. It is believed that the studied structure will be useful in designing resonant tunneling structure or for fabricating ohmic contacts without metal layer.

KEY WORDS: resonant tunneling, resonance condition, novel single-barrier structure

Introduction

During these thirty years resonant tunneling phenomena have been carried out both theoretically and experimentally, extensively for the double-barrier structures[1-6] which have been a basis for understanding and utilizing resonant tunneling effects. The triple-barrier structures have been interested because of the coupled well characterictics[7,8] and the quadruple-barrier structures because of having two independent resonance conditions [9,10]. However, it seems to be overlooked that a rectangular single-barrier system has a resonance condition which leads to unity transmission coefficient, if an outer well is added to a single barrier structure both in front and behind.

In this work, the theoretical study of the resonant tunneling in the rectangular single-barrier with asymmetrical outer wells has been carried out by taking into account the effective mass difference in each region. We have derived the analytical expressions for the tunneling transmission coefficient and the resonance condition. It has been also obtained that the studied structures show about a score femto-second dwell time and a favorable current density for low DC vias voltages, which is promising for designing resonant tunneling structures or for fabricating ohmic contacts between semiconductor devices without metal layer.

Tunneling Transmission Coefficient and Resonance Condition

As a model potential, we consider the rectangular single-barrier structure with asymmetrical outer wells as shown in Fig. 1. The six regions are specified by the coordinates $(x_1, x_2, x_3, x_4,$ and $x_5)$: The well region is described by the even number (2 and 4). The structure is composed of the left-hand side well with the width L_{w1} and the potential V_{w1}, the central barrier with width L_b and potential height V_b, the right-hand side well with the width L_{w2} and the potential V_{w2}, and the region

1 and the region 5. The energy origin is taken at the conduction band edge of the region 1 material.

We assume that an electron with energy E is incident from the left and transmits to the right along the x-direction. Then the wave function for the electron in the j-th region ($j=1, 2, \cdots, 5$) is written in the following form.

$$\psi_j(x) = A_j \exp(ik_jx) + B_j \exp(-ik_jx) \ ,$$
(1)

where we have

$$k_j = [2m_j(E - V_j)]^{1/2}/\hbar \ ,$$
(2)

m_j and V_j are the electron effective mass and the potential value in j-th region, respectively, and $\hbar(\equiv h/2\pi)$ is the reduced Planck constant. Using the transfer matrix method, we derive the following transmission coefficient:

$$T_{1aw} = [1 + (\Lambda_1^2 + \Lambda_2^2)/(T_1T_2T_3)]^{-1} \ ,$$
(3)

where

$$\Lambda_1 = [R_1^{\frac{1}{2}} + R_3^{\frac{1}{2}}]\cos[(\Phi_{w1} + \Phi_{w2})/2]$$
$$+ [R_2^{\frac{1}{2}} + R_1^{\frac{1}{2}}R_2^{\frac{1}{2}}R_3^{\frac{1}{2}}]$$
$$\times \cos[(\Phi_{w1} - \Phi_{w2})/2],$$
(4)

$$\Lambda_2 = [R_1^{\frac{1}{2}} - R_3^{\frac{1}{2}}]\sin[(\Phi_{w1} + \Phi_{w2})/2]$$
$$- [R_2^{\frac{1}{2}} - R_1^{\frac{1}{2}}R_2^{\frac{1}{2}}R_3^{\frac{1}{2}}]$$
$$\times \sin[(\Phi_{w1} - \Phi_{w2})/2].$$
(5)

$R_1 = 1 - T_1$, $R_2 = 1 - T_2$, $R_3 = 1 - T_3$: T_1, T_2, and T_3 are the (tunneling) transmission coefficients between region 1 and region 2, between 2 and 4, and between 4 and 5, respectively. They are given as follows:

$$T_1 = [1 + (k_1m_2 - k_2m_1)^2/4k_1k_2m_1m_2]^{-1},$$
(6)

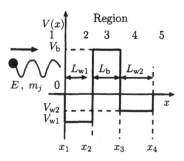

Figure 1: Potential energy diagram of asymmetrical rectangular single-barrier system.

$$T_2 = [1 + (k_2m_4 - k_4m_2)^2/4k_2k_4m_2m_4$$
$$+ (k_2^2m_3^2 + \kappa^2m_2^2)(k_4^2m_3^2 + \kappa^2m_4^2)$$
$$\times (\sinh \kappa L_b)^2/4k_2k_4\kappa^2m_2m_3^2m_4]^{-1} \ ,$$
(7)

$$T_3 = [1 + (k_4m_5 - k_5m_4)^2/4k_4k_5m_4m_5]^{-1} .$$
(8)

The characteristic phase differences, Φ_{w1} and Φ_{w2}, are given as follows:

$$\Phi_{w1} = 2k_2L_{w1} + \phi_1 + \phi_2 + \pi/2 \ ,$$
(9)

$$\Phi_{w2} = 2k_4L_{w2} + \phi_1 - \phi_2 + \pi/2 \ ,$$
(10)

where

$$\kappa = -ik_3 = [2m_3(V_3 - E)]^{1/2}/\hbar \ .$$
(11)

Then we derive the resonance condition which leads to the unity transmission coefficient, i.e., $T_{1aw} = 1$: Both $\Lambda_1 = 0$ and $\Lambda_2 = 0$ are required simultaneously in Eq. (1). Therefore, the resonance condition is rewritten as

$$\tan^2 \frac{\Phi_{w1}}{2} = [R_{13} + 2(R_1R_2R_3)^{\frac{1}{2}}][R_{13} - 2R_3^{\frac{1}{2}}]$$
$$/[R_{13} - 2R_2^{\frac{1}{2}}][R_{13} - 2R_1^{\frac{1}{2}}]$$
(12)

and

$$\tan^2 \frac{\Phi_{w1}}{2} = [R_{13} + 2(R_1 R_2 R_3)^{\frac{1}{2}}][R_{13} - 2R_1^{\frac{1}{2}}]$$
$$/[R_{13} - 2R_2^{\frac{1}{2}}][R_{13} - 2R_3^{\frac{1}{2}}],$$

(13)

where

$$R_{13} = R_1^{\frac{1}{2}} + R_2^{\frac{1}{2}} + R_3^{\frac{1}{2}} - R_1^{\frac{1}{2}} R_2^{\frac{1}{2}} R_3^{\frac{1}{2}}.$$

(14)

When the structure has symmetrical outer wells, we obtain the transmission coefficient and the resonance condition: $\Phi_{w1}=\Phi_{w2}$, $\phi=\phi_1$, $\phi_2=0$, and $T_1=T_3$. The transmision coefficient T_{1sw} is given by

$$T_{1sw} = [1 + \Lambda^2/T_1^2 T_2^2]^{1/2}.$$

(15)

Consequently, the resonance condition is $\Lambda = 0$, i.e.,

$$\Lambda = 2R_1^{\frac{1}{2}} \cos(\Phi_w) + R_2^{\frac{1}{2}}(1 + R_1) = 0,$$

(16)

where

$$\Phi_w = 2k_2 L_{w1} + \phi + \pi/2.$$

(17)

Thus, we have derived the tunneling transmission coefficient and the resonance condition: the right hand side of Eq.(12) and Eq.(13) is not negative.

Tunneling Transmission Characteristics

We investigate here the energy variation of the transmission coefficient in the rectangular single-barrier structure with asymmetrical outer wells. At first, let us design a resonant tunneling single-barrier structure by using the resonance conditions, (12) and (13), which determine the values of the relevant parameters.

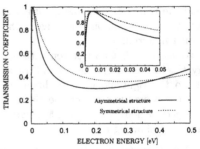

Figure 2: Transmission coefficient versus electron energy ($E = 0.005$ [eV], V_b =0.3 [eV], $V_{w1} = -0.2$[eV], $V_{w2} = -0.1$[eV], $L_{w1} = 1.28$[nm], $L_{w2} = 2.16$[nm]).

The procedure is as follows:
1. We select the materials for the system: The values of the potential and the effective mass are determined.
2. We specify the resonance energy, E, such a way that it is lower than the potential height V_b.
3. The values of the outer well layers, the left-hand well width L_{w1} and the right-hand well width L_{w2}, are determined by using the conditions, (12) and (13).

As a typical example, let us construct the GaAs/In$_{0.2}$Ga$_{0.8}$As/Al$_{0.3}$Ga$_{0.7}$As/ In$_{0.1}$Ga$_{0.9}$As/GaAs system according to the above procedures.
1. We specify $V_b= 0.3$ [eV], $V_{w1}=-0.2$ [eV], $V_{w2}=-0.1$[eV], and $m_1=m_5=0.063m_0$ [kg] for GaAs, $m_2=0.0558m_0$[kg] for In$_{0.2}$Ga$_{0.8}$-As, $m_3 = 0.0891m_0$ [kg] for Al$_{0.3}$Ga$_{0.7}$As, $m_4 = 0.0594m_0$ [kg] for In$_{0.1}$Ga$_{0.9}$As. Here m_0 is the free electron mass.
2. For example, we select a resonance energy at $E=0.005$ [eV].
3. The values, $L_b=2.0$[nm], $L_{w1}=1.28$[nm], and $L_{w2}=2.16$[nm], are obtained from (12) and (13).

The energy variation of the transmission coefficient is shown by the solid line for $E = 0.005$[eV] in Fig. 2. It is seen that unity resonance occurs at $E = 0.005$ [eV] as expected. The energy variation of the transmission coefficient for the symmetrical single-barrier structure with outer wells is shown by the broken line simultaneously. It is seen that the resonant transmission spectrum of the asymmetrical structure is sharper than that of the symmetrical one, though the former characteristic is similar to the latter one both qualitatively and quantitatively.

Probability Density and Dwell Time

Here let us calculate the probability density and the dwell time for the electron in the asymmetrical single-barrier structure with outer wells. The probability density for the electron wave function at the unity resonance state ($E = 0.005\,[\text{eV}]$) is depicted by the solid line in Fig. 3: the same values are used as in Fig. 2. The potential energy diagram of the single-barrier structure with outer wells is shown by the broken line. The value of the probability density shows under unity, which is similar to that in the quantum well system as shown in Fig. 4. This phenomenon expects short dwell time to us because the electron can pass fast through the three regions between region 2 and region 4 in Fig. 3.

Next, we calculate the dwell time [11] by assuming that the amplitude of the incident wave is unity. It is seen in Fig. 3 that both the amplitude of the incident wave and the amplitude of the transmitted wave are unity, and that the confining in the well region containing the barrier is not strong: this phenomenon is different from that for the usual double-barrier structure. The energy variation of the dwell time for the asymmetrical single barrier structure is shown in Fig. 5. The peak value appears near the resonance energy and is about 23[fs], which is favorable and satisfactorily fast as high speed electron device behavior.

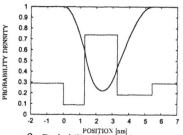

Figure 3: Probability density in asymmetrical single-barrier system.

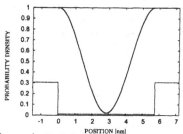

Figure 4: Probability density for unity transmission (at $E = 0.005\,[\text{eV}]$) in the quantum well system.

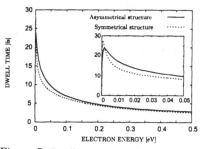

Figure 5: Dwell time versus electron energy in asymmetrical single-barrier system.

Current Density

In this section we calculate the current density for the studied structure whose size is determined in the above section. We assume for treating the idealized case that the effect of the space charge built up in the well is neglected, that the voltage drop occurs only across the three regions (i.e., from the region 2 to the region

4), and that the conduction band edge of the regions 1 and 5 is flat with zero field. The voltage drop in the left hand side well, that in the right hand one, and that in the barrier region, (i.e., the values of the voltage drop on the three regions), are calculated by taking into account the difference in each dielectric permittivity. Moreover, we assume only the tunneling current and use the equation for current density in the reference[1]. It is assumed at 77K that the donor density in the region 1 is 10^{23} [m^{-3}] and the Fermi level is $E_F \approx 0.004$ [eV] above the conduction band. The current density versus the applied volltage is shown in Fig. 6. It is seen from the curve that comparatively large current density is obtaind at very low voltage, which is favorable, for example, for fabricating ohmic contacts without metal layer.

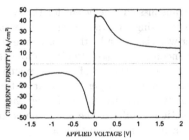

Figure 6: Current density versus applied dc voltage in single-barrier system.

for fabricating ohmic contacts without metal layer for connecting semiconductor devices.

Discussion and Conclusion

We have obtained the analytical expression for the transmission coefficient and the resonance condition in the asymmetrical single-barrier system with outer wells, and shown that this structure leads to short dwell time. Here the dwell time method is employed for estimating the tunneling time. It is confirmed that both the asymmetrical structure and the symmetrical one have the resonance state even when the electron energy is lower than the barrier potential. This is favorable for fabricating devices because in general asymmetrical structure is obtained even if we expect to make up a perfect symmetrical structure. It is obtained, moreover, that the structure studied leads to short dwell time and shows the high current density for low applied voltages.

It is believed that the studied single-barrier structure with asymmetrical outer wells may be favorable and useful in designing resonant tunneling structure and

REFERRENCE

1. R. Tsu and L. Esaki, Appl. Phys. Lett. **22**, 562 (1973).
2. L.L. Chang, L. Esaki, and R. Tsu, Appl. Phys. Lett. **24**, 593 (1974).
3. B. Ricco and M.Ya. Azbel, Phys. Rev. B, **29**, 1970 (1984).
4. H.Yamamoto, Appl. Phys. A **42**, 245 (1987).
5. X.D. Zhao, H. Yamamoto, and K. Taniguchi, Appl. Phys. A, **60**, 369 (1995).
6. K. Miyamoto and H. Yamamoto, J.Appl. Phys. **84**, 311 (1998).
7. M.C. Payne, J. Phys. C **18**, L879 (1985).
8. H. Yamamoto, Y. Kanie, and K. Taniguchi, Phys. Status Solidi B **167**, 571 (1991).
9. H. Yamamoto, H. Sano, Y. Kanie, and K. Taniguchi, Superlattices and Microstructures **13**, 29 (1993).
10. T. Waho, S. Koch, and T. Mizutani, Superlattices and Microstructures **16**, 205 (1994).
11. e.g., A.P. Jauho, "Hot Carriers in Semiconductor Nanostructures", edited by J. Shah (Academic, 1992) p.121.

Nonlinear Analysis of Large Deflections of Isotropic Rectangular Clamped Plate using Hybrid Method

Yen-Liang Yeh[1], Ming-Jyi Jang[2] and Cheng. Chi. Wang[3]

Department of Automation and Contral[1,2], (E-mail:yehyl@cc.fec.edu.tw)

Department of Mechanical Engineering[3],

Far East College, Tainan, Taiwan, 744, Republic of China

Abstract

This paper analyses the large deflections of an isotropic rectangular clamped thin plate. A hybrid method which combines the finite difference method and the differential transformation method is employed to reduce the partial differential equations describing the large deflections of the plate to a set of algebraic equations. The simulation results indicate that significant errors are present in the numerical results obtained for the deflections of the plate in the transient state when a step force is applied. The magnitude of the numerical error is found to reduce, and the deflection of the plate to converge, as the number of sub-domains considered in the solution procedure increases. The load-deflection curves converge as the aspect ratio of the plate is reduced. The current modeling results confirm the applicability of the proposed hybrid method to the solution of the large deflections of a rectangular isotropic clamped plate.

Keywords: Differential transformation, Plate, Large deflection, Finite difference method

Introduction

Plates are employed in many engineering structures and thin-walled structural components play a fundamental role in a diverse range of engineering applications. Accordingly, the large deflections of thin elastic plates have attracted considerable attention. In recent years, researchers have employed various numerical methods to characterize the distinct dynamic behaviors of these components as they undergo large deflections. These numerical methods include the double Fourier series, the generalized Fourier series, the perturbation technique, Galerkin's method, Ritz's method, and similarity methods [2]. When these methods are used to solve three-dimensional partial differential equations, the series coefficients must be obtained by performing term-by-term integration of the corresponding solution series. However, when the system is complex, this integration operation becomes difficult. When the finite differential method is applied to the solution of partial differential equations, the truncation errors must be carefully controlled. When the finite difference method is used to solve initial value problems, accumulative truncation errors may also arise. Therefore, the finite difference method is generally applied to the solution of static systems.

The differential transformation method was first applied in the engineering domain by Zhou [5] and is commonly used for the solution of electric circuit problems. The differential transformation method is based on the Taylor series expansion and constructs an analytical solution in the form of a polynomial. The traditional high-order Taylor series method requires symbolic computation. However, the differential transformation method obtains a polynomial series solution by means of an iterative procedure. The finite difference method expands the space variable into separated coordinates and the differential transformation method can then be used to solve the initial value problems of all the coordinates simultaneously [3, 4]. When solving initial value problems, the truncation error produced by the finite difference method is greater than that produced by the differential transformation method. Accordingly, this paper develops a hybrid method which combines the differential transformation method and the finite difference method. The proposed method has the advantage that the solution can be obtained using a simple iterative procedure.

The objective of this study is to investigate and characterize the large deflection behavior of an isotropic rectangular clamped plate using the developed hybrid method. In order to investigate the accuracy of the solutions, the large deflections of the plate are compared for various numerical parameters, including the number of sub-domains specified in the solution procedure, the aspect ratio of the plate, and the lateral force applied.

Mathematical model of plate

This study considers large deflections of the rectangular plate shown in Figure 1. The plate has a thickness "h" and edge lengths "a" and "b" in the x- and y-directions, respectively. Let O_{xyz} be a Cartesian coordinate system which lies in the mid-plane of the plate and has its origin at the corner. The lateral loading on the

plate is denoted by $p(t)$. Under these conditions, the equations of motion for the plate (Timoshenko and Woinowsky-Krieger [1]) are given by:

$$\frac{\partial^2 u}{\partial x^2} + d_1 \frac{\partial^2 u}{\partial y^2} + d_2 \frac{\partial^2 v}{\partial x \partial y} = -\frac{\partial w}{\partial x}(\frac{\partial^2 w}{\partial x^2} + d_1 \frac{\partial^2 w}{\partial y^2}) - d_2 \frac{\partial w}{\partial y}\frac{\partial^2 w}{\partial x \partial y} \quad (1)$$

$$\frac{\partial^2 v}{\partial x^2} + d_1 \frac{\partial^2 v}{\partial y^2} + d_2 \frac{\partial^2 u}{\partial x \partial y} = -\frac{\partial w}{\partial y}(\frac{\partial^2 w}{\partial y^2} + d_1 \frac{\partial^2 w}{\partial x^2}) - d_2 \frac{\partial w}{\partial x}\frac{\partial^2 w}{\partial x \partial y} \quad (2)$$

$$DV^4 w + \rho h \frac{\partial^2 w}{\partial t^2} + \delta \frac{\partial w}{\partial t} = p(t) + \frac{Eh}{1-\mu^2}[(\frac{\partial u}{\partial x} + \frac{1}{2}(\frac{\partial w}{\partial x})^2)(\frac{\partial^2 w}{\partial x^2} + \mu \frac{\partial^2 w}{\partial y^2})$$
$$+ (\frac{\partial v}{\partial y} + \frac{1}{2}(\frac{\partial w}{\partial x})^2)(\frac{\partial^2 w}{\partial y^2} + \mu \frac{\partial^2 w}{\partial x^2}) + (1-\mu)\frac{\partial^2 w}{\partial x \partial y}(\frac{\partial u}{\partial y} + \frac{\partial v}{\partial x} + \frac{\partial w}{\partial x}\frac{\partial w}{\partial y})] \quad (3)$$

where: $d_1 = \frac{1-\mu}{2}$, $d_2 = \frac{1+\mu}{2}$, $D = \frac{Eh^3}{12(1-\mu^2)}$, and

$\nabla^4 = \frac{\partial^4}{\partial x^4} + 2\frac{\partial^4}{\partial x^2 \partial y^2} + \frac{\partial^4}{\partial y^4}$. Furthermore, $w(x,y,t)$ is the deflection of the neutral plane of the plate, $u(x,y,t)$ and $v(x,y,t)$ are the displacements of the neutral plane of the plate in the x- and y-directions, respectively. Additionally, ρ is the density of the plate material, h is the plate thickness, and E, μ, and δ are the Young's modulus, Poisson ratio, and damping coefficient of the plate material, respectively.

The current study assumes that clamped and immovable boundary conditions are imposed at the plate edges. Under these conditions, the deflection of the neutral plane, w, satisfies the following boundary conditions:

$$w = \frac{\partial w}{\partial x} = u = v = 0 \text{ at } x = 0, a \quad (4)$$

$$w = \frac{\partial w}{\partial y} = u = v = 0 \text{ at } y = 0, b \quad (5)$$

In order to reduce the order of the system dynamic equation, this study introduces the following velocity function:

$$g = \frac{\partial w}{\partial t} \quad (6)$$

The system dynamic equation is then given by:

$$\frac{\partial w}{\partial t} = g \quad (7)$$

$$DV^4 w + \rho h \frac{\partial g}{\partial t} + \delta g = p(t) + \frac{Eh}{1-\mu^2}[(\frac{\partial u}{\partial x} + \frac{1}{2}(\frac{\partial w}{\partial x})^2)(\frac{\partial^2 w}{\partial x^2} + \mu \frac{\partial^2 w}{\partial y^2})$$
$$+ (\frac{\partial v}{\partial y} + \frac{1}{2}(\frac{\partial w}{\partial y})^2)(\frac{\partial^2 w}{\partial y^2} + \mu \frac{\partial^2 w}{\partial x^2}) + (1-\mu)\frac{\partial^2 w}{\partial x \partial y}(\frac{\partial u}{\partial y} + \frac{\partial v}{\partial x} + \frac{\partial w}{\partial x}\frac{\partial w}{\partial y})] \quad (8)$$

Taking the differential transform of the

system equation with respect to time, it can be shown that:

$$\frac{k+1}{H}W(x,y,k+1) = G(x,y,k) \qquad (9)$$

$$(10)$$

$$\frac{k+1}{H}G(x.y.k+1) = \frac{P(k)}{\rho h} - \frac{\delta}{\rho h}G(x.y.k) - \frac{D}{\rho h}\nabla^4 W(x.y.k) + \frac{Eh}{1-\mu^2}[(\frac{\partial U(x.y.k)}{\partial x}$$
$$+\frac{1}{2}(\frac{\partial W(x.y.k)}{\partial x})^1 \chi \frac{\partial^2 W(x.y.k)}{\partial x^2} + \mu \frac{\partial^2 W(x.y.k)}{\partial y^2}) + (\frac{\partial V(x.y.k)}{\partial y} +$$
$$\frac{1}{2}(\frac{\partial W(x.y.k)}{\partial x})^1 \chi \frac{\partial^2 W(x.y.k)}{\partial y^2} + \frac{\partial^2 W(x.y.k)}{\partial x^2})$$
$$+(1-\mu)\frac{\partial^2 W(x.y.k)}{\partial x \partial y}(\frac{\partial U(x.y.k)}{\partial y} + \frac{\partial V(x.y.k)}{\partial x} + \frac{\partial W(x.y.k)}{\partial x}\frac{\partial W(x.y.k)}{\partial y})]$$

where $W(x,y,k)$, $G(x,y,k)$, $U(x,y,k)$ and $V(x,y,k)$ are the differential transforms of $w(x,y,t)$, $g(x,y,t)$, $u(x,y,t)$ and $v(x,y,t)$, respectively.

Taking the fourth-order accurate central finite difference approximation with respect to x and y, the system dynamic equation can be obtained. By applying differential transformation and the finite difference approximation, the associated boundary conditions are transformed to:

$W(1,j,k) = 0$, $W(i,1,k) = 0$,

$W(m-1,j,k) = 0$, $W(i,n-1,k) = 0$ (15)

$U(1,j,k) = 0$, $U(i,1,k) = 0$,

$U(m-1,j,k) = 0$, $U(i,n-1,k) = 0$ (16)

$V(1,j,k) = 0$, $V(i,1,k) = 0$,

$V(m-1,j,k) = 0$, $V(i,n-1,k) = 0$ (17)

$\frac{W(2,j,k)-W(0,j,k)}{2h_x} = 0$, $\frac{W(i,2,k)-W(i,0,k)}{2h_y} = 0$, (18)

$\frac{W(m,j,k)-W(m-2,j,k)}{2h_x} = 0$, $\frac{W(i,n,k)-W(i,n-2,k)}{2h_y} = 0$ (19)

i is the node number of the sub-domain in the x-direction, and j is the node number of the sub-domain in the y-direction.

Simulation results

In investigating the dynamic motion and large deflections of the isotropic rectangular plate, this study initially considered the case of a plate with $\frac{D}{\rho h} = 1$ and $\frac{\delta}{\rho h} = 10$, subjected to a variable lateral load of $\frac{P}{\rho h}$. The dynamic motion and the large deflections were solved using the proposed hybrid method combining the finite difference method and the differential transform method. Simulations were performed with $H=0.01$, $k=5$, $a=1.0$, $b=1.0$, and $\nu = 0.316$. The edges of the plate were divided into ten equal units such that $m=n=11$. It was assumed that the edges of the plate were all clamped and that a lateral step force load of $\frac{P}{\rho h} =100.0$ was applied.

Figure 2 shows the dynamic motion of the center of the plate at x=0.5 and y=0.5. It can be seen that a significant error exists between the present results and those of Chia [2] in the large deflection of the plate. Furthermore, the plate oscillates during the initial transient phase before stabilizing to a steady state deflection of 1.062 at the center of the plate. The steady state deflection result is in reasonable agreement with that of Chia [2] (w=0.9333). Figure 3 illustrates the displacements (w) of the plate in the z-direction. The figure show that the displacement (w) of the plate in the z-direction has axial-symmetry characteristics. These results are consistent with the findings reported by Leissa [7].

In order to investigate the large deflections of the isotropic rectangular clamped plate under a variable lateral force, the lateral force, $\frac{P}{\rho h}$, was increased from 100 to 500 in intervals of 100. The corresponding deflections of the center of the plate are shown in Figure 4. It can be seen that the deflection varies non-linearly with the lateral force. Furthermore, it is apparent that the current deflection results are in good general agreement with those of Chia [2]. It can be seen that the numerical error between the present results and those of Chia [2] increases as the lateral force $\frac{P}{\rho h}$ increases, but reduces as the number of sub-domains increases. In order to investigate the effect of the number of sub-domains on the accuracy of the solution, this study calculated the deflection of the neutral plane of the plate

55

using various values of *m=n*. The corresponding results are presented in Figure 5, in which it can be seen that as the number of sub-domains increases to infinity, the maximum deflection of the plate converges. Specifying 31 sub-domains in the solution procedure, the deflection at the center of the plate is found to be 1.0054.

Figure 6 shows the effect of the aspect ratio (*a/b*) on the maximum deflection of the clamped rectangular plate (*a=1*) under a variable lateral load, $\frac{pa^4}{Eh^4}$. As the aspect ratio is reduced, the maximum deflection of the plate increases and the stiffness of the plate decreases. Comparing the load-deflection curves for different values of *a/b*, it is observed that the curves converge when $\frac{a}{b} \le \frac{1}{2}$. Moreover, when the aspect ratio of the plate is reduced to $\frac{a}{b} \le \frac{1}{2}$ for a constant lateral uniform load, the maximum deflection value of the plate converges because the plate edge length, *a*, is fixed. In general, when the maximum deflection of the plate increases, the membrane force and the bending moments also increase. For a plate with a small aspect ratio and a fixed edge length, the membrane force and the bending moments in the x-direction become particularly large.

Conclusion

This paper has solved the large deflection motion of a clamped isotropic rectangular plate using a hybrid method combining the finite difference method and the differential transformation method. The investigated parameters include the number of sub-domains, the lateral force applied, and the aspect ratio of the plate. The following conclusions can be drawn:
(a) Significant errors are present in the numerical results obtained for the large deflections of the plate in the transient state when a step force is applied.
(b) The rectangular isotropic plate oscillates during the initial transient phase and then stabilizes to a steady state deflection of 1.062 at the center of the plate.
(c) The numerical error reduces as the number of sub-domains considered in the solution process increases.
(d) When the number of sub-domains increases to 31, the maximum deflection of the plate converges to 1.0054.
(e) When the aspect ratio decreases to $\frac{a}{b} \le \frac{1}{2}$, the load-deflection curves converge.
(f) When the plate has a small aspect ratio and a fixed edge length, the membrane force and the bending moments in the x-direction increase significantly.

Acknowledgement

The financial support provided to this study by the National Science Council of Taiwan under Grant No. NSC 95-2221-E-269-012 is gratefully acknowledged.

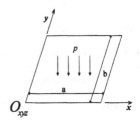

Figure1. Plate model

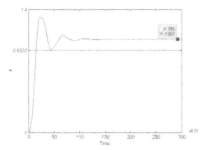

Figure2. Deflection of center of plate under applied lateral load of $\frac{pa^4}{Eh^4}=100$

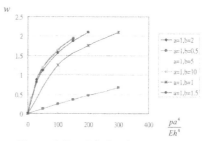

Figure 6. Load-deflection curves for clamped rectangular plate with various aspect ratios under increasing uniform lateral load.

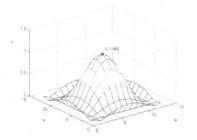

Figure 3. Displacement (w) of plate with applied lateral load of $\frac{pa^4}{Eh^4}=100$ in z-direction

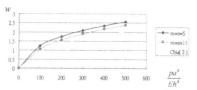

Figure 4. Load-deflection curves for clamped rectangular plate under increasing uniform lateral load.

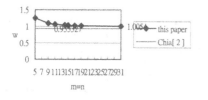

Figure 5. Deflection of center of plate for increasing number of sub-domains

References

[1] Timoshenko S. and Woinowsky-Krieger S., Theory of Plates and Shells. McGraw-Hill, New York, 1959.

[2] Chia C. Y.,"Nonlinear Analysis of plates", Mc Graw-Hill, New Youk, 1980.

[3] Yu L.T., Chen C.K., Application of Taylor transform to Optimize Rectangular Fins with Variable Thermal Parameters, Applied Mathematical Modeling 22(1998) 11-21.

[4] Yu L.T., Chen C.K., The solution of the Blasius Equation by the Differential Transform Method, Math. Comput. Modeling Vol. 28, No. 1,pp.101-111,1998.

[5] J. K. Zhou, Differential Transformation and its Applications for Electrical Circuits. Huarjung University Press, Wuuhahn, China, 1986 (in Chinese)

[6] Chen, Cha'o-Kuang; Ju, Shin-Ping ,"Application of differential transformation to transient advective–dispersive transport equation", Applied Mathematics and Computation, Vol. 155, No.1, pp. 25-38 , 2004.

[7] Leissa W., "Vibration of Plates", NASA SP-160, 1969.

Two-dimensional Boundary Element Analysis of Edge Cracked Plate using Near-tip Solution

Toshio FURUKAWA*

* Division of Mechanical and System Engineering
Graduate School of Engineering and Technology
Kyoto Institute of Technology
Goshokaido-cho, Matsugasaki, Sakyo-ku, Kyoto, 606-8585 Japan
(E-mail: furukawa@kit.ac.jp)

ABSTRACT

The extended method of solution for two-dimensional crack problems is discussed. The first proposed method has been the combination of near-tip solution and boundary element method with point symmetry. A domain to be analyzed is devided into two regions: the near-tip region, which is circular in shape and centered at the crack-tip, and the outer region. The displacements and stresses in the near-tip region are represented by the truncated infinite series of the eigenfunction with unknown coefficients. The stress intensity factors of mode I and mode II are represented by one of the corresponding coefficients, respectively. The outer region is formulated by the boundary elements. Using the domain decomposition method, this method is extended from the point symmetry problem to the problem without symmetry. The slant edge cracked rectangular plate under a uniform tension is treated and the calculated dimensionless stress intensity factors are in good accuary.

KEY WORDS: Elasticity, Stress Intensity Factor, Crack, Boundary Element Method, Near-Tip Solution

NOMENCLATURE

A_{1n}, A_{11n} : unknown coefficient
a : .radius of virtual boundary
C_{ij} : .configuration coefficient
c : .crack length
F_1, F_{11} : dimensionless stress intensity factor
$f_{1n}^{(i)}, f_{11n}^{(i)}$: function of angle θ
H : height of cracked plate
$h_{1n}^{(i)}, h_{11n}^{(i)}$: function of angle θ
K_1, K_{11} : stress intensity factor
Me : total number of elements
N : truncated term number
S : boundary
T_{ij}, U_{ij} : fundamental solution
t_i : traction

u_i : displacement
u_{i0} : rigid body displacement
V : domain
W : width of cracked plate
μ : rigidity

INTRODUCTION

It is well known that Boundary Element Method (BEM) is more efficient method comparing with Finite Element Method (FEM) and Finite Difference Method (FDM) and widely applied to a lot of problems. By the way, some ideas are necessary in the crack problem to obtain an appropriate solution as well as the other numerical calculation methods because of the stress singularity at the crack-tip.

There are many methods to obtain the stress intensity factors, such as, the extrapolation method based on stress and displacement near the crack-tip [1] and the method introducing the singular element, such as quarter point element [2-5]. The element division near the crack-tip is required in these methods and severe ideas are required to obtain the good accurate solution. Then, authors proposed the method by which the stress intensity factors can be obtained in good accuracy without element division near the crack-tip [6]. A virtual area including the crack-tip is introduced. In that area, we use general solutions for displacements and stresses shown by the infinite series that satisfies the boundary conditions on the crack-tip. A usual boundary element method is used in remaining major area. Moreover, the condition that satisfies the continuities of displacements and stresses is added on the boundary in two areas. The stress intensity factors are obtained by solving the equations from the discretized boundary integration equation. In this paper we consider slant edge cracked rectangular plate under uniform tension without symmetry. It is shown that the calculated results are very good accuracy.

ANALYSIS

Boundary integral equations
After the limit operation to Somigliana's equations, the boundary integral equations for our problem is expressed as

$$C_{ij}(P)u_j(P) + \int_S T_{ij}(P,Q)u_j(Q)dS = \int_S U_{ij}(P,Q)t_j(Q)dS \quad (1)$$

Discretized boundary integral equations
When we discretize the boundary S to boundary element S_i ($i=1,2,\ldots,M$), the boundary integral equations are changed to the following matrix equation

$$\begin{bmatrix} H_{11} & H_{12} & \cdots & \cdots & H_{1M} \\ H_{21} & H_{22} & \cdots & \cdots & H_{2M} \\ \vdots & \vdots & \ddots & & \vdots \\ \vdots & \vdots & & \ddots & \vdots \\ H_{M1} & H_{M2} & \cdots & \cdots & H_{MM} \end{bmatrix} \begin{Bmatrix} u_1 \\ u_2 \\ \vdots \\ \vdots \\ u_M \end{Bmatrix}$$

$$= \begin{bmatrix} G_{11} & G_{12} & \cdots & \cdots & G_{1M} \\ G_{21} & G_{22} & \cdots & \cdots & G_{2M} \\ \vdots & \vdots & \ddots & & \vdots \\ \vdots & \vdots & & \ddots & \vdots \\ G_{M1} & G_{M2} & \cdots & \cdots & G_{MM} \end{bmatrix} \begin{Bmatrix} t_1 \\ t_2 \\ \vdots \\ \vdots \\ t_M \end{Bmatrix} \quad (2)$$

or briefly

$$[H]\{u\} = [G]\{t\} \quad (3)$$

The domain V is divided into two regions V_1 and V_2. The corresponding boundaries put as S_1 and S_2 and new interface boundary S_3. When we use the continuity conditions for displacements and tractions at the interface, the final matrix equation becomes

$$\begin{bmatrix} H_1 & H_3(1) & 0 & -G_3(1) \\ 0 & H_3(2) & H_2 & G_3(2) \end{bmatrix} \begin{Bmatrix} u_1 \\ u_3(1) \\ u_2 \\ t_3(1) \end{Bmatrix}$$

$$= \begin{bmatrix} G_1 & 0 \\ 0 & G_2 \end{bmatrix} \begin{Bmatrix} t_1 \\ t_2 \end{Bmatrix} \quad (4)$$

where the number in the parenthesis implies the corresponding region.

Near-tip solution

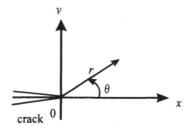

Figure 1 Coordinate system near the crack

As shown in Figure 1, we use the polar coordinate (r, θ) centered at the crack-tip. The near-tip solutions of displacements and tractions for two-dimensional elastic body are well known and expressed as follows for virtual boundary radius $r=a$.

$$\begin{Bmatrix} u_x \\ u_y \end{Bmatrix} = \sum_{n=1}^{\infty} \frac{A_{1n}}{2\mu} a^{n/2} \begin{Bmatrix} f_{1n}^{(1)}(\theta) \\ f_{1n}^{(2)}(\theta) \end{Bmatrix}$$
$$- \sum_{n=1}^{\infty} \frac{A_{11n}}{2\mu} a^{n/2} \begin{Bmatrix} f_{11n}^{(1)}(\theta) \\ f_{11n}^{(2)}(\theta) \end{Bmatrix} + \begin{Bmatrix} u_{x0} \\ u_{y0} \end{Bmatrix} \quad (5)$$

$$\begin{Bmatrix} t_x \\ t_y \end{Bmatrix} = \sum_{n=1}^{\infty} A_{1n} \frac{n}{2} a^{(n/2)-1} \begin{Bmatrix} h_{1n}^{(1)}(\theta) \\ h_{1n}^{(2)}(\theta) \end{Bmatrix}$$
$$- \sum_{n=1}^{\infty} A_{11n} \frac{n}{2} a^{(n/2)-1} \begin{Bmatrix} h_{11n}^{(1)}(\theta) \\ h_{11n}^{(2)}(\theta) \end{Bmatrix} \quad (6)$$

The stress intensity factors of mode I, K_I, and mode II, K_{II}, are expressed as

$$K_I = \sqrt{2\pi} A_{11}, \quad K_{II} = -\sqrt{2\pi} A_{III} \quad (7)$$

Combination of near-tip solution and boundary element method

The equations (5) and (6) are truncated by first N terms. The final matrix forms are

$$\{U\} = \begin{Bmatrix} u_x \\ u_y \end{Bmatrix} = \begin{bmatrix} \mathbf{F}^{(1)}(a, \theta) \\ \mathbf{F}^{(2)}(a, \theta) \end{bmatrix} \{A\} \quad (8)$$

$$\{T\} = \begin{Bmatrix} t_x \\ t_y \end{Bmatrix} = \begin{bmatrix} \mathbf{H}^{(1)}(a, \theta) \\ \mathbf{H}^{(2)}(a, \theta) \end{bmatrix} \{A\} \quad (9)$$

where the order of elements of vector $\{A\}$ are A_{1n} ($n=1,2,\ldots, N$), A_{11n} ($n=1,2,\ldots, N$), u_{x0}, and u_{y0}.

The discretized boundary integral equation for the body excluding the virtual circular region is

$$\begin{bmatrix} \mathbf{H}_R & \mathbf{H}_V \end{bmatrix} \begin{Bmatrix} \mathbf{U}_R \\ \mathbf{U}_V \end{Bmatrix} = \begin{bmatrix} \mathbf{G}_R & \mathbf{G}_V \end{bmatrix} \begin{Bmatrix} \mathbf{T}_R \\ \mathbf{T}_V \end{Bmatrix} \quad (10)$$

In this expression, the subscripts R and V denote the real and virtual boundaries, respectively. The boundary conditions on these two boundaries are leaded from the continuity conditions for displacements and tractions and are expressed as

$$\mathbf{U}_i' - \mathbf{U}_{Vi} = \mathbf{0}, \quad \mathbf{T}_i' + \mathbf{T}_{Vi} = \mathbf{0} \quad (11)$$

where $\mathbf{U'}_i$ and $\mathbf{T'}_i$ are the discretized i-th term nodal displacements and tractions, respectively.

Domain decomposition method

To treat the problem with no symmetry, we introduce the domain decomposition method. We decompose the original configuration to two domains along the crack surface. We combine the near-tip solutions and usual boundary element method for domains I and II, respectively. Then we use the combination conditions for displacements and tractions

$$\mathbf{u}(1) = \mathbf{u}(2), \quad \mathbf{t}(1) + \mathbf{t}(2) = \mathbf{0} \quad (12)$$

The final system of linear algebraic equation is

$$[\mathbf{A}]\{\mathbf{x}\} = \{\mathbf{f}\} \quad (13)$$

NUMERICAL RESULTS

We consider the slant edge cracked rectangular plate under uniform tension σ_0 with width W and Height H, crack length c, and the slant angle α as shown in Figure 2. We decompose the plate to two parts. The boundary conditions of these domains are shown in Figure 3.

The dimensionless stress intensity factors are defined as

$$F_I = \frac{K_I}{\sigma_0 \sqrt{\pi c}}, \quad F_{II} = \frac{K_{II}}{\sigma_0 \sqrt{\pi c}} \quad (14)$$

Now we determine the parameters.

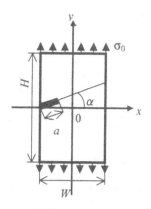

Figure 2 Slant edge cracked plate

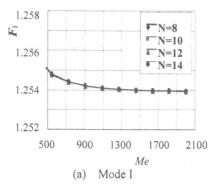

(a) Mode I

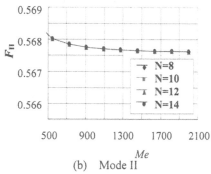

(b) Mode II

Figure 4 Variations dimensionless stress intensity factors with total element number

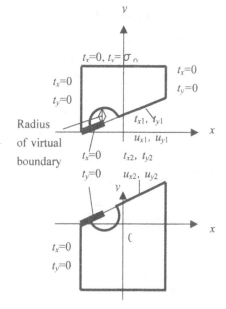

Figure 3 Domain decomposition

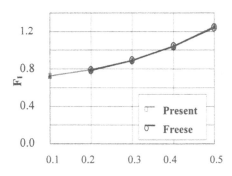

Figure 5 Variations dimensionless stress intensity factor F_I with crack length c/W

Figure 4 shows the variations dimensionless stress intensity factors F_I and F_{II} with total element number Me for the case that slenderness $H/W=2$, slant angle $\alpha = \pi/4$, crack length $c/W=0.5$ and radius of virtual boundary $a/c=0.1$. From these figures, we see that stress intensity factors converge monotonically.

To compare with the other result, we compute for slenderness $H/W=2$ and slant angle $\alpha = \pi/4$. Figure 5 shows the variations dimensionless stress intensity factor F_1 with crack length c/W. From this figure, we see that present method has almost identical results compared with other ones. The tendency of dimensionless stress intensity factor F_{II} is similar to F_1.

To test the accuracy, we take the crack length c/W as 0.01. This case is almost same as the semi-space with slant edge crack [7, 8]. Figures 6 and 7 is the comparison of present solution and Nisitani's solution. From these figures, present results have a good accuracy.

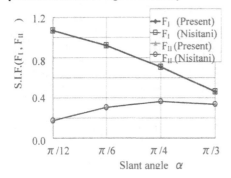

Figure 6 Relations between dimensionless stress intensity factors and slant angle

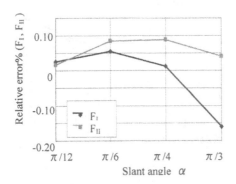

Figure 7 Relations between relative errors of dimensionless stress intensity factors and slant angle

CONCLUDING REMARKS

A highly accurate and simple solution method related to boundary element method has been presented. The numerical results discussed for slant edge cracked rectangular plate with no symmetry are in good agreement with the available results in the literature.

ACNOWLEDGEMENTS

Author sincerely expresses his gratitude to the late professor Hiroshi Nakanishi for the contribution of this manuscript.

REFERENCES

1. For Example: Tanaka, M., Hamada, M., and Iwata, Y., Computation of a two-dimensional stress intensity factor by the boundary element method, Ingenieur Archiv, 1982, 52-1&2, pp.95-104.
2. Jia, Z.H., Shippy, D.J., and Rizzo, F.J., 1988, International Journal for Numerical Methods in Engineering, , pp.2739-2753.
3. Liu, S. B. and Tan, C. L., Two-dimensional boundary element contact mechanics analysis of angled crack problems, Engineering Fracture Mechanics, 1992, 42-2, pp.273-288.
4. Dong, Y., Wang, Z., and Wang, B., On the computation of stress intensity factors for interfacial cracks using quarter-point boundary elements, Engineering Fracture Mechanics, 1997, 57-4, pp.335-342.
5. Mukhopadhyay, N.K., Maiti, S.K. and Kakodkar, A., Effect of modelling of traction and thermal singularities on accuracy of SIFS computation through modified crack closure integral in BEM, Engineering Fracture Mechanics, 1999, 64-2, pp.141-159.
6. Nakanishi, H., Furukawa, T., and Honda, T., A method of analysis for two-dimensional crack problems by the boundary element method, Transactions of the Japan Society of Mechanical Engineers, A, 2004, 70-692, pp.560-566.
7. Nisitani, H., Stress Intensity Factor for the Tension of a Semi-Infinite Plate Having an Oblique or a Bent Edge Crack, Transactions of the Japan Society of Mechanical Engineers, 1975, 41-344, pp.1103-1110.
8. Murakami, Y. (Ed.), Stress Intensity Factors Handbook, Vol. 1, Pergamon Press, Oxford, 1987, pp.118-119.

Robust Controlling Chaos for Unified Chaotic Systems via Sliding Mode Control

Tsung-Ying Chiang*, Meei-Ling Hung** and Jun-Juh Yan*

*Department of Computer and Communication
Shu-Te University
Kaohsiung 824, Taiwan, R.O.C.
(E-mail: jjyan@mail.stu.edu.tw)
** Department of Electrical Engineering
Far-East College
Tainan 744, Taiwan, R.O.C.

ABSTRACT

This study investigates the stabilization problem for uncertain unified chaotic systems with input nonlinearity. A sliding mode control technique is adopted to facilitate the robustness of controlled systems and an adaptive switching surface is newly proposed to simplify the task of assigning the stability of the closed-loop system in sliding motion. This controller is robust to the nonlinear input and guarantees the occurrence of sliding motion of the controlled unified chaotic systems with uncertainties. Incidentally, in the sliding mode, the investigated uncertain chaotic system with input nonlinearity still possesses advantages of fast response, good transient performance and insensitive to the uncertainties as the systems with linear input.

KEY WORDS: Input nonlinearity, Sliding mode control, Adaptive switching surface

INTRODUCTION

It has been well known that a chaotic system is a very complex dynamical nonlinear system and its response possesses some characteristics, such as excessive sensitivity to initial conditions, broad spectrums of Fourier transform and fractal properties of the motion in phase space. Also, it has been found to be useful in analyzing many problems, such as information processing, power systems collapse prevention, high-performance circuits and device, etc..

In 2002, Lü et al. introduced a unified chaotic system [1], which contains the Lorenz and Chen systems as two extremes and the Lü system as a transition system between the Lorenz and Chen systems [1, 2].

Recently, several papers have been published for the control problem [3], drive-response synchronization [4] and secure communication schemes [5] of unified chaotic systems. On the other hand, the control schemes can be realized by electronic components such as operational amplifier (OPA), resistor, and capacitor, etc. or by electromechanical actuators. However, in practice, there always exist nonlinearities in the control input including saturation, backlash and dead-zone in OPA or electromechanical devices. Furthermore, it is impossible to maintain the values of resistance and capacitance due to the uncontrollable environmental conditions. It has been shown that input nonlinearity can cause a serious degradation of the system performance, a reduced rate of response, and in a worst-case scenario, system failure if the controller is not well designed. Therefore, it is clear that the effects of input nonlinearity must be taken into account when analyzing and implementing a control scheme for the unified chaotic systems. However, a review of the published literature suggests that the problem of controlling chaotic systems subject to input nonlinearity has received relatively little attention.

Accordingly, this study presents a control scheme for uncertain unified chaotic systems with input nonlinearity. A sliding mode control technique is adopted to facilitate the robustness of controlled systems. An adaptive switching surface is newly proposed to simplify the task of assigning the stability of the closed-loop system in sliding motion. This controller is robust to the nonlinear input and guarantees the occurrence of sliding motion of the controlled unified chaotic systems with uncertainties. Incidentally, in the sliding mode, the investigated uncertain chaotic system with input nonlinearity still possesses advantages of fast response, good transient performance and insensitive to the uncertainties as the systems with linear input.

SYSTEM FORMULATION

With the consideration of system's uncertainties and input nonlinearity, the unified chaotic system can be expressed by

$$
\begin{aligned}
\dot{x} &= (25\alpha + 10)(y - x) \\
\dot{y} &= (28 - 35\alpha)x + (29\alpha - 1)y - xz \\
&\quad + p(x, y, z, d) + \psi(u(t)) \\
\dot{z} &= xy - \frac{8 + \alpha}{3}z
\end{aligned}
\tag{1}
$$

where $p(x, y, z, d)$ is the parameter uncertainty and external disturbance

applied to the system. Without loss of generality, it is assumed that $p(x, y, z, d)$ is bounded by

$$
|p(x, y, z, d)| \leq \beta_x |x| + \beta_y |y| + \beta_z |z| + d;
\tag{2}
$$

where $\beta_x, \beta_y, \beta_z$ and d are known positive constants. $u(t) \in R$ is the control input, $\psi(u(t))$ is a continuous nonlinear function and $\psi(0) = 0$, where $\psi : R \to R$ with the law $u(t) \to \psi(u(t))$ and inside sector $[\beta_1, \beta_2]$ that β_1 and β_2 are nonzero positive constants, i.e.

$$
\beta_2 u^2(t) \geq u(t)\psi(u(t)) \geq \beta_1 u^2(t)
\tag{3}
$$

A scalar nonlinear function $\psi(u)$ is illustrated in Figure 1.

The control goal considered in this paper is that for any given uncertain unified chaotic systems subject to uncertainties and input nonlinearity, a sliding mode controller is designed such that the closed-loop system is stabilized.

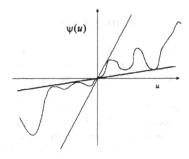

Figure 1 A scalar nonlinear function $\psi(u)$ inside sector $[\beta_1, \beta_2]$

SWITCHING SURFACE AND SLIDING MODE CONTROLLER DESIGN

First, a novel adaptive switching surface design is defined as

$$\sigma(t) = y(t) + g(t) = y(t) + \int_0^t \rho(\tau)d\tau \qquad (4)$$

where $\sigma(t) \in R$ and $g(t)$ is an adaptive function given by

$$\dot{g}(t) = \rho(t) = (25\alpha + 10)x + zx + ry \qquad (5)$$

where r is a positive constant specified by the designer. According to the works in [6, 7], when the system operates in the sliding mode, the following equations hold:

$$\sigma(t) = \dot{\sigma}(t) = 0 \qquad (6a)$$

i.e.

$$\dot{y}(t) = -\dot{g}(t) = -(25\alpha + 10)x - zx - ry \qquad (6b)$$

Therefore, from (6b) we obtain the following sliding mode dynamics as

$$\begin{aligned}
\dot{x} &= (25\alpha + 10)(y - x) \\
\dot{y} &= -(25\alpha + 10)x - zx - ry \\
\dot{z} &= xy - \frac{8+\alpha}{3}z
\end{aligned} \qquad (7)$$

In the following, we analyze the stability of the sliding mode dynamics (7) based on the Lyapunov stability theory. The Lyapunov function is selected as $v(t) = 0.5(x^2 + y^2 + z^2)$, which leads to

$$\begin{aligned}
\dot{v}(t) &= x\dot{x} + y\dot{y} + z\dot{z} \\
&= -(25\alpha + 10)x^2 - ry^2 - \frac{8+\alpha}{3}z^2 \\
&\leq 0
\end{aligned} \qquad (8)$$

Thus, according to Lyapunov stability theory, it is seen that $v(t) = 0.5(x^2 + y^2 + z^2)$ will converge to zero and the stability of the sliding motion on the sliding manifold is guaranteed.

Having established the appropriate switching surface (4), as described above, the next step is to design a sliding mode

control scheme to drive the system trajectories onto the sliding mode $s = 0$ even when input nonlinearity is present.

The reaching condition of the sliding mode is given below.

Lemma 1: The motion of the sliding mode is asymptotically stable, if the following reaching condition is held

$$\sigma(t)\dot{\sigma}(t) < 0 \quad \text{for all } \sigma(t) \neq 0 \qquad (9)$$

Theorem 1: For a class of unified systems subjected to uncertainty and input nonlinearity given in (3), if the control input $u(t)$ is suitably designed as:

$$u(t) = -\omega\lambda[sign(\sigma(t))], \quad \omega > \frac{1}{\beta_1} \qquad (10)$$

where

$$\lambda = |(38 - 10\alpha)x + (29\alpha - 1 + r)y| + \beta_x|x| + \beta_y|y| + \beta_z|z| + d \qquad (11)$$

, then the trajectory of the closed-loop system converges to the sliding mode.
Proof: By substituting (1), (2) and (4) into the derivative of $\sigma(t)\dot{\sigma}(t)$, it yields

$$\begin{aligned}
&\sigma(t)\dot{\sigma}(t) \\
&= \sigma(t)[\dot{y}(t) + \rho(t)] \\
&\leq |\sigma(t)||(38 - 10\alpha)x + (29\alpha - 1 + r)y| \\
&\quad + |\sigma(t)|(\beta_x|x| + \beta_y|y| + \beta_z|z| + d) \\
&\quad + \sigma(t)\psi(u(t)) \\
&= \lambda|\sigma(t)| + \sigma(t)\psi(u(t))
\end{aligned} \qquad (12)$$

Furthermore, form (3), we have

$$-\omega\lambda[sign(\sigma(t))]\psi(u(t)) \geq \beta_1\omega^2\lambda^2[sign(\sigma(t))]^2 \qquad (13)$$

Since $\sigma^2(t) \geq 0$, we have

$$-\omega\lambda\sigma^2[sign(\sigma(t))]\psi(u(t)) \geq \beta_1\omega^2\lambda^2\sigma^2[sign(\sigma(t))]^2 \qquad (14)$$

Furthermore, using the fact of $\sigma \cdot sign(\sigma) = |\sigma|$, it yields

$$\sigma(t)\psi(u(t)) \le -\beta_1|\sigma(t)|\omega\lambda \qquad (15)$$

By placing (15) to (12), we get

$$\sigma(t)\dot{\sigma}(t) \le |\sigma(t)|\lambda(1-\beta_1\omega) \qquad (16)$$

Since $\omega > 1/\beta_1$ has been specified in (10), we have $\sigma(t)\dot{\sigma}(t) < 0$. The proof is completed.

AN ILLUSTRATIVE EXAMPLE

In this section, to verify and demonstrate the effectiveness of the proposed method, we discuss the simulation result for the case of Lorenz system. In simulation experiments, values of uncertain parameters are chosen as follows:

$$|p(x,y,z,d)| \le (0.1|x| + 0.3|y| + 0.85|z| + 0.1)$$

In numerical simulation, the left parameters are given as $\beta_1 = 0.2$, $\beta_2 = 0.8$, $\omega = 6$, $r = 1 > 0$. The simulation result of the Lorenz $(\alpha = 0)$ system is shown in Figure 2. The initial condition of Lorenz system is given as $(x(0), y(0), z(0), \rho(0)) = (0.1, 0.2, 0.3, 0.2)$. In Figure 2, for the first two seconds, the system is uncontrolled and, therefore, all of its state trajectories are chaotic. Then, the control input is turned on at $t = 2$ second for regulating nonlinear gyro to the desired states. Figure 2 shows that states of controlled system are regulated to zero rapidly in about 1.5 seconds after the control input is turned on at $t = 2$ second. From the simulation result, it shows that the proposed sliding mode controller works well for the chaotic Lorenz system.

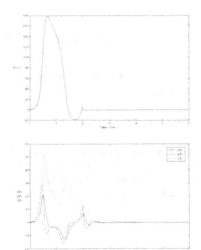

Figure 2 $\sigma(t)$ and state responses with $\alpha = 0$; the controller is turned at 2 second.

CONCLUSION

A novel sliding mode control scheme capable of guaranteeing the globally stabilization of uncertain unified chaotic systems subject to input nonlinearity is demonstrated in above study. The results show that the proposed adaptive switching surface can determine the stability of systems in the sliding mode motion. The scheme also shows a fast convergence rate can be achieved by selecting appropriate design parameters in the controller.

REFERENCES

1. J. Lü, G. Chen, D.Z. Cheng, S. Celikovsky, "Bridge the gap between the Lorenz system and the Chen system," Int J Bifurcat Chaos, vol. 12, pp. 2917-2926, 2002.
2. G. Chen, J. Lü, "Dynamics of the Lorenz system family: analysis, control and synchronization," Beijing: Science Press, 2003.
3. C. Hua, X. Guan and P. Shi, "Adaptive feedback control for a class of chaotic systems," Chaos Solitons and Fractals, vol. 23, pp. 757-765, 2005.

4. C. Tao, H. Xiong and F. Hu, "Two novel synchronization criterions for a unified chaotic system," Chaos Solitons and Fractals, vol. 27, pp. 115-120, 2006.

5. C. Hua, B. Yang, G. Ouyang and X. Guan, "A new chaotic secure communication scheme," Physics Letters A, vol. 342, pp. 305-308, 2005.

6. U. Itkis, Control system of variable structure. Wiley, New York, 1976.

7. V.I. Utkin, Sliding mode and their application in variable structure systems. Mir Editors, Moscow, 1978.

Simulation and Application of Soft Measurement Method Based on Process Neural Network

Zaiwen LIU, Xiaoyi WANG and Lifeng CUI
School of Information Engineering
Beijing Technology and Business University
Beijing, 100037, China
(E-mail: liuzw@th.btbu.edu.cn)

ABSTRACT

Soft measurement is a method by modeling mathematic model for some undetected parameters in control system A new algorithm of soft measurement based on process neural network (PNN) was studied. A time aggregation operator was introduced to process neuron, and it made the neuron network has the ability to deal with the information of space-time two dimensions at the same time, so the data processing enginery of biological neuron was imitated better than traditional neuron. PNN with the structure of three layers in which hidden layer was process neuron and inputs and output were common neurons was discussed. The soft measurement based on PNN may be used to fulfill measurement of the effluent BOD from wastewater treatment system , and a good training result of soft measurement was obtained by simulation with MATLAB.

KEY WORDS: Soft measurement , Neural network, Wastewater treatment, Simulation, Algorithm

NOMENCLATURE

PNN: Process Neural Network.
DO: Dissolved Oxygen.
COD: Chemical Oxygen Demand.
BOD: Biochemical Oxygen Demand
MLSS: Mixed Liquor Suspended Solid.

INTRODUCTION

Soft measurement based on PNN is a new method by modeling mathematic model for time-varying system. Most of soft measurement models adopt traditional artificial neural network model, whose inputs are constants independent of time[1]. Every input is instantaneous in the form of geometrical point, however, wastewater treatment process is a reaction process associated with time nearly ,and the inputs of its neural network are dependent on time[2]. Time accumulation of inputs is neglected by traditional neural network, so there are big errors on prediction and the values of prediction can not be applied well in practical production. PNN is an extension of traditional neural network, in which the inputs and outputs are time-variation, and it shows that PNN can be brought into the soft measurement of variables in wastewater treatment process.

MODEL OF PNN

1) Process neuron

Process neuron consists of three parts: weighting function, converge and energizing threshold[3-4]. The relation between inputs and outputs of process neuron can be written as:

$$Y=F((w(t) \oplus x(t)) \otimes K(t)- \theta) \qquad (1)$$

Where $x(t)$ is process neuron input, $w(t)$ is connection weighting, and $\oplus$ represents

68

one of space-converge operations, $\otimes$ is time-converge operation, $k(.)$ is time-converged function, $f(.)$ is energizing function.

$$w(t) \oplus x(t) = \sum w_i(t) x_i(t), i = 1, 2 \ldots \quad (2)$$

$$A(t) \otimes k(.) = \int A(t) k(t) dt \quad (3)$$

2) Model of process neural network

PNN is an artificial neuron system based on certain topological structure, which is made of some process neurons and commonly no time-varying neurons. The soft measurement structure in wastewater treatment adopts the three-layer network, and according to the theory of neural network, it can approach any nonlinear function. Fig.1 is its configuration.

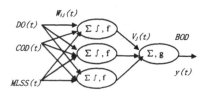

Fig.1 Three layers of PNN for sewage disposal

Seen from Fig.1, input layer has three nodes: DO, COD, MLSS. Let hidden layer have m nodes, so the reflection between input and output of network is defined as follows:

$$y = g \left\{ \sum_{j=1}^{m} v_j f \left[\int_0^T \left(W_{ij}(t) x_i(t) \right) dt - \theta_j^i \right] - \theta \right\} \quad (4)$$

Where v_j is the connection weighting value form hidden layer node to output-layer node, θ_j^i is the energizing threshold of hidden layer node J, $[0,T]$ is sampling period, f, g are energizing functions. S function should always be adopted in wastewater treatment process. θ is the threshold of output node. Equation (4) is the forward-time and space accumulation values of a group of training data.

TRAINING ALGORITHM

The calculation of PNN is more complicated. Meanwhile, because the form of network connection weighting and the parameter contained are random, the connection weighting function is very hard to be confirmed by the training of learning sampling basis without the common form of functions.

Input functions are transformed into limited series of this group by given precision. Meanwhile, network weighting functions are expressed as the expanded forms in the same group of basis functions whose orthogonality can be used to simplify the complexity of process neuron about time-aggregation operation. The application shows that this algorithm has not only simplified the operation of PNN but also increased the stability and convergence in network learning. There are many kinds of methods to choose function orthogonal basis. Basis function can be chosen as Multinomial function, Fourier basis function, Walsh function etc.

Based on the predigesting algorithm mechanism, the algorithm of soft measurement in wastewater treatment process is as following steps:

1) Data acquisition and processing

First the sampling interval of input variables should be obtained and the detailed interval can be decreased according to the increasing changing current of data. The form of one group of sampling data is:

$$X(t, DO, TOC, MLSS) = f(0, DO_1, TOC_1, MLSS_1; 1, DO_2, TOC_2, MLSS_2; \ldots 8, DO_8, TOC_8, MLSS_8) \quad (5)$$

Data like (5) is fitted into the form of fifth order multinomial in sampling circle so that a group of training sampling can be obtained as follows:

$$X = \left(\sum_{i=0}^{5} a_{1i} x^i, \sum_{i=0}^{5} a_{2i} x^i, \sum_{i=0}^{5} a_{3i} x^i \right). \quad (6)$$

Because fifth order multinomial can

69

approach any function by fitting, this fitting can be adopted to show and gather the space geometrical points of input parameters in sampling circle.

Selecting a group of orthogonal trigonometric basis functions: $1, sin(x), cos(x), sin(2x), cos(2x), ... sin(nx), cos(nx)$. The number of basis functions can be adjusted according to the precision requirement of approaching function and the ability of generalization after network training. Do not choose many basis functions or the calculation will be increased largely. It goes against the network training.

Based on the orthogonal basis functions selected, the fitting fifth-order multinomial of input can be transformed into Fourier series with $[0, T]$:

$$x = (\sum_{i=0}^{L}(a_{1i}\cos(ix) + b_{1i}\sin(ix)), \sum_{i=0}^{L}(a_{2i}\cos(ix)$$
$$+ b_{2i}\sin(ix)), \sum_{i=0}^{L}(a_{3i}\cos(ix) + b_{3i}\sin(ix))) \quad (7)$$

Where L is the number of orthogonal basis, a_{li}, b_{li} are expanding coefficients of orthogonal basis. There are many kinds of expanded forms of Fourier series and the Fourier series with dissymmetrical interval is adopted in this algorithm. There are $2*L+1$ items in the expanded coefficient which should be noticed in programming. To simplify the following formula, let the form of orthogonal basis selected be $b_1(t), b_2(t) ... ... b_l(t)$, so equation (7) is transformed into (8):

$$X = (\sum_{l=1}^{L}a_{1l}b_l(t), \sum_{l=1}^{L}a_{2l}b_l(t), \sum_{l=1}^{L}a_{3l}b_l(t)) \quad (8)$$

There is big difference among orders of coefficient magnitudes in expanded orthogonal basis. To prevent the saturation output of neuron because of the big absolute value of net input and to prevent the weighting regulation to come to the even area of error curved surface, the coefficient a_{1i}, a_{2i}, a_{3i} of (8) should be treated as a whole. The data coefficients are changed in the range of $[-1,1]$ to complete pre-treatment of the data.

2) Initialize network parameters

Calculating the learning speed of weighting from input layer to hidden layer, hidden layer threshold, the number of basis functions, error precision of network, and the biggest times of network circulations, weighting and threshold are initialized in term of the network structure of Fig.1. The structure of no time-varying neuron is adopted from hidden layer to output layer, so let the initialized value of weighting V_j be a tiny random number between $[0,1]$ or normal distribution random number whose average is 0 and variance is 1. The neural threshold of hidden layer and output layer are initialized as the way of V_j. Because $W_{ij}(t)$ is functions about time, for the convenience of calculation, weighting functions are expanded in the form of basis functions in the same group:

$$W_{ij}(t) = (\sum_{l=1}^{L} w_{ij}^{(l)} b_l(t)) \quad (9)$$

Where $w_{ij}^{(l)}$ is the connection weighting from input node i to hidden layer node j relative to $b_l(t)$. Given the number of hidden layer nodes is m, the weighting matrix can be expressed as:

$$w = \begin{bmatrix} \sum_{l=1}^{L} w_{11}^{(l)} b_l(t), \sum_{l=1}^{L} w_{12}^{(2l)} b_l(t), ..., \sum_{l=1}^{L} w_{1m}^{(ml)} b_l(t) \\ \sum_{l=1}^{L} w_{21}^{(l)} b_l(t), \sum_{l=1}^{L} w_{22}^{(2l)} b_l(t), ..., \sum_{l=1}^{L} w_{2m}^{(ml)} b_l(t) \\ \sum_{l=1}^{L} w_{31}^{(l)} b_l(t), \sum_{l=1}^{L} w_{32}^{(2l)} b_l(t), ..., \sum_{l=1}^{L} w_{3m}^{(ml)} b_l(t) \end{bmatrix}$$

Where $w_{1m}^{(ml)}$ is the expanded coefficient of the first input neuron and m_{th} hidden layer neuron under basis function $b_l(t)$.

3) Calculate forward outputs and errors

Group training algorithm is employed to complete the calculation of errors in this algorithm. If there are K groups of training samplings, according to the gradient descent algorithm, the output and error in Fig.1 are obtained as:

$$y = g\left\{ \sum_{j=1}^{m} v_j f\left[\sum_{i=1}^{3}\sum_{l=1}^{L} a_{il}^{(k)} w_{ij}^{jl} - \theta_j^{(l)} \right] - \theta \right\} \quad (10)$$

$$E = \sum_{k=1}^{K} (y_k - d_k)^2 \quad (11)$$

$$= \sum_{k=1}^{K}\left\{ g\left\{ \sum_{j=1}^{m} v_j f\left[\sum\sum a_{il}^{(k)} w_{ij}^{jl} - \theta_j^{(l)} \right] - \theta \right\} - d_k \right\}^2$$

In (9), $d_{il}^{(k)}$, which is relative to $b_l(t)$ based on expanded basis function, is the expanded coefficient of i_{th} input neuron in group k of training sample. Equation(10) can be stated as the total error of group training. d_k is the expected output of k_{th} training. Equation (10), (11) are the simplified results of calculation based on orthogonal basis.

4) Regulate learning speed of network based on gradient descent algorithm

The equations of network weighting value and threshold regulated are:

$$v_j = v_j + a\Delta v_j, \quad j=1,2\ldots\ldots m \quad (12)$$

$$w_{ij}^{jl} = w_{ij}^{jl} + b\Delta w_{ij}^{jl}, i=1,2,3,l=1,2\ldots, (13)$$

$$\theta_j^1 = \theta_j^1 + \Upsilon\Delta\theta_j^1 \quad j=1,2\ldots m \quad (14)$$

a, b, Υ are learning speed. To make the expression and calculation more convenient, let

$$u_{kj} = \sum_{i=1}^{3}\sum_{l=1}^{L} a_{il}^{(k)} w_{ij}^{(jl)} - \theta_j^1 \quad (15)$$

$$z_k = \sum_{j=1}^{m} v_j f\left(\sum_{i=1}^{3}\sum_{l=1}^{L} a_{il}^{(k)} w_{ij}^{(jl)} - \theta_j^1 \right) - \theta \quad (16)$$

$$\Delta v_j = -2\sum_{k=1}^{K}\left[(g(z_k) - d_k)g'(z_k)f(u_{kj}) \right] \quad (17)$$

$$\Delta w_{ij}^{(jl)} = -2\sum_{k=1}^{K}\left[(g(z_k) - d_k)g'(z_k)f'(u_{kj})a_{il}^{(k)} \right] (18)$$

$$\Delta\theta_j^1 = -2\sum_{k=1}^{K}\left[(g(z_k) - d_k)g'(z_k)f'(u_{kj})(-1) \right] (19)$$

Because both f and g use *Sigmoid* function, $f'(x) = f(x)(1 - f(x))$ is brought into (17), (18), (19) to simplify the calculation. The subscript coefficient of this formula is as same as the one of (12)~ (14).

5) Check error precision and biggest circulation time to meet the expectation

If error $E < \varepsilon$ or training times $S < N_{max}$, the expectation of network has been achieved. Turn to step 6). Otherwise, the value of circulation times is added 1, then back to step 3).

6) Output learning results and end training

Save network weighting, threshold and error regulated every time.

APPLICATION AND SIMULATION

According to the data requirements and network structure of PNN, 5 groups of training data are selected to simulate network convergence and error curve. MATLAB programming can be used to realize the network training algorithms. Last M profile function is defined as:

```
[W, V, E, EN, YCYZ, SCCYZ]
=process_neural (x, d, T, hidnum,
funnum, Nmax, e, s1, s2, s3 ).
W=srcdycqzcsh(n,m,l);
// initialization    function of hidden layer
weighting value.
V=ycdsccqzcsh(M);
//initialization function of output layer weighting
value.
YCYZ=rand(1,M)*0.2;
// hidden layer threshold.
SCCYZ=rand(1)*0.2;
//output layer threshold.
E=zeros(1,Nmax);
// initialization error.
wtiao1=cell(N,M);
//momentum initialization.
```

Where E is error value of every training, x is sampling basis of training, d is signal from tutor, T is sampling cycle, *hidnum* is the number of hidden-layer neurons, *funnum* is the number of basis functions,

N_{max} is the biggest time of training, e is training precision, $s1, s2$ and $s3$ are the learning speed of weighting value from input layer to hidden layer, of threshold in hidden layer, and of weighting value from hidden layer to output layer respectively. Based on the condition of $hidnum=12$; $e=0.01$; $s1=0.38$; $s2=0.3$; $s3=0.4$; $N_{max}=1000$, the regulation of momentum item and fixed learning speed, neural network is trained to obtain the error curve as following:

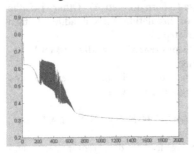

Fig.2   Curve of error convergence

Fig.3 is an error convergence curve obtained through the algorithm of changing learning speed.

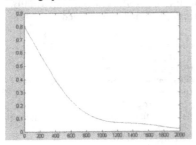

Fig.3 Error curve of changing learning speed

Seen from the figures, the convergence speed of network can be accelerated by changing learning speed, however, according to other groups of training curves, it is hard to find a balance point between the regulation value of coefficient in momentum items and learning speed. Especially, the oscillation can be brought into the beginning of network through raising learning speed. The oscillation decreases along with the increase of training times and the convergence speed of network error curve turns slowly. The improving learning algorithm of BP network can be introduced to the PNN completely. Error function can be optimized to accelerate the convergence of network. The training speed of network is affected obviously by the initialization of network weighting function.

CONCLUSION

Considering the technical requirements of time varying system, the algorithm of process neural network for soft measurement is tried to introduce into the soft measurement of wastewater treatment process. From the point of biology, PNN is fit for the operation mechanism of organic neuron furthermore. Many process input problems, such as wastewater treatment process, in relative to time can be settled by PNN.

ACKNOWLEDGEMENTS

This study is supported by the Beijing Education Committee(No.200589) and the Beijing Nature Science Foundation Committee(No.4062011). Those supports are gratefully acknowledged.

REFERENCES

1. L. Luccatini, E Porra, A Spagni, Soft sensors for control of nitrogen and phosphorus removal from wastewaters by neural networks. War Sic Tech, London,2002,45(4-5),pp.101-107.
2. Zaiwen LIU, Xiaoqin LIAN, Research and Application of Artificial Intelligence for Water Environment Protection , 2006 International Conference on AI(ICAI'06), Beijing ,Aug.2006
3. He Xingui, Liang Yongzhen, Training of process neural network and its application, China Engineering Science, Apr. 2001,pp.31~35.
4. Xu Shaohua, He Xingui, Learning algorithms of expanded process neural network based on orthogonal basis, Computer Transaction, May 2004, pp.:645~650.

A Model Reference Adaptive Control Scheme Based on Neural Network

Hu HONGJIE*, Miao YUQIAO*

* Automatic Control Department, Beihang University
Beijing, 100083 China
(E-mail: hhj@buaa.edu.cn, maahoo13@gmail.com)

ABSTRACT

This paper presents a new model reference control method based on a neural network. The widely used projection algorithm is used as iterative algorithm for the neural network to automatically adjust the parameters online. The neural network PI controller is designed to minimize the differences between the reference model and the plant which is influenced by parameter variation and disturbance. Simulation results show that the proposed control scheme can reduce the plant's sensitivity to parameter variation and disturbance.

KEY WORDS: Model reference, Neural network, Projection algorithm

INTRODUCTION

Servo system, for example, flight simulator can be considered as a closed-loop system which is always implemented by motor. As a typical position servo system, flight simulator has a lot of nonlinearities caused by mechanical friction and distortion of transmission shaft, besides, there are some uncertain factors in system, such as non-balance load factor, inertia coupling between axes, the vary of electrical parameters, disturbances of environment and other un-modeling factors etc. Considering the realizability, the model of the plant is always expressed by a linear differential equation. However, with the continuous increasing of system performance, the effect of nonlinearity and uncertainty on system will become more and more serious.

The ability of a multi-layer perceptron type neural network to learn a large class of nonlinear function is well known [1]. There have been numerous examples where dynamic systems have been controlled through neural network. The Back propagation and the Radial Basis Function are two of most widespread iterative algorithms [2]. Although both of them have excellent ability to infinitely approximate any function, the algebraic operation (exponential) is much too complex to implement in real-time control system. Based on reference frame theory, some robust speed control scheme is used for controlling motor [3], and in that paper the

73

load torque estimator become an important argument.

This paper proposes a model reference control scheme based on a neural network PI controller, it does not need the load torque estimator to observe the load torque and just use the compensation controller to improve the performance of the system. The widely used projection algorithm is used as iterative algorithm for the neural network to automatically adjust the parameters of the neural network PI controller. The neural network PI controller is used to minimize the differences between the reference model and the plant which is influenced because of parameter variation and disturbance, so that the differential output signal of the plant can accurately follow the output signal of model, whose transfer function is linear and certain equation. So using the traditional control methods can make the system have perfect dynamic and steady-state performance, at the same time the traditional control theory guarantee the stability.

MODEL OF PLANT

The dynamic model of the motor speed can be expressed as

$$K \times I_c - M_z = J\frac{d\omega_r}{dt} + B \times \omega_r \qquad (1)$$

By using Laplace transformation, the transfer function for (1) is

$$\omega_r(s) = \frac{K \times I_c(s) - M_z(s)}{Js + B} \qquad (2)$$

Where J and B denote the motor inertia and viscous friction coefficient respectively, M_z is the disturbance load torque, ω_r is the motor load-shaft actual velocity, I_c is the output of the controllers. K is the gain.

Figure 1 the structure of plant's model

NEURAL NETWORK CONTROL SCHEME

The block diagram for the proposed model reference control scheme is shown in Fig.2, there are three controllers in it. The neural network PI controller is used to reduce the influence of non-linear and uncertain factors which influence the performance of the plant, it makes use of the error between the output of the reference model and the differential output the plant and the other measurable signals such as its input. The model of plant can be attained approximately by experiment method in practice, and this approximate model of plant can be used as the nominal model in the control scheme. Then the neural network iterative algorithm updates the parameters of the neural network, and adjusts the output of the neural network PI controller. By doing this, the output of the plant can accurately follow the track of the nominal model. This is the plant has a characteristic of linear and certain, whose dynamic performance is just interrelated with the nominal model's. So using the traditional control methods can make the system have perfect dynamic and steady-state performance, at the same time the traditional control theory can guarantee the stability. Based on the theory of the linear system control, the parameters of the speed controller and the position controller can be designed by the reference model, and make the plant have an excellent performance.

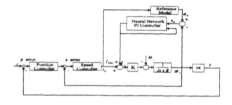

Figure 2 Block diagram of the model reference control scheme

Firstly, the transfer function of neural network PI controller can be expressed as:

$$I_{NNC}(s) = (Kp_{NNC} + \frac{Ki_{NNC}}{s})e_m(s) \qquad (3)$$

Where Kp_{NNC} and Ki_{NNC} denote the proportion and the integral of the neural network PI controller.

e_m is the error between the output of the reference model and the

plant($e_m = \omega_m - \omega_r$).

Using Tustin transformation $s = \frac{2}{T_s}\frac{(z-1)}{(z+1)}$ the transfer function for (3) is

$$I_{NNC}(k) = I_{NNC}(k-1) + Kp_{NNC}(e_m(k) - e_m(k-1))$$
$$+ \frac{T_s}{2}Ki_{NNC}(e_m(k) + e_m(k-1)) \qquad (4)$$

Then constructing the neural network as Fig.3, in which the neural network has three input nodes and one output node, the input vector is defined as:

$$\phi(k-1) = [I_{NNC}(k-1), e_m(k) - e_m(k-1), e_m(k) + e_m(k-1)]^T \qquad (5)$$

Also, the weight vector is defined as:

$$W(k-1) = [1, Kp_{NNC}, \frac{T_s}{2}Ki_{NNC}] \qquad (6)$$

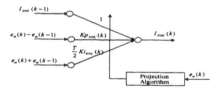

Figure 3 The structure of neural network

In order to update the weights online, the projection algorithm is used. The input-output characteristic of a wide class of linear and nonlinear deterministic dynamical system can be described as following simple from:

$$y(t) = \phi(t-1)^T * W_0^T \qquad (7)$$

Where $\phi(t-1)$ is the system's function vector of the input and output, W_0^T denotes a idea parameter vector.

Projection algorithm can be expressed as:

$$\hat{W}(t)=\hat{W}(t-1)+\frac{\phi(t-1)^T}{\phi(t-1)^T\phi(t-1)}[y(t)-\phi(t-1)^T\hat{W}(t-1)] \qquad (8)$$

The projection algorithm results from the optimization problem. Given $\hat{w}(t-1)$ and $y(t)$, determine $\hat{w}(t)$ so that the index is defined as:

$$J=\frac{1}{2}\|\hat{W}(t)-\hat{W}(t-1)\|^2 \qquad (9)$$

is minimized subject to

$$y(t)=\phi(t-1)^T * \hat{W}(t) \qquad (10)$$

However, a potential problem with the basic algorithm (8) is that there is the (remote) possibility of division by zero. So this lead to the following slightly modified from the algorithm:

$$\hat{W}(t)=\hat{W}(t-1)+\frac{a\phi(t-1)^T}{c+\phi(t-1)^T\phi(t-1)}[y(t)-\phi(t-1)^T\hat{W}(t-1)^T]$$

(11)

Where the choice of a is usually such that $0<a<2$,the constant c is to avoid dividing zero.

The projection algorithm is globally exponentially convergent to W_0^T provided that

$$\sum_{i=0}^{l-1}\frac{\phi(t+i)\phi(t+i)^T}{\phi(t+i)^T\phi(t+i)}\ge cI, \quad c>0$$

for all t and some fixed $l>0$[4], it means that the stability of neural network can be guaranteed if the initial weight vector of neural network is chosen appropriately. Since the parameter of speed controller and position controller are designed by the theory of pole assignment, the whole closed-loop system's stability can be guaranteed.

In this paper, the iterative algorithm of the weight is:

$$W(k)=W(k-1)+\frac{g\phi(k-1)e_m(k)}{h+\phi^T(k-1)\phi(k-1)} \qquad (12)$$

The output of the neural network can be expressed as:

$$I_{NNC}(k)=W(k-1)\phi(k-1) \qquad (13)$$

The neural network PI controller is used to reduce the error ($e_m=\omega_m-\omega_r$) online, so the plant can be considered as a certain and linear system. Then using traditional control theory, the parameters of speed controller and position controller can be designed, and they can make the system have a perfect performance.

SIMULATION RESULTS

In this paper, Simulation data are chosen as follow:

Sampling period: Ts=0.001s, Simulation

time 10s. (10000 steps)

The transfer function of reference model is expressed as:

$$\omega_r(s) = \frac{0.45}{6.88e\text{-}4s + 5.15e\text{-}4} I_p(s)$$

The parameters of plant are as follow: $J = 2.7 * 10^{-3} + 0.001 * \sin(2 * pi * 0.05 * t)$,

B=6.9e-3 , K=1.8.

Disturbance signal: $M_t = 0.58 * \sin(2 * pi * 1 * t)$.

The initial weight vector for (6) are chosen to be $W(0) = [1,1,0.5]$, where $Kp_{NNC}(0) = 1$, $Ki_{NNC}(0) = 1000$.

Parameters of speed controller: Kp_v=0.265, Ki_v=0.0185.

Parameters of position controller: Kp_p=15, Ki_p=0.1.

Position command signal: 0.5sin(t).

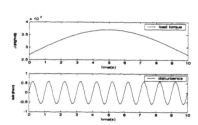

Figure 4 Variation of the inertia and disturbance signal

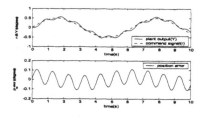

Figure 5 Response and position error of conventional control scheme

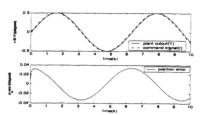

Figure 6 Response and position error of proposed scheme

CONCLUSION

This paper proposed a reference model adaptive control scheme based on neural network. The projection algorithm is used as the Iterative Algorithm, which automatically adjust the parameters of neural network PI controller and effectively reduced the system's sensitivity due to both parameter variations and disturbances. Hence according with the theoretical analysis and the simulation results we can concluded that the proposed control scheme have a lot of value on engineering control.

REFERENCES

1. K. S. Narendra and K. Parthasarathy. Identification & control of dynamical systems using neural network. IEEE Transactions on Neural Network. 1990.pp 4-27.
2. Cybenko, G. Approximation by superpositions of a sigmoidal function. Math. Control Signal System. 1998, pp.303-314.
3. Tien-Chi Chen. Model Reference Neural Network Controller for Induction Motor Speed Control. IEEE. 2002, pp 157-163.
4. G.C.Goodwin K. S. Sin. Adaptive Filtering Prediction and Control.Prentice-Hall, Inc. Englewood Cliffs, New Jersey.1984.pp 68-72.

Robust Fuzzy Tracking Control Simulation of Medium-speed Pulverizer

Minrui FEI and Jian ZHANG

Shanghai Key Laboratory of Power Station Automation Technology
School of Mechatronics and Automation
Shanghai University, Shanghai 200072, China
(Email: mrfei@staff.shu.edu.cn, jianzhang668@163.com)

ABSTRACT

This paper presents a novel robust fuzzy tracking control method of medium-speed Pulverizers (MSP) and develops the corresponding design and simulation software. To facilitate the control system design, the T-S fuzzy model of MSP is proposed based on improving the nonlinear mathematical model firstly. Then the design procedure of robust fuzzy tracking control system is illustrated. In succession, the Robust Fuzzy Tracking Control Platform of MSP (RFTCM) is developed. It makes the design process of robust fuzzy tracking control system of MSP modularized and become easy. Simulation results based on the platform show that the control system can track the desired trajectory asymptotically.

KEY WORDS: Robust fuzzy tracking control, Medium-speed pulverizer, T-S fuzzy model, Internal model principle.

INTRODUCTION

Pulverised coal preparation systems are the important auxiliary system in the thermal power plants. It had significant effect on the security and reliability of the thermal power units. The medium speed pulverizer is the heart of the pulverised coal preparation system. Fast pulverizer response is desired to maintain boiler pressure and temperature of a thermal power unit. However pulverizer responses could not always satisfy the dynamic requirements of a thermal power unit because the control system is not designed under considering the nonlinear dynamic characteristic of MSP fully.

So far, several pulverizer mathematical models have been developed [1-3]. However, these models are too complicated to apply. It is very hard to design control system of the pulverizer with good performance because of the complexity and nonlinearity of these models.

T-S Fuzzy modeling can solve this problem by using some fuzzy inference methods. In this type of fuzzy model, local dynamic characteristic in different state-space regions is represented by linear models. The overall model of the nonlinear system is achieved by fuzzy "blending" of those linear models through nonlinear fuzzy membership functions. The blended models can approximate the nonlinear system very well if the membership functions are appropriate. Thus controllers with good performance to every linear system and the whole nonlinear system can be designed by parallel distributed compensation.

Based on the T-S fuzzy model of MSP, a hybrid robust fuzzy tracking controller is introduced to track the desired trajectory.

The tracking performance of this controller is better than other controllers [4-10] whose tracking error only can be attenuated below some certain level. The hybrid robust fuzzy tracking controller is designed based on the internal model principle. It can track the desired trajectory asymptotically.

To facilitate engineers with basic control theory to design the proposed control system, we develop the Robust Fuzzy Tracking Control Platform of MSP (RFTCM). With the aid of RFTCM, an engineer can design the control system of an actual MSP served in a commercial power plant. The simulation results show that the control system has good performance. It can track the reference input signal asymptotically.

MATHEMATICAL MODEL OF MEDIUM SPEED PULVERIZERS

The pulverizer mathematical model in [1] is described by several differential and algebraic equations as follows:

$$\begin{cases} \dot{M}_c = W_c - K_{11}M_c \\ \dot{M}_{pf} = K_{11}M_c - W_{pf} \\ \dot{T}_{out} = (K_1 T_{in} + K_2)W_{air} + K_3 W_c - (W_{air} + W_c)(K_4 T_{out} + K_5) \\ \Delta P_{mill} = K_8 \Delta P_{pa} + K_9(M_{pf} + K_{10}M_c) \\ W_{pf} = K_{12}\Delta P_{pa}M_{pf} \\ P = K_6(\Delta P_{mill} - \Delta P_{pa}) + K_7 \end{cases}$$

$$(1)$$

where
M_c mass of coal in pulverizer
M_{pf} mass of pulverized coal in pulverier
T_{out} outlet temperature of pulverizer
ΔP_{mill} pulverizer differential pressure
W_{pf} mass flow rate of pulverized coal
P pulverizer power consumed
ΔP_{pa} primary air differential pressure
W_c mass flow rate of coal into pulverizer
T_{in} inlet temperature of pulverizer
W_{air} primary air flow into pulverizer
K_i the constant coefficients of the pulverizer model, $i=1,2,3,\cdots,12$.
The whole mathematic model of a pulverizer can be obtained after identifying the coefficients in equation set (1) by the improved GA. However, it is not convenient to design the control system of the pulverizer. So the above model needs to be converted into a T-S fuzzy model based on analysing the operation mechanism.

To minimize the design effort, we try to use as few rules as possible with guarantee of the accuracy of the T-S fuzzy model. Let the primary air differential pressure ΔP_{pa} and the primary air-flow into pulverizer W_{air} be the premise variables of T-S fuzzy model. W_{air} and the product of T_{in} and W_{air} $T_{in}W_{air}$ are the input variables. W_{pf}, ΔP_{mill}, T_{out}, P-K_7 are the output variables. Then the nonlinear model can be converted into an equivalent T-S fuzzy model of the pulverizer as follows:

Plant Rule i:

IF ΔP_{pa} is P_i and W_{air} is W_i,
THEN

$$\dot{x} = A_i x + B_i u$$
$$y = C_i x + D_i u \qquad i = 1,2,3,4$$

where

$$x = \begin{bmatrix} M_c \\ M_{pf} \\ T_{out} \end{bmatrix}, \quad u = \begin{bmatrix} W_{air} \\ T_{in}W_{air} \end{bmatrix}, \quad y = \begin{bmatrix} \Delta P_{mill} \\ T_{out} \\ W_{pf} \\ D - K_7 \end{bmatrix}$$

Blending linear models (1)~(4) through the above nonlinear fuzzy membership functions $\mu_i^j (i=1,2; j=1,2,3,4)$, the T-S fuzzy model of the pulverizer can be obtained as follows:

$$\dot{x}(t) = \sum_{i=1}^{4} h_i \left[A_i x(t) + B_i u(t) \right]$$
$$y(t) = \sum_{i=1}^{4} h_i \left[C_i x(t) + D_i u(t) \right]$$

$$(2)$$

where

$$h_i = \frac{\mu_1^i \mu_2^i}{\sum_{i=1}^{4} \mu_1^i \mu_2^i}$$

It is composed of four linear models that are blended through nonlinear membership functions. Controllers with good performance to every linear system and the whole nonlinear system can be designed based on the T-S fuzzy model easily. So the T-S fuzzy model is suitable for designing the control system of the pulverizer.

ROBUST FUZZY TRACKING CONTROL OF MEDIUM SPEED PULVERIZERS

After obtaining the T-S fuzzy model of MSP, the hybrid robust fuzzy tracking controller based on the internal model principle can be designed to track the desired trajectory. Consider a reference model as follows:

$$x_r(t) = A_r x_r(t)$$
$$r(t) = C_r x_r(t) \tag{3}$$

where
  $r(t)$ reference input
  $x(t)$ reference state
  A_r specific asymptotically stable matrix
  $\{A_r \; C_r\}$ are observerable
It is assumed that $r(t)$, for all $t \geq 0$, represents a desired trajectory.
According to the Internal Model Principle, the following servo-compensator can be designed:

$$x_c = A_c x_c + B_c (r - y)$$
$$y_c = x_c \tag{4}$$

Then the state equation of every fuzzy subsystem can be represented as follows:

$$\begin{bmatrix} \dot{x} \\ \dot{x}_c \end{bmatrix} = \begin{bmatrix} A_i & 0 \\ -B_c C_i & A_c \end{bmatrix} \begin{bmatrix} x \\ x_c \end{bmatrix} + \begin{bmatrix} B_i \\ 0 \end{bmatrix} u + \begin{bmatrix} 0 \\ B_c \end{bmatrix} r$$

$$\tilde{y} = [C_i \quad 0] \begin{bmatrix} x \\ x_c \end{bmatrix}, \; i = 1, 2, \cdots, g \tag{5}$$

Eigenvalues of the subsystem (5) can be placed randomly by the following state feedback controller:

$$u_i = [K_i \quad K_{ci}] \begin{bmatrix} x \\ x_c \end{bmatrix} = K_i x + K_{ci} x_c \tag{6}$$

Let us denote

$$\tilde{x}(t) = \begin{bmatrix} x(t) \\ x_c(t) \end{bmatrix}, \quad \tilde{A} = \begin{bmatrix} A_i & 0 \\ -B_c C_i & A_c \end{bmatrix}, \quad \tilde{B} = \begin{bmatrix} B_i \\ 0 \end{bmatrix},$$

$$\tilde{B}_r = \begin{bmatrix} 0 \\ B_c \end{bmatrix}, \quad \tilde{C} = [C_i \quad 0], \quad \tilde{K}_i = [K_i \quad K_{ci}]$$

Therefore, the augmented system in (5) can be expressed as the following form:

$$\begin{bmatrix} \dot{x} \\ \dot{x}_c \end{bmatrix} = \begin{bmatrix} A_i & 0 \\ -B_c C_i & A_c \end{bmatrix} \begin{bmatrix} x \\ x_c \end{bmatrix} + \begin{bmatrix} B_i \\ 0 \end{bmatrix} [K_j \quad K_{cj}] \begin{bmatrix} x \\ x_c \end{bmatrix}$$

$$+ \begin{bmatrix} 0 \\ B_c \end{bmatrix} r = \tilde{A}_i \tilde{x} + \tilde{B}_i \tilde{K}_j \tilde{x} + \tilde{B}_r r = (\tilde{A}_i + \tilde{B}_i \tilde{K}_j) \tilde{x} + \tilde{B}_r r$$

$$\tilde{y} = [C_i \quad 0] \begin{bmatrix} x \\ x_c \end{bmatrix} = \tilde{C}_i \tilde{x}, \; i, j = 1, 2, \cdots, g$$

$$\tag{7}$$

that is

$$\dot{\tilde{x}} = (\tilde{A}_i + \tilde{B}_i \tilde{K}_j) \tilde{x} + \tilde{B}_r r$$
$$\tilde{y} = \tilde{C}_i \tilde{x}, \; i, j = 1, 2, \cdots, g \tag{8}$$

The overall fuzzy tracking control system can be expressed as follows:

$$\dot{\tilde{x}}(t) = \sum_{j=1}^{g}\sum_{i=1}^{g} h_i(\tilde{x}(t)) h_j(\tilde{x}(t))\left(\tilde{A}_i + \tilde{B}_i \tilde{K}_j\right)\tilde{x}(t) + \tilde{B}_r r \quad (9)$$

$$\tilde{y}(t) = \sum_{i=1}^{g} h_i(\tilde{x}(t))\tilde{C}\tilde{x}(t)$$

If the fuzzy system contains uncertainties, then the system can be expressed as follows:

$$\dot{\tilde{x}}(t) = \sum_{i=1}^{g}\sum_{j=1}^{g} h_i h_j\left(\tilde{A}_i + \Delta\tilde{A}_i + (\tilde{B}_i + \Delta\tilde{B}_i)\tilde{K}_j\right)\tilde{x}(t) + \tilde{B}_r r$$

$$\tilde{y}(t) = \sum_{i=1}^{g} h_i(\tilde{x}(t))\tilde{C}_i\tilde{x}(t) \quad (10)$$

If the system (10) is stable, then the output y can track the desired trajectory $r(t)$. The closed-loop eigenvalues can be chosen according to the performance requirement of nominal closed-loop system. Then the controller $\tilde{K}_1, \tilde{K}_2, \cdots, \tilde{K}_g$ can be obtained.

SIMULALTION RESEARCH

After obtaining the T-S fuzzy model of MSP, the hybrid robust fuzzy tracking controller based on the internal model principle can be designed to track the desired trajectory. To simplify the design of robust fuzzy tracking controller, the whole process can be decomposed into four steps: (1) Accept the coefficients of MSP; (2) Allocate the poles of closed-loop system; (3) Solve the poles of all subsystems; (4) Enter the simulation. They make the design process of robust fuzzy tracking control system modularized. Based on these steps, Matlab/simulink is adopted to develop the design and simulation system software of robust fuzzy tracking control, i.e., Robust Fuzzy Tracking Control Platform of MSP (RFTCM). A person who has basic control theory can design the robust fuzzy tracking control system easily and accomplish simulation to test the control results by RFTCM.

Four steps of design process are embodied on the visual man-machine interface of RFTCM. It is developed by GUIDE (graphical user interface development environment) in Matlab. The GUIDE provides a set of tools for creating GUIs. These tools greatly simplify the process of laying out and programming a GUI. The Man-machine interface is shown as Fig. 1.

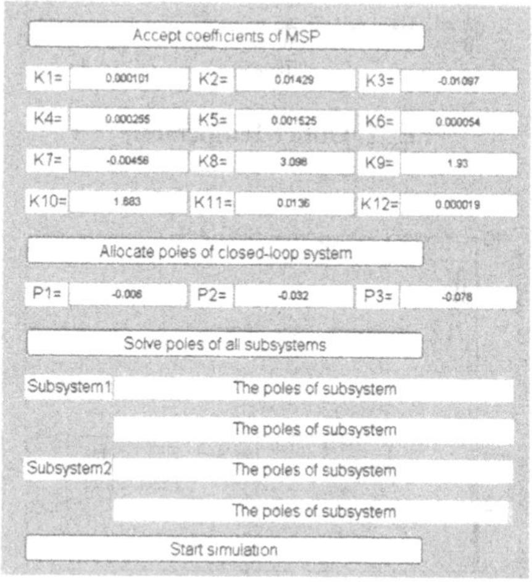

Fig. 1. Man-Machine Interface of RFTCM

The main function of Man-machine interface of RFTCM is to prompt the designer to input information and to display the results that simulation software has produced. The Man-machine interface also implies the steps of design robust fuzzy tracking control systems.

After designing the robust fuzzy tracking control system according to the hint of Man-machine interface, the simulation results can be achieved: the transient curve of outlet temperature and the transient curve of mass flow rate of pulverized coal as shown in Fig. 2 and Fig. 3. These curves indicate that tracking performance of Robust Fuzzy Tracking (RFT) control system is better than PID control.

81

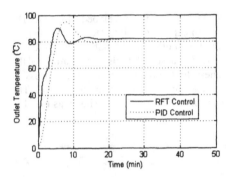

Fig. 2. Outlet Temperature

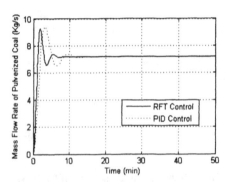

Fig. 3. Mass Flow Rate of Pulverized Coal

CONCLUSION

In this paper, we have proposed the robust fuzzy tracking controller based on IMP to control the MSP. Because the internal model of the desired trajectory is embedded in the control system, the robust fuzzy tracking controller can track the desired trajectory asymptotically.

Furthermore, the Robust Fuzzy Tracking Control Platform of MSP (RFTCM) is developed to facilitate the controller design. Thus an engineer can design robust fuzzy tracking controllers of MSP easily. Simulation results show that the desired trajectory for MSP can be tracked via the proposed method asymptotically.

ACKNOWLEDGEMENT

This work is supported by Key Project of Science & Technology Commission of Shanghai Municipality (04JC14038 and 04DZ11008), Doctoral Program Foundation of Science & Technology Special Project in University (20040280017), Program for New Century Excellent Talents in University (NCET-04-0433), and Shanghai Leading Academic Disciplines (T0103).

REFERENCES

1. Zhou G, Si J and Taft CW, Modeling and simulation of C-E deep bowl pulverizer, IEEE Transactions on Energy Conversion, 3 (2000), pp. 312-322.
2. Zhang YG, Wu QH, Wang J, Matts D and Zhou XX., Pulverizer modeling by machine learning based on onsite measurements, IEEE Transactions on Energy Conversion, 4 (2002), pp. 549-555.
3. Tanaka S., Kurosaki Y., Teramoto T., and Murakami S., Dynamic simulation analysis of MPS mill for coal fired boiler and application of its results to boiler control system, IFAC Symposium of Power Plant and Control, 1997.
4. El, H. A. and Bentalba, S., Fuzzy path tracking control for automatic steering of vehicles. Robotics and Autonomous Systems, 4 (2003) pp. 203-213
5. Tseng, C.-S., Chen, B.-S. and Uang, H.-J., Fuzzy tracking control design for nonlinear dynamic systems via T-S fuzzy model, IEEE Transactions on Fuzzy Systems, 3 (2001), pp. 381-392.
6. Kim, E., Output feedback tracking control of robot manipulators with model uncertainty via adaptive fuzzy logic, IEEE Transactions on Fuzzy Systems, 3 (2004), pp. 368-378.
7. Tong, S.-C., Wang, T., and Li, H.-X., Fuzzy robust tracking control for uncertain nonlinear systems. International Journal of Approximate Reasoning, 2 (2002), pp. 73-90.
8. Guan, X. and Chen, C., Adaptive fuzzy control for chaotic systems with H infinity tracking performance. Fuzzy Sets and Systems, 1 (2003), pp. 81-93.
9. Yu, W.-S., H infinity tracking-based adaptive fuzzy-neural control for MIMO uncertain robotic systems with time delays. Fuzzy Sets and Systems, 3 (2004), pp. 375-401.
10. Chang, Y.-C., Robust tracking control for nonlinear MIMO systems via fuzzy approaches. Automatica, 10 (2000), pp. 1535-1545.

DDDAS M&S Reference Framework Based on PADS

Shoupeng HAN, Xiaogang QIU and Kedi HUANG

Laboratory of Simulation, College of Mechaeronics Engineering and Automation
National University of Defense Technology
Changsha, 410073 China
(E-mail: hspself@163.com)

ABSTRACT

Dynamic Data Driven Application System (DDDAS) is a new paradigm for research of interdisciplinary complex problems which entails the ability to incorporate additional data into an executing simulation application and, in reverse, the ability of applications to dynamically steer the measurement process. It needs the support of online simulation to assist decision makers to complete their tasks in time. To facilitate the building of such environments, levels of adaptability and challenging technologies of collaborative DDDAS environment are analyzed and a DDDAS M&S reference framework based on parallel and distributed simulation (PADS) is proposed. Realization mechanism relating to this framework, including multi-paradigm modeling based on Discrete Event System Specification (DEVS), dynamic reconfiguration based on flexible points binding, component substitution and dynamic compilation are also discussed.

KEY WORDS: Dynamic Data Driven Application System, Multi-Paradigm Modeling, Parallel and Distributed Simulation, Dynamic Reconfiguration, Discrete Event System Specification

NOMENCLATURE

DDDAS: Dynamic Data Driven Application System
PADS: Parallel and Distributed Simulation
SBD: Simulation Based Decision
CAMPaM: Computer Automated Multi-Paradigm Modeling
DEVS: Discrete Event System Specification
HLA: High Level Architecture

INTRODUCTION

Dynamic Data Driven Application System (DDDAS) is a new research paradigm of multidisciplinary large complex system. It entails the ability to incorporate additional data into an executing simulation application (these data can be archival or collected online) and, in reverse, the ability of applications to dynamically steer the measurement process [1] [2]. The DDDAS concept offers the promise of improving application models and methods and augmenting the analysis and prediction capabilities of application simulations and the effectiveness of measurement systems. To facilitate design and development of DDDAS system, a domain-independent and adaptive reference integrated modeling and simulation environment which can support the requirements of inverse computation and simulation based decision (SBD) by evaluating different alternatives in time is needed.

DDDAS M&S ENVIRONEMENT

Concept of DDDAS

Accurate analysis and prediction of the

behavior of a complicated system is difficult. Today, simulations of systems are fairly complex, but they still lack the ability to accurately describe such systems. This situation is accentuated in cases where real-time dynamic conditions exist. Application simulations that can, at execution time, dynamically incorporate new data, archival, or from online measurements of the actual systems offer the promise of more accurate analysis, more accurate predictions, and more precise controls. These capabilities are fostered with the DDDAS concept (see Figure1).

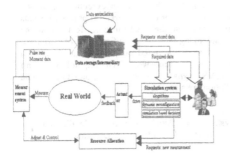

Figure 1 Structure of DDDAS

DDDAS offers the promise of improving modeling methods, augmenting the analysis and prediction capabilities of application simulations, improving the efficiency of simulations and the effectiveness of measurement systems. It can be viewed as a methodology to counterbalance incompleteness in model and capability to enhance the application models by imparting additional information into the model as runtime additional data are used to selectively enhance or refine the original model. It can also be used to reduce the time to derive the simulation results.

Multi-Paradigm Modeling in DDDAS

DDDAS aims to address complicated problems which can not be dealt with effectively using traditional methods. These problems are usually interdisciplinary. Different aspects of a problem need to be solved with most suited methods in associating domain. So, how to weave these interdisciplinary methods together to solve given question is a core problem DDDAS needs to be faced with. Multi-paradigm modeling is a kind of technique to address this requirement which has been successfully applied in the field of software architectures, control system design, model-integrated computing, and tool interoperability. The emerging field of Computer Automated Multi-Paradigm Modeling (CAMPaM) [3] aims to achieve this by addressing and integrating three orthogonal directions of research:

Model abstraction: deals with the different levels of detail of models and the relationship between these models;

Multi-formalism modeling: deals with coupling of and transforming between the manifold of formalisms used;

Meta-modeling: deals with the description of modeling formalisms and their domain-specific aspects.

Integrating CAMPaM into DDDAS M&S is necessary and it can improve efficiency of system development. Because DDDAS is a dynamic variable environment, there are also some special aspects should be addressed in order to make CAMPaM useful in DDDAS. The core of these aspects is to equip models with dynamic adaptabilities, which will be discussed detailedly in following chapters.

Adaptability of DDDAS M&S

Simulation subsystem is the core of a DDDAS. It should be able to assist Subject Matter Experts (SMEs) to make decision about how to control and adapt the running of the whole system. Because DDDAS environment is changing dynamically, to fulfill its role, the simulation subsystem also must be able to adapt to this changing environment. These adaptabilities can be divided into three levels:

Application-level: First, a number of models at different resolutions or different formalizations (discrete, continuous, etc.) maybe available to describe the nature of a given problem. DDDAS simulation code should be able to switch adaptively between such models to trade off accuracy for computational time and resources. In addition, there are also requirements to add, modify and remove components from existing simulation according to external dynamic data.

Algorithm-level: First, DDDAS simulation needs algorithms adaptive to a wide range varying conditions; Second, there may be many algorithms for implementing a desired functionality (e.g., direct and iterative solvers for linear systems), and it may be advantageous to switch between them according to different conditions.

Infrastructure-level: Changes in the computational environment (such as hardware failures, load balancing etc.) may require a simulation system to be adaptive at the Infrastructure-level. Because every kind of simulation system has its specificity, so some special adaptive mechanism is needed to be investigated in addition to adaptive mechanisms of common software.

Dynamic Reconfiguration

It is notable that DDDAS simulation should gain these adaptabilities at runtime. This is because DDDAS is dynamic environment, and it is not permitted to record current state, stop current simulation running, reconstruct a simulation from scratch and rerun simulation again. So, DDDAS simulation must be equipped with dynamic adaptabilities at various levels discussed above. The function of this kind of dynamic reconfiguration is also the core of DDDAS simulation system.

Because of the dynamic and adaptive features it has, DDDAS is a effective research paradigm for complex system. Currently, advanced modeling and simulation technology is one of the important measures to investigate complex problems. How to make DDDAS built upon advanced parallel and distributed simulation (PADS) is a realistic problem. Because of its requirement of dynamic adaptability, DDDAS needs to combine model, simulation runtime monitor and control, decision making activities of SMEs into a tightly closed loop.

COLLABORATIVE DDDAS M&S BASED ON PADS

Levels of Collaborative Environment

Because of its requirement of dynamic adaptability, DDDAS needs to combine modeling activity, simulation runtime monitor and control, decision making activities of SMEs and various resources into a tightly closed loop. This requires building a collaborative environment for specific DDDAS, which can integrate modeling, simulation, decision making and adaptation activities effectively. In terms of multi-paradigm modeling and dynamic adaptability discussed in above section, we propose a layered structure of this kind of collaborative environment (see Figure 2).

Collaboration
workflow management
Decision
Evaluation, Exploray analysis, Optimization
Search
Model base, Heuristic search
Modeling
Multi-Paradigm modeling based on DEVS
Simulation
Paraell and distributed simulation
Network
Workstation, Distributed OS, Cluster, Grid

Figure 2 Levels of DDDAS Collaborative Environment

In this layered structure, network layer is the base of the whole computation system.

Collaboration layer is on the top of this structure, and it should confront to some kind of workflow restriction, which will make people with different roles work together more efficiently. The middle four layers are the core of this environment; they construct a bidirectional closed loop: first, we should build a system model and apply it to specific simulation system to build a simulation execution; when the simulation execution can't complete our requirement, we should use meta-data of model to search more suited model composition; result of this search should be examined by SMEs who will make decision about how to adjust simulation execution; if searched result cannot fulfill the requirement, new models or new modules may also be built and inserted into simulation execution at runtime; at the end, this decision will be applied to current simulation execution and this closed loop starts again. So, how to make activities according with different layers interoperating effectively is critical for building a DDDAS environment proposed here.

Flexible Point Binding

All the adaptabilities of a DDDAS should relate to some elements which are adaptable. So, when a model is built, we should be able to identify the adaptable elements from its metadata. In consistent with literate [4], we call these adaptable elements flexible points here. These flexible points bridge multiple layers in DDDAS collaborative environment proposed above together to complete needed adaptation dynamically. These flexible points are described when a model is built, and they may bind to different values for a specific simulation execution. When current running simulation cannot fulfill users' requirements, decision makers would collect current flexible points and their bindings together and seek for better flexible points to fulfill users' requirements. To use these flexible points easily, we describe them as XML files

formally. Part of this XML schema is shown in Figure 3. At current, they are classified into four kinds: algorithm, integer, numeric and boolean flexible points. When a model is embedded into a simulation, its associating flexible point bindings are also formally provided and can be observed and changed at runtime, this formal description can assure model be adjusted in correct restriction.

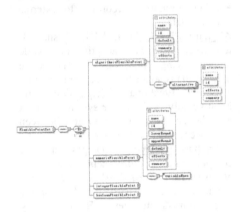

Figure 3 Flexible Point Description

Reference Framework based on PADS

To build DDDAS environments on advanced modeling and simulation technology effectively, we proposed a DDDAS reference framework based on PADS (see Figure 4). What is most different from ordinary simulation system is DDDAS simulation in this framework provides an online decision making mechanism which can help SMEs make adaptations to simulation execution or resource allocation semi-automatically. The core of this mechanism is simulation adaptation based on optimization. There are three kinds of adaptation in this framework: dynamic flexible points binding, component substitution, and dynamic compilation. Except from flexible points discussed in above section, component substitution allows one component replaced by another alternative component at runtime. Dynamic compilation allows new component or module be inserted into simulation without stopping current execution.

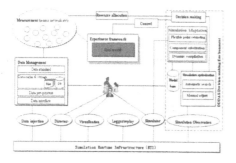

Figure 4 DDDAS Reference Framework Based on PADS

OUR ONGOING WORK

Multi-paradigm Modeling Based on DEVS

DEVS is a well defined formalism which can be used to specify a model in a hierarchical, modular form. It can be used to describe discrete event system, continuous system, and hybrid system effectively. DEVS can be viewed as not only a modeling formalism but also a foundation of simulation because each module in DEVS has the feature of time. Furthermore, because DEVS is built on common system theory, many domain specific modeling formalism such as state-chart, Petri net etc. can be mapped into DEVS formalism. In our research, DEVS is selected as the intermediate layer to tie multi-paradigm model and simulation together. This includes two parts of work: one is to map domain specific model into DEVS formalism; the other is map DEVS model into model compatible with specific simulation runtime infrastructures. Our work involves two kinds of simulation infrastrtures: real-time simulation based on shared-memory network and HLA.

DDDAS Compatible Simulation Infrastructures

We build a hard real-time simulation infrastructure based on shared-memory network in which model is based on DEVS formalism and communication and time management mechanism are custom defined. We are also building a DEVS/HLA modeling environment in which model is compatible with DEVS and bottom time management and data communication mechanism is through HLA/RTI.

We are extending these two simulation infrastructures with dynamic adaptabilities now. Aspect-Oriented Programming (AOP) is selected as the method to define adaptable elements (such as flexible point) and weave them into simulation execution at runtime.

Furthermore, we are exploring simulation cloning as a special dynamic adaptation and an assistant mechanism for decision. Simulation cloning entails the ability to produce multiple similar simulation scenarios from an origin scenario and allow them execute parallelly in one simulation execution. This will be a useful tool for SMEs to judge the actual effect of different configurations.

REFERENCES

1. DDDAS Workshop Report [R]. NSF Workshop Report, January 2006. www.cise.nsf.gov/dddas
2. Frederica Darema, Dynamic Data Driven Applications Systems: New Capabilities for Application Simulations and Measurements, Proceedings ICCS'05, Atlanta, USA, May 2005, pp. 610-615.
3. Pieter J. Mosterman, Computer Automated Multi-Paradigm Modeling: An Introduction, SIMULATION, 2004, **80**-9, pp.433-450.
4. Yannick Loitiere, Y., David C. Brogan, and Paul F. Reynolds, Simulation Coercion Applied to Multiagent DDDAS, Proceedings ICCS'04, Kraków, Poland, June 2004 ,pp.789-796.

Research on the Combined Simulation and Its Application of the Virtual Prototype Based on Multi-platforms

Liao Ying*, Li Changjiang*, Feng Xiangjun*, Pan wanghua*, Liao Chaowei*

*College of Aerospace and Material Engineering, National University of Defense Technology, Changsha 410073, China
(E-mail: liaoying1104@yahoo.com.cn, pwh2008_79@163.com)

ABSTRACT

The combined simulation method on the virtual prototype model based on multi-platforms was given here. As an example, the method was used on the validation of the virtual prototype of the two-axes position mechanism for satellite antennas. Firstly, the "3D" solid model of the two-axes position mechanism was built by use of the software platform Pro/Engineer. Based on the solid model, we made the virtual prototype model of the two-axes position mechanism on ADAMS. Then, the simulation model based on the mathematic model of the two-axes position mechanism was built on Matlab/Simulink. The mathematic model was combined with the virtual prototype model, and then the combined simulation model was gained. Through the analysis and the comparison of simulation results between the mathematic model and the combined model of the system, the reliability of the virtual prototype of the two-axes position mechanism for satellite antennas was preliminarily evaluated.

Keywords: Virtual Prototype, Combined Simulation, Reliability Evaluation, Two-axes Position Mechanism

1 PRESENT OF THE QUESTION

Presently the study on the technology of virtual prototype mostly focuses on the constitution technology and the simulation realization of virtual prototypes. There are few reports on the elementary evaluation to the results of modeling and simulation of virtual prototypes. In some special instances, such as the research stage of physical prototype, the costly manufacture of physical prototype, the unpractical experiment conditions etc., we lack the data of experiment. In such case, we can not evaluate the reliability of virtual prototype model effectively by use of the traditional evaluation methods. So we need to develop some new methods. The paper introduced a combined simulation method on the virtual prototype model based on multi-platforms. As an example, it was used on the validation of the virtual prototype of the two-axes position mechanism for satellite antennas. Through

88

the analysis and the comparison of the simulation results between the mathematic model and the combined model of the system, we finished the elementary evaluation to the reliability of the virtual prototype of the two-axes position mechanism for satellite antennas.

2 THE COMBINED SIMULATION METHOD BASED ON MULTI-PLATFORMS

2.1 The Combined Simulation Method

At the case of lacking the data of experiment, we can build the mathematic model and the virtual prototype model of the system. Through the comparison on the simulation results of the mathematic model and the virtual prototype model of the system, we finished the elementary evaluation to the reliability of the virtual prototype [1]. But the advantages of these models could not be combined in this method. Moreover, it was difficult for us to judge if the results were correct. So we had a reasonable imagination: we built both the virtual prototype model and the mathematic model. And the mathematic simulation model provided the driving signal to the virtual prototype by state variables. Then, we made a combined simulation model. At last we got the conclusion which we had wanted by comparing the results of the mathematic model and the combined model. That's the combined simulation method based on multi-platforms we discussed in this paper. Obviously, this method was reasonable and credible.

2.2 The Virtual Prototype Model of the Two-axes Position Mechanism

In this paper, we built 3D solid model on the platform Pro/Engineer[2]. Then the mechanism was analyzed and defined with the multi-body dynamics on the platform ADAMS. At last we built the virtual prototype model of the two-axes position mechanism on the platform ADAMS shown in Fig 1. The control torque of the vertical motor was equal to the holding torque of stepper motor (1500*2/pi N*mm) while the vertical motor was electrified and was not to run. At the electrifying moment, the control torque mutated as involving torque (539 N*mm).The control torque of cross motor was 1500*2/pi N*mm, and the involving torque was 245 N*mm. The numerical values, such as 1500, 539 and 245, were the measured data of the stepper motor. And we set the damp coefficient between the stators and the rotors as 0.3.

So we built the whole virtual prototype of the two-axes position mechanism that is shown in Fig 1.

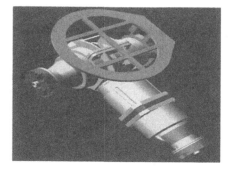

Fig 1 The virtual prototype of the two-axes position mechanism

2.3 The Mathematic Simulation Model of the Two-axes Position Mechanism

The principle diagram of the two-axes position mechanism is shown in Fig 2. The mathematic model of the two-axes position mechanism was built, including modeling

89

of the two-axes load sub-system, the stepper motor sub-system, the harmonic transmission sub-system, the space disturbing torques sub-system. Because of the space limit of this paper, we didn't enumerate the models here. At last, these sub-systems were combined into a collective model of the two-axes position mechanism based on physical quantities exchanged in each sub-system. The simulation of the mathematic model of the two-axes position mechanism was achieved on the platform MATLAB. The simulation model is shown in Fig 3.

by state variables [3]. In the platform ADAMS, we defined the control torque of the virtual prototype as import state variable T_out. And we defined two output state variables for the virtual prototype: azimuth_position (rotate angle) and rotor_velocity (rotate angle velocity). So the control module in the platform ADAMS created the multi-body dynamical simulation model of the two-axes position mechanism. It is shown in Fig 4.

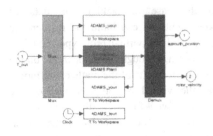

Fig 4 The multi-body dynamical simulation model of the two-axes position mechanism

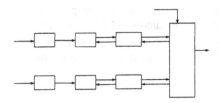

Fig 2 The principle diagram of the two-axes position mechanism

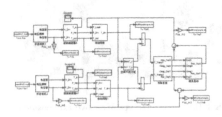

Fig 3 The simulation model of the two-axes position mechanism

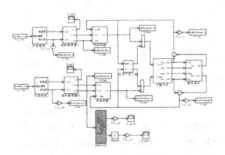

Fig 5 The combined simulation model of the virtual prototype of the two-axes position mechanism

2.4 The Combined Simulation Model of the System
The mathematic simulation model provided the driving signal to the virtual prototype

We used the control torque of the stepper motor, as shown in Fig 3, as the input of the dynamical simulation model of the two-axes position mechanism. Then we

90

could realized the combined simulation on the platforms of ADAMS and MATLAB. For example, we simulated the direct-axis of the two-axes position mechanism. As shown in Fig 5, the adams_sub is the multi-body dynamical simulation model of the two-axes position mechanism on the platform ADAMS. Then the mathematic model drives the virtual prototype of the two-axes position mechanism.

2.5 Realization of the Combined Simulation

In order to realize the combined simulation, we must analyze the different structures and characteristics of the mathematic model and the virtual prototype model. Taking the combined simulation of the two-axes position mechanism as an example, the mathematic simulation model provided the driving signal to the virtual prototype by state variables. Then, we made a combined simulation model and could begin the combined simulation test.

3 ANALYSIS ON THE RESULTS OF COMBINED SIMULATION

3.1 Parameter Setting of the Combined Simulation

Because we lacked the data of experiment, we adopted the simplified mathematic model of the stepper motor. According to the initiative design project, we set step angle 0.2°, normal pulse velocity 100pps, drive ratio 202 and drive clearance 6′(0.001745rad). And we set the two axes pointing range ±8° according to the requirement of system. Because the system was under the open-loop control, we could control the stepper motor availably through controlling the input impulses.

3.2 Analysis on the Results of Combined

Simulation

After we set the parameters, we studied the vertical axis of the two-axes pointing mechanism as an example. The results of combined simulation and mathematic simulation (rotate angle and rotate velocity) are shown in Fig 6 to Fig 9. We can know that the result of combined model simulation was accordant with the result of mathematic model simulation in the change way of rotate velocity.

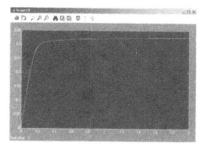

Fig 6 The rotate velocity of vertical axis
(The result of combined model simulation)

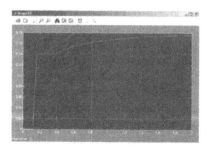

Fig 7 The rotate velocity of vertical axis
(The result of mathematic model simulation)

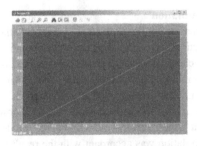

Fig 8 The point placement of vertical axis
(The result of combined model simulation)

Fig 9 The point placement of vertical axis
(The result of mathematic model simulation)

There were two different points between the two kinds of simulation results that are shown in Fig 6 and Fig 7. Firstly, the change of rotate velocity hadn't time delay in the combined simulation. On the contrary, the change of rotate velocity had time delay in the mathematic simulation. The clearance was the reason to this differentia. Because the clearance was the non-key characteristic, we didn't consider its effectiveness in the combined simulation. Secondly, the steady value of rotate velocity was 0.325rad/s in the combined simulation, while 0.175rad/s in the mathematic simulation. Because we neglected some non-key factors, such as the space disturbing torques, the shafting

shake etc., the steady value of rotate velocity in the combined simulation was bigger than that in the mathematic simulation.

As shown in Fig 8 and Fig 9, we can know that the point placement of vertical axis increased linearly. So the rotate velocity of motor was constant while the input impulse speed is 100pps. The results of combined simulation and mathematic simulation were accordant on the movement law.

So we made a conclusion that the results of the combined model simulation and mathematic model simulation were accordant on the movement law. Taking into account the influences of some unimportant factors, we made a conclusion that the virtual prototype model of the two-axes position mechanism was credible.

4 CONCLUSION

The study of this paper showed that we can use the combined simulation as a kind of credibility valuation method on the design of virtual prototype. So, the method has the important practical value in the design phase of complicated products.

REFERENCES

1. Chen Dingfang etc, Virtual design[M], Beijing: China Machine Press, 2002, pp.18-106.
2. Zhang Yishan etc, The basic to enter PRO/E[M], Beijing: China Machine Press, 2002, pp.332-376.
3. Wang Guoqiang etc, Virtual prototype technology and its practice on ADAMS[M], Xi'an: Northwestern University of Technology Press, 2002, pp.219 -227.

Research on High Level Modeling Method for Complex Simulation System

Peng Wang*, Bo Hu Li* ,Xudong Chai** ,Yanqiang Di*

*Scholl of Automation Science and Electronic Engineering,
Beihang University
Beijing 100083, China
(E-mail: pennywang@vip.163.com)
** The Second Academy, China Aerospace Science and
Industry Corp.
Beijing 100854, China

Abstract

The development of virtual prototype for complex product is a complicated system engineering involving multi-disciplines, multi-departments and multi-levels models. For rapidly organizing development and reducing the cost of complex product, system high level modeling method is provided for describing the system's structure and behavior which helps the system and model information to be translated among different development stages, tools and persons. High level modeling method and its usage in development process of complex system engineering are introduced in this paper.

KEY WORDS: System Simulation, High Level Modeling, Complex System

Introduction

The development of virtual prototype for complex product is a complicated system engineering involving multi-disciplines, multi-departments and multi-levels models.[1] For rapidly organizing development and reducing the cost of complex product, system high level modeling method is provided for describing the system's structure and behavior which translates the models' information among different development stages, tools and persons. This method is independent with platform and programming language that provides specification of elements, rules and methodology. It's mainly used at domain of complex distributed and interactive system and interdisciplinary engineering system.

System High Level Modeling Method

Concept

High level modeling(HLM) technology is a modeling method for constructing and describing complex system based on interdiscipline models which models complex system's structure and behavior at system level and interdependency between interfaces of subsystems and subsystems. Structure model includes all the components and relationship between them and behavior model includes the scene of system running and all the responses to any external things under any conditions.

The basic requirements for high level modeling technology are:

1) Supporting modeling multidiscipline virtual prototype at system level and developing complex simulation system by system engineering development method;

2) Supporting modeling continuous, discrete and hybrid system;

3) Unified and symbolic modeling method which is easy to communicate information and knowledge among different experts;

4) Independent with platform and realized by platform-dependent models through mapping to specific platform;

5) Including rigorous executable semantics which can validate system's interfaces and behavior at concept stage;

HLM method is based on system formalism theory and system engineering theory in which system decomposition and composition are of great importance.

Complex system is divided into Compound Model (CM) and Atomic Model (AM) in HLM method. AM is the basic component of structured system that realizes a minimal function. CM is composed of sub-models, couplings between models, behavior models. System's structure is show as follows:

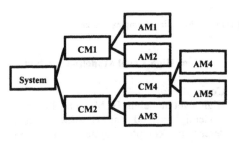

Figure 1 System hierarchal models specification in HLM

Atomic Model

HLM specification is port based system specification in which ports are the interactive channel between models. AM formalism and CM formalism is the main specification with which the discrete, continuous and hybrid system are modeled. AM is defined as follow:

$AM =< iP_N, oP_N, iE_N, oE_N, fsm_0, pars >$

iP_N is input ports set,

$iP_N = \{(ip_1, ip_2, \cdots, ip_n) \mid ip_1 \in X_1, ip_2 \in X_2, \cdots, ip_n \in X_n\}$

X_i is the value set of ports ip_i. oP_N is output ports set,

$oP_N = \{(op_1, op_2, \cdots, op_n) \mid op_1 \in Y_1, op_2 \in Y_2, \cdots, op_n \in Y_n\}$

iE_N, oE_N is model's input events set and output events set,

$iE_N = \{ie_1, ie_2, \cdots ie_N\}$

$oE_N = \{oe_1, oe_2, \cdots oe_N\}$.

fsm_0 is model's basic behavior state machine,

$fsm_0 = < S, S_0, iE, \delta >$

$S = \{("START", A_1), ("INIT", A_2), ("RUN", A_3),$
$("STOP", A_4), ("PAUSE", A_5), ("EXIT", A_6)\}$

A_i is the action of S_i as well as AM's scheduled simulation algorithm.

$iE = \{evRun, evInit, evPause, evStop,$
$evTimeAdvance\}$

$iE_0 \in iE_N$, $\delta : S \times iE \to S$, fsm_0 is showed as statechart[4] in figure 2:

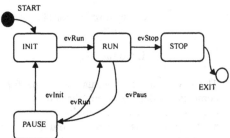

Figure 2 fsm_0's states and state transition

$pars$ is parameter set including name-value pairs of model's configurable parameters and attributes.

$pars = \{(p_1, v_1), (p_2, v_2), \cdots, (p_n, v_n)\}$

Compound Model

$CM =< iP_N, oP_N, iE_N, oE_N, D,$
$\{M_d \mid d \in D\}, CPLs, FSM >$

D is index set of submodel, $\{M_d \mid d \in D\}$ is submodels set of CM,

$M_d = < iP_N, oP_N, iE_N, oE_N, fsm_0, pars >$

$CPLs$ is internal coupling set of CM.

$CPLs = \{cpl_0, cpl_1, \cdots, cpl_n\}$

$cpl_i = \{(M_a, oP_j) \to (M_b, iP_k) \mid a, b \in D \cup \{FSM\} \cup \{CM\}\}$

Finite state machine FSM is defined as follows:

$FSM = < iP_N, iE_N, oE_N, fsms, R_{sf} >$

$fsms = \{fsm_0, fsm_1, \cdots, fsm_n\}$

$R_{sf} : S_{ij} \to fsm_j$, $i \neq j$, $S_i \in fsm_i$, State ("RUN", $fsm_{i,i\neq0}$) in fsm_0 is a compound state, other states have the same meanings as fsm_0 of AM ;

$fsm_{i,i\neq0} = < S, S_c, iE, S_0, C, \delta >$.

Others have the same meanings as those AM

iP_N is the input ports set of fsm. iP_N couples fsm with output ports of CM or M_d which is input variables set of fsm's state transition guard conditions. iE_N is the input events set which is input as trigger events of state transitions. oE_N is the output events set that schedules CM's submodels as input events.

The relationship between structure models and behavior model is show in figure 3:

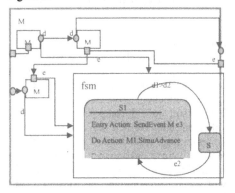

Figure 3 The relationship between structure

models and behavior model

The coupling relationship in CM includes external input with submodels, external input with fsm, fsm with external output, submodels with fsm and submodels. When coupling the models two types constraints should be considered. One is syntax constraint which keeps service type, I/O type and data type match those are attributes of source ports and destination ports of models' couplings. The other is semantic constraint which includes data meaning, unit, update frequency, data coding.

Specification for Model Document Format

HLM is a system level formalism specification which may be documented to XML format. HLM XML document parsed by specific software module may be translated between different CAD tools that showed in figure 4.

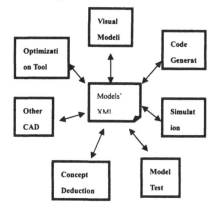

Figure 4 The relation between HLM models' XML documentation and tools

System Development Process

MDA and High Level Modeling Method

Object Management Group (OMG) introduced model driven architecture (MDA)[5][6] which is provided as a framework to support collaboration of OMG standards including CORBA, UML and so on. Platform independent model (PIM) is model described by UML that is independent with programming language. PIM is mapped into platform specific model (PSM) dependent with specific platform which includes design and realization detail. HLM method is a platform-independent and visual modeling method that separates system's application rules and implementation rules. System defined by HLM method will also separate the application model and communication model (adaptor) that makes the system run distributedly. The relationship between high level model and MDA is showed in figure 5.

HLA/RTI adaptor which realizes the connection from data ports to object classes and the interaction between event ports and interaction classes. The AM in HLM method may be mapped into a Matlab/Simulink model when data ports are connected to Simulink's variables through its API.

Model Driven System Development

HLM method is applied for modular complex system with loose coupling at stages of concept design, detail design, implementation, model and system integration and model test. In common the development of complex system conforms to process like figure 6.

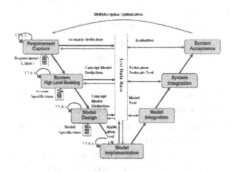

Figure 6 Development process of complex system

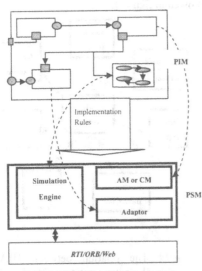

Figure 5 HLM Specification and MDA

In figure 5 the adaptor is the PSM (HLA/RTI, Grid/Globus et al.) mapped from PIM. For example, the PSM is a

After capturing the requirement of simulation system HLM method will assist to decompose the system to structure models and behavior models according to system's function, processes or data flow. The result of decomposition can be validated and verified by executing the system's high level models as its concept model. In system design and implementation stages high level model will be the integration specification and interfaces specification of each model. When integrating models and subsystems these modules will be tested individually and integrated into system framework generated by high level model information.

Development Environment

COSIM [7][8] is an integrated development platform for complex simulation system. HLM IDE is a service-oriented and problem-oriented modeling environment of COSIM tool suite by which the complex simulation system is modeled in form of visual symbols. In HLM IDE the behavior models is represented by state chart. The HLM IDE graphic interface is showed in figure 7.

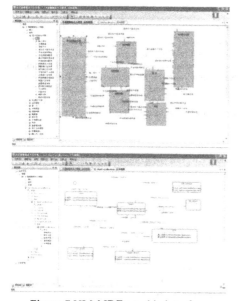

Figure 7 HLM IDE graphic interface

Conclusion

HLM method is mainly applied to distributed and hybrid simulation system such as multi-discipline virtual prototype and battlefield simulation system. Rigorous excutable syntax specification of HLM method is needed researched further.
For supporting collaboration of experts and interdiscipline HLM language needs to enrich its specification and extend to application domain.

Reference

1. Bo Hu Li, Xudong Chai, Guangleng Xiong et al. Research and Primary Practice on Virtual Prototyping Engineering of Complex Product, Journal of System Simulation, 2002,14(3), pp. 336-341.
2. Bernard P. Zeigler, Herbert Praehofer, Tag Gon Kim, Theory of Modeling and Simulation: Integrating Discrete Event and Continuous Complex Dynamic Systems. San Diego, CA: Academic Press, 2000.
3. Rajarishi Sinha, Vei Chung Liang et al. Modeling and Simulation Methods for design of engineering systems, http://www-2.cs.cmu.edu/~compsim/articles/JCISE01.pdf, 2002.
4. David Harel, Statecharts: A visual formalism for complex systems, Science of Computer Programming, 1987(8), pp.231--274.
5. OMG, UML Specification 2.0, http://www.omg.org, 2003, 11.
6. OMG, Model Driven Architecture, A Technical Perspective. http://www.omg.org ab/2001-02-05.
7. Peng Wang, Bo Hu Li, Xudong Chai et al. Collaborative Modeling Technology of Virtual Prototype for Complex Product. Journal of System Simulation .2004.16(2), pp.274-277.
8. Peng Wang, Bohu Li, Xudong Chai et al. Research on Collaborative Simulation Technology Based Multidiscipline Virtual Prototype Modeling and Optimization Design Method, Proceedings of 2005 Asia Simulation Conference, Beijing, China: World Publishing Corporation. 2005, pp.347-351.

Seamless Integration of Both System and Engagement Levels Simulation of EW

Weihua ZHANG, Haiquan QIAO and Kedi HUANG

College of Mechatronics Engineering and Automation
National University of Defense Technology
Changsha, Hunan, 410073 China
(E-mail: fly2high@126.com)

ABSTRACT

While simulations for both the military and commercial industry are geared toward the development of high-fidelity component models that accurately predict system performance, scenario and damage assessments, EW Test and Evaluation (T&E) domains call for some Joint Synthetic Battlespace, that is, to test and evaluate the performance of EW systems under all kinds of threats and complex environment, an integrated M&S environment connecting analysis and training and tying together many types of simulations is in great demand. Object-Oriented (OO) techniques have been examined as effective solutions for complex systems such as radars, EW equipments and Synthetic Nature Environment (SNE) simulations. By presenting a standard object-oriented RF environmental framework with an extended signal representation and target signature model, a practicable solution for seamless integration of both system and engagement levels simulation of EW is given. The impact such standard framework would have on the EW model developers is also discussed.

KEY WORDS: object oriented, engagement simulation, EW, Test and Evaluation, RF environment

INTRODUCTION

Simulations for both the military and commercial industry are geared toward the development of high-fidelity component models that accurately predict system performance, scenario and damage assessments, which require system and component/circuit level design and analysis for Radar and Electronic Warfare (EW) equipments [1]. On the other hand, the increasing needs from EW Test and Evaluation (T&E) domains call for a Joint Synthetic Battlespace - an integrated M&S environment connecting analysis and training and tying together many types of simulations. More exactly, to test and evaluate the performance of EW weapon systems under all kinds of threats and complex environment, not only natural environment but also man-made environment (such as jammer interfere), engagement-level simulation of EW is in great demand. Traditionally simulations like radar system-level simulations, are narrowly focused; do not fully meet joint simulation needs; are lack of interoperability and reusability with each other; and are not easily maintainable and extensible. In order to address all these issues, simulation efforts have examined Object-Oriented (OO) techniques as effective solutions. For software developers, OO software address three major problems: iterative development, reuse, and maintenance [2,3]. Using OOD

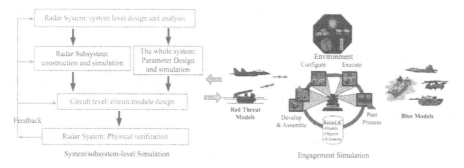

Figure 1   Radar and EW system design and T&E flow

methodology, a large and complicated entity/object can be decomposed into multiple individual components or subsystems, which implies that any complex system can be modeled with any resolution and any fidelity depended on actual requirements. Thus, OO technology combined with standard software architecture and model interfaces make the concept "software plug-and-play" realizable [4]. By presenting a standard object-oriented RF environmental framework with an extended signal representation and target signature model, this paper gives a practicable solution for seamless integration of both system and engagement levels simulation of EW. The impact such standard framework would have on the EW model developers is also discussed.

DESIGN, TEST AND EVALUATION OF RADAR AND EW SYSTEMS

To yield very accurate simulation results, high fidelity radar and EW equipments system-level design is required. David and Shiyang Li have presented a lot of valuable work and perfect solutions [5,6]. A typical radar system design flow is shown in Figure 1. First, each component of radar system is designed/modeled and tested by spectrum analyzer (like Vector Signal Analyzer, VSA). Then hardware circuits are created or just bought from a vendor to replace the corresponding component model. It is

important that the demo system model should be incorporated into the Joint Synthetic Battlespace to predict and evaluate system performance under expected complex battlespace. Only after the model is verified, validated and accredited (VV&A) and the demo system passes physical verification, can real radar system be manufactured and produced.

As shown as Figure 1, either for design or for T&E purpose, validated and high fidelity environment models are indispensable. Mostly red threat models validated by defense intelligence agency should be incorporated into the scenario, too. Since all kinds of EW weapon models may interact with the Environment model, standard definition of model interfaces are key techniques for integration signal and engagement simulation of EW seamlessly.

EXTENDED TARGET MODEL AND SIGNAL SIMULATION

To get high fidelity results, signal simulation is always needed. The classical target model shown as follows [7]:

$$\gamma = \sqrt{\sigma}\, e^{j\phi} \qquad (1)$$

where γ denotes the complex reflectance of a point target; ϕ is the phase term; and $\sigma = |\gamma|^2$ denotes target's RCS. It is too simple to carry more informaton about the target and environment which may be very useful for some advanced radar systems like Phased Arrays/ESA, polarization radar, Pulse Doppler (PD) radar, etc. To keep up with the great development of modern radar technology, some extensions to the normal one (Eq.1) ought to be made in both time and space domains. The actual extensions involve polarization, antenna pattern, S-parameters, angular glint, Jet Engine Modulation (JEM) effect, and so on. To compute polarization missmatch in 3D space, some necessary coordinates calculations also need to be taken into account.

Polarization and antenna pattern[8]

Because a real radar signal is always polarized by the antenna of most modern radar systems, the polarization and antenna pattern must be introduced into the new representation. By two complex voltages (horizontal_voltage and vertical_voltage) and two complex antenna gain (gain.horizontal and gain.vertical), all necessary polarization information can be derived.

Polarmetric RCS

When the signal is propagated off of a reflector the RCS is applied. The reflected signals relate to the impinging signals as follows [9]:

$$\begin{bmatrix} V_{ref} \\ H_{ref} \end{bmatrix} = \begin{bmatrix} S_{vv} & S_{vh} \\ S_{hv} & S_{hh} \end{bmatrix} \begin{bmatrix} V_{imp} \\ H_{imp} \end{bmatrix} \qquad (2)$$

It is important that because the polarization behavior is not ideal in the sidelobes for most antennas, good polarmetric measurement data is needed for RCS, antennas, and terrain effects to completely handle polarization.

Glint and JEM data [10]

Target angular glint and Jet Engine Modulation effects are also known as taget noise. To describe glint characteristic two quantities should be provided to the radar models for internal use: the max target extent L(t) in the perpendicular field of view from the observer's perspective and the total target rotational rate $\omega(t)$ relative to the observer. It is sensor models that determine whether or not use the information. So do the JEM datas, not discussed here for saving pages.

Coordinates computations

The important thing to keep track of is what "horizontal" and "vertical" mean. Each antenna, target, etc., has its own body-fixed idea of vertical and expects the signal in its coordinate frame. When the signal is propagated off of a reflector, the signal must be rotated from the transmitter frame of reference to the reflector frame of reference, the RCS is applied and then the signal is rotated to the receiver frame of reference for reception. Remember that the signal is represented by two complex voltages: one is horizontal and the other is vertical.

COMMON RF ENVIRONMENTAL FRAMEWORK

Based on the extended signal description and target model discussed above, an object-oriented common RF environmental framework with standard EW model interfaces is presented as Figure 2, where class *RFSignalObject* defines a radar signal to be propagated, with all transmit signal properties and data structs to store information filled by target and environment models along the signal path, such as clutter, return, glint and JEM data, and so forth. Radar model use all or part of the information depended on model fidelity. The base classes *ClutterModelBase/ MultiPathModelBase/TransmissionModel-Base* define standard model interfaces for effects model developers. A *RFPathObject* at least contains three *RFPathNodeObject*s: EmitterObject, ReflectorObject and CollectorObject and may contains one or more *GroundPatchObject*s and/or *SpecularReflectObject*s. Instances of *RFPathObject* class are processed by actual effect models and the signal processing flow is displayed in Figure 3 [11].

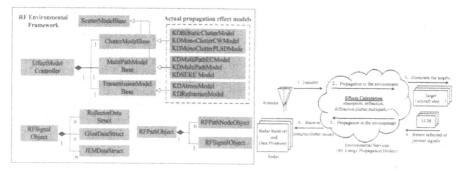

Figure 2   RF Environmental Framework   Figure 3   Signal processing flow

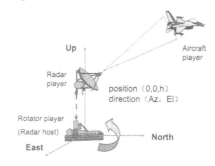

Figure 4   Radar vs. Aircraft scenario

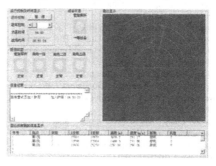

Figure 6   Simulation results

SIMULATION

In this section, an example of joint modeling and simulation of radar vs. aircraft will be demonstrated [12,13].

As shown in Figure 4, there are three players in the simulated scenario where a pulse Radar is attached to a 360° Rotator which means the Radar moves along with the Rotator. The Aircraft players are independent of these two players. The components of Radar and Aicraft players are shown in Figure 5.

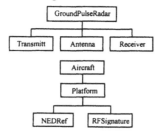

Figure 5   Components of Radar & Aircraft

Among the components *RFSignature* is used to model the fluctuatation of target RCS which can be Swerling I~IV statistical distribution or N-piont model. Some of the simulation results are displayed in the Figure 6.

CONCLUSIONS

A common object-oriented RF environmental framework with standard EW model interfaces is proposed in this paper, as well as a practicable solution for seamless integration of both system and engagement levels simulation of EW. The design given here will standardlize and simplify model interfaces with the environment by allowing a single set of interfaces for all RF effects. Through the standard environmental interfaces, the responsibility of RF effect model developers and EW weapon model developers will be insulated from the complexities of integrating correctly with the synthetic environment framework. Environment experts can build RF effects model focused on the physics rather the software architecture.

REFERENCES

1. Robert McGraw, Joseph Clark & Allyn Treshansky. Abstract Modeling Demonstration[R]. AFRL-IF-RS-TR-2001-149 Final Technical Report, 2001.
2. William K. McQuay, The New Vision for Modeling and Simulation In the DOD Acquisition Process[C], Digital Avionics Systems Conference Proceedings, 1997.
3. Kenneth R.Allen & William K.McQuay, Modeling And Simulation Under The Standard Architectures:How Will DoD Organizations Make It Happen[J], IEEE, 1997.
4. Joint Modeling and Simulation System (JMASS) Joint Initial Requirements Document (JIRD)[R]. Washington DC: OUSD(A&T)/DTSE&E/TFR , 1997.
5. David Leiss. Microwave chirp radar design: combining virtual and physical hardware performance analysis[EB/OL]. August 2003. http://www.rfdesign.com.
6. ShiyangLi. Radar system design[EB/OL]. 2005. http://www.ansoft.com/converge/li_ansoft.pdf.
7. Richard L. Mitchell. Radar Signal Simulation[M]. USA: Artech House, INC. 1976.
8. IRE Standards on Radio Wave Propagation (definition of terms)[S]. Supplement to Proc. IRE, 1942:2.
9. Huang P K. Radar Target Signature [M]. Beijing: Publishing House of Electronics Industry, 2005.
10. Dunn J H, Howard D D. Radar Target Amplitude, Angle and Doppler Scintillation from Analysis of the Echo Signal Propagating in Space[J]. IEEE Trans. On MYY, 1968, 16(9): 715~728.
11. Kim J. Allen, Thomas Tisler. Standard Multispectral Environmental and Effects Model (STMEEM) [J]. IEEE Trans. 1997.
12. Jeffrey P.Bacso & Russell F.Moody, Project Amber: Re-engineering A Legacy Ground Radar Modeling System into A Standards Based Object Oriented Architecture[J], IEEE, 1988.
13. Bassem R.Mahafza & Atef Z.Elsherbeni, MATLAB Simulations for Radar Systems Design, Chapman & Hall/CRC CRC Press LLC, 2004.

Multi-approach Simulation Modeling: Challenge of the Future

Timofey POPKOV*, Maxim GARIFULLIN**

*XJ Technologies Company
Nepokorennykh pr. 49, office 410, St.Petersburg, Russia
(e-mail: tim@xjtek.com)

**XJ Technologies Company
Nepokorennykh pr. 49, office 410, St.Petersburg, Russia
(e-mail: maxim@xjtek.com)

ABSTRACT

In today's fast-paced world everything changes fast and new challenges requires new solutions, which should be more universal, flexible and provide more possibilities to react to the continuous changes. The same situation is with simulation modeling solutions and tools. To effectively address new issues and challenges simulation modeling tools should be more flexible, more powerful and provide seamless integration of various simulation approaches.

KEY WORDS: Multi approach simulation modeling, agent-based, system dynamics, discrete-event, abstraction levels

INTRODUCTION

Simulation models are trying to address more and more complex problems and as a result sooner or later simulation professionals come to the situation when they can't do the model using only one simulation modeling approach. Let's consider an example with simulation modeling of IT infrastructure of a telecom operator. The cost of the hardware is very high, it can be up to tens of millions of US dollars, and before purchasing it is needed to estimate what kind of hardware we really need. At first it seems that discrete-event approach is well suited in this case but telecom IT infrastructure consists of thousands of servers, hundreds of applications, tens of switches and millions transactions per second - none of discrete-event simulation tools will be able to handle so much events per second. The way out is to model the whole system at global level using system dynamics approach to identify the parts of IT infrastructure with possible bottlenecks and simulate them at more precise level using discrete-event approach to get more accurate results.

If we consider simulation modeling by modeling paradigm (approach) there will be four basic paradigms: discrete event, system dynamics, agent-based and dynamic systems. The first three approaches are widely used for simulation modeling in various areas from urban-planning and healthcare to business and finance, while the last one is mainly used for engineering purposes. In this paper we will leave dynamic system simulation modeling out of our consideration because of it is used for a special application area which we don't discuss in the paper.

Each of those paradigms may be used at appropriate level(s) of abstraction (see Figure 1) which mean how many details we count when we develop a model. For example, developing model of subway station we would like to optimize the space inside. In this case we should count details like layout dimensions, people dimensions, individual people behaviors, how people influence each other, crossing flows of people etc., so we should develop a rather precise model which count a lot of physical details (physical level) while if we are interested in simulation of how workload of this subway station will be changing during some year we will operate with things like passengers per day and will not consider physical dimensions at all (strategy or operational level).

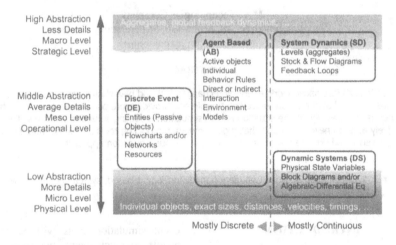

Figure 1 Simulation modeling approaches by abstraction level

As one could see on the Figure 1 system dynamics and discrete event approaches are mainly used at high abstraction or middle abstraction levels appropriately while agent based approach can be used almost at any level of abstraction but it does not mean agent-based simulation modeling is a cure for all "diseases". Sometimes it is easier to use system dynamics, sometimes flow-chart based modeling, sometimes agent-based – the choice of an approach(es) depends on problem definition, model requirements and how you formalize the model.

Farther in the paper we will explain some underlying mathematics of multi-approach simulation modeling and give an example of mixed system dynamics and agent-based simulation model.

MULTI-APPROACH SIMULATION MODELING: MATHEMATICAL BACKGROUND

Simulation models of any types are mathematical objects used to model real life objects whose state changes over time. From mathematical point of view System Dynamics and Dynamic Systems approaches work with continuous systems meaning systems evolving as continuous functions $F(t)$. Whereas Agent Based and

Discrete event approaches are systems which evolve over the time by representing changes as separate events or which is the same as jumping from one event to another. In discrete systems we abstract away from any continuous processes and consider only events - nothing is happening in between.

On figure below there are three charts; first of them displays different processes occurring in a system. Each process is described with a variable; some of them are changing continuously, some of them – only at certain moments of time. Considering only continuous processes we obtain a continuous system which is shown on the second chart. Third chart on the picture shows discrete process where variable is changed only when an event occurs.

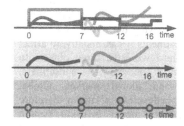

Figure 2 Hybrid, continuous and discrete processes

Coming back to approaches we propose the following correspondence. System Dynamics applied on high abstraction level where large amounts of discrete objects are represented as amounts and behave like continuous processes. Physical processes are also typically represented with equations. Therefore System Dynamics and Dynamic Systems are mostly continuous whereas Agent Based and Discrete event approaches are mostly discrete event systems which evolve over

the time by representing changes as separate events.

Mixing the approaches means seamless integration of continuous and discrete event behaviors and those systems are called hybrid. To model hybrid systems and to get accurate and reliable results from simulation we obviously need an executable language describing hybrid behavior, and a simulation tool capable of simulating discrete events interleaved with continuous time processes.

For modeling of hybrid system we use a combination of a set of algebraic-differential equations with state machines or statecharts (enhanced UML state machines). Each state in a statechart may have its own equation system and equation variables may be used in conditions on transitions. This way when a statechart switches to new state as a result of a discrete event, the continuous behavior may also be changed. Vice versa continuous behavior may trigger a transition in a statechart by means of using variables in trigger conditions. This mechanism is implemented in simulation tool AnyLogic.

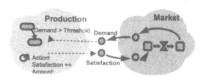

Figure 3 Seamless integration of continuous and discrete systems

On the picture above stock and flow diagram of a market produces demand variable ("Demand" in the middle). The "Demand" affects production which in turn influences "Satisfaction", which is the part of the system dynamics diagram. This mechanism is implemented in multi-approach simulation tool AnyLogic.

AnyLogic engine takes the model specification and executes it. The model execution is a sequence of steps of two types: time steps - when variables are being changed continuously and event steps - when an event is executed that may change the system state.

Classical example of a system with hybrid behavior is a bouncing ball. AnyLogic description of that system is presented on a picture below. The movement dynamics is described with differential equations located on the left part. Statechart on the right part observes Y coordinate and changes direction of movement if the ball hits a surface.

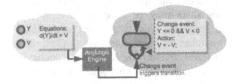

Figure 4 Model of bouncing ball

On the picture below there are timed charts for ball coordinate Y. Oval is the change event which occurs when Y becomes equal to zero, this event changes the direction of ball speed.

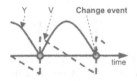

Figure 5 Chart of bouncing ball altitude

MIXED AGENT-BASED AND SYSTEM DYNAMICS MODEL OF TELECOM MARKET

Let's consider a multi-approach simulation model example on the base of a telecom market model. We assume there are some telecom operators which sell e.g. ADSL equipment and plans, we are one of them and we should choose our marketing strategy. The model should help to analyze reaction of customers to marketing activities, migration of subscribers churn between operators and tariffs, dynamic for new subscribers, average Internet traffic consumption etc.

The analysis of global dependences on telecom market shows that subscribers activities depends on average salary level while salary level depends on global country market parameters like inflation, profitableness, risk level etc. For operator the most effective time to invest in marketing is the time when subscribers activity is growing but if operator do too much investments it can negatively affect market. Thus, we have three objects to model and simulate – subscribers, operators and global market. Global market dependencies are known therefore it is easier to model it using system dynamics approach while subscribers and operators are easier to model using agent-based approach as soon as we know "local behavioral rules" of those objects whereas global dependencies are unknown. So, system dynamics part of the model simulates market and provide some input to agent-based part (e.g. inflation level, stagflation, average salary level) agent based part also provide some outputs to system dynamics part (e.g. investments, innovation level), this way the parts work in the loop.

Let's have a little bit deeper inside into the model implementation to better understand how various approaches can be integrated. As we mention above operators and subscribers are modeled as agents - they communicate with each other, take "local" decisions like "Well, I will by this package" and provide some aggregated parameters which is being collected during simulation to system dynamics part as an input and also read some parameters from market model. On the picture below the part of mixed model is shown.

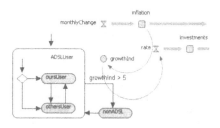

Figure 6 Mixed model of telecom market

As one can see statechart use an expression with variable "growtInd" on a transition while this variable is the part of system dynamics diagram – this is one of the ways of integration of various approaches (applicable only for AnyLogic).

CONCLUSION

Multi-approach simulation modeling is new technology and it is being actively developed. The range of application areas where the technology is successfully used is increasing daily, and more and more simulation professionals look this way. Besides the fact multi-approach simulation modeling tools allow to address more complex problems there is also an advantage which is probably even more obvious – simulation professional may use one tool for developing various types of models instead of using various tools for various models.
All this makes think that multi-approach simulation modeling tools are coming

thing and they will drive traditional simulation tools out of a market providing more possibilities, more power and flexibility.

REFERENCES

1. Astrom, J., Emqvist, H., Mattson, S.E.: Evolution of Continuous-time Modeling and Simulation. In: Proceedings of the 12th European Simulation Multiconference, ESM'98, Manchester, UK (1998)
2. Forrester, Jay. 1958. Industrial Dynamics: A Major Breakthrough for Decision Makers. Harvard Business Review, Vol. 36, No. 4, 37-66.
3. Forrester, Jay. 1961. Industrial Dynamics. Cambridge, MA: MIT Press
4. Sterman, John. 2000. Business Dynamics: Systems Thinking and Modeling for a Complex World. McGraw Hill.
5. Gordon, Geoffrey. 1961. A General Purpose Systems Simulation Program. McMillan NY, Proceedings of EJCC, Washington D.C., 87-104.
6. Schelling, Thomas. 1978. Micromotives and Macrobehavior. W. W. Norton and Co.
7. Schieritz, Nadine, and Milling, Peter. 2003. Modeling the Forest or Modeling the Trees - A Comparison of System Dynamics and Agent-Based Simulation. The 21st International Conference of the System Dynamics Society, New York, USA.
8. Schieritz, Nadine, and Grosler, Andreas. 2003. Emergent Structures in Supply Chains – A Study Integrating Agent-Based and System Dynamics Modeling. The 36th Annual Hawaii International Conference on System Sciences, Washington, USA.
9. Solo, Kirk, and Paich, Mark. 2004. A Modern Simulation Approach for Pharmaceutical Portfolio Management. International Conference on Health Sciences Simulation (ICHSS'04), San Diego, California, USA. Available from http://www.simnexus.com/SimNexus.PharmaPortfolio.pdf.
10. Keenan, Philip, and Paich, Mark. 2004. Modeling General Motors and the North American Automobile Market. The 22nd International Conference of the System Dynamics Society, Oxford, England
11. Borshchev, A.V., Kolesov, Yu.B., Senichenkov, Yu.B.: Java Engine for UML Based Hybrid State Machines. In: Proceedings of the Winter Simulation Conference 2000, WSC'00, De-cember 10-13, Orlando, FL, USA (2000)
12. UML – The Unified Modeling Language. http://www.uml.org.

Application of MRTR Method for Solving Complex Symmetric Linear Systems

Akira SHIODE*, Kuniyoshi ABE**, Seiji FUJINO***

*Graduate School of Information Science and Electrical Engineering, Kyushu University
(E-mail: shiode@zeal.cc.kyushu-u.ac.jp)
**Department of Economics and Infomation, Gifu Shotoku Gakuen University
***Computing and Communications Center, Kyushu University

ABSTRACT

The MRTR method has been recognized as an effective iterative method for singular systems of linear equations. The MRTR method is based on the three-term recurrence formula of the CG method and the algorithm is proven to be mathematically equivalent to the CR method. This paper will describe the algorithm of the cs_MRTR method for solving complex symmetric linear systems, and prove that this method is mathematically equivalent to the COCR method. Numerical experiments indicate that the cs_MRTR method convergences more stably compared with the COCR method.

KEY WORDS: cs_MRTR method, singular systems, minimum residual norm

1 Introduction

Consider the solution of singular complex symmetric linear systems of the form

$$Az = b, \quad (1)$$

where A and b stand for an n-by-n non-Hermitian symmetric matrix ($A = A^T \neq A^H$) and a vector($b \in C^n$), respectively. The vector z is a solution vector. If the vector b is in an image space of the matrix A, a unique solution of the system (1) doesn't exist in theory.

In fact, when solving the system (1) in finite floating point arithmetics, the vector b itself has numeric errors in some cases due to the rounding operations. As a result, none of the solutions of the system (1) exist. Here, the least squares problem

$$\min_{z \in C^n} \|b - Az\|_2 \quad (2)$$

is solved instead of the system (1). The corresponding residual $\hat{r} = b - A\hat{z}$ is always unique, where $\hat{z}$ denotes a solution of the system (2).

We consider to apply the original Conjugate Gradient (CG) [3] and Conjugate Residual (CR) methods [2] to the system (2) with the matrix A of singular real symmetric matrix. In this case, the residual norm ($\|\hat{r}\|_2$) of the CG method oscilates greatly and diverges eventually. Moreover the CR method attains the minimum residual norm, but cannot maintain at the level of the minimum residual norm because of effect of rounding errors [1]. In contrast, the MRTR method [1] can maintain at the level of the minimum residual norm.

Next we consider to apply the Conjugate Orthogonal CG (COCG) method and Conjugate Orthogonal CR (COCR) method [5] to the system (2). In this case, the COCG and COCR methods have unfavorable convergence property from the analogy of the above behavior of CG and CR methods. Therefore, it needs to develop the MRTR method for complex symmetric linear systems. We refer to as the cs_MRTR method.

This paper describes the cs_MRTR method for solving complex symmetric linear systems. The algorithm of the cs_MRTR method is introduced and proved to be mathematically equivalent to the COCR method. The COCG, COCR and cs_MRTR methods are applied to the systems (2) with the matrix A of singular complex symmetric matrix. Then it is shown that the cs_MRTR method has preferable convergance among the three methods. Namely the COCG and COCR methods cannot solve the systems (2) with singular matrix. In contrast, the cs_MRTR method outperforms.

2   cs_MRTR method

This section reviews the cs_MRTR algorithm. The cs_MRTR algorithm implements new parameters ξ_k, η_k ($\in R$) and designs the polynomial $H_k(\lambda)$ satisfying the following three-term recurrence formula such as the MRTR algorithm[1].

$$H_0(\lambda) = 1, \quad H_1(\lambda) = (1 - \zeta_0\lambda)H_0(\lambda), \quad (3)$$
$$H_{k+1}(\lambda) = (1 + \eta_k - \zeta_k\lambda)H_k(\lambda)$$
$$-\eta_k H_{k-1}(\lambda). \quad (k = 1, 2, \ldots) \quad (4)$$

The residual of the cs_MRTR method is defined as $r_k := H_k(A)r_0$. The polynomial $H_k(\lambda)$ with the formulas (3)-(4) satisfies $H_k(0) = 1$ for all k, leads to $H_{k+1}(0) - H_k(0) = 0$. Moreover, using a new polynomial $G_k(\lambda)$ as $G_k(\lambda) = \{H_k(\lambda) - H_{k+1}(\lambda)\}/\zeta_k\lambda$, the formulas (3)-(4) are converted into

$$H_0(\lambda) = 1, \quad G_0(\lambda) = 1, \quad (5)$$

$$\zeta_k\lambda G_k(\lambda) = \zeta_k\lambda H_k(\lambda) + \zeta_{k-1}\eta_k\lambda G_{k-1}(\lambda), \quad (6)$$
$$H_{k+1}(\lambda) = H_k(\lambda) - \zeta_k\lambda G_k(\lambda). \quad (7)$$
$$(k = 1, 2, \ldots)$$

By introducing an auxiliary vector $\boldsymbol{y}_k$ as

$$\boldsymbol{y}_k = \zeta_{k-1}AG_{k-1}(A)\boldsymbol{r}_0, \quad (8)$$

the formulas (5)-(7) imply the residual $\boldsymbol{r}_{k+1}$ calculated as

$$\boldsymbol{y}_{k+1} = \eta_k\boldsymbol{y}_k + \zeta_k A\boldsymbol{r}_k, \quad (9)$$
$$\boldsymbol{r}_{k+1} = \boldsymbol{r}_k - \boldsymbol{y}_{k+1}. \quad (10)$$

In the cs_MRTR algorithm the recurrence coefficients ξ_k, η_k are determined by the condition

$$|(\bar{\boldsymbol{r}}_{k+1}, \boldsymbol{r}_{k+1})| = \min_{\zeta_k, \eta_k} |(\bar{\boldsymbol{r}}_k - \bar{\boldsymbol{y}}_{k+1}, \boldsymbol{r}_k - \boldsymbol{y}_{k+1})|. \quad (11)$$

The recurrence coefficients ξ_k, η_k satisfying the condition (11) are expressed by

$$\zeta_k = \frac{(\bar{\boldsymbol{y}}_k, \boldsymbol{y}_k)(\bar{\boldsymbol{r}}_k, A\boldsymbol{r}_k) - (\bar{\boldsymbol{y}}_k, A\boldsymbol{r}_k)(\bar{\boldsymbol{r}}_k, \boldsymbol{y}_k)}{(\bar{\boldsymbol{y}}_k, \boldsymbol{y}_k)(\bar{A}\bar{\boldsymbol{r}}_k, A\boldsymbol{r}_k) - (\bar{\boldsymbol{y}}_k, A\boldsymbol{r}_k)(\bar{\boldsymbol{y}}_k, A\boldsymbol{r}_k)},$$
$$\eta_k = \frac{(\bar{A}\bar{\boldsymbol{r}}_k, A\boldsymbol{r}_k)(\bar{\boldsymbol{y}}_k, \boldsymbol{r}_k) - (\bar{\boldsymbol{y}}_k, A\boldsymbol{r}_k)(\bar{A}\bar{\boldsymbol{r}}_k, \boldsymbol{r}_k)}{(\bar{A}\bar{\boldsymbol{r}}_k, A\boldsymbol{r}_k)(\bar{\boldsymbol{y}}_k, \boldsymbol{y}_k) - (\bar{\boldsymbol{y}}_k, A\boldsymbol{r}_k)(\bar{A}\bar{\boldsymbol{r}}_k, \boldsymbol{y}_k)}$$

, respectively. Also, the condition (11) reveals the orthogonalities for the vectors $\boldsymbol{r}_k$ and $\boldsymbol{y}_k$ as

$$(\bar{\boldsymbol{r}}_{k+1}, A\boldsymbol{r}_k) = 0, \quad (12)$$
$$(\bar{\boldsymbol{r}}_{k+1}, \boldsymbol{y}_k) = 0. \quad (13)$$

The formulas (10), (13) imply $(\bar{\boldsymbol{r}}_k, \boldsymbol{y}_k) = (\bar{\boldsymbol{y}}_{k+1}, \boldsymbol{y}_k)$, while the formulas (9), (12) and (13) lead to $(\bar{\boldsymbol{r}}_k, \boldsymbol{y}_k) = 0$. Hence, the vectors $\boldsymbol{r}_k$ and $\boldsymbol{y}_k$ are generated by enforcing the orthogonality properties

$$(\bar{\boldsymbol{r}}_k, \boldsymbol{y}_k) = (\bar{\boldsymbol{y}}_{k+1}, \boldsymbol{y}_k) = 0. \quad (14)$$

Since the formulas (9)-(10) and the orthogonalities (12)-(14) imply

$$(\bar{\boldsymbol{y}}_k, \boldsymbol{y}_k) = \zeta_{k-1}(\bar{\boldsymbol{r}}_{k-1}, A\boldsymbol{r}_{k-1}). \quad (15)$$

Therefore, the calculation for the recurrence coefficients ζ_k and η_k can be carried out through

$$\zeta_k = \frac{\zeta_{k-1}(\bar{\boldsymbol{r}}_{k-1}, A\boldsymbol{r}_{k-1})(\bar{A}\bar{\boldsymbol{r}}_k, \boldsymbol{r}_k)}{\zeta_{k-1}(\bar{A}\bar{\boldsymbol{r}}_k, A\boldsymbol{r}_k)(\bar{\boldsymbol{r}}_{k-1}, A\boldsymbol{r}_{k-1}) - (\bar{\boldsymbol{y}}_k, A\boldsymbol{r}_k)(\bar{\boldsymbol{y}}_k, A\boldsymbol{r}_k)},$$
$$\eta_k = \frac{-(\bar{\boldsymbol{y}}_k, A\boldsymbol{r}_k)(\bar{A}\bar{\boldsymbol{r}}_k, \boldsymbol{r}_k)}{\zeta_{k-1}(\bar{A}\bar{\boldsymbol{r}}_k, A\boldsymbol{r}_k)(\bar{\boldsymbol{r}}_{k-1}, A\boldsymbol{r}_{k-1}) - (\bar{\boldsymbol{y}}_k, A\boldsymbol{r}_k)(\bar{\boldsymbol{y}}_k, A\boldsymbol{r}_k)}.$$

Furthermore, by introducing a new auxiliary vector $\boldsymbol{p}_k$ as

$$\boldsymbol{p}_k := G_k(A)\boldsymbol{r}_0, \qquad (16)$$

the formulas (5)-(7) are converted into

$$\boldsymbol{p}_k = \boldsymbol{r}_k + \frac{\zeta_{k-1}}{\zeta_k}\eta_k\boldsymbol{p}_{k-1}, \qquad (17)$$

$$\boldsymbol{r}_{k+1} = \boldsymbol{r}_k - \zeta_k A\boldsymbol{p}_k. \qquad (18)$$

However, the formula (10) was used instead of (18). Moreover, the approximation $\boldsymbol{x}_{k+1}$ is updated by

$$\boldsymbol{x}_{k+1} = \boldsymbol{x}_k + \zeta_k\boldsymbol{p}_k. \qquad (19)$$

The cs_MRTR is defined as follows:

Algorithm 1 (cs_MRTR):

$\boldsymbol{x}_0$ is an initial guess, $\boldsymbol{r}_0 = \boldsymbol{b} - A\boldsymbol{x}_0$,

for $k = 0, 1, \dots$ until $\|\boldsymbol{r}_{k+1}\|_2/\|\boldsymbol{r}_0\|_2 < \epsilon$ do :

begin

$$\zeta_k = \frac{\nu_k(\bar{A}\bar{\boldsymbol{r}}_k, A\boldsymbol{r}_k)}{\nu_k(\bar{A}\bar{\boldsymbol{r}}_k, A\boldsymbol{r}_k) - (\bar{\boldsymbol{y}}_k, A\boldsymbol{r}_k)(\bar{A}\bar{\boldsymbol{r}}_k, \boldsymbol{y}_k)},$$

$$\eta_k = \frac{-(\bar{\boldsymbol{y}}_k, A\boldsymbol{r}_k)(\bar{A}\bar{\boldsymbol{r}}_k, \boldsymbol{r}_k)}{\nu_k(\bar{A}\bar{\boldsymbol{r}}_k, A\boldsymbol{r}_k) - (\bar{\boldsymbol{y}}_k, A\boldsymbol{r}_k)(\bar{A}\bar{\boldsymbol{r}}_k, \boldsymbol{y}_k)},$$

if $k = 0$, then $\zeta_k = \frac{(\bar{A}\bar{\boldsymbol{r}}_k, \boldsymbol{r}_k)}{(\bar{A}\bar{\boldsymbol{r}}_k, A\boldsymbol{r}_k)}, \quad \eta_k = 0,$

$$\nu_{k+1} = \zeta_k(\bar{\boldsymbol{r}}_k, A\boldsymbol{r}_k),$$

$$\boldsymbol{p}_k = \boldsymbol{r}_k + \frac{\zeta_{k-1}}{\zeta_k}\eta_k\boldsymbol{p}_{k-1}, \quad \boldsymbol{x}_{k+1} = \boldsymbol{x}_k + \zeta_k\boldsymbol{p}_k,$$

$$\boldsymbol{y}_{k+1} = \eta_k\boldsymbol{y}_k + \zeta_k A\boldsymbol{r}_k, \quad \boldsymbol{r}_{k+1} = \boldsymbol{r}_k - \boldsymbol{y}_{k+1}$$

end.

3 Equivalent Relation

This section proves that the cs_MRTR method is mathematically equivalent to the COCR method. The COCR algorithm is defined as follows[5],

Algorithm 2 (COCR):

$\boldsymbol{x}_0$ is an initial guess, $\boldsymbol{r}_0 = \boldsymbol{b} - A\boldsymbol{x}_0$, $\beta_{-1} = 0$,

for $k = 0, 1, \dots$ until $\|\boldsymbol{r}_{k+1}\|_2/\|\boldsymbol{r}_0\|_2 < \epsilon$ do :

begin

$$\boldsymbol{p}_k = \boldsymbol{r}_k + \beta_{k-1}\boldsymbol{p}_{k-1}, \qquad (20)$$

$$A\boldsymbol{p}_k = A\boldsymbol{r}_k + \beta_{k-1}A\boldsymbol{p}_{k-1}, \qquad (21)$$

$$\alpha_k = \frac{(\bar{\boldsymbol{r}}_k, A\boldsymbol{r}_k)}{(\bar{A}\bar{\boldsymbol{p}}_k, A\boldsymbol{p}_k)}, \qquad (22)$$

$$\boldsymbol{x}_{k+1} = \boldsymbol{x}_k + \alpha_k\boldsymbol{p}_k, \qquad (23)$$

$$\boldsymbol{r}_{k+1} = \boldsymbol{r}_k - \alpha_k A\boldsymbol{p}_k, \qquad (24)$$

$$\beta_k = \frac{(\bar{\boldsymbol{r}}_{k+1}, A\boldsymbol{r}_{k+1})}{(\bar{\boldsymbol{r}}_k, A\boldsymbol{r}_k)}, \qquad (25)$$

end.

The following lemmas 1-2 are proved first.

Lemma 1: When A is an n-by-n non-Hermitian symmetric matrix, the residual $\boldsymbol{r}_k$ and the auxiliary vector $\boldsymbol{p}_k$ of the COCR algorithm satisfy the equation

$$(\bar{\boldsymbol{r}}_k, A\boldsymbol{p}_k) = (\bar{\boldsymbol{r}}_k, A\boldsymbol{r}_k).$$

Proof. The eqn. (20) is converted into

$$\boldsymbol{p}_k = \boldsymbol{r}_k + \frac{(\bar{\boldsymbol{r}}_k, A\boldsymbol{r}_k)}{(\bar{\boldsymbol{r}}_{k-1}, A\boldsymbol{r}_{k-1})}\boldsymbol{p}_{k-1} = \sum_{j=0}^{k}\frac{(\bar{\boldsymbol{r}}_k, A\boldsymbol{r}_k)}{(\bar{\boldsymbol{r}}_j, A\boldsymbol{r}_j)}\boldsymbol{r}_j.$$

As the residual $\boldsymbol{r}_k$ satisfies the following condition[5]

$$\boldsymbol{r}_k \perp \bar{A}K_k(\bar{A}; \bar{\boldsymbol{r}}_0), \qquad (26)$$

this leads to $(\bar{\boldsymbol{r}}_k, A\boldsymbol{r}_i) = 0$ $(i < k)$. Hence, an inner product $(\bar{\boldsymbol{r}}_k, A\boldsymbol{p}_k)$ is converted into $(\bar{\boldsymbol{r}}_k, A\boldsymbol{r}_k)$. Then the lemma is proved. ∎

Lemma 2: When A is an n-by-n non-Hermitian symmetric matrix, the recurrence coefficient β_k of the COCR algorithm satisfies the equation

$$\beta_k = \frac{(\bar{\boldsymbol{r}}_{k+1}, A\boldsymbol{r}_{k+1})}{(\bar{\boldsymbol{r}}_k, A\boldsymbol{r}_k)} = -\frac{(\bar{A}\bar{\boldsymbol{r}}_{k+1}, A\boldsymbol{p}_k)}{(\bar{A}\bar{\boldsymbol{p}}_k, A\boldsymbol{p}_k)}.$$

Proof. By the eqns. (22), (24) an inner product $(\bar{A}\bar{\boldsymbol{r}}_{k+1}, \boldsymbol{r}_{k+1})$ is converted into

$$(\bar{A}\bar{\boldsymbol{r}}_{k+1}, \boldsymbol{r}_{k+1}) = (\bar{A}\bar{\boldsymbol{r}}_{k+1}, \boldsymbol{r}_k)$$
$$- (\bar{\boldsymbol{r}}_k, A\boldsymbol{r}_k)\frac{(\bar{A}\bar{\boldsymbol{r}}_{k+1}, A\boldsymbol{p}_k)}{(\bar{A}\bar{\boldsymbol{p}}_k, A\boldsymbol{p}_k)}. \qquad (27)$$

Moreover, the condition (26) satisfies $(\bar{A}\bar{\boldsymbol{r}}_{k+1}, \boldsymbol{r}_k) = 0$ and clearly speaking, we know $(\bar{A}\bar{\boldsymbol{r}}_{k+1}, \boldsymbol{r}_{k+1}) = (\bar{\boldsymbol{r}}_{k+1}, A\boldsymbol{r}_{k+1})$. Hence, the formula (27) is converted into

$$-\frac{(\bar{A}\bar{\boldsymbol{r}}_{k+1}, A\boldsymbol{p}_k)}{(\bar{A}\bar{\boldsymbol{p}}_k, A\boldsymbol{p}_k)} = \frac{(\bar{\boldsymbol{r}}_{k+1}, A\boldsymbol{r}_{k+1})}{(\bar{\boldsymbol{r}}_k, A\boldsymbol{r}_k)}(= \beta_k).$$

Then the lemma is proved. ∎

In the preceding section, we noted that the formulas (5)-(7) were converted into the formulas (17)-(18). As the recurrence coefficient ζ_k satisfies the condition (11), it is expressed by

$$\zeta_k = \frac{(\bar{r}_k, Ap_k)}{(A\bar{p}_k, Ap_k)}. \qquad (28)$$

By the formulas (8) and (16), the formula (14) is converted into

$$(A\bar{p}_k, Ap_{k-1}) = 0. \qquad (29)$$

Hence, by the formulas (17) and (29) the parameter $\frac{\zeta_{k-1}}{\zeta_k}\eta_k$ is expressed by

$$\frac{\zeta_{k-1}}{\zeta_k}\eta_k = -\frac{(A\bar{r}_k, Ap_{k-1})}{(A\bar{p}_{k-1}, Ap_{k-1})}. \qquad (30)$$

Here the lemma 1 satisfies $\zeta_k = \alpha_k$ and the lemma 2 satisfies $\frac{\zeta_{k-1}}{\zeta_k}\eta_k = \beta_{k-1}$, the formulas (17)-(19), (28) and (30) can be applied to the COCR algorithm. Therefore, the following theorem can be stated:

Theorem 1: The cs_MRTR method is mathematically equivalent to the COCR method.

4 Numerical results

This section presents numerical experiments on a model problem with singular matrix, and compares the convergence of the cs_MRTR method with that of the COCG and COCR methods. All computations are carried out in double-precision floating-point arithmetic on a PC with an Intel Pentium 4 (3.8GHz) processor equipped with an Intel Fortran compiler. All codes were compiled with the -O3 optimization option. In all cases the iteration was started with $x_0 = 0$.

The model problem is treated as well as [4]. Applying 5-point central differences to 2-D Poisson equation

$$\frac{\partial^2 u}{\partial x^2} + \frac{\partial^2 u}{\partial y^2} = f(x, y), \quad 0 < x, y < 1, \qquad (31)$$

over the unit square $\Omega = (0, 1) \times (0, 1)$ with the Neumann boundary condition $\frac{\partial u}{\partial n}|_{\partial\Omega} = g$ yields a singular system with a symmetric coefficient matrix. The functions $f \in L^2(\Omega)$ and $g \in L^2(\partial\Omega)$ are assumed to satisfy the compatibility condition $\int_\Omega f\,dx\,dy = \int_{\partial\Omega} g\,ds$. The mesh size is chosen as $1/(m-1)$ in both directions of Ω, so that the resulting system has the following n-by-n coefficient matrix, where $n = m^2$:

$$B := \begin{bmatrix} \frac{1}{2}D_m & -E_m & & & \\ -E_m & D_m & -E_m & & \\ & \cdots & \cdots & \cdots & \\ & & -E_m & D_m & -E_m \\ & & & -E_m & \frac{1}{2}D_m \end{bmatrix}.$$

Here D_m and E_m are the m-by-m matrices given by

$$D_m := \begin{bmatrix} 2 & -1 & & & \\ -1 & 4 & -1 & & \\ & \cdots & \cdots & \cdots & \\ & & -1 & 4 & -1 \\ & & & -1 & 2 \end{bmatrix}$$

and $E_m := \mathrm{diag}(1/2, 1, \ldots, 1, 1/2)$. Here "diag" means diagonal matrix.

When expressing a matrix $A = B + \sqrt{-1} \times B$, the matrix A is n-by-n non-Hermitian complex symmetric matrix. For the matrix A the identity $Ae = A^T e = 0$ holds, so that $\mathrm{Null}(A) = \mathrm{Null}(A^T) = \mathrm{Span}\{e\}$, where $e := (1, \ldots, 1)^T$. Hence, the matrix A is a singular matrix.

Finally, the vectors $b_R \in \mathrm{Range}(A)$ and $b_N \in \mathrm{Null}(A^T)$ can be chosen so that the right-hand side vector is expressed as $b = b_R + b_N$. A perturbed system with the matrix A can be solved under the following conditions: First, the unperturbed right-hand side vector is taken from the range space of A by substituting a random vector $\hat{x}$ into the equation $b_R = A\hat{x}$. Second, a perturbation is made to yield the right-hand side vector $b_R + \delta\frac{e}{\|e\|_2}$. Consequently the system

$$Ax = b_R + \delta\frac{e}{\|e\|_2}$$

is solved for x by using the COCG, COCR and cs_MRTR methods. Here, we note that the numerical computation was carried out for $m = 100$ and $\delta = 10^{-6}$. The numerical results for the model matrix are displayed in Figure 1-2. In Figure 1 the convergence plots show the iteration counts (on the horizontal axis) versus the residual 2-norm ($\log_{10}\|r_k\|_2$). Here the residual r_k is recursively updated in these algorithms. In Figure 2 the convergence plots depict the iteration counts (on the horizontal axis) versus the true residual 2-norm ($\log_{10}\|b - Ax_k\|_2$).

From these Figures the observations are made.

- The COCG method oscilates violently and diverges.

- The COCR method attains once at the level of the minimum residual norm. After that, however, it oscilates fairly beyond 1300 iterations and converges misleadingly below the level of the minimum residual norm. Moreover, a significant difference can be seen between the residual norm and true residual norm of the COCR method.

- On the other hand, the cs_MRTR method can keep the residual at the level of its theoretical minimum. Furthermore, the true residual 2-norm history is close to the residual 2-norm history.

5 Conclusions

We derived an extended MRTR method for solving complex symmetric linear systems. The cs_MRTR method is proven to be mathematically equivalent to the COCR method. Moreover, the numerical experiments indicate that, for a singular system, the cs_MRTR method keeps at the level of the minimum residual norm, while the COCR method does not keep.

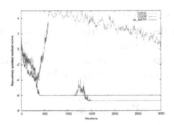

Figure 1 The residual 2-norm ($\log_{10}\|r_k\|_2$) history of three iterative methods for the model problem.

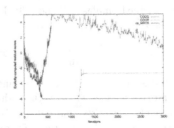

Figure 2 The true residual 2-norm ($\log_{10}\|b - Ax_k\|_2$) history of three iterative methods for the model problem.

REFERENCES

1. Abe, K., et al., MRTR method: An iterative method based on the three-term recurrence formula of CG-type for non-symmetric matrix, JSIAM, 7(1997), 37-50.
2. Eisenstat, S.C., et al., Variational iterative methods for nonsymmetric systems of linear equations, SIAM J. Numer. Anal., 20(1983), pp.345-357.
3. Hestenes, M.R. and Stiefel, E., Methods of conjugate gradients for solving linear systems, J. of Research of NBS, 49(1952), pp.409-436.
4. Kaasschieter, E.F., Preconditoned conjugate gradients for solving singular systems, J. of Comput. Appl. Math., 24 (1988), pp.265-275.
5. Sogabe, T., Zhang, S., A COCR method for solving complex symmetric linear systems, Proc. of SCAN2004, (2004), p.107.

Absolute Diagonal Scaling Preconditioner of COCG Method for Symmetric Complex Matrix

Moethuthu*, Noriko Okamoto**, Akira Shiode *, Seiji Fujino***, Toru Otsuru****

*Graduate School of Information Science and Electrical Engineering, Kyushu University
**Venture Business Laboratory, Oita University
***Computing and Communications Center, Kyushu University
****Department of Architecture, Faculty of Engineering, Oita University

ABSTRACT

The iterative method, i.e., Conjugate Orthogonal Conjugate Gradient (COCG) method included in the Krylov Subspace methods, can solve a linear system of equations $Ax = b$. This COCG method is well known to solve by the system with large sparse matrix arises for realistic problems by FEM. The characteristic of the matrix is that the diagonal entries only are complex besides real nondiagonal entries. In this paper, we propose new preconditioner for a matrix with complex diagonal entries only and real nondiagonal entries. We refer to as an absolute diagonal scaling (A-D-s) technique. This method can reduce computation times and amount of memory compared with nondiagonal scaling method.

KEY WORDS: ADs_COCG method, symmetric complex matrix, minimum residual norm

1 Introduction

There are a great many of iterative methods for solving a linear system of equations $Ax = b$, where A denotes an n-by-n complex symmetric coefficient matrix $A = A^T$ ($A \neq A^H$ non-Hermitian) and x, b stand for solution vector and righhand side vector of order n, respectively. Matrix A which arises from discretization by FEM for realistic problems is usually large and sparse matrix. Then large amount of computation times and memory are needed in order to solve efficiently the problems.

Therefore, various iterative methods included in the Krylov Subspace methods have been proposed to reduce computation times and necessary memory.

Among the iterative methods, Conjugate Orthogonal Conjugate Gradient (COCG) methods by van der Vorst et al. is well known [6]. Moreover CO-Conjugate Residual (COCR) method was proposed by Sogabe et al.[5]. Recently the authors proposed newly CO-Minimized Residual method based on the Three-term Recurrence (**cs_MRTR**) method for solving symmetric complex matrix [1].

In this paper, we are mainly concerned with a particular preconditioning technique of the CG method for linear systems which stem from problem in the field of sound analysis discretized by FEM approach. Roughly speaking, a preconditioner is an explicit (implicit) modification of an original coefficient matrix that makes it easier to solve linear systems by an adequate iterative methods. Often used diagonal scaling all rows of a linear system to make the diagonal entires equal to one. The resulting system can be solved by an iterative method, and require a fewer number of iterations until convergence than the original system. We propose a particular preconditioning technique suited to a matrix with complex diagonal entries only of matrix A and real nondiagonal entries of matrix A.

The outline of the paper is as follows: In section 2, we review briefly sound analysis and discretization by FEM. Section 3 contains conventional diagonal scaling preconditioning and also a particular diagonal scaling preconditioning for acoustic analysis. In section 4, some typical results of numerical experiments for various frequencies, are given. Finally, in section 5, we make some concluding remarks.

2   Acoustic Analysis by FEM

We treat with the following linear systems which can be gained by the standard Finite Element Method (FEM) for sound field analysis of regularly shaped reverberation room [4]. The notation of matrices below is written according to that of application fields in this section.

$$[M]\{\ddot{p}\} + [C]\{\dot{p}\} + [K]\{p\} = \rho\omega^2 u\{W\}. \quad (1)$$

Here $\{p\}$, ρ, ω and u are sound pressure vector, air density, angular frequency and displacement, respectively. With shape function $\{N\}$, and normal surface impedance z_n, the acoustic element matrices that construct global matrices in the equation (1) are given by

$$[K]_e = \int_e (\{\frac{\partial N}{\partial x}\}\{\frac{\partial N}{\partial x}\}^T + \{\frac{\partial N}{\partial y}\}\{\frac{\partial N}{\partial y}\}^T$$
$$+ \{\frac{\partial N}{\partial z}\}\{\frac{\partial N}{\partial z}\}^T)dV, \quad (2)$$

$$[M]_e = \frac{1}{c^2}\int_e \{N\}\{N\}^T dV \quad (3)$$

$$[C]_e = \frac{1}{c}\int_{e'} \frac{1}{z_n}\{N\}\{N\}^T dS. \quad (4)$$

Here matrix $[C]$ is refered to as the lumped dissipation matrix. In the frequency domain, equation (1) can be represented as

$$[A]\{p\} = \{f\} \quad (5)$$

where $\{f\}$ and $[A]$ denote external force vector and coefficient matrix. $[A]$ is a complex symmetric non-Hermitian matrix. However, in case of the lumped dissipation matrix, diagonal entries only of matrix $[A]$ are complex, and nondiagonal entries of matrix $[A]$ are real.

3   Preconditioning

The idea of preconditioning is based on consideration of a linear system with the same solution as the original equation. The problem is that each preconditioning technique is suited for a different type of problem. Until current days, no robust preconditioning technique appears for all or at least much types of problems. A popular preconditioned technique is described subsequently in the next section.

3.1   A usual case of all entries of complex number

A commonly used and useful preconditioning technique is to scale the original matrix A, i.e., to choose the left-hand and right-hand preconditioned matrix S of diagonal matrix as

$$\tilde{A}\tilde{x} = \tilde{b} \quad (6)$$

where $\tilde{A} = (S^{-1/2}AS^{-1/2})$, $\tilde{x} = (S^{-1/2}x)$, $\tilde{b} = (S^{-1/2}b)$ are defined, respectively. The resulting entries of scaled matrix $\tilde{A}$ is written as follows:

$$\tilde{a}_{ij} = \begin{cases} 1 & \text{if } (i = j) \\ \frac{a_{ij}}{\sqrt{a_{ii}}\sqrt{a_{jj}}} & \text{if } (i \neq j). \end{cases} \quad (7)$$

Scaling technique is cheap and easy to implement. It may result in a quite better successful convergence in case of the problems with simplicity and/or equilibrium of nature. The choice of preconditioned matrix is an underlying factor for solving efficiently linear systems [7].

However, when we solve problems with the lumped dissipation matrix, diagonal entries only of original matrix A are complex, and nondiagonal entries of original matrix A are real. As a result of usual scaled preconditioning, nondiagonal entries of preconditioned matrix change from real number to complex number. Consequently much memory are necessary for storage of nondiagonal entries.

3.2 A particular case of complex diagonal entries only

Here we treat with the matrix A with particular characteristics as

$$
A = \begin{bmatrix} c_{11} & & & \text{real} \\ & \ddots & & \\ & & \ddots & \\ \text{real} & & & \ddots \\ & & & & c_{nn} \end{bmatrix} \quad (8)
$$

where diagonal entries c_{ii} only are complex numbers and all nondiagonal symmetric entries a_{ij} $(= a_{ji})$ are real numbers[2] [3]. Therefore it needs for the preconditioning technique that the characteristic of nondiagonal entries as real number is kept. For the purpose of preserving the merit of real nondiagonal entries, we propose the following diagonal scaling technique as

$$
a'_{ij} = \begin{cases} \dfrac{a_{ii}}{|a_{ii}|} & \text{if } (i = j) \\[2ex] \dfrac{a_{ij}}{\sqrt{|a_{ii}|}\sqrt{|a_{jj}|}} & \text{if } (i \neq j). \end{cases} \quad (9)
$$

The diagonal entries of preconditioned matrix A' may not become one, but the absolute value of the diagonal entries become surely one. Furthermore, it is of consequence that nondiagonal entries preserve as they are real numbers. Indeed, it is a great saving of memory. We refer to this scaling technique as the **absolute diagonal scaling** preconditioning.

We present briefly characteristics of used arrays in the implementation of CG method in Table 1. We remark that array "A-nd" for nondiagonal entries of matrix A is real array of eight bytes.

Table 1 Characteristics of used arrays in the implementation of CG method.

array	description	A-D-s (v.1)	A-D-s (v.2)
A	matrix	complex	not used
A-d	diagonal	–	complex
A-nd	nondiagonal	–	**real**
x	solution	complex	complex
b	R.H.S.	complex	complex

4 Numerical Experiments

4.1 On serial computer

In this section numerical results will be presented. We are primarily concerned with the COCG and cs_MRTR methods. All computations were done in complex double precision floating point arithmetics (16 bytes), and performed on PC with CPU of 3.2GHz clock and main memory of two Gigabytes. Fortran compiler ver. 8.0, and optimization option -O3 were used. The right-hand side of vector b was imposed from the physical load conditions. The stopping criterion for successful convergence of the iterative methods is less than 10^{-8} of the relative residual 2-norm $||r_{n+1}||_2/||r_0||_2$. In all cases the iteration was started with the initial guess solution $x_0 = 0$. The maximum iteration is fixed as same as the dimension of each matrix. CPU times are written in sec. and iteration counts of the iterative method are displayed in parenthesis. "freq." means frequency of sound, "Non-s" means non-scaling, "D-s" means usual diagonal scaling, "A-D-s (v.1)" means implementation v.1 of the absolute diagonal scaling, and "A-D-s (v.2)" means implementation v.2 of the absolute diagonal scaling, respectively. In Table 1 we will sketch used arrays for diagonal and nondiagonal entries of matrix A. In Tables the bold figures of CPU time denote the results of the absolute diagonal scaling of implementation v.2. Implementation v.1 means that arrays for entries of matrix are entirely complex (16 bytes). Implementation v.2 means that arrays for diagonal entry only of matrix are also complex (16 bytes).

Tables 2-3 show CPU time and iterations of four preconditioners of the COCG, COCR and cs_MRTR methods for acoustic problem when a sound source is located in the center of reverberation room. From these Tables, the following observations are made obviously.

- A-D-s (v.2) performs well, e.g., at frequency 125Hz, reduction of CPU time of non-scaling preconditioner is about 33% in case of the absolute diagonal scaling preconditioner.

- Between frequency 125Hz and 250Hz, the COCG, cs_MRTR methods are competitive. However, at frequency 315Hz, the cs_MRTR method does not work slightly well compared with the COCG method.

Figure 1 exhibit history of residual 2-norm of absolute diagonal scaling COCG and cs_MRTR methods at frequency 125Hz and 315Hz when a single sound source is located in the center of room. From Figure, the residual of COCG method oscilates violently compared with that of the cs_MRTR method. The cs_MRTR

Table 2 CPU time and iterations of four preconditioners of the **COCG** method for acoustic problem.

freq.	Non-s	D-s	A-D-s(v.1)	A-D-s (v.2)
125Hz	15.46 (1784)	12.42 (1249)	11.28 (1260)	**10.21** (1260)
160Hz	24.83 (2872)	19.71 (2008)	17.97 (2026)	**16.39** (2026)
200Hz	40.43 (4648)	31.52 (3203)	28.45 (3206)	**26.00** (3206)
250Hz	58.45 (6773)	46.36 (4708)	42.23 (4730)	**38.26** (4730)
315Hz	93.73 (10798)	71.31 (7345)	65.96 (7436)	**59.97** (7436)

Table 3 CPU time and iterations of four preconditioners of the **cs_MRTR** method for acoustic problem.

freq.	Non-s	D-s	A-D-s(v.1)	A-D-s (v.2)
125Hz	16.78 (1880)	11.63 (1302)	11.61 (1300)	**10.76** (1300)
160Hz	26.13 (2937)	18.43 (2069)	18.59 (2080)	**17.20** (2080)
200Hz	43.16 (4844)	29.26 (3281)	29.15 (3266)	**26.98** (3266)
250Hz	62.23 (6983)	42.53 (4766)	42.75 (4786)	**39.59** (4786)
315Hz	120.49 (13539)	72.05 (8074)	70.79 (7920)	**65.52** (7920)

method oscillates slightly at the late stage of iteration process.

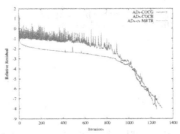

Figure 1 History of residual 2-norm of the absolute diagonal scaling COCG, COCR and cs_MRTR methods at frequency 125Hz.

4.2 On parallel computer

As for computational conditions on parallel computer, if there is not a specified description, they are as same as those on serial computer. Computations were performed on IBM eServer p5 with CPU of 1.9GHz clock and main memory of 48GB. Fortran compiler ver.9.1, and optimization option -O3 -qarch=pwr5 -qtune =pwr5 -qhot was used. OpenMP was used as a parallel library. The results are taken as average times of three trials of computations.

Table 4 compares the elapsed times in sec. of usual D-s preconditioner and A-D-s(v.2) preconditioner of the COCG method. A-D-s(v.2) preconditioner can outperform not only on serial computer but also on parallel computer. From Table 4, the following observations are made.

- A-D-s(v.2) preconditioner can convergence faster than usual D-s preconditioner. e.g., in Table 4(b) with eight threads, the elapsed times of A-D-s_COCG method reduces to 59% of that of D-s_COCG method.

- In Table 4(a) cache miss can cause hardly because of small size. In contrast, in Table 4(b), cache miss can be seen because of large size. Namely the number of threads increases, occurrences of cache miss decreases. As a result, speedup of computations was attained.

- Many nonzero entries of matrix of A-D-s preconditioner can store in cache memory compared with those of usual D-s preconditioner. Consequently, the proposed preconditioner can save memory and elapsed times on parallel computer.

5 Conclusions

We have demonstrated the effectiveness of absolute diagonal scaling preconditioner for the CG method. For the matrix of which diagonal entries only are complex number, it is especially attractive that the proposed absolute diagonal scaling preconditioner is effective on serial and parallel computers from the viewpoint of reduction of both memory and computation times.

Table 4 Elapsed times of preconditioners of the COCG method for small and large size problems.

Th	D-s	A-D-s(v.2)	ratio	speedup
1	13.01	7.11	0.54	1.00
2	5.48	3.53	0.64	2.01
4	2.90	1.79	0.61	3.97
8	1.58	0.98	0.62	7.25

(a)125Hz_S1 (size=24,255 D.O.F.)

Th	D-s	A-D-s(v.2)	ratio	speedup
1	284.98	193.57	0.67	1.00
2	149.62	94.76	0.63	2.04
4	73.60	38.68	0.52	5.00
8	31.00	18.55	0.59	10.44

(b)125Hz_S1_big (size=183,885 D.O.F.)

References

[1] Abe, K., Zhang, S.-L., Mitsui, T., Jin, C.: A variant of the ORTHOMIN(2) method for singular linear systems, Numerical Algorithms Vol.36, pp.189-202, 2004.

[2] Freund, R.W.: Conjugate gradient-type methods for linear system with complex symmetric coeficient matrices, SIAM Sci. Comput., Vol.13, pp.425-448, 1992.

[3] Made, M., Beauwens, R. and Warzee, G.: Precondition of discrete Helmholtz operators perturbed by a diagonal complex matrix, *Commun. Numer. Meth. Engrg.*, Vol.16, pp.801-817, 2000.

[4] Okamoto, N., Otsuru, T. et al.: Relationship between Sound Field and Convergence Characteristic of Iterative Methods in Finite Element Sound Field Analysis of Rooms, The 33rd Int. Congress and Exposition on Noise Control Engineering, 2004.

[5] Sogabe, T., Zhang, S.-L.: COCR methods for solving complex symmetric linear systems, The Proc. of SCAN2004, p.107, Fukuoka, 2004.

[6] van der Vorst, H.A., Melissen, J.: A Peterov-Galerkin type method for solving $Ax = b$, where A is symmetric complex, IEEE Trans. on Magnetics, Vol.26, No.2, pp.706-708, 1990.

[7] Weiss, R., Parameter-Free Iterative Linear Solvers, Akademie Verlag, 1996.

The Fluid-Structure Interacting Simulations with the Immersed Interface Method on a Cartesian Grid

Satoshi II , Feng XIAO and Kenji ONO

Department of Energy Sciences,
Tokyo Institute of Technology,
4259 Nagatsuta, Midori-ku, Yokohama, 226-8502, Japan
(E-mail: d06ii@es.titech.ac.jp, xiao@es.titech.ac.jp,)
VCAD System Research Program,
RIKEN,
2-1 Hirosawa, Wako-shi, Saitama, 351-0198, Japan
(E-mail: keno@riken.jp)

ABSTRACT

We simulated fluid-structure interaction problems using the immersed interface method on a Cartesian grid. The immersed interface method allows explicit specification of the jump conditions across the fluid-structure interface, yielding high order accuracy. We in this study evaluated the jump condition with one-side stencil over the interface. The resulting formulation is able to deal with structures even smaller than mesh size. We use local-based and high-order numerical scheme which involves the derivative jump conditions to get high-order accuracy. The present numerical method were verified by some numerical examples.

KEY WORDS: Fluid-Structure Interaction, Immersed Interface Method, IDO-SC Scheme.

INTRODUCTION

Fluid-Structure interactions are found in various natural phenomena, for example, blood flow, swimming microorganism, frying insect and many others. Usually, unstructured grids have been used to simulate the fluid-structure interactions with geometrically complex shapes. However, it is necessary to reconstruct the numerical grids at every step in case of moving structure or interface. This requires extra computational cost, moreover, the numerical results are highly dependent on the quality of the re-meshed grids especially when the interfaces experience violent motions or topological changes.

On the other hand, numerical methods that use Cartesian grids have also been proposed and used in dealing with the moving interfaces in CFD. Peskin [7] has introduced the immersed boundary method (IBM) for simulating blood flow through heart valves. Goldstein [1] has extended IBM to a rigid boundary. However, the IBMs are usually of first-order accuracy, and the numerical solutions are smeared near the interface. A high-order approach, namely immersed interface method, has been proposed by LeVeque and Li for elliptic problems [4] and extended to the incompressible Navier-Stokes equations [5]. In this method, the interface is explicitly treated as a discontinuity where the jump conditions are evaluated by a singular force. Generally, high-order derivatives of the jump conditions are required to obtain a high-order accuracy. However, it is not easy to obtain the high-order derivatives of the jump conditions from a singular force. Recently, a more practical method has been devised by Linnick [6], in which he evaluated the jump conditions by one-side stencils and extended the scheme to the two-dimensional incompressible flow with a formulation in terms of stream function and vorticity.

Our numerical method for treating the

irregular interface on a Cartesian grid is based on Linnick's method. It is suitable for simulating the interaction of fluid and thin-structure like a flapping flag. In his method, the compact finite-difference scheme [3] is used to obtain a high-order accuracy. Regarding the spatial discretization, we use the interpolated differential operator-stable coupling (IDO-SC) scheme of Imai [2], which is a high-order scheme in primitive variables on the collocated Cartesian grid. The discontinuities on the interface have been then well resolved. We will show some numerical examples of the interactions between fluid and moving rigid body.

NUMERICAL APPROACH

We use IDO-SC scheme [2] for a discretization, and immersed interface method [4, 5, 6] for treatment of complex geometric boundary on a Cartesian grid.

Numerical formulation

The two-dimensional incompressible Navier-Stokes equations are given by following the continuous equation and the momentum equation,

$$\nabla \cdot \mathbf{u} = 0, \qquad (1)$$
$$\rho \frac{\mathbf{u}}{t} + (\mathbf{u} \cdot \nabla)\mathbf{u} = -\nabla p + \mu \nabla^2 \mathbf{u}. \qquad (2)$$

where $\mathbf{u} = (u, v)$ are velocity for x and y components, p the pressure, ρ the density and μ is the viscosity.

We use fractional-step technique and apply the fourth-order Runge-Kutta time-integration to advection-diffusion terms.

$$\mathbf{u}^{l+1} = \mathbf{u}^l + \Delta t \left(\frac{1}{\rho}(\mathbf{u}^l \cdot \nabla)\mathbf{u}^l + \frac{\mu}{\rho}\nabla^2 \mathbf{u}^l \right),$$
$$(3)$$

for $(l = 0, 1, 2, 3)$. Where, $\mathbf{u}^0 = \mathbf{u}^n$, $\mathbf{u}^3 = \mathbf{u}$.

Then, we solve following Poisson equation for pressure,

$$\nabla^2 p^{n+1} = \frac{\nabla \cdot \mathbf{u}}{\Delta t}, \qquad (4)$$

and project the velocity as follows,

$$\mathbf{u}^{n+1} = \mathbf{u} - \Delta t \, \nabla p^{n+1}. \qquad (5)$$

In two-dimensional IDO-SC scheme, four types of moments or variables are defined as the prognostic variables, i.e. point value, first-order derivative for x and y respectively and second-order cross derivative of x and y. All of these quantities are updated independently in time. The governing equations of the derivative moments are derived by differentiating Eqs. (3)-(5). Compared to others, this formulation needs compact stencils and gives high-order accuracy (for detail in [2]).

Modified Taylor series expansion

We introduce the physical variable (x). The modified Taylor series expansion over a domain which includes an interface at $x \in [x_i, x_{i+1}]$ are written as

$$(x_{i+1}) = \sum_{m=0} \frac{(\Delta x)^m}{m!} \frac{\partial^m}{\partial x^m}\bigg|_{x_i} + J ,$$
$$J = \sum_{m=0} \frac{(\Delta x_i^+)^m}{m!} \left[\frac{\partial^m}{\partial x^m}\right]_{x_\alpha}, \qquad (6)$$

where Δx is a grid space, and $\Delta x_i^+ = x_{i+1} - x$. Jump condition is denoted as

$$\left[\frac{\partial^m}{\partial x^m}\right]_{x_\alpha} \equiv \left(\frac{\partial^m}{\partial x^m}\right)_{x_\alpha^+} - \left(\frac{\partial^m}{\partial x^m}\right)_{x_\alpha}. \qquad (7)$$

In IDO-SC scheme, we can construct fifth-order interpolation function over two cells with point value and first-order derivative defined as moments. Therefore, modified Taylor series expansion for first-order derivative is written as

$$x(x_{i+1}) = \sum_{m=0} \frac{(\Delta x)^m}{m!} \frac{\partial^{m+1}}{\partial x^{m+1}}\bigg|_{x_i} + J_{x_\alpha}, \qquad (8)$$

Analogously, in case that an interface is located at $x \in [x_{i\ 1}, x_i]$, modified Taylor series expansion for point value and first-order derivative are given by

$$(x_{i\ 1}) = \sum_{m=0} \frac{(-\Delta x)^m}{m!} \frac{\partial^m}{\partial x^m}\bigg|_{x_i} - J , \qquad (9)$$

$$x(x_{i\ 1}) = \sum_{m=0} \frac{(-\Delta x)^m}{m!} \frac{\partial^{m+1}}{\partial x^{m+1}}\bigg|_{x_i} - J_{x_\beta}. \qquad (10)$$

From Eqs. (6)-(10), we can evaluate the first, second and third derivatives for updating the Navier-Stokes equations.

Treatment of jump condition

Our approach for treatment jump condition is similar with Linnick's approach [6]. We assume that an interface exists at $x \in [x_i, x_{i+1}]$ and the left side of the interface is fluid while the right side is the immersed body. Then, point value or first-order derivative on right side is evaluated directly as,

$$x_a^+ = f \quad \text{for Dirichlet BC,}$$

$$\left(\frac{\partial}{\partial x} \right)_{x_a^+} = g \quad \text{for Neumann BC,}$$

where f and g are the boundary conditions. Other high-order derivatives on right side are set to zero.

The point value and the derivatives on the left side (fluid side) of the interface are evaluated by the left-side stencils. The interpolation reconstruction is conducted in the outward normal direction of the interface.

NUMERICAL EXAMPLES

Flow past a circular cylinder

We computed an incompressible flow passing a circular cylinder with $Re = 100$. The computational domain is $[0, 10] \times [0, 8]$, and grid number is 100×80. Lagrangian points of a circular cylinder are shown in Figure 1.

Figure 1   Lagrangian points.

Figure 2 shows the velocity field at non-dimensional time $t = 100$. The effects of the circular obstacle is well resolved. Moreover, we plotted the time histories of the drag and the lift coefficients in Figure 3. Figure 4 shows the bird's eye views of the flow field around a half circle. We can obtain high-resolution results near the interface.

Rotation of a circle in static field

Next, we compute a rotating circular cylinder in a initially static viscous flow

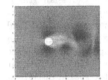

(a) Global	(b) Around cylinder

Figure 2   Velocity vector. $t = 100$.

Figure 3   Drag and Lift coefficients. $Re = 100$.

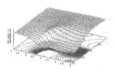

(a) Velocity u

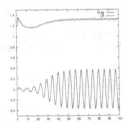

(b) Velocity v

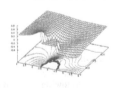

(c) Pressure p

Figure 4   Bird's eye view around the half cylinder. $t = 100$.

with $Re = 100$. The computational domain is $[0, 1] \times [0, 1]$ and grid number is 100×100.

We show the time evolution of velocity field in Figure 5. A rotating flow field is well developed due to the rotational motion of the central circle that has a non-slip boundary with the fluid.

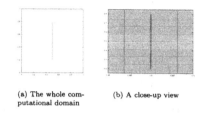

(a) The whole computational domain

(b) A close-up view

Figure 6   The computational domain of the cavity flow with an embedded thin plate.

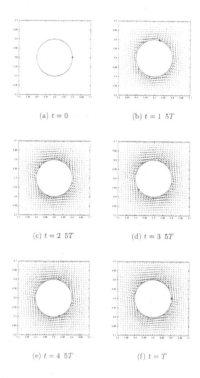

(a) $t = 0$ (b) $t = 1\ 5T$

(c) $t = 2\ 5T$ (d) $t = 3\ 5T$

(e) $t = 4\ 5T$ (f) $t = T$

Figure 5   Time evolution of the velocity field. T is the periodic time.

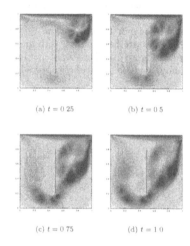

(a) $t = 0\ 25$ (b) $t = 0\ 5$

(c) $t = 0\ 75$ (d) $t = 1\ 0$

Figure 7   Time evolutions of velocity. $Re = 1000$.

Cavity flow with a thin structure

We carry out cavity flow with a thin embedded structure whose thickness is less than the mesh size (Figure 6). The computational domain is $[0, 1] \times [0, 1]$ and grid number is 100×100.

From Figure 7, we can find the thin plate affects substantially the whole velocity field in the cavity. It reveals that the present scheme works well with structure of a subgrid scale. The pressure around the interface is closed up in Figure 8. We obtained a sharp jump in the pressure field around the interface.

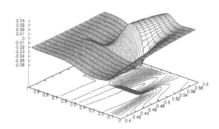

Figure 8   Pressure distribution around the interface at $t = 0\ 5$.

A free-falling rigid body in gravity field

Finally, we present a test for interactions between fluid and a rigid body. A motion

121

of the rigid body is governed by

$$m\frac{\mathbf{u}}{t} = \int_\Gamma \mathbf{F} d\Gamma, \qquad (11)$$

$$\frac{(I)}{t} = \int_\Gamma \mathbf{F} \times \mathbf{r} d\Gamma, \qquad (12)$$

where Γ is the surface of the rigid body, m the mass, $\mathbf{u}$ the velocity, $\mathbf{F} = (F_x, F_y)$ the force imposing on the body, I the inertial moment, ω the angular velocity and $\mathbf{r} = (r_x, r_y)$ the position vector in respect to the mass center of the body.

The computation is carried out over $[0, 1] \times [0, 1]$ with 50×50 grid points, and $Re = 200$. We show the time evolution of the rigid body in Figure 9. The velocity and the pressure fields at $t = 0.16$ are depicted in Figure 10. The swing motion of the falling body is reasonably captured.

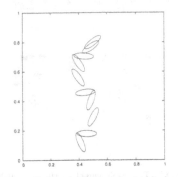

Figure 9   Time evolutions of a rigid body.

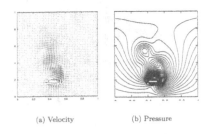

(a) Velocity   (b) Pressure

Figure 10   Instant values at $t = 0.16$.

CONCLUSIONS

We proposed an accurate scheme for fluid-structure interaction using the IDO-SC scheme and immersed interface method on a Cartesian grid. By using IDO-SC scheme, we can construct high-order formulation with local stencils. As the immersed interface method, Linnick's approach is used for the treatment of the jump conditions across the fluid-structure interface. The interface is numerically formulated with adequate accuracy even for sub-grid structures.

As the future work, the present method will be implemented to more general fluid-structure interactions including the elastic effects of the structure.

REFERENCES

1. D. Goldstein, R. Handler, L. Sirovich, Modeling a no-slip flow boundary with an external force field, J. Compute. Phys. **105** (1993) 354.

2. Y. Imai, T. Aoki, Stable coupling between vector and scalar variables for the IDO scheme on collocated grid, J. Compute. Phys. **215** (2006) 81.

3. S. K. Lele, Compact finite difference schemes with spectral-like resolution, J. Compute. Phys. **103** (1992) 16.

4. R. J. LeVeque and Z. Li, The immersed interface method for elliptic equations with discontinuous coefficients and singular sources, SIAM J. Numer. Anal. **31** (1994) 1019.

5. Z. Li and M. C. Lai, The Immersed Interface Method for the Navier-Stokes Equations with Singular Forces, J. Compute. Phys. **171** (2001) 822.

6. M. N. Linnick, H. F. Fasel, A high-order immersed interface method for simulating unsteady incompressible flows on irregular domains, J. Compute. Phys. **204** (2005) 157.

7. C. S. Peskin, Flow Patterns Around Heart Valves: A Numerical Method, J. Compute. Phys. **10** (1972) 252.

Design of Fuzzy Logic Controller for Chaos Synchronization

Her-Terng Yau, Cheng-Shion Shieh

Department of Electrical Engineering, Far-East College, No 49,
Jung-Hwa Road, Hsin-Shih Town Tainan 744, Taiwan, R.O.C.
(Email: pan1012@ms52.hinet.net)

ABSTRACT

The design of a rule-based controller for a class of master-slave chaos synchronization is presented in this paper. In traditional fuzzy logic control (FLC) design, it takes a long time to obtain the membership functions and rule base by trial-and-error tuning. To cope with this problem, we directly construct the fuzzy rules subject to a common Lyapunov function such that the master-slave chaos systems satisfy stability in the Lyapunov sense. Unlike conventional approaches, the resulting control law has less maximum magnitude of the instantaneous control command and it can reduce the actuator saturation phenomenon in real physic system. The example of Duffing-Holmes system is presented to illustrate the effectiveness of the proposed controller.

KEY WORD: chaos synchronization, fuzzy logic control, Lyapunov function, Duffing-Holmes system

INTRODUCTION

Over the past decades, chaos plays a more and more important role in nonlinear science field. Synchronization of chaotic systems has received a significant attention, since Pecora and Carroll presented the chaos synchronization method to synchronize two identical chaotic systems with different initial values in 1990 [1]. Generally the two chaotic systems in synchronization are called drive system and response system, respectively. Nowadays, chaos and its synchronization have found a lot of useful applications in many field of engineering and science such as in secure communications, chemical reactions, power converters, biological systems, and information processing. Many methods have been presented for the control and synchronization of chaotic system [2, 6, 7]. Generally speaking, the synchronization phenomenon has the following feature: the output of the drive system is used to control the response system so that the output of the response system follows the output of

123

the drive system asymptotically.

The fuzzy logic control (FLC) schemes have been widely developed for almost 40 years, and have been successfully applied to many applications [3]. Besides, the adaptive fuzzy controller had also been used to control and synchronize the chaotic systems [4]. However, it takes a long time to obtain the membership functions and rule base by trial-and-error tuning in traditional FLC design.

To overcome the trail-and-error tuning of the membership functions and rule base, we directly construct the fuzzy rules subject to a common Lyapunov function [5] such that the error dynamics satisfies stability in the Lyapunov sense in this paper. The Duffing-Holmes systems is presented in this study to show that the feasibility of the proposed controller.

SYSTEM DESCRIPTION

In this section, Duffing-Holmes is presented for synchronizing by fuzzy rule-based controller. Consider a master-slave Duffing-Holmes systems as follows

$$\begin{cases} \dot{x}_1 = x_2 \\ \dot{x}_2 = -p_1 x_1 - px_2 - x_1^3 + q\cos(\omega t) \end{cases}, \quad (6)$$

$$\begin{cases} \dot{y}_1 = y_2 \\ \dot{y}_2 = -p_1 y_1 - py_2 - y_1^3 + \Delta f(y) \\ \quad + d(t) + q\cos(\omega t) + u(t) \end{cases} \quad (7)$$

The control input $u(t)$ is attached to the second equation of the slave system (7). In the followings, we will give an explicit and simple procedure to construct the FLC to guarantee the synchronization of two Duffing-Holmes systems, such that

$$\lim_{t \to \infty} \|x(t) - y(t)\| \to 0, \quad (3)$$

where $\|\cdot\|$ is the Euclidean norm of a vector.

FUZZY CONTROLLER DESIGN FOR CHAOTIC SYNCHRONIZATION

For the synchronization systems (6) and (7), let the error states are $e_1 = y_1 - x_1$ and $e_2 = y_2 - x_2$. Subtracting (6) from (7) yields the synchronization error dynamics as

$$\begin{cases} \dot{e}_1 = e_2 \\ \dot{e}_2 = -p_1 e_1 - pe_2 - y_1^3 + x_1^3 \\ \quad + \Delta f(e,x) + d(t) + u(t) \end{cases} \quad (8)$$

Let the control input $u(t) = u_{eq} + u_L$ and $u_{eq} = y_1^3 - x_1^3$, then the error dynamics becomes

$$\begin{cases} \dot{e}_1 = e_2 \\ \dot{e}_2 = -p_1 e_1 - pe_2 + \Delta f(e,x) + d(t) + u_L \end{cases} \quad (9)$$

Here, we use the signal (e_1, e_2) in (9) as the antecedent part of the proposed FLC to design the control input u_L that will be used in the consequent part of the proposed FLC i.e.:

$$u_L = FLC(e_1, e_2), \quad (10)$$

where the FLC accomplishes the objective to stabilize the error dynamics (9). The fuzzy rule is listed in Table 1 in which the input variables in the antecedent part of the rules are e_1 and e_2, and the output variable in the consequent is u_{Li}. Using P, Z and N as input fuzzy sets representing 'postive', 'zero' and 'negative', respectively, we obtain the membership function shown in Fig. 1. The centriod defuzzifier evaluates the output of all rules as follows

$$u_L = \frac{\sum\limits_{i=1,\mu_i \neq 0}^{n} \mu_i \cdot u_{Li}}{\sum\limits_{i=1,\mu_i \neq 0}^{n} \mu_i}, \mu_i = \min(\mu_{x1}(e_1), \mu_{x2}(e_2)). \quad (11)$$

The $u_{L1}, u_{L2}, \cdots, u_{L9}$ in Table 1 are the output from the ith-If Then rule and will be discussed in the followings.

From system (9), we select a Lyapunov function such that:

$$V = \frac{1}{2}(e_1^2 + e_2^2), \quad (12)$$

The corresponding requirement of Lyapunov stability is $\dot{V} = e_1\dot{e}_1 + e_2\dot{e}_2 < 0$, that is

$$\dot{e}_2 < -\frac{e_1\dot{e}_1}{e_2}. \quad (13)$$

According the Lyapunov stability condition (13), the following case will satisfy all the stability conditions.

Case1: $e_2 < 0$

For $e_2 < 0$, the Eq.(13) becomes to

$$\dot{e}_2 > -e_1. \quad (14)$$

Substituting Eq.(14) into Eq.(9) yields
$-p_1e_1 - pe_2 + \Delta f + d(t) + u_L > -e_1$,
hence $u_L > (p_1 - 1)e_1 + pe_2 - \Delta f - d(t)$. It is assumed that the uncertainty term Δf and external disturbance are bounded, that is, $|\Delta f + d(t)| \le \alpha$, where $\alpha > 0$ is given. We can define that

$$(p_1 - 1)e_1 + pe_2 + \alpha = u_1^*. \quad (15)$$

Case2: $e_2 > 0$

For $e_2 > 0$, the Eq.(13) becomes to

$$\dot{e}_2 < -e_1. \quad (16)$$

Substituting Eq.(16) into Eq.(9) yields
$\dot{e}_2 = -p_1e_1 - pe_2 + \Delta f + d(t) + u_L < -e_1$,
hence $u_L < (p_1 - 1)e_1 + pe_2 - \Delta f - d(t)$. It is defined that

$$(p_1 - 1)e_1 + pe_2 - \alpha = u_2^*. \quad (17)$$

If the system satisfies the case1 and case 2, then $\dot{V} < 0$ and the error state will be asymptotically driven into zero. In order to achieve this result, we will design u_L by rule table in the next work in this paper. For rules 1, 4 and 7 in Table 1, the error state e_2 is positive, and $\dot{e}_2 < -e_1$ and $u_{L1} = u_{L4} = u_{L7} = u_2^*$. The corresponding derivative of the Lyapunov function in (13) is $\dot{V} = e_1\dot{e}_1 + e_2\dot{e}_2 = e_2(e_1 + \dot{e}_2) < 0$.

Similarly, for rules 3, 6 and 9 in table 1, the error state e_2 is negative, and $\dot{e}_2 > -e_1$ and $u_{L3} = u_{L6} = u_{L9} = u_1^*$. The corresponding derivative of the Lyapunov function in (12) also satisfies $\dot{V} < 0$.

Case3: $e_1 > 0$ and $e_2 \in$ zero

For rule 2 in table 1, the error state e_1 is positive and e_2 is zero. If the corresponding derivative of the Lyapunov function needs to be still kept negative in (14), then it needs to be satisfied

$e_1 + \dot{e}_2 = -\text{sgn}(e_2)$, where $\text{sgn}(e_2) = \begin{cases} 1; e_2 > 0 \\ -1; e_2 < 0 \end{cases}$.

Because of e_1 is positive, then

$$\dot{e}_2 < -\text{sgn}(e_2). \quad (18)$$

Substituting equation (18) into equation(9) yields
$-p_1e_1 - pe_2 + \Delta f + d(t) + u_L = \dot{e}_2 < -\text{sgn}(e_2)$.
The above equation can be rewritten as
$u_L < -\text{sgn}(e_2) + p_1e_1 + pe_2 - \Delta f - d(t)$,

and it is defined that

$$u_{L2} = -\text{sgn}(e_2) + p_1 e_1 + p e_2 - \alpha. \qquad (19)$$

Case4: $e_1 < 0$ and $e_2 \in$ zero
The controller u_{L8} in rule 8 will be discussed similarly to rule 2 in table 1. In this case, it is defined that

$$u_{L8} = -\text{sgn}(e_2) + p_1 e_1 + p e_2 + \alpha. \qquad (20)$$

Case5: $e_1 \in$ zero and $e_2 \in$ zero
For rule 5 in table 1, the error states e_1 and e_2 is zeros. This condition is included in the other rules, and we define $u_L = u_{L5} = 0$ in this rule.

Hence, all of the rules in the FLC can lead to Lyapunov stable subsystems under the same Lyapunov function (12). That is, the states (e_1, e_2) guarantee convergence to zero and the Duffing-Holmes systems is synchronized.

AN ILLUSTRATIVE EXAMPLE

For the overall control systems (6) and (7), the parameters are $p_1 = -1$, $p = 0.25$, $q = 0.3$ and $\omega = 1.0$, the master system (6) displaces chaotic behavior [2]. It is supposed that the uncertainty term

$\Delta f(y) = -0.05 y_1$ and the disturbance $d(t) = 0.2 \cdot \cos(\pi t)$. The simulation results with initial conditions $x_1(0)=0.1$, $x_2(0)=0.1$, $y_1(0)=-0.5$, and $y_2(0)=0.5$ are shown in Figures 2-4. In Fig. 2, it shows that the slave system and the master system can reach synchronization with control operation. In addition, the time responses of error states and control input are shown in Figs. 3-4.

CONCLUSION

In this paper, nonlinear FLC theory has been exploited in this paper to design a controller for chaos synchronization with system uncertainties and disturbance. To overcome the trail-and-error tuning to obtain the membership functions and fuzzy rules, a Lyapunov-based robust FLC of chaos synchronization is studied in this paper. From simulation results, the error dynamics of Duffing-Holmes synchronization systems are regulated to zero asymptotically in spite of the overall system is undergoing uncertainty and disturbance. The other types of chaotic synchronization systems could also be synchronized by using the same control scheme proposed in this study.

Table 1. Rule-table of FLC

Rule	Antecedent		Conseque.
	e_1	e_2	u_{Li}
1	P	P	u_{L1}
2	P	Z	u_{L2}
3	P	N	u_{L3}
4	Z	P	u_{L4}
5	Z	Z	u_{L5}
6	Z	N	u_{L6}
7	N	P	u_{L7}
8	N	Z	u_{L8}
9	N	N	u_{L9}

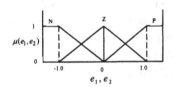

Fig. 1. Membership functions

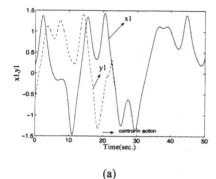

(a)

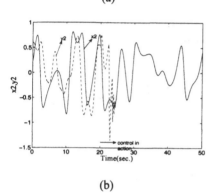

(b)

Fig. 2. Time responses of Duffing-Holmes chaos synchronization: master and slave system outputs are x_1, x_2, (solid) and y_1, y_2, (dashed), respectively.

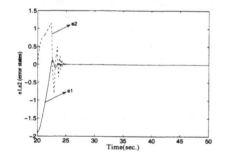

Fig. 3. The time response of error states.

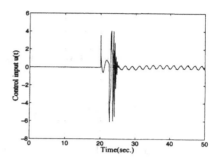

Fig. 4. The control action versus time. The control u(t) is activated at t=20 sec.

Reference

1. Pecora LM, Carroll TL. Synchronization in chaotic systems. Phys. Rev. Letter 1990; 64(8):821-824.
2. Chen G, Dong X. From chaos to order: methodologies, perspectives and applications. Singapore: World Scientific; 1998.
3. Zadeh, LA. Fuzzy logic. IEEE Computer 1988; 21(4), 83-93
4. Feng G, Chen G. Adaptive control of discrete-time chaotic systems: a fuzzy control approach. Chaos Solitons & Fractals 2005; 23, 459-467.
5. Shieh CS. Nonlinear rule-based controller for missile terminal guidance. IEE Proc.-Control Theory Appl. 2003; 150(1), 45-48
6. Yau HT. Design of adaptive sliding mode controller for chaos synchronization with uncertainties. Chaos Solitons & Fractals 2004; 22, 341-347.
7. Yau HT, Lin JS and Yan JJ. Synchronization control for a class of chaotic systems with uncertainties. Int. J. Bifurcation and Chaos 2005; 15(7), 2235-2246.

Design of an Evolutionary-based Fuzzy System

Yi-Pin Kuo*, Ming-Tang Liu**, Juing-Shian Chiou**

*Department of Electronic Engineering, Far East University of Technology
No.49, Chung Hua Rd., Hsin-Shih, Tainan County 744, Taiwan, R.O.C
(E-mail: ypkuo@mail2000.com.tw)
**Department of Electrical Engineering, Southern Taiwan University of Technology,
1Nan-Tai St. Yung-Kung, Tainan County 710, Taiwan, R.O.C

ABSTRACT

This paper presents the application of evolutionary genetic algorithm (GA) in the design of the fuzzy system, in which the membership function shapes and types and the fuzzy rule set, including the number of rules inside the rule set are evolved by GA to create a complete fuzzy controller. In addition, the genetic parameters of the evolutionary algorithm are adapted by using fuzzy system. The simulation results of second-order system show that our approach is effective.

KEY WORDS: Fuzzy system, genetic algorithms

I. INTRODUCTION

Fuzzy systems are being used successfully in an increasing number of application areas. In the design of fuzzy system, the definition of the membership functions, modeled by fuzzy sets and the rule sets are most important considerations; them also constitute the main difficulty [1,2]. Many researchers have been applied GAs to fuzzy system, include encoding all the rules into the chromosome while the membership functions are fixed [3,4]. Karr et al. [5] use GAs to adjust the membership functions. Homaifar et al. [6] use GAs to tune the membership functions and evolve the rule set at the same time but all possible rules are encoded into the chromosomes. Similarly, Lee et al. [7] encode membership functions and all the rules into the chromosome, but also have

constrains at the input range. Shi et al. [8] have been solved the problems of above-mentioned methods, however, the length of the chromosome is represented as 226 integers long, its cost is lost the computationally efficiency. In this paper, we utilize GA to construct an optimal fuzzy system, and the length of chromosome in the GA is shorter which means the better computationally efficiency.

In GA, there are two main reproduction operators, namely crossover and mutation. The choice of the probabilities of crossover and mutation is known to critically affect the behavior and the performance of GA, and a number of guidelines are existing in the literature for choosing them [9]. Instead of having fixed probabilities of crossover and mutation, a fuzzy-controlled crossover and mutation probabilities is presented in this paper. The basic concept is based on considering the useful knowledge and human expertise. For example, if the best fitness value of the individual does not change during several generations, the mutation rate should be increased to prevent the system premature convergence. When the fitness value of the individual grows up obviously and continuously, we should emphasize the crossover rate but the mutation rate should be reduced to keep the convergence of system. By using fuzzy system can assist GA to adjust the evolution parameters such as crossover rate and mutation rate.

This paper presents intelligent fuzzy logic-based genetic algorithms by using genetic algorithm and FLC system are discussed in which the membership function shapes and types and the fuzzy rule set including the number of rules inside it are evolved using a GAs. In addition, crossover and mutation are two critical genetic parameters (operators). We use fuzzy control to dynamic adjustment the crossover rate and mutation rate to enhance the efficiency of evolution.

II. CHROMOSOME ENCODING METHODS

GAs are search algorithms modeled after the mechanics of natural genetics. They are useful approaches to problems requiring effective and efficient searching In an optimally designed application, GAs can be used to obtain an approximate solution for single variable or multivariable optimal problems. While stochastic in nature, GAs perform a highly effective search of the problem hyperspace, efficiently directing the search to promising regions. So GAs work with a population of points rather than a single point. The analogy between biological evolution and a binary GA, it is required to encode values as individual chromosomes. The GA begins, like any other optimization algorithm, by defining the optimization variables, the fitness function, and the error amount. It ends like other optimization algorithms too, by testing for convergence.

For the object is to optimize the number of fuzzy sets, which is the problem of membership function's distributing in fields, so fixing on membership function's shape is considered firstly. In order to properly represent the space distributing of fields, each membership function is determined by the start point x_1 and the end point x_2. Theoretically, each fuzzy variable can have different fuzzy sets with its own membership function, but commonly used are three, five, seven, or nine fuzzy sets for each fuzzy variable, and the membership function can be linear or nonlinear. In this paper, we adopt six membership functions for the fuzzy set; they are left triangle, right triangle, triangle, Gaussian, and sigmoid functions, respectively. The equations of these membership functions are described as follows:

$$f_{left\_triangle} = \begin{cases} 1, & if\ x < x_1 \\ \dfrac{x_2 - x}{x_2 - x_1}, & if\ x_1 \leq x \leq x_2 \\ 0, & if\ x > x_2 \end{cases} \quad (1)$$

$$f_{right\_triangle} = \begin{cases} 0, & if\ x < x_1 \\ \dfrac{x - x_1}{x_2 - x_1}, & if\ x_1 \leq x \leq x_2 \\ 1, & if\ x > x_2 \end{cases} \quad (2)$$

$$f_{triangle} = \begin{cases} 0, & if\ x < x_1 \\ 2\dfrac{x - x_1}{x_2 - x_1}, & if\ x_1 \leq x \leq \dfrac{x_2 + x_1}{2} \\ 2\dfrac{x_2 - x}{x_2 - x_1}, & if\ \dfrac{x_2 + x_1}{2} \leq x \leq x_2 \\ 0, & if\ x > x_2 \end{cases} \quad (3)$$

$$f_{Gaussian}(x) = e^{-0.5y} \text{ where } y = \dfrac{8(x - x_1)}{x_2 - x_1} - 4 \quad (4)$$

$$f_{sigmoid}(x) = \frac{1}{1+e^{(-y+6)}} \quad \text{where} \, y = \frac{12(x-x_1)}{x_2-x_1} \quad (5)$$

$$f_{reverse\_sigmoid}(x) = 1 - f_{sigmoid}(x) \qquad (6)$$

From the definitions, the membership function of each fuzzy set can be described as three evolution parameters which are denoting the start point x_1, the end point x_2 and the function type value respectively. In this paper, all these evolutionary parameters are coding with real number, a total of six types of functions are used as the membership function candidates; each is represented by an integer from 0 to 6, zero is useless, one is the Triangle, two is the Left_triangle, three is the Right_triangle, four is the Gaussian, five is the Sigmoid and six is the Reverse_sigmoid. In order to have a homogeneous chromosome, integers are chosen to represent the start point x_1 and the end point x_2 instead of real values. If the fuzzy membership functions are uniformly distributed over the range with half-way overlap as shown in Figure 1, then the center point $c_i (i = 1,...,7)$ of the ith membership function is located at

$$c_i = x_{i1} + \frac{x_{i2} - x_{i1}}{2} \qquad (7)$$

In this paper, the fuzzy numbers 1~7 in the fuzzy rule table represent the linguistic values *NL, NM, NS, ZE, PS, PM,* and *PL,* respectively. The total length of the chromosome representing the system is

$$(3\times7)+(7\times7)=70$$

and the system can be represented as:

$C_1 C_2 C_3 .... C_{21} C_{22} C_{23} C_{24} .... C_{68} C_{69} C_{70}$
where $C_1 C_2 C_3 .... C_{21}$ represents (start point, end point, type), C_{22} to C_{70} represent the fuzzy rules.

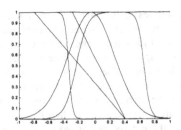

Figure 1 Six uniformly distributed membership functions.

III. ADAPTIVE GENETIC ALGORITHM

Crossover and mutation are two critical operators; they facilitate an efficient search and guide the search into new regions. They can be varied during the running, usually starting out by running the GA with a relatively higher value for crossover and lower value for mutation, then tapering off the crossover value and increasing the mutation rate toward the end of the evolution. In order to make GA can explore the potential solutions in the searching field as soon as possible, the mutation rate and crossover rate should be duly adjusted during the evolution. Although there is no a rule for how to adjust these evolutionary parameters, but by using human experience can help us to achieve this purpose. For example, when the best fitness did not increasing after a few generations of the evolution, it means that the system could be stuck at a local minimum, so the system should probably concentrate on exploiting rather than exploring; in another word, the crossover rate should be decreased and the mutation rate should be increased. According to this kind of knowledge, we use fuzzy system to adjust the crossover and mutation rates. The best fitness (BF), the number of generations for unchanged best fitness (UN), and the variance of fitness (VF) are the input variables, and mutation rate (MR) and crossover rate (CR) are the output variables of the fuzzy system. The examples of the fuzzy control rules based on the linguistic description of the fuzzy implications are stated as

If UN is *high* and VF is *medium*, then MR is *high*.

If UN is *high* and VF is *medium*, then CR is *low*.

For simplicity, each variable has three fuzzy sets: Low, Medium, and High. The variation of BF is [0,4], VF is [0,5], UN is [0,10], MR is [0.005,0.1] and CR is [0.5,0.9]. The fuzzy rules table is shown in Table 1. After the fuzzy inference, we can obtain the dynamic crossover and mutation rates which are used in the evolution. The flowchart of adaptive genetic algorithm is shown in Figure 2.

IV. SIMULATION

In this paper the system simulation uses the following evolutionary-based fuzzy control system shown as Fig. 3. The input variables of the fuzzy controller are error e and error's derivative $\dot{e}$, and the output variable is control u. The transfer function of the controlled plant is a second-order system and described as following [10]:

$$G(s) = \frac{1}{s(s+1)} \qquad (8)$$

Using the genetic algorithms presented in this paper to optimize the number and shape of fuzzy sets in fields of e, $\dot{e}$ and u, the number of fuzzy rules is decided. The fitness function F is defined as follow:

$$F = w_1 * F_1 + w_2 * F_2 \qquad (9)$$

where $F_1 = \sum_{i=0}^{200} (e_i)^2$, $F_2 = \sum_{i=200}^{1000} (e_i)^2$ and

w_1, w_2 are the weighting number which values are 3 and 2, respectively. The sampling time in this simulation is 0.01.

Table 1 Fuzzy rule table for CR and MR

(MR,CR)		BF			VF		
		L	M	H	L	M	H
UN	H	(L,H)	(H,H)	(H,H)	(H,L)	(H,L)	(L,L)
	M	(L,H)	(M,M)	(M,M)	(H,M)	(H,M)	(L,M)
	L	(L,H)	(L,H)	(L,H)	(H,H)	(M,H)	(L,H)

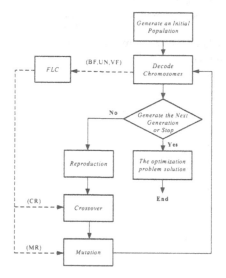

Figure 2 Flow chart of the adaptive genetic algorithm.

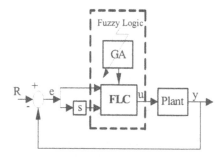

Figure 3 Structure of the evolutionary-based fuzzy system

131

We compare three kinds of different methods. One is the traditional PID control, another one is fuzzy system with GA which crossover rate and mutation rate are fixed [10], and the third is fuzzy system with GA which crossover rate and mutation rate are dynamic adjusted by using fuzzy logic. The time response of these methods for a second-order system is depicted in Figure 4, and the comparison of their performance is listed in Table 2. The computer simulations demonstrate that the proposed scheme achieves much better performance compared with the traditional PID control and Fuzzy with GA control.

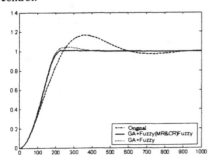

Figure 4 Time response to a second-order system

Table 2 Performance compared of three methods

Control Method	PID control	Fuzzy with GA [10]	Fuzzy with adaptive GA
Settling Time (improvement %)	9.67' (0%)	3.8' (60.70%)	2.19' (77.35%)
Maximum Overshoot (improvement %)	1.1650 (0%)	1.0432 (10.45%)	1.0103 (13.28%)

V. CONCLUSION

In the study of evolutionary-based fuzzy system have been discussed in which the membership function shapes and types and the fuzzy rule set, including the number of rules inside the rule set, are evolved using a GA. In addition, the crossover rate and mutation rate of GA are dynamic adjusted by fuzzy system. The GA can help the fuzzy logic system to reach the optimization by using GA's powerful searching ability, moreover, utilize the advantage of fuzzy logic can assist GA to increase the efficiency of evolution. The computer simulations demonstrate that the effectiveness for our proposed scheme.

REFERENCES

1. Jang, J. R., Self-Learning Fuzzy Controllers Based on Temporal Back Propagation, IEEE Transactions on Neural Networks, 3-5, 1992, pp.714-123.
2. Kropp, K. and Baitinger, U. G., Optimization of Fuzzy Logic Controller Inference Rules Using a Genetic Algorithms,.EUFIT'93-First Technologies, 1993, pp.1090-1096.
3. Thrif, P., Fuzzy logic synthesis with genetic algorithms, in Proc. 4th Int. Conf. Genetic Algorithms, San Diego, CA, July 1991, pp.509-513.
4. Hwang, W. R. and Thompson, W. E., Design of intelligent fuzzy logic. controllers using genetic algorithms, in Proc. IEEE Int. Conf. Fuzzy Syst., Orlando, FL, June 1994, pp.1383-1388.
5. Karr, C. L. and Gentry, E. J., Fuzzy control of pH using genetic algorithms, IEEE Trans. Fuzzy Syst., 1, 1993, pp.46-53.
6. Homaifar, A. and McCormick, Ed., Simultaneous Design of Membership Functions and Rule Sets for Fuzzy Controllers Using Genetic Algorithms, IEEE Transactions on Fuzzy Systems, 3-2, 1995, pp.129-139.
7. Lee, M. A. and Takagi, H., Dynamic control of genetic algorithms using fuzzy logic techniques, in Proc. Int. Conf. Genetic Algorithms, Urbana-Champaign, IL, July 1993, pp. 76-83.
8. Yuhui Shi, Russell Eberhart, and Yaobin Chen, Implementation of Evolutionary Fuzzy Systems, IEEE Transactions on Fuzzy Systems, 7-2, 1999, pp.109-119.
9. Grefenstette, J. J., Optimization of control parameters for genetic algorithms, IEEE Trans. Syst., Man, Cybern., 16, 1986, pp.122-128.
10. GUO, X., ZHOU, Y. and GONG, D., optimization of fuzzy sets of fuzzy control system based on hierarchical genetic algorithms, Proceedings of IEEE TENCON'02. 2002, pp. 1463-1466.

Evaluation of a New Backtrack Free Path Planning Algorithm for Multi-arm Manipulators

Md. Nazrul Islam, Tomoya Murata, Shinsuke Tamura and Tatsuro Yanase
Faculty of Engineering
University of Fukui
3-9-1, Bunkyo, Fukui 910-8507, Japan
E-mail: h5n_islm@radio.fuis.fukui-u.ac.jp (or) nazrul.02@gmail.com

ABSTRACT

This paper evaluates a newly proposed back track free path planning algorithm for Multi-Arm Manipulators. To reduce computation volume and enable path planning for manipulators with many arms, the proposed algorithm calculates paths that avoid obstacles by searching Euclidean space directly. The performance of the algorithm is evaluated while changing the number of arms and obstacles, and location of obstacles. In the experiment, collision free paths were found within less than few seconds. The computation volume of the algorithm is almost the same as the theoretical one even for complicated cases.

KEY WORDS: Backtrack Free, Path Planning, Manipulator, Off-line, Real-time.

INTRODUCTION

A manipulator is a mechanism in which a sequence of arms are connected by joints i.e. fulcrums, which are located between neighboring arms, and it can changes its attitudes by varying angles of these joints to handle and convey things. The path planning is a process to find paths that bring initial attitudes of manipulators to their goal attitudes while avoiding collision with obstacles. It had been considered that computation time and memory space of calculating collision free paths increase exponentially with the number of arms, i.e. they are the order of R^N [1, 2]. Here, it is assumed that positions in the workspace of manipulators are approximated by finite number of grid points, and N is the number of arms and R is the maximum number of grid points on the moving range of individual arms located at a point. Therefore usual planners adopt heuristics that are not adequate for real time applications, i.e. sometimes they cannot find paths even

they exist, and it is not possible to estimate path calculation times in advance. The new path-planning algorithm [3] reduces computation time and memory space to the order of NMR (increases linearly with the number of arms). Here M is the number of grid points included in the work area of the manipulator.

THE ALGORITHM TO BE EVALUATED

This section describes the path planning algorithm to be evaluated. In the following a manipulator consists of N arms is considered, and the fulcrums of individual arms are called their joints and other end positions are called their movable ends. The joint position of the 1st (base) arm in Euclidian space is fixed, and the movable end of the n-th arm coincides with the joint of the (n+l)-th arm.

Definition of Terms

Location and attitude of an arm: A location of the n-th arm is represented by the grid point occupied by its joint. An attitude of the n-th arm is represented by a pair of grid points (X, Y). Here, X and Y are grid points occupied by the joint and the movable end of the n-th arm, respectively.

Feasible attitude set (FAS): Attitude (X, Y) of the N-th arm (N is the maximum arm number) is called feasible when the N-th arm does not collide with any obstacle. Also attitude (X, Y) of the n-th arm $(n < N)$ is called feasible when the n-th arm does not collide with any obstacle and there exists at least one feasible attitude (Y, Z) of the $(n+1)$-th arm. A feasible attitude set (FAS) of the n-th arm at X is a set of grid points that are occupied by the movable end of feasible attitudes of the n-th arm located at X and denoted as $A(X, n)$.

Successive attitudes: A pair of attitudes of the n-th arm (X_1, Y_1) and (X_2, Y_2) is called successive, when X_1 and Y_1 are equal or adjacent to X_2 and Y_2, respectively

Connecting point pair: Any grid point pair P and Q included in $A(X, n)$ and $A(Y, n)$ is called a connecting point pair of a FAS pair $A(X\ n)$ and $A(Y, n)$, when attitudes of the n-th arm (X, P) and (Y, Q) are successive.

n-connectivity: Adjacent grid points X_1 and X_2 are called N-connective(N is the total number of arms), when they are not occupied by any obstacle. Adjacent grid points X_1 and X_2 are called $(n-1)$-connective, when a FAS pair $A(X_1, n)$ and $A(X_2, n)$ has at least one connecting point pair (Y_1, Y_2) such that Y_1 and Y_2 are n-connective.

n-reachable set: n-reachable set $R(n)$ is a set of grid points that are reachable from H_n, the initial position of the movable end of the n-th arm, by chaining grid points, which are mutually n-connective.

[Theorem] Under the assumptions that individual FAS $A(X, n)$ are connective sets in terms of n-connectivity and collisions of arm themselves are allowable, the necessary and sufficient condition for the existence of collision

free paths of a manipulator from its initial attitude $H = \{H_0, H_1, H_2, ----, H_N\}$ to the goal attitude $D = \{D_0 = H_0, D_1, D_2, ----, D_N\}$ is that $R(n)$ and $A(D_{n-1}, n)$ includes D_n for each n $(= 1, 2, ---, N)$. Also when collision free paths from H to D exist, L_0, the locus of the joint of the 1st arm is the point $\{H_0\}$, and L_n the locus of the movable end of the n-th arm can be determined without backtracks based on L_{n-1}. Here H and D, initial and goal positions of the arms, are represented as sets of initial and goal positions of movable ends of individual arms, i.e. $H = \{H_0, H_1, H_2, ----, H_N\}$ and $D = \{D_0 = H_0, D_1, D_2, ----, D_N\}$.

```
/* off-line part */
calculate R(N), a set of grid points to which
the movable end of the N-th arm can reach
from the initial position as a single point
n=N
while (n > 0) {
find feasible attitude set A(X, n) of the n-th
arm at each point X in the 2-d or 3-d grid
calculate R(n-1), a set of points, which
are reachable by the joint of the n-th arm
from its initial position, based on feasible
attitude sets calculated in the above
n=n-1
}
/* real-time part */
if ( D_n ∈ R(n), and D_n ∈ A(D_{n-1}, n) for all n) {
n=1
while (n=<N) {
find the locus of the movable end of the n-th
arm that connects its initial position to its
goal position
n=n+1
}
else {there is no collision free path}
```

Figure 1. Overall structure of the algorithm

Based on the theorem a back track free path planning algorithm can be constructed easily. Figure 1 shows the overall structure of the algorithm. The algorithm consists of two parts, off-line and real-time parts. The off-line part calculates $R(N)$, and for each n beginning from $n = N$ to 1, it finds feasible attitude sets of the n-th arm at individual points, and based on them, it calculates $R(n-1)$. The real-time part generates loci of individual arms sequentially from the first (base) to the last (N-th) arm when the goal attitude is given to the manipulator. Here existence of paths is ensured when $D_n \in R(n)$ and $D_n \in A(D_{n-1}, n)$ are satisfied for all n at the beginning of the real-time part, and loci of individual arms are calculated, without any backtrack. Here, $D_n \in A(D_{n-1}, n)$ means that the attitude of the n-th arm, of which joint and movable end are located at its goal positions, is feasible.

The algorithm is effective under the assumption that collision of arms themselves are allowable, and FAS of the n-th arm at each position is n-connective, i.e. arms can rotate without collision from one attitude to any other attitude within their FAS at every point. The former assumption can be satisfied easily by the local adjustments of arm positions, because there are enough free spaces around collision free attitudes. To make path planning problems satisfy the later assumption, the algorithm defines copies of points at points where the assumption is not satisfied. Namely, when a FAS has multiples disjoint connected components at a point, multiples copies of that point are generated corresponding to different connective components of the FAS. Therefore the computation time and memory space, which are the order of NMR when no obstacle exists, increases when obstacle allocations are complicated, moreover copies generated for the higher arms reproduce copies for lower arms as follows. In Fig.2 the (n+2)-th arm collides with obstacles when it rotates around P, therefore A(P, n+2) has multiple connected components P_A, P_B, P_C and P_D, corresponding to areas A, B, C and D, and copies P_A, P_B, P_C and P_D of gird point P that occupy the same position as P are created in F(n+2) (F(n) is the work area on which movable end of the n-th arm is located). Moreover, copies P_A, P_B, P_C and P_D are not (n+1)-connective because their corresponding FASs are disjoint, then copies corresponding to P_A, P_B, P_C and P_D are also generated at point Q.

As a conclusion, A(P, n+2) has 4 disjoint (n+2)-connective sets, therefore grid point P has 4 copies in F(n+1). Then, A(Q, n+1) has 5 disjoint (n+1)-connective sets that correspond to area E and 4 copies of P in area D, and this means that Q has 5 copies in F(n). In this way, copies generated in higher arm analyses propagate to lower arm analyses, and increase computation complexity of the algorithm. However it can be expected that the number of copies can be suppressed to relatively small value, and the computation volume can be maintained at almost the order of NMR. Namely, in many cases, this propagation terminates, because usually there is an arm position with a FAS that includes points connecting all copies. In the figure, A(R, n) includes V, from which the movable end of the n-th arm can be moved to every copy of Q, because the (n+1)-th and (n+2)-th arms can possess any kind of attitudes at V. Then A(R, n) is a connective set that includes all copies of Q, and therefore, R does not need to have its copy. Even when all arms have G copies at all grid points and the copy propagation does not terminate, total number of copies can be limited to $G^N M$.

In the following sections, the computation volume of the algorithm is evaluated while considering effects of these copies.

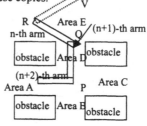

Figure 2. Copy propagation

EVALUATION OF THE ALGORITHM

In this section the performance of the

algorithm is evaluated under various scenarios. The execution time of off-line part, real-time part, total execution time, the total number of copy points and the maximum number of copies at a point are evaluated. Figure 3 shows the obstacle placement used in the evaluation scenarios. It also explains behaviors of arms. A 5-armed manipulator is changing its attitudes from the initial to the goal ones. In order to avoid collision, the first arm firstly rotates to P_1 and then rotates back to P_2 because the 2nd arm can change its direction only at P_1.

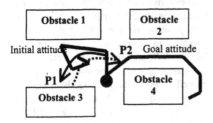

Figure 3. Obstacle allocation

The computation volume and the number of arms

This sub section evaluates the relation between number of arms and the computation volume of the algorithm. The obstacle placement is fixed as shown in Fig.3. Table 1 shows the relation between computation time and number of arms. In the table TET, OLPET and RTPET represent the total execution time, off-line part execution time and real-time part execution time, respectively. A5, A4, A3, A2 and A1 are manipulators with 5 arms, 4 arms, 3 arms, 2 arms and 1 arm, respectively. The numbers in the table are computation time measured in seconds.

According to Table 1, the computation time of off-line part is linearly increasing with the number of arms, when the number of arms are greater than 2. And real-time part execution time is smaller than off-line part execution time, it can

be expected that the computation volume for real-time part can be reduced, so that it can be neglected compared with that of off-line part.

Table 1. Number of arms and the execution time

	A5	A4	A3	A2	A1
TET	3.225	3.024	3.084	2.844	2.103
OLPET	2.220	2.213	2.133	2.043	2.003
RTPET	1.004	.811	.951	.80	.10

Table 2 shows the relation between number of arms and the number of copy points generated. In the table TNCP is the total number of copies, and MNC 1st A, ---, MNC 3rd A are the maximum number of copies generated for single points in F(1), F(2) and F(3), respectively (F(n) is the work area on which movable end of the n-th arm is located).

According to the table, the copy points generated is less than 5% of the total grid points and maximum number of copies is 10. (The total number of grid points is 80 x 80 x number of arms). This means that the actual computation volume does not increase so much compared with the theoretical one.

Table 2. Number of arms and copy points

	A5	A4	A3	A2	A1
TNCP	1086	1082	626	12	0
MNC 1st A	10	10	7	3	0
MNC 2nd A	3	3	2	0	0
MNC 3rd A	1	1	0	0	0
Rest of arms have no copy.					

The computation volume and the obstacle placement

This sub section evaluates the relation between obstacle placement and the computation volume of the algorithm for planning paths of a 5 arms manipulator.

Table 3 shows the relation between computation time and obstacle placement. O5, O4, O3, O2 and O1 correspond to obstacle placements where 5, 4, 3, 2 and 1 obstacle are allocated, respectively. Basic layout is shown in Fig.3.

According to the table, the computation times does not increase much even the number of obstacles is increasing, especially for off-line part.

Table 3. Number of obstacles and the execution time

	O5	O4	O3	O2	O1
TET	3.285	3.225	3.164	3.044	2.904
OLPET	2.223	2.220	2.218	2.214	2.200
RTPET	1.034	1.004	.846	.830	.694

No obstacles exist then TET, OLET and RTET is 2.694, 2.434 and 0.26 sec respectively.

Table 4 shows the relation between obstacle placement and the number of copy points generated. According to the table, although the total number of copies increases as the number of obstacles increase, the maximum copy number does not increase so much. This means that the algorithm is applicable also to cases where many obstacles are located.

Table 4. Number of obstacles and copy point

	O5	O4	O3	O2	O1
TNCP	1318	1086	507	40	2
MNC 1st A	10	10	3	1	1
MNC 2nd A	3	3	1	0	0
MNC 3rd A	1	1	1	0	0

Rest of arm have no any copy and copy is not generated when no obstacle exists.

CONCLUSION

The performance of the new path planning algorithm is discussed. This algorithm is backtrack free and required computation time and memory space are the order of NMR. Here, M and N are the number of grid points that cover the work area of the manipulator, and the number of arms, respectively. R is the upper bound of the number of grid points on surfaces of spheres constituted by the moving ranges of individual arms. According to the numerical result the number of copies is less than 5% of the total number of grid points. This means that the actual computation volume is the same as the theoretical one. Actually collision free paths are found within less than 3.2sec under various scenarios by using a usual PC.

REFERENCES

1. Arjang Hourtash, et. al., Manipulator Path Planning by Decomposition: Algorithm and Analysis, IEEE Transactions on Robotics And Automation, 2001, **17**-6, pp 842-856.
2. Santosha, K. D. and Peter Eberhard, Dynamic analysis of flexible manipulators, a literature review, Mechanism and Machine Theory, 2006, **41**, pp. 749-777.
3. Shinsuke Tamura, Tatsuro Yanase, Md. Nazrul Islam, Takafumi Ito and Hikari Miyashita, A New Path Planning Algorithm for Manipulators, IEEE International Conference on Systems, Man and Cybernetics. Waikoloa, Hawaii, October 2005, pp 2242-2247.

Application of Multi-agent System in Virtual Prototype Engineering for Complex Product

Zhu-yaoqin, Wu-huizhong, Chen-xueqin and Chen-shenglei

Lab 603, Department of Computer Science
Nanjing University of Science & Technology, 210094 Nanjing, China
E-MIAL:zhuyaoqin@163.com

ABSTRACT

Because of the vehemence of market competence, the individuation and diversification of consumer's demands and the complexity of products, the virtual prototyping technology for complex product becomes one of studying and applying hotspots in current simulation technology. The paper proposes a novel organization structure of multi-agent system for virtual prototype engineering, thus to support the life-cycle collaboration roundly and effectively. Then the paper discusses the four types of agents---information agents, service agents, platform agents and application agents in detail. And the paper illustrates the relations among types of agents. At last, it proposes two key techniques of MAS: the internal structure of agent and agent communication language. All these prove that MAS is effectively and extendable when applying to virtual prototype engineering.

KEY WORDS: Multi-agent system, Complex product, Virtual prototype

INTRODUCTION

Virtual prototype (shorted as VP) is a digital model which will resemble the physical product as closely as possible, it can decrease the cost, shorten the cycle, support agile process, easy modification and concurrent engineering[1]. The research on virtual prototype has been hotspots for several years, and the basic techniques on virtual prototype develop rapidly, there are a few applications so far, for example, the Boeing 777 is a success case. However, the research on collaborative virtual prototype for complex product is still immature, there are still several obstacles, one of them is lack of collaborative management to support full life-cycle and different domains. From the lengthways viewpoint, the development of virtual prototype for complex product involves participants from conceptual design, detail design, analysis, testing, manufacturing, evaluating and maintenance etc; from the widthways viewpoint, the development of virtual prototype for complex product includes several subsystem, such as mechanics subsystem, electronics subsystem, dynamics subsystem [2]. It needs all numbers from different domains develop collaboratively. So it becomes a key problem to manage the virtual prototype roundly and full life-cycle. Multi-agent system (shorted as MAS) emphasizes on harmony and cooperation among agents each of which is independent but correlative among them in distributed environment. So these agents that cooperate interactively in complex and dynamic environment can be the same with collaborative management of virtual prototype roundly and for full life-cycle.

RELEVANT CONCEPTION

Multi-agent system is a branch in distributed artificial intelligence (shorted as DAI). It refers to the federation composed of multi agents that can collaborate and serve reciprocally to realize a goal jointly. Each agent is self-governing and independent, its goal and action are not limited by other agents. It harmonizes and resolves the inconsistencies or conflicts among agents by means of competence and negotiation. [3] The agent of MAS is an entity which has the goal, knowledge and ability, the ability of agent includes apperceive, action, reasoning, learning, communicating and cooperating etc. The term agent represents a hardware or (more usually) software based computer system that has the properties of autonomy, social ability, reactivity, and pro-activeness. A stronger notion of agent adopts mentalistic notions, such as knowledge, belief, intention, and obligation. [4]

STRUCTURE OF MULTI-AGENT SYSTEM APPLYING TO VP FOR COMPLEX PRODUCT

It is a pivotal tache of how to organize the agents in multi-agent system. If all the agents in the system are equal and at the same level, the management of them will be more complicated and difficult. On the other hand, the communication among agents will increase rapidly thus to pull heavy burden on network. So we shall manage agents layered that can adapt to collaborative management of virtual prototype. We adopt multi-agent system as virtual prototype infrastructure to support collaborative management in a highly distributed environment. According the architecture of virtual prototype, we classify the agents into four types: information agent, service agent, platform agent and application agent. They cooperate with each other to support the development of virtual prototype and to decrease the time & cost, increase the quality of the product meanwhile. Figure 1 denotes the structure of MAS in detail:

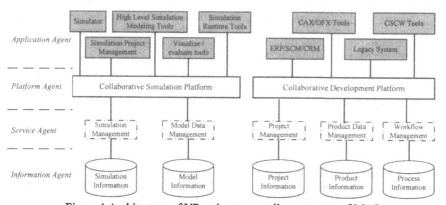

Figure 1 Architecture of VP and corresponding structure of MAS

Information agent

Information agents represent all kinds of information, which includes simulation information, model information, project information, product information, workflow information and resource information etc.

They also answer for the integrality and consistency of the information. Accessing information is controlled by the information agents. Because of the distribution of the integrated product development teams, the information agents are distributed too.

Service agent

Service agents[5] mainly represent different services offered by kinds of management systems, such as simulation run-time management service and simulation schedule service offered by simulation management system, model check-in and check-out service offered by model data management system, critical path calculation service and project duration calculation service offered by project management system, product data check-in and check-out service offered by product data management, and workflow engine service offered by workflow management. In order to manage the service agents effectively, we divide the service agents into five groups: simulation service agent group, model service agent group, project service agent group, product service agent group and workflow service agents group. Each group has detailed service agent, figure 2 illustrates the composition of project service agents group:

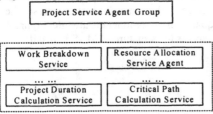

Figure 2 Composition of project service agent group

Here the critical path calculation service agent (shorted as CPSA) in distributed project management is illustrated. Because of the distribution, the technology of mobile agent is used in developing this service. First, the CPSA sends mobile agents to collect tasks' information (include task duration, task definition, tasks' relation etc.). Then CPSA can construct DAG (Directed acyclic Graph) from the tasks' relation information. According DAG, different path's duration will be calculated separately. At last, the longest path is recorded. This is the critical path.

Service agents get information by information agents, but the information agents are distributed, it is critical to communication among agents so that the service agents can cooperated with information agents distributed and interactively. Through the communication, they can access, transform and exchange the distributed information collaboratively. Service agents are small and single functioned. They are stand-alone packages and can be utilized both manually and as other agents. If standards are open, anyone can program a service agent and provide one kind of service to anyone else.

Platform agent

The responsibility of platform agents is to manage other agents, such as registration, generation, scheduling and release of the agents. Platform agents are agency of service agents and application agents. Because of the unavoidable conflicts among service agents, another main function of platform agents is to resolve the conflicts. For example, if there is task scheduling service agent in project management system, while the workflow management system offers workflow instantiation service agent and they are not coherent, the platform agent should unify the task logic and process logic so as to realize the process integration between project management and workflow management.

Application agent

The application agents are responsible for starting, hang-up of the application and transfer the interoperation between users and application, so they are user-faced. They also guarantee the application/tool integration with the virtual prototyping engineering framework. In order to support application/tool integration widely in distributed environment, application agents also assimilate the techniques of middle ware, COM and CORBA.

Relations among different types of agents

MAS system architecture influences information exchanging patterns and relationships between individual agents. One of the advantages of MAS comes from the cooperation among agents, which enables better solutions to problems that cannot easily be solved by centralized method. Conflicts are inevitable in cooperation process because of different opinions from individual agents. Negotiation is believed a promising method to resolve conflicts in MAS environment. They can make big success through cooperation. Here we analyze the relations among different types of agents, so that different types of agents can work together effectively. Figure 3 shows the relations among different types of agents.

Figure 3 Relations among different types of agents

First of all, the application agents propose service request to platform agents, then the platform agents will call services provided by service agents that interoperate with information agents to access, achieve, gather or transfer distributive information. After that, the platform agents return the service results that are offered by service agents to application agents. Figure 4 illustrates the flow of the cooperation among kinds of agents when they breakdown the project in the earlier phase of developing virtual prototype.

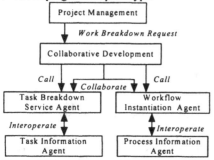

Figure 4 Flow of cooperation among agents for project breakdown

KEY OF IMPLEMENTATION

Internal structure of agent

Although each agent has different functions and the functions should be defined when an agent is developed, they have common characteristics in some sense. We abstract these common characteristics to construct the internal structure of agent (illustrated in figure 5). The basis of agents' action is apperception. Using owned knowledge and apperception, the agent can reason and solve compound problems, and pull affection to the objects by effector. The communication part is the interface to exchange information between agent and outer environment.

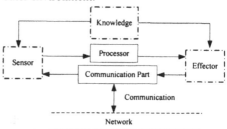

Figure 5 Internal Structure of Agent

The structure is not so special, but we must construct different knowledge module for this system. For example, there must be knowledge to be shared for task information agents. When task is assigned resources, we can get the knowledge about which resource is good at this kind of task.

Communication among agents

Cooperation embodies the sociality of agent, while communication is the base of cooperation. The isomeries are impersonal among agents, but because of the intelligence of agents, they needn't master the internal infrastructure of each agent to cooperate. They can cover up the details of internal realization when communicating. So the agent communication language (shorted as ACL) should independent to the domain knowledge and it should be in high level. They also can effect their action by the language.

During the communication process, ontology is very important[6], because different field agents must understand each other. For example, agents of project management and workflow management have different understandings on term "resource", so there must be interpreter between them, that's why ontology arises. And KIF (Knowledge Interchange Format) can act as ontology between project management and workflow management.

CONCLUSION AND FUTURE WORK

In this paper, we apply the techniques of multi-agent system to support the development of virtual prototype. From the viewpoint of system organization, we propose a novel structure for the MAS. And agents correspond not only to physical objects, but also to logistic objects. Four types of agents are defined and they jointly or separately can represent any object. Therefore, this structure is suitable to all applications. The MAS can support the members from different domains and phases to develop the virtual prototype interactively and collaboratively, thus to decrease the time and cost of developing virtual prototype and increase the quality of virtual prototype.

Here are three interfaces about the prototype of this MAS system applied virtual prototyping for complex product.

Figure 6 Interfaces about the system

One of the future work focuses is the schedule method for service agents. Because all the service agents in the system are distributed and can be created or destroyed dynamically. Other cases, such as the collaboration of service agents from different domains or subsystems should be analyzed. And the conflict mediation is interesting topics.

REFERENCES

1. Zhu Yaoqin, Wu Huizhong etc., Information Management of Virtual Prototype in General Design Phase, Journal of System Simulation (in Chinese), 2003,15-10, pp. 1497-1499

2. Xiong Guangleng, Li Bohu and Chai Xudong, Virtual Prototyping Technology, Journal of System Simulation (in Chinese), 2001,13-1. pp.114-117

3. Zhao Longwen, Hou Yibin, Architecture of Multi-agents system and Cooperation, Computer Engineering and Application (in Chinese), 2000,10, pp.59-61

4. M. Wooldridge, N. Jennings, Intelligent agents: Theory and practice, Knowledge Engineering Review, 1995.10-2, pp:115-152.

5. Ivan Madjarov, Omar Boucelma and Abdelkader Betari, An Agent and Service-Oriented e-Learning Platform, Advances in Web-Based Learning, Third International Conference, Beijing, China, August, 2004, pp. 27-31

Optimization of a Process Control System using OO Approach with Matlab-Modelica Environment

Borut Zupančič

Laboratory for Modelling, Simulation and Control
University of Ljubljana, Faculty of Electrical Engineering
Tržaška 25, 1000 Ljubljana, Slovenia
(E-mail: borut.zupancic@fe.uni-lj.si)

ABSTRACT

The paper deals with an optimization of a process control system – three tank hydraulic system. As most advanced control strategies are usually model based the appropriate environment which enables efficient modelling, simulation and optimization, is very important. In spite of the fact that Matlab is a very common tool in process and control engineering, its simulation environment Simulink is due to the lack of object orientation not very effective. A very efficient environment is the combination of Matlab Simulink and a Modelica based OO environment Dymola. Modelica is used for OO physical modelling. In our case a library of hydraulic components was developed in Modelica. Simulink is on the other hand a very efficient tool for control systems modelling. In such cases all Matlab possibilities for control system design and optimization can be used. The efficiency of the environment is demonstrated on a control of the hydraulic laboratory set up. Two different control strategies are demonstrated: a single loop PID controller and a cascade controller, which assure appropriate level in a tank by controlling a flow by a pump. The parameters of the control system were determined by optimization using Matlab optimization toolbox.

KEY WORDS: OO modelling, Modelica, control system, optimization

INTRODUCTION

Standardization of languages for modelling and simulation was always very important in the history. However the last standard that was really accepted was CSSL standard in 1967 [6]. From then all attempts were more or less unsuccessful. Nowadays perhaps the most promising activities are in conjunction with the so called Modelica activities [3, 5] (www.modelica.org).

A lack of object-oriented properties, which disables the reuse of already build models, is another disadvantage of many modelling and simulation tools. Modelica [3,5] (with appropriate working environment e.g. Dymola [1,2]) represents an advanced OO modelling tool. Using such modelling environments the modelling effort is reduced considerably since model components can be reused and tedious and error-prone manual manipulations which are needed when using conventional tools (e.g. Matlab-Simulink), are not needed.

IMPORTANT FEATURES OF OO M&S ENVIRONMENTS

Some most important features of modern OO M&S environments (e.g. Dymola with Modelica) are:

- Modelling of various kinds of physical systems with object oriented approach.

143

- General-purpose tool, equivalently usable for modelling of mechanical, electrical, chemical, thermo dynamical and other systems.
- Possibilities to reuse already built models (model libraries).
- Acausal model building.
- Description of processes through physical laws (differential equations) irrespective to the type and purpose of a model.
- Easy and efficient way for submodels connections through connectors (more general then input-output connections known in conventional block oriented simulation tools).
- Symbolical and numerical solving of systems of equations - algebraic formula manipulation.
- Algebraic loops solving.

The appropriate complexity of the implementation of connections between model building blocks is probably the most important property of OO M&S tools. Connections between submodels are based on variables, which define proper relations and influences between movements, angles, currents, pressures, etc. It is similar as when real systems are built. Fig. 1 shows how three hydraulic subsystems are connected. Three physical variables are presented in connections (connectors in Modelica): q_i (hydraulic flow), p_i (hydraulic pressure), T_i (temperature).

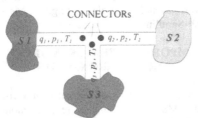

Figure 1. Connection of hydraulic subsystems

There are two types of variables, which

are defined in CONNECTORs: variables that become equal in connection points, in our example temperature and pressure (ACROSS variables e.g. potential, temperature, pressure,...) and variables which sum equals zero (THROUGH variables, e.g. current, momentum, force, prefix FLOW in Modelica).

The efficiency of the described advanced modelling environment will be shown on a modelling of a control system for three tank hydraulic process.

THREE TANK HYDRAULIC SYSTEM AS AN EXAMPLE

Process systems are dynamical systems dealing with physical quantities like level, flow, temperature, pressure, ph. Appropriate control strategies in such systems are very important. As all modern and sophisticated control methods are model based, the appropriate M&S environment is very important. In the past we used more or less Matlab-Simulink environment. It is extremely efficient for the design of control schemes. However due to the lack of object orientation the modelling of the process to be controlled is inefficient.

The process which was used for demonstration is a three tank laboratory set-up which is shown in Fig. 2.

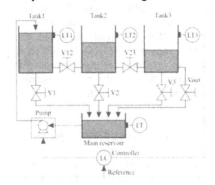

Figure 2. Process scheme of the three tank laboratory set up

For modelling the Dymola-Modelica environment, which has all previously described features, was used. The combination of Dymola-Modelica and Matlab-Simulink was also examined. Modelica was used to model the physical part - hydraulic process. The whole process was then used in Simulink as a Dymola block. So the complete Matlab environment can be used for control system design (e.g. the usage of Control toolbox, Optimization toolbox, ...).

Dymola 5.3 includes several Modelica libraries: electrical systems, mechanical systems, control systems, multibody systems,... However for hydraulic systems a new library which supplements the basic configuration was developed [7]. The building blocks of the hydraulic systems library were divided into four groups:

Table 1. Components in the Hydraulic systems library

1st group	Components, which define output pressure in their equations	• Reservoir • Pump • Controlled pump • Reference pressure
2nd group	Components, that based on a pressure difference define a flow	• Valve • Controlled valve • Flow element
3rd group	Sources	• Constant volume flow • Controlled volume flow
4th group	Interfaces between hydraulic and control signals	• Linear signals transducer • Flow measurement

Elements of the first and the second group must be alternatively used when building a model. So an element of the second group which is used behind an element of the first group, determines the flow. The reservoir and the pump can be directly connected, but then a flow element should be used in order to define the flow.

The library was developed using icon, diagram and text layers in Dymola-Modelica. So low level components are described with textual Modelica programs and appropriate icons were defined. These components can later be used when designing more complex models with graphical approach.

The process was then modelled with our Modelica library. The appropriate Modelica model is shown in Fig. 3.

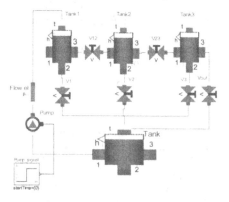

Figure 3. Scheme of the hydraulic system in Modelica

The modelling data were the following: Tank 1, Tank 2 and Tank 3 are the same with the cross section area $0.0154m^2$, maximal level is 0.63m and initial levels are 0. The main reservoir Tank has the cross section area $1m^2$, initial level is 0.2m. The valves V12, V23 and Vout are fully opened with the valve constants $0.0001m^2$. The valves V1 and V3 are shut, the valve V2 has the valve constant $0.0001m^2$ with the opening 0.1 (10%). The flow element has the cross section area 0.00002 m². The controlled pump has the maximal pump level 10m (control signal 0-10) and it has to pump to the level 1.37m.

OPTIMIZATION OF THE HYDRAULIC CONTROL SYSTEM

To confirm the efficiency of the combination of the Matlab-Simulink and Dymola-Modelica we modelled the following control system: with controlled pump the level in the Tank 3 must be controlled to the level 0.1m. At time t=0 the reference step change 0.1 appeared and at time t=200s there was a disturbance: the valve V1 was opened for 20%.

A PI controller and a cascade controller with Matlab Optimization Toolbox (function fminsearc for multidimensional unconstrained nonlinear minimization (Nelder-Mead)) were developed. The objective function was

$$Of = \int_0^{400} t \left| e(t) \right| dt$$

where $e(t)$ is the difference between the desired and actual level in Tank 3.

Fig. 4 shows the model, which was prepared in Dymola-Modelica for the use in Matlab-Simulink as a Dymola block. The connectors (input and outputs) between Dymola-Modelica and Matlab-Simulink were defined.

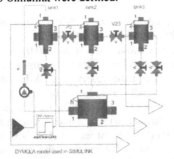

Figure 4. Dymola-Modelica model prepared for Matlab-Simulink

Fig. 5 depicts the Simulink model for the cascade control system which includes also the Dymola block as the physical part.

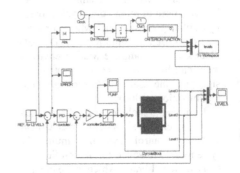

Figure 5. Simulink model which includes Dymola block

The first closed loop study was however made with a single loop PI controller, which was optimized for the reference step change in the interval 0-200s. The optimization calculated the following parameters for the proportional and integral gains: K_p= 105.6 and K_i=1.06. Fig. 6 presents all three levels as results to the reference change and the disturbance.

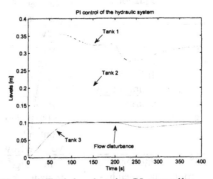

Figure 6. Tank levels using PI controller

We can notice a very good performance for the reference signal (time interval 0-200s) but the disturbance elimination is very slow (time interval 200-400s).

Such results were expected as the controller was optimized for the reference step change.

In the next study we optimized the cascade controller with the main (PI) and auxiliary (P) controllers. The optimization was performed on the interval 0-400s with the presence of reference and disturbance signals. The following parameters were calculated: for the main PI controller- K_{p1}=85.6, K_{i1}=0.92, for the auxiliary P controller- K_{p2}=1.24. The simulation results are presented in Fig. 7.

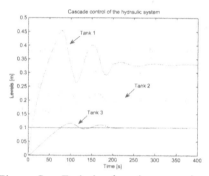

Figure 7. Tank levels using cascade controller

As expected the cascade control is very efficient in the disturbances elimination. The reference response shows a small overshoot but the flow disturbance influence to the level in Tank 3 is so small that it can hardly be observed from Fig. 7.

CONCLUSIONS

Traditional simulation tools (e.g. Matlab-Simulink, ACSL,...) are not object oriented so it is very difficult or even impossible to built fully reusable models or components. Modelica language on the other hand enables true object oriented support and as equations are algebraically pre-processed during model translation, this means also a strong modelling support as there is no need to define a model in the state space form.

A Modelica library for modelling and simulation of hydraulic systems was developed. This is a library with eleven components, very suitable for control system design but also for modelling and simulation in education. Namely it is possible to develop quite complex models without profound understanding and knowledge from the area of modelling and simulation.

Our experiments also confirm the efficiency of the possibility that Dymola-Modelica models can be included in Matlab-Simulink environment. All advantages of both environments can be used: Dymola-Modelica for efficient object oriented modelling and Matlab-Simulink for complex experimentations. In our example optimization was used to calculate the parameters of the controllers.

REFERENCES

1. Cellier, F.E., Continuous System Modelling, Springer - Verlag, NY, USA, 1991.
2. Dymola, Dynamic Modelling Liboratory, Users Manual, ver. 5.3, Dynasim Ab, Lund, Sweden, 2005.
3. Fritzson, P., Principles of Object Oriented Modelling and Simulation with Modelica 2.1. IEEE Press, John Wiley&Sons, Inc., Publication, NY, USA, 2004.
4. Matko, D., Karba, R. and Zupančič, B. (1992), Simulation and Modelling of Continuous Systems: A Case Study Approach, Prentice Hall Int., NY, USA, 1992.
5. Modelica Association,. Modelica- A Unified Object-Oriented Language for Physical Systems Modelling: Language Specification Version 2.1, 2003.
6. Strauss, J.C. 1967. 'The SCi continuous system simulation language". Simulation, no.9, 281-303.
7. Zupančič, B.,Zauner, G., Breitenecker, F., Modelling and Simulation in Process Technology with Modelica, Proceedings of the 2005 Summer Computer Simulation Conference, Cherry Hill, New Jersey, USA, pp. 207-212, 2005.

Simulation and Estimation for Internet-based Equipment Sharing System with the Novel Entropy-driven Arithmetic

Yabo LUO*, Li ZHENG**

* School of Mechanical and Electrical Engineering, Wuhan University of Technology, Wuhan, 430070 P.R..China
(E-mail: luoyabo@tsinghua.org.cn)
** Department of Biology and Light Industry, Changsha University of Science and Technology, Changsha, 410076 P.R.China

ABSTRACT

Manufacturing network platform is a crucial approach to share manufacturing resource overcoming the difficulties of poor transparency and low efficiency. Firstly, based on the previous research works involving theory and development of virtual manufacturing system/ enterprise, a formal definition and architecture for a networked manufacturing system are proposed. Secondly, based on the systems analysis of the Internet-based sharing workflow, the novel entropy-driven tactics for estimation of sharing cost is presented. Finally, with the entropy-driven tactics, the simulation and estimation methodologies for Internet-based equipment sharing system are developed.

KEY WORDS: Networked manufacturing, Simulation, Resource sharing

INTRODUCTION

Virtual manufacturing has been a populate research area in recent years [1]. However, currently virtual manufacturing technology is affordable only to selective gigantic international enterprises. It is indeed difficult for middle or small-sized enterprises to apply the virtual manufacturing technology to develop products with its limited internal resources. In today's competitive business environment, companies cannot afford to be second-rate in any aspect of their business offerings. Companies have come to realize that focusing on their core competencies and outsourcing the rest is probably the best way forward when budgets are tight and economic difficulties require flexibility of the business model [2]. On the background, networked manufacturing is a burgeoning advanced manufacturing technology [3] combining the advantages of both the virtual manufacturing and the virtual enterprise.

Networked manufacturing benefits middle and small-size enterprises particularly in developing countries. The competitive advantage of some still-developing countries over other countries, particularly the developed ones, is its low-cost-based production made possible by employing labor at low cost. However, considering a global competitive environment today, the advantage of low cost labor is losing. Networked manufacturing is a feasible method to integrate the advantages of the middle and small-size enterprise groups to improve the competency of an enterprises alliance.

148

THE ARCHITECTURE OF NETWORKED MANUFACTURING

Though many primary networked manufacturing platforms are available [4], there is a lack of a rigorous formal definition and characterization of networked manufacturing. Furthermore the vagueness or even the disagreement about what constitutes a networked manufacturing platform, make the gap between theories and practices quite evident. In this paper, based on the previous research works on the theories and developments of virtual manufacturing, virtual enterprise, and networked manufacturing [5], the definition and constitutions of a networked manufacturing are addressed as follows.

As an advanced manufacturing technology, networked manufacturing integrates the advantageous resources of enterprises group, including the design resources, manufacturing resources, intelligence resources, and the market resources, to improve the overall integrated competency of the enterprises group, using cooperative product design, virtual manufacturing, and the cooperative product commerce technologies.

Networked manufacturing integrates the internal and external resources of an enterprise, with resource sharing as its core task. In the past years, research works on resource sharing concentrates on database-based information sharing technologies. In the viewpoint of varying inputs, the resource sharing technologies of networked manufacturing are classified as the software sharing, equipment sharing, and the information sharing. The architecture of networked manufacturing is divided into 2 layers as showed in Figure 1.

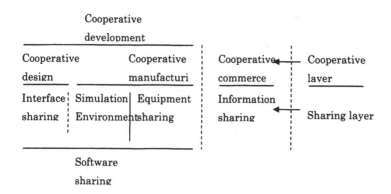

Figure 1 The architecture of networked manufacturing

The software sharing, which is the foundation of cooperative design and equipment sharing, includes the software interface sharing employed to implement the cooperative design, and the equipment simulation environment sharing employed to simulate the shared equipment. Cooperative design aims at intelligence sharing. Product diversification and individual requirements lead to complex product design with multi-functional considerations requiring strong integrated design competencies in diverse domains. For example, the automobile bodywork design involves functional design, manufacturing process design, safety endurance design, vision design, human engineering design, etc. However, apparently companies need not be high-class in all domains, while being competitive in their core capabilities. Cooperative design provides a possibility to call professionals from different companies, departments or from diverse professional domains together to integrate their intelligence resources including the design knowledge and experience into integrated product design.

Information sharing is the foundation of cooperative product commerce. Shared information includes the equipment resources information, intelligence resources information and particularly the market information. Cooperative design and cooperative manufacturing make up the cooperative product development, while cooperative product commerce improves the agility of the product to the market.

This research work focuses on equipment sharing, an integral part of cooperative manufacturing. Often, some large-size enterprises that possess costly equipments fail in acquiring order forms due to the slow reaction to the market, while some middle or small-size enterprises which acquire production orders due to the agile reaction to the market, have limited production capabilities. In such situations the middle and small-size enterprises have to forego some orders because it is unwise to invest on costly equipments for small-lot tasks with the consideration of maximizing profit, while the large-size enterprises leave their costly equipment unused. Equipment sharing is thus a good solution to overcome such conflicting requirements for agile manufacturing and improving the production capability.

Key technologies for sharing different

equipment are discrepant due to the distinct ways of running. CNC machine tool is typically an equipment to be shared [6]. CNC machine offers flexibility into programming and more particularly editing, therefore is a good solution for automation while ensuring manufacturing accuracy required by the modern information-enabled manufacturing practices that requires higher flexibility and agility. It is normal for a company to embark on a cost-benefit study prior to the purchase of any capital equipment such as a CNC machine tool. Generally a middle or small-size enterprise would not invest in a costly CNC machine tool involving familiarization cost for a short-dated task. Sharing through the way of hiring is a feasible solution for middle or small-size enterprises to avoid the acquisition cost of assets, maintenance cost, and the familiarization cost, while for large-size enterprises it lowers the machine idle costs. Based on the results from previous research works in virtual CNC machine domain [5], this research considers the CNC machine tool as a case study for common technologies of equipment sharing.

ENTROPY-DRIVEN SIMULATION AND ESTIMATION

The virtual equipment is diverse according to the different real equipment. CNC machine tool sharing involves the common technologies of equipment sharing such as the net topology structure and the distinct technologies such as the virtual machining. Therefore, study of the CNC machine tool sharing is significant for common equipment sharing technologies. A virtual CNC machine tool, which is a typical application in the virtual manufacturing technology, has been developed in the previous research [5]. The virtual CNC machine tool can simulate and optimize NC programs in a vision-rich virtual environment, check for collisions and interferences in real time using the web-based real-time rendering technology. It can also be used to train operators on new machines to help increase productivity. Apparently when launching new machining task, a virtual CNC machine tool ensures machining costs remain low.

The analysis of the workflow for CNC machine tool sharing is necessary to construct entropy-driven simulation and estimation. The workflow is as shown in figure 2. Firstly, a hirer searches for adequate CNC machine tool providers on the networked manufacturing platform over the Internet, and then decides on an advisable provider according to the published performance and cost criteria. Secondly, the virtual CNC machine tool is run to verify and optimize the NC codes for minimizing the cost. Thirdly, an agent is defined to represent the task for Internet-based bidding. Finally the defined agent together with the optimized task is submitted to the queue for machining.

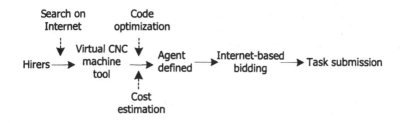

Figure 2 the internet-based sharing workflow

The cost components of Internet-based bidding are different from general cost estimation. Costs in Internet-based bidding can be classified as the calculable costs and the negotiation cost. The calculable costs in the Internet-based bidding are relative with the time and urgent of the tasks. The paper proposes an entropy-driven tactics for sharing cost estimation employing agent technology.

The Internet-based bidding system is a complex distributed components system. Agents and multi-agent systems (MASs), which can seamlessly integrate these independent components into a single system, can mutually cooperate to complete a decision-making task through intelligent information flows via Internet.

The elementary tactics for scheduling and resources assignments are first-come first-do and charge balance, meanwhile negotiations between agents are approved to minimize the total non-effective ahead time of enterprises alliance. If a task is estimated to be completed before the anticipated time according to the current position in the queue, it is a good practice to rearrange the task to make the time of completing the task as close as possible to the anticipated point of time, so that the resource can be fully utilized due to minimization of the total non-effective ahead time.

The elements direct correlative to the actions of an agent are the input information, output information, and the decision-making mechanism. The input information is the reflection of some requirements from other agents with the feedbacks of environment state. The decision-making mechanism takes the input information as variables to make appropriate decisions to output information based on specific feedback requirements. In the Internet-based bidding system, agents are defined to realize automation and intelligence via online negotiation. The decision-making mechanism is the core part of the agent definition. In order to measure the status of an agent in the dynamic information environment, such that provide evidences for decision-making, the concept of the entropy of agent is proposed. In the dynamic information environment, the typical information flows are abstracted as variables to decide on the entropy of an agent, by which an agent's status can be measured to make decision automatically. Since the negotiation cost is correlated to the arrangement of resources and scheduled tasks, it is advisable to take the value of negotiation cost considered in the entropy of agent.

$$\text{Entropy= time cost- negotiation cost} \tag{1}$$

The time cost is defined as the increased cost due to the delay. Negotiation cost is defined as the cost for changing the schedule. When the entropy is a positive number, the schedule changing will be accepted. Taking CNC sharing as case study, every task is associated with an agent. Through the above negotiation mechanism, the valid machining time can be fully utilized most efficiency. The benefit balance and cost distributed among the enterprises maximize the benefit of the enterprises group.

CONCLUSIONS

Equipment sharing is a crucial component in the networked manufacturing platform. Taking the CNC machine tool as the study case, this paper details the common technologies of equipment sharing, such as the net topology structure and the entropy-driven tactics for simulation and estimation, which realizes the automation and intelligence of equipment sharing and consequently is an effective method to increase equipment utilization, lower the cost, and improve the competitiveness of the integrated enterprises alliance.

ACKNOWLEDGEMENTS

This paper is supported by the Hubei province Natural Science Fund for young elitist (No.2005ABB023), Wuhan city dawn plan (No.20055003059), and the Wuhan city ZhaoYang plan from Wuhan association for science and technology.

REFERENCES

1. Luo, Y. B., Chen, D. F., Xiao, T. Y., A Distributed Image-based Virtual Prototyping System with Novel Rendering Tactics, International Journal of Advanced Manufacturing Technology, 2005, 26, pp.236-242.
2. Stanescu, A. M., Dumitrache, I., Curaj, A., Caramihai, S. I. and Chircor, M., Supervisory Control and Data Acquisition for Virtual Enterprise, International Journal of Production Research, 2002, 40(15), pp.3545-3559.
3. Cloutier, L., Frayret, J.M., Sophie, D.A., Espinasse, B., and Montreuil, B., A Commitment-oriented Framework for Networked Manufacturing Co-ordination, International Journal of Computer Integrated Manufacturing, 2001, 14(6), pp.522-534.
4. Wang, C.G., Zhang, Y., Song, G.N., Yin, C.W., Chu, C.B., An Integration Architecture for Process Manufacturing Systems, International Journal of Computer Integrated Manufacturing, 2002, 15(5), pp.413-426.
5. Luo,Y.B., Ong,S.K., Chen,D.F., and Nee,A.Y.C., An Internet-enabled Image- and Model-based Virtual Machining System, International Journal of Production Research, 2002, 40(10), pp.2269-2288.
6. Jywe, W., The Development and Application of A Planar Encoder Measuring System for Performance Tests of CNC Machine Tools, International Journal of Advanced Manufacturing Technology, 2003, 21(1), pp.20-28.

Applying Modeling and Simulation Technology to Context-aware Web Services

Heejung Chang* and Kangsun Lee*

* Department of Computer Engineering,
MyongJi University
38-2 San, Namdong, YongIn, Kyunggi-Do, Korea 449-728
(E-mail: ksl@mju.ac.kr)

ABSTRACT

Context-Aware Services are emerging as a promising technology for the pervasive computing environments. Unfortunately, development of successful CASs (Context-Aware Services) still remains as a hard task. In this paper, we propose SIMP4P (Simulation-based Personalization Web Services Composer for Pervasive Computing), a simulation-based development framework for context-aware services. SIMP4P framework (semi-) automates the development process of CAS, including context management, CAS composition, and validation. In this framework, all or parts of the comprising web services are simulated to efficiently test out the resulting CAS before actual deployment.

KEY WORDS: Context-Aware Services, Pervasive Computing, Modeling and Simulation

1. INTRODUCTION

CASs (Context-Aware Services) are the kind of web services that provide users with a customized and personalized behavior [1,2]. The CASs are getting attention to many software developers as internet applications and services are available to many ubiquitous computing devices (e.g. PDAs, 3G mobile phones). Despite the increasing popularity of CASs, development of successful CASs still remains as a hard task partly due to the following reasons:

■ There is no standard way to formally model CASs and (semi)automatically generate their executable implementation from the formal description. Therefore CAS development requires high cost and time.

■ There are many kinds of contexts to consider for personalization- location, previous activities, users preferences, execution constraints in terms of execution time and execution location, and current status of resources. However, management tasks on context collection, dissemination, and usage are manually done by engineers. [3]

■ Pervasive computing environment can be characterized as nondeterministic and complex inter-networking environment where contexts change dynamically with time (e.g. temperature, humidity etc.). Unexpected events always occur (e.g. sudden unavailability), as we manage context information. It is almost impossible to efficiently test out CASs with realistic context data before their actual deployment, even if failures of the CASs are critical to users.

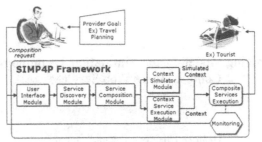

Figure 1 SIMP4P Methodology

In this paper, we propose SIMP4P (Simulation-based Personalization web Services Composer for Pervasive Computing), a simulation-based development framework for context-aware services. SIMP4P framework (semi-)automates the development process of CAS, including context management, CAS composition, and validation. In this framework, all or parts of the comprising web services are simulated to efficiently test out the validity of the resulting CAS before actual deployment.

This paper is organized as follows: Section 2 proposes SIMP4P with some explanations on how we can benefit from simulation technologies to efficiently develop CAS. Section 3 illustrates our framework with an example. Section 4 concludes this paper with future works to achieve.

2. SIMP4P FRAMEWORK

In the CAS environment, a context contains any information that can be used by a Web service to adjust its execution and output [1]. Examples of contexts are information about physical characteristics (such as location and temperature), users preferences (such as privacy and presence), and systems (such as available services). Context information can be provided by the sources:

- *Context Provision Services*: Contexts are provided by context providers. For example, we can acquire weather information by weather forecast web services (e.g.

http://www.webservicex.net/WeatherForecast.asmx).

- *Context Simulation Models*: We can substitute *Context Simulation Models* for *Context Provision Services* to reduce development cost. For example, we can acquire weather information by weather simulation models instead of the weather forecast web services.

The CAS environment is nondeterministic and complex inter-networking environment. Therefore, it is almost impossible to efficiently test out CASs with realistic context data before their actual deployment. To solve this problem, we propose a simulation-based development framework for context-aware services. As shown in figure 1, SIMP4P is performed with the following steps:

Step 1: A user defines how CASs are formed into a new web process. User Interface Module provides the graphical interface to describe a workflow of CASs with BPMN (Business Process Modeling Notation) representation [4]. While specifying a web process, a user determines necessary contexts of each CAS and context sources. *Context Provision Service* and *Context Simulation Model* can be context sources. After the web process is defined, a user sets context generation parameters (e.g. type and range of contexts) and evaluation parameters (e.g. testing frequency).

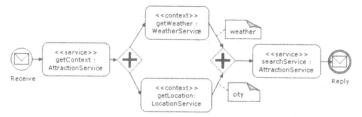

Figure 2 *Travel Planner* Process

Step 2: Service Discovery Module discovers the web services for satisfying user goal.

Step 3: Service Composition Module composes the selected web services into the web process.

Step 4: SIMP4P collects and disseminates contexts. The contexts are collected from *Context Provision Services* and *Context Simulation Models*. If a user determines to use *Context Simulation Models* for efficiently testing out CASs, Context Simulator Module generates suitable simulation models and performs simulations. Then it provides context information to the CASs.

Step 5: Composite Services Execution dynamically invokes and executes the web services. Then, SimP4P reports test results.

3. Example

In this section, we illustrate SIMP4P with an example of *Travel Planner*. Suppose *Travel Planner* gives users suggestions on where to visit in their current location, depending on weather condition (e.g. temperature). Figure 2 shows BPMN representation of *Travel Planner*. *Travel Planner* consists of AttractionService for making suggestions on where to visit and WeatherService and LocationService for getting contexts. WeatherService provides weather information. LocationService provides

detailed user location (e.g. city name). In figure 2, <<service>> represents CASs and <<context>> represents *Context Provision Services*. SIMP4P allows a user to choose a method of getting contexts for evaluating the CASs. As shown in figure 3, we can evaluate the CASs with the following multi-resolution:

- Low-resolution: All of the comprising *Context Provision Services* are simulated (see Figure 3-(d)).
- High-resolution: All of the comprising *Context Provision Services* are actually invoked and executed (see Figure 3-(a)).
- Mid-resolution: Figure 3-(b) and (c) show possible combinations. Some *Context Provision Services* are simulated, and others are actually invoked and executed.

We compare (a) and (b) in figure 3 to show how a user can benefit from SIMP4P to efficiently develop the CASs. For the high-resolution, we use a weather forecast web service of the US national Weather Service (http://www.nws.noaa.gov). For the mid-resolution, we use a weather simulation model instead of the weather forecast web service. The simulation model is based on the historical weather data sets. For *Context Simulation Models*, SIMP4P provides the user interface for setting up contexts. As shown in figure 4, a user can set conditions for weather contexts. For example, figure 4 shows maximum, minimum, and average temperature on July 31, 2006. To produce the accurate estimation data, it requires the validity of the simulation model. Figure 5 shows the monthly average temperature forecast of New York from the weather web service and the weather simulation model. The graph shows our weather simulation model is accurate enough to evaluate the resulting *Travel Planner*. Figure 6 shows how we can save development cost by simulation technologies. The solid line presents the total test time of *Travel Planner* by using the weather simulation model, while the dotted line represents the same measurements from the weather forecast web service. As shown in figure 6, we can save more time as the number of tests increases. This is because simulation technologies can save time for invoking and executing the actual web services and receiving execution results from the web services.

Figure 4 User Interface of the simulation-based context generation

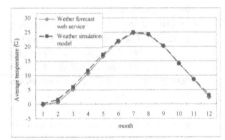

Figure 5 Monthly average temperatures in New York

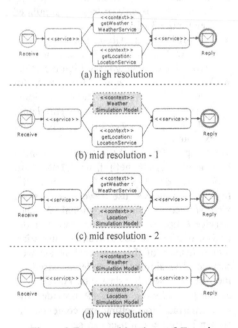

(a) high resolution

(b) mid resolution - 1

(c) mid resolution - 2

(d) low resolution

Figure 3 Four combinations of *Travel Planner*

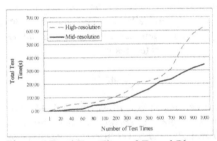

Figure 6 Total Test Time of *Travel Planner*

4. CONCLUSION

In this paper, we introduced SIMP4P, a simulation-based development framework for context-aware services. The key to our framework is to use simulation technology to efficiently development CASs. SIMP4P discovers appropriate CASs and composes the CASs into the web process. Then contexts are collected either from actual web services or simulations. Once simulation models are validated against the actual web services, the web process can be test out without actually invoking the web services; contexts are generated from simulations with satisfiable accuracy. In this way, we can develop various web processes with less cost and time in SIMP4P. We will develop various context simulation models and apply them to our framework.

REFERENCES

1. QuanZ. Sheng and Boualem Benatallah, ContextUML: a UML-based modeling language for model-driven development of context-aware Web services, In Proceedings of the International Conference on Mobile Business, 2005, pp.206-212.

2. T. Buchholz, M. Krause, C. Linnhoff-Popien, and M. Schiffers, CoCo: Dynamic Composition of Context Information, In Proceedings of the First Annual International Conference on Mobile and Ubiquitous Systems: Networking and Services, Boston, USA, August 2004

3. Zakaria Mammar, Ghazi AlKhatib, Soraya Kouadri Mostéfaoui, Context-based Personalization of Web Services Composition and Provisioning, In Proceedings of the 30th EUROMICRO Conference, 2004, pp.396-403.

4. OMG, Business Process Modeling Notation Specification 1.0, http://www.omg.org/docs/dtc/06-02-01.pdf

Workflow Simulation Scheduling Model with Application to a Prototype System of Cigarette Factory Scheduling

Xingquan ZUO*, Yushun FAN**, Huiping LIN**, Yimin SHEN**, Hongjun SUN**

* School of Information Engineering, Beijing University of Posts and Telecommunications, Beijing, 100876, P. R. China
(E-mail: zuoxq@tsinghua.edu.cn)
** Automation Department, Tsinghua University, Beijing, 100084, P. R. China

Abstract

Production scheduling is very significant for improving the enterprise efficiency and reducing the production supply periodicity. The scheduling problems have become more and more complex in recent years, and how to model the complex scheduling problems is a key problem. This paper uses a workflow simulation scheduling model to model the complex scheduling environment of cigarette factory. Then, a heuristic algorithm is designed that is integrated with the model to allocate resources for each active of the multi-process model. Based on the scheduling model and the heuristic algorithm, a prototype system of cigarette factory scheduling is developed. The system can well model the practice scheduling environment and generate feasible scheduling schemes successfully.

KEY WORDS: Production scheduling, Workflow technology, Scheduling model, Cigarette factory, Heuristic algorithm

Introduction

Production scheduling is very significant for improving the enterprise efficiency and reducing the production supply periodicity [1]. The scheduling problems have become more and more complex in recent years, and how to model the complex scheduling environment is a key problem.

Scheduling problems can be modeled by analytic models or simulation models. Analytic models are based on mathematical methods, including programming equations, disconnected charts and Petri net methods; however, analytic models are very difficult to describe a complex practice scheduling problem because of its large complexity. The simulation models of scheduling problems can well describe a practice complex scheduling environments. The models first collect data through the simulation on a practice scheduling system, and then uses those data to analysis (or evaluate) the performances of a scheduling scheme. But the traditional simulation model is not a universal model, and a special simulation model is needed to be developed for each practice scheduling problem. So the cost of developing a simulation model is too high [2].

Workflow technology is a new information technology that is developed rapidly along with the maturation of computer, internet and data base technology [3]. Workflow technology has been successfully applied to the areas of library, hospital, bank and insurance company etc. Workflow model is a kind of process model that can describe complex production processes roundly, and has a clear and distinct modeling structure that can be understood by customers easily, so it has nice capability of modeling complex manufacture processes [4].

In this paper, we use workflow models to model complex scheduling environments, and a workflow simulation scheduling model is introduced. The model is applied to modeling complex scheduling environment of cigarette factory. A heuristic algorithm is designed to integrate with the model to generate scheduling scheme. Based on the workflow simulation scheduling model and the heuristic algorithm, a prototype system of cigarette factory scheduling was developed. The system can well model the practice scheduling environment and generate a feasible scheduling scheme successfully.

Workflow Simulation Scheduling Model

The workflow simulation scheduling model (WSSM) [5], utilizing workflow model to describe scheduling problems, has nice conversional and is capability of describing all kinds of scheduling problems. The model is composed of process model, resource model, transaction model and workflow controlling data.

Process model
The process model consists of multi-processes that are independent one another. Each of these processes describes the manufacturing procedures of a classification of jobs, and the process model defines the manufacturing procedures of all classifications of jobs. The process model can define job shop scheduling, flow shop scheduling, and hybrid scheduling problems easily, so the workflow simulation scheduling model is a universal model.

Each process of the model has several actives, and an active is defined as an operation of a job. The logic relationship of actives in a process, i.e., the restriction of processing order of the job, is defined by the process.

Resource model
Resource model defines resource entities used in a manufacturing process, and is used to describe the resource restriction of a scheduling problem. The resource entities mainly include manufacture devices, transportation devices, and storage devices etc. Two kinds of resources are defined, i.e., resource entities and resource pools. The resource entities refer to real equipments and a resource pool is a classification of resource entities that has some same functions. The resource model is related to the process model by the mapping between the actives in the process model and the resource entities in the resource model.

Transaction model
Jobs are considered as transactions. According to transaction model, the scheduling system generates transactions and enables process instances to execute on the workflow simulation scheduling system.

Workflow controlling data
The workflow controlling data is used to identify and control the states of each process or active instance, and select the next process or active instance that should be executed. Hence, the workflow controlling data controls the execution of process instances and realizes the navigation of actives.

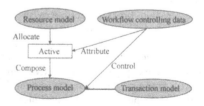

Figure 1 Workflow simulation scheduling model

The four models above compose the workflow simulation scheduling model, which is shown in Figure 1. The model has some merits, such as clear model structure, powerful describing capability, and fitness for modeling large scale scheduling problems.

Modeling the Scheduling Problems of Cigarette Factory by the WSSM

In this part, we use the workflow simulation scheduling model to model the complex scheduling problems of cigarette factory, i.e., describe the process of transporting and processing of cut tobacco on the primary processing line, cut tobacco silos, shaking discs and cigarette making machines. We briefly introduce the process model and resource model of the WSSM used to model the cigarette factory scheduling.

Process model
The process model describes the manufacturing process of cut tobacco. There are several process models, and the number of shaking discs used in a batch plan is considered as the number of processes. Each of these processes consists of two kinds of actives. The first active is "cut tobacco entering cut tobacco silo", and the resource used is primary processing line; the second active is "cigarette making machine processing cut tobacco", and the resources used are cigarette making machines.

Resource model
There are two kinds of resources in the resource model, i.e., primary processing line and cigarette making machines. The resource model adheres to process model through the mapping between actives and resource entities. The resource model is composes of the states and attributes of each resource entity, especially the sharing states for the resources of cigarette making machines.

The WSSM based cigarette factory scheduling model has some characteristics and merits:
(1) Model flexible and easy to expand. One primary processing line can be easily expended to tow primary processing line, and the cut tobacco silos and cigarette making machines can be configured arbitrarily;
(2) Powerful model description capability. The model can describe the cigarette factory scheduling environment expediently and intuitionally, and has powerful model description capability.

The WSSM utilizes a multi-process workflow model to describe the practice scheduling process of cigarette factory. The workflow simulation engine uses this model to drive instances to simulate and run. During the simulation, there are resource conflict phenomena, and resource allocation algorithm is needed to solve these conflicts. Hence, the cigarette factory scheduling problem is converted into a resource allocation problem of workflow simulation on the multi-process model.

A Heuristic Algorithm Integrated with the WSSM

Heuristic algorithms are also called dispatching rules [6], and are used in engineering practices widely. The cigarette factory scheduling problem is modeled by WSSM, and a workflow simulation engine uses this model to simulate. During the simulation, a designed heuristic algorithm is used to allocate the resources for each active in the multi-process of the model. So a feasible scheduling scheme can be generated.

The cigarette factory scheduling problem has there decision points. The designed heuristic algorithm is given as follows to make decision on the three decision points.
(1) The processing order of cut tobacco on the primary processing line:
a) If a cut tobacco silo is empty, then the kind of cut tobacco that should enter into the silo is arrayed on the primary processing line.
b) If there are several empty cut tobacco

silos, and each silo correspond to a kind of cut tobacco. The kind of cut tobacco that has the most uncompleted cut tobacco should be arrayed on the primary processing line.

c) If there are several empty cut tobacco silos, and the uncompleted cut tobacco for each silo is similar, then the kind of cut tobacco whose silos has the quickest output speed is arrayed on the primary processing line.

(2) Which cut tobacco silo should the cut tobacco enter:

a) If there are several empty cut tobacco silos, then the kind of cut tobacco should enter the silo that has the most uncompleted cut tobacco.

b) If there are several empty cut tobacco silos, and the uncompleted cut tobacco for each silo is similar, then the kind of cut tobacco should enter the silo whose output speed is quickest.

(3) From which shaking disc should the cut tobacco processed on the cigarette making machine come.

If a cigarette making machine connects two shaking disc, then the cut tobacco processed on the cigarette making machine is determined by following rules:

a) If a kind of cut tobacco is completed, then the cigarette making machine processes the cut tobacco from the other shaking disc.

b) The cigarette making machine should process the kind of cut tobacco whose uncompleted amount is the most.

Prototype System of Cigarette Factory Scheduling

Based on the WSSM of cigarette factory scheduling and the designed heuristic algorithm, a prototype system was developed, which is shown in figure 2. This prototype system can configure the cigarette factory scheduling environment easily, for example, setting the number of cut tobacco silos; setting the connection

relation between shaking discs and cigarette making machines. The system can generate a feasible and optimal scheduling scheme automatically according to a given batch scheduling plan. By using the obtained scheduling scheme, the system can give a vivid simulation of scheduling process.

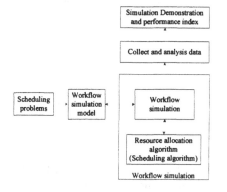

Figure 2 The prototype system of cigarette factory scheduling based on WSSM

The input and output of the prototype system

In cigarette factory, the annual production plan is decomposed into month production plans. Further, each month plan is divided into several batch production plans. A batch plan includes the production plans of several cigarette brands. The prototype system is to decide how to schedule and process a batch plan.

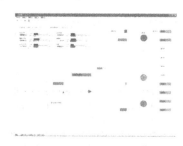

Figure 3 The simulation demonstration of the scheduling scheme obtained

The input of the prototype system is a batch plan (time is about 5-15 days). The output of the system is a table of scheduling scheme including the decision information. By using the table, the Gantt chart for each device, the statistic performance indexes and simulation demonstration for the scheduling scheme can be illustrated.

Figure 4 The scheduling scheme table of the primary processing line

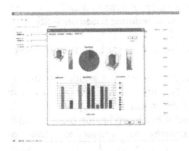

Figure 5 The performance indexes of the scheduling scheme

The interfaces of the prototype system

A batch plan can be inputted in the input interface. Then a heuristic algorithm is used to generate a feasible scheduling scheme automatically. Utilizing the scheme, the prototype is capable of performing visual simulation to demonstrate the obtained scheduling scheme (see Fig.3). The generated scheduling scheme can also be illustrated in the form of table shown in Fig.4. In order to evaluate the performances of the scheduling scheme, the statistical performance indexes can be given in Fig. 5.

Conclusion

In this paper, a workflow simulation scheduling model is used to model cigarette factory scheduling problems, and a heuristic algorithm is designed to integrate with the model to generate scheduling scheme automatically. Based on the model and algorithm, a prototype system of cigarette factory scheduling was developed. The system has some merits, such as nice capability of configuring scheduling environment, clear and friendly interfaces, and nice expanding capability.

Acknowledgements

This work was granted financial support from the National Natural Science Foundation of China (No. 60504028)

References

1. Brucker, P., Scheduling Algorithms. Berlin, Heidelberg: Springer-Verlag, 1998.
2. Chin, S. C., Appa, I. S., Robert, G., Simulation-based Scheduling for Dynamic Discrete Manufacturing, Proceedings of the 2003 Winter Simulation Conference, 2003, pp.1465-1473.
3. Fan, Y. S., Luo H. B., Lin H. P., Workflow Management Technology Foundation. Beijing: Tsinghua University Press, Springer-Verlag, 2001.
4. Li, J. Q., Fan, Y. S., Zhou, M. C., Performance Modeling and Analysis of Workflow, IEEE Transactions on Systems, Man, and Cybernetics-Part A: Systems and Humans, 2004, 34-2, pp. 229-242.
5. Lin, H. P., Fan, Y. S., Loiacono, E. T., A Practical Scheduling Method Based on Workflow Management Technology, International Journal of Advance Manufacture Technology, 2004, 24-11, pp. 919-924.
6. Shutler, P. M. E., A Priority List Based Heuristic for the Job Shop Problem: Part 2 Tabu Search, Journal of Operational Research Society, 2004, 55-7, pp. 780-784.

A Research Review on Dynamic Performance Analysis of Supply Chain System

Wei Lingyun*, Chai Yueting* ,Ren Changrui** and Dong Jin**

* National CIMS Engineering Research center, Tsinghua University,
Beijing 100084, P. R. China;
(E-mail: weily@tsinghua.edu.cn)
** IBM China Research Lab, Beijing, 100094, P. R. China.

ABSTRACT

The paper presents a research topic of supply chain dynamic performance analysis, which focuses on analyzing the casual relationships among various key factors in supply chain through simulation method to learn more about the supply chain operational mechanism and complex behaviors and then optimize the key factors for improving the supply chain performance. The presented topic consists of the following three areas: (1) identification of key factors affecting supply chain performance and casual relations among key factors; (2) development of simulation model (casual model) quantitatively describing casual relationships among key factors; (3) development of dynamic performance optimization methods. The paper provides a focused review of literature in above three areas. Some suggestions are made for future research finally.

KEY WORDS: Supply chain, Casual relations, Casual model, System thinking, System dynamics

INTRODUCTION

Supply chain is enterprise network system, which includes suppliers, manufacturers and dealers, involving flow of material, flow of capital, flow of information. Main aim of supply chain management is to achieve a simultaneous increase in customer service and profitability. Effective management of the total supply chain is regarded as an essential ingredient for business success in a global market. Two key challenges to supply chains in the 21st Century are fragmentation of demand and shorter product life-cycles. Agility in the supply chain is a prerequisite to cope with rapid changes in volume and mix, with the development of new products and with promotional activities. So the supply chain system manifests significant dynamic characteristics. Namely, Supply chain and its management need to keep adjusting for properly and rapidly respond to changes, coming from inside as well as outside the system.

In practice, managers often found that they have to face the following problems. What is the root cause of a significant increase in inventory level of some product in this month? What factors should be adjusted if we want to maintain the appropriate inventory levels? If the lead time is changed, which factors are influenced and how? What is casual relationship between sales promotion plan and profit increment? At present, performance measurement systems are main tools to deal with these problems. However, far too many enterprises often design their measurement systems without understanding the dynamic interdependencies between measures and ultimately the process underlying performance generation [1]. Consequently, it is difficult for performance measurement systems to solve these problems involved with multiple interrelated factors.

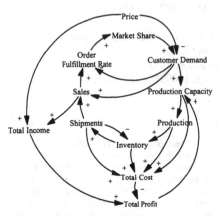

Fig.1 Casual relationships among some key factors in supply chain

The complexity essence of supply chain and the ever-changing market environment have bearing on lots of dynamic, uncertain and complex factors affecting supply chain performance [2]. However, managers mostly pay their attention to some critical performance measure and key variables, such as order fulfillment rate, inventory level, production capacity, Today's market place is increasingly dynamic and volatile. So these factors often change over time. Moreover, there are many feedback loops within these factors (as shown in Fig.1), which cause complex interrelationships and complex behaviors in supply chain [2]. It is much difficult for supply chain managers to clearly understand various problems in supply chain operations and make appropriate decisions within limited time to improve supply chain performance. Actually, there is at present little known on

how these factors drive effective supply chain management, and even less on how they drive each other, let alone on what drives them in turn[3]. What are the right levers to pull and buttons to push in the organizational change effort [3]? In other words, we do not yet have causal relationships between the various factors driving effective supply chain management and their interrelations with performance improvements in areas like inventory management, supply chain costs, and customer satisfaction [3].

Therefore, we presents a research topic of supply chain dynamic performance analysis, which focuses on analyzing the casual relationships among various key factors in supply chain through simulation method to learn more about the supply chain operational mechanism and complex behaviors and then optimize the key factors for improving the supply chain performance. The presented research topic consists of the following three areas: (1) identification of key factors affecting supply chain performance and casual relations among key factors; (2) development of simulation model (casual model) quantitatively describing casual relationships among key factors; (3) development of dynamic performance optimization methods. Obviously, it is very helpful to realize quantitative management of supply chain and provide managers theoretical foundation for decision making, so that achieve continuous performance improvement and collaborative operations of supply chain. In the following sections, the paper first provides a focused review of literature in above three areas. Then some suggestions are made for future research in the topic.

THE REVIEW ON KEY FACTORS AND CAUSAL RELATIONS AMONG KEY FACTORS

Identification of key factors' set and casual

relationships among key factors are the first and critical step in supply chain dynamic performance analysis. As mentioned above, there exist lots of dynamic, uncertain and complex factors in supply chain management [2]. However, managers mostly focus on some key factors, such as order fulfillment rate, inventory level, gross profit rate and so on. Obviously, key factors not only include KPI and measurement indicators, but also contain some key state variables, such as gross profit rate, inventory and so on. Moreover, other strategic, tactical and operational variables, which reflect the manager's decision-making intention, may also be regarded as key factors.

Till now, few works on identification of key factors' set have been done [4]. Actually, the identification of appropriate performance measures for supply chain is still undertaking. However, the principles and methods of performance measurement frameworks are very helpful to identify the key factors set. Some important performance measure systems, such as Balanced Scorecard (BSC) [5], Supply Chain Operations reference (SCOR) may be used to find out key factors set. BSC is regarded as one of the most comprehensive performance systems. BSC mainly choose measures in four different areas: the financial, customer, internal-business-process and learning and growth perspectives [5]. It contains outcome measures (financial measures) and the performance drivers of outcomes, linked together in causal relations. BSC described detailedly causal relations among performance measures [5]. SCOR model is based on five management processes to describe supply chains, namely, plan, make, source, deliver and return. SCOR Model describes supply chains in five dimensions: deliver reliability, responsiveness, flexibility, cost, and efficiency in asset utilization. The core of SCOR is to identify the performance measures from supply chain processes. Moreover, Other frameworks, such as ROI (Resource, Output and Flexibility) [6], are also helpful to identify key factors. However, these performance measurement systems seldom consider the dynamic nature of the performance measures.[7]

At present, performance measurement frameworks mostly focus on design and choice of performance measures. Little literature on causal relations among key factors is available. However, some researcher recognized that causal relations appear to be pivotal to the success of performance measurement model (PMM) [8]. Mary and Frank [8] mentioned three related reasons for the importance of cause and effect in PMM: predictive ability of business models, organizational communication and learning, and motivation and evaluation of personnel. Causal relations should be an important PMM design criterion. [8]. There are many tools and methods to identify relationships among key factors. Suwignjo [7] suggested the use of cognitive maps and Kaplan and Norton [5] the use of strategy maps. Sergo etc. [1] used Causal Loop Diagrams (CLDs) to identify the performance measure and causal relations among key factors. Sergo [1] pointed out that CLDs are an important tool for identifying and representing feedback loops. They may prove very effective in helping to identifying appropriate performance measures and to understand their dynamic relationships. Actually, CLDs are key tools of System Thinking for showing the causal relationships among a set of variables operating in a system [1]. System thinking method, which has its origins in System Dynamics, is considered as a good method for identification of casual relations among key factors [9]. The method gives the basic principles and methods building casual relationship network of complex system in a system view [9].

165

THE REVIEW ON QUANTITATIVELY DESCRIBING CASUAL RELATIONS AMONG KEY FACTORS

The identified casual relationships of key factors need to be qualitatively described for learning more about the complex behaviors of supply chain and realizing the quantitative management [10]. Due to the fact that supply chain system contains many complex non-linear relationships, these relationships are difficult to model analytically in a mathematical model [10]. So these methods, like operational methods and differential equations[11], which are difficult to deal with dynamic, nonlinear and stochastic factors, are not suitable to describe the casual relationships of key factors. System Dynamics is a computer-aided approach, whose essence is to use casual relation loops to model how system variables drive each other [1]. It can easily deal with complex factors and is often used to understand the behavior modes of complex system and design policies for improving system performance [10]. Actually, System Dynamics has been applied successfully in some supply chain topic, such as, inventory decision and policy development, time compression, demand amplification, supply chain design and integration, and international supply chain management, etc [10]. So System Dynamics is regarded as the main method that builds a quantitative supply chain causal model and quantitatively describes the causal relations among key factors. However, due to the complex interrelationships of key factors, single method or theory are difficult to exactly build quantitative models for supply chain. Wang [12] suggested that System Dynamics should combine with other methods, such as data mining, statistical analysis and fuzzy inference, to better describe the casual relationships network among key factors.

THE REVIEW ON SUPPLY CHAIN DYNAMIC PERFORMANCE OPTIMIZATION

The main objective of supply chain dynamic performance analysis is to optimize the key factors for constantly improving the supply chain performance based on the quantitative casual model of key factors in whole supply chain. Sergo[1] point out that the achievement of high levels of performance on one measure can only obtained at the expense of performance on one or more other measures. It is inevitable to make trade-offs among these measures [1]. Moreover, the goals of supply chain management, which is to achieve a simultaneous increase in customer service and profitability, are also conflicting. Anyway, optimizing the structure and function of economic systems through adjusting key factors has increasingly received attention [12]. However, few efforts have been done in this area. There are two reasons. First, the quantitative casual model of whole supply chain is still undertaking and the relationships within key factors are uncertain. Second, the performance optimization problem often is a nonlinear multi-objective programming problem with mixed variables [12]. In general, key factors in supply chain consist of continuous variables and discrete variables. Objective function and constraint functions are highly nonlinear and non-convex because of nonlinear casual relations among key factors in supply chain [12]. Traditional nonlinear programming algorithms generally require a convex optimization model and are trapped into local optimum. So feasibility and practicability of traditional methods are limited. Consequently, there is a pressing need to use a simple and effective global optimization method to easily solve the performance optimization problem. Genetic algorithms (GAs), which are probabilistic global optimization techniques inspired by natural selection process and population genetics theory, provide a general architecture for solving complex optimization problems. It can uniformly express the mixed variables in some coding and have no requirement for optimization model [13]. So it is suitable to solve the nonlinear programming problem with mixed variables. Wang [12] proposed a general solution for policy optimization of social systems with GAs and system dynamics. However, GAs usually suffer from a certain inefficiency in optimizing complex problems because of their well-known drawbacks, premature convergence and weak exploitation capabilities. Consequently, GAs generally need to be modified for solving the optimization problem effectively.

DISCUSSION AND CONCLUTION

The paper first presents a research topic of supply chain dynamic performance analysis, which consists of the following three areas: (1) identification of key factors affecting supply chain performance and casual relations among key factors; (2) development of simulation model (casual model) quantitatively describing casual relationships among key factors; (3) development of dynamic performance optimization methods. Then the paper gives a literature review on above three areas. Obviously, some suggestions could be made for future research through above reviews. Namely, System thinking [10] combined with Balanced Scorecard is a good method for identifying key factors and casual relations among key factors. Whereas, System Dynamics combined with other method and theory, may be effective way to quantitatively describe the causal relations among key factors. Genetic algorithm, which is a simple and effective global optimization method solving complex optimization problem, may be used to optimize the key factors for obtaining better supply chain dynamic performance.

REFERENCES

1. Santos S P, Belton V, Howick S. Adding value to performance measurement by using system dynamics and multicriteria analysis. International Journal of Operations & Production Management, 2002, 22-11, pp. 1246-1272.
2. Richard Wilding. The supply chain complexity triangle. International Journal of Physical Distribution & Logistics Management, 1998, 28-8, pp. 599-616.
3. Akkermans H A, Bogerd P, Vos B. Virtuous and vicious cycles on the road towards international supply chain management. International Journal of Operations & Production Management, 1999, 19-(5-6), pp. 565-581
4. Benita M. Beamon, supply chain design and analysis: models and methods, int. J. Production Economics, 1998, 55, pp.281-294
5. Kaplan, R.S. and Norton, D.P., The Strategy-Focused Organization –How Balanced Scorecard Companies Thrieve in the New Business Environment, Harvard Business School Press, Boston, MA. , 2001
6. Benita M Beamon. Measuring Supply Chain Performance. International Journal of Operations & Production Management, 1999, 19-3, pp. 275-292.
7. P. Suwignjo, U.S Bititci, A.S Carrie, Quantitative models for performance measurement system, Int. J. Production Economics, 2000,64, pp.231-241
8. Mary A. Malina, Frank H. Selto. Causality in Performance Measurement Models. http://www -bus.colorado.edu/faculty/selto/home.html, 2004.
9. Dennis Sherwood, Seeing the Forest for the Trees: A Manager's Guide to Applying Systems Thinking, 2002
10. Angerhofer B J, Angelides M C. System Dynamics Modeling in Supply Chain Management: Research Review. In: Joines J A, Barton R R, Kang K, et al., eds. Proceedings of the 2000 Winter Simulation Conference, 2000, pp.342-351.
11. C. E. Riddalls, S. Bennett and N. S. Tipi, Modeling the dynamics of supply chain, Int. J. of systems science, 2000, 31-8, pp 969-976
12. Wang Q. F., Li X., Social system policy and optimizaiotn based on system dynamics, science and technology review, 2004,5, pp.34-36 (In Chinese)
13. Goldberg, D.E., Genetic Algorithm in Search, Optimization and Machine Learning, Addison-Wesley, New York, 1989

Study the Demand Information Sharing in Supply Chain with Process Modeling and Simulation

Huiping Lin[*], Yushun Fan[*]

Department of Automation, Tsinghua University,

Beijing, China, 100084, P.R.China

(E-mail: linhp@tsinghua.edu.cn)

ABSTRACT

The impacts of information sharing between supply chain partners had been studied for many years due to its importance in supply chain management. Although there is no doubt that information should be shared between partners, to what extent should individual enterprises share their information is still an open topic. In literature, usually analytic methods are used to understand the behavior of the chain and the effects of information sharing. The analytic method has solid mathematical base, however it is not easy for industrial users to understand. In this paper, a Process-information Model is built to describe the information sharing process. A simulation based analysis framework is then proposed to consider three aspects such as market environments, information sharing levels (frequent, aggregate, and no demand information sharing) and companies' production process. Finally, a case study is given to show how the proposed method works.

Key Words: Supply Chain, Information sharing, Modeling, Analyzing

INTRODUCTION

Supply chain is a network of suppliers, factories, warehouse, distribution centers and retailers through which materials are required, transformed and delivered to customers. The impact of information sharing between supply chain partners had been a research topic for many years due to the fact that the successful integration of the entire supply chain process depends heavily on the availability of accurate and timely information that can be shared by all members of the supply chain.

In literature, many research efforts about information sharing address the questions such as what kind of information should be shared, how they can be shared, and the impact of information sharing on supply chain performance. The five categories of information such as order and demand, inventory, sales, shipment, and production information are considered typical information chosen for sharing and analyzing, among which the analysis of demand and inventory information is most often seen. For example, Wikner et al. (1991), Wu and Meixell (1998), Lee et al. (2000), Beamon and Chen (2001), Thonemann (2002), Milner (2002), and Raghunathan (2003) analyzed the value of demand information sharing between supply chain members and studied how and under what circumstances that the supply chain member could benefit greatly. Lin et al. (2002) simulated and analyzed the buyer-seller correlation in order, inventory, and demand information sharing through multi-agent simulation system and indicated that such an information sharing could reduce the demand uncertainty. Baganha and Cohen(1998), Cachon and Fisher (2000), and Yu et al. (2001) study the results of inventory information sharing. Mak et al. (2002), etc proposed a systematic framework for investigating the impact of sharing production information. There is no doubt that information should be shared between partners to achieve better supply chain performance, however, to what extent should individual enterprises in the supply chain share product information is still an open topic (Huang et al. 2003).

Besides, the modeling of the information in supply chain needs further research. When analyzing the information sharing in supply chain, usually the mathematical models are established to understand the behavior of the model and the effects of information sharing (Lee et al. 2000). It has solid theory base and is suitable for computing, however, it is not easy for industrial users to understand how the information passes through the chain and affects the chain performance.

In order to provide graphic view of process and the information flow within it, as well as providing dynamic analysis capability, a new Process-Information Model (PIM) is proposed based on workflow modeling technology(Workflow Management Coalition, 1994 and Fan et al. 2001) for manufacturing supply chain. The corresponding simulation-based analyzing method is put forward to choose the appropriate demand information sharing level according to the market environment and product process. The paper is organized as follows. First, the structure and elements of the PIM are discussed in detail. The related simulation-based analyzing method is provided followed. Finally, a case study is given.

PROCESS-INFORMATION MODEL

Due to the complexity of real supply chain system, it is very difficult to contain all the important elements in a single model. PIM is a compound model that is made up of Process and information View, Resource View and Order View (Figure 1). Different view describes different aspects of the chain.

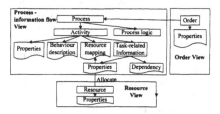

Figure 1 Model structure

The process and information view describes the business process and information flow within it. Each process is composed of activity, process logic. For each activity, we have four kinds of description: property, behavior description, resource mapping, and task-related information.

- Property definition: Describing the basic property of each activity, such as activity ID, processing time, and so on.
- Behavior description: Defining the execution of activities by ECA rules, which is formed as "if Event and Condition then Action".
- Resource mapping: Allocating resources to activities.
- Task-related information: Defining the information needed for activity's operation (input information), the information generated by the activity (output information), and the existing dependency between input and output information.

Resource view describes the resources participate in the process such as people, equipment, and so on. Order view describes the properties of orders and demand, which includes the orders and demands' arrival time, product type, batch size, due date, late penalty cost, and so on.

SIMULATION BASED ANALYSIS

Simulation is an effective way to study the dynamic properties of the complex system. In this paper, a simulation-based analyzing method is developed to study how the demand information sharing policy affects supply chain performance under certain market environment. Three aspects are considered: market environment, Demand sharing mode and production process (Table 1).

Table 1 Analysis dimension

Order	Share Mode	Production
Frequency	Frequent	Process
Batch	Aggregate	Time
Due date	None	Storage Cost
Late penalty		

Although many factors could be counted in market environment, in order to limit the analysis scope reasonably, only four basic ones such as order frequency, batch size, due date, and late penalty cost are considered in our method. Eight kinds of markets are identified as follows:
- frequent order with small batch size and tight due date;
- frequent order with large batch size and loose due date;
- frequent order with large batch size and tight due date;
- loose order with small batch size and loose due date;

- loose order with small batch size and tight due date;
- loose order with large batch size and loose due date;
- loose order with large batch size and tight due date.

Demand sharing mode defines the relationship between demand and previous order and forecasting demand. It determines the frequency and content of the demand information. Three types of demand sharing policy are considered:
- Frequent demand sharing: demand is shared at the same time when the order arrives;
- Aggregate demand sharing: the interval between demands is longer than that between orders;
- No demand sharing.

When considering production process, process, total processing time and early storage cost taken in account. The "process" that defines the how the product is manufactured is included in the process-information view. We outlined total processing time because it is an important index when we consider "urgencies" of an order. Definition of early storage cost associate with each product is necessary for performance measurement.

CASE STUDY

Consider a two level supply chain that consists of a manufacturer and N retailers. External orders and demands forecasting for the products occur at retailers. The manufacturer organizes the production according to the orders. The production of each item includes five serial tasks such as T1, T2, T3, T4, and T5. Three machines M1, M2, and M3 are available for the production (Table 2).

Table 2 Task-resource relation

Activity	T1	T2	T3	T4	T5
Resource	M1	M2	M1	M3	M2

When the product is completed before its due date, it will be stored in warehouse until being released on due date. If the product is finished after its due date, it will be released immediately when it is done.

Suppose the process time of activity T1, T2, T3, T4 and T5 is drawn from a uniform distribution between 3.0 and 4.0 hours. The interval between orders is draw from a normal distribution of $N(\sigma, \varepsilon)$ days, the order batch is uniformly distributed from A to B, the order date $T_{duedate} = a * ETPK$, where the ETPK stands for the estimate total processing time of an product and a is the due date coefficient. Then the eight different markets can be expressed Table 3.

For the frequent demand sharing, the demand comes at the same when the order arrives. For the aggregate demand sharing, the demand interval time is draw from a normal distribution of N (7, 0.5) days.

Total Cost (TC) is used to test the effectiveness of our methods. It is the sum of the total early storage cost and late penalty cost.

With the definition of order and demand, 24 situations are considered in our case study. For each situation we have 50 simulation runs and the performance result is the average of all 50 runs. The simulation result is shown in table 4

From the simulation result we can see when the order batch size is small, especially when the order has rather loose due date, the manufactory does not benefit from demand information sharing when TC are considered. However, when the order batch size is large, the demand information sharing became to improve the performance of average TC. Generally, frequent demand information sharing plays better than aggregate demand sharing. Under the extremely "tight" situation (frequent order with large order batch), the effect of frequent demand sharing is much more significant than with aggregate demand sharing and no demand sharing. However, when the interval between orders is large and the order batch size is large, aggregate demand sharing has better performance than the frequent one does.

CONCLUSIONS
In this paper, a process modeling and simulation based analyzing method is proposed to study the effect of different demand information sharing level on supply chain performance. It shows the demand sharing mode has different impact on supply chain performance. It is important for the enterprise to choose the appropriate demand sharing policy according to its production and market situations.

Table 3 Definition of market environment

No	Interval, Batch, Due date coefficient	No	Interval, Batch, Due date coefficient
1	N(3,0.5), U[5,10], a=1.5	5	N(6,0.5), U[5,10], a=1.5
2	N(3,0.5), U[5,10], a=3.5	6	N(6,0.5), U[5,10], a=3.5
3	N(3,0.5), U[15,20], a=1.5	7	N(6,0.5), U[15,20], a=1.5
4	N(3,0.5), U[15,20], a=3.5	8	N(6,0.5), U[15,20], a=3.5

Table 4 Simulation Results of *TAD* and *cost*

Market Type	Demand Sharing Level	Average TAD	Average Cost	Market Type	Demand Sharing Level	Average TAD	Average Cost
1	a	20.34	1.02	5	a	16.75	1.07
	b	21.23	4.25		b	18.83	8.01
	c	16.68	0.83		c	16.44	0.82
2	a	47.45	2.61	6	a	38.36	2.29
	b	43.69	4.95		b	42.44	8.44
	c	18.15	0.36		c	18.65	0.37
3	a	71.66	11.35	7	a	60.53	7.07
	b	88.87	9.47		b	55.13	10.45
	c	212.76	12.64		c	87.44	13.33
4	a	76.39	7.64	8	a	48.33	3.77
	b	122.69	11.69		b	47.43	9.86
	c	177.97	15.9		c	52.36	12.26

REFERENCES

1. Baganha, M.P. and Cohen, M.A., 1998, The stabilizing effect of inventory in supply chains, Operations Research, 46, 72-83

2. Beamon, B.M. and Chen, V., 2001, Performance analysis of conjoined supply chain, International Journal of Production Research 39(14), 3195-3218

3. Cachon, G. and Fisher, M., 2000, Supply chain inventory management and the value of shared information, Management Science 46(8), 1032-1048

4. Fan, Y., Luo, H., Lin, H., and etc., 2001, Fundamentals of Workflow Management Technology. Tsinghua University Publisher, Springer Publisher.

5. Huang G.Q., Lau, J.S.K. and Mar, K.L., 2003, The impacts of sharing production information on supply chain dynamics: a review of the literature, International Journal of Production Research 41(7), 1483-1517

6. Lee, H.L., So, K.C. and Tang, C.S., 2000, The value of information sharing in a two-level supply chain, Working paper, Management science 46, 626-643

7. Lin, F., Huang, S. and Lin, S., 2002, Effects of information sharing on supply chain performance in electronic commerce, *IEEE Transactions on Engineering Management* 49(3), 258-268

8. Mak, K.L., Lau, J.S.K. and Huang, G.Q., 2002, Web-based simulation portal for investigating impacts of sharing production information on supply chain dynamics from the perspective of inventory allocation, Integrated Manufacturing Systems 13(5), 345-358

9. Milner, J. M., 2002, On the complementary value of accurate demand information and production and supplier flexibility, Manufacturing and Service Operations Management 4(2), 99-113

10. Raghunathan, S., 2003, Impact of demand correlation on the value of and incentives for information sharing in a supply chain, European Journal of Operational Research 146, 634-649

11. Thonemann, U.W., 2002, Improving supply-chain performance by sharing advance demand information, European Journal of Operational Research 42(1), 81-107

12. Workflow Management Coalition. The workflow reference model. WFMC TC00-1003, 1994.

13. Wikner, J., Towill,D.R. and Naim, M., 1991, Smoothing supply chain dynamics, International Journal of Production Economics 22(3), 231-48

14. Wu, S.D. and Meixell, M.J., 1998, Relating demand behavior and production policies in the manufacturing supply chain, Lehigh University, Bethlehem, PA.

15. Yu, Z., Yan, H. and Cheng, T.C.E., 2001, Benefits of information sharing with supply chain partnerships, Industrial Management & Data Systems 101(3), 114-11

The Cost Valuation Model for Reverse Supply Chain using System Dynamics

Hyunjong JEONG*, Jiyoun KIM* and Jinwoo PARK**

* Department of Industrial Engineering, Seoul National University
(E-mail: conan617@hanmail.net)
** Department of Industrial Engineering, Faculty of Engineering
Seoul National University,
Shillim-dong, Kwanak-ku, Seoul, 151-742 Korea

ABSTRACT

Due to some recent environmental regulations in developed countries, industrial companies are forced to consider recycling systems more seriously. However, there are very few studies on the economic justification on the implementation of recycling systems. In this paper, we propose a model to evaluate the environmental costs of a reverse supply chain. The model uses the concept of ABC(Activity-Based Costing) to assess the cost of each activity in a supply chain and identifies the consumption of resources. We represent a reverse supply chain from a new point of view based on the I/O(Input/Output) structure. A simulation model was developed based on the classic system dynamics concept, and simulation experiments were conducted to validate our model. Enterprises as well as governments can carry out various analyses using the developed model to obtain a better understanding of the strategic and operational aspects of a recycling system.

KEY WORDS: Simulation, Reverse Supply Chain, ABC, System Dynamics

INTRODUCTION

Recently, issues such as the depletion of natural resources and environmental pollution have attracted much attention to the importance of a reverse supply chain. A reverse supply chain can be defined as a series of activities required to retrieve a used-product from a customer for either the recovery of its left-over market value or disposal of it[6]. The economic effect of a reverse supply chain can be classified into direct factors such as raw material acquisition and cost reduction, or indirect factors such as 'green image' improvement. However, because these factors are qualitative rather than quantitative, it is difficult to convince an enterprise of the necessity of a reverse supply chain.

In this paper, we propose a model to evaluate the environmental benefit and the costs of the reverse supply chain over the life cycle of a product, based on the assumption that environmental regulations are imposed fairly on the whole supply chain. We expect that the model will be used as a good reference for setting environmental policies.

This text is organized as follows. Section 2 presents a literature review about the assessment of the cost of a supply chain. Section 3 presents the framework for the assessment of the cost. Section 4 develops a simulation model based on the suggested framework and the result of the simulation is presented. Section 5 summarizes the work and suggests future researches.

LITERATURE REVIEW

A reverse supply chain has been widely

studied lately. In this section, we review related researches and analyze their strengths and weaknesses.

Life Cycle Assessment(LCA) is a methodology that examines, identifies, and evaluates the relevant environmental implications of a material, process, product, or system across its life span [9]. Clift et al. evaluated the supply chain of a cell phone by using OBIA(Overall Business Impact Assessment), a modified methodology based on LCA. However, the suggested environmental impact did not show relation to monetary value.

Azapagic et al. proposed an approach to improve a system applying multiobjective optimization. Although this method is a quantification of the LCA, it had limited application for a large scale problem.

Life Cycle Cost(LCC) analysis provides a framework for specifying the estimated total incremental cost of developing, producing, using, and retiring a particular item[1]. Jan proposed the LCC analysis methodology based on ABC, whose benefits as a process-based assessment was maintained.

Finally, McLaren et al. studied the reverse supply chain of a cell phone from the point of view of energy consumption, rather than the economic benefits of a reverse supply chain.

THE DEVELOPMENT OF A FRAMEWORK FOR A REVERSE SUPPLY CHAIN

In this section, a reverse supply chain framework and input/output structure of an activity in the supply chain are presented. First of all, ABC is introduced in the next subsection.

Activity-Based Costing(ABC)

ABC assesses the cost of a product by measuring the amount of resources the product consumes. In this research, we apply the ABC method to evaluate the cost for managing a reverse supply chain. In this case, the product to be assessed is a reverse supply chain, and the activities are the functions of the members in the supply chain. Translated into societal terms, the activities in the reverse supply chain are the mining of raw material, manufacturing, delivery, etc. In the next section, we present a definition of resources.

The Definition of Resources

Materials that affect the environment have been widely researched in the field of industrial ecology. Based on such researches, resources for cost assessment can be defined. In industrial ecology, the resources that mankind possesses are classified into five groups: atmosphere, hydrosphere, geosphere, biosphere and anthrosphere. Geosphere is the solid in the earth, such as the continental and the oceanic crust, and stratum. Anthrosphere includes everything constructed by mankind, such as a plant or a building.

Let us define resources using the classification cited above. Raw material consumes the geosphere, and exhaust gas can be considered to consume the atmosphere as it pollutes the air. We listed the material that consumes each resource.

An Extended Reverse Supply Chain Framework

Existing studies on reverse supply chain framework mainly focus on specific parts. By examining past works, 8 different activities were extracted: collection of the used product, inspection, reuse, refurbishment, disassemble, remanufacture, recycling and disposal[4]. However, in this list, the mining activity, which represents a large share of the total energy use, is excluded and the possibility of materials being transferred to another supply chain needs to be considered. We, therefore, propose an extended reverse supply chain framework in Fig. 1, accounting for such shortcomings.

174

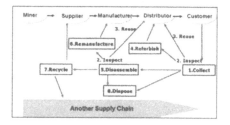

Figure 1 an Extended Reverse Supply
Chain Framework

We develop a model to evaluate the environmental costs based on this framework. In the next subsection, the I/O structure of an activity is presented.

Input/Output Structure of an Activity

To define cost elements in a reverse supply chain, we analyzed the activities of 10 participants in the suggested framework. The cost of transportation was not included because of the diverse modes of transportation and the product collection policy. As shown in Fig. 2, we developed a structure of the input and output of a system by referring to the I/O structure of LCA and the resources of ABC. Although emitting pollutants is an output of a system, it can be regarded as an input because it consumes related resources when we consider cost. Following Fig. 3 depicts the I/O structure of a supplier on a supply chain. The process of energy acquisition is also shown.

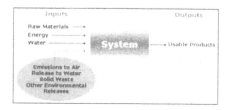

Figure 2 Input/Output Structure of
an Activity

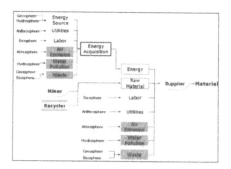

Figure 3 I/O Structure of a Supplier

SIMULATION MODELING

Model Design

The formulation of a simulation model by system dynamics methodology is described by two-phase[7]. In the first stage, the influence of each object on another is shown by the influence diagram. Subsequently, mathematical interrelation among objects is represented by a flow diagram, and finally, a quantitative result is derived by simulation. Fig. 4 shows the influence diagram based on the reverse supply chain framework in Fig. 2.

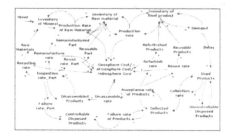

Figure 4 an Influence Diagram of a
Reverse Supply Chain Framework

A quantitative model based on the influence diagram in Fig. 4 is shown in Fig. 6 in the next subsection.

Experiment Result & Application

Due to the lack of the data on the environmental cost of various materials, we focus on the way to utilize the model rather than calculate the exact cost. If we compare the cost of a reverse supply chain with the cost of a supply chain without reverse activities, assuming that all other conditions are the same, the difference in cost can be calculated. In this context, we make a comparative study and show how the result can help in decision making.

Let us imagine the scenario in which the government earmarks subsidy for the installment of metal recycling equipment. In this case, the economic value or the cost of the equipment becomes essential information. In the steel industry, a manufacturer, supplier, distributor is the steel company. We only include recycling of steel, for steel is rarely refurbished or remanufactured. During the simulation, CO_2(carbon dioxide) as atmosphere consumption, and coal and iron ore as geosphere consumption are considered. The cost of each material is also examined. CO_2 incurs $4.02 per kilogram when released to the air. The costs of coal and iron ore are $125 and $47, respectively. We simulate the model using these data above, assuming that the collection rate of scrap iron is 80% and the ratio for the scrap iron to be accepted for recycling is 60%. The results are shown in Fig.5 and Fig.6.

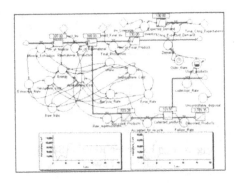

Figure 6 Simulation Results: a Reverse Supply Chain

Comparing Fig. 5 and Fig. 6, we can see the huge difference in Atmosphere Cost and Geosphere Cost. When there is only a forward supply chain, environmental cost keeps increasing until it converges. On the other hand, in a reverse supply chain environment, the cost goes up and down before convergence, according to the procurement of the recycling material. The total cost decreases because mineral consumption and CO_2 emission of the recycling process are less than those of production. The results are summarized in Table 1.

Table 1 Simulation Results

	Atmosphere Cost	Geosphere Cost
w/ a Reverse Supply Chain	$150,000	$18,000
w/o a Reverse Supply Chain	$92,000	$13,000
Cost Reduction	39%	28%

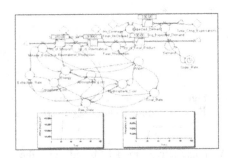

Figure 5 Simulation Results: Without a Reverse Supply Chain

Based on this information, policy makers can appropriate subsidy for recycling equipment as stated below.

Maximum subsidy
= ($150,000 -$92,000+$18,000-$13,000)
+ other environmental costs
- costs for the installment of equipment

We compared the cost of a supply chain with and without a reverse supply chain in the case of the steel industry and based upon this comparison, briefly presented the logic behind a policy decision. In addition, we expect that the cost assessment method suggested in this study can be utilized in various situations. Although the value added increases as a product reaches the end of a supply chain, environmental cost decreases. In this case, our model can be utilized to distribute the responsibility fairly among the objects over a whole supply chain. We can also analyze the change of cost according to the component ratio of reverse supply chain activities such as refurbishing, remanufacturing and recycling to regulate or support a specific activity.

CONCLUSION AND FURTHER RESEARCH

This study presents the framework of the environmental cost of reverse supply chain from a social viewpoint by taking into account the Activity-Based Costing as well as the results of past studies and determines the environmental cost by modeling and simulating the framework using system dynamics.

The proposed cost analysis model is expected to be an excellent reference to policy makers. The calculated cost could validate to the companies the need for a reverse supply chain and be used as basic information for deciding on all kinds of subsidy payments. With this model, the whole cost structure of the supply chain can be studied, and the load arising from the restriction can be fairly distributed.

Also, the proposed model could be useful for the simulations needed for various scenario comparisons. For example, deciding on what course of action we are going to take to collect, reuse, reproduce, or recycle a product can be an important issue and the simulation could prove to be useful regarding this issue. The result of analyzing the methods of collecting or transporting products by scenarios could be a good reference in the decision-making process.

However, for the proper use of the proposed model, a few more points must be added. For accurate cost distribution, we must determine what sorts of materials consume what sorts of resources, and study the costs arising from pollution by each pollutant.

REFERENCES

1. Asiedu, T. and Gu, P., Product life cycle cost analysis: state of the art review, International Journal of Production Research, 1998, 36- 4, pp.883-908.
2. Azapagic, A. and Clift, R., Life cycle assessment and multiobjective optimisation, Journal of Cleaner Production, 1999, 7-2, pp.135-143.
3. Clift, R. and Wright, L., Relationships Between Environmental Impacts and Added Value Along the Supply Chain, Technological Forecasting and Social Change, 2000, 65- 3, pp.281-295.
4. Lim, C., Development of Reference Model and Strategic Road Map for the Implementation of a Reverse Supply Chain, 2005.
5. McLaren, J., Wright, L., Parkinson, S., Jackson, T., A Dynamic Life-Cycle Energy Model of Mobile Phone Take-back and Recycling, Journal of Industrial Ecology, 1999, 3-1, pp.77-91.
6. Pochampally, K.K. and Gupta, S.M., A multi-phase mathematical programming approach to strategic planning of an efficient reverse supply chain network, IEEE International Symposium on Electronics and the Environment, 2003, pp.72-78.
7. Towill, D., Industrial dynamics modeling of supply chains, Internation Journal of Physical Distribution and Logistics Management, 1995, 26-2, pp.23-42.
8. Emblemsvag, J., Life-Cycle Costing: Using Activity-Based Costing and Mote Carlo Methods to Manage Future Costs and Risks, Wiley, 2003.
9. Graedel, T. E. and Allenby, B. R., Industrial Ecology, Prentice Hall, 2003.

Experimental and Simulation Design of an Engineering Scheduling Problem Based on Molecular Computing Approach

Mohd Saufee MUHAMMAD and Osamu ONO

Institute of Applied DNA Computing, Meiji University, 1-1-1 Higashi-mita, Tama-ku
Kawasaki-shi, Kanagawa-ken, JAPAN 214-8571
(E-mail: {msaufee, ono}@meiji.isc.ac.jp)

ABSTRACT

An in vitro experimental implementation of an engineering scheduling problem in the case of an elevator travel path optimization using molecular computing approach has been successfully presented in our previous research. Experimental result obtained verifies that this approach can be well-suited to solve such real-world problem of this nature. For a larger scale problem, the experiment design involves a high DNA oligonucleotides cost. In order to eliminate errors during the design process, we successfully developed a simple Visual Basic platform software program capable of simulating the DNA computing process of parallel overlap assembly and polymerase chain reaction. This software program capability is unlimited where problem of any size and complexity can be simulated before the actual experimental work is carried out, thus saving cost due to possible errors during the DNA oligonucleotides design process.

KEY WORDS: In vitro experiment, DNA computing, simulation software, parallel overlap assembly, polymerase chain reaction

INTRODUCTION

The practical possibility of using molecules of Deoxyribonucleic Acid or DNA as a medium for computation was first demonstrated in 1994 by Leonard M. Adleman [1] to solve a directed Hamiltonian Path Problem (HPP). Since then, many research results of similar combinatorial problems which are mainly in the realm of computer science and mathematics have been presented [2, 3, 4, 5]. The application in solving engineering related problems however, has not been very well established. A proposed method on how DNA computing approach can be used to solve an engineering scheduling problem in the case of an elevator travel path optimization for a typical building of N floors with M elevators has been presented [6] based on the researches mentioned.

Although an in vitro experimental work has been carried out successfully for the case of an elevator travel path optimization problem, a mechanism for implementing the DNA computing approach for a much larger and complex problem is needed. Therefore, the aim of this research is to develop a simulation program that is capable of simulating the DNA computing process before the actual experiment is carried out. Since the complexity and costs of the DNA oligos increases for complex and larger problem, this software program will provide a helpful guide for the DNA computing implementation as to eliminate errors during the design process. In this paper, we first give an overview of the elevator scheduling problem and its DNA computing solution design. We then discuss about the software program developed, and shows that the DNA computing solution for this type of problem is well suited for any problem scale and complexity.

ELEVATOR SCHEDULING PROBLEM OVERVIEW

Consider a typical building with 2 elevators and 6 floors as illustrated in Table 1.

Table 1 Scheduling Problem Example

Floor No	Elevator A	Elevator B	Hall Call
6		(3 , 2)	
5			
4			↑
3			↓
2			
1	(3 , 5)		

These elevator travel paths can be represented using a weighted graph by representing each elevator position at floors 1, 2, ... , 5, 6 with nodes $V_1, V_2, ... , V_5, V_6$ respectively. The weight between each node representing the elevator's travel time between each floor can be formulated as

$$\omega|_{j-i}| = (|j-i|) T_C + T_S \qquad (1)$$

where

- i, j — elevator's present and destination floor
- $|j-i|$ — total number of floors of elevator's movement
- T_C — elevator's traveling time between consecutive floors
- T_S — elevator's stopping time at a floor

Now, assume that $T_C = 5$ s, $T_S = 15$ s, and representing 5 s of time with 10 units we have from (1)

$\omega 1 = 40, \quad \omega 2 = 50, \quad \omega 3 = 60$
$\omega 4 = 70, \quad \omega 5 = 80$

The minimum total traveling time of both elevators thus gives the optimal elevator travel path, i.e.

Optimal Travel Path = $\sum \omega|_{j-i}|$
$$= G(A, B)_{min} \qquad (2)$$

DNA COMPUTING SOLUTION

First, the elevator movements are represented as a weighted graph that indicates the start, intermediate and end nodes, and also to differentiate the nodes of different travel path combinations as depicted in Figure 1. The nodes are then assigned with a specific DNA sequence [7]. All the possible travel path combinations of the elevator are synthesized so that the sequence length will directly represent the weight between the nodes based on the initial condition requirements as tabulated in Table 2. Parallel overlap assembly (POA) [8] is then employed for initial pool generation to generate all the possible travel path combinations, and polymerase chain reaction (PCR) [9, 10] for the amplification of the required optimal path. Finally, gel electrophoresis [11] is performed to separate all the possible travel path combinations according to its length, and the image is captured where the DNA duplex representing the shortest path could be visualized representing the required optimal path solution of the problem as illustrated in Figure 2. The PCR gel image shows 4 bands indicating all the 4 possible travel paths, i.e. $G(A, B)_3 = 230bp$, $G(A, B)_1 = 250bp$, $G(A, B)_4 = 280bp$ and $G(A, B)_2 = 300bp$. This confirms the expected result that the optimal elevator's travel path is given by $G(A, B)_3 = 230bp = 115$ s.

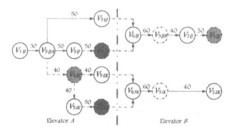

Figure 1 DNA computing weighted graph

179

Table 2 Synthesized DNA Sequences

Node V_i	DNA sequences (5' – 3')
$V_{1SJ} \rightarrow V_{3IJ}$	CGGCGGTCCACTAAATACTAaggtcgtttaa ggaagtacgCACTCTTTGTGAACGCCTTC
$V_{3IJ} \rightarrow V_{4IK}$	CACTCTTTGTGAACGCCTTCacgtcgtgta acgaagtcctGTGGGTTAGAGGTAGTCCGG
$V_{3IJ} \rightarrow V_{5IJ}$	CACTCTTTGTGAACGCCTTCccgtcggttaagcaa gtaatgtactatgctTGAACCGGCCCTTTATATCT
$V_{3IJ} \rightarrow V_{5EJ}$	CACTCTTTGTGAACGCCTTCgcgtcgctta ccgaagcacgCTATAAGGCCAAAGCAGTCG
$V_{4IK} \rightarrow V_{5IK}$	GTGGGTTAGAGGTAGTCCGGcgctcgttga agccagtaccCCGCTGATCCTTGCTAAGTA
$V_{4IK} \rightarrow V_{5EK}$	GTGGGTTAGAGGTAGTCCGGgcgtc ttttaATGCCTGGCTAAAGTGAGAC
$V_{5SJ} \rightarrow V_{3EJ}$	TGAACCGGCCCTTTATATCTacgtgtttta cccaagtcagTCATTCGAGTTATTCCTGGG
$V_{5IK} \rightarrow V_{3EK}$	CCGCTGATCCTTGCTAAGTAgcggcgtgtc acgaactacgAAATGACCTTTTTAACGGCA
$V_{3EJ} \rightarrow V_{6SJ}$	TCATTCGAGTTATTCCTGGG GGACCTGCATCATACCAGTT
$V_{5EJ} \rightarrow V_{6SJ}$	CTATAAGGCCAAAGCAGTCG GGACCTGCATCATACCAGTT
$V_{3EK} \rightarrow V_{6SK}$	AAATGACCTTTTTAACGGCA TGCACGCAAAACTATTTCAT
$V_{5EK} \rightarrow V_{6SK}$	ATGCCTGGCTAAAGTGAGAC TGCACGCAAAACTATTTCAT
$V_{6SJ} \rightarrow V_{3IJ}$	GGACCTGCATCATACCAGTTacgtggtttaaggaa gtacggtactatgctCACTCTTTGTGAACGCCTTC
$V_{6SK} \rightarrow V_{3IK}$	TGCACGCAAAACTATTTCATccgtgggttaaagaa gtcctgtactctcctTCTGCACTGTTAATGAGCCA
$V_{2IJ} \rightarrow V_{4EJ}$	AAAGCCCGTCGGTTAAGTTAggtcttttaa tcaactaatgGGAATCCATTGATCGCTTTA
$V_{3IJ} \rightarrow V_{2IJ}$	CACTCTTTGTGAACGCCTTCacgtcgctgc aagaactacgAAAGCCCGTCGGTTAAGTTA
$V_{3IK} \rightarrow V_{2EK}$	TCTGCACTGTTAATGAGCCAacgtcttgtc CTACGGATAGGTGTCTGGGA

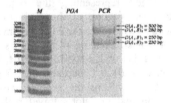

Figure 2 Gel electrophoresis image output

SIMULATION SOFTWARE DESIGN

The DNA computing implementation involves oligos sequences design to represent both the problem and solution. As the problem grows larger, the complexity of the oligos design gets complicated. In order to assist in the design, we developed a simple simulation program that is able to simulate the expected DNA process during the computational stage.

The Microsoft Visual Basic platform software program developed is able to simulate the POA and PCR physical processes of the computation. The flowchart of the designed software program is shown in Figure 3. It is a simple user friendly program that allows the user to choose between the two processes as shown in Figure 4.

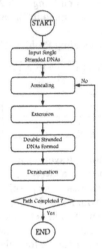

Figure 3 Simulation software flow chart

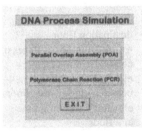

Figure 4 Simulation software process menu

Once the process is chosen, a new menu appears that guides the user to enter the input data, start the simulation process and save the results. For simulation convenience, the weighted graph of Figure 2 is relabeled as shown in Figure 5.

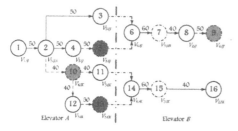

Elevator A | Elevator B

Figure 5 Simulation software weighted graph

The simulation result is stored in the MS Access database and can be manipulated using the MS Excel. The simulation result for the POA and PCR processes of the

problem discussed is shown in Figure 6 and Figure 7 respectively. Here, it can be seen that after 4 cycles of POA, all the possible travel path combinations of the elevator are generated, and the length of the DNA oligos representing the travel time shown. This verifies the theoretical as well as the in vitro experimental result of the problem. Finally, for the PCR simulation process, as expected, after 2 cycles of PCR process, $2^2 = 4$ sequences are replicated that will represent the DNA computational output of the problem.

Path	DNA Sequence	Cycle	Length
1-2	CGGCGGTCCACTAAATACTAaggtcgtttaaggoagtacgCACTCTTTGTGAACGCCTTC	1	60
2-3	CACTCTTTGTGAACGCCTTCgcgtcgcttaccgoagcacgCTATAAGGCCAAAGCAGTCG	1	60
2-4	CACTCTTTGTGAACGCCTTCccgtcggttaagcaagtaatgtactatgcttGAACCGGCCCTTTATATCT	1	70
4-5	TGAACCGGCCCTTTATATCTacgtgtttacccoagtcagTCATTCGAGTTATTCCTGGG	1	60
3-6	CTATAAGGCCAAAGCAGTCGGGGACCTGCATCATACCAGTT	1	40
5-6	TCATTCGAGTTATTCCTGGGGGACCTGCATCATACCAGTT	1	40
6-7	GGACCTGCATCATACCAGTTacgtggtttaaggoagtacggtactatgctAAGCAATGTGGTTGTAGGGA	1	70
7-8	AAGCAATGTGGTTGTAGGGAacgtcgctgcaagoactacgAAAGCCCGTCGGTTAAGTTA	1	60
8-9	AAAGCCCGTCGGTTAAGTTAggtcttttaatcaactaatgGGAATCCATTGATCGCTTTA	1	60
2-10	CACTCTTTGTGAACGCCTTCacgtcgtgtaacgoagtcctGTGGGTTAGAGGTAGTCCGG	1	60
10-11	GTGGGTTAGAGGTAGTCCGGgcgtcttttaATGCCTGGCTAAAGTGAGAC	1	50
10-12	GTGGGTTAGAGGTAGTCCGGcgctcgttgoagccagtaccCCGCTGATCCTTGCTAAGTA	1	60
12-13	CCGCTGATCCTTGCTAAGTAgcggcgtgtcacgoactacgAAATGACCTTTTAACGGCA	1	60
11-14	ATGCCTGGCTAAAGTGAGACTGCACGCAAAACTATTTCAT	1	40
13-14	AAATGACCTTTTAACGGCATGCACGCAAAACTATTTCAT	1	40
14-15	TGCACGCAAAACTATTTCATccgtgggttaaagoagtcctgtactctccttCTGCACTGTTAATGAGCCA	1	70
15-16	TCTGCACTGTTAATGAGCCAacgtcttgtcCTAATTTTAGAAATGGCGCG	1	50
1-2-3-6-7-8	CGGCGGTCCACTAAATACTAaggtcgttta . . . aagoactacgAAAGCCCGTCGGTTAAGTTA	4	210
1-2-4-5-6-7	CGGCGGTCCACTAAATACTAaggtcgttta . . . gtactatgctAAGCAATGTGGTTGTAGGGA	4	220
2-3-6-7-8-9	CACTCTTTGTGAACGCCTTCgcgtcgctta . . . tcaactaatgGGAATCCATTGATCGCTTTA	4	210
2-4-5-6-7-8	CACTCTTTGTGAACGCCTTCccgtcggtta . . . aagoactacgAAAGCCCGTCGGTTAAGTTA	4	220
4-5-6-7-8-9	TGAACCGGCCCTTTATATCTacgtgttta . . . tcaactaatgGGAATCCATTGATCGCTTTA	4	210
1-2-10-11-14-15	CGGCGGTCCACTAAATACTAaggtcgttta . . . gtactctccttCTGCACTGTTAATGAGCCA	4	200
1-2-10-12-13-14	CGGCGGTCCACTAAATACTAaggtcgttta . . . TTTAACGGCATGCACGCAAAACTATTTCAT	4	200
2-10-11-14-15-16	CACTCTTTGTGAACGCCTTCacgtcgtgta . . . acgtcttgtcCTAATTTTAGAAATGGCGCG	4	190
2-10-12-13-14-15	CACTCTTTGTGAACGCCTTCacgtcgtgta . . . gtactctccttCTGCACTGTTAATGAGCCA	4	210
10-12-13-14-15-16	GTGGGTTAGAGGTAGTCCGGcgctcgttga . . . acgtcttgtcCTAATTTTAGAAATGGCGCG	4	200
1-2-3-6-7-8-9	CGGCGGTCCACTAAATACTAaggtcgttta . . . tcaactaatgGGAATCCATTGATCGCTTTA	4	250
1-2-4-5-6-7-8	CGGCGGTCCACTAAATACTAaggtcgttta . . . aagoactacgAAAGCCCGTCGGTTAAGTTA	4	260
2-4-5-6-7-8-9	CACTCTTTGTGAACGCCTTCccgtcggtta . . . tcaactaatgGGAATCCATTGATCGCTTTA	4	260
1-2-10-11-14-15-16	CGGCGGTCCACTAAATACTAaggtcgttta . . . acgtcttgtcCTAATTTTAGAAATGGCGCG	4	230
1-2-10-12-13-14-15	CGGCGGTCCACTAAATACTAaggtcgttta . . . gtactctccttCTGCACTGTTAATGAGCCA	4	250
2-10-12-13-14-15-16	CACTCTTTGTGAACGCCTTCacgtcgtgta . . . acgtcttgtcCTAATTTTAGAAATGGCGCG	4	240
1-2-4-5-6-7-8-9	CGGCGGTCCACTAAATACTAaggtcgttta . . . tcaactaatgGGAATCCATTGATCGCTTTA	4	300
1-2-10-12-13-14-15-16	CGGCGGTCCACTAAATACTAaggtcgttta . . . acgtcttgtcCTAATTTTAGAAATGGCGCG	4	280

Figure 6 POA process simulation showing all the possible travel path combinations

Path	DNA Sequence	Cycle	Length
1-2-3-6-7-8-9	CGGCGGTCCACTAAATACTAagggtcgttta … tcaactaatgGGAATCCATTGATCGCTTTA	1	250
1-2-3-6-7-8-9	CGGCGGTCCACTAAATACTAagggtcgttta … tcaactaatgGGAATCCATTGATCGCTTTA	1	250
1-2-4-5-6-7-8-9	CGGCGGTCCACTAAATACTAagggtcgttta … tcaactaatgGGAATCCATTGATCGCTTTA	1	300
1-2-4-5-6-7-8-9	CGGCGGTCCACTAAATACTAagggtcgttta … tcaactaatgGGAATCCATTGATCGCTTTA	1	300
1-2-10-11-14-15-16	CGGCGGTCCACTAAATACTAagggtcgttta … acgtcttgtcCTAATTTAGAAATGGCGCG	1	230
1-2-10-11-14-15-16	CGGCGGTCCACTAAATACTAagggtcgttta … acgtcttgtcCTAATTTAGAAATGGCGCG	1	230
1-2-10-12-13-14-15-16	CGGCGGTCCACTAAATACTAagggtcgttta … acgtcttgtcCTAATTTAGAAATGGCGCG	1	280
1-2-10-12-13-14-15-16	CGGCGGTCCACTAAATACTAagggtcgttta … acgtcttgtcCTAATTTAGAAATGGCGCG	1	280
1-2-3-6-7-8-9	CGGCGGTCCACTAAATACTAagggtcgttta … tcaactaatgGGAATCCATTGATCGCTTTA	2	250
1-2-3-6-7-8-9	CGGCGGTCCACTAAATACTAagggtcgttta … tcaactaatgGGAATCCATTGATCGCTTTA	2	250
1-2-3-6-7-8-9	CGGCGGTCCACTAAATACTAagggtcgttta … tcaactaatgGGAATCCATTGATCGCTTTA	2	250
1-2-3-6-7-8-9	CGGCGGTCCACTAAATACTAagggtcgttta … tcaactaatgGGAATCCATTGATCGCTTTA	2	250
1-2-4-5-6-7-8-9	CGGCGGTCCACTAAATACTAagggtcgttta … tcaactaatgGGAATCCATTGATCGCTTTA	2	300
1-2-4-5-6-7-8-9	CGGCGGTCCACTAAATACTAagggtcgttta … tcaactaatgGGAATCCATTGATCGCTTTA	2	300
1-2-4-5-6-7-8-9	CGGCGGTCCACTAAATACTAagggtcgttta … tcaactaatgGGAATCCATTGATCGCTTTA	2	300
1-2-4-5-6-7-8-9	CGGCGGTCCACTAAATACTAagggtcgttta … tcaactaatgGGAATCCATTGATCGCTTTA	2	300
1-2-10-11-14-15-16	CGGCGGTCCACTAAATACTAagggtcgttta … acgtcttgtcCTAATTTAGAAATGGCGCG	2	230
1-2-10-11-14-15-16	CGGCGGTCCACTAAATACTAagggtcgttta … acgtcttgtcCTAATTTAGAAATGGCGCG	2	230
1-2-10-11-14-15-16	CGGCGGTCCACTAAATACTAagggtcgttta … acgtcttgtcCTAATTTAGAAATGGCGCG	2	230
1-2-10-11-14-15-16	CGGCGGTCCACTAAATACTAagggtcgttta … acgtcttgtcCTAATTTAGAAATGGCGCG	2	230
1-2-10-12-13-14-15-16	CGGCGGTCCACTAAATACTAagggtcgttta … acgtcttgtcCTAATTTAGAAATGGCGCG	2	280
1-2-10-12-13-14-15-16	CGGCGGTCCACTAAATACTAagggtcgttta … acgtcttgtcCTAATTTAGAAATGGCGCG	2	280
1-2-10-12-13-14-15-16	CGGCGGTCCACTAAATACTAagggtcgttta … acgtcttgtcCTAATTTAGAAATGGCGCG	2	280
1-2-10-12-13-14-15-16	CGGCGGTCCACTAAATACTAagggtcgttta … acgtcttgtcCTAATTTAGAAATGGCGCG	2	280

Figure 7 PCR process simulation for 2 cycles

CONCLUSIONS AND DISCUSSIONS

A proposed method to solve an elevator scheduling problem using DNA computing with an in vitro experiment to verify the expected result has been presented and discussed. In order to assist in designing the oligos for a larger and complex problem, a simulation program capable to simulate the POA and PCR processes is developed. With this successful DNA computing design, in vitro experimental implementation and simulation software to simulate and verify the expected result, the applicability and feasibility of DNA computing approach could therefore be extended into many more complex problems of this type of nature.

REFERENCES

1. L.M. Adleman, "Molecular computation of solutions to combinatorial problems," Science, vol. 266, pp. 1021-1024, 1994.
2. Narayanan, and S. Zorbalas, "DNA algorithms for computing shortest paths," Proceedings of Genetic Programming, pp. 718-723, 1998.
3. Y. Yamamoto, A. Kameda, N. Matsuura, T. Shiba, Y. Kawazoe, and A. Ahochi, "Local search by concentration-controlled DNA computing," International Journal of Computational Intelligence and Applications, vol. 2, pp. 447-455, 2002.
4. J.Y. Lee, S.Y. Shin, S.J. Augh, T.H. Park, and B.T. Zhang, "Temperature gradient-based DNA computing for graph problems with weighted edges," Lecture Notes in Computer Science, Springer-Verlag, vol. 2568, pp. 73-84, 2003.
5. Z. Ibrahim, Y. Tsuboi, O. Ono, and M. Khalid, "Direct-proportional length-based DNA computing for shortest path problem," International Journal of Computer Science and Applications, vol. 1, issue 1, pp. 46-60, 2004.
6. M. S. Muhammad, Z. Ibrahim, O. Ono, and M. Khalid, "Direct-Proportional Length-Based DNA Computing Implementation for Elevator Scheduling Problem", Proceedings of the IEEE International Region 10 Conference (TENCON2005), 2005.
7. F. Udo, S. Sam, B. Wolfgang, and R. Hilmar, "DNA sequence generator: A program for the construction of DNA sequences," Proceedings of the Seventh International Workshop on DNA Based Computers, pp. 23-32, 2001.
8. P.D. Kaplan, Q. Ouyang, D.S. Thaler, and A. Libchaber, "Parallel overlap assembly for the construction of computational DNA libraries," Journal of Theoretical Biology, vol. 188, issue 3, pp. 333-341, 1997.
9. J.Y. Lee, H.W. Lim, S.I. Yoo, B.T. Zhang, and T.H. Park, "Efficient initial pool generation for weighted graph problems using parallel overlap assembly," Preliminary Proceeding of the 10th International Meeting on DNA Computing, pp. 357-364, 2004.
10. J. P. Fitch, Engineering Introduction to Biotechnology, SPIE Press, 2001.
11. G. Paun, G. Rozenberg, and A. Salomaa, "DNA computing: New computing paradigms," Lecture Notes in Computer Science, Springer-Verlag, vol. 1644, pp. 106-118, 1998.

Exploring an Online Method of Vehicle Route Planning for Low Altitude Flight

XIA Jie, GAO Jinyuan, CHEN Zongji

Department of Automatic Control, BeiHang University,
Beijing, 100083, China
(E-mail: xiaj@buaa.edu.cn)

ABSTRACT

In this paper, an online method of vehicle route planning for low altitude flight is presented. The route divides into three segments: glide, low altitude follow and climb. By using the uniform down velocity method, an elementary route could be obtained in glide segment. The fastest up algorithm is used to plan the elementary route in climb segment,. These routes are modified with the altitude beneath the elementary routes. In the low altitude follow segment, an elementary route can be obtained by used of the improved grid A* heuristics search algorithm. In the algorithm, using bevel-length as the heuristic factor could reduce the searching area and raise the searching rate. Simulation results are presented which prove that the algorithm is effective.

KEY WORDS: real-time planning, route planning, low altitude flight, heuristics algorithm

INTRODUCTION

The low flight security is ensured by terrain following which reduces the probability coming to light and enhance the unmanned aerial vehicle (UAV) system efficiency. For this reason, the low flight mode is often used in modern aerial defense [1]. The motivation of route planning for low altitude flight is to maximally used terrain and environment, considerate the UAV maneuverability, plan a route with maximum survival probability [2].

The general process of low altitude flight for UAV is: (1) gliding down to an appointed clearance height; (2) terrain follow, terrain avoidance and threat avoidance; (3) climb up to a suitable height for next mission. The route planning for low altitude flight divides into three segments: glide, low altitude follow and climb.

Each segment has different motivation which leads to use different planning method. These methods were synthesized to generate whole low altitude flight route. Several plan routes and one track course were given at the end of the paper.

GLIDE SEGMENT PLAN

The motivation of this segment is to enter the low altitude safely and rapidly. A lot of factors should be considerate, which include original flight direction, permitted descend speed, roll angle limit and terrain beneath the route.

Glide segment divides to two sections: glide and level-off. In glide section, the vehicle works with minimums thrust. In level-off section, the vehicle works with normal thrust in low altitude. The terrain only affects in the last part of the glide and the level-off section.

In order to assure the longitudinal maneuverability in glide segment, the lateral maneuverability should be strictly limited.

Combined the permitted descend speed, the uniform down velocity method is used to control the vehicle glide from high to low altitude. We can get the relationship among the height, speed in high altitude and the length which needs for the vehicle to glide. The glide section elementary route can be planed as a line whose length is determined by this relationship.

Bases on the vehicle's longitudinal load limit, we obtain the longitudinal minimize radius Rgmin which can be used to plan the route of level-off section. The glide segment route was shown in Fig.1. Furthermore, a simplification can be made which leads to the glide route becomes a fold line, shown in Fig.2.

The clearance between elementary route and terrain should be checked carefully. If the clearance is less than the expect clearance, the elementary route should run-up which leads to final glide route.

LOW ALTITUDE FOLLOWING SEGMENT PLAN

In this segment, the vehicle has the original flight direction and exiting direction. The motivation of this segment is to plan a 3D flyable route with terrain follow, terrain avoidance and threat avoidance.

An elementary route can be obtained by used of the improved grid A* heuristics search algorithm. The maneuverability is used to smooth the route in horizontal plane and in longitudinal plane.

Plan elementary route for low altitude

The based idea of the A* search algorithm is to design an appropriate heuristics function and evaluate the cost of each node to be expanded [3]. The node with the least cost should be expanded. This process went on until the target node is expanded.

The evaluating cost of node m can be written as

$$f(m) = g(m) + h(m) \qquad (1)$$

where $g(m)$ is the real minimize cost from the start to m, $h(m)$ is heuristics cost from m to the target.

The plan route should be terrain avoiding, atrocious weather avoiding and threat avoiding. The used fuel corresponds to the flight length, so the consume fuel can convert to the function of the flight length.

Suppose the real minimize cost route from the start to m pasts through n, then $g(m)$ can be written as

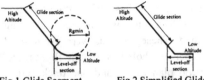

Fig.1 Glide Segment   Fig.2 Simplified Glide
Elementary Route   Segment Route

$$g(m) = g(n) + k_1 P_{th}(m) + k_2 D_n(m) + k_3 H(m)$$

$$(2)$$

where $g(n)$ is the real minimize route cost from the start to n. $P_{th}(m)$ is the probability attacked by weapons and fatal flight in atrocious weather during the route from n to m. $D_n(m)$ is the minimize cost route length from n to m. $H(m)$ is the altitude of the landform which can be obtained from numerical-map. $k_i(i = 1,2,3)$ is the weight for above item.

The acceptance of A* search algorithm can be express as

$$h(m) \le h_{\min}(m) \qquad (3)$$

Where $h_{\min}(m)$ is the minimize cost from m to the target and $h(m)$ is defined above.

The heuristics cost from m to the target was common abstained as

$$h(m) = \mu \cdot D_2(m) \qquad (4)$$

where $D_2(m)$ is the distance from m to the target.

When grid A* algorithm is realized, all the calculated nodes and expanded nodes are grid nodes. Hence, the shortest length from the calculate node to the target node is calculated alone grid line or grid diagonal. The shortest length is not equal to the distance.

Definition: the shortest length between two nodes is their bevel-length, which denote as D_{bevel}.

For square grid, we denote the bevel-length between node (x_i, y_i) and node (x_j, y_j) as $D_{bevel}(i,j)$, which can be expressed according to the following equations:

$$L_{\min}(i,j) = \min\{| x_i - x_j |, | y_i - y_j |\}$$

$$L_{\max}(i,j) = \max\{| x_i - x_j |, | y_i - y_j |\}$$

$$D_{bevel}(i,j) = [L_{\max}(i,j) - L_{\min}(i,j)] + \sqrt{2} \cdot L_{\min}(i,j) \qquad (5)$$

It is showed that the shortest route length is the bevel-length between start and target without any threat and atrocious weather.

The bevel-length from m to the target denotes as $D_{bevel}(m)$, which can be used to modify Eq.(4). Then,

$$h(m) = \mu \cdot D_{bevel}(m) \qquad (6)$$

It is evidence that using bevel-length to instead of distance could satisfy the acceptance of A* search algorithm, improve the heuristics cost, reduce the searching area and raise the searching rate.

In order to satisfy the limits of original direction and exiting direction, we add three virtual threat circles with high cost in the opposite direction (shown in Fig.3 and Fig.4)[4].

Fig.3 virtual circles for original direction

Fig.4 virtual circles for exiting direction

The radius of virtual circle equals to minimum flyable radius which correspond to the lateral maneuverability. Thus, the plan route avoids these virtual threats and would be flyable.

The Eq.(4) could modify as follows

$$g(m) = g(n) + k_1 P_{th}(m) + k_2 D_n(m) \\ + k_3 H(m) + k_4 Vir(m) \qquad (7)$$

Based on the A* algorithm with Eqs.(5)-(7) and (1), a elementary route for low altitude flight could be easily made out which takes into account the environment and terrain for the vehicle.

Smooth the route

Flight at low altitude needs a refine route. In most occasions, the distance between two border points is less than 300 m. Route smoother works in two aspects: longitudinal plane and horizontal plane.

Base on the lateral maneuverability, we can get the minimum flyable radius. The lateral smoother works with the minimum flyable circle to adjust the elementary route in the lateral plane. By used of the lateral smoother, we obtain a route satisfied lateral maneuverability.

The elementary route in height is not smooth as it follows the landform of the rugged earth. The correctional route in height is adjusted based on the longitudinal characteristic of the vehicle.

CLIMB SEGMENT PLAN

In this segment, the vehicle climbs to the demanded height with maximum thrust. The motivation for this segment is to fleetly climb up under the condition of limited power and the characteristic of the vehicle.

In this segment, an elementary route can obtain based on the fastest up algorithm[5]. The relationship between the climb height and speed could be obtained off-line which determined by the flight characters (especially the power) of the vehicle. This relationship is used to guide the climb planning. The altitude beneath the elementary route should be considerate. A suitability raise in height may be done to improve the security for this segment which leads to final climb route. In order to assure the longitudinal maneuverability, the lateral maneuverability should be strictly limited.

SIMULATION RESULTS

The algorithm is programmed with VC++ and runs in PC with 2.4GHz processor. Each planning time is less than 2 seconds. We describe the threat as a circle in horizontal plane. Two simulation examples are provided to illustrate the plan routes for low altitude flight. These examples were produced in the globe longitude latitude reference frame. The first example has 5 threats located in plan range and the result shows in Fig.5 and Fig.6. In Fig.6, S is the start point and T is the target point. The second example's result shows in Fig.7. Fig.8 gives a plan route and its tracking course.

CONCLUSIONS

In this paper, an online method of vehicle route planning for low altitude flight is presented. By using bevel-length as the heuristic factor, the grid A* heuristics search algorithm reduces the searching area and raise the searching rate. Adding virtual threat circles helps to satisfy the limits of original direction and exiting direction. Simulation results validate that the algorithm is effective. The planning time is not more than 2 seconds which means the algorithm could run in real-time. Track flight experiment shows that the planning route is flyable.

REFERENCES

1. QIU Xiaohong. Research on Core Technology for Tactical Mission Integrated Flight Management System. Beijing: Beijing University of Aeronautics and Astronautics, 1995(in China)
2. LI Qing, GAO Pan, SHEN Chunlin, Design of TF/TA2 Flight Control System--Problems and Methods, Journal of Nanjing University of Aeronautics and Astronautics, 1998, 30-5,pp.562-568
3. Iris Hong Yangy, Yiyuan J. Zhao, Real-time trajectory planning for autonomous aerospace vehicles amidst static obstacles[J] , AIAA-2002-3421, University of Minnesota, Minneapolis, MN 55455
4. XIA Jie , GAO Jin-yuan ,Real-Time Flight Path Planning for Combat Mission, Journal of Beijing University of Aeronautics and Astronautics, 2004, 30-2,pp.95-99
5. ZHANG Minglian, Flight Control System, Beijing Aeronautics industry Press, 1994(in China)

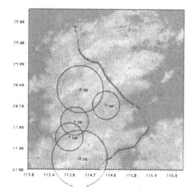

Fig.5 Plan route 1 in horizontal plane

Fig.6 Plan route 1 in 3D

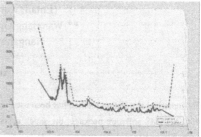

Fig.7 Plan route 2

Fig. 8   Plan route and track course

Numerical Simulation for an Automotive Shock Absorber and Its Integration into Vehicle Virtual Prototype

Weiqun REN*, Sheng HUANG* and Jie ZHANG**

* CAD Center, School of Mechanical Science and Engineering
Huazhong University of Science and Technology
Wuhan 430074, China
(Email: wqrencn@yahoo.com)
** Wanxiang Group Technology Center
Hangzhou 311215, China

ABSTRACT

The numerical simulation method has been used to build a detailed model of an automotive shock absorber. In MSC.ADAMS software package, the shock absorber model has been built using ADAMS/Hydraulics. The model has been validated using test data and the precision is above 90%, which can fulfill the engineering requirement. The model has been integrated into a full vehicle virtual prototype, which can support a systematic research for the effects of shock absorber on full vehicle behaviors.

KEY WORDS: Automotive shock absorber, Numerical simulation, Vehicle virtual prototype, MSC.ADAMS

INTRODUCTION

The design of an automotive shock absorber, especially its functional aspect, plays a very important role in vehicle dynamics behaviors, such as ride and handling. Traditional method for the absorber design is apt to an empirical one. Designers make sure the absorber design parameters using their experience, and the physical prototype of the absorber has been made out to test its performance and its effect for the full vehicle dynamics behaviors. This empirical method based on physical prototypes is more time-consuming, and the high cost process cannot get the optimized design.

Therefore numerical simulation method becomes an indispensable methodology for analyzing, predicting, optimizing and assessing the absorber's dynamics performance, especially its damping behavior. The modeling method includes the "Black- box model" based on the relation between the input and the output [1, 2], and the detailed mechanism model based on the inner structure [3, 4]. The simulation can be finished before the physical prototype is built up, which can reduce the time and the cost and can give a clue to a more rational design for the shock absorber furthermore.

While MSC.ADAMS is widely used in vehicle dynamics simulation, the absorber modeling should use a similar method so that it can be integrated into the full vehicle model and the effect of its structure parameters on vehicle behaviors can be assessed directly. Here the shock absorber model has been built using ADAMS/ Hydraulics so as to be integrated into the full vehicle ADAMS model conveniently. The implementation of the absorber model is supported by Wanxiang Group Companies, one of the most famous Chinese automotive component manufacturers. The numerical simulation approach is used on Wanxiang absorbers' development for the front suspension of a certain Chinese brand compact car.

1 SHOCK ABSORBER STRUCTURE AND WORKING PROCESS

An automotive shock absorber is typically a hydraulic system, shown as Figure 1. It includes the damping fluid, three basic chambers for holding the fluid, and some valve sets between the chambers. The basic chambers include the upper chamber I, the lower chamber II and the equivalent chamber III. The reserve valve set between chamber I and II include the reserve valve and the flow valve. The flowing area includes these two valve orifice (A5_15, A19), two set of notches in valve seat (A20, A21) and the open orifice of the valves under the flowing pressure (A_{res}, A_{flow}). The compression valve set between chamber II and III include the compression valve and the equivalent valve. The flowing area includes these two valve orifice (A1_4,

A16), two set of notches in valve seat (A17, A18) and the open orifice of the valves under the flowing pressure (A_{comp}, A_{equ}).

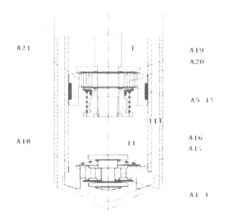

Figure 1 An automotive shock absorber's basic structure

The shock absorber's working process includes two cases. (a) When the valve piston moves down, the fluid flows from chamber II to I, and some leakage fluid flows from II to III. At this time the compression valve (A_{comp} and A1_4) and the flow valve (A_{flow} and A19) open. (b) When the valve piston moves up, the fluid flows from chamber I to II, and some equivalent fluid flows from III to II. At this time the reserve valve (A_{res} and A5_15) and the equivalent valve (A_{equ} and A16) open. In these two cases, different flowing path due to different valve sets opening makes the damping force different. This is the hysteretic characteristics for the damping force.

2 SHOCK ABSORBER MODELING

From the basic structure above, some assumptions are made before modeling. The flowing is assumed to be quasi-static, and the pressure inside the chambers is assumed to be uniform. The chamber wall's flexibility, the heat transfer and the leakage due to the piston pole are ignored. is also ignored. Then the shock absorber can be expressed as a physical model in Figure 2. It includes mechanical system (the basic chambers and the piston, etc.) and hydraulic system (the damping fluid and the valve sets, etc.).

orifices or notches opening constantly can be modeled as laminar orifices. The hydraulic system connected to the mechanical system, and the numerical simulation model is shown as Figure 3.

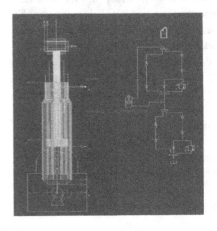

Figure 3   The numerical simulation model of the shock absorber

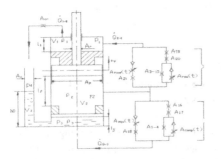

Figure 2   The physical model of the shock absorber

This physical model can be easily transferred into MSC.ADAMS software package. The mechanical system can be modeled as parts and constraints. And the movement of the piston can be expressed as MOTION for the translational joint between the joint and the chamber wall. Using ADAMS/ Hydraulics plug-in, the hydraulic system can be modeled as fluid, cylinders and valve sets. The valves which can just open in one direction under the flowing pressure (in case a, A_{comp}, A_{flow} and case b, A_{res}, A_{equ}) can be modeled as check valves or pressure relief valves. The other

This numerical simulation model can be used for predicting the damping force as a function of the absorber's displacement and velocity. This model can relate the model inner components' parameters, such as valve opening area and valve stiffness, directly to the absorber's damping force behavior. It can provide the necessary insight in the absorber physics and can be easily integrated into a full vehicle model.

3 MODEL VALIDATIONS

The shock absorber model should be validated by the experimental data. The experiment has performed in a dynamometer (such as MTS 849 shock absorber test rig) with different frequencies, and the damping force has been recorded in the real test as a function of the absorber's displacement and velocity. After that a virtual test has been performed under the same boundary condition as in real test. The damping force simulation result related with the displacement and velocity has been compared to the real test result. The virtual test result is shown as Figure 4.

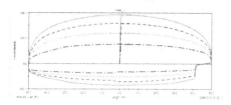

Figure 4 Simulation result in different frequencies (10.4Hz, 7.8Hz, 5.2Hz, 2.6Hz)

The comparing of the max and min value between the test data and the simulation result is shown as Table 1.

Table 1 Compare for the test and the simulation result

		Simula-tion	Test	Relative error%
10.4	Max	962.86	959.08	0.39%
	Min	422.26	409.12	3.21%
7.8	Max	789.00	762.12	3.53%
	Min	358.64	365.79	2.00%
5.2	Max	598.98	565.73	5.88%
	Min	269.41	280.40	3.92%
2.6	Max	373.20	340.95	9.46%
	Min	186.70	172.21	8.41%

As shown above, the simulation result has good agreement with that of the test data. Thus the engineering accuracy of the numerical simulation model can be validated. The effectiveness and practicability of the model can also be made sure.

4 INTEGRATING THE SHOCK ABSORBER MODEL INTO THE FULL VEHICLE MODEL

The validated absorber model can be implemented in the full vehicle simulation. The full vehicle virtual prototype has been built up based on the Multi-Body System dynamics theory and the corresponding software packages MSC.ADAMS. As the shock absorber model is also built up in MSC.ADAMS, it can be integrated into the full vehicle ADAMS model conveniently. The full vehicle virtual prototype with the absorber's ADAMS/Hydraulics model is shown as Figure 5.

Figure 5 The full vehicle virtual prototype with the shock absorber model

Then the full vehicle virtual prototype with the absorber model can be used for the measure of ride and handling. For example, the vehicle virtual prototype runs along a give stochastic road surface, and the virtual proving ground simulation can be run for assessing the ride behavior. The vehicle body acceleration and its power spectrum density can be used for the measurement.

Using the full vehicle virtual prototype with the absorber model, the vehicle behavior can be related directly to the absorber's inner parameters, such as the valve opening area, valve stiffness and inner spring stiffness. Thus the shock absorber parameters can be optimized facing to improve the vehicle behavior. The vehicle ride behavior (i.e. vehicle body acceleration) can be set as the design objective, and the absorber parameters (i.e. valve opening area, valve stiffness and inner spring stiffness) can be set as the design variables. Then the absorber parameters can be optimized to obtain better ride properties, using ADAMS/ Insight as a helpful optimization tool.

As the shock absorber model is integrated into the full vehicle virtual prototype, its inner parameters are optimized directly in the full vehicle level context. From these results, the vehicle behavior can be characterized directly by the absorber's inner parameters. The full vehicle level simulation can give some penetrated guidance for shock absorber design.

5 CONCLUSION

(1) The numerical simulation method and MSC.ADAMS software package can be used to build a detailed model of an automotive shock absorber efficiently and conveniently.

(2) The model precision can fulfill the engineering requirement, which has been validated using test data.

(3) The model can be integrated into a full vehicle virtual prototype conveniently. And the systematic research for the effects of shock absorber on full vehicle behaviors is helpful for the absorber design.

REFERENCES

1 Duym, S., Schoukens, J., Guillaume, P.. A local restoring force surface method[C]//Proceedings of the 13th International Modal Analysis Conference. Nashville, Tennessee, 1995: 1392-1399.

2 Fash, J.. Modeling of shock absorber behaviour using artificial neural networks [C]//SAE paper 940248, 1994.

3 Duym, S.. Simulation tools, modeling and identification, for an automotive shock absorber in the context of vehicle dynamics [J]. Vehicle System Dynamics (ISSN 0042-3114), 2000, 33: 261-285.

4 Herr, F., Mallin, T., Roth, S.. A shock absorber model using CFD analysis and Easy5[C]//SAE Steering and Suspension Technology Symposium. 1999: 267-281

Mission Planning Integrating in
UAV Synthetic Simulation Environment (UAVSSE)

WU Jiang*, CHEN Zongji*

* School of Automation Science and Electrical Engineering
Beijing University of Aeronautics and Astronautics
Beijing, China, 100083
(E-mail: wujiang@buaa.edu.cn)

ABSTRACT

A service oriented method is presented to the mission planning integrating in the context of UAVSEE which is a System-of-Systems (SoS) simulation environment for Unmanned Air Vehicles (UAVs). The architecture of UAVSSE is introduced, and an integrating framework based on SOA (service oriented architecture) is designed to integrate common mission planning for the simulated vehicle and ground control system in UAVSEE. Mission planning module is abstracted as a service, and encapsulated as common mission planning service through Web Services technology. Planning function can be dynamically integrated in simulation without changing other systems, and one planning system simultaneously can serve multi vehicles and ground control systems in simulation. At last, related technologies are demonstrated through prototype simulation system. The experimental result shows that service oriented integrating of mission planning will provide more efficient and effective integrating ability for UAVs simulation.

KEY WORDS: Service oriented architecture (SOA), Mission planning, Integrating framework, Simulation

INTRODUCTION

The challenge for UAV implementation recently raises the need for intelligent functionality of UAV systems. The difference between conventional and developing UAVs is the autonomy mission ability that means the UAVs can accomplish the task according to pilot's mission instruction automatically, other than controlled by pilot all the time. Therefore, the mission planning/replanning research need some simulation means to test and demonstrate their imagines and techniques before flight testing.

Much discussion has focused on the need of using simulation to assess UAV technologies and simulation tools [1][2]. Through modeling and simulating, we can demonstrate methods and algorithms in studying of UAV autonomy mission ability. The UAVs simulation should provide an integrating technique, in order to enable the UAVs' researchers to dynamically configure mission planning and implementing model of UAV. Mission planning function should be integrated as parts of UAV ground control system into a simulation system to view the UAV's functional status and mission result.

This paper focuses on UAVs mission planning simulation integrating in UAVSSE, which is a SoS simulation environment for multi UAVs. A method of service oriented integrating is presented in the context of the previously mentioned simulation environment. Necessary and feasibility of service integrating method on heterogeneous systems and simulations are analyzed.

OVERVIEW OF UAVSSE INTEGRATING

UAV Synthetic Simulation Environment

UAVSSE is a composiable simulation environment for UAVs, in which UAVs researchers can dynamically visualize the result and effect of their algorithms and designs. It can provide possible solutions for UAVs simulation requirements and infrastructures to compose a system or mission level simulation.

UAV is considered as the complex system with characteristics of SoS, UAVSSE also has the characteristic of SoS.

UAVSSE is combined with a set of element systems which can implement a self-contain and complete function of simulation. Each element system is also combined with a set of simulation components, model, or real system, some of which are inherited and developed for different purpose, with different development team, in different development environment. Thus the UAVSSE is inherently a heterogeneous and loosely coupled system.

We designed the hybrid infrastructure architecture for UAVSSE, which can make inter-system and intra-system communication adapt to element systems interactive specifications. The architecture can provide a common backplane that allows "plug-and-play" UAV simulations from various sources for algorithms demonstration, simulation result visualization, data access and management for simulated or real UAV flight control, etc. The architecture and interaction mechanism of UAVSSE can support simulations with HLA/RTI based federates and other communication infrastructure. The proposed architecture uses a number of components and interfaces. Standards are needed for the architecture, interaction, and formats of text and graphics files. Figure 1 depicts the architecture of UAVSSE.

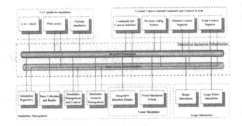

Figure 1 Architecture of UAVSSE

Integrating methods in UAVSSE

Different simulation systems and components need different integrating methods to make them parts of the whole simulation environment. Three levels of systems integrating methods are adapted in UAVSSE , including: code module or programmed segment integrating; component integrating; system or simulation integrating. Figure 2 illustrates the hierarchy integrating framework.

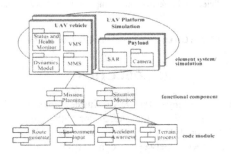

Figure 2 Three levels integrating in UAVSSE

Code module/programmed segment integrating: Some basic algorithms are packaged with program code module to provide the necessary structural elements for other simulation components. For example, route planning is a basic module in mission planning algorithm component.

Component integrating: Component integrating is to deal with kinds of software wrappers, some of which wraps third-party software component as a function

194

component of simulation. For example, some vehicle simulations are provided by different vehicle dynamics models, mostly encapsulated into COMs or DLLs. UAV platform simulation program can dynamically configure different COM or DLL to construct different UAV vehicle models.

System/simulation integrating: According to simulation scenarios, different element systems can be composed into a specific simulation execution.

Previous mission planning in UAVSSE mainly be integrated into UAV vehicle simulation as a code module or component, because the researchers need to survey whether the algorithm support the vehicle flight effectively. However, current interests of UAV system research need the mission planning system can be dynamically tailored to satisfy different algorithm complication. For example, both vehicle and its ground control station (GCS) have a mission planning element system, and each mission planning system may obtain different situation input. On the other hand, mission planning system of GCS may be developed as an independent mission planning system to provide preplanned mission information for multi UAV vehicles or GCS. A uniform integrating module of mission planning in a UAV simulation is quite appropriate.

Although High Level Architecture (HLA) succeeded in salvaging reuse and interoperability of simulations, it is not obvious that HLA is the best solution for the new need. The main problem HLA must be faced with in UAVSSE is about SoS system integrating, such as integrating of mission planning/replanning element system, as well as integrating real system (GCS segment) with UAV simulation. We adopt service oriented mechanism to organize and combine systems/simulations similar with mission planning.

MISSION PLANNING SERVICE

Mission Planning
Simulated UAVs should track the route and execute tasks according to the planning result. GCS and UAV vehicle need the result of planning/replanning result, not the computing capability of planning. Both on-board Mission Management System (MMS) and GCS need mission planning and replanning function. "Planning" and "Replanning" call the same planning algorithm component with different parameters. Therefore, relative algorithms of mission planning can be abstracted as an independent planning service to provide common mission planning system.

Service Oriented method in mission planning integrating
As a part of technology and methodology orientations in the evolution of UAVSSE, service oriented paradigm, namely SOA, is adopted to address high level system integrating.

SOA is business process centric rather than technology centric, a service usually represents a business task. A formal definition of service is "a contractually defined behavior that can be provided by a component for use by any component, solely based on the interface contract"[3]. By adopting standard architecture, interactive mechanism, interface, and protocols of SOA, mission planning/replanning function module can be decupled with UAV platform and GCS applications, and can be easily integrated of individual and common Mission Planning Console in GCS in future.

In a system of SOA, each component or participant may play three possible rules: services consumer, services provider and services broker/registry. Service provider is discovered dynamically from a service Registry rather than statically coded in the client program.

In UAVSSE, a mission planning service is a logical component or application with well-defined interface, which can provide planning computing capability to other elements of simulation. Mission planning service is also a paradigm of system of systems integrating. Planning function is abstracted as a service, and interactive entities are abstracted as consumer or provider. The mission planning service paradigm in UAVSSE is shown in figure 3.

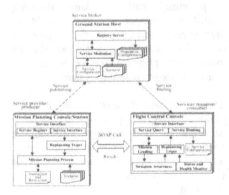

Figure 3 Mission planning service paradigm

Planning service integrated in UAVSSE make the nodes of simulation system exchange high level service or function rather than low level data each other. SOA provides UAV simulation application with certain architectural characteristics and benefits: 1) providing location independence, i.e. services need not be associated with a particular system on a particular network; 2) protocol-independent communication framework; 3) offering better adaptability and faster response rate for changing simulation mission or composing; 4) loosely coupled system architecture allows easily integrating by operational UAVs applications; 5) easily constructing large scale UAVs simulation, etc.

SERVICE INTEGRATION OF MISSION SYSTEM

Mission planning service implementation
We will go through three phases of service oriented integrating in UAVSSE in order to ensure validity of new methods. In first phase, we have achieved binding mission planning service to the GCS through a registry server. Now, we are ongoing the exploration of automatically combining of multi service roles, such as multi GCSs and UAV vehicles. In the future, publish/subscribe mechanism will be adopted for service combination.

Protocols and interactions adapted in Mission planning service
Different standards may be used for implementation of service oriented applications. Web Services technology is the adopted technology of SOA based integrating in UAVSSE, which consists of a group of communication and interoperability protocols, including HTTP, XML, SOAP, WDSL, UDDI, etc.. Service developing in UAVSSE is implemented with Microsoft.Net platform.
In first phase, we designed different "service interface" module for planning requester and producer application in UAVSSE. Service interface is a "shell" or middle layer between mission planning logical components and communication infrastructure. The layered framework is designed to construct service interface application, as shown in figure 4.

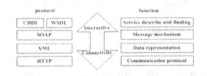

Figure 4 Protocols adopted in UAVSSE planning service

Typical interaction procedure of mission planning in UAVSSE using standard protocols is shown in figure 5.

Figure 5 Typical planning procedure

Simulation demonstration

The prototype system configuration for mission planning in simulation is shown in figure 6.

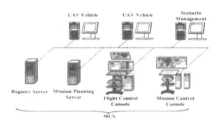

Figure 6 Element systems in prototype simulation

Mission planning server runs Windows XP IIS. Registry server runs Windows 2003 UDDI. Screen capture of GCS is shown in figure 7. Planning result derived from a mission planning server is to upload to vehicle before mission starting. Mission execution is presented in a scrolling map interface.

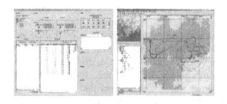

Figure 7 Mission result from planning server in GCS

Screen capture of UAV interface is shown in figure 8. The planning result may be downloaded from GCS, and also can be derived from a mission planning server.

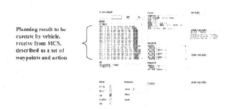

Figure 8 Mission result executed by vehicle

CONCLUSION AND FUTURE WORK

Simulation practice demonstrated that service oriented method can provide a mechanism for integrating multi level mission planning into UAVSSE, and support common mission planning system integrating in simulation. The result and experiences should provide strategy and reference for future UAVs distributed simulation.

Future work on UAVSSE will include self-combining service integrating, and the methods necessary to allow real systems be integrated into UAVSSE as specific simulation services.

REFERENCES

1. Erik D. Jones, Randy S. Roberts, T.C.Steve Hsia, STOMP: A Software Architecture for the Design and Simulation of UAV-based Sensor Networks, Proceedings of the 2003 IEEE International Conference on Robotics & Automatics, Taipei, Taiwan, September 14-19, 2003.
2. S. Rasmussen and P. Chandler, MultiUAV: A Multiple UAV Simulation for Investigation of Cooperative Control, Proceedings of the 2002 Winter Simulation Conference, San Diego, CA, December 2002.
3. Global Information Grid Core Enterprise Services Strategy, Draft Version 1.1a, Office of the Assistant Secretary of Defense for Network and Information Integration/DoD Chief Information Offer, 2003.

A Multi-crossover Genetic Algorithm for Parameters Estimation of a Two-link Robot

Jian Liung CHEN* and Wei-Der CHANG**

*Department of Electrical Engineering
Kao Yuan University
Kaohsiung 821, Taiwan
(E-mail: clchen@cc.kyu.edu.tw)
** Department of Computer and Communication
Shu-Te University
Kaohsiung 824, Taiwan
(E-mail: wdchang@mail.stu.edu.tw)

Abstract

In this paper, we propose a novel multi-crossover genetic algorithm (GA) to identify the system parameters of a two-link robot. It is well known that the ordinary form of GA used for solving a given optimization problem is a binary encoding during operating procedures. However, our proposed algorithm is different from the binary GA, which is a real-valued encoding. It is more suitable to directly represent genes as real values for most of real optimization problems during genetic operations. Finally, the simulation result will be illustrated to show that the more accurate estimations can be achieved by using our proposed method.

KEY WORDS: System identification, Parameters estimation, Multiple crossover, Real-coded genetic algorithm

INTRODUCTION

The work of system identification is very important and essential for the control system engineering. According to a known mathematical or an estimated model for system, a controller will then be designed by using a lot of different control techniques such that the certain output response of system can be satisfied. The mathematical representation of a two-link robot is a highly nonlinear dynamic equation. Under many physical situations, exact mathematical models can't be easily obtained especially for the system parameters of a two-link robot. In the paper, a multi-crossover genetic algorithm (GA) is developed for identifying system parameters of a two-link robot.

The GA method has been proven as a powerful tool for solving optimal or near optimal solution for an given optimization problem [1,2,3]. It provides better searching capability over the traditional gradient method. Because the gradient method searches for a problem solution only from a single direction, while GA method is from multiple directions due to its crossover and mutation operations. This means that it is highly possible to escape from a local minimum [4]. In the binary GA [5,6], all parameters of interest must be encoded as binary digits (genes) and then collect these binary digits to be a string (chromosome). In contrast to the binary GA, another kind of real-coded GA has been also introduced to a wide variety of applications as in [7,8,9]. All genes in the chromosome are now encoded as real numbers. For most real optimization problems, this type of real-coded GA has more advantages over the conventional binary GA. For example, the length of a chromosome used in the real-coded GA becomes much shorter than that of the binary GA, and it is easier to implement the real-coded GA into the computer programs.

Unlike the general crossover operation by using two chromosomes, a multi-crossover operation will be proposed in this paper. We use the improved real-coded GA to identify the system parameters of a two-link robot. All of unknown parameters are collected as a chromosome, and a population of these chromosomes will be evolved by using genetic operations of reproduction, multiple crossover, and mutation.

PROBLEM FORMULATION

Consider the nonlinear dynamic equation for a two-link robot [10], which is shown in Fig. 1, described as follow

$$M(\theta)\ddot{\theta} + N(\theta,\dot{\theta}) + G(\theta) = \tau. \qquad (1)$$

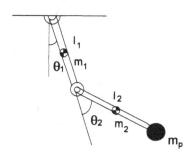

Figure1: A two-link robot system.

Note that,

$\theta = [\theta_1, \theta_2]^T$ is the output vector,

$\tau = [\tau_1 \ \tau_2]^T$ is the two-dimensional torque input vector,

$M(\theta) = \begin{bmatrix} M_1 & M_2 \\ M_2^T & M_4 \end{bmatrix}$ is the symmetric inertia

matrix and is the positive definition for all $\theta \in \Re^2$, which

$$M_1 = \tfrac{1}{3}m_1 l_1^2 + \tfrac{1}{2}m_2 l_2^2 + m_2(l_1^2 + \tfrac{1}{4}l_2^2) + m_p(l_1^2 + l_2^2) + (m_2 + 2m_p)l_1 l_2 \cos\theta_2$$

$$M_2 = \tfrac{1}{2}m_2 l_2^2 + \tfrac{1}{4}m_2 l_2^2 + m_p l_2^2 + \tfrac{1}{2}(m_2 + 2m_p)l_1 l_2 \cos\theta_2$$

$$M_4 = \tfrac{1}{2}m_2 l_2^2 + \tfrac{1}{4}m_2 l_2^2 + m_p l_2^2$$

$N(\theta,\dot{\theta}) = [N_1 \ N_2]^T$ accounts for centrifugal and Coriolis forces, which

$$N_1 = -(m_2 + 2m_p)l_1 l_2 \dot{\theta}_1 \dot{\theta}_2 \sin\theta_2 - \tfrac{1}{2}(m_2 + 2m_p)l_1 l_2 \dot{\theta}_2^2 \sin\theta_2$$

$$N_2 = (\tfrac{1}{2}m_2 + m_p)l_1 l_2 \dot{\theta}_1 \sin\theta_2$$

$G(\theta) = [G_1 \ G_2]^T$ accounts for gravity forces, which

$$G_1 = (\tfrac{1}{2}m_1 l_1 + m_2 l_2 + m_p l_1)g \sin\theta_1 + (\tfrac{1}{2}m_2 l_2 + m_p l_2)g \sin(\theta_1 + \theta_2)$$

$$G_2 = (\tfrac{1}{2}m_2 + m_p)l_2 \, g \sin(\theta_1 + \theta_2).$$

For convenience, let

$$[x_1 \ x_2 \ x_3 \ x_4] = [\theta_1 \ \dot{\theta}_1 \ \theta_2 \ \dot{\theta}_2].$$

Since $M(\theta)$ is the positive definition for all $\theta \in \Re^2$, we set

$$M^{-1}(\theta) = \begin{bmatrix} M_1 & M_2 \\ M_2^T & M_4 \end{bmatrix}^{-1} = \begin{bmatrix} \varphi_1 & \varphi_2 \\ \varphi_2^T & \varphi_4 \end{bmatrix}.$$

The nonlinear dynamic equation of (1) can be represented as the state equation

$$\begin{bmatrix} \dot{x}_1 \\ \dot{x}_2 \\ \dot{x}_3 \\ \dot{x}_4 \end{bmatrix} = \begin{bmatrix} x_2 \\ -\varphi_1(N_1 + G_1) - \varphi_2(N_2 + G_2) \\ x_4 \\ -\varphi_2^T(N_1 + G_1) - \varphi_4(N_2 + G_2) \end{bmatrix} + \begin{bmatrix} 0 & 0 \\ \varphi_1 & \varphi_2 \\ 0 & 0 \\ \varphi_2^T & \varphi_4 \end{bmatrix}\tau \qquad (2)$$

and output equation

$$\begin{bmatrix} y_1 \\ y_2 \end{bmatrix} = \begin{bmatrix} 1 & 0 & 0 & 0 \\ 0 & 0 & 1 & 0 \end{bmatrix} \begin{bmatrix} x_1 \\ x_2 \\ x_3 \\ x_4 \end{bmatrix}.$$

In this paper, we use the novel multi-crossover genetic algorithm to identify the system parameters $(l_1,\ l_2,\ m_1,\ m_2)$ of a two-link robot.

A MULTI-CROSSOVER GENETIC COMPUTATION

To describe our proposed modified real-coded GA, let $\Gamma = [\gamma_1, \gamma_2, \cdots, \gamma_m]$ be an unknown parameter vector in the two-link robot system. From the evolutionary point of view, Γ is called a chromosome and all γ_i, for $i \in \underline{m}$ and $\underline{m} = \{1, 2, \cdots, m\}$, are called genes. To execute the genetic operations, a performance index or an objective function should be defined in the beginning. In GA, it only requires the computation of the objective function to guide its search, and there is no requirement for its differentiation, which may be usually needed in the traditional optimal method. A summation of squared error (SSE) is chosen as the objective function in this study defined by

$$SSE = \sum_{k=1}^{T} \left[(y_1(k) - \hat{y}_1(k))^2 + (y_2(k) - \hat{y}_2(k))^2 \right]$$
$$= \sum_{k=1}^{T} \left[e_1^2(k) + e_1^2(k) \right] \qquad (3)$$

where T is the number of given sampling steps, y_1 and y_2 are the actual outputs, $\hat{y}_1$ and $\hat{y}_2$ are the evaluated outputs. Our purpose is to find the optimal model parameter vector Γ by using the proposed method such that the SSE in (4) is minimized.

The parameters estimation of system using a multi-crossover GA starts with a population with many chromosomes Γ which are generated randomly. Each chromosome in the population represents a set of possible solution to the optimization problem of parameters estimation. The chromosomes Γ are then evolved to generate better offspring according to the values of SSE by applying three genetic operations. Before introducing three genetic operations, a search space for Γ is first defined by

$$\Omega_\Gamma = \left\{ \Gamma \in \mathfrak{R}^m \,\middle|\, \gamma_{1min} \leq \gamma_1 \leq \gamma_{1max}, \gamma_{2min} \leq \gamma_2 \leq \gamma_{2max}, \cdots, \gamma_{mmin} \leq \gamma_m \leq \gamma_{mmax} \right\}$$
$$(4)$$

All of genes, i.e., γ_i for $i \in \underline{m}$, in the chromosome will be evolved in the constrained space Ω_Γ during the genetic operations. The upper and lower bounds of γ_i should be considerably given by designer or be cited from other reference articles, if possible. Generally speaking, if we construct a larger search space, it would need more time for computations and the convergence of search may become very slow. Conversely, if the search region is set too small, the optimal system parameters probably are not included. Once a generated chromosome by genetic operations goes beyond Ω_Γ, the original chromosome will be retained. Let N represent the number of chromosomes in the population, i.e., the size of population, and parameters P_r, P_c, and P_m are referred to as probabilities of reproduction, crossover, and mutation, respectively. In addition, it is noteworthy that throughout the paper we will assume a uniform probability distribution for all used random values. The detailed descriptions of these operators are stated as follows.

A. Reproduction

For the reproduction operation there are two well-known selection mechanisms: the roulette wheel and tournament selections. The roulette wheel selection can be visualized by imagining a wheel where each chromosome occupies an area that is related to its value of objective function. When a spinning wheel stops, a fixed marker determines which chromosome will be selected to reproduce [7]. This kind of selection mechanism needs more numerical computations. However, the tournament selection is simpler than the roulette wheel selection. In this selection $p_r \times N$ chromosomes with better SSE values are duplicated into the population, and the same amount of chromosomes with worse SSE values are discarded from the population. This keeps the same population size.

B. Multiple crossover

Unlike the traditional crossover by using only two chromosomes, a novel crossover formula that contains three parent chromosomes is proposed in this study. We assume that chromosomes Γ_1, Γ_2, and Γ_3 are selected from the population randomly and $SSE(\Gamma_1)$ is the smallest among three SSE values. Also, let c be a random number selected from $[0,1]$. If $c \geq p_c$, then the following multiple crossover are performed to generate new chromosomes

$$\Gamma_1 \leftarrow \Gamma_1 + \rho(2\Gamma_1 - \Gamma_2 - \Gamma_3),$$
$$\Gamma_2 \leftarrow \Gamma_2 + \rho(2\Gamma_1 - \Gamma_2 - \Gamma_3), \quad (5)$$
$$\Gamma_3 \leftarrow \Gamma_3 + \rho(2\Gamma_1 - \Gamma_2 - \Gamma_3),$$

where $\rho \in [0,1]$ is a random value determining the crossover grade of these three. If $c < p_c$, no crossover operation is performed. It is clear from Fig. 2 that the resulting adjusted vector $(2\Gamma_1 - \Gamma_2 - \Gamma_3)$ is a combination of vectors $\Gamma_1 - \Gamma_2$ and $\Gamma_1 - \Gamma_3$.

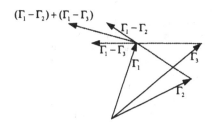

Figure2: A modified adjusting vector by using the proposed multiple crossover.

C. Mutation

The mutation operation follows the crossover and provides a possible mutation on some chosen chromosomes Γ. Only $p_m \times N$ chromosomes in the population will be randomly selected to mutate. The formula of mutation operation for the selected Γ is given by

$$\Gamma \leftarrow \Gamma + s \times \Phi, \quad (6)$$

where s is a positive constant and $\Phi \in \Re^m$ is a random perturbation vector producing a small effect on Γ.

Performing the above three evolutionary operations for the whole population one time is called a generation. The algorithm stops if the desired value of SSE is satisfied or the pre-specified number of generations is achieved. Notice again that if a generated chromosome during genetic operations is outside the search space Ω_Γ, then the original chromosome will be retained. The overall design steps for parameters estimation of nonlinear system using the proposed GA can be summarized as follows.

Data: Nonlinear system of (1), number of sampling steps p in (3), parameters γ_{1min}, γ_{1max}, γ_{2min}, γ_{2max}, $\cdots$, γ_{mmin}, and γ_{mmax} in (4) for Ω_Γ, population size N, probabilities of reproduction p_r, crossover p_c, and mutation p_m, parameters s and Φ in (6), and number of generations G (or the SSE tolerance ε).

Goal: Search for parameters of nonlinear system such that the value of SSE in (3) is minimized.

1. Create a population with the size of N chromosomes, in which all of genes are randomly generated from Ω_Γ.
2. Evaluate the value of SSE in (3) for each chromosome in the population.
3. If the pre-specified number of generations G is reached or there is a chromosome in the population with SSE value less than ε, then stop.
4. Carry out operations of reproduction, multiple crossover in (5), and mutation in (6). If the resulting chromosome during operations is outside the Ω_Γ, then the original one is retained.
5. Go back to Step 2.

SIMULATION RESULT

In this section, an illustrative example is given to demonstrate the feasibility of the proposed method. Consider a two-link robot system of (1) with the actual parameters $l_1 = 0.5$, $l_2 = 0.5$, $m_1 = 3.24$, $m_2 = 2.16$, and $m_p = 1$.

The proposed multi-crossover GA is applied to parameter identification of system (1) for $[l_1, l_2, m_1, m_2]$. For simulations, the sampling time is set to be 0.005, and both torque inputs τ_1 and τ_2 in (1) are generated from the interval $(-1,1)$ at random. The related variables used in GA operations are given as follows:

$$[r_l, r_u] = [0, 10], \quad T = 20,$$
$$N = 20, \quad G = 3000,$$
$$p_r = 0.2, \quad p_c = 0.4,$$
$$p_m = 0.1, \quad s = 0.05.$$

All of initial chromosomes are randomly created from the searching interval. Each element of noise vector Φ in (6) is randomly chosen from $[-0.01, 0.01]$. After performing our proposed GA method, we obtain the resulted system parameters

$$[\hat{l}_1 \quad \hat{l}_2 \quad \hat{m}_1 \quad \hat{m}_2] = [0.5 \quad 0.5 \quad 3.2399 \quad 2.16].$$

It is almost the same with the actual parameters.

CONCLUSION

In this paper, a modified real-coded GA with a multiple crossover is proposed and uses it to estimate the unknown system parameters. These parameters are viewed as genes and evolved by three genetic operations of reproduction, multiple crossover, and mutation operations, respectively. Based on it, the parameters of a two-link robot can be estimated. To demonstrate the performance of the proposed method, a simulated example is illustrated. From the final result, it is easily seen that our proposed method is effective.

ACKNOWLEDGEMENT

This work was supported in part by the National Science Council of Taiwan under Grant NSC 94-2218-E-244-002.

REFERENCES

1. Davis, L., Handbook of Genetic Algorithms, Van Nostrand, New York, 1991.
2. Montiel, O. C., Sepulveda, R., and Melin, P., Application of a breeder genetic algorithm for finite impulse filter optimization, Information Sciences, 2004, 161, pp. 139-158.
3. Tang, Y. C. and Xu, Y., Application of fuzzy Naive Bayes and a real-valued genetic algorithm in identification of fuzzy model, Information Sciences, 2005, 169, pp. 205-226.
4. Huang, Y. P. and Huang, C. H., Real-valued genetic algorithm for fuzzy grey prediction system, Fuzzy Sets and Systems, 1997, 87, pp.265-276.
5. Kristinsson, K. and Dumont, G. A., System identification and control using genetic algorithms, IEEE Transactions on Systems, Man, and Cybernetics, 1992, 22, pp. 1033-1046.
6. Jiang, B. and Wang, B. W., Parameter estimation of nonlinear system based on genetic algorithm, Control Theory and Applications, 2000, 17, pp.150-152.
7. Blanco, A., Delgado, M. and Pegalajar, M. C., A real-coded genetic algorithm for training recurrent neural networks, Neural Networks, 2001, 14, pp.93-105.
8. Lu, H. C. and Tzeng, S. T., Design of two-dimensional FIR digital filters for sampling structure conversion by genetic algorithm approach, Signal Processing, 2000, 80, pp.1445-1458.
9. Xu, D. J. and Daley, M. L., Design of optimal filter using a parallel genetic algorithm, IEEE Transactions on Circuits and Systems-II: Analog and Digital Signal Processing, 1995, 42, pp.673-675.
10. Spong, M. W. and Vidyasagar, M., Robot Dynamics and Control, Wiley, New York, 1989.

Parametric Time-frequency Modeling of Nonstationary Signals by Adaptive Decomposition Based on Time-shearing Gabor Atoms

Shiwei MA, Zhongjie LIU, Weibin LIANG

School of Mechatronical Engineering & Automation
Shanghai University
Shanghai 200072, P.R.China
(E-mail: swma@mail.shu.edu.cn)

ABSTRACT

A kind of localized four parameters Gabor atom (dialating, time-shearing, modulating and translating of Gaussian function) was derived. Based on it, a parametric adaptive time-frequency distribution (PAD) is proposed by using adaptive signal decomposition method in frequency domain, which is a non-negative energy distribution and free of cross-term interference for multi-component signals and is suitable to model the dispersion components of localized time-varing nonstationary signals. A method of using zooming-like approximation for estimating the four parameters at each decomposisition step was proposed. Numerical simulation results manifested the effectiveness of the approach in time-frequency representation applications.

KEY WORDS: Gabor atom, time-shear, adaptive signal decomposition, time-frequency distribution

1. INTRODUCTION

Modeling of nonstationary signal in time-frequency plane is of great importance for signal processing and system analyzing applications. Signal having limited time and frequency support can be represented by an image of time-frequency distribution (TFD), whose effects depend in a great measure on the properties of employed elementary anlysis function (known as time-frequency atom, or atom in short), such as wavelet, Gaussian function (Gabor atom). The atoms should match the local time and frequency structures of signal handled as much as possible. Mann[1] and Mihovilovic[2] independently suggested using multiple-parameters "chirplet" atom, derived from a dilating, translating, modulating, frequency shearing version of a single window function to match signal's scale-varying, time-shift, frequency-shift and linear frequency modulation properties in time-frequency plane, respectively.

Meanwhile, there has been considerable interests in developing parametric adaptive TFD (PAD) techniques to represent signal by the linear combination of localized simple atoms. The "matching pursuit" proposed by Mallat[3] and the "adaptive spectrogram" proposed by Qian[4] are two typical approches, which expand signal onto a few of best matched atoms that are selected from a redundant dictionary of three parameters Gabor atom (dilating, translating and modulating of Gaussian function) by using adaptive signal subspace decomposition method.

In this work, a kind of four parameters time-shearing Gabor atom was derived. The adaptive signal decomposition based on this kind of atom and its implementation in frequency domain was proposed, the related PAD and some numerical simulation results are presented.

2. TIME-SHEARING GABOR ATOM

Gabor atom is given as

$$g_s(t) = (\pi s^2)^{-0.25} e^{-0.5(t/s)^2} \qquad (1)$$

where dilating (or scale) parameter $s > 0$, determines its time duration and frequency bandwidth. Taking a time-shearing operator[1] M_η to it, yield a time-shearing Gabor atom, denoted as

$$\begin{aligned} g_{s,\eta}(t) &= M_\eta g_s(t) \\ &= g_s(t) * \sqrt{0.5/(\pi\eta)} e^{i0.5t^2/\eta} \end{aligned} \qquad (2)$$

where * means convolution in time, $\eta \in \{R^+\}$ is a time-shearing parameter. Its Fourier transform $G_{s,\eta}(\omega)$ is found as

$$G_{s,\eta}(\omega) = (4\pi s^2)^{0.25} e^{-0.5\omega^2(s^2+i\eta)} e^{0.25i\pi} \qquad (3)$$

It is suitable to be manipulated in frequency domain with $\eta \in \{R\}$. Then taking modulating operator M_{ω_c} and translating operator M_{t_c} to it successively, yield a set of four parameters time-shearing Gabor atoms, denoted as $\hat{\Psi} = \{G_\chi(\omega)\}$ in frequency domain, i.e.

$$G_\chi(\omega) = G_{s,\eta}(\omega - \omega_c) e^{-it_c\omega} \qquad (4)$$

where $\chi = \{s, \eta, \omega_c, t_c\} \in (R^+ \times R^3)$ is parameter set.

It has been proved that three parameters (s, ω_c, t_c) Gabor atom set, which is a subset of $\hat{\Psi}$ when $\eta = 0$, is complete in $L^2(R)$ space[3]. Therefore, $\hat{\Psi}$ is an over complete set in $L^2(R)$ and conveys more information though it is more redundant.

By taking Wigner-Ville Distribution[5]

(WVD) to $G_\chi(\omega)$, one can get the TFD (WVD type) of the derived atom, i.e.

$$WVD_{g_\chi}(t,\omega) = 2e^{-\{t-t_c-\eta(\omega-\omega_c)\}^2/s^2 - s^2(\omega-\omega_c)^2} \qquad (5)$$

It is a nonnegative TFD function whose energy distributes in the vicinity of a time-frequency center (t_c, ω_c) within an elliptic area (the shape is determined by η and s) shearing in time orientation along its instantaneous frequency curve $t = t_c + \eta(\omega - \omega_c)$, as depicted in Figure 1. When $\eta \neq 0$, the time duration increasing with the increasing of η, but the bandwidth remains unchanged.

The physical consideration of this modification is to match the dispersion properties of localized nonstationary signals, such as those passing through inhomogeneous media.

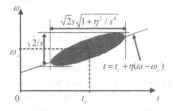

Figure 1 Schematic diagram of TFD of a time-shearing Gabor atom

3. ADAPTIVE SIGNAL DECOMPOSITION AND PAD

Assume $\{g_{\gamma_n}(t)\}_{\gamma_n \in \Gamma} \in L^2(R)$ a set of atoms, Γ its parameters set. Any signal $f(t) \in L^2(R)$ can be decomposed as[3,4]

$$f(t) = \sum_{n=0}^{\infty} c_n g_{\gamma_n}(t) \qquad (6)$$

where c_n is expansion coefficient which

can be obtained by

$$c_n = \langle R^n f(t), g_{\gamma_n}(t) \rangle \qquad (7)$$

The signal residual is given by

$$R^n f(t) = R^{n-1} f(t) - c_{n-1} g_{\gamma_{n-1}}(t) \qquad (8)$$

which is a procedure of adaptive signal subspace decomposition. Let the iteration starting at $R^0 f(t) = f(t)$ and search a best matched atom from $\{g_{\gamma_n}(t)\}_{\gamma_n \in \Gamma}$ at each iterative step by the criterion

$$|c_n|^2 = \max_{\gamma_n \in \Gamma} \left| \langle R^n f(t), g_{\gamma_n}(t) \rangle \right|^2 \qquad (9)$$

It had been proved that, with the iteration continuous, signal energy contained in residual will decay monotonically and converge to zero eventually[3,4]. And the PAD of the signal was given as the weighted summation of atom's WVD[3,4]

$$PAD_f(t,\omega) = \sum_{n=0}^{\infty} |c_n|^2 WVD_{g_{\gamma_n}}(t,\omega) \qquad (10)$$

Assuming $\Gamma = \chi = \{s, \eta, \omega_c, t_c,\} \in (R^+ \times R^3)$, then $\gamma_n = (s_n, \eta_n, \omega_{cn}, t_{cn}) \in \chi$, which give four parameters of the derived time-shearing Gabor atom obtained at the nth step. Then the PAD of a signal based on time-shearing Gabor atoms can be readily obtained. Obviously, it is also a nonnegative TFD function and free of cross-term for multi-component signal.

The above adaptive decomposition can also be carried out in frequency domain and the coefficient can be obtained by

$$c_n = \frac{1}{2\pi} \langle R^n F(\omega), G_{s_n, \eta_n}(\omega - \omega_{cn}) e^{-it_{cn}\omega} \rangle \qquad (11)$$

where, $R^n F(\omega)$ is the Fourier transform of signal residual $R^n f(t)$. It should satisfy

$$|c_n|^2 = \max_{s_n, \eta_n, \omega_{cn}, t_{cn}} \left| \frac{1}{2\pi} \int R^n F(\omega) G_{s_n, \eta_n}{}^*(\omega - \omega_{cn}) e^{it_{cn}\omega} d\omega \right|^2 \qquad (12)$$

Given an error threshold ε, so that

$$\|F(\omega)\|^2 - \sum_{n=0}^{N-1} 2\pi |c_n|^2 \leq \varepsilon \cdot \|F(\omega)\|^2 \qquad (13)$$

As a result, one can get

$$F(\omega) = \sum_{n=0}^{N-1} c_n G_{\gamma_n}(\omega) \qquad (14)$$

$$PAD_f(t,\omega) = 2\sum_{n=0}^{N-1} |c_n|^2 e^{-\{t - t_{cn} - \eta_n(\omega - \omega_{cn})\}^2 / s_n^2 - s_n^2(\omega - \omega_{cn})^2} \qquad (15)$$

which indicate that signal and its TFD can be approximate represented and reconstructed by using only a few of atoms and corresponding expansion coefficients obtained by adaptive decomposition.

4. A METHOD FOR PARAMETERS ESTIMATION

The key issue of the proposed adaptive decomposition and PAD is to find four parameters (s, η, t_c, ω_c) according to Eq.(12) at each iterative step. Since four parameters space χ is overcomplete and redundant, global searching among whole set is quite difficult and impractical. So, the searching should be done in approximate ways, i.e. to reduce the searching space into one or two parameters and estimate their values at each step.

Since the time-frequency energy center of signal residual at each step is independent of the atom selected, one can first find it in time-frequency plane and use its coordinates as (t_c, ω_c). Then, search the other two parameters (s, η) in its vicinity. In order to reduce redundant and accelerate searching speed.

Analogue to a zooming-like procedure (as in wavelet transform), one can use a few discrete dilating values, as

$$s = a^k, k = -k_0, -k_0 + 1, \cdots, 0, 1, \cdots, k_0 \quad (16)$$

where, k_0 and a are constant, $a > 1$ and can be chosen according to practical requirement. Then, Eq.(12) is equivalent to matching signal residual with Gaussian windows of multiple scales. Since the effective time duration and frequency bandwidth of a Gabor atom depend on dilating parameter, one can only use a few discrete values for (t_c, ω_c), i.e. $t_c = p\Delta T$ and $\omega_c = q\Delta\Omega$, where $p, q \in Z$, ΔT and $\Delta\Omega$ are sampling intervals in time and frequency respectively determined by s. Hence, at the nth step, the calculation of expansion coefficient, inner product at the right side of Eq.(11), can be rewritten as

$$c_n(p,q) = \frac{1}{2\pi} \cdot \quad (17)$$
$$\int R^n F(\omega) G_{s_n,\eta_n}{}^*(\omega - q\Delta\Omega_n) e^{ip\Delta T_n \omega} d\omega$$

It is just the short time Fourier transform (STFT) of signal residual implemented in frequency domain and can be effectively computed using IFFT.

As a result, at the nth step, one can take following procedure to search four parameters: (a) first let $\eta_n = 0$ and $s_n|_{k=-k_0}$, find a rough value of (t_{cn}, ω_{cn}) within a larger area in time-frequency plane, then adjust η_n to make $|c_n(p,q)|^2$ maximum; (b) let $s_n|_{k \leftarrow k+1}$ and find a finer (t_{cn}, ω_{cn}) within a shrinkage area in the vicinity of last obtained time-frequency center to make $|c_n(p,q)|^2$ increasing again, then adjust η_n to make $|c_n(p,q)|^2$

maximum; (c) repeat (b) until $|c_n(p,q)|^2$ no longer increasing, then stop the searching and get $(s_n, \eta_n, t_{cn}, \omega_{cn})$ the approximated best matched parameters and $c_n(p,q)$ the expansion coefficient.

Obviously, after finding (t_{cn}, ω_{cn}), the adjusting of η_n turns to be a problem of one dimensional optimization and can be solved by simple method, for example golden section method was used in the simulation experiment and found it converged rapidly.

Define a ratio of signal to noise SNR_n as a measure of reconstruction accuracy

$$SNR_n = -10\log\left\{\frac{\|F(\omega)\|^2}{\|R^{n+1}F(\omega)\|^2}\right\}(dB) \quad (18)$$

which is equivalent to Eq.(13). Hence, after finished the nth step, store coefficients and parameters, then compute residual $R^{n+1}F(\omega)$ and judge SNR_n: if it is less than a prescribed threshold, finish decomposition, otherwise continue the $(n^{th} + 1)$ step until it is satisfied.

5. SIMULATION RESULTS

Simulations were conducted using MATLAB programs. The simulated signal composed of three time-shearing Gaussian signals with different local properties. Figure 2 gives this signal waveform and Figure 3 its PAD. Each component of the signal is depicted clearly in time-frequency plane with its time-frequency location, orientation and energy distribution.

The adaptive decomposition and PAD to white noise polluted versions of the simulated signal with different signal-noise-ratio, i.e. 5dB, 0dB and -5dB, were compared. Results are given in Figure 4. As observed, residual energy decrease rapidly for original clean signal but slowly for noise polluted signal, which indicate that most of the original signal energy was decomposed during initial steps but noise energy in the follow-up steps. Figure 5 gives obtained PAD of the white noise polluted signal with -5dB signal-noise-ratio, in which three signal components were clearly depicted in different locations though white noise scattered over whole time-frequency plane.

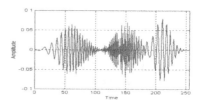

Figure 2 Simulated signal

6. CONCLUSION

The derived four parameters time-shearing Gabor atom can be used for time-frequency modeling of nonstationary signals having localized dispersion properties. The adaptive decomposition based on this atom and related PAD can be implemented in frequency domain by using a zooming-like approximation to estimate four parameters at each iterative step. Numerical simulation results manifested its effectiveness in time-frequency representation applications.

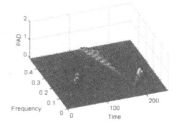

Figure 3 PAD of simulated signal

Acknowledgements
Authors acknowledge the support of the National Science Foundation of China under Grants 60472102 and Shanghai Leading Academic Discipline Project Foundation under Grants T0103.

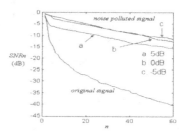

Figure 4 Residual energy reductions

REFERENCES

1. Mann S., Haykin S, 'Chirplet' and 'wavelet': novel time-frequency methods, Electronic Letters, 1992, 28-2, pp.114-116
2. Mihovilovic D, Brachewell R N, Adaptive chirplet representation of signal on time-frequency plane, Electronics Letters, 1991, 27-13, pp.1159-1161
3. Mallat S G, Zhang Z F, Matching pursuits with time-frequency dictionaries, IEEE Transaction on Signal Processing, 1993, 41-12, pp.3397-3415
4. Qian S E, Chen D P, Signal representation using adaptive normalized Gaussian functions, Signal Processing, 1994, 36-1, pp.1-11
5. Cohen L, Time-frequency distributions—a review, Proceedings of IEEE, 1989, 77, pp.941-981

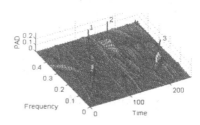

Figure 5 PAD of noise polluted signal (SNR=-5dB)

The Hybrid Meta-heuristics Method
by Reflecting Recognition of Dependence Relation
among Design Variables for The Multi-peak Problems

Hiroshi HASEGAWA*, Hiroto SASAKI** and Hiroyasu UEHARA***

* Department of Machinery & Control Systems, Faculty of Systems Engineering
Shibaura Institute of Technology
307 Fukasaku, Minuma-ku, Saitama-shi, Saitama 337-8570, Japan
(E-mail: h-hase@sic.shibaura-it.ac.jp)
** Nippon Telegraph and Telephone East Corp.
3-19-2, Nishi-shinjuku, Shinjuku-ku, Tokyo 163-8019, Japan
*** PENTAX Corp.
2-36-9, Maeno-cho, Itabashi-ku, Tokyo 174-8639, Japan

ABSTRACT

In this paper, a new hybrid meta-heuristics method has been proposed to solve multi-peak optimization problems with multiple dimensions by reflecting the recognition of dependence relation among design variables. The proposed method is applied to some benchmark functions to evaluate its performance, and it has been confirmed that this method reduces the computational cost and improves the convergence up to the optimal solution. Furthermore, for assistance in vehicle design, we investigate the optimization of spot weld positions using the proposed method. The validity of the proposed method is discussed through the optimization of the benchmark functions and spot weld positions.

KEY WORDS: Meta-heuristics method, GA, SA, Local search method, Multi-peak problems, Vehicle design

NOMENCLATURE

X : Design variable vectors (DVs)
X^{Gene} : Integer-type DVs coded into genes
β : Coding factor of DVs
sd : Number of selections of DVs.
u : Uniform random number $u \in [0, 1]$
SP_p : Matrix of step size
mr : Maximum range size of DVs
nr_0 : Initial neighborhood ratio
AD_1 : Total number of $sd = 1$ was accepted
AD_2 : Total number of $sd = 2$ was accepted

INTRODUCTION

Meta-heuristics methods require huge computational costs for obtaining stability in the convergence to the optimal solution. To reduce the cost and improve stability, a hybrid approach becomes necessary, which combines global and local search abilities. The most popular approach is the combination of the global search ability of a Genetic Algorithm (GA) [1] with the local search ability of Simulated Annealing (SA) [2]. This approach has been applied to major benchmark functions and has been reported to be valid [3]–[6]. It is believed to be both locally and globally efficient. However, major multi-peak benchmark functions with multiple dimensions, i.e., Rastrigin (RA) and Griewank (GR) functions, require about 10^6 function calls for arriving at the optimal solution. Furthermore, GR functions with multiple dimensions cannot achieve the optimal solution. Generally, when the optimal problem exhibits a dependence on DVs and the steepness of the objective function is small in the feasible space of DVs, it is difficult to obtain an optimal solution.

To overcome these difficulties, we propose a new meta-heuristic method by automatically reflecting the recognition of dependence relation among DVs.

Hybrid meta-heuristic method

The proposed method (PM)
PM has three search abilities—multi-search ability (MSA), local search ability (LSA), and neighborhood optimal search ability (NOSA); these include a new strategy to enhance the search ability in the neighborhood of the optimal solution.

MSA: GA is used to search multiple points in a wide range of design space, and a good optimal solution can be obtained by estimating the fitness function by using the GA operation.

LSA: A design space may possess more than one optimum solution. Therefore, a local search of the individuals uses a stochastic method to prevent from falling into the local optima. LSA is realized by using an acceptance criterion in a metropolis loop of SA for varying values of DVs.

NOSA: NOSA is realized by a direct search process (DSP), which is an intuitive method. DSP generates a new neighborhood point X_{renew} by adding a step size to the current search point X. This generation process reflects the recognition of a dependence relation among the DVs, which are calculated by trial and error using the LSA strategy. If a fitness function is improved, the value of X is modified to the value of X_{renew}. This process is iterated, and the search point X arrives at the optimal solution.

Algorithm of PM: The conceptual process of PM is shown in Figure 1. PM uses GA as the MSA strategy to control all the

processes. The generation process of MSA uses the LSA or NOSA strategy for a self-change in the values of DVs. The LSA strategy is adopted until the terminal temperature of the cooling schedule is attained. In the LSA strategy, one individual adopts only the NOSA strategy during each generation process in order to ensure variety. As the temperature reaches the terminal temperature, the generation process adopts the NOSA strategy. The hybrid MSA and NOSA strategies are iterated; finally, the search point arrives at the optimal solution.

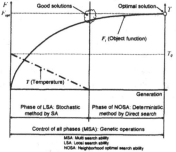

Figure 1 Conceptual process of PM

GA for the MSA strategy
DVs are individually coded into a string. This string represents an integer value of DV. The population size is 20 individuals. Selection is performed by using roulette wheel selection. Crossover is performed only between the variables, as shown in Figure 2. An elite strategy is adopted during each generation process. Mutation is not considered.

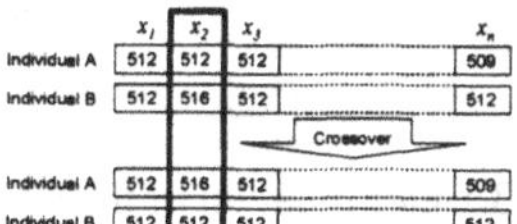

Figure 2 Crossover

SA for the LSA strategy
The LSA strategy is adopted in a metropolis loop of the SA process [2]. It is the same as that of conventional SA.

Independence and dependence relations: This strategy introduces the following equation in order to determine the dependence relation among DVs:

$$sd = \begin{cases} 1 & if \ 0 \le u < 0.5, \\ 2 & if \ 0.5 \le u \le 1.0. \end{cases} \quad (1)$$

Equation (1) randomly calculates $sd = 1$ or $sd = 2$. The former implies that an independence relation exists among the DVs, where only one design variable x_i changes. The latter implies that a dependence relation exists among the DVs, where two design variables x_i and x_{i+1} change.

Direct search for the NOSA strategy

Now, we introduce the direct search process (DSP). DSP is based on an intuitive method, which changes the value of DVs step by step through a series of step sizes. This strategy has three processes: generation, acceptance criterion, and change in step size. Furthermore, DVs are selected on the basis of sd. The generation process generates a new neighborhood point X_{renew} from the current search point X according to the following iteration formula:

$$X_{renew} = X + SP_p. \quad (2)$$

$SP_p = [sp_{p,1}, \ldots, sp_{p,n}]$ $(p = 1, \ldots, ps;$ ps is the population size) is updated using the activity chart, as shown in Figure 3, step by step during the iteration process.

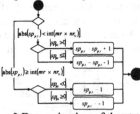

Figure 3 Determination of the step size

Independence and dependence relations:

The independence and dependence relations of DVs—$sd = 1$ and $sd = 2$—are modified during every iteration by using the following equation.

$$sd = \begin{cases} 1 & if \ 0 \le u < AD_1/(AD_1 + AD_2), \\ 2 & if \ AD_1/(AD_1 + AD_2) \le u \le 1.0. \end{cases} \quad (3)$$

In the LSA strategy, sd is randomly assumed by Equation (1), and the accepted or rejected values of sd are recorded. In the NOSA strategy, this archive is utilized in Equation (3) as learned knowledge from the LSA strategy.

Numerical experiments

Benchmark problems

PM estimates the stability of convergence to the optimal solution by using RA, Ridge (RI), GR, and Ackley (AC) functions in the numerical experiments. The benchmark functions have 20 dimensions. The optimization problem is formulated. DVs and the objective function are defined as follows:

DVs:

$$X_i = \beta \cdot \left(X_i^{Gene} - 512 \right) \quad (4)$$

Objective function:

$$F_i(X_i) = -f_i(X_i) \rightarrow Max \quad (5)$$

Range of DVs:

$$0 \le X_i^{Gene} \le 1024. \quad (6)$$

If the search point attains an optimal solution or a current generation process reaches the terminal generation, the search process is terminated. The terminal generation is 30,000th generation. The metropolis loop at the LSA strategy and the loop at the NOSA strategy are two loops. The parameters, ranges of DVs, and characteristics of the benchmark functions are listed in Table 1.

Table 1 Parameters and characteristics

Functions	Range of DVs	β	Dependence relation among DVs	Multi-peak	Steep
RA	$-5.12 \le X_i \le 5.12$	0.01	No	Yes	Average
RI	$-51.2 \le X_i \le 51.2$	0.10	Yes	No	Average
GR	$-512 \le X_i \le 512$	1.00	Yes	Yes	Small
AC	$-51.2 \le X_i \le 51.2$	0.10	No	Yes	Average

Discussion
Independence and dependence relations:

In this section, the numerical experiment is performed by using the RA and GR functions. Figure 4 shows the results of the acceptance ratios. Figures 4 (a) and (b) show the acceptance ratios of the RA and GR functions, respectively. The acceptance ratio AR_1 of the independence relation (i.e., $sd = 1$) is calculated as $AR_1 = AD_1 / (AD_1 + AD_2)$, and the acceptance ratio AR_2 of the dependence relation (i.e., $sd = 2$) is calculated as $AR_2 = 1 - AR_1$. In this experiment, PM switches from the LSA strategy to the NOSA strategy at the 459th generation. For the LSA strategy, AR_1 appears to approach 0.7, as shown in Figure 4 (a). For the NOSA strategy, the selection probability of sd is not uniform, as stated in Equation (3), and AR_1 tends to be about 0.7. Therefore, $sd = 1$ is selected with a high probability. As shown in Table 1, these DVs exhibit an independence relation. Therefore, by means of this experiment, we could confirm that the independence and dependence relations are reflected in the generation process of DVs. The result in Figure 4 (b) shows that both acceptance ratios AR_1 and AR_2 tend to be about 0.5 for the LSA strategy; AR_1 approaches 0.6 in the NOSA strategy after prolonged generations. As a result, AR_1 and AR_2 become 0.6 and 0.4, respectively. As shown in Table 1, the GR function requires a combination of the independence and dependence relations of DVs. Based on these acceptance ratios, we could confirm that the independence and dependence relations are reflected in generation process of DVs.

Based on the experimental results of the RA and GR functions, we believe that

- PM can distinguish between the independence and dependence relations of DVs by using Equations (1) and (3)
- DSP can reflect the independence or dependence relation of DVs in generation process by using an archive of sd.

<u>Convergence to the optimal solution:</u> The numerical experiments are performed 10 times for every benchmark function. The initial seed number is randomly varied during every trial. Table 2 lists the results from four benchmark functions. The solutions of all the benchmark functions

reach their optima during every trial. Therefore, the success ratio of PM becomes 100%. We assume that this can optimize the complex or multi-peak optimization problems with multiple dimensions, which exhibit the dependence relation of DVs.

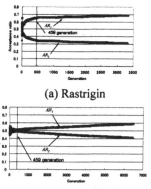

(a) Rastrigin

(b) Griewank

Figure 4 Acceptance ratio and generation

Table 2 Final generation to optimal solution

	RA	RI	GR	AC
1	3439	21246	2805	3864
2	3525	15333	6875	3944
3	4084	15996	5357	3181
4	3914	23486	13373	2557
5	3404	11739	6775	5035
6	3298	23698	14594	1755
7	3857	16335	22681	2409
8	2723	16657	6704	3782
9	3835	17063	8475	3380
10	4217	15306	2394	3179
Ave	3629.6	17685.9	9003.3	3308.6

Optimal design of the spot weld positions
We investigate the optimization of the spot weld positions on the front fender of a white body for assisting in the core technology of vehicle design. An FEM model of the front fender is shown in Figure 5. A static analysis is performed by using MSC.Nastran. The boundary conditions are shown in this figure. The spot weld point is modeled by the beam element between the panels [7]. The initial spot weld positions are indicated by the white circles. The spot weld numbers are denoted as $Weld_1$, $Weld_2$,...$Weld_{15}$. This optimal problem is formulated as follows:

DVs:
$$X^{Gene} = [x_1,...,x_{15}], \quad 0 \leq X^{Gene} \leq 1024, \quad (7)$$

$$A = \beta \cdot X^{Gene} \quad , \quad A = [a_1,...,a_{15}], \qquad (8)$$

$$a_i = \begin{cases} 0 & if \ 0 \leq a_i \leq 10, \\ a_i & if \ 10 < a_i \leq 102.4, \end{cases} \qquad (9)$$

$$Weld_i \in \begin{cases} 0 & if \ a_i = 0, \\ 1 & if \ a_i > 0, \end{cases} \qquad (10)$$

Objective function:

$$F = \sum_{i=1}^{15} Weld_i + \gamma \sum_{j=1}^{2} \{max(g_j, 0)\} \to Min, \qquad (11)$$

Constraint functions:

$$g_1 = \begin{cases} 0 & if \ S_{max} \leq S_a, \\ \dfrac{S_{max}}{S_a} & otherwise, \end{cases} \qquad (12)$$

$$g_2 = \sum_{i=1}^{15} g_{i,2}, \quad g_{i,2} = \begin{cases} 0 & if \ \tau_i \leq \tau_a, \\ \dfrac{\tau_i}{\tau_a} & otherwise, \end{cases} \qquad (13)$$

where A, S_{max}, $S_a = 225.5 \ [MPa]$, τ_i, and $\tau_a = 212.0 \ [N]$ denote the cross-section vector of the spot weld points, maximum stress on the panels, allowable stress on the front fender, shared component of the axial force at $Weld_i$, and allowable axial force at the spot weld point, respectively. Further, the 200th generation is the terminal generation.

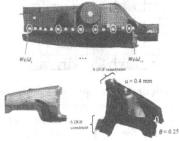

Figure 5 Front fender of the white body

Discussion of the optimal positions
The obtained optimal solutions are indicated by the elliptical symbols in Figure 5. The number of evaluations required to find the optimal solution is 360. The number of optimal positions is reduced from 15 points to 6 points. At its position, $Weld_1$ experiences an axial force that occurs due to torsional deformation at the nose. $Weld_9$ and $Weld_{10}$ transfer the axial forces that occur due to the tensile deformation at

the front strut. $Weld_{14}$ experiences the axial force that occurs due to the reaction force at the A-pillar. Therefore, it can be concluded that these points, related to the force and constraint conditions, are necessary to ensure stiffness and strength. Furthermore, it is not necessary to consider other spot weld points.

CONCLUSION

A new hybrid meta-heuristic method by reflecting the recognition of dependence relation among DVs has been proposed. The proposed method is applied to four benchmark functions and the optimal design of spot weld positions in order to evaluate its performance, and its validity confirms that the method can reduce the computational cost and improve the stability of convergence to the optimal solution.

REFERENCES

1. Goldberg, D. E., Genetic Algorithms in Search Optimization and Machine Learning, Addison-Wesley, 1989.
2. Rosen, B. E. and Nakano, R., Simulated annealing—basics and recent topics on simulated annealing, Proceeding of JSAI, 1994, 9–3, (in Japanese).
3. Kawada, H., Uehara, H. and Kawamo, K., Development of General-purpose Optimization Engine and Test Run, Journal of JSST, 2003, 21–4, pp. 280–288, (in Japanese).
4. Uehara, H., Kawada, H. and Kawamo, K., Numerical Experiments on Optimal Points Searching Using Hybrid Method of Genetic Algorithm and Simulated Annealing, Japan NCTAM-52, 2003, pp. 280–288, (in Japanese).
5. Hiroyasu, T., Miki, M. and Ogura, M., Parallel Simulated Annealing using Genetic Crossover, Proceedings of the ISCA 13th International Conference on PDCS-2000, 2000.
6. Ong, Y. S. and Keane, A. J., Meta-Lamarckian Learning in Memetic Algorithms, IEEE transactions on evolutionary computation, 2004, 8–2, pp. 99–110.
7. Rupp, A., Storzel, K. and Grubisic, V., Computer Aided Dimensioning of Spot-Welded Automotive Structures, SAE TECHNICAL PAPER, 1995, 95071.

Hierarchical Response Surface Methodology for Parameter Optimization: Efficiency of a Hierarchical RSM with a Hessian Matrix

Teppei TANAKA, Koji SAKAI, Yukiko YAMASHITA, Naohisa SAKAMOTO, and Koji KOYAMADA

Graduate School of Engineering, Kyoto University
Yoshidahonmahi, Sakyoku, Kyoto-shi, Kyoto-Fu, Japan

ABSTRACT

We propose a hierarchical response surface methodology (hRSM) for parameter optimization. In this hRSM, a target domain is subdivided recursively based on the coefficient of determination (COD). However, deciding whether to execute subdivision based only on the COD results in a time-consuming technique. To solve this problem, we implemented hRSM with a Hessian matrix (hRSM-Hm) to determine whether a target domain is to be subdivided. To evaluate our proposed technique, we compared hRSM-Hm with a genetic algorithm (GA) in terms of computation time by using various numerical functions. From the results, the hRSM-Hm reduced the computation time by 25% compared with the GA on some functions. If the approximated shape of a function is similar to a quadric surface, even though there are many local minima, the hRSM-Hm could find an optimal set of parameters with very few computational cycles.

KEY WORDS: RSM, GA, Parameter optimization, Hessian matrix

INTRODUCTION

With the dramatic improvement in computational power over the last decade, there have been significant developments in numerical simulation, and optimization techniques have come to play a crucial role in advances in science and technology. When we simulate something, we often assume a simplified model of the object to understand the primary issues and to limit the computational resources required. Sometimes, however, the results are greatly influenced by the way in which this simplifying (modeling) is done. Therefore, we have to optimize the model. In this way, optimization is indispensable to achieve more accurate models.

There are several parameter optimization techniques, including the method of steepest descent, genetic algorithms (GAs), response surface methodology (RSM), and so on. RSM is used widely in quality engineering fields, such as in optimization of product processes or reducing product variability. RSM is frequently used with quadratic polynomials for fitting curves. We can construct a model function using RSM when we know the shape of the solution space. However, in general, the numerical simulations employed in scientific fields are usually complex and involve non-linear functions. It is therefore challenging to construct an approximate model.

To solve this problem, we propose a hierarchical RSM (hRSM). In this hRSM, we distinguish the degree of adaptation of a model using the coefficient of determination (COD), which is used for determining the accuracy or suitability of the model. When the COD is low, we divide the target domain into small subspaces and construct a response surface again. We continuously search for the optimal parameter (this technique is based on the divide and conquer approach). However, when we determine the optimal parameter only from the COD, we cannot know whether that point is a local minimum, a local maximum, or a saddle point. In other words, because hRSM searches a space which has no optimal set of parameters, it is computationally intensive. Therefore, we implemented hRSM with a Hessian matrix (hRSM-Hm) and used it to search only a space that has local minima.

RELATED WORK

To obtain an accurate heat simulation model, Koyamada et al. [1] used a compact model based on a GA. For the same problem, Kuzuno et al. [2] used a GA with RSM to obtain converged values with reduced simulation time. However, they had less-accurate results. Therefore, they proposed two ways to raise the accuracy. One was to narrow the target domain and apply a new GA-based RSM method [3]. The other was to increase the number of points constructing the response surface. In this paper, we propose hRSM-Hm to obtain the optimum parameter set efficiency.

PROPOSED TECHNIQUE

We propose a hierarchical optimization technique which subdivides the target

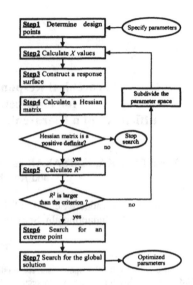

Figure 1. Recursive subdivision optimization process.

region recursively. In Step 1, the user should first specify the parameters and their valid ranges, and then the design points are determined via DOE. In Step 2, the association measure (X) of the test function is calculated. In Step 3, a response surface is constructed. In Step 4, eigen decomposition of the Hessian matrix of the response surface is performed. If all eigenvalues of the Hessian matrix are positive, i.e. the Hessian matrix is a positive definite matrix, then this indicates the existence of a minimum value at the verified area, and the process goes to Step 5. If one of the eigenvalues is not positive, then the searching process is stopped in the subspace. In Step 7, the COD (R^2) is calculated by the following equation:

$$R^2 = 1 - \frac{RSS \ /(k - p - 1)}{TSS \ /(k - 1)},$$

where k and p denote the number of parameters and responses, respectively, and *RSS* and *TSS* denote the regression sum of squares and the total sum of squares, respectively. If the obtained R^2 value exceeds a predetermined criterion, the process goes to Step 6. If this calculated R^2 value is smaller than the predetermined criterion, then the search space is subdivided and the process returns to Step 2. This process is recursively executed until a satisfactory R^2 value is found. We divided each of the parameters being analyzed into two. Figure 2 illustrates subdivision of the target space. In Step 6, the extreme points are searched to solve the function generated with the RSM. When the entire parameter space is searched, the optimal set of parameters is determined by comparing the local extreme points with each other (Step 7).

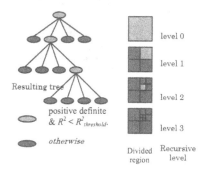

Figure 2. Tree structure.

EXPERIMENT

We compared our proposed hRSM-Hm with a GA. We assumed that the functions for simulation were very complicated and that one computation cycle takes a long time. We assumed that we could ignore the time to compute a Hessian matrix itself. Therefore, we compared not only computation time but also the time required to assess conversion of parameters of the object

function (we call this the "evaluation time").

RSM was applied to target functions with 25 design points, a maximum depth of 4, and $R^2 = 0.999$. The evaluation times for GA were (population × generations) of genes. The results of the GA experiment were the average of five cycles.

Test Functions

1. *Bohachevsky Function*

$f(x) = x_1^2 + 2x_2^2 - 0.3\cos(3\pi x_1) - 0.4\cos(4\pi x_2) + 0.7$, where $-10 \le x_i \le 10$, has many local minima. The global minimum is $f_0 = 0$ at $x_0 = (0, 0)$.

2. *Branin Function*

$f(x) = (1 - 2x_2 + \frac{1}{20}\sin(4\pi x_2) - x_1)^2 + (x_2 - \frac{1}{2}\sin(2\pi x_1))^2$, where $-10 \le x_i \le 10$, has 23 local minima, and 5 of them are global minima. The global minima are $f_0 = 0$ at $x_0 = (1, 0)$, (0.149, 0.402), (0.403, 0.287), (1.597, -0.287), and (1.851, -0.402).

3. *Six Hump Camel Function*

$f(x) = (4 - 2.1x_1^2 + \frac{x_1^4}{3})x_1^2 + x_1 x_2 + (-4 + 4x_2)x_2^2$, where $-3 \le x_1 \le 3$, and $-2 \le x_2 \le 2$, has 6 local minima, and 2 of them are global minima. The global minima are $f_0 = 0$ at $x_0 = $ (0.0898, -0.7127), (-0.0898, 0.7127).

4. *Easom Function*

$f(x) = \cos(x_1)\cos(x_2)\exp(-(x_1 - \pi)^2 - (x_2 - \pi)^2)$, where $-10 \le x_i \le 10$, has many local minima. The global minimum is $f_0 = -1$ at $x_0 = (\pi, \pi)$.

5. *Himmeblau Function*

$f(x) = (x_1^2 + x_2 - 11)^2 + (x_1 + x_2^2 - 7)^2 + 1$, where $-5 \le x_i \le 5$, has 4 local minima. The global minimum is $f_0 = 0$ at $x_0 = (3, 2)$.

Table 1. Result of experiments.

function No.	global solution	RSM		GA	
		evaluation (times)	obtained solution	evaluation (times)	obtained solution
1	(0, 0)	125	(0.000, 0.000)	550	(0.001, 0.000)
2	(1, 0)	125	(1.000, 0.000)	440	(1.002, -0.001)
3	(π, π)	1225	(3.139, 3.139)	650	(3.138, 3.141)
4	(3, 2)	3225	(3.001, 2.001)	1000	(3.578, -1.841)
				1800	(3.000, 2.002)
				1150	(-2.805, 3.128)
5	(0.0898, -0.7127)	4525	(0.090, -0.722)	350	(0.089, -0.714)
	(-0.0898, 0.7127)		(-0.090, 0.722)	625	(-0.088, 0.712)

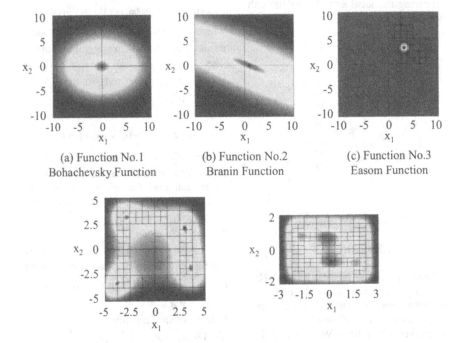

(a) Function No.1
Bohachevsky Function

(b) Function No.2
Branin Function

(c) Function No.3
Easom Function

Figure 3. Search process and obtained solution with hRSM-Hm.

RESULTS AND DISCUSSION

Table 1 shows the results of the evaluation times and the obtained solutions. Figure 3 show the exploration results of the test functions. The points in Fig. 3 indicate the obtained points (minimum) using hRSM-Hm. The lines show the recursive subdivision process with hRSM-Hm; only spaces having a local minimum were searched.

The results of exploration of the minima of the Bohachevsky function and the Branin function showed that the evaluation times with hRSM-Hm were approximately 25% less than those with GA. Since the genes of GA were initially set randomly in the domain, GA had to search in the entire target domain, which inevitably increased the computation time. However, if the Hessian matrix is positive, hRSM-Hm does not need to calculate the design points in the searched domain. If most searched spaces have a positive Hessian matrix, the evaluation times will be very short.

In the cases of the Easom function, the Himmeblau function, and the Six Hump function, the evaluation times were longer than those for GA. However, the results of those functions did not fall into the local minima, like the GA did. Figure 3 (c), (d), and (e) show that the hRSM-Hm explored only the spaces having local minima. This indicates that the hRSM-Hm could explore only the local minima, in accordance with our aim. To improve the ability of hRSM-Hm, it is necessary to introduce a way of selecting a space including a specific local minimum, without searching all local minima.

CONCLUSION

In this paper, we propose a hierarchical RSM (hRSM) with a Hessian matrix (hRSM-Hm) for parameter optimization. One feature of the proposed hRSM-Hm is to use the coefficient of determination (COD), which shows the degree of adaptation of a response surface, in order to decide whether to proceed with further subdivision. Another feature is to use a Hessian matrix, which can verify whether or not there is an extreme point. The results of comparison with GA showed that hRSM-Hm could operate effectively on the approximated shape of a function similar to a quadric surface, and it did not fall into a local minimum. However, the hRSM-Hm required a long evaluation time for some test functions.

In our future work, we will reconsider our hRSM-Hm algorithm and the threshold of the COD to reduce the evaluation time.

REFERENCES

1. Koyamada K., Yamada S., Nishio T., and Kotera H., Compact Modeling Approach using GA for Accurate Thermal Simulation, JSME, 1999, Vol. 65, pp. 1370-1376.
2. Kuzuno M., Nishio T., and Koyamada K., Compact Modeling for Thermal Simulation Using Response Surface Methodology, International Symposium on Computational Technologies, 2001, PVP-Vol. 424-2, pp. 57-63.
3. Koyamada K., Sakai K., and Itoh T., Parameter Optimization Technique Using The Response Surface Methodology, 26th Annual International Conference of the IEEE EMBC, 2004, pp. 2909-2912.
4. Kuzuno M., Nishio T., and Koyamada K., A thermal compact modeling method using Response Surface Methodology with Genetic Algorithm, PDPTA, CISST & IC-AI International Conferences, 2000, pp. 627-634.
5. Mammadov, M. A., A new global optimization algorithm based on a dynamical systems approach, 6th International Conference on Optimization, 2004.
6. Iba M., Bioinformatics Series: Genetic Algorithm, Igaku-Shoin Ltd., 2002.
7. Montgomery D. C., Design and Analysis of Experiments, 4th edition, 1996, John Wiley & Sons Inc

An ASP-based Distributed Collaborative Design System

ZHANG Linxuan, XIAO Tianyuan, LIANG CE, HU Changchang, FAN Wenhui

National CIMS Engineering Research Center
Department of Automation, Tsinghua University
Beijing 100084, China
(E-mail: lxzhang@tsinghua.edu.cn)

ABSTRACT

Collaborative design is the most important task of all activities at the lifecycle of product development under Networked Manufacturing (NM) environment. Application Service Provider (ASP) is a practical service style of informationization and ASP-based system is a effective approach to NM platforms. In this paper, combined industrial requirements with our efforts in some research projects funded by *Hi-Tech R&D Program of China* and *Beijing Municipal Sci-Tech Program*, an ASP-based distributed collaborative design system namely Co-Design is proposed to support remote collaboration among enterprises. Architecture of the system is presented and some key techniques of collaborative design are researched. Now the proposed Co-Design system has been implemented and used as ASP tools to help several small and medium enterprises to accelerate their product development and typical application examples shows that substantial benefits can be achieved by reducing of collaboration expenditure, development cost and shortening time to market.

KEY WORDS: collaborative design, application service provider (ASP); networked manufacturing (NM)

INTRODUCTION

The main purpose of Networked Manufacturing (NM) is to carry out generalized product manufacturing via the Internet/Intranet, i.e., to undertake tasks such as collaborative product design, product manufacturing and some other related activities, though various definitions of NM have appeared in these years. Design of a product is usually regarded as the origin of its formation to a great extend. Therefore, undoubtedly, collaborative design can be regarded as the most important task of all NM activities at the whole lifecycle of product development. In order to achieve collaborative design under NM environment, many attempts have been made by researchers from both of universities and enterprises[1~5]. And Application Service Provider (ASP) is a

well accepted practical technique of these attempts and has become a fashion of enterprise informationization both in China and abroad.

ASP-based system has proved to be a highly effective approach to NM platforms. Drawing lessons from the idea of intensive management, ASP acts as a service mode that the professional service company provides centralized management of costly high level software systems and their related technique supports meanwhile small and medium enterprises rent ASP services to implement normal business management and to achieve high level informationization at an easy rate. This kind of service mode can lower the threshold of high level informationization dramatically and hence it has won the favor of enterprises, especially those who have not enough money for hardware and software

218

investments and lack professional IT engineers. In China, about 99 percent of companies are small and medium enterprises (whose production value is less than 100 million Yuan and employees are less than 300), and they create 40 percent of the whole production value of all companies[5]. Consequently we can foresee that ASP-based system will become a dominant direction of informationization development for small and medium enterprises henceforward and in the meantime large amounts of small and medium enterprise users will provide a huge latent market for the ASP technique development.

Nowadays, some large scale commercial collaborative design supported systems such as PTC Windchill, EDS TeamCenter, Dassault Enovia, MatrixOne eMatrix, etc., have been developed by world-leading companies. However, these systems seem to share the following character flaws:

1) They are designed mainly for large scale enterprise. They seem to be perfect by providing all kinds of excellent functions for enterprises, but they are too expensive to suit small and medium enterprise.

2) The integration with CAD systems should be further enhanced. Usually a system offers seamless integration only with CAD system(s) from the same company as itself but not from other companies.

On the other hand, some small support tools which realize collaborative design through terminal service, such as PC Anywhere, Exceed, VNC, etc., have the following shortcomings:

1) Sharing only one session and supporting only one user to login at a certain time.

2) Not supporting three dimensional solid graphics.

3) High request for bandwidth to insure network speed.

4) Supporting only one operating system at client, not allowing multi-operating systems.

5) Due to C/S structure, software must be installed at client.

6) Mechanism of authority control is not flexible.

Currently, according to the need of domestic informationization construction, several ASP-based collaborative design systems suitable for small and medium enterprises have been developed by researchers in China[1~5]. In this paper, combined with our efforts in some research projects funded by *Hi-Tech R&D Program of China* and *Beijing Municipal Sci-Tech Program*, an ASP-based distributed collaborative design system based on web is introduced. Its framework is presented and some key techniques of system implementation and their solutions are researched. And then practice of the system is described.

SYSTEM ARCHITECTURE

Architecture of General ASP System

The architecture of a general ASP system can be illustrated by a three-level structure shown as in Figure 1, i.e., *Web Browser*, *Web Server* and *Application Server*. Where, service management and scheduling system is constructed between *Web Server* and *Application Server*.

Features of ASP system can be summarized as following[5]:

- Application services can be provided to clients by renting. It means no need of large investment on equipments, software and human resource, and, hence, reduction of investment risk.
- Centralized management is employed to application services. In general, ASP services are managed at a center, and clients access specified application via the Internet.

- Diversity of requirements and application services. As the most prominent feature, it means that diversity of consumers creates diversity of requirements, hence, diversity of application styles, shared resources, commercial manner, as well as complexity of security and charging.

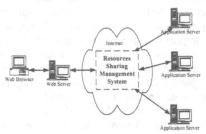

Figure 1   Architecture of general ASP system

Architecture of the Proposed System

Combining industrial requirements with our efforts in some research projects, we have developed an ASP-based collaborative design system, namely *Co-Design*. The proposed system support distributed real-time product design via the Internet/Intranet. Its aim is to build a virtual Computer Supported Cooperative Work (CSCW) environment, and makes it possible that we can design a product at the same time but from different places. Furthermore, it provides friendly interfaces with some resource libraries, such as mechanical component library, electronic component library, etc., to help engineers to design product more efficiently by utilizing these resources. Real-time collaborated design means the designer in collaborative design environment can perceive others' action in time. This collaborative method makes the design task be explored among the designers who are in different places and can satisfy the need of collaborative design of enterprises.

Figure 2 shows the general architecture of the proposed Co-Design system. The system is composed of four levels of functional modules: three fundamental levels, i.e., service-portal level, service-enable level and administrative level, and a common resource level. Where, service-enable level and administrative level form the core of the ASP-base distributed collaborative design system meanwhile the other two levels, i.e., service-portal level and resource level, are optional modules for NM-oriented informationization according to the needs of enterprises. However, if all of the above four levels are joined together, an integrated NM-oriented distributed collaborative ASP platform can be formed. Functions of the four levels are summarized in the following.

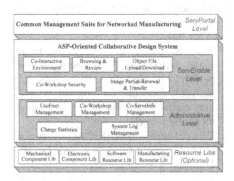

Figure 2   Architecture of Co-Design system

1) Service-portal Level
It is a portal administration module which provides universal application-independent service portal for the NM-oriented ASP platform. Main functions of the portal are as follow: providing entrance of single-sign-on authentication; providing entrance of integrated navigation for various applications and services; and supporting user-defined webpage set-up.

2) Service-enable Level

It is a collection of core modules which make collaborative design services available for end users. These modules, mainly used by common Co-Design users, are arranged to provide a virtual interactive workspace for distributed engineers to fulfill collaborative design activities. The five functional modules are listed as follows:

- Collaborative Interactive Environment
- Browsing & Review
- Object File Upload/Download
- Collaborative Workshop Security
- Image Partial-Renewal & Transfer

3) Administrative Level

It is a collection of core modules which make Co-Design administrations available for two kinds of administrators. One is for collaborative team leaders to manage design workspace, usufruct, resources, etc. Another is for system administrators to manage and maintain the system itself. The five functional modules are listed as follows:

- Usufruct Management
- Collaborative Workshop Management
- Collaborative ServiceInfo Management
- Charge Statistics
- System Log Management

4) Resource Libs

It is a collection of common resource libraries which facilitate collaborative design activities by utilizing these resources, such as selecting standard mechanical parts and/or electronic elements from libraries directly. Where, these mechanical parts and electronic elements can be stored as specified parametric templates in libraries and be instantiated to get actual form and dimensions at product design. The four libraries are listed as follows:

- Mechanical Component Library
- Electronic Component Library
- Software Resource Library
- Manufacturing Resource Library

KEY TECHNIQUES OF IMPLEMENTATION

Synchronization Mechanism of Distributed Collaboration

During the process of collaborative design, it needs cooperation among the geographically distributed designers. So we must have a concurrent control mechanism to guarantee that all users develop their goal in special orders otherwise there will be impossible to achieve their common goal because of the inefficiency. During the implementation of the collaborative design system, we adopt the method of token control to achieve our concurrent control function.

Autoadaptive Image Compression and Transferring

The geographically distributed real-time collaborative design system can run not only in the situation of the Internet but also in the Intranet. Because of restriction of the unbalance of network development in our country, we adopt two kinds of image compression method, i.e., JPG-based method and PNG-based method respectively, to implement the system in order to adapt to the different network situations. The compression method, JPG format or PNG format, is adopted autoadaptively according to bandwidth of the Intranet/Internet. Only 512K bandwidth is enough to implement the real-time synchronization in interactive collaborative design.

APPLICATIONS OF THE SYSTEM

Now the proposed Co-Design system has been applied to several networked manufacturing platform in some industrial informationization projects. For example, it has been used as an application service tool on the *Networked Manufacturing Platform of the Beijing Electronic Zone* (Beijing Electronic Zone Incubator Co., Ltd., URL. http://mapp.bez.com.cn/easp_ecm_view/dis playecm2/) and used as collaborative product development system on the *Networked Manufacturing Platform of Beinei Incubator* (Beijing Beinei Manufacturing High-tech Incubator Co., Ltd., URL. http://www.bjzzy.com.cn/). Figure 3 shows an example of product collaborative design via Beinei Platform.

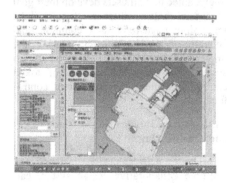

Figure 3 Industrial application example
of Beinei Incubator NM Platform

The effects of the system application can be summarized as follows:
- Small and Medium enterprises can use the big advanced manufacturing equipments and software and realize the informationization without expensive expenditure that is used to construct infrastructure of network and buy equipments and software.
- Searching for collaborators in wide range makes the collaborative designing and developing easy and effective, which upgrades the development ability of small and medium enterprises.
- Typical applications of the system were more than 16 enterprises, and were spread more than 200 enterprises, which have produced substantial social and economic benefits by reducing of collaboration expenditure, development cost and shortening time to market.

CONCLUSIONS

ASP-based system is a highly effective approach to NM platforms. In this paper, an ASP-based distributed collaborative design system is proposed to support remote collaboration. Architecture of the system is presented and some key techniques of collaborative design are researched. Now the system has been used as ASP tools to help several small and medium enterprises to accelerate their product development and typical application examples shows it can bring substantial benefits.

REFERENCES

[1] ZHANG Cheng, WANG Yunli, XIAO Tianyuan, Research on Distributed Real Time Collaborated Design Environment, Computer Engineering and Applications, 2002, 38(14), pp.61-63

[2] WANG Yunli, Research on Key Technologies in Internet-based Manufacturing and Supported Platform, Postdoctoral Research Report, Beijing: Tsinghua University, 2002

[3] LUO Ya-bo, XIAO Tian-yuan, Correlation-based Methodology for Resource Scheduling in Synchronal Cooperative Design System, Computer Integrated Manufacturing Systems, 2004,10(4), pp399-403

[4] GUO Cheng, LIAO Linrui, XIAO Tianyuan. Distributed Real Time Collaborative Design System Based on Intelligent Agent, Europe-Asia International Conference on advanced Engineering Design and manufacture for globalization, Xi'an China, April 2004

[5] WU Cheng , XIAO Tianyuan, ASP Platform and Its Federation Integration Based on Internet Used in Networked Collaborative Design and Manufacturing, 2006 10th International Conference on CSCW, May 2006, Nanjing, China, pp9-13

Incremental Reorganization
for Distributed Index System

Ken HIGUCHI*, Hidenori NOMURA*, and Tatsuo TSUJI

*Graduate School of Engineering,
University of Fukui,
Bunkyo 3··9··1, Fukui·city, Fukui, 910—8507, Japan
(E-mail: {higuchi, hidenori, tsuji}@pear.fuis.fukui-u.ac.jp)

ABSTRACT

In recent years, database systems have to manage large-scale and complex data and more rapidly response is desired. For these purpose, we proposed the distributed index system for complex objects. In our index system, an index of references between complex objects is constructed using the multi-index technique. The index is divided and managed on a shared-nothing parallel computer. By processing queries in parallel, good response time would be expected. Furthermore, the on-line modification and the on-line reorganization schemes were proposed. But on-line reorganization is expensive and degrades the turn-around times of other operations. In order to overcome this deterioration, we propose new reorganization scheme, called incremental on-line reorganization scheme. In our new scheme, reorganization operation is divided into small ones, and other operations are inserted between then. The experimental result on simulator proves the improvement of the turn-around times of other operations and the efficiency of our new scheme.

KEYWOED: object oriented database, distributed index system, on-line reorganization

INTRODUCTION

In recent years, database systems have to manage large-scale and complex data such as multimedia data, XML-document, etc. Furthermore, more rapidly response is desired. For these purposes, in an object-oriented database, a set of complex objects which have complex reference relation internally are managed, and the technique for rapidly retrieving them is desired. And, many kinds of large indexes are constructed for rapidly response. While index improves the response time for retrieval, index degrades the response time for data modification. In order to overcome this disadvantage, the distributed index for complex objects was proposed in Refs.7 and 8. In this system, an index of references between objects is made using the multi-index technique. And, the index is divided and managed on a shared-nothing parallel computer, and our system retrieves the final result along the specified retrieval path expression. By processing queries in parallel, good response time would be expected.

However, if the tendency of retrieval queries changes or a large amount of index modification queries occurs, response time would be often degraded. In order to overcome such a situation, index reorganization is needed. There are many reorganization schemes for database (Refs.1, 3, 4, 5, 6). But these techniques can be adapted effectively. Then, in Ref. 8, the incremental reorganization scheme was proposed. However, the reorganization keeps the influence on other processing even if it is on-line operation. In our new system, reorganization is divided into small ones and they are processed successively with other operations. By scheduling other operations among divided reorganize operations, response time of other operations are improved.

DISTRIBUTED INDEX SYSTEM

In this section, we summarize the index distributed system for complex objects. For detail of it, see Refs 7 and 8.

Before describing the distributed index system, we describe path expression and index. Path expression is the description for query condition. It is sequence of attributes of objects. Retrieval query contains the path expression and a set of objects. By traversing according to the path expression from specified objects, the result of query is computed. Therefore, according to path expression, the index elements are made from data objects. The distributed index system uses multi-index technique. Its index elements are made from parent-child relationships between objects.

The distributed index system divides the index constructed using multi-index technique (Ref. 2) into small indexes, and manages these divided indexes on shared nothing parallel computer.

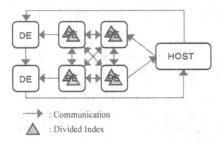

——▶ : Communication
▲ : Divided Index

Figure 1 The distributed index system

In the distributed index system (Figure 1), there are three kinds of processor elements (PE), which are retrieval PE (RPE), HOST, and DETECTOR (DE).

RPE is the PE which actually manages the divided index. Retrieval is processed by traversal among RPE using its index and communication according to the path expression. The retrieval scheme in RPE is the followings:

(1) RPE receives query.
(2) RPE retrieves the objects using query conditions and the index.
(3) If the result of (2) are the objects which belong to the class of the end of the path expression, the result send to HOST as result of query.
(4) If the result of (2) are not the objects which belong to the class of the end of the path expression, the result send to HOST as query of next step.

HOST is the PE which transmits retrieval/modification requests to RPEs. Furthermore, HOST aggregates the results of query from RPEs.

DE is the PE which decides whether the each step of request is finished or not. From above mentioned retrieval scheme, retrieval process is divided into small steps corresponding to the path expression. Each step of retrieval corresponds to an attribute in the path expression. And the retrieval steps are processed in fixed order. This is the property of multi-index. By using this property, DE decides the termination of the step of retrieval. One DE decides the termination of one step of retrieval by the information of the number of communications and the number of received and processed messages (see [] for details). For this purpose, RPE and HOST send this information to DE. Furthermore, DE decides the timing of modification and reorganization by the information of the termination of requests.

The performance of the distributed index system depends on the index partition. In [], hash function is used for deciding the index partition, and the reorganization consist of the change of hash function and the migration of index elements.

The features of the distributed index system are the followings:

(a) It can make history of operation equal to specified order.
(b) The modification scheme is on-line.
(c) It is independent from data storing system.
(d) It need no aborting for concurrency control
(e) The reorganization scheme is based on on-line modification, and on-line.

INCREMENTAL REORGANIZATION

In Ref. 8, we proposed on-line reorganization scheme for distributed index system. However, since reorganization is high cost operation and needs a large amount of index modifications, the advantage of on-line operation is not much as that of modification. Then, the reorganization degrades the turn around times of other operations which are processed in parallel with the reorganization. That is, while throughput is improved by on-line reorganization, the turn around times of other operations are not improved. Thus, new approach that improves turn around times of other operation is needed.

On the other hands, since reorganization needs a large amount of index modifications, the cost of locking the index for reorganization is relatively small. Then, if reorganization can be divided into several small reorganizations, it is expected that the cost of whole reorganization is nearly equal to the summation of the divided reorganizations. Furthermore, if other operations can be inserted between the divided reorganizations and can be processed by this order, it is expected that the turn around times of these inserted operations are improved. In this paper, this reorganization technique is called incremental. The distributed index system can apply the incremental technique because it fulfills these requirements.

EXPERIMENTS

To show the advantage and disadvantage of our incremental on-line reorganization scheme, we evaluate the performance of it by experiments on simulator. Our simulator is virtual simulator. In our simulator, each PE can process only one operation at a time in order of sending on HOST.

Experiment Environments

The target indexes are the followings.

(a) The length of path expression is 9. That is, the number of steps of query is 8, and the number of class is 9.
(b) The number of instances of each class is 1000000. Each object has no reference, 1, or 2 references at random.
(c) We constructed three indexes for simulation.

The parameters of simulation are the followings:

(d) The system consists of 16 RPEs, 4 DEs, and 1 HOST.
(e) Let Cs be the it initial set uptime needed at the beginning of communication, let Ct be the time needed for transferring a single object ID for request, and let Tr be the time necessary for retrieving a single index element. The ratio of these times is assumed to be Cs:Ct:Tr = 100:1:100\$.
(f) The probability that each object is included in one query is 0.01.
(g) The 10th request is the reorganization request.
(h) Two hash functions are used for index partition:.
type A : IID mod 64
type B : (IID mod 8) $\times$ 8 + CID - 1
Here, CID is ID for class and IID is ID for instance in same class. And type A is changed to type A' and type B is changed to type B' by reorganization request:
type A' : (IID + IID/64) mod 64
type B' : ((IID + IID/64) mod 8) $\times$ 8 + CID - 1

The reorganization form type A to type A' is called ROA, and that form type B to type B' is called ROB.

For each conditions and index, five times of simulation are executed, and the average of then is adapted as result. On the incremental on-line reorganization system, the numbers of elements in one part of divided reorganization are nearly equal to each other.

By simulation, our incremental on-line reorganization system is compared with the non-incremental on-line reorganization system, non-incremental off-line reorganization system, and incremental off-line reorganization..

Results of Experiments

Table 1 shows the total execution times, and Table 2 shows the average of turn round times for retrieval request. Figure 2 and Figure 3 show the turn around times for each retrieval requests in one sequence of simulation. The measure of them is Ct. Here, ION, ON, OFF, and IOFF show the incremental on-line reorganization system, non-incremental on-line reorganization system, the non-incremental off-line reorganization system, and the incremental off-line reorganization system respectively. On this experiment, the reorganization is divided into five parts, and 10 retrieval requests are inserted between them.

From Figure 2, Figure 3, and Table 2, ION and IOFF have steps, and the turn around times of the inserted retrieval requests between divided reorganizations are improved. It is reflected by incremental technique. From Table 2, ION is best of 4 systems for average of turn around times. From Table 1, for ROB, the differences between the total execution times of the incremental systems and the non-incremental systems are little. However, for ROA, the total execution times of incremental systems are degraded slightly. But these differences are nearly equal to the execution time for two retrieval requests. Then, this deterioration is not the serious disadvantage. On the comparison between the on-line systems and the off-line systems, the on-line systems are better than off-line systems except ION for ROA. But this deterioration is little relatively. Hence, the incremental on-line reorganization improves turn round time while it doesn't degrade throughput.

Table 1 Total execution time

	ROA	ROB
ION	57787171	51107052
ON	57462360	51112552
OFF	57531268	52060521
IOFF	57845358	51968506

Table 2 Average of turn round time

	ROA	ROB
ION	30613386	27489170
ON	44919596	40880081
OFF	44981305	41759893
IOFF	30665756	28295771

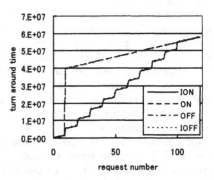

Figure 2 Turn around time (ROA)

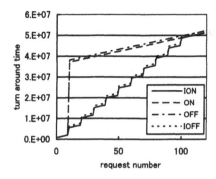

Figure 3 Turn around time (ROB)

CONCRUSION

We proposed the new reorganization scheme for the distributed index system, called the incremental on-line reorganization scheme. By simulation results, the turn around times of other request are improved by our new scheme. Then, it is effective. For future works, we need to examine in real system and real reorganization

REFERENCES

1. Salzberg, B., and Dimock, A., Principles of Transaction-Based On-line Reorganization, Proc. of 18th International Conf. on Very Large Data Bases, pp. 511-520, 1992.
2. Bertino, E., A survey of indexing techniques for object-oriented database systems, in Query Processing for Advanced Database, Freytag, J.C., Maier,D and Vossen, G.(Eds.), Morgan Kaufmam, pp. 383--418, 1995.
3. Achyutuni, K., Omiecinski, E., and Navathe, S., Two techniques for on-line index modification in shared nothing parallel database, Proc. of the 1996 ACM SIGMOD International Conf. on Management of Data, pp. 124-136, 1996.
4. Omiecinski, E., Concurrent File Reorganization: Clustering, Conversion and Maintenance, Data Engineering Bulletin, 19, 2, pp 25-32, 1996.
5. Zou, C. and Salzberg, B., Safely and Efficiently Updating References During On-line Reorganization, Proc. of 24th International Conf. on Very Large Data Bases, pp. 512-522, 1998.
6. Lakhamraju, M. K., Rastogi, R., Seshari, S., and Sudarshan, S., On-line Reorganization in Object databases, Proc. of the 2000 ACM SIGMOD International Conf. on Management of Data, pp.58-69, 2000.
7. Higuchi, K. and Tsuji, T., and Hochin, T., On-line Reorganization for Distributed Index System for Complex Objects, IPJS Trans. of Databases, 43, SIG12(TOD16), pp.64--79, 2002.
8. Higuchi, K. and Tsuji, T., On-line Reorganization for Distributed Index System for Complex Objects, IPSJ Trans. of Database, 45, SIG10(TOD23), pp 1-17,2004.

Containerization Algorithms for Multidimensional Arrays

Teppei Shimada   Tong Fang*   Tatsuo Tsuji   Ken Higuchi

Graduate School of Engineering, University of Fukui
3-9-1 Bunkyo, Fukui-shi, 916-8507, Japan
(E-mail: {shimada,touhou,tsuji,higuchi}@pear.fuis.fukui-u.ac.jp)

ABSTRACT

Multidimensional arrays used in MOLAP are often sparse. They also suffer from the problem that the time consumed in sequential access to array elements heavily depends on the dimension along which the elements are accessed. In this paper, we resolve the problem of this further dimension dependency.

KEY WORDS: MOLAP, chunk, container, extended chunk, Z-order

INTRODUCTION

Multidimensional arrays employed in MOLAP (Multidimensional On-Line Analytical Processing) systems have the following two problems:

(1) They are sparse in which empty elements occupy the greater part of the whole array.

(2) The time consumed in sequential access to array elements heavily depends on the dimension along which the elements are accessed.

The second problem stems from the way that the array elements are allocated to actual storage. That is, they are arranged linearly based on pre-determined order of dimensions. Sequential access that proceeds along this order is fast, but the access that does now follow this order would be slow. For example, the response time of aggregation computation for a slice of an array might greatly differ depending on the sliced dimension. To have a uniform treatment for all the dimensions, we can *chunk* the array [1]. Chunking is a way to divide an *n*-dimensional array into small size *n*-dimensional chunks and stores each chunk as a contiguous page on secondary storage. By chunk array, the dimension dependency above can be moderated.

In MOLAP systems, a chunk is the basic unit of data administration [2] [3]. The simple way of chunk allocation on secondary storage is the traditional scheme that allocating chunks linearly in a predetermined order of dimensions. This would produce further dependency. By using a constructed simulator, we will prove that our algorithms are really effective against the dependency problem.

Coping with the Dimension Dependency

The order in which the elements of a large array are accessed can have a considerable impact on performance. The usual method of storing a multidimensional array is *liner allocation* whereby the array is laid out linearly by a nested traversal of the axes (i.e. dimensions) in some predetermined order. This strategy does not cause serious problem when arrays are stored in a main memory, but can lead to disastrous on a

---

*Currently with Graduate School of Science and Engineering of Waseda Univ.

secondary storage. Unlike main memory accessing, a secondary storage is accessed based on page fetching. If array elements are accessed in the predetermined order, retrieving array elements can be performed very efficiently; i.e., the number of page fetches can be minimized. But all other accessing order would be inefficient due to the increasing number of page fetches.

It would be a big problem in MOLAP that retrieval performance thus depends on the ordering of dimensions along which array elements are allocated in secondary storage. One of the major objectives of OLAP system is to provide an interactive environment of multidimensional analysis of large volume data, and the response time is expected not to be damaged. If the viewpoints of a user's data analysis are changed, the response time might greatly deteriorate. Such situation is absolutely undesirable. It is very important for MOLAP system to respond to every demand of data analysis from various viewpoints within a tolerable constant time.

Chunk and its compression

In order to solve the performance dependency on the order of dimensions, a multidimensional array will be divided into *chunks* that are stored and retrieved together. A chunk of an *n* dimensional array is also an *n* dimensional array. The size of a chunk is within a single *page* and the element of the chunk occupies contiguous disk storage. So a chunk can be loaded on main memory by one page fetch procedure from secondary storage.

By chunking an array, we can have a uniform treatment for all the dimensions. Slicing an *n*-dimensional array along some dimension and aggregating the data on the sliced out *n-1* dimensional array are quite common operations in MOLAP. The number of times to access a disk page will be averaged regardless of the slicing direction. This is due to the fact that many

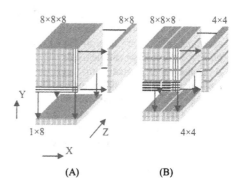

Figure 1: Chunk

data adjacent in every direction can be obtained by a single page fetch.

For example, Fig.1 (B) shows a three dimensional array of size 8×8×8 divided into 64 chunks of size 2×2×2. A single disk page is assumed to be able to contain 8 elements of the array. Fig.1 (A) is a usual case where the array elements are allocated contiguously along X axis. In (A), 8, 64, and 8 disk pages should be accessed to fetch all the elements sliced out by X-Y, Y-Z, and X-Z planes respectively. On the contrary, in (B), 16 disk pages are accessed for the elements sliced out by any plane. Note that both of the average number of the disk pages to be accessed and the standard deviation of the number are greater in (A) than in (B). This proves that the chunking is effective for alleviating the dimension dependency.

This averaging of disk page accesses is effective if the multidimensional array is occupied by dense chunks filled out with nonempty elements. The arrays employed in MOLAP are often sparse, so compressing is necessary to allocate only nonempty data. But compressing chunk data might produce further performance dependency on the order of dimensions. Our research aims to propose a disk allocation strategy for large multidimensional array by which chunk data compression does not introduce further performance dependency. Some appropriate compressing techniques, such as *chunk-offset* compression [3] or simple *bitmap* compression can be used.

A chunk is a logical unit and its size coincides with one disk page size. The size of the physical storage for a chunk is smaller than one page unless all the chunk elements are filled out with nonempty data. If more than one chunk involves many empty elements, they can be compressed and packed into one disk page. A disk page that involves such compressed chunks will be called a *chunk container* or simply as a *container*.

The combination of the compressed chunks packed into the same container should be determined deliberately. If they are packed in specific dimension order, a further problem of performance dependency on the dimension order might be caused. The aim of this paper is to propose a better chunk containerization strategy to alleviate this further dependency.

Containerizing Schemes

In this section, we propose several schemes (algorithms) of containerizing chunks in order to meet the requirement stated in the previous section. Fig.2 shows the sketch of these schemes. In the following, the memory buffer used for containerization will be called a *container buffer*, whose size is a single disk page size.

[A] Static order (S-ordering)
As in a non-chunked ordinary array, the compressed chunks are packed into the container buffer linearly according to the predetermined order of dimensions. If the container buffer is filled up with chunks, the buffer is output to the container file on the secondary storage. This containerization procedure is repeated until the last chunk in the order will be packed and output.

[B] Extended Chunk
An *extended chunk* is a chunk whose size is

flexibly determined according to the density of the effective elements involved in the related part of the array. The chunk used in the other algorithms is classified as the *base chunk*. An extended chunk is an array of base chunks. Each dimension of an extended chunk is same sized, and the size is 2^n ($n \geq 0$) times of that of the base chunk. Here n is called as the *rank* of the extended chunk. The containerization algorithm using extended chunks is two phased.

1. Rank determination phase
1) The origin chunk that is the start of checking rank up possibility is selected in predetermined order.
2) The filling rate of the neighbor chunks of the origin chunk are checked to know the rank up possibility.
3) If the neighbor chunks can be stuffed in the containerization buffer, rank up is possible and the region covered by the neighbor chunks becomes a new rank upped extended chunk. Then the above 2) is repeated. Otherwise, all the chunks in the region are not ranked up.
4) If above processes finished, a new origin (extended) chunk is selected and the rank up process continues until any rank up would not occur.

2. Combining phase
1) First we select the extended chunk that is the origin of this phase.
2) The dimension order of combining extended chunks is randomly determined. According to the order, the extended chunks in neighbor of the origin extend chunk are combined if the total size is under 1 page.
3) The above 1) and 2) are performed on the whole array to obtain the final containers in the output container file.

[C] Z-ordering
Z-ordering is studied and utilized in data engineering field. This algorithm arranges array elements recursively in the order of Z-curve. See Fig.2. We employ this algorithm as a containerization scheme. In this scheme, chunks are selected in the

order of Z-curve, and packed into the container buffer like in S-ordering. Employing Z-ordering contributes to avoid growing along specific directions and to preserve the neighborhood well. This feature leads to alleviate the further dimension dependency.

In Z-ordering scheme, the container buffer may contain the chunks in different Z-curves that are distantly located from each other. Such situation is not desirable for preserving proximity. One of the methods to avoid this situation is to consider the *level* of Z-ordering. The level of minimum region of Z-curve is called Lv0, the level of double sized region is called Lv1, and quadruple sized region is called Lv2, and so on. The whole array is partitioned into the same level regions, and even if the container buffer is not full, it is output to the secondary storage when the last chunk of the region is encountered. The region level should be determined based on the density of chunks.

Evaluation

Simulation experiment

We have constructed a simulator to evaluate the containerization algorithms proposed in the previous section. The evaluated chunk array is five dimensional. Its size is 18 chunks in every dimension, so the total number of chunks is $18^5 = 1,889,568$. Each chunk in the array is assumed to have uniform data density. Its filling rate is changed for 0.01% to 0.1% by the width 0.01%. The five dimensional chunk array will be containerized. From the produced containerized array A, we get an i-dimensional slice of A ($i = 1,..., 4$), which means the set of the containers involved in an i-dimensional cross section of A. The total number of the i-dimensional slices of A can be computed as:

$$_5C_i \times 18^{(5-i)}$$

We measure the average number of

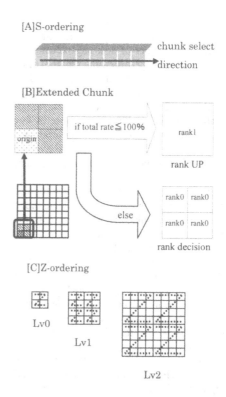

Figure 2: Containerization

containers involved in an i-dimensional slice and the standard deviation of the number. The smaller the standard deviation is, the less the performance dependency on the dimension order is.

Simulation results and comparison

Fig.3 shows the number of produced containers corresponding to the filling rate of the container. Fig.4 and Fig.5 show the average number of containers involved in a 3 dimensional slice and the standard deviation of the number. The total number of the produced containers in S-order is smaller, but the standard deviation is larger than in any other schemes due to the dimension dependency discussed in Section

"Chunk and its compression".

In Lv0, since total number of containers is larger, the number of disk page accesses is much larger in Z-ordering. On the other hand, we can see that the numbers in Lv1 and Lv2 Z-orderings are small. This is due to that the Lv0's region (unit of container-ization) is the smallest, so number of low filling rate containers would be produced. In Lv1 and Lv2 Z-orderings, the average number of containers and the standard deviation are rather small. This is due to that the Lv1 and Lv2 have larger regions than Lv0, so each container can have much more base chunks. This means that the filling rate of each container is higher than Lv0. The standard deviation of Lv1 is proved to be the smallest. This means that the number of containers in the slice of each dimension is well averaged. So Lv1 is proved to be the best method in this point.

In extended chunk, the number of produced containers is less than Lv1, and the standard deviation is also better. Since an extended chunk consists of the lower rank extended chunks that are closely located logically, the number of containers in a slice can be well averaged.

In consequence, we can conclude that the Lv1 Z-ordering is recommended in both of the low average number of the disk page accesses and the less access performance dependency on the dimension order.

Conclusion

This paper presented an implementation scheme of large scaled multidimensional arrays for MOLAP system. Several kinds of algorithm for packing and arranging compressed chunks into a container were proposed and evaluated. These algorithms reduce the performance dependency on the dimension order in which array elements are allocated on the secondary storage, while suppressing the storage cost.

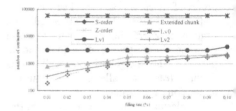

Figure3: Total number of containers

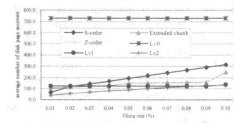

Figure4: Average number of disk page access of three dimensional slices

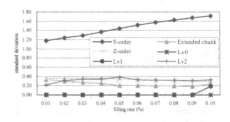

Figure5: Standard deviation of three dimensional slices

REFERENCES

1. S.Sarawagi, M.Stonebraker, Efficient Organiza-tion of Large Multidimensional Arrays, Proc. of ICDE, 1994, pp.328-336.
2. Sanjay Goil, Alok Choudhary, A Parallel Scalable Infrastructure for OLAP and Data Mining, International Data Engineering and Applications Symposium, AZ, 1999, pp.159-170.
3. Yihong Zhao, Prasad M.Deshpande, Jeffry F.Naughton, An Array-Based Algorithm for Simultaneous Multidimensional Aggregates, Proc. of SS- DBM, 1994, pp.218-227

A Mechanism for Anonymous Auction

Kazem HASSAN*, Shinsuke TAMURA** and Tatsuro YANASE**

* Department of Computer Engineering, Faculty of Engineering
Ittihad University
Ras Al Khimah, P.O.Box 2286 United Arab Emirates
(E-mail: hassanishome@hotmail.com)
** Department of Information science, Faculty of Engineering
University of Fukui
3-9-1 Bunkyo, Fukui, 910-8507 Japan

ABSTRACT

Most of current technologies that enable secure information sharing assume that entities that share information are mutually trustworthy. However, in recent applications this assumption is not realistic. As applications become sophisticated, information systems are required to share information securely even among untrustworthy entities. This paper discusses one kind of problem about information sharing among untrustworthy entities, i.e. anonymous auction. The problem is to keep the entities' identities confidential while ensuring detecting the dishonesty such as deadbeat bidders, sellers not selling to auction winners.

KEY WORDS: Security, Anonymous, Authentication, Auction, Passwords

NOMENCLATURE

$A, B, ...$: The name of the clients(bidders).
S : Seller's blind signature; a function to sign on token without knowing its value.
Ec :The encryption function used by clients to veils their token.
i: The number of the auction round and its range is from $0,1$ to m ; m is the final round.
$(^b)$: Encryption key used in blind signature at the client's side.
$(^b)$: Encryption key used in blind signature at the seller's side.
$V(T_i)$: *Veiled Token;* . i.e.: set of data (Token) encrypted (Veiled) by encryption function Ec.

INTRODUCTION

The current online auctions are bringing great benefits but the privacy policy is subject to be discussed; and it will be a great achievement if it would be possible to maintain data and identities of individuals secret. This paper proposes a mechanism for anonymous auctions that enable the above achievement to increase the trust and use of online auctions.

The auction proceeds as follow: a seller announces its service and a starting bid price online, then clients (bidders) after visiting the site and opening accounts anonymously announce their bid price. The bidding is repeated while clients are increasing their bids according to their strategies and limits. There will be a winner who will get the appointment to exchange its bid price with the service.

There are many difficulties in developing such systems when bidders are anonymous, for example: the winner might not come to the appointment (deadbeat bidder), the seller might not sell, the seller might bid in its own auction, or bidders might conspire. This research is trying to mitigate these difficulties.

The requirements for such a system are:

1. Bidders can know the current price and the winning price.
2. Bidder is anonymous to the seller and other bidders.
3. The seller sells to the highest bidder.
4. Deadbeat bidders (Bidders who wins but don't appear to appointment) can be identified.
5. Detect seller's dishonesty.

In order to satisfy these requirements, the mechanism proposed in this paper uses two methods i.e. anonymous authentication and blind signature

ANONYMOUS AUTHENTICATION

The anonymous authentication mechanism enables entities to be authenticated as authorized ones without disclosing their identities, based on password selection strategy. In the mechanism a seller determines whether a client, which is characterized by its identification code (ID) and password pair, is an authorized one or not. Different from conventional mechanisms, according to password selection strategy, the client dose not show its ID and password pair. The client finds its password in the password list, which is generated by the seller, and declares whether its password is included in the list or not in the following way.

Firstly, the client generates D, a list of IDs that includes the ID of the client itself. Also the client memorizes the position where its own ID is located in D, and the

client sends D to the server. After that, the seller registers all passwords that correspond to items in D to the password list P, while maintaining their order in the list as designated by the client. Then the seller encrypts each password p in P by using secret random bit pattern r, that is, each password p is replaced by $\underline{p}$ = p XOR r (exclusive-or of p and r). At the same time the seller calculates $\underline{r}$ = E(r,K) and send P and $\underline{r}$ to the client. Here, E a one-way encryption function and K is its encryption key. Then, the client finds out its encrypted password p in P (it is possible because items in P are ordered as designated by the client), and calculates r' as the result of XOR of $\underline{p}$ and the password that the client is memorizing. Also the client calculates r* = E(r', K) while using the same encryption function E and key K as the seller, and send r' back to the seller, when it confirms that $\underline{r}$ = r* . Finally the seller authenticates the clients when r = r'

It is easy to prove that the seller can authenticate authorized clients while not knowing their identities by the above procedure. Namely, the facts that 1) only clients that have authorized ID and password pairs are authenticated, and 2) all clients that know their ID and password pairs can be authorized.

BLIND SIGNATURE

Blind signature shown in Fig.1, works as follow:

The client prepares a message n, encrypts it with the random bit number r and public encryption key (^{b}) and sends the result as a veiled token to the seller. Then the seller blindly signs on the token i.e. encrypt it again with the encryption key (^{b}) ($\underline{b}$ is defined so that ($^{b*\underline{b}}$ =1) is satisfied), and sends the signed token back to the client. The client can calculate m=n$^{\underline{b}}$ since it knows (r), which is the signed message of the seller. Namely the seller can verify m by decrypting n^b by the public key b. The benefits of this technique is to allow data to be shared and verified without disclosing its meaning.

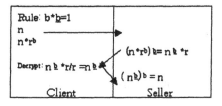

Fig.1 Blind signature

PROCEDURES OF THE ANONYMOUS AUCTION

Authentication
When the auction starts, the only authorized clients can join the succeeding phases of anonymous auction, this is achieved through the anonymous authentication mechanism.

Initial token preparation

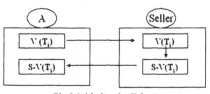

Fig.2 Initiating the Token

Figure 2 shows the procedures in the initial token preparation phase. Each client prepares its preferable but unique *Veiled Token* $V(T_i)$ and sends it to the seller. Then the seller blindly signs on it and saves it in its records and sends the result i.e. S-V(T_i) to the client for its future use. Then the auction moves to the next phase.

Bidding phase
At this point as shown in Fig.3, the seller discloses the initial bid price for the item,

then every client tries to bid to the seller with valid (blindly signed)-(veiled token) S-V(T_i). At the same time the client sends a new veiled token $V(T_{i+1})$; to be signed by the seller in order to be used for the next round.

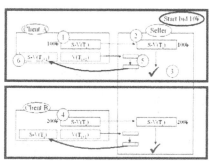

Fig.3 Bidding phase

The seller rejects tokens, which are not signed or are used repeatedly. Concerning the $V(T_{i+1})$ it will be changed into S-V(T_{i+1}) i.e. signed by the seller and sent to the client whenever another client bids. When no client bids within duration pre defined, the auction moves further to the next phase.

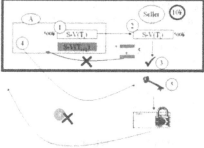

Fig.4 Final Round

At final round as shown in Fig.4, once one client (A) remains with the heights bid and no other client (B) bids during the round time limits (A) becomes the winner.

235

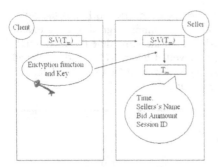

Fig.5 Identifying winner

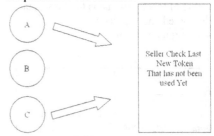

Seller Check Last
New Token
That has not been
used Yet

Fig.6 Exclude deadbeat bidder

At this stage we assume that the token contains some important information such as the name of the seller and the bid amount as shown in Fig.5. Therefore when the winner A appears, the seller and clients can challenge (A) to disclose its encryption key that was used for its final token $S\text{-}V(T_m)$, so that they will be able to decrypt $S\text{-}V(T_m)$ which contains the highest bid amount, seller's name and etc. It's not possible that two winners appear because no client can forge the token that includes the winning price with the seller's signature; i.e. at each round only one round winner is being validated by the seller's blind signature and at each round the used token is saved in all entities' records. When the winner is identified the seller exchange appointment with the client and this can be done with any convenient key exchange method like *Diffie-Helman Key Exchange.*
At this stage the requirements 1,2 and 3 are satisfied.

Deadbeat bidder detection phase
A bidder might win the auction but never appear which affect the seller's reputation. The last token of clients can be used to detect such behavior as shown in Fig.6, i.e. the seller requests all clients to disclose their last valid (not being used yet)) token and only the deadbeat bidder (B), fails to respond to this challenge because it didn't receive valid token when it was identified as an auction winner. And at this point

Dishonest seller detection phase

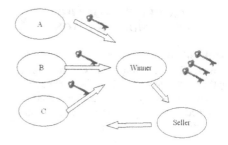

Fig.7 Detect server's dishonesty

When the auction is closed and the winner had been anonymously identified, the winner requests the seller to prepare appointment using the key that had been exchanged in winner identification phase. Here, the winner can challenge the seller by disclosing his key, and all other clients can verify that the disclosed key can decrypt the appointment. It is also possible to force the seller to attend the appointment and excluding seller's dishonesty by using the techniques as shown in Fig.7, i.e. the seller responds to the challenge of proving his attendance the appointment by disclosing a secret words known to all other clients but not known to it. Namely the winner sends a secret word SW1 to client A and a secret word SW2 to client B …and SW3, SWn in advance, and when the seller appears the client disclose all those secret words to the seller so that the seller can responds to the challenge of proving attendance to the auction entities then requirement 5 is satisfied.

EVALUATION AND CONCLUSION

The proposed procedures satisfy the requirements as follows.

- The clients had disclosed no identification information, therefore their privacy is maintained i.e. authentication is anonymous, token had no identification information, it had private key but its value is random and can't be used to identify clients and also with the assumption the network is anonymous.
- The seller in every round discloses current price and the round's wining price, and when the auction is closed it discloses the final winning price.
- The seller can identify the winner anonymously using the winner's last used token.
- Excluding the deadbeat bidder is satisfied anonymously.
- Detecting the seller's dishonesty is satisfied.
- It is possible to use the password selection strategy for anonymous account creation. As future works, more research could be done to apply the mechanism to more open environments where large numbers of clients and mutually unknown clients are involved.

REFERENCES

1. F.Stajano: "Security for Ubiquitous Computer," John Wiley & Sons, pp. 153-160 (2002)
2. S.Tamura, T.Yanase: "Information Sharing among untrustworthy entities," IEEJ Trans. EIS, Vol. 125, No. 11,2005
3. S.Tamura, K.Kouro and T.Yanase "Expenditure Limits in Anonymous Credit Card Systems," IEEESMC 2006.

A Web System for Dynamic Displays of Special Functions in a Mathematical Software Package

Toshiki Sando*, Yohsuke Hosoda*, Yousuke Takada* and
Takemitsu Hasegawa*
*Department of Information Science,
University of Fukui,
Fukui, 910-8507, Japan

ABSTRACT

A mathematical software package NUMPAC includes many routines for computing special functions of single or double variables. To view each special function in 2D or 3D graphics, we have constructed a system on the Web. This system enables users to display special functions in 3D graphics dynamically as well as interactively.

keyword: Online system, WWW, 3D dynamic display, special functions, mathematical software package

1 Introduction

NUMPAC is a mathematical software package constructed at Nagoya University, which has been installed in a number of computers in Japanese universities since 1970's and has been used by a large number of users. NUMPAC consists of around 1000 subroutines written in FORTRAN with their manuals for performing various numerical computations, say, linear systems of equations, nonlinear equations, eigenvalue problems, interpolations, integrations, differential equations, special functions.

To make numerical computations with NUMPAC routines avaliable to lots of users we have constructed a system on the WWW, NetNUMPAC [2], which provides users on the Web with several useful facilities, such as retrieving online manuals, template interface to facilitate users to compute with NUMPAC routines, displaying the computed results in 2D or 3D graphics and so on.

In this paper we describe one of the facilities above in NetNUMPAC, namely, a facility to display computed results in 3D graphics, in particular, a dynamic and interactive display system on the Web for a variety of special functions such as Bessel functions and interpolations of bivariate functions or of two-dimensional data as well as for functions defined by users. No other systems seem to exist on the Web for computing mathematical functions like special functions and displaying them in 3D graphics dynamically and interactively.

2 NUMPAC

NUMPAC is a general-purpose numerical subroutine library constructed by the members of Numerical Analysis Group at Nagoya Univerisity since 1971. NUPAC has been installed in more than fifty major universities in Japan, whereas in 1998 it was installed in Hitachi supercomputer SR2201 at Polish-Japanese Institute of Computer Techniques in Warsaw, Poland.

NUMPAC covers a wide range of numerical computations as follows (the numerals in parentheses denote the numbers of members included): system of linear equations (40), eigenvalue analysis (29), nonlinear equation (14), interpolation (25), Fourier analysis (34), numerical quadrature (38), ODE (4), special function (148) as well as semi-numerical processing (20) like sorting. Each member consists of single and double precision versions at least and sometimes even complex value and quadruple precision versions, too, as well as some versions tuned for supercomputers of Fujitsu, Hitachi and NEC.

The richest part of NUMPAC programs is the field of special function (148). Indeed typical ones are Bessel functions of integer or real order and real or complex argument and their related integrals and zeros; inverse hyperbolic functions; Struve functions; Kelvin functions; exponential integrals; Gamma function of complex argument; incomplete Gamma functions; incomplete Beta function; Dawson's integral; Clausen's integral; integral of the complementary Error function; Riemann Zeta function; solutions of Thomas-Fermi equation and Blasius equation and their derivatives; Abramowitz functions; Langevin function; orthogonal polynomials and so on.

3 NetNUMPAC

NetNUMPAC system aims at making the NUMPAC routines and their manuals accessible to anyone who can access to the WWW but doesn't want to use the mainframe computers which have accommodated the NUMPAC routines. In fact, NetNUMPAC provides users on the Web with facilities as follows,

1. online manuals written in HTML for each subroutine,

2. downloading the source programs in NUMPAC,

3. retrieving manuals and corresponding subroutine programs; each manual is arranged in a hierarchical structure, that is, in a tree structure similar to the classification scheme of scientific software GAMS[1],

4. computing with given test programs call-

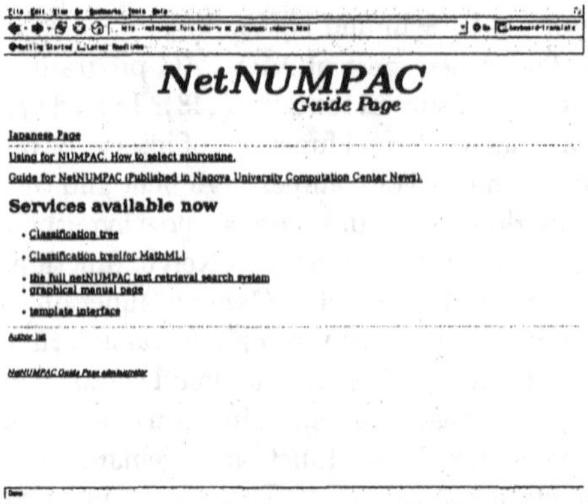

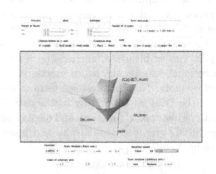

Figure 1: Top page of the NetNUMPAC sysytem

Figure 2: 3D display of Spence function with input forms to specify the figure position

ing MUNPAC routines,

5. simple interfaces to facilitate the use of NUMPAC routines without knowledges of any programming languages,

6. graphical interfaces to display computed results in 2D or 3D graphs, in particular, for special functions or interpolations.

In the next section the last facility above will be described in some details. Fig 1 shows the top page of NetNUMPAC.

4 Graphical display system

This section explains a 3D graphics system for NUMPAC. Each NUMPAC routine has its own test program to illustrate the use of the routine and computed (numerical or graphical) results. To demonstrate the graphical

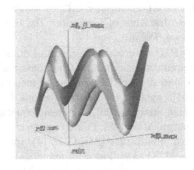

Figure 3: 3D display of Hermite interpolation

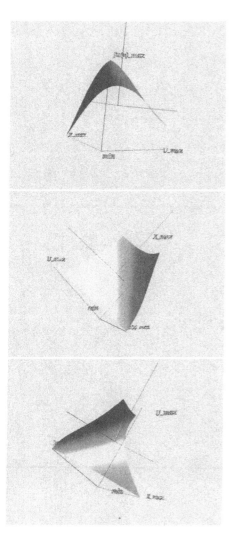

Figure 4: Displays of automatic roration of Bessel function with complex argument around an axis specified by the user.

results, NetNUMPAC provides a graphic system, that displays the computed results in 2D or 3D graphics on Web pages. To this end Java is useful, in particular for the dynamical and interactive display on Web pages, where client users set values of arguments of subroutines and the ranges of coordinate axes for displaying figures, see Fig 2. In this connection, the client-server system is also used to communicate between both client and server machines so that figures may be displayed on the client machine after the computations are performed on the server machine installing NUMPAC routines to prepare the data required to produce graphics.

Now, twenty three special functions of NUMPAC routines are availble to be diplayed in 3D graphics on Web pages, where clients can choose the function name of special functions above and the way of displaying, namely the addition of the contour map and/or the grid mesh and/or the automatic rotation of the figure displayed. In the facility of the automatic rotation above users can choose the rotation axis arbitrarily as well as rotational speed, see Figs 3 and 4. In addition the mouse operation enables users to translate, rotate or enlarge the displayed graphics. These operations are possible by using Java3D as follows:

1. Function to specify rotational angle

This function is achieved by using Thread class of Java3D. When users input the numerical value to the text field and start rotation, the figure rotates by a given angle and then stop.

2. Automatic rotation around a given axis

This function is achieved by using addChild

and removeChild method. When users specify values of 3D vector for an axis around which users wish to rotate the figure, it rotates automatically around the given axis.

3. Function to operate solid figure with mouse

This function is achieved by using MouseBehavior class. The figure rotates, zooms and moves by dragging mouse buttons on the left, the center and the right, respectively.

5 Outlook

The problems left are to display more than one objects on the same screen and to display a section of the objects.

References

[1] R. F. Boisvert, S. E. Howe and D. K. Kahaner, GAMS: A framework for the management of scientific software, ACM Trans. Math. Soft., 11 (1985) 313–355.

[2] T. Hasegawa, T. Sando, Y. Sato, Y. Hatano and I. Ninomiya, An online system NetNUMPAC for NUMPAC and its performance test on supercomputers, Memoir of Fukui University, 48 (2000) 193–214.

Study of Nonlinearity of Pneumatic Servo Table System

Takashi MIYAJIMA*, Taro OGISO**, Toshinori FUJITA***, Kenji KAWASHIWA****
and Toshiharu KAGAWA****

* Department of Computational Intelligence and Systems Science, Tokyo Institute of
Technology
R2-46 4259 Nagatsuta-cho, Midori-ku, Yokohama, Kanagawa, 226-8503 Japan
(E-mail: miyajima@k-k.pi.titech.ac.jp)
** Department of Mechano-Micro Engineering, Tokyo Institute of Technology
*** Department of Machinery System Engineering, Tokyo Denki University
2-2, Kanda-Nishiki-cho,Chiyoda-ku, Tokyo, 101-8457 Japan
**** Precision and Intelligence Laboratory, Tokyo Institute of Technology

ABSTRACT

Pneumatic servo table system is one of a precise positioning system using air power. We have derived the
linearized model of the pneumatic servo table system and have designed the controller and the observer
based on the derived linear model. On experimental results, the servo table system shows tracking error
on the linear model based control. This tracking error comes from the discrepancy between the actual
system and the linear model.
In this paper, we design a nonlinearity compensation method to reduce this tracking error. Then, we
confirm that the accuracy of the trajectory tracking is greatly improved in the nonlinear simulation by
using the nonlinearity compensation method. Finally, we apply this controller to the actual system and
confirm the effectiveness experimentally. The controllability of the system is improved both the nonlinear
simulation model and the experimental results.

KEY WORDS: Pneumatic Servo System, Precise Positioning, Nonlinearity Compensation

NOMENCLATURE

A_p	area of pressured wall	$[m^2]$
b	critical pressure ratio	[-]
G	mass flow rate	[kg/s]
K_a	acceleration feedback gain	$[V\ s^2\ /m]$
K_f	mass flow rate coefficient	[s/m]
K_n	system gain	[m/(V s)]
K_p	proportional gain	[V/m]
K_{sv}	valve gain	$[m^2/V]$
K_v	velocity feedback gain	[V s/m]
l_t	slider stroke	[m]
M_t	slider mass	[kg]
P	pressure	[Pa]
R	gas constant	[J/(kg K)]
s	Laplace operator	$[s^{-1}]$
t	time	[s]
u	control input	[V]
V	chamber volume	$[m^3]$

x	slider position	[m]
δ	non-choke coefficient	[-]
κ	specific heat ratio	[-]
θ	temperature	[K]
ω_n	natural frequency	[rad/s]

Subscripts
0	equilibrium point
1,2	chambers
a	atmosphere
s	supply
lin	nonlinearity compensation
ref	reference

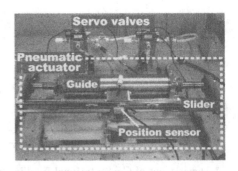

Fig. 1: External view of Pneumatic Servo Table

INTRODUCTION

Pneumatic servo systems are used in many fields, such as pneumatic robot systems[1], aspherical glass molding machines, and vibration isolation systems. Because air has a number of advantages, including compressibility, high power ratio, and low heat generation. Also air is non-magnetic and is a clean energy source. Recently, pneumatic servo systems are also applied to precise positioning systems.

The pneumatic servo table system is one of pneumatic precise positioning systems which have an air bearing to reduce friction force [2]. To design a controller of this system, the linear model of the system is required. The model is used to tune the control gains and to calculate the feedfoward control parameters.

The derived model of the servo table system under appropriate assumptions becomes 3rd-order delay system. The controller uses position of the servo table, velocity of it and acceleration of it to calculate a feedback signal. The velocity and the acceleration are obtained using a Kalman filter. For the control gains calculation, a gain-phase margin diagram of 3rd order is used. The closed loop transfer function has a steady state velocity error. To compen-

sate for this velocity error, a feedfoward compensator has been added to the control system. We have confirmed that the position error of the linear model based control is 5.0 [μm].

In this paper, a nonlinearity compensator is derived and applied to the servo table system to improve the position controllability.

We confirmed that the accuracy of the trajectory tracking is greatly improved in the nonlinear simulation. Then, we applied this controller to the real system and measured it experimentally.

PNEUMATIC SERVO TABLE

The pneumatic servo table system is one of precise positioning systems using air power. Figure 1 and 2 shows the external view and the the schematic diagram pneumatic servo table system.

This system is constructs from a pneumatic actuator and a pair of servo valves. The pneumatic actuator consists of a slider and a guide. The slider is the moving part of the actuator. The pressured wall is attached to the slider; consequently, the slider is driven by the pressure difference at both sides of the pressured wall. The pressured wall forms two chambers between the guide

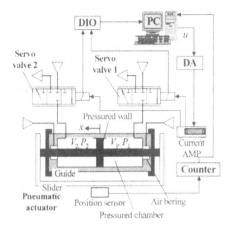

Fig. 2: Schematic Diagram of Pneumatic Servo Table

and the slider. Mass flow rate to each chamber is controlled by a High-Performance Pneumatic Servo Valve (HPPSV) [3]. Between the slider and the guide, air bearings are attached. The slider can move under zero friction force condition by the air bearings.

The HPPSV is a direct drive 3-port spool valve. This valve has higher dynamic characteristic than commercially available servo valve.

The position of the pneumatic actuator is measured by an optical position sensor of resolution 0.05[μm]. The position are stored in a personal computer with real-time operating system. The personal computer calculates a control input and sends the control input to servo valves.

Modeling

The governing equations of the system are an equation of motion, a state equation of ideal gases and a flow equation. In this study, these equations are written under the following assumptions to derive a linear model of the system.

The influence of the pipes is neglected. The friction force is negligible because of the air bearings. From these assumptions, the equation of motion is given by:

$$M_t \ddot{x} = A_p(P_1 - P_2) \tag{1}$$

It is assumed that the slider moves only right to left in Fig. 2. It follows that the chamber 1 is charging and the chamber 2 is discharging. The state change of the gas is assumed to be an isothermal condition. From these assumptions, the total differentiation of the state equation of ideal gases is linearized around the equilibrium point:

$$\frac{dP_1}{dt} = \frac{R\theta_0}{V_0}G_1 - \frac{P_0 A_p}{V_0}\dot{x}$$
$$\frac{dP_2}{dt} = \frac{R\theta_0}{V_0}G_2 + \frac{P_0 A_p}{V_0}\dot{x} \tag{2}$$

The air leakage from air bearings is negligible. The characteristic between the effective area and the servo valve input can be assumed as a linear. The pressure of both chambers at equilibrium point is slightly higher than atmosphere pressure. Hence, the mass flow to chamber 1 is choked and that of chamber 2 is non-choked. From these assumptions, the flow equation is given by:

$$G_1 = K_f K_{sv} P_s u$$
$$G_2 = -\delta K_f K_{sv} P_s u \tag{3}$$
$$K_f = \sqrt{\frac{\kappa}{R\theta_0}\left(\frac{2}{\kappa+1}\right)^{\frac{\kappa+1}{\kappa-1}}}$$
$$\delta = \sqrt{1 - \left(\frac{P_a/P_0 - b}{1 - b}\right)^2}\frac{P_0}{P_s}$$

From Eq. (1) - (3), the open loop transfer function from the servo valve input u to position of the actuator x given by:

$$P_n(s) = \frac{K_n \omega_n^2}{s(s^2 + \omega_n^2)} \tag{4}$$
$$K_n = \frac{(1+\delta)K_f K_{sv} P_s R\theta_0}{2A_p P_0}$$
$$\omega_n = \sqrt{\frac{2A_p^2 P_0}{M_t V_0}}$$

245

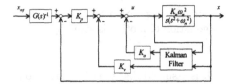

Fig. 3: Block Diagram of Linear Model

Control Method

Linear Model Based Control

A PDD^2 control method is used to control this system. The PDD^2 control method feedbacks the position, the velocity and the acceleration.

The velocity and the acceleration are not detectable. To estimate these value, The Kalman filter is used. The feedback gains are selected from gain-phase margin diagram adequately. The closed loop transfer function has a steady state velocity error. To compensate for this velocity error, a feedfoward compensator has been added to the control system.

The maximum acceleration of the servo table is restricted by the maximum effective area of the servo valve. Therefore, the acceleration reference trajectory is designed not to saturate the servo valve. Then, the position reference trajectory became the 3rd order curve. Figure 3 shows the block diagram of the system under the linear model. In Fig. 3, $G(s)^{-1}$ shows the feedfoward compensator of the system.

Nonlinearity Compensation

The experimental results by using the linear model based control show tracking error in the large acceleration moving and the large stroke moving.

The causes of this tracking error is the discrepancy between the actual system and the linear model. To reduce this tracking error, nonlinearity compensator is designed.

The chamber volume changes according to the variation of the position of the actuator. In the linearized model, the chamber volume is fixed at equilibrium point value. In large stroke moving, this modeling error causes tracking error. From the position of the slider, The chamber 1 volume is given as:

$$V_1 = A_p(l_t + x) + V_m \qquad (5)$$

Then, Eq. (2) including the variation of the chamber volume given by:

$$\frac{dP_1}{dt} = \frac{R\theta_0}{V_1}G_1 - \frac{A_pP_0}{V_1}\dot{x} \qquad (6)$$

From Eq. (2) and (6), the nonlinearity of the chamber can compensate by adjusting the mass flow rate. The compensated mass flow rate G_{lin} given by:

$$G_{1lin} = \frac{V_1}{V_0}G_{1ref} - A_pP_0\left(\frac{V_1}{V_0} - 1\right)\dot{x} \qquad (7)$$

From Eq. (2), (7), the compensated control input is given:

$$u_1 = \frac{V_1}{V_0}u - \frac{P_0A_p}{K_fK_{sv}P_s\sqrt{R\theta_0}}\left(\frac{V_1}{V_0} - 1\right)\dot{x} \qquad (8)$$

Hence, the tracking error could be improved by using compensated control input u_1.

SIMULATION RESULTS

The effectiveness of the nonlinearity compensation is confirmed by using a nonlinear simulation model. The nonlinear simulation model considered the nonlinearity of flow equation, the temperature variation and the nonlinear characteristics of the servo valve. Figure 4 shows the simulation results of the position response and the tracking error of the pneumatic servo table system.

From Fig. 4 the tracking error of the linear model base control increases according to the slider movement. On the other hand, the result of the nonlinearity compensation control does not increase. It is clear that the nonlinearity compensation is effective to improve tracking error.

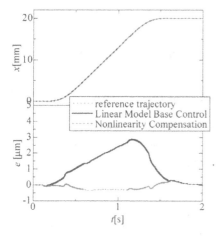

Fig. 4: Nonlinear Simulation Results

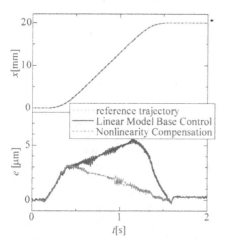

Fig. 5: Experimental Results

EXPERIMENTAL RESULTS

Figure 5 shows the experimental results of the tracking control of the pneumatic servo table system.

From Fig. 5, The tracking error of the nonlinear compensation is significantly improved compared with that of the linear model based control. The tracking error of the system become under $3[\mu m]$ at 20[mm] stroke.

The experimental results of the linear model based control shows good agreement with the simulation result in Fig. 4. On the other hand, the experimental results of the nonlinearity compensation method shows large tracking error compared with the simulation result. One reason of this error is considered as the delay of the servo valve response.

CONCLUSION

We proposed a control method to compensate nonlinearity characteristics of a pneumatic servo table system. By using this control method, the effect of the volume change of pressurized chambers were compensated.

The effectiveness of this control method was confirmed in a nonlinear simulation model. The experimental results indicate that the position controllability is improved. As a result, the tracking error of the system become under $3[\mu m]$.

REFERENCES

[1] Liu S. and Bobrow J.E. An analysis of a pneumatic servo system and its application to a computer-controlled robot. 1988, ASME J. Dyn. Syst. Meas., and Control, 110:228-235

[2] Kagawa, T. et al., Accurate positioning of a pneumatic servo system with air bearings, 2000, Power Transmission and Motion Control: 257-268.

[3] Miyajima, T. et al., Development of a Digital Control System for High-performance Pneumatic Servo Valve, 2006, Precision Engineering,(to appear in)

Modelling of a 4-port Nozzle-flapper Type Pneumatic Servo Valve

Tao WANG, Kenji KAWASHIMA and Toshiharu KAGAWA

Precision and Intelligence Laboratory, Tokyo Institute of Technology
4259 Nagatsuta-cho, Midori-ku, Yokohama, Kanagawa, 226-8503, Japan
(E-mail: wangtao@k-k.pi.titech.ac.jp)

ABSTRACT

In many precise pneumatic control systems, nozzle-flapper type servo valves are widely used as proportional elements neglecting the torque motor dynamics and flow force on the flapper inside the servo valve. In this study, a nonlinear dynamic model for a 4-port servo valve with dual fixed orifices and dual nozzles is derived. This includes the dynamics of the torque motor, the flow rate characteristics of the fixed orifices and variable nozzle-flappers, and the flow force on the flapper. In order to validate the derived model, we establish a simulation system using Matlab/Simulink software. It is confirmed that the static and dynamic responses of both the simulated and experimental results shows good agreement. a practical linear model is derived from the complete nonlinear model. It is showed that the applicable range of the linear model is about ±30% of the rate input current.

KEY WORDS: nozzle-flapper type pneumatic servo valve, nonlinear model, linear model

NOMENCLATURE

A : Area of nozzle
B_f : Damping coefficient
b : Critical pressure ratio
C : Sonic conductance
F_f : flow force at flapper
G : Mass flow rate
i : Input current
J : Armature-flapper moment
K_a : Rotational stiffness of flexure tube
l_a : Distance from nozzle to centre of rotation
m : Subsonic index.
P : Pressure
V : Volume of control chamber
x : Displacement of flapper
x_f : Distance from flapper tip to each nozzle at zero input current
α : Armature-flapper deflection
θ : Temperature of air

INTRODUCTION

In pneumatic position and force control systems, nozzle-flapper type servo valves are normally used for obtaining precise, quick-response control due to their simple construction, high sensitivity, and wide frequency range. Pneumatic control systems with nozzle-flapper elements are generally approximated as a first-order lag system assuming isothermal state change for the air in the load chamber. Nozzle-flapper type servo valves are usually treated as a proportional element by neglecting the torque motor dynamics and flow force on the flapper. Currently, there is no general mathematical model to describe a 4-port nozzle-flapper type electronic-pneumatic servo valve [1]. Especially, in some high precision pressure control systems, e.g. exposure apparatuses that are actively isolated using air-springs, an accurate model of the servo valve is required for the design of the system dynamics. Therefore, in this paper, general nonlinear and linear models are proposed that include the torque motor dynamics and the flow force.

CONSTRUCTION AND OPERATION

The basic construction of a 4-port nozzle-flapper type servo valve with dual fixed orifices and dual nozzles is shown in (a) of Figure 1. The armature flapper is moved by a torque motor consisting of a coil and vertically arranged magnets. Movement of the flapper changes the distance between it and both nozzles. This creates different pressures, P_{c1} and P_{c2}, on the control sides. Based on its construction and characteristic, we proposed a new symbol for the nozzle-flapper type servo valve in (b) of Figure 1.

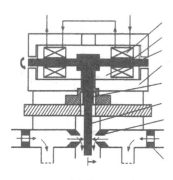

(a) Construction

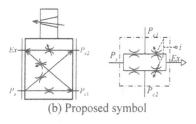

(b) Proposed symbol

Figure 1 The basic construction of a 4-port nozzle-flapper type pneumatic servo valve

DYNAMIC MODEL

Torque motor and armature-flapper

We consider the servo valve is completely symmetrical. For a one-degree-of-freedom model of the armature-flapper [2], the current in the coil generates a torque driving the armature flapper. The relationship between the input current and the torque, including the influence of eddy currents, is given by:

$$T_e \dot{T}_t + T_t = K_m \alpha + K_i i \qquad (1)$$

The torques on the armature flapper are caused by a flex-tube, acting as an elastic support, and flow forces generated by the air jet from the two nozzles as follows:

$$T_s = K_a \alpha \qquad (2)$$

$$T_f = (F_1 - F_2) l_a \qquad (3)$$

Summing moments about the centre of rotation yields:

$$J \ddot{\alpha} = T_t - T_s + T_f - B_f \dot{\alpha} \qquad (4)$$

The flapper tip displacement depends on the inclinations and deflections of the flex tube and of the flapper as:

$$x = \alpha l_a + K_e (F_{f1} - F_{f2}) \qquad (5)$$

Flow rate characteristics

The flow through the fixed orifice and through the nozzle flapper can be either sonic or subsonic, depending on the upstream/downstream pressure ratio. The mass flow rate through a restriction is a function of geometric parameters and of the upstream and downstream pressures. The mass flow rate can be expressed as:

$$G = C \rho P_u \varphi(P_u, P_d) \qquad (6)$$

where

$$\varphi(P_u, P_d) = \begin{cases} 1 & P_d/P_u \leq b \\ \left\{1 - \left(\dfrac{P_d/P_u - b}{1-b}\right)^2\right\}^m & P_d/P_u > b \end{cases} \quad (7)$$

C_0, b_0, and m_0, represent the corresponding constants for fixed orifices. We assume a constant critical pressure-ratio, b_n and a constant subsonic index, m_n for the nozzle flapper. The sonic conductance, C_n, is approximately proportional to the gap between the nozzle and the flapper and can be expressed as:

$$C_n = \begin{cases} C_{n0}(x_f + x)/x_f; & \text{for right nozzle - flapper} \\ C_{n0}(x_f - x)/x_f; & \text{for left nozzle - flapper} \end{cases} \quad (8)$$

where C_{n0} is the sonic conductance of the nozzle flapper at zero input current.

Flow force on the flapper
Applying momentum theory for the control surface in the nozzle-flapper and neglecting the velocity of the flapper tip, the air velocity reaches a maximum value up to the local speed of sound at exit of the nozzle. The flow force, F_f, acting on the flapper can be approximately expressed as:

$$F_{f1} = \left(1 - f\left(\frac{x_f + x}{x_f}\right)^3\right) P_c A \quad (9)$$

$$F_{f2} = \left(1 - f\left(\frac{x_f - x}{x_f}\right)^3\right) P_c A \quad (10)$$

where f is flow force coefficient related to nozzle physical geometrics.

Air dynamics in the control chamber
The servo valve construction shows that when the control ports are closed, there are small chambers (V_1 and V_2) between the

fixed orifice and the nozzle. The air temperature change inside the chamber is assumed to be isothermal. The flow rate change in the chamber can be determined from the air state equation and continuity equation as:

$$G_c = \frac{\dot{P}_c V}{R\theta} = G_o - G_n \quad (11)$$

G_c, V, P_c, G_o, and G_n for the left and right sides of the flapper are expressed by substituting the subscripts for these parameters with the subscripts 1 and 2, respectively.

Simulations and experiment verification

Simulation structure
From the above analysis, we can establish a resulting model of the servo valve from Eqs. (4)-(8) and (11) as shown in Figure 2.

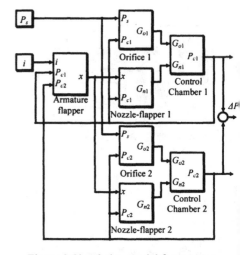

Figure 2 Simulation model for a 4-port nozzle-flapper type pneumatic servo valve

The input is the current, i, and the outputs are either the pressures, P_{c1} and P_{c2}, or ΔP. Of the model parameters, the torque motor and the armature-flapper dynamic coefficients, T_e, B_f, and K_e were compared with the experimental results. The coefficient in the flow force Eqs. (9) and (10) were estimated by using the experimental approach. The coefficients in the flow rate Eqs. (6)-(8), C_o, b_o, and m_o, C_{n0}, b_n, and m_n, were determined according to the flow rate measurement method. The other parameters were determined from the physical properties of the valve.

Simulation and experiment conditions

To validate the model, a Matlab/Simulink model of the servo valve shown in Figure 2 was constructed and solved for various operating conditions. The simulation results were compared with experimental results for the same operating conditions. In addition, to clarify the influence of flow force, a model was also formulated that excludes the flow force.

Steady-state results

Figure 3 shows the measured and simulated steady-state pressures, P_{c1}, P_{c2} and ΔP, vs. input current, i (no load flow rate) with both of the control ports closed.

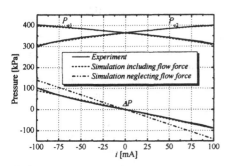

Figure 3 Output pressure vs. input current

It shows good agreement between measured and simulated results, despite some hysteresis and a slight deviation at both ends of the curve representing the measured results. For the simulation results neglecting the flow force, the change of ΔP with respect to i was in excess of the experimental results. This can be explained

by noting from Eqs. (4) and (5) that neglecting the flow force on the flapper leads to larger displacements of the flapper than for the real system.

Dynamic response results

Various step input currents were applied to the model and to the experimental setup with both control ports closed. The input current was varied using step-up signals with magnitudes of ±20% and ±40% of the rated current. Figure 4 shows ΔP vs. t for these conditions. As shown in Figure 4, the measured and simulated results that include the flow force are in good agreement. However, neglecting the flow force produces a steady-state error of about 30% between the simulated and measured results. This shows that the flow force reduces the pressure gain of the servo valve.

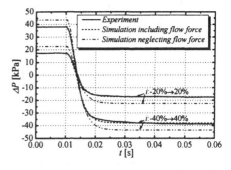

Figure 4 Step response of the differential pressure to different step-up inputs

Linear model

In servo system design, linear models are often more useful than nonlinear models. Therefore, we derived a linear model to approximate the nonlinear model described in the previous section as shown in Figure 5. The linear model approximation is made with respect to the equilibrium state corresponding to blocked control flow with $i = 0$.

Because the two control pressures at

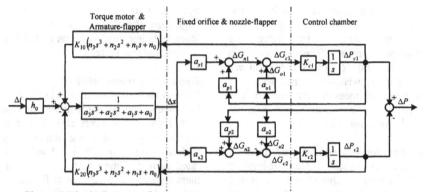

Figure 5 Block diagram of a 4-port pneumatic nozzle-flapper type servo valve

equilibrium are not zero, the pressure and flow rate variation dynamics to the input current variation have the forms shown in Figure 5. This block diagram shows that a 4-port pneumatic nozzle-flapper type servo valve including the control chambers can be represented by an approximate fourth-order model.

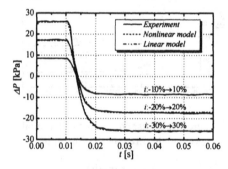

Figure 6 Step responses by nonlinear and linear models

To verify that the linear model correctly capture the fundamental dynamics of the servo valve, the responses to the various step input currents were simulated using the nonlinear and linear model. Because the input range for the actual control system was ±30% of the rated input current, the amplitude of the change in input current

was set to $i=\pm10$, ±20, and ±30 mA.

Figure 6 shows the experimental and simulated results for the response of the differential pressure of both the models. The linear model agrees well with the nonlinear model and the experiment. Figure 6 also clearly demonstrates that for changes in input current up to ±30 mA, there is close correlation between the linear model and the nonlinear model.

CONCLUSION

A nonlinear model of a 4-port pneumatic nozzle-flapper type servo valve is proposed, which includes motor dynamic and the flow force on the flapper. Static and dynamic responses of both the simulated and actual systems are in good agreement. And the influence of the flow force was demonstrated. A linear model was derived from the nonlinear model, and is applicable over a range of about ±30% of the rated input current.

REFERENCES

1. Urata, E. and Yamashina, C. 1998. Influence of Flow Force on the Flapper of a Water Hydraulic Servovalve, *JSME International Journal*, Series B, Vol. 41, No. 2, pp. 278-285
2. Urata, E. 2004. One-degree-of-freedom Model for Torque-motor Dynamics, *International Journal of Fluid Power*, Vol. 5, No. 2, pp. 35-42.

Dynamical Model of Leak Measurement by Pneumatic Pressure Change

Laksana Guntur HARUS*, Maolin CAI**, Kenji KAWASHIMA** and Toshiharu KAGAWA**

* PhD student of Mechano-Micro Engineering Department, Tokyo Institute of Technology
4259 Nagatsuta Chou, Midori-Ku, Yokohama, 226-8503 Japan
(E-mail: harus@k-k.pi.titech.ac.jp)
** Precision and Intelligence Laboratory, Tokyo Institute of Technology
4259 Nagatsuta Chou, Midori-Ku, Yokohama, 226-8503 Japan

ABSTRACT

We developed a leak detector based on pressure change measurement using a leak-tight master and test chamber, modeled the system and simulated the pressure responses. As the heat transfer tend to be different between master and test chamber, imbalance of temperature recovery will occur when the required temperature recovery time is not satisfied and produce unexpected pressure difference despite leak tight. This will increase the inaccuracy of the leak detector. The mathematical model was established and the heat transfer coefficient of the master is set to be slightly different with the test chamber to show the phenomena. The results showed that inadequate temperature recovery time produces unexpected pressure difference and reduce the accuracy. The results were verified experimentally and showed a good agreement.

KEY WORDS: Leak, Temperature recovery, Pressure change, accuracy

NOMENCLATURE

b : Critical pressure ratio []
C : Sonic conductance [m^3/(s.Pa)]
C_p : Specific heat at constant pressure [J/(kg.K)]
C_v : Specific heat at constant volume [J/(kg.K)]
G : Mass flow rate [kg/s]
h : Heat transfer coefficient [W/(m^2.K)]
κ : Ratio of specific heat []
m : Mass [kg]
P : Pressure [Pa]
ΔP : Differential pressure [Pa]
Q_L : Leak rate [m^3/s]
R : Ideal gas constant [m^2/(s^2.K)]

S_h : Heat effective area [m^2]
T_h : Thermal-time constant [s]
T_r : Temperature recovery time [s]
V : Volume [m^3]
W : Air mass [kg]
θ : Temperature [K]
$\Delta\theta$: Differential temperature [K]
ρ_o : Air density at standard conditions [kg/m^3]

Subscripts
m : Master
t : Test
in : Inflow

out : Outflow

INTRODUCTION

Leak is unexpected problem in many fields since it causes energy losses, hazard to human health, inefficiency and low performance. Leak and its measurement becomes a very important research field nowadays, not only due to the wide application in industry, but also due to the wide range of leak size that needs several methods to handle [1-3].

Detecting leak by measuring the pressure change between two identical components (master and test component) is one of widely used method in leak detector industry [1]. This will include a charging process of air/gas in to the components/chambers before starting leak detection. Kagawa *et al* demonstrated in his paper that pressure response of a charged chamber is affected by the heat transfer between the chamber wall and the environment [4]. Higher charged pressure and bigger volume take longer temperature recovery time that must be considered when the pressure change technique is used for leak detector [5].

When two chambers are charged simultaneously, imbalance of temperature recovery between the chambers occurs due to a minute difference of heat transfer coefficient and produces unexpected pressure difference. To minimize the effect of imbalance of temperature recovery to the leak detection, providing sufficient temperature recovery time is one of the solutions [5].

In the present research, we modeled the system, simulated the effect of imbalance of temperature recovery time between master and test components to the leak detection, and verified experimentally the result.

THEORETICAL ANALYSIS AND SIMULATION

Charging in to a leak-tight chamber

When a chamber is charged with air, as shown in Figure 1, in to a certain level of pressure, the temperature within the chamber increases and recovers to the environment temperature. To illustrate the phenomena, the state equation of ideal gas is derived as follows:

$$PV=WR\theta \tag{1}$$

$$\frac{dP}{dt} = \frac{P}{\theta}\frac{d\theta}{dt} + \frac{R\theta}{V}G \tag{2}$$

And from the conservation of energy, the following equation is obtained:

$$C_v m\frac{d\theta}{dt} = C_v G(\theta_a - \theta) + RG\theta_a + q \tag{3}$$

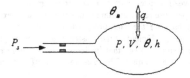

Figure 1 Air charged in to a chamber

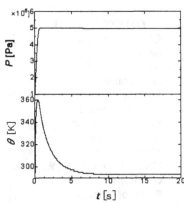

Figure 2 Simulated pressure and temperature response when air charged in to a chamber

As the atmosphere temperature is maintained constant at a certain level θ_a, the heat transfer rates passing through the chamber wall of the charging-discharging

254

process can be expressed as:

$$q = hS_h(\theta_a - \theta) \quad (4)$$

Based on Eq. (1), Eq. (2) and Eq. (3), the pressure and temperature change inside the chamber during charging process, can be expressed utilizing the following equations:

$$\frac{dP}{dt} = \frac{R}{C_v V}\left[G(C_p\theta_a - C_v\theta) + hS_h(\theta_a - \theta)\right] + \frac{R\theta}{V}G \quad (5)$$

$$\frac{d\theta}{dt} = \frac{R\theta}{C_v PV}\left[G(C_p\theta_a - C_v\theta) + hS_h(\theta_a - \theta)\right] \quad (6)$$

Where the mass flow rate in to the chamber is expressed as:

$$G_{in} = \begin{cases} C\rho_o P\sqrt{1 - \left(\dfrac{P/P_s - b}{1-b}\right)^2} \dots \dfrac{P}{P_s} > b \\[4mm] C\rho_o P \dots \dots \dots \dots \dots \dots \dots \dfrac{P}{P_s} \le b \end{cases} \quad (7)$$

During charging process $G=G_{in}$ for both leak and leak-tight chamber, neglecting the leak rate G_{out} which is pretty small compared to the charging rate G_{in}.
Figure 2 shows the simulated pressure and temperature responses when a $140 \times 10^{-6}\text{m}^3$ of chamber is charged up to 500kPa of pressure.

Charging in to two leak-tight chambers
In a pressure change measurement based leak detector, as shown in Figure 2, two leak-tight chambers are charged simultaneously to supply pressure before starting leak detection. Owing to Eq. (5) and (6), the pressure and temperature distribution inside the chambers are expressed as:

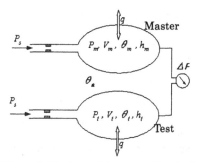

Figure 3 Air charged in to two identical chambers

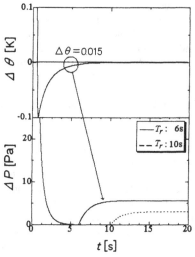

Figure 4 Simulated differential temperature and pressure response

$$\frac{dP_m}{dt} = \frac{P_m}{\theta_m}\frac{d\theta_m}{dt} + \frac{R\theta_m}{V_m}G_m \quad (8)$$

$$\frac{dP_t}{dt} = \frac{P_t}{\theta_t}\frac{d\theta_t}{dt} + \frac{R\theta_t}{V_t}G_t \quad (9)$$

$$\frac{d\theta_m}{dt} = \frac{R\theta_m}{C_v P_m V_m}\left[G_m(C_p\theta_a - C_v\theta_m) + h_m S_h(\theta_a - \theta_m)\right] \quad (10)$$

$$\frac{d\theta_t}{dt} = \frac{R\theta_t}{C_v P_t V_t}\left[G_t(C_p\theta_a - C_v\theta_t) + h_t S_h(\theta_a - \theta_t)\right] \quad (11)$$

The imbalance of temperature recovery between the two chambers and the induced pressure difference can be expressed by:

$$\frac{d\Delta P}{dt} = \frac{dP_t}{dt} - \frac{dP_m}{dt} \tag{12}$$

$$\frac{d\Delta\theta}{dt} = \frac{d\theta_t}{dt} - \frac{d\theta_m}{dt} \tag{13}$$

When the charging process is stopped, G_{in} is equal zero.

Temperature recovery time T_r is defined as a period of time from start charging to stop charging or start leak detection. Figure 4 shows the simulated differential temperature and pressure responses of two identical leak-tight chambers, $140\times10^{-6}\mathrm{m}^3$, charged up to 500kPa, at two different T_r, 6s and 10s. As the heat transfer tend to be different between master and test chamber, in the simulation, the heat transfer coefficient is set at $30\mathrm{W(mK)}^{-1}$ and $30.08\mathrm{W(mK)}^{-1}$ for master and test chamber respectively.

As shown in the upper part figure, imbalance of temperature recovery occurs due to a minute difference of heat transfer coefficient between master and test chamber. When the leak detection is started during the imbalance of temperature recovery (e.g. at T_r=6s), unexpected pressure difference occurs. The results show, the longer the T_r, the smaller the unexpected pressure difference is.

Temperature affected inaccuracy

To demonstrate the effect of the temperature affected pressure to the accuracy of leak detection, the simulation on leak test chamber is conducted. When the test chamber in Figure 3 is leaking, the leak rate $G_{out} \neq 0$ though it is pretty small in the order of $10^{-12}\mathrm{m}^3\mathrm{s}^{-1}$. Owing to the state equation of ideal gas equation, the relation between leak rate and pressure change can be derived as follows:

$$\frac{dW_m}{dt} = \frac{V_m}{R\theta_m}\frac{dP_m}{dt} - \frac{P_m V_m}{R_m\theta_m^2}\frac{d\theta_m}{dt} \tag{14}$$

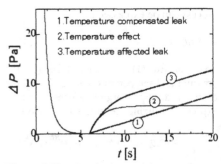

Figure 5 Simulated pressure changes due to leak

$$\frac{dW_t}{dt} = \frac{V_t}{R\theta_t}\frac{dP_t}{dt} - \frac{P_t V_t}{R_t\theta_t^2}\frac{d\theta_t}{dt} \tag{15}$$

$$\rho Q_L = \frac{dW_t}{dt} - \frac{dW_m}{dt} \tag{16}$$

If the two chambers are equal in temperature, volume and undergo identical thermal fluctuations, then the leak rate is:

$$Q_L = \frac{1}{\rho}\left(\frac{V}{R\theta}\frac{d\Delta P}{dt} - \frac{\Delta P V}{R\theta^2}\frac{d\theta}{dt}\right) \tag{17}$$

The real leak or the temperature compensated leak can be expressed by:

$$Q_L = \frac{Vd\Delta P}{\rho R\theta.dt} \tag{18}$$

Figure 5 shows the simulated results of the temperature compensated leak, the temperature affected leak and the temperature effect/the unexpected temperature difference. The real leak is set at $0.57\mathrm{Pa.s}^{-1}$. When the required T_r is not satisfied, imbalance of temperature recovery produces unexpected pressure difference that can decrease the accuracy of the leak detection.

EXPERIMENTAL VERIVICATION

Responses of leak-tight chamber
Figure 6 shows the simulated and experimental temperature affected pressure

differences of two identical leak-tight chambers, $140 \times 10^{-6} m^3$, charged up to 500kPa, at two different T_r, 6s and 10s. Both the simulated and experimental results show, the longer the T_r, the smaller the unexpected pressure difference is.

Leak detection
It has been illustrated theoretically the phenomena of imbalance of temperature recovery and its effect to the accuracy of leak detection. Figure 7 shows the leak detection results when $8.33 \times 10^{-10} m^3 s^{-1}$ of leak rate was generated form the test chamber ($V_t = 140 \times 10^{-6} m^3$) at 500kPa of applied pressure. Inaccuracy of leak detection occurs affected by temperature due to inadequate temperature recovery time.

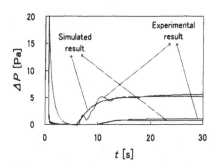

Figure 6 Simulated and experimental temperature affected pressure difference

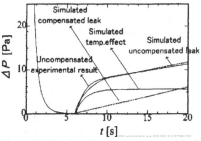

Figure 7 Simulated and experimental leak detection

CONCLUDING REMARK

A leak detector based on pressure change measurement using a leak-tight master and test chamber was developed and the mathematical model was established. The simulated results show that the imbalance of temperature recovery occurs when the required temperature recovery time is not satisfied and produces unexpected pressure difference despite leak tight. It produces inaccuracy to the leak detector. The simulated results were verified experimentally and in a good agreement.

REFERENCES

1. Leak tester : http://www.directindustry.com
2. Witness, M. and Sarah, L.G., Leak Detection in Pipes by Frequency Response Method, Journal of Hydraulic Engineering,2001, Vol.127, p.134-147.
3. Lee, I.D., Smith, O.I. and Karagozian, A.R., Hydrogen and Helium Leak Rates from Micromachined Orifices, Journal of AIAA (American Institute of Aeronautics and Astronautics), 2003, Vol.41, p.457-464.
4. Kagawa, T. and Shimizu, M., Non dimensional Pressure Responses of Pneumatic RC Circuit Considering Heat Transfer, Proceeding of Hydraulic and Pneumatic, 1988, Vol.19 p.306-311.
5. Harus,L.G. et al, Determination of Temperature Recovery Time in Differential-pressure-based Air Leak Detector, Transaction of Measurement Science and Technology, Institute of Physics Publishing, England, 2006, Vol.17, pp.411-418.

Simulation for Energy Savings in Pneumatic System

Maolin CAI* and Toshiharu KAGAWA**

* School of Automation Science and Electrical Engineering
Beihang University,
Xueyuan-road 37, Haidian District, Beijing, 100083 China
(E-mail: caimaolin@buaa.edu.cn)
** Precision and Intelligence Laboratory
Tokyo Institute of Technology
4259 Nagatsuta-cho, Midori-ku, Yokohama, 226-8503 Japan

ABSTRACT

Energy saving is very important for pneumatic system since it is not efficient. Simulation technology makes it possible to save energy by three measures. They are analysis of energy distribution inside a component, optimization of component selection and rationalization of pressure supply. In this paper, the necessity and utilization of simulation technology in the three measures are discussed respectively. The simulation objects include pneumatic cylinder, solenoid valve and pipe, etc. Dynamic behavior of these components is calculated by simulation and the results are used for energy distribution analysis, component selection and control of optimal pressure supply.

KEY WORDS: Energy saving, Pneumatic system, Air power, Energy distribution, Pneumatic cylinder

NOMENCLATURE

$\dot{E}$: rate of mechanical work
P : air power
p : absolute pressure
Q : volumetric flow rate
Subscript
a : atmosphere

INTRODUCTION

It is known that pneumatic system is not efficient and it consumes 10% to 20% of the total electricity in manufacturing factories. A significant portion of the energy consumed by pneumatic system is wasted due to improper settings and operation, as well as inappropriate equipment [1]. This is because that a pneumatic system is generally designed with less consideration of energy consumption. For securing the desired system performance, some components are selected over necessary specifications and pressure is outputted at compressor far higher than in terminal equipment. The system built in this way inevitably leads to lots of unnecessary energy consumption. Furthermore, a pneumatic component such as cylinder is always designed without any energy distribution analysis. Therefore, analyzing energy distribution inside a component, optimizing component selection and making pressure supply reasonable are essential for minimizing energy costs of a pneumatic system.

To do these, we must obtain dynamic behavior of a component and a system, and then calculate energy distribution inside a component or confirm system performance after selecting a component. Simulation technology becomes necessary for calculating the dynamic behavior. This paper introduces how simulation technology is used for the three energy saving measures mentioned above.

SIMULATION FOR ENEGY DISTRIBUTION ANALYSIS

What is Air Power?

In the previous study, air power was proposed to represent the energy flux of flowing compressed air that can be theoretically converted to mechanical power [2]. Given Q and Q_a as the volumetric flow rate under the compressed state and the atmospheric state respectively, Air power can be expressed as

$$P = pQ \ln \frac{p}{p_a} = p_a Q_a \ln \frac{p}{p_a} \qquad (1)$$

at the atmospheric temperature.

From Eq. (1), it is visible that air power has a unit of Watt just like electric power. This makes it easy to discuss the power supply and its distribution in a pneumatic system just like in an electric system.

Energy Distribution in Pneumatic Cylinder

Among pneumatic equipment, it is considered that cylinder and compressor result in low energy transformation efficiency. Large quantities of cylinders are used in automatic production lines. It is an important project to establish a method to make clear energy distribution in a cylinder. Figure 1 shows a vertically actuating cylinder lifting a load. The cylinder behavior at one actuation cycle can be simulated with the mathematic model of cylinder, which has been proved by lots of experiments [3]. With the simulated behavior including piston displacement,

piston velocity, chamber pressures in driving and returning sides, etc, energy rate distributed to the following parts can be calculated [4].

$\dot{E}_1$: work done against external forces

$\dot{E}_2$: increased energy conserved in the driving chamber

$\dot{E}_3$: work done against external air pressure

$\dot{E}_4$: energy loss at supply passage

$\dot{E}_5$: work done against internal forces

$\dot{E}_6$: work done for acceleration

$\dot{E}_7$: energy loss resulted from irreversible factors such as heat transfer, etc

The distributed energy during one actuation cycle may be calculated by the following integration.

$$E_{sub} = \oint_{1cycle} \dot{E}_{sub} dt \qquad (2)$$

There are two typical control circuits in cylinder actuating systems: meter-out and meter-in circuits. Simulation and energy calculation was conducted in these two circuits. The results are shown in Figure 2. It is clear that the supplied energy is mainly distributed to the work for lifting the load, the energy conserved in the driving chamber and the work done against the pressure in the discharging side and the atmospheric pressure. The work done for piston acceleration and the energy loss resulted from irreversible factors is very little. The sum of them is even not larger than 3% of the supplied.

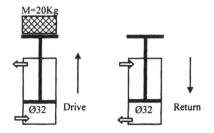

Figure 1   A vertically actuating cylinder

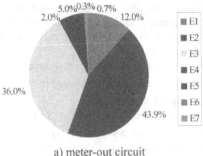

a) meter-out circuit

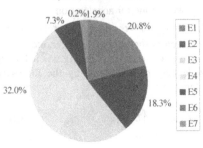

b) meter-in circuit

Figure 2   Energy distribution during one
cycle of a vertically actuating cylinder

From the above calculation example, we
know that it becomes possible to clarify
energy distribution in a pneumatic
component using the similar method based
on simulation.

SIMULATION FOR COMPONENT SELECTION

When constructing a pneumatic system, it is
not easy to determine model or size of
components such as cylinder, solenoid
valve and pipe. In the past, these
components were usually selected by
experience. But a number of components
larger than required were selected. Today,
simulation technology is helping us to
pursue an optimal selection.

Cylinder Actuating System

On the basis of cylinder actuation model,
flow rate characteristics of solenoid valve

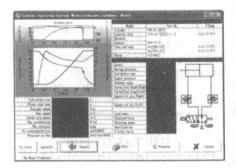

Figure 3   Component selection software

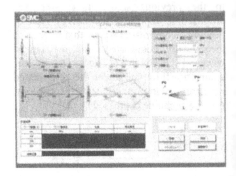

Figure 4   Nozzle size determination
software

and model of air flow inside a pipe, it is
possible to build a simulation system to
calculate the dynamic characteristics of a
simple cylinder actuating system. Figure 3
shows the window of the simulation system.
In the system, the dynamic characteristics
will be given by simulation after all the
components are selected. According to the
results, a customer can change size of
components to obtain the desired actuation.
Simultaneously, a customer can input a
desired actuation such as full stroke time,
maximum speed, etc., and make the system
automatically determine components. The
first selection is completed based on an
expert database. Then the selected
component will be changed automatically
by inquiring whether the desired actuation
is obtained [4].

With this component selection system, we can easily determine components with a size just required.

Air Blowing System

Air blowing system is widely used in factories for draining water off parts, blowing dust off slot and so on. It is reported that almost half of supplied air is consumed by air blowing system in an automobile assembly plant. However, many blowing nozzles used in plants are inappropriate to their applications. This is because airflow around nozzle is so complicated that it is not an easy work to determine a proper one.

The simulation tool shown in Figure 4 can solve this problem [4]. Based on desired blowing force inputted manually, the tool can optimally determine nozzle size, supply pressure and blowing distance to make air consumption the minimum.

SIMULATION FOR OPTIMAL PRESSURE SUPPLY

What is Optimal Pressure Supply?

Generally, compressor is controlled to keep the pressure in a buffer tank, mounted nearly after compressor, in a narrow range. Because pressure loss along supply pipe changes largely in various conditions, the pressure in the tank is always set far higher than that required in the terminal equipment. The unnecessary pressure will be reduced at the terminal by a regulator.

As shown in Figure 5, an optimal pressure supply is a system where the pressure at the terminal is fed back to the controller in real time and compressor only works to secure the minimum pressure supply at the terminal. In the system, pressure losses are considered and compensated in the control.

Control Realization

Because there is long pipe between the compressor and the terminal, the control system is nonlinear and it has a large delay.

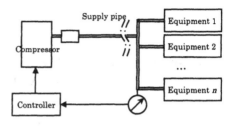

Figure 5 An optimal pressure supply

Furthermore, it is difficult to describe pipe dynamics with a transfer function. Because simulation should be faster than actual pressure transfer, simulation in real time can compensate the delay due to pipe. We are trying to propose a fast-calculated model for pipe.

CONCLUSION

This paper introduces the following three simulation applications used for energy savings in pneumatic system.
1. Energy distribution analysis inside a pneumatic component
2. Component selection tool for cylinder actuating system and air blowing system
3. Control of optimal pressure supply system

REFERENCES

1. Advices of Energy Conservation for Compressors, Japan Society of Industrial Machinery Manufacturers, 2000.
2. Maolin Cai, Kenji Kawashima, Toshiharu Kagawa, Power Assessment of Flowing Compressed Air, Journal of Fluids Engineering, Transactions of the ASME, 2006, 128-2, pp.402-405.
3. L.R. Tokashiki, Toshinori Fujita and Toshiharu Kagawa, Dynamic Characteristics of Pneumatic Cylinders including Pipes, Proceeding of the 9th Bath International Fluid Power Workshop, 1996, pp.382-396.
4. Naotake Oneyama, The Actual Situation and Problems on Energy Savings of Pneumatic System, Journal of Fluid Power System, 2001, 32-4, pp.231-236.

A Novel Prediction Method for Vehicle and Satellite Interaction in the Simulation with GPS Signals Collected

Masato TAKAHASHI

University of Tokyo
Tokyo, 1138656 Japan
(E-mail: mtakahash@cyber.rcast.u-tokyo.ac.jp)
National Institute of Information and Communications Technology
Tokyo, 1848795 Japan
(E-mail: mtakahash@nict.go.jp)

ABSTRACT

A novel scheme is proposed and demonstrated where satellite visibility viewed from running vehicle is economically and effectively estimated by a new style simulation with data from such low-cost GPS receivers like automobiles are equipped with. Our preliminary experiment articulated even economical L1 GPS receivers can create enough precise database of ground feature blockage, compared to fisheye photograph method, if only two statistical parameters we propose are adequately set. Integrating the series of our efforts on this research field, the author concluded it is feasible to develop an automatic database creation system in cooperation with the government and the civil with low-cost GPS receivers. The blockage database can be an indispensable layer to discriminate whether the vehicular satellite link is blocked or not by ground features. It will play an essential role to predict the state-transition of the link and to make a handover for seamless satellite communications in future.

KEY WORDS: Global Positioning System, Blockage, Satellite Communications, Land Vehicle, Handover

INTRODUCTION

As one of high elevation satellite systems for land mobile satellite communications, QZSS (Quasi-Zenith Satellite System) has been discussed. QZSS uses inclined geostationary orbits. When observed from an adequate service area such like middle latitude areas, a satellite of QZSS traces a "figure of eight" pattern in the sky and provides elevation angles as high as 70 degrees or more

for eight hours a day. Thus, when three or more satellites are placed in adequate orbits, minimum elevation angle of as high as 70 degrees or more are available continuously. In this background it comes to be important to comprehend and evaluate the status quo of blocking by ground features such like buildings or mountains while vehicles drive on actual roads. However there was no adequate method to realize the demand in cost effective and simple way.

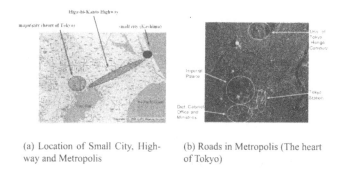

(a) Location of Small City, High-way and Metropolis

(b) Roads in Metropolis (The heart of Tokyo)

Figure 1: Evaluated Areas for Vehicular Satellite Communication Simulations

METHODOLOGY

From this standpoint, at first, a novel scheme was proposed and demonstrated by the author where satellite visibility viewed from running vehicle is economically and effectively evaluated with such low cost GPS receivers like those equipped in automobiles. He showed the geographical features of the satellite visibility on three areas.

Secondly the author opened the door to the new style of simulation on the intermitted blockage estimation based on the GPS signal strength data. In this simulation, blockage database on each ground point plays the key role. However, it is created by data of GPS satellite signal strengths which were collected by a vehicle, moving along the interested route about forty kilometers in Tokyo metropolitan in weeks, equipped with GPS receiver and recorder. The database on blockage on each ground point of the interested route is effectively used to analyze intermittent blockage phenomena between the vehicle and the supposed satellite on any supposed orbit, including QZSS. In this framework, the vehicle movement can correctly reflect the reality of the real traffic including traffic jams and go-stop effects.

EXPERIMENT

The specifications of Antenna in this experiment are as follows: A micro-stripped plane antenna of Right-Handed Circular Polarization (RHCP) is used, which has its sensitivity of -130 dBm. The size and weight is 54 (w) x 15.5 (H) x 58 (D) mm and 0.12kg respectively. The specifications of GPS receiver in this experiment are as follows: L1-band 1575.42MHz Coarse and Acquisition (C/A) code GPS standard positioning service receiver is used, which have parallel tracking ability of eight channels. The weight is about 0.55kg. The output is created at every second and it includes latitude, longitude, height, GPS Time, orientation of the vehicle, satellite ID, satellite elevation, satellite azimuth, signal strength. These antenna and receiver specifications are one of the most common specifications for the civil use GPS apparatus.

With the road map matching mechanism, acceleration and velocity detectors, and a gyroscope, the GPS chipset made by Trimble is used. The apparatus used is one of most prevailing compositions for the civil use for vehicle navigation system based on L1 C/A GPS satellite signals. As the latest position and almanac data are stored as well, warm

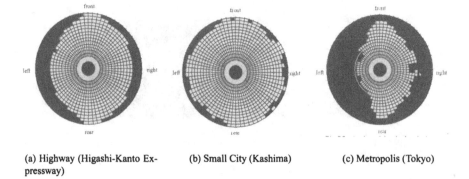

(a) Highway (Higashi-Kanto Expressway)   (b) Small City (Kashima)   (c) Metropolis (Tokyo)

Figure 2: Projections of the sky hemisphere where the blocking probability is less than 5 %

start condition is presumed whenever the vehicle starts the experiment. Latitude, longitude, altitude, GPS time and orientation of the vehicle are recorded every second, as well as GPS satellite ID, signal strength, elevation and azimuth as a result of positioning calculations.

RESULTS

In three areas the GPS signal strength data was gathered. As a major city, a highway and a small city, the heart of Tokyo, Higashi-Kanto Highway and Kashima city were selected respectively. The locations of the areas are illustrated in the map described below. The length of the horizontal width of the map itself corresponds to about 140km long. The left-side driving rule is applied to all three areas.

Highways are often bordered by barricades for noise protection, and due to the left-side driving rule in Japan, the effective elevation angle viewed from the vehicle is greater on the left side than on the right. The result shows that tendency. The blocked region on the left (15 to 30 degrees) is greater than that on the right (5 to 15 degrees). It is based on the data taken along a typical Highway,

connecting between Tokyo and a small city, about 100km long.

The result in a small city is also characteristic as indicated by the result. It is anticipated that reliable or 95 percent acquisition can be achieved in all directions for geostationary and QZSS satellites. The data of the result is taken at the small city "Kashima" which has the population of about 62000, located at 100km east from Tokyo. There is no specific blockage tendency which strongly depends on any specific azimuth orientation. This blockage tendency reflects lower artificial buildings and housings and wider roads in the area than the large city.

In large cities, except the orientations along and against the heading, satellite visibility is extremely limited especially in both sides. In other words, blocking is expected to be severe due to high-rise buildings on both sides of a vehicle at ground level. The result indicates this character well. The 95 percent clear path elevation's limit on the graph are closer to the zenith on the left and right (25 to 55 degrees) than at front and rear (10 to 30 degrees). This characteristic may be called metropolis-type blocking.

Although being simple method, this frame-

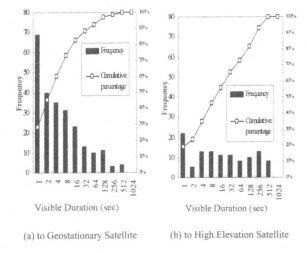

Figure 3: Histogram of Visible Durations from Vehicle estimated by novel style GPS simulation

work enables us to evaluate the satellite visibility at the sky above vehicles moving in real roads in a city, an expressway and a rural area. There are considered to be geographical patterns of satellites' visibility at the sky above vehicles running in those areas respectively. To be common to any cases, however, QZSS is more suitable for landmobile satellite communications than a geostationary satellite in terms of fewer blockages by features on the ground.

This blockage database framework has characteristics extendable for the study on durability of vehicle satellite communication link at a specified road in a time span. It has the merit to be able to reflect the real traffic jam and go-stop effects in the roads. This method has another merit to be able to analyze the tendency of the future's vehicle satellite communications based on real satellite signal before the launch. This scheme provides an excellent simulation platform to discuss the feasibility of future's vehicular

satellite communication systems and its design choice as it can include the real vehicle movement as well.

As a result of such a framework to the heat of Tokyo of 40 km circular route in Japan, histogram of continuous connection (visible) time of a geo-stationary satellite viewed from running vehicle is shown in Fig.3(a), and that of QZSS in Fig.3(b). The distribution of QZSS-vehicle links shows much stability than GEO-vehicle links .The average of continuous connection time of QZSS-vehicle links is 57.8sec, about three times longer than that of GEO-vehicle links.

DISCUSSION and CONCLUSION

A series of GPS blockage experiments articulated even economical L1 C/A 1.5GHz GPS receivers can create enough precise database of ground feature blockage, compared to fisheye photograph method, if only two statistical parameters; the first threshold and the second threshold. Integrating the series of efforts on this research field, the author concluded it is feasible to develop an automatic database creation system by the cooperation of the government and the civil with low cost GPS receivers. The block diagram for the plan and the requirements will be demonstrated. Besides, the blockage database is very useful for the near future's Land Vehicle Satellite Communication society oriented toward seamless interoperability, allowing us with the proposed real-time simulation to predict the possible blockage with the precise blockage database semi-automatically created with cooperation of the civil and the government, to realize effective hand-over for seamless interoperability in vehicular satellites communications and to support meaningful design choice on such key technologies like data-compression and error-correction algorithms in them by this novel simulation scheme using GPS signal strengths data.

REFERENCES

1. Scott Pace, et al, "The Global Positioning System", prepared for the Executive Office of the President, Office of Science and Technology Policy, Published by RAND, U.S., 1995

2. Global Positioning System Standard Positioning Service Signal Specification, 2nd Edition, June 2, 1995

3. Hiroyuki Miyata, Masato Takahashi, Hiroyuki Takano and Kazuhiro Aoyama, Dynamic Scheduling Algorithms of Real-Time Signal Processing on Ring-Based Multiprocessor Systems, in: Journal of Information Processing Society of Japan, Vol.39 Noh.7, 1998

4. Masato Takahashi, Masato Tanaka, Noriaki Obara, Shinichi Yamamoto and Kazuhiro Kimura, An Evaluation Method on Path Ratio to High-Elevation Satellites using GPS Signals, in: IEICE General Conference Proceedings, B-3-29, Keio Univ., 1998

5. Masato Takahashi, et al., A New Method to Evaluate Blocking Probability on High Elevation Satellites Viewed from Land Vehicles, in: Proceedings of IEEE 49th International Vehicular Technology Conference, p.p. 170 -174 , Huston, United States, 1999

6. Masato Takahashi, et al., An effective method to evaluate intermittent blocking on land vehicle satellite communications, in: Proceedings of IEEE 50th International Vehicular Technology Conference, pp.2735-2739, Amsterdam, Netherlands, 1999

7. Masato Takahashi, et al., A new evaluation method of intermittent blockage on land mobile satellite comm., in: European Space Agency Millennium Conf. on Antennas and Propagation, Davos, Switzerland, 2000

8. Masato Takahashi, Kazuhiro Kimura and Masato Tanaka, A Novel Evaluation Method of Blockage by Ground Features on land vehicle satellite communications, in: Proceedings of IEEE 51st International Vehicular Technology Conference, Tokyo, pp. 1810-1814, 2000

9. Masato Takahashi, Geographical Patterns of Satellites Visibility viewed from Running Vehicle, in: proc. of American Inst. Aeronautics and Astronautics 21st Intern. Communications Satellite Systems Conference, (AIAA 21st IC-SSC), Yokohama, Japan, 2003

10. Masato Takahashi, Vehicle and Satellite Interactivity, in: proceedings of American Institute Aeronautics and Astronautics 24th International Communications Satellite Systems Conference, AIAA-2006-5444, (AIAA 24th IC-SSC), San Diego, United States, 2006 (to be appeared)

11. Masato Takahashi, et al, "Geographical Features of Satellite Visibiliity viewed from running Vehicles", IEEE 17th Annual International Symposium on Personal, Indoor and Mobile Radio Communications, Helsinki, Finland, September 2006 (to be appeared)

12. Masato Takahashi, et al, "Vehicle Satellite Interactivity Database with GPS Blockage Collected in the Civil Activities", IEEE 17th Annual International Symposium on Personal, Indoor and Mobile Radio Communications, Helsinki, Finland, September 2006 (to be appeared)

13. Masato Takahashi, Patent Granted, "Method of Gathering Information on Clear-Path Coverage in the Sky Hemisphere", Japan Patent Office, Patent Registered Number 2963994 , August 1999

Simulation and Performance Analysis for Decentralized Signal Control on Four Intersections in Malaysia Traffic Systems

Mohd Nazmi* Nadiah Hanim**, Sadao TAKABA***

* Department of Electrical and Computer Engineering,
International Islamic University Malaysia
P.O. Box 10, 50728 Kuala Lumpur, Malaysia
(E-mail: mnazmi@iiu.edu.my)
*Graduate School of Computer Science, Tokyo University of Technology
1404-1 Katakura, Hachioji, 192-0982 Tokyo, JAPAN
** Department of Computer Science, Tokyo University of Technology
1404-1 Katakura, Hachioji, 192-0982 Tokyo, Japan

ABSTRACT

This research is to propose and develop the new signal control system which is to be integrated into Malaysia Traffic System. The control system obtains information from image detectors which are installed inside the intersection; predict the future traffic flows at various levels and conditions. A dynamic network system could capture the problem of the network traffic congestions, estimates the information on each particular link (neighboring intersection), in terms of vehicles flow and traffic can be calculated. Referring to the network flow control, the information data let the system to set the parameter itself then allow the system to allocate green time for each different demand pattern and each phase. These decisions are determined not at a central system but at the intersection control system. Simulation is done to find any difficulty of the system.

KEY WORDS: Decentralized Intersection, Signal Control System, Traffic Flows, Simulation System

INTRODUCTION

In traffic control, the split, cycle length, and offset timing parameters are continuously and incrementally adjusted by the control system. Traffic control requires a sensor that monitors traffic in real time. As traffic changes, the splits, offsets, and cycle lengths are adjusted by several seconds. In network intersection, the importance is to know the neighboring intersections conditions are very important to know. Four network intersections have been selected to be a model for our new traffic controller system. The controller system were expected to be use in order to fix up the recent system.

RESEARCH OBJECTIVES

In this research, we are focused to control the four neighboring intersection. The decentralized system are been proposed for this method. The algorithm and the model of the traffic signal control have been designed and the model can generate the real-time traffic control system such as the calculation, predicting time simulation and memorizing the new data. In this system, the performance of it will be similar to the traffic main center system. The detector and the traffic control grant the safety and orderly movement of the traffic to resolve conflicts between vehicles and also maintaining the system in related junctions.

267

TRAFFIC DETECTOR

Nowadays, the detectors are mainly located outside of the intersection and this type of detector can only provide small and limited traffic information. If the detector were set to detect the movement inside the intersections, the information of this movement could provide the information to the next intersections. The other intersections could prepare for the changing signal cycles especially in heavy traffic. To improve the traffic information by using our research method, we find that the traffic information could be added such as the flow, situation and direction of vehicle.

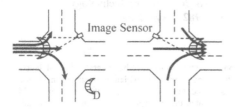

Figure 1 Flow-in and Flow-out Measurement

PREDICTION CONTROL

Prediction Control System is identified to be most important in the system. For heavy traffic, it is important to predict arriving vehicle, turning probabilities and queues at intersection, in order to calculate phase timing that optimize a given measure of effectiveness. The prediction of the arrival at the downstream intersection, the signal timing pattern represents the number of vehicles from the upstream intersection to arrive in fixed time intervals. This arrival patterns are identical until the signal control has decided whether to control this approach or to control another approach. The traffic demand occurs directly at the downstream system. In this case, there will be also a little demand immediately following to the neighboring control system and greater demands should be predict in the future.

SYSTEM CALCULATIONS

Calculations for this research are use mathematical analysis for traffic flow, stop and queue equation. Our basic idea is to calculate the flow-in and flow-out inside the intersection as in figure 2. In the downstream intersection, the saturation flow-out rate of flow-in vehicle (from east) is $S1(i, j)$.

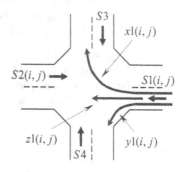

Figure 2 Flow-in Analyses

The ratio of vehicle that flow into the intersection and make a right turn to the north is $x1(i, j)$ and the vehicle that make a left turn ratio to the south is $y1(i, j)$. $z1(i, j)$ is for the ratio of flow-out vehicle that go straight to the west. Equation (1) shows how to calculate the saturation flow-out vehicle.

$$x1(i, j) + y1(i, j) + z1(i, j) = 1 \qquad (1)$$

Correspondingly, the inflow car from the west, the north, and the south also define from the below percentage.

$$S2(i, j), x2(i, j), y2(i, j), z2(i, j) \qquad (2)$$
$$S3(i, j), x3(i, j), y3(i, j), z3(i, j) \qquad (3)$$
$$S4(i, j), x4(i, j), y4(i, j), z4(i, j) \qquad (4)$$

The green time for the intersection in figure 2 for the flow from east to west is $G(i, j)$ and the green time for south to north flow will be $C - G(i, j)$, where C is the cycle time length.

Twin Intersection
From figure 3, the downstream (west) intersection (i, j) length queue is lq and the upstream (east) intersection $(i, j + 1)$ is lq'. The distance between 2 intersection is L.

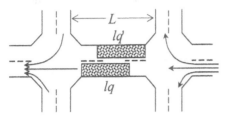

Figure 3 Twin Intersection Analysis

Let say that the congestion level 1 is light traffic and congestion level 2 is moderate traffic. The index that gives the boundary of congestion level 1 and 2 is assumed to be β. It will fulfill the requirement of congestion level by the below condition where $0 < \beta < 1$,

$$lq < \beta L \qquad (5)$$
$$lq' < \beta L \qquad (6)$$

Four Intersections.
In figure 4, L_e, L_w, L_n, L_s are the lengths between the intersections. The queue vehicle of N_E, N_W, N_N, N_S are multiply with an a to carry out the queue length. To calculate the flow of vehicle from intersection $(i, j + 1)$ to L_e street in 1 cycle

$$\frac{S1(i,j+1)z1(i,j+1),G(i,j+1)+\{C-G(i,j+1)\}}{\{x3(i,j+1)S3(i,j+1)+y4(i,j+1)S4(i,j+1)\}} \qquad (7)$$

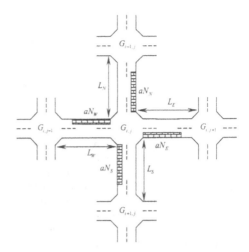

Figure 4 Analysis for Intersection (i, j)

Where the queue vehicle at the east side of intersection (i, j) will flow out to be

$$S1(i, j)G(i, j) \qquad (8)$$

Therefore, the time of t_e until it is turn into congestion level 2 at the east street is calculated as equation (9).

$$t_e = \frac{C(\beta_e L_E - aN_E)/a}{S1(i,j+1)z1(i,j+1)G(i,j+1)+\{C-G(i,j+1)\}}.$$
$$\overline{\{x3(i,j+1)S3(i,j+1)+y4(i,j+1)S4(i,j+1)\}-S1(i,j)G(i,j)} \qquad (9)$$

The street for the west, the north and the south also calculate in the same way. Equation (10, (11), (12)

$$t_w = \frac{C(\beta_w L_W - aN_W)/a}{S2(i,j-1)z2(i,j-1)G(i,j-1)+\{C-G(i,j-1)\}}.$$
$$\overline{\{x4(i,j-1)S4(i,j-1)+y3(i,j-1)S4(i,j-1)\}-S2(i,j)G(i,j)} \qquad (10)$$

$$t_n = \frac{C(\beta_n L_N - aN_N)/a}{S3(i-1,j)z3(i-1,j)\{G(i-1,j)\}+G(i-1,j)\{x2(i-1,j)\}}.$$
$$\overline{S2(i-1,j)+y1(i-1,j)S1(i-1,j)\}-S3(i,j)\{C-G(i,j)\}} \qquad (11)$$

269

$$t_s = \frac{C(\beta_r L_s - aN_s)/a}{S4(i+1,j)z4(i+1,j)\{C - C(i+1,j)\} + C(i+1,j)\{x1(i+1,j)}$$

$$\overline{S1(i+1,j) + y2(i+1,j)S2(i+1,j)\} - S4(i,j)\{C - C(i,j)\}}$$

(12)

SIMULATION

ARENA System Simulation tool has been used to carry out the traffic problem in Japan and the models are developed. Meanwhile, for the Malaysia traffic control system, the simulation for traffic flow is using the C++ programming language. The model requirements are exactly same as Japanese traffic condition model but for the traffic signal parameter's setting are different. More important thing is the new developed simulator is able to use the memory & database system to recall the previous signal parameter, so the system will be able to calculate and set the signal parameter more effectively.

Model Construction

Four connected intersections are used to be the simulation model. The simulation scenarios designed are aimed at analyzing the impact of traffic flow at four neighboring intersection when one of the intersection are congested. The simulation system simulates every intersection without integrated to each others. When, the traffic become heavy, the system will communicate with neighboring intersection to locate the finest signal parameter. The same techniques of the traffic main center method are used for the real-time decentralized intersection system. The maximum times for the signal until the congestion level change for each street are use from the evaluated equation (10) to (12). Figure 5 shows the model of four intersections by using the Arena Simulation System.

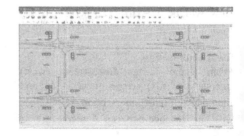

Figure 5 Simulation Model of 4 Junctions

Simulation Result

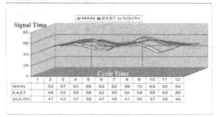

Figure 6 Simulation Result

Figure 6 shows one of the simulation results. The red line shows the maximum extended green time at the congested intersection. The result also shows the alteration of green time at the east and south intersection when signal parameter change in main.

CONCLUSION

The relation may not always the same as the site and situation change. Simple relation between flow-in traffic volume and occurrence of stopping vehicles inside the intersection gives useful suggestions on signal control to prevent traffic jam.

REFERENCES

1. M. Higashikubo, T. Hinenoya, K. Takeuchi, "Traffic Queue Length Measurement Using an Image Processing Sensor", The 3rd ITS World Conference, 1996.
2. Mohd Nazmi, Nadiah Hanim, Sadao Takaba, "Simulation and Evaluation for Solving The Traffic Flows Problem at Four Intersection in Malaysia", Proc for The 24rd JSST Conference, July 2005

Performance and Reliability of Image Traffic Sensor in Malaysia Traffic Dilemma Control Systems

Nadiah Hanim*, Mohd Nazmi**, Sadao TAKABA***

*Graduate School of Computer Science, Tokyo University of Technology
1404-1 Katakura, Hachioji, 192-0982 Tokyo, JAPAN
(E-mail: mnazmi@iiu.edu.my)
** Department of Electrical and Computer Engineering,
International Islamic University Malaysia
P.O. Box 10, 50728 Kuala Lumpur, Malaysia
***Department of Computer Science, Tokyo University of Technology
1404-1 Katakura, Hachioji, 192-0982 Tokyo, Japan

ABSTRACT

The use of image traffic sensor is proposed to determine the microscopic control during the dilemma zone time. The light traffic flow especially at night is applied as the drivers intense to increase the speed of their vehicles in this situation. In order to implement the system to the Malaysia Traffic Signal System, we build the model which can fit to Malaysia traffic condition. Our main goal is to find a problem and to solve it by using the investigation data. This objective is accomplished by using image detectors to monitor vehicle existence in the dilemma zone and then extending the phase until the dilemma zone is cleared or until a maximum green is reached. The control systems described have additional objectives that are intended to provide other safety or operational benefits. Arena simulations are used to determine the existence of vehicle in the dilemma zone.

KEY WORDS: Dilemma Control System, Zone Detection, Image Sensor, Simulation, Microscopic Control.

NOMENCLATURE

I : Inter-green interval (yellow + all red) [sec]
t : Driver perception-reaction time [sec]
v : Vehicle approaching speed [m/sec]
W : Intersection width [m]
L : Length of vehicle [m]
f : Coefficient of friction
G : Roadway grade [percent/100]
g : Acceleration of gravity [m/sec^2]
V_{Ni} : Minimum speed of Vehicles [m/sec]
V_{xi} : Maximum speed of Vehicles [m/sec]
Δt_i : The time after perception and by present of vehicles ($t - \Delta t_i$ is vehicles perception time)
L : Distance from a sensor to a stop line
L_{Si} : Distance from the upper end of the dilemma zone made applicable to official approval to Vehicles to a stop line

L_{Ei} : Distance from the down-stream end of the dilemma zone made applicable to official approval to vehicles to a stop line

INTRODUCTION

The yellow interval in traffic signal timing is designed to allow drivers to decide either to stop or to drive through the intersection before the following red interval begins. When the speed and the location of the vehicle is such that the driver cannot stop and also cannot drive through in time, the vehicle is said to be in a dilemma zone. For a fixed speed v, there is a minimum distance before the vehicle can stop (the stopping sight distance), and there is a maximum distance that the vehicle can

271

travel through during the yellow interval (the clearing distance). If the vehicle's current distance to the intersection is smaller than the stopping sight distance but larger than the clearing distance, then it is in the dilemma zone. The simulation shows the proposed adaptive signaling strategy that significantly reduces the number of vehicles in a dilemma zone.

OVERVIEW OF DILEMMA ZONE

The location of the dilemma zone on a typical approach is shown in figure 1. The vehicle should not go passed through the stop line while facing the yellow signal for its safety.

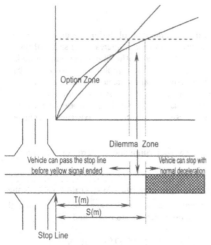

Figure 1 Dilemma Zone Characteristic

Dilemma Zone[1]
If the vehicle can not stop and have to go through the intersection while yellow signal is also permitted but must stop at the stop line if the signal is changed to red. Therefore, when the driver who faced the yellow signal cannot stop whether it can stop safely by the stop line, even before a red signal starts, driver will make a judgment about the ability to go into an intersection. A dilemma zone is the domain

that cannot make such a judgment. In order to stop by the stop line, vehicle is required to be located in an upstream side at least from upstream $S_{(m)}$ (of a stop line) at the time of a yellow signal start (figure 1). Moreover, even before a red signal starts, in order to go into a intersection, it is required to be located in a downstream side from upstream (of a stop line) $T_{(m)}$ at least. At the time of yellow signal starts, the vehicles which exist in the range of T and S can not make a decision whether to stop at the stop line or go into the intersection even before a red signal starts. In this area, the driver can suddenly decrease the vehicle speed or increase the speed when exceeding the stop line when red signal start. At this condition, the possibility for vehicle to face the incident is high.

IMAGE DETECTOR[2]

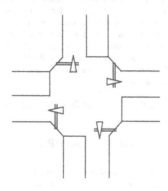

Figure 2 Optimal Camera Locations

Camera location is an important factor influencing detection accuracy. Multifunction image sensor describes an optimal location as one that provides a stable, unobstructed view of each traffic lane on the intersection approach. Moreover, the view must include the stop line and extend back along the approach for a distance equal to that needed for the desired detection layout. An example of an optimal camera location is identified in Figure 2.

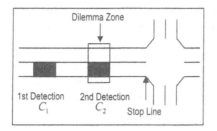

Figure 3 Dilemma Zone Detection Range

The first detection is located before entering the dilemma zone (C_1). A second detection is then located between the first detection and the stop line (C_2). The location of these intermediate detectors is resolute through reflection of the speed distribution and the controller passage-time setting (figure 3). Detection zone layout is an important factor influencing the performance of the intersection.

DILEMMA CONTROL SYSTEM[2]

Basic Function

When there are vehicles exist in the dilemma zone, dilemma zone control will continuous the green signal but if there is no vehicle exist in the dilemma zone, the system will changes the green signal to yellow signal. The present time of induction within the limits is set to t. Time between $t-T$ to t where all vehicles are detected (figure 4). Below, whether (i) or (ii) condition is fulfilled, control system will end a green light signal and changes it to a yellow signal. If at least one vehicle is detected, control system will continue a green light signal. In addition, vehicles shall run within speed range (min - max as shown below).

(i) Even run at minimum speed, has to pass through the end of downstream dilemma zone.

$$V_{Ni}\Delta t > L - L_{Ei} \qquad (1)$$

(ii) Even run at maximum speed, has not arrived at a dilemma zone upstream end.

$$V_{xi}\Delta t_i < L - L_{Si} \qquad (2)$$

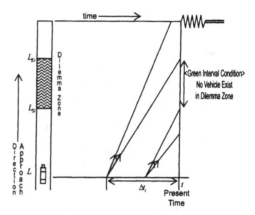

Figure 4 Basic of Dilemma Zone Control

RELIABILITY OF DILEMMA ZONE PROTECTION

The existence of C_1 and C_2 distances is dynamic respond to the safe design and operation of the intersection. An analysis is needed on study the impact of C_1 and C_2 and evaluates the effectiveness of the detectors on dilemma zone. The variations of dilemma zone can be caused by traffic, geometric, roadway, and driver characteristics in an estimate process. A reliability analysis is well suited for this purpose and has been undertaken in this research. The limit state equation to be analyzed is formed as

$$I = t + \frac{\upsilon}{2g(f \pm G)} + \frac{W + L}{\upsilon} - I\upsilon \qquad (3)$$

The reliability analysis investigates the probability of dilemma zone protection considering stochastic changes in the parameters of equation (3). Simulations are done by using the above equation.

SIMULATION

Arena simulation is an effective way to understand the underlying principles of traffic system. The importance of differentiated service levels helps us to create dilemma detection zone system simulation.

Simulation Model

One model with two detection zone has been designed for the dilemma detection systems. The simulation model is simply use to detect the existence of vehicle in dilemma zone, detect the vehicle approach the intersection when the signals in yellow, detect the vehicle flow into the intersection when the signal is in yellow time and detect the vehicle flow into the intersection when the signal is in all red time.[1] Figure 5 and 6 shows the dilemma detection logic program and simulation model with scanning system. All the simulation, simulate by using the investigation data that have been collected in Malaysia and Japan

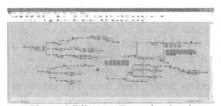

Figure 5 Dilemma Detection Logic

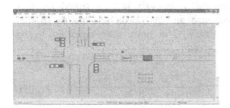

Figure 6 Simulation Model with Scanning

Simulation Result

Simulation result shows that we could detect the vehicle existence in the dilemma

zone matching with the investigation data. The simulation can construct a various condition of vehicle movement when approaching the intersection in difference speed. The simulation results by using the investigation data in Malaysia (figure 7) and Japan (figure 8) are shown. The number of vehicle flow into the intersection when the signal turn into the yellow time and all red time are taken.

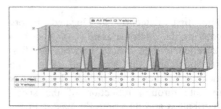

Figure 7 Simulation Result (Malaysia)

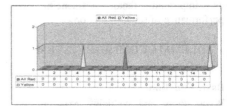

Figure 8 Simulation Result (Japan)

CONCLUSIONS

Dilemma zone control, manage the signal to modify the signal time (extend the yellow time) depend to the speed of vehicle. In order to control the signal parameter, the results are very valuable. In order to organize the signal parameter, these results are very valuable.

REFERENCES

1. Nadiah Hanim, Mohd Nazmi, Sadao Takaba, "Simulation for Image Traffic Sensor in Malaysia Traffic Dilemma Control System", Proc. For Asia Simulation Conference 2005, Oct 2005, Beijing, China.
2. Nadiah Hanim, "Application of the Traffic Image Sensor in Dilemma Zone Control", Master Thesis, Tokyo University of Technology, 2004

Performance Analysis for Priority Signal Control of Fast Emergency Vehicle Preemption Systems (FAST) in Malaysia

Mohd Nazmi*, Sadao TAKABA**, Mohd Nazaruddin Yusoff***

* Department of Electrical and Computer Engineering,
International Islamic University Malaysia
P.O. Box 10, 50728 Kuala Lumpur, Malaysia
(E-mail: mnazmi@iiu.edu.my)
** Department of Computer Science, Tokyo University of Technology
1404-1 Katakura, Hachioji, 192-0982 Tokyo, Japan
***Faculty of Public Management and Law,
University Utara Malaysia
06010 Sintok, Kedah Darul Aman, Malaysia

ABSTRACT

Malaysia traffic systems need to have the latest research of signal clearance system. Our research is proposing a method of Fast Emergency Vehicle Preemption System (FAST) which can be fit to Malaysia traffic conditions. A traffic signal preemption system is a system that allows a traffic control signal to respond uniquely to the approach emergency vehicle at intersection. Such systems are designed to increase safety, reduce emergency response times and enhance public transit operations. One method for priority signal control in FAST system in the traffic signal control has been proposed in order to implement into the Malaysia Traffic Control System. The objective is to provide safe and fast driving environment for emergency vehicles to reach the destination at the earliest possible time.

KEY WORDS: Priority Signal Control, Preemption System, Light Traffic, Heavy Traffic, Simulation.

NOMENCLATURE

ρ_l : Traffic density at heavy traffic
ρ_{max} : Maximum traffic density
u_l : Speed of vehicle at heavy traffic
u_{max} : Maximum speed of vehicle at heavy traffic
t_s : Stop time until vehicle starts to move

INTRODUCTION

Fast Emergency Vehicle Preemption System (FAST) requires the installation of a device at the road to receive a data from specific authorized vehicles (emergency vehicle). These systems proposed to be used for the preemption of normal traffic control signal operation by the approach of emergency vehicles and to modify the length of the green time to allow for more efficient transit operation. FAST systems generally allow vehicles traveling in the same direction as the emergency vehicle to receive, or continue to receive, a green indication. In the case of emergency vehicle preemption, the green indication provides an opportunity for other vehicle to clear the road ahead of the advancing emergency vehicle. If the remote signal from the source is interrupted or terminated for any reason, normal traffic control signal operation will continue. FAST systems may respond to different vehicles or types of vehicles in recognition of different vehicle priorities. The researches in FAST system have been proposed by Japan National Police Agency in 2000. Malaysia traffic conditions are parallel to Japan traffic and formulate us to implement in Malaysia traffic systems. Figure 1 shows the FAST system layout.

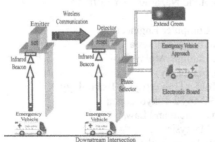
Figure 1 FAST Image System Layout

RESEARCH OBJECTIVES

The ultimate goal of the proposed research is to develop a dynamic route clearance system for efficient and safe operations of emergency vehicles. Our research is to reach the position where signal clearance strategies can be automatically generated and implemented in real time. For Fast Emergency Preemption Systems, three system objectives were identified.
(a) The system shall reduce response time to emergency vehicles.
(b) The system shall improve the safety and health of emergency personnel by reducing accidents, relieving stress or both.
(c) The system shall reduce accidents between non-emergency vehicles related to responding emergency units at intersections where it is installed.

The FAST Difficulty
Most of the problem of FAST will occur
(a) In the rush hour time, most of vehicle will block the emergency vehicles especially at the one lane road, and emergency vehicles can not run smoothly,

(b) Even the emergency vehicle will slow down the speed of vehicle when the signal at the intersection is red, and it will give more time loss for them.
(c) Emergency vehicle may run without obey the signal, and will cause a danger to other vehicles or pedestrians.

SIMULATIONS

Priority Signal Control (PSC) is realized at the time of an emergency vehicle's approach into the intersection with direct optical communication between the vehicle and the roadside signal controller. Effectiveness of priority signal control depends on miscellaneous traffic situations. Traffic volume along the arterial is the principal factor. In the heavy traffic, long queue of other vehicles preceding the emergency vehicle takes a long time to pass the intersection which disturbs smooth passage of the emergency vehicle. Priority usage of the vacant space at the center of the road or at the opposite lane by the emergency vehicle depends on the length of queue as well as the width of the vacant zone. These situations are modeled and evaluated with simulation.

Simulation Conditions
The simulation was performed by nine condition of heavy traffic by using Arena Simulation software. Below, the nine condition for heavy traffic.
① Single sided and one lane passing
② Without any trespassing
③ Never runs through the opposite lane
④ Ignore any vehicle acceleration
⑤ The initial traffic density at the time of light traffic is ρ_0
⑥ The initial traffic density at the time of heavy traffic is ρ_1
⑦ $\rho_0 < \rho_1$
⑧ The time of 1 cycle of the signal is t_s ($t_s = 120$ sec)
⑨ 50% split time for each red time and green time (60 sec each)

Model Constructions

Two models have been constructed to simulate the FAST system regarding to Malaysia traffic condition. Simulation data was taken from the investigation results at the Gombak Road and Setapak Road in Malaysia. We created the simple model for the road to intersection where the vehicles run only on the single lane. On heavy traffic, we concerned the effect of traffic flow where the signal will form a queue of vehicle and it is increasing every cycle. The lengths of the queue vehicle are calculated as follows. When the signal time is red, the speed of vehicles will increase at

$$\frac{\rho_1 u_1}{\rho_{max} - u_1} \tag{1}$$

When the signal time become green, the speed of vehicles will decrease at

$$u_{max} - \frac{\rho_1 u_1}{\rho_{max}} \tag{2}$$

The length of the queue which occurs from the above condition in 1 cycle of signal is

$$\left\{ \frac{\rho_1 u_1}{\rho_{max} - u_1} - \left(u_{max} - \frac{\rho_1 u_1}{\rho_{max}} \right) \right\} \frac{t_s}{2} \tag{3}$$

The length of this queue will become longer depend on the time.

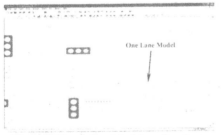

Figure 2 Simulation Model on One Lane

Figure 2 shows the simulation model for the heavy traffic condition on one lane. When the emergency vehicle occurred at the queue, the signal will perform the Priority Signal System (PSC) to give a way for the emergency vehicle to escape from congestion.

Figure 3 Position of Emergency Vehicle

Figure 3 shows the position of emergency vehicle caught at the congestion in the first simulation model. When the emergency vehicle is detected, the signal will perform the PSC and the traffic volume is counted until the emergency vehicle can pass trough the downstream intersection. Figure 4 shows the volume of vehicle which flow under the PSC time.

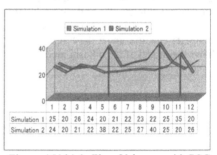

	1	2	3	4	5	6	7	8	9	10	11	12
Simulation 1	25	20	26	24	20	21	22	23	22	25	35	20
Simulation 2	24	20	21	22	38	22	25	27	40	25	20	26

Figure 4 Vehicle Flow Volumes with PSC

The volume of vehicle could flow more from usual when using the PSC at simulation 1 on phase 11 where the volume is 38 vehicle and simulation 2 phase 5 and phase 9 where the vehicle number are 38 and 40 at each phase.

Oikoshi (Overtaking) Model

This model is created to find the time of emergency vehicle that could escape from the congestion when the signal is in red. One lane has been added into the model to give a way for the emergency vehicle to go straight into the intersection by using the signal parameter condition (figure 5).

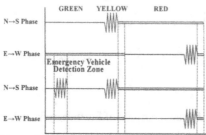

Figure 5 Signal Parameter Modify on PSC

When the detector detects the emergency vehicle, it will change the green time to the yellow time in the North-South phase. The vehicles from that side have to aware of the approaching vehicle from East-West way. The oikoshi lane model has been construct to fulfill the condition when the detector detecting the emergency vehicle. The emergency vehicle will use the oikoshi lane to escape the intersection when the parameter changes under the PSC. Figure 6 shows the model of the oikoshi model.

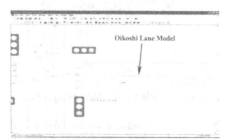

Figure 6 The Oikoshi Lane Model

Figure 7 shows the emergency vehicle (red) using the oikoshi lane to escape from the congestion and the time are recorded.

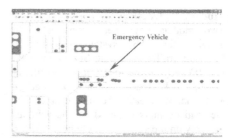

Figure 7 Simulation Using Oikoshi Lane

Figure 8 shows the result of time escape for emergency vehicle in heavy traffic by using the oikoshi lane model. By using the oikoshi lane, the time to escape is shorter than using the normal signal time.

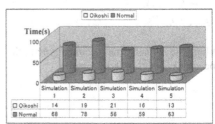

Figure 8 Time Escape Comparisons

CONCLUSION

The FAST system study is mainly to find any problem which will happen to the signal control system where there are interruptions from the user side. The study of signal parameter setting for Malaysia traffic system gives us to know a problem and different between Japan and Malaysia. The research is proposed to Malaysia government in order to implement in Malaysia Traffic System.

REFERENCES

1. Mohd Nazmi, Kouhei Nishizawa, Shinichi Nakamura, Sumio Ohno, Sadao Takaba, "Priority Signal Control in FAST Emergency Vehicle Preemption System", Proceeding of The 22nd Japan Society for Simulation Technology Conference (JSST), Tokyo, pp 351-354, 2003.6

Using KD-FBT to Implement the HLA Multiple Federations System

Han Chao, Hao Jianguo and Huang Kedi

Institute of Electromechanical Engineering and Automation
National University of Defense Technology
Changsha, Hunan, 410073 China
(E-mail: nudthc@yahoo.com)

ABSTRACT

The interconnection of HLA multiple federations is essential for the large scale simulation, especially for the simulation on the wide area network. Using the Bridge Federate is one of the approaches to interconnect HLA multiple federations. Following the principle of the Bridge Federate, we have developed the software "KD-FBT" which can interconnect multiple federations rapidly by creating bridge federate automatically. Eleven federations distributed in several cities in China have been interconnected by using the software KD-FBT. This paper describes the design principle and architecture of the software. A scenario tests the performance of the software.

KEY WORDS: HLA, Multiple Federations, Bridge Federate, KD-FBT

INTRODUCTION

To promote interoperability between simulations and aiding the reuse of models in different contexts, the High Level Architecture (HLA) has been developed to provide a common architecture for distributed modeling and simulation. In its original form the HLA allows a number of simulations to be joined together into a federation using a single run time infrastructure. The reusability and scalability of the HLA determine that multiple developed federations can be interconnected to enlarge the simulation scale quickly. The interconnection of HLA multiple federations is essential for the large scale simulation, especially for the simulation on the wide area network.

Using the Bridge Federate is one of the approaches to interconnect HLA multiple federations. The Bridge Federate is composed of a Surrogate Component for each federation linked using the bridge, a Transformation/Mapping Specification that specifies the associations between object attributes and interaction of each federation being linked, and a Transformation Manager that transforms and communicates attribute values and interactions between the linked federations.

Following the principle of the Bridge Federate, we have developed the software "KD-FBT" which can interconnect multiple federations rapidly by creating bridge federate automatically. Now, it has been used successfully in a multiple federations system which interconnecting eleven federations distributed in several cities in China. Each federation can be based on heterogeneous RTI, such as DMSO_RTI, pRTI, MAKRTI, KD-RTI and so on. Section 2 provides some background on multiple federations. Section 3 describes the architecture of the software KD-FBT and its implementation class structure. A scenario tests the performance of the software in section 4.

MULTIPLE FEDERATIONS BACKGROUND

A multiple federation (or multi-federation) is defined as a set of more than one currently executing federations to which one or more federates are simultaneously joined. Multi-federations may include one or more FOMs. This logically gives rise to a new term, a Federation Community. In a federation community, intra-federation federate communication would utilize a common FOM, while inter-federation communications could embody several different FOMs and mechanisms that otherwise in some way use the events of one execution to influence events in another.

Federation connectivity, which gives rise to a federation community, falls into one of 4 fundamental combinations of homogeneous and heterogeneous federations and RTI. Each of which can be spanned by either a Gateway, a Bridge Federate, a Broker, or an "on-the-wire" protocol [1].

The concept of the Bridge Federate is an extension of the DMSO's work on the issue of multi-level security and its impact on HLA federations. Such a federate would act as a mediator, passing events between the two federations. The bridge federate would appear to be an ordinary federate to both federations, effectively encapsulating the federation substructure on each side. Furthermore the bridge could handle the various filtering and event translation needs to "match impedances" of the joined federations or enforce security restrictions. The use of a bridge federate is architecturally attractive for a number of reasons. Since it simply looks like any other federate, multiple federations could be joined transparently to the joined federations. Furthermore, in principal the use of a bridge would require no changes to the current HLA specification: by using existing services and event subscriptions a bridge should be able to update each side appropriately.

The combined federation execution as shown in Figure 1 shows two federation executions interoperating through the support of a Bridge Federate. The Bridge Federate participates in multiple federations. It has several internal components: surrogates (one for each federation in which it participates) and a transformer manager (TM) that coordinates among the surrogates. The communication of this combined federation execution is achieved without requiring any one federate to understand each and every FOM. Each federation execution (fedex) can communicate with other fedexs using its own FOM through the corresponding surrogates provided by the Bridge Federate. Each federate has no knowledge that it is, in fact, interoperating within multiple federation executions. The specification for how objects, attributes, and interaction are mapped throughout the combined federation execution is defined by the FOM Mappings/Transformations specification (FOMAT in Figure 1) [2, 3, 4].

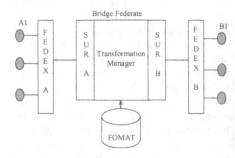

Figure 1 Bridge Federate Components

RESEARCH AND IMPLEMENTATION OF KD-FBT

KD-FBT ARCHITECTURE

When operating as a data filter, the Bridge Federate may not be the ideal architecture when the simulation is geographically dispersed. As the Bridge Federate is a single process application it can be local to at most one federation, thus, data generated by remote federations traverse the potentially large distances between LANs only to filtered; the same situation as for the single federation simulation. The notion of distributing the Bridge Federate and having a component local to each federation is briefly introduced in Hao [5]. Following the principle of DBC (Distributed Bridge Federate Component), the KD-FBT is designed as shown in figure 2.

The information process model for the KD-FBT is as follows:

1) The surrogate component of KD-FBT participates within its joined FEDEX as a federate on behalf of all other federation executions.

2) The Surrogate$_1$ receives RTI messages through the Federate Ambassador services.

3) The TM$_1$ transforms the messages to the specific format according to the FOM mapping file, then sends the message to the other TM$_2$ by point to point communication.

4) The Surrogate$_2$ calls the specific RTI Ambassador function.

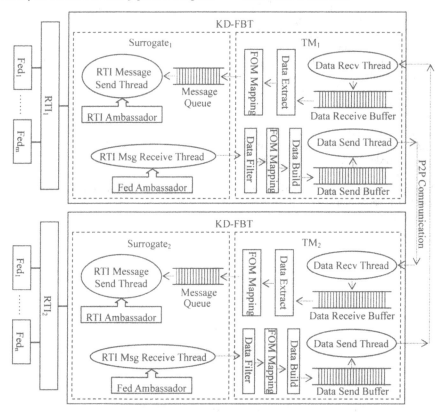

Figure 2 Architecture of KD-FBT

281

By this, the message is transferred from one federation to the other.

The software KD-FBT assigns four threads for above four steps. KD-FBT is also competent for more than two federations, described in Figure 3. The RTI of each federation can be not only homogeneous but also heterogeneous.

CLASS STRUCTURE

The UML Class Diagram as shown in figure 4 illustrates the core infrastructure classes used to implement the KD-FBT.

- Transformation Component Class: This class is used to achieve the function of Transformation Manager of Bridge Federate.
- Association Mapping Class: All the interfaces of FOM Mapping between each federation are implemented in this class, including reading FOM mapping file, mapping the handle of object instance handle, etc.
- Surrogate Class: This class is used to achieve the function of Surrogate of Bridge Federate.
- Federate Ambassador Class: Every HLA federate should overload this class in order to get messages from RTI.
- Wizard Class: By configuring correlative parameters, KD-FBT can be fit for heterogeneous RTI.

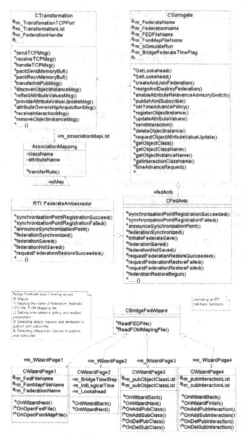

Figure 4 UML Class Diagram

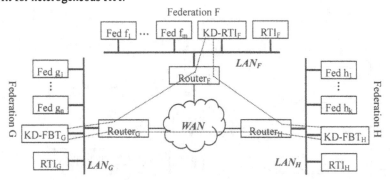

Figure 3 Interconnection of Multiple Federations

PERFORMANCE MEASUREMENT

Using the definitions and methods introduced in Sun [6], this section measures the one-way latency between two federate distributed in one/two federations. The scenario is shown in figure 5. All the federations are based on KD-RTI which is used widely in China. The test was conducted using six computers. Each computer was a single 2.4GHz P4 and equipped with 100BaseT Ethernet, running Windows 2000. The computers distributed in one LAN were connected through a 100Mbs hub. The two LANs were connected through a router Cisco 2600.

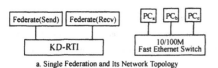

a. Single Federation and Its Network Topology

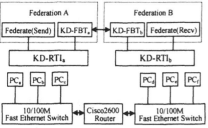

b. Multiple Federations and Their Network Topology

Figure 5 Test Scenario

A simple Federation Object Model (FOM) and two test federates were developed. The FOM consisted of a single class containing a data attribute. The attribute was best effort transport. The size of the data attribute could be set to 4/128/256/1024/2048 bytes. The test result is shown in figure 6.

CONCLUSION

The interconnection of HLA multiple federations is essential for the large scale simulation, especially for the simulation on the wide area network. This paper has provided a brief overview of the software KD-FBT which following the principle of Bridge Federate. It has shown that through the use of KD-FBT it is possible to interconnect multiple federations.

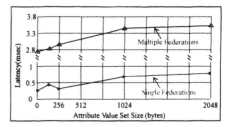

Figure 6 Test Result

REFERENCES

1. Michael D. Myjak, Sean T. Sharp, Implementations of Hierarchical Federations, 1999 Fall Simulation Interoperability Workshop.
2. Wesley Braudaway, Reed Little, The High Level Architecture's Bridge Federate, 1997 Fall Simulation Interoperability Workshop.
3. Juergen Dingel, David Garlan and Craig A. Damon, A Feasibility Study of the HLA Bridge, Technical Report CMU-CS-01-103, School of Computer Science, Carnegie Mellon University, 2001.
4. Han Chao, Hao Jianguo, Huang Jian, Huang Kedi, Research on the Architecture of HLA Multiple Federations Interconnected by Bridge Federate, Journal of System Simulation, Vol.18 Suppl.2, 2006, China.
5. Hao Jianguo, Huang Jian, Han Chao, Huang Kedi, Research on Implementation of HLA Multi-Federations, Journal of System Simulation, Vol.16 No.5, 2004, China.
6. Sun Shixia, Huang Kedi, Testing and Analysis of Run-Time Infrastructure Performance, Journal of System Simulation, Vol.17 No.4, 2005, China.
7. Mr. Terrell Burks, Mr. Tom Alexander, Mr. Kurt Lessmann, Mr. Kenneth G. LeSueur, Latency Performance of Various HLA RTI Implementations, 2001 Spring Simulation Interoperability Workshop.

Study on the Design and Implement Technology of

the STK-RTI Middleware

JIANG Li-li, Wang Da, HUANG Jian, Qiu Xiao-gang, HUANG Ke-di

College of Mechatronics Engineering and Automation, National University of Defense
Technology, Changsha 410073, China

ABSTRACT

The support of HLA has been the trend of distributed interactive simulations, as the abundance and development of specific field applications, it is necessary to integrate these specific applications with HLA-based simulation systems. Through analyzing different kind of techniques of connecting specific applications with HLA, we come to a conclusion that middleware is a better way. The program flow chart is given in the paper.

KEYWORDS: DIS, HLA, STK, Middleware

SUMMARIZE

Today's High Level Architecture (HLA) has improved the Distributed Interactive Simulation (DIS) and been used a lot in business and utilities [3]. As HLA/RTI [1] is becoming the support applications of more and more simulation systems in the past few years, it is important to find a way to integrate those specific applications which already existed with HLA-based simulation systems.

In the area of spaceflight, the Satellite Tool Kit (STK) is advanced system analysis applications software. STK is used to analyze complicated spaceflight, navigation, earth and sea missions. The potential utilization is quite great. In order to expand the application field and enhance the using and meet the demands of simulation system construction, we need to reconstruction STK into simulation applications which is becoming to distribute interactive simulation. The paper gives a detailed description on the design and realization of the STK-RTI Middleware. It is a reference to the common technical to built HLA middleware.

The paper analyzes different kinds of techniques of connecting specific applications with HLA. The whole design and realization scheme are also given in the paper.

ANALYZING ON THE TECHNIQUES TO INTEGRATE THE SPECIFIC APPLICATIONS WITH HLA

Integration

Integration means repacking the data send by the specific applications into HLA Data Standardization for the use of HLA system. When receives data from HLA, it repacks the data for the use of the specific applications.

Because it doesn't need another computer as the transformation, the delay is comparable less. However, as it needs a code level modification and the modification can only on the network interface, it can't make the modified applications totally elaborate the advantage of HLA.

Switcher/Gateway

This method needs to develop independent applications. It doesn't need to modify the original non-HLA simulation system. It also realizes a degree of compatibility. The shortage is that the data transportation from the original node to the object node needs another computer as the switcher, it has great network delay. The reliability will be seriously overload infected if the quantity of data is too much.

Middleware

The middleware is independent system applications or a service program. The Distributed Application shares the resource between different techniques in dependence on the middleware. The middleware is located on top of the operating system of Client/Service. It manages computation resource and network communication. For example, NAWCTSD developed the simulation middleware SMOC. It is used to apply ModSAF into HLA simulation systems. The important usage of middleware is to integrate applications developed on different periods or on different operation system, make them work in coordination with each other. It can't be done by operation system or database management itself.

By way of inserting middleware between simulation applications and RTI, some common functions of simulation applications and some special services which RTI provides can realize in the middleware [4]. The middleware can reduce the cost of development of simulation systems and reduces the time of realizing simulation applications. It also enhanced the flexibility and common usage of simulation applications. Besides, as the demands of simulation applications are improved, the RTI service functions can be extended though the middleware method.

Table 1 Comparison of the advantage and disadvantage of the techniques in common use

Items	Techniques		
	Integration	Switcher/Gateway	Middleware
The number of processors	1	2	1
Consuming	high	low	Middling

Conversion time	Long	short	Middling
Running speed	fast	Slow	fast

DEVELOPMENT OF STK-RTI MIDDLEWARE SOM

As a federate of the HLA federation, the STK-RTI middleware participates in the entire simulation process (Figure 1) [2].

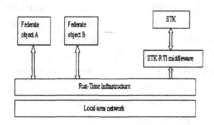

Figure 1 System Frame

The way STK-RTI middleware interacts with the third applications is sending STK/Connect commands to STK and returning the STK answer. SOM interaction classes are designed as commands which STK/Connect module can receive.

The SOM object classes of STK-RTI middleware include and public all possible scenario objects and their attributes.

REALIZATION OF STK-RTI MIDDLEWARE

As STK-RTI middleware is a Federate of HLA Federation, the services HLA Interface Standard prescribes should be realized as much as possible.

Federation Management

The STK-RTI middleware may create Federation Execution or just join Federation Execution. The STK-RTI middleware realizes some Federation Management Functions, such as: Create Federation Execution, Join Federation Execution, Resign Federation Execution, Destroy Federation Execution.

Declaration Management

In order to communicate with HLA simulation system, STK-RTI middleware should be able to declare the data it needs and data it can produce. The STK-RTI middleware realizes all the Declaration Management Functions.

Time Management

As the 2D and 3D Scenario Animation of STK are base on the time step, in order to elaborate the powerful Scenario Animation functions, STK-RTI middleware uses step based time advance.

STK joins Federation by way of middleware. It is necessary to actualize the logical time synchronization of STK scenario and the middleware. We build up the mechanism of logical time synchronization of STK scenario and STK-RTI middleware. First, use the logical time that STK-RTI middleware join the federation to initialize STK Scenario. Second, every time STK-RTI middleware requests time advance, use the same time step to advance STK 2-D, 3-D Graphic Animation. When STK-RTI middleware request time advance by timeAdvncedRequest() service, the middleware call a function which is used to advance STK 2-D,3-D Scenario Graphic Animation.

Object Management

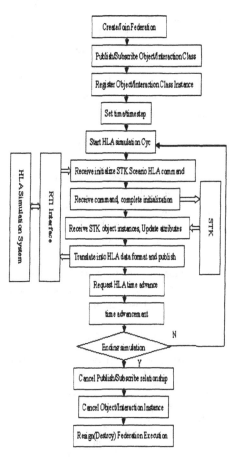

Figure 2 Program Flow

STK-RTI middleware SOM defines HLA Object Classes and Interaction Classes which is corresponding one by one with the object classes and STK/Connect command of STK. The operation on STK through STK-RTI middleware becomes operation on HLA Object Class or Interaction Class. STK-RTI middleware realizes functions such as the register of object instance, register of interaction instance, updating

object attribute, deleting object instance, sending interaction, receive interaction and so on.

The STK-RTI middleware this paper describes doesn't support Federation/Federate Save/Restored. The system it works in doesn't need these services at present.

GENERAL DESIGN

The main thought of general design is to build a flexible, easy-use, good expansibility middleware which connect STK with HLA/RTI. The design is according to these aspects.

Federate agent mode
As Figure 1 shows, STK-RTI middleware interacts with other federates straight through HLA/RTI. STK-RTI middleware is a HLA federate essentially. On the other hand, STK-RTI middleware runs on the server node of STK, STK has to join Federation via STK-RTI middleware, so it can be considered as an agent member. The agent member interacts with STK, sends simulation control messages, outside simulation object messages and incident messages to STK, acquires inside simulation object messages and incident messages from STK.

Invoke STK/RTI services
As STK-RTI middleware is a federate essentially, it uses standard services such as Federation Management, Declaration Management, Object Management, Time Management, Ownership Management and Data Distribution Management which HLA/RTI provides to realize the interaction between agent member and other federates.

Module Constitute

STK-RTI middleware is realized base on the module technique. The whole middleware composed of STK/Connect command encapsulation module, client simulation application module, agent member module. Using STK Client Simulation applications support, STK Object Module joins into the Agent member and produce proper coupling with Fed, FedAmbassador, Pub, Sub, and other assistant classes.

Other Problems

As the STK functions are enhanced and the client demands are more and more complicated and diversification, the expansibility of STK-RTI middleware must be good for the client use and the applications upgrade.

The expansibility is acquired by dynamic-link library of STK/Connect command functions and STK-RTI middleware object class SOM design. The link library packs many STK/Connect functions for the client to use them easily. The upgrading and modifying becomes much easier. It doesn't need to change the STK-RTI middleware itself a lot.

STK-RTI middleware object class SOM includes all scenarios and all objects' attributes STK probably produces. STK-RTI middleware publishes STK scenario and all objects' attributes no matter there are other federates subscribes or not. The clients can set weather the object and the objects' attributes are published or not through STK-RTI middleware flexibly. Besides, during the designation of STK-RTI middleware, the modules of the applications are designed to be functional simplification, they are realized as independent modules. The applications' upgrading in the future will be much easier because of it.

THE ENDING

The paper analyses several HLA middleware techniques in common use, explains the realization and the general design techniques of STK-RTI middleware. The research and application shows that STK-RTI middleware this paper develops has abundance functions and convenient uses. It can satisfy the need of connecting STK and HLA-based simulations.

REFERENCES

1. The Department of Defense. High Level Architecture Interface Specification, version 1.3. http://hla.dmso.mil/
2. ZHOU-Yan, DAI Jian-wei, Designation Of HLA Simulation Applications, Publishing House Of Electronics Industry, 2002.
3. HUANG Ke-di, System Simulation Technology, Publishing House Of National University of Defense Technology, Changsha, China, 1998.
4. WANG Da, Study On STK-RTI Middleware Based Modeling and Simulation of Space-Ground Integrated Combat, Journal Of System Simulation, Feb. 2005.

A Resolution Converter for Multi-resolution Modeling/Simulation on HLA/RTI

Su-Youn Hong* and Tag Gon Kim*

* Department of EECS, KAIST
373-1 Kusong-dong, Yusong-gu
Daejeon, Korea 305-701
Tel: +82-42-869-3454
Fax: +82-42-869-8054
syhong@smslab.kaist.ac.kr, tkim@ee.kaist.ac.kr

ABSTRACT

Multi-Resolution Modeling (MRM) represents a real system as a set of models at different resolution in different abstraction levels from the view point of simulation objectives. The main problem for distributed simulation of multi-resolution models is resolution mis-matching in communication between simulators (processes) for different resolution models. Aggregation and disaggregation are methods for conversion of high-to-low resolution and low-to-high resolution, respectively. This paper describes design and implementation of a resolution converter in multi-resolution modeling of discrete event systems and distributed simulation of such models on HLA(High Level Architecture)/RTI(Run Time Infrastructure). A simple multi-resolution queuing model with multi-servers and multi-queues is developed and proved to be correctly behaved.

KEY WORDS: Resolution Converter, Multi-resolution Modeling/Simulation, HLA/RTI

INTRODUCTION

The DMSO on-line M&S (Modeling & Simulation) glossary defines resolution as "the degree of detail and precision used in the resolution real word aspects in a model or simulation."[4] MRM represents a real system as a set of models at different resolution in different abstraction levels from the view point of simulation objectives. The main purpose of such modeling is to save computing resources as well as to reduce simulation time at the cost of simulation accuracy. If resolutions of two communicating simulators are different resolution conversion should be made.

Aggregation and disaggregation are methods for conversion of high-to-low resolution and low-to-high resolution, respectively.

This paper describes design and implementation of a resolution converter which manages data format converting and time synchronization in multi-resolution modeling of discrete event systems and distributed simulation of such models on HLA/RTI. It can be implemented either within one simulator process or as a separate process. In this paper, we assume that the resolution converter is implemented as a single process which is connected to the DEVS simulator via TCP/IP and it uses

HLA/RTI as a communication tool for data exchange.

Figure 1 shows the proposed architecture for MRMS on HLA/RTI.

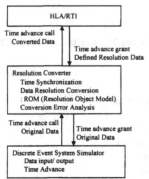

Figure 1 Proposed Architecture for MRMS on HLA/RTI

The paper is organized as follows: Section 2 briefly reviews multi-resolution modeling, High Level Architecture and the simulation interoperation layer [1]. The design of a resolution converter is described in Section 3. Section 4 presents the implementation of the resolution converter. Section 5 shows an example, the GBP model which has multi-queues and multi-servers. Finally Last section concludes the paper and proposes the future work.

BACKGROUND

HLA & Simulation Interoperation Layer

The HLA is a specification for interoperation among distributed heterogeneous simulations. The standard consists of two parts; Federate Interface Specification and Object Model Template (OMT) [4]. Federate Interface Specification defines essential services. The RTI is an implementation of HLA Federate Interface Specification. OMT is a documentation format for shared objects and message types by which simulators exchange events. OMT is used to describe Federation Object Model (FOM) and Simulation Object Model (SOM).

The Simulation Interoperation Layer manages mapping between HLA services and DES simulation messages used in DEVS abstract simulation algorithm. [1] The main function of the Simulation Interoperation Layer is to provide communication interface between HLA and the DEVS simulator which is to be interoperated with other simulators through HLA services.

Multi-Resolution Modeling

Multi-resolution Model is a simulation model which has various levels of resolution. The kinds of multi-resolution modeling can be divided two types when the simulators use resolution conversion: Static vs. Dynamic.

Static multi-resolution modeling is that the resolution level which the objects are simulated is fixed when the simulation is constructed [3]. It does not need resolution conversion because these simulators do not exchange the data when the simulation runs, so this paper will not consider this approach.

Dynamic multi-resolution modeling permits an object to switch levels of resolution during the course of the simulation [3]. This approach can be divided into two types. *Replacement* means that the whole data of one simulator with some resolution level is converted to a different resolution level data format and transferred to the other simulator with that resolution level. The both simulators are mutually exclusive at time.

Interoperation is the data exchange among simulators with different resolution level while the simulation is constructed. For one simulator, before data inputs are accepted from another simulator, it needs to be converted into the resolution level of simulator itself.

MULTI-RESOLUTION CONVERTER ON HLA/RTI

This section describes design of a resolution converter in multi-resolution modeling of discrete event systems and distributed simulation of such models on HLA/RTI.

Data Resolution Conversion

In a dynamic multi-resolution modeling, the data resolution of one simulator needs to be converted to different resolution level. What should be specified in the resolution converter? There are three categories: definition of resolution levels, registration of data with specified resolution, and converting rule. Figure 2 shows the relation of three categories.

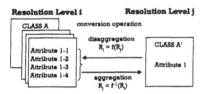

Figure 2 Data Resolution Conversion

For defining the static data format as a resolution level, this paper suggests the Resolution Object Model (ROM). ROM which is analogous to SOM, FOM approach, defines a resolution level, an object class name and attributes for each object group.

```
(Object Group
  (Resolution Level
    (Class Name
      (Object Group ID)
      (Attribute Name Type Default-Value)
    )
  )
)
```

Figure 3 Resolution Object Model (ROM) Format

Because the proposed architecture uses RTI as a communication tool, the objects of simulators are converted as a resolution level defined by FOM at first. The simulator of high resolution sends data to converter, and the resolution converter transforms the data to FOM and reverse. Therefore the proposed resolution converter assumes only two resolution levels.

Time Synchronization

In the interoperation, the simulators need to convert data resolution while simulation is constructed. A resolution converter supports time synchronization because simulators have different time resolution levels. Because the proposed architecture is based on HLA/RTI, a resolution converter is designed to manage time synchronization using RTI time management.

Conversion Error Analysis

A typical multi-resolution converting problem is the error which occurs while aggregation and disaggregation. A typical aggregation problem is to summarize various data into one or less data. The aggregated data contains less information; therefore the simulator looses some information in the aggregation process. Disaggregation is a reverse process, i.e. extracting information from low resolution level to high resolution level. In the ideal case, a resolution converter cannot generate error in these processes. The converting functions are defined as $R_i = f(R_j)$ and $R_j = f^{-1}(R_i)$, therefore $R_i = f(f^{-1}(R_i)) = R_i$. But in practical, f^{-1} cannot be the complete reversed function of f because of the information loss. Multi-resolution converting cannot avoid these errors. Developers analyze these error and determines whether within or without a permissible range.

Federation Management

Federation management includes such tasks as creating federations, joining federates to federations observing federation-wide synchronization points, effecting federation - wide saves and restores, resigning federates from federations and destroying federations. These services are usually not considered in each simulator. The multi-resolution converter needs to provide an easy way for users to use these services because it uses HLA/RTI as a communication tool.

IMPLEMENTATION: MULTI-RESOLUTION CONVERTER

KHLAAdaptor library is the implementati -on of core library for the Simulation Interoperation Layer. A resolution converter uses KHLAAdaptor library for supporting HLA/RTI managements, and adds a resolution converting component. A resolution converting component handles conversion among different resolution level.

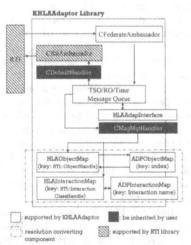

Figure 4 Architecture of KHLAAdaptor

Figure 4 shows the architecture of a multi-resolution converter. This section laid emphasis on the implementation of data resolution conversion. The implementation of time management is explained in [1].

Data Resolution Conversion

The resolution conversion component provides schemes for automatic conversion between two different resolution levels. HLAObject/interaction means the data format defined by FOM and ADPObject/interaction is described in ROM. Developers need to implement actual conversion functions used in the library.

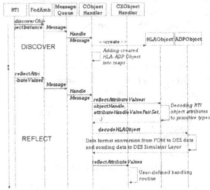

Figure 5 Discover and Reflect Attribute Values

EXAMPLE: THE GENERATOR-BUFFER-PROCESSOR MODEL

The resolution converter is applied to development of simple multi-resolution queuing model with multiple queues and multiple servers as shown in Figure 6, called MGBP (Multi-resolution Generator-Buffer-Processor) model. The MGBP model is separated as a two part. The GB model generates customer by poisson distribution and sends it when the P model is idle. The P model calculates a waiting time of a customer by poisson distribution and sends it to the result model.

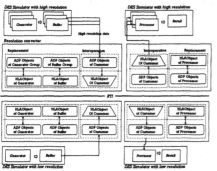

Figure 6 Multi-resolution Queuing Model

The GB and P Models convert resolution level while simulation is run. Figure 7 shows the number of generated messages and interoperated messages.

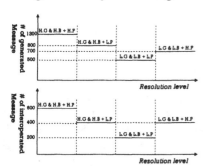

Figure 7 Multi-resolution Simulation Experiment

Because the simulation scale is too small, the MGBP example does not show predominant performance improvement. But the decrease of the message number can be surmised a speedup in the case of an enough large scale simulation.

In the resolution converting process, resolution converters execute resolution converting according as a mathematical equation. The mean parameter r of a low resolution generator is the sum of the mean parameters of high resolution generators. Reversely, the mean parameters m, n and p is equal to the mean parameter r. If m, n and p are different, they cannot be restored in aggregation and disaggregation. But as mathematical equation and experimental result showed, waiting times were identical.

CONCLUSION AND FUTURE WORK

A resolution converter for Multi-resolution Modeling/Simulation on HLA/RTI was designed and implemented. A ROM format is defined for resolution definition of multi-resolution objects, which can be used by conversion functions. Implementation provides an automated environment of a whole resolution conversion process.

This paper only considers a resolution converter on HLA/RTI. But a fixed communication interface sets limits to the utility of a resolution converter. Therefore future research should be aimed at data resolution converting component independent from HLA/RTI.

REFERENCES

[1] Jae-Hyun Kim, Su-Youn Hong and Tag Gon Kim, "Design and Implementation of Simulators Interoperation Layer for DEVS Simulator" in *Proceedings of the Summer Computer Simulation Conference*, Calgary, Canada, July 2006, pp.95-100.

[2] Bernard P. Zeigler, Herbert Praehofer, and Tag Gon Kim, *Theory of Modeling and Simulation*, Academic Press, 2000.

[3] Anand Natrajan, Paul F. Reynolds Jr. and Sudhir Srinivasan "MRE: A Flexible Approach to Multi-Resolution Modeling", in *Proceedings of Parallel and distributed system 11th workshop*, Lockenhaus, Austria, June 1997, pp.156-163.

[4] Science Applications International Corporation Technology Research Group, *High Level Architecture Run-Time Infrastructure RTI 1.3-Next Generation Programmer's Guide Version 5*, DMSO, 1999.

A Simulation Platform of Integrated Logistics Support System Based on HLA /DEVS

Wenhui FAN, Tianyuan XIAO, Guangleng XIONG and Bin GUO

The National CIMS-ERC, Automation Department of Tsinghua University,
Tsinghua Garden, Haidian district, Beijing, 100084,China

ABSTRACT

The methods and key techniques of distributed ILSS simulation platform based on HLA and DEVS are studied. Firstly, according to features and demands of ILSS, the distributed simulation architecture is proposed based on HLA and DEVS. Secondly, a modeling method based on HLA and DEVS is discussed. Thirdly, to improve the extendibility of DEVS simulation mechanism, time synchronization algorithms between DEVS and HLA are studied, and the simulation engine framework is discussed. Finally, an ILSS distributed simulation platform is designed and implemented.

KEYWORDS: High Level Architecture (HLA); Discrete Event System Specification (DEVS); Integrated Logistics Support System (ILSS); Distributed Simulation Platform

1 INTRODUCTION

In the process of modern weapon design, reliability, maintainability, and supportability (RMS) have become important specification that have a marked influence on efficiency, maneuverability and maintenance costs of weapon. So the Integrated Logistics Support System (ILSS) has become an important part of modern weapon system. The ILSS is a typical kind of complex, dynamic and stochastic system, due to its large scale, complex structure, and many factors needed to be considered.

At present, there are a few of commercial ILSS simulation tools. These RMS simulation tools generally make a united model by some simulation language (such as SimscriptII),

then transfer it into simulation program. Classic ILSS models include LOCM, OPUSI, SIMLOX, SALOMO and SCOPE et al. [1] However, these models mostly run at a single computer. For a large ILSS, the united model and its simulation mechanism aren't provided with enough extendibility and maneuverability. Distributed simulation technology can be used to study the ILSS system. It can conveniently describe the complex relationship among distributed models by time synchronization and data exchange, realize the integration among simulation models, and improve reusability of simulation models.

2 HLA/DEVS SIMULATION ARCHITECTURE

The High Level Architecture (HLA)

tandard mandated Department of Defense of
e United States for simulator interoperability
]. The Discrete Event System Specification
DEVS) formalism introduced by Zeigler
rovides a means of specifying a mathematical
bject called a system [3]. A system has a time
ase, inputs, states and outputs, functions for
etermining next state and outputs given
urrent states and inputs. The DEVS model can
upport for hierarchical, modular construction
nd repository reuse [4].

he ILSS can be taken as a complex discrete
vent dynamic system. The behavior of system
driven by missions, and its performance
epends on interact rules and modes among
b-systems. Simulation of ILSS needs several
ey technologies to be surmounted
ommendably: generating fault event,
mulating the process of repair, queue and
ochastic factors.

ccording to features and demands of ILSS,
e distributed simulation architecture is
oposed based on HLA and DEVS (Figure
.The architecture integrates DEVS and HLA
order to realize reusable simulation
odeling and large-scale distributed
mulation, and provides an integrated and
neric reference for large-scale ILSS
mulation platform in programming,
signing, implementing and applying.

OS services provide file transportation and
network communication by various network
protocols, which include FTP, TCP/IP and
HTTP et al.
In the level of service, there are three parts:
simulation runtime service, modeling service
and platform management service.
HLA/DEVS engine provides a distributed
simulation environment. DEVS models are
linked to become a large model via it.
FOM/XML data integration framework defines
a set of specifications to describe simulation
model, simulation data, evaluation algorithm
model and other information.
In the level of tools, the platform offers users a
suit of software, which can support the whole
life-cycle of ILSS simulation to enhance
efficiency of modeling and execution.

3 DISTRIBUTED SIMULATION MODEL TECHNOLOGY

In HLA terms, an individual simulation is
referred to as a federate. A group of federates
that intend to interoperate with one another
form a federation.
A distributed simulation based on HLA is
composed of three kinds of models: virtual
model (I), federate model (II) and algorithm
model (III) (Figure 2). Virtual model describes

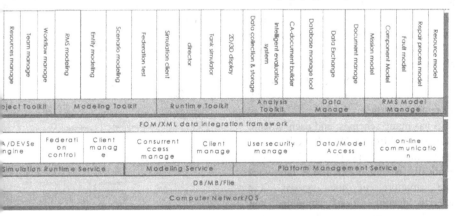

Figure 1 the architecture of HLA/DEVS distributed simulation platform

high level structure of simulation system to help engineers to understand. A federate model specifies a HLA federate, and is in charge of mapping events to objects or interactions. Algorithm model is described by DEVS formalism. Simple models are coupled to complex models, Partition line is boundary between I and II. It can flexibly move to make different federation topology.

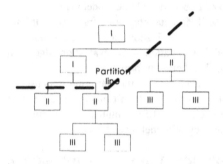

Figure 2 the structure of HLA simulation system

Based on DEVS formalism, a HLA/DEVS modeling is proposed. A HLA simulation system is referred as a HLA/DEVS model. A virtual model is a DEVS couple model; its component models denote federates and their relationship. A federate model is a extend DEVS model (Figure 3). HLA Agent model communicates with HLA/RTI. In the other words, it receives events from other federates, and sends events to other federates. Common service specifications provide an approach to share data among DEVS models in a federate model. There is no need for DEVS models to store redundancy common information, because required data can be accessed by service request interface.

An ILSS has many schemes, and each scheme is made up of different DEVS models. The System Entity Structure (SES) can systematically be organized into a family of possible structure of the system, and characterize decomposition, coupling, and taxonomic relationships among DEVS models [5].

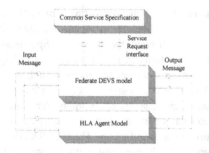

Figure 3 extended DEVS model

4 THE FRAMEWORK OF SIMULATION ENGINE

The HLA/DEVS model is not an executable program. So users need a simulation environment to parse and execute the model. We present a framework of simulation engine to mapping HLA/DEVS models into federate (Figure 4).

In the framework, HLA agent carries on data mapping according as virtual models; each algorithm model is handled by its own simulator; a federate model is mapped to a coordinator, which is in charge of synchronizing its component simulators and handling of external events. Each simulator has a set of service ports, which provide comprehensive data access functions, for example, function getFaultInfo returns information of a specified fault.

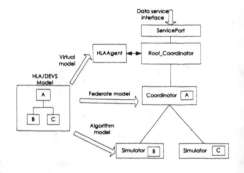

Figure 4 mapping model to federate

ach federate has a local logical time (THLA), ach federate DEVS model has its own time (DEVS). In order to correctly synchronize HLA and TDEVS, a time advance algorithm presented as follow:

ep 1: each federate initializes HLA, set timing rule and time constraint, set THLA = 0;

ep 2: each federate initializes DEVS models, set TDEVS = 0, tL= tN=0;

ep 3: if simulation is end, go to Step 8; or compute tN, advance TDEVS to tN;

ep 4: acquire output events, send events to other federates via SendInteraction or UpdateObject of HLA Agent service;

ep 5: use NextEventRequest to advance THLA to TDEVS;

ep 6: process RO and TSO events received by LRC, until timeAdvanceGrant is returned;

ep 7: map RO and TSO events to DEVS event, send events to each federate DEVS model, go to Step 3;

ep 8: each federate resign simulation federation.

EXAMPLE

ccording to demands of ILSS of certain tank, ILSS distributed simulation platform is signed and implemented. The platform is veloped with VC++, and DMSO RTI1.3NG ith the help of this platform, users can ickly build federate model of tank, depot, d repair shop, such as a repair shop model own in Figure 5. According to simulation issions of ILSS, federate models are coupled a complete scenario model (Figure 6). mulation Director controls a scenario ecution, watches all federates' state (Figure

CONCLUSION

e Integrated Logistics Support System .SS) is a typical kind of complex, dynamic

and stochastic system. HLA/DEVS-based distributed simulation technology can be used to study the integrated logistics support system, which can conveniently describe the complex relationship among distributed models by time synchronization and data exchange, realize the integration among simulation models, and improve reusability of simulation models. HLA/DEVS-based ILSS simulation platform is developed.

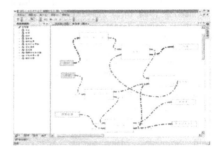

Figure 5 federate modeling

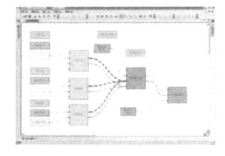

Figure 6 scenario modeling

Figure 7 simulation director

REFERENCE

1. CAO Junhai. The Application of Collaborative Simulation in Virtual Prototype and Integrated Logistics Support Simulation. Beijing: Department of Automation, Tsinghua University, 2005.
2. IEEE-SA Standards Board. IEEE Std 1516-2000, IEEE Standard for Modeling and Simulation (M&S) High Level Architecture (HLA) —Object Model Template (OMT) Specification[S], New York: The IEEE Inc. 2000.
3. Arturo I. Concepcion, Bernard P. Zeigler. DEVS Formalism: A Framework for Hierarchical Model Development. IEEE Transactions on Software Engineering. 1988, 14(2): 228~241.
4. Bernard P. Zeigler, George Ball, Hyup Cho et al. Implementation of the DEVS Formalism over the HLA/RTI: Problems and Solutions. Simulation Interoperability Workshop, 1999.
5. Bernard P. Zeigler, Herbert Praehofer, Tag Gon Kim. Theory of Modeling and Simulation: Integrating Discrete Event and Continuous Complex Dynamic System. San Diego, CA: Academic, c2000.
6. . Hironori Hibino, Yoshiro Fukuda, Yoshiyuki Yura, Keiji Mituyuki, Manufacturing Adapter of Distributed Simulation Systems Using HLA, Proceedings of the 2002 Winter Simulation Conference, 1099~1107, (2002)

Research on Simulation Resource Service Framework in Simulation Grid

Baocun Hou*, Bo Hu Li*, Xudong Chai**

* School of Automation Science and Electrical Engineering
Beijing University of Aeronautics and Astronautics
Beijing, 100083 China
(E-mail: houbc2002@yahoo.com.cn)
** Beijing Simulation Center
Beijing, 100854 China

ABSTRACT

To solve the problem about the limitations in the dynamic sharing, reuse, fault tolerant and collaboration of simulation resources, the simulation resource service framework is put forward. It provides discovery, composition, scheduling, fault tolerant and data transfer services based on the simulation resource description framework, and establishes "resources service bus" for simulation gird. Furthermore, the latest research results of simulation resource service framework are introduced in detail, which include the service-oriented, MDA (Model Driven Architecture)-complied and semantics-based simulation model resource description framework, the simulation model discovery service based on semantics and the simulation resource dynamic fault tolerant and migration service. At last, the typical application cases are presented. The further works are also given.

KEY WORDS: networkitized M&S, simulation grid, semantic, service discovery, fault-tolerant and migration

INTRODUCTION

Now, there are still some shortcomings in current networkitized M&S system, especially the limitations in the dynamic sharing, autonomy, fault tolerant and collaboration of simulation resources and the security application mechanism. The simulation grid [1] employs grid technology to fetch up these limitations.
In the research on simulation grid, the simulation resources including simulation models and tools software, which are most important and useful for simulation applications, can not realize good sharing, reuse and cooperation by current grid resource management middleware, due to their collaborative-work characteristic and complex interface requirements. To solve this problem, the simulation resource service framework, for short, SRSF is put forward and studied by authors.

SIMULATION RESOURCE SERVICE FRAMEWORK

SRSF is the important part of the collaborative run supporting services provided by the simulation application oriented core services layer in simulation grid. Based on the simulation resource description specification, SRSF provides five core services, including discovery, composition, scheduling, fault-tolerant and migration, and data transfer for simulation resources, as shown in Figure 1.

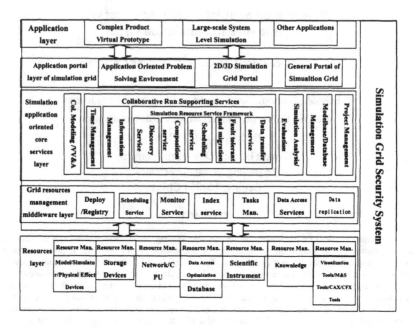

Figure 1 The architecture of simulation grid and SRSF

SRSF fetches up the limitations of current grid resource management middleware in supporting the simulation applications. Its design and development are simulation application-oriented and based on semantics. Significantly, SRSF supports the collaborative work and time-space consistency. It establishes "resources service bus" for simulation gird.

The remainder of this paper introduces the phased research achievements in detail. Section 3 presents simulation model description framework, which is main content of simulation resource description specification. Section 4 discusses simulation model discovery service. Section 5 introduces simulation resource fault tolerant and migration service. These services are important parts provided by SRSF.

SIMULATION MODEL DESCRIPTION FRAMEWORK

By introducing ontology technology [2], Simulation Model Description Framework (SMDF) establishes simulation model description ontology to realize semantic description for simulation models. The simulation model description ontology is composed of the simulation model service ontology and a series of simulation model domain ontologies, as shown in Figure 2.

The simulation model service ontology defines the conceptions used to describe simulation models, and their relationships. It is extended from OWL-S [3], and modified based on the description requirement of simulation models. It includes ModelProfile, ModelBehavior and ModelInterface.

(1) ModelProfile, which defines the basic

information, and the characteristic information used to match and discovery simulation model, especially including model input/output parameters.

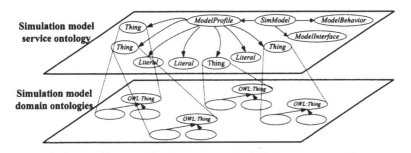

Figure 2 The simulation model description ontology

(2) ModelBehavior, which only exists in the descriptions of composed models, and describes the static structure and dynamic behavior of them. It is provided to simulation model composition service [4] to realize the composition and scheduling of atomic models in those composed models.

(3) ModelInterface, which is the standard description for the visit interface of simulation models. It not only provides the lift-cycle operations, but also standardizes these operations into application-independent and universal form.

The simulation model domain ontologies define the conceptions used to describe the characteristic information of ModelProfile, and their relationships. It is the foundation for the semantic description and matching of simulation models. The simulation model domain ontologies are modeled by the mature ontology modeling means [5] with certain simulation application background.

SIMULATION MODEL DISCOVERY SERVICE BASED ON SEMANTICS

At present, the discovery method provided by the grid resource management middleware is based on name-contrast and lacks the matching of the semantic context of the resources. So it is difficult to efficiently and intelligently discover simulation models in large-scale, trans-section, trans-organization simulation applications. To solve the problem, with the research on SMDF, the authors improve the semantic matching degree definition given in reference [6], and define the semantic matching degree for input/output parameters of simulation models. Based on this definition, the semantic matching algorithm for input/output parameters based on the ontology inference is studied and has gained well achievements [7].

The simulation model discovery service based on semantics is shown in Figure 3. The inference machine employs the semantic matching algorithm above to match the requests and simulation models registered.

SIMULATION RESOURCE FAULT TOLERANT AND MIGRATION SERVICE

The simulation resource fault tolerant and migration service not only has responsibility to watch simulation

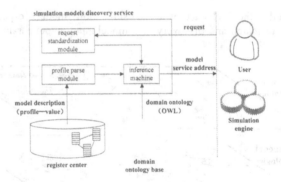

Figure 3 The simulation model discovery service based on semantics

resources states and save/restore checkpoints, but also must keep simulation time consistent during task migration, that is not required in other situations.

In the research, the authors adopt reflective software analyze and modeling method [8-9]. The simulation resource fault tolerant and migration model put forward is illuminated in Figure 4. When resource watch-control module is aware of a fault on simulation resource R1 (shown in step 1), it return the information to simulation resource composition and scheduling service. Then the simulation system stops and the new simulation resource R2 is discovery (shown in step 2), and scheduling interceptor is informed to alter resource address (shown in step 3). At the same time, the scheduling interceptor employs resource watch-control module to restore task states on simulation resource R2 (shown in step 4 and 5). So the simulation system advances again (shown in step from 6 to 15). During each advance period, the simulation resource is detected (shown in step 7 and 8) and task states are saved (shown in step 14 and 15).

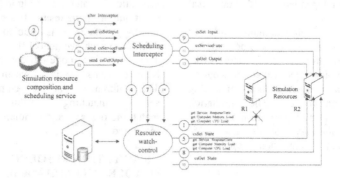

Figure 4 The simulation resource fault tolerant and migration model

APPLICATIONS

One of the typical application cases is the collaborative simulation system for undercarriage based on simulation grid. In this system, SRSF achieves well validation as the "resource service bus", as shown in

302

Figure 5.

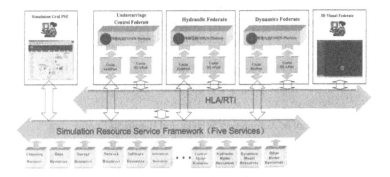

Figure 5 The collaborative simulation system for undercarriage based on simulation grid

In building phase of this simulation system, the control, hydraulic, dynamics models for undercarriage are developed according to SMDF, and deployed in distributed regions. The users employ simulation model discovery service to match and discover the right models according to simulation task requirement. Then federates are dynamically constructed by composing the simulation models discovered. In running phase, the federates communicate FOM data through HLA/RTI, at the same time, use simulation resource fault tolerant and migration service to detect simulation resource states and migrate simulation tasks when required.

FURTHER WORKS

Further works include to consummate key technologies of SRSF, especially to model the simulation application oriented universal domain ontology and to deeply research on the inference rules and algorithm in semantic matching; and to increase application scale of SRSF to improve SRSF function and performance, etc.

REFERENCES

1. Bo Hu Li, Xudong Chai, Baocun Hou, et al, A new infrastructure of networkitized M&S, the Proceedings of ICSC2005, 2005, pp.1-8.
2. O'Leary D E, Using AI in Knowledge Management: Knowledge Bases and Ontologies, IEEE Intelligent Systems, 1996, pp.34-39.
3. OWL-S 1.1 Release, 2006[2006-4-20], http://www.daml.org/services/owl-s/1.1/.
4. Di Yanqiang, Li Bo hu, Chai Xu dong, et al, Research on collaborative modeling & simulation platform for multi-disciplinary virtual prototype and its key technology, Computer Integrated Manufacturing Systems, 2005, 11-7, pp.901-908. (in Chinese)
5. Jing Li, Study on the Theory and Practice of Ontology and Ontology-based Agricultural Document Retrieval System--Floricultural Ontology Modeling, Dissertation for Doctor, Beijing, Graduate University of Chinese Academy of Sciences, 2004. (in Chinese)
6. M. Paolucci, T. Kawmura, T. Payne, et al, Semantic Matching of Web Services Capabilities, the Proceedings of the First International Semantic Web Conference, 2002.
7. Baocun Hou, Bo Hu Li, Xudong Chai, Model Resource Discovery Technology Based on Semantic for Simulation Grid, Accepted by Journal of Beijing University of Aeronautics and Astronautics. (in Chinese)
8. Huang Xiaodong, Reflective software development approaches for adaptive software with applications in distributed interactive simulation. Yantai, Naval Aeronautical Engineering Institute, 2005. (in Chinese)
9. Gordon S. Blair, Geoff Coulson, Anders Andersen, et al. The design and implementation of open ORB V2, IEEE Distributed System Online, 2001, 2-6.

Research and Application on Virtual Prototying Engineering Grid

Bo Hu Li*, Xudong Chai**, Wenhai Zhu**, Baocun Hou*,
Guoqiang Shi*, Peng Wang*, Runmin Yin*

* School of Automation Science and Electrical Engineering
Beijing University of Aeronautics and Astronautics
Beijing, 100083 China
(E-mail: bohuli@moon.bjnet.edu.cn)
** Beijing Simulation Center
Beijing, 100854 China

ABSTRACT

This paper firstly concisely introduces the research background of Virtual Prototyping Engineering Grid (VPEG), and presents the connotation of VPEG. Then, combined with authors' ongoing project, the phased research achievements of VPEG are introduced in detail, including the prototyping system and some solved key technologies, some typical application demonstration systems of VPEG. It is known from the primary practice that: (1) VPEG is a new supporting platform for VPECP. It can realize the dynamic sharing and reuse of various resources in VPECP safely, the whole life cycle team/organization/project/process/product management and optimization, the collaborative modeling/simulation/evaluation/VR, dynamic composition, scheduling and execution of VPECP applications, etc.(2) The prototyping system of VPEG developed by authors achieves technical innovations in architecture, portals, web-based RTI, service virtualization, model discovery based on semantics technologies.(3) VPEG expands the application fields of grid technology. Finally, the conclusion and some further works are given.

KEY WORDS: virtual prototyping engineering, complex product, grid computing

INTRODUCTION

Virtual prototyping technology for complex product is the expansion of CAx/DFx technologies [1]. At present, facing lots of new challenges raised to traditional virtual prototyping technology, the authors and their colleagues consider that the development of virtual prototype for complex product has become a systematic engineering, named Virtual Prototyping Engineering for Complex Product (VPECP).
The implementation of VPECP requires a supporting platform to provide platform/tools suits to support the management and optimization of the whole life cycle team/organization, project/process/product and technologies, to support the integration of the multidisciplinary tools and application systems, to support the collaborative modeling/simulation/evaluation/VR, and to support the sharing, reuse and cooperation of various resources. But current supporting platforms for VPECP have some limitations to these requirements, such as no mechanisms for

dynamic management and scheduling for resources, no capability for self-organization and fault tolerant of application systems, limited interoperation and reuse capability for resources and systems, no security mechanisms for system execution, etc. On the other hand, grid computing [2] has matured significantly in the past few years. It is aiming to fulfill the sharing and collaborative application among all kinds of network resources.

The Virtual Prototyping Engineering Grid (VPEG) put forward by authors is a new supporting platform for VPECP. It synthetically applies specialistic technologies related to product itself, modeling and simulation technology, information technology, multimedia/virtual reality technology, grid technology, AI technology, system technology and management technology, etc., to realize the dynamic sharing and reuse of various resources in VPECP safely, the whole life cycle team/organization/project/process/product management and optimization, the

collaborative modeling/simulation/evaluation/VR, dynamic composition, scheduling and execution of VPECP applications, etc., to support the various activities in whole life cycle (from argumentation, research, design, development, test, execution, evaluation to maintenance and disposal) for existing or tentative complex system/project/product in VPECP field.

From the view of grid technology, VPEG is different from other grids, and characterized to support such tight/loose coupling and collaborative task as distributed, collaborative virtual design/manufacturing and large-scale argumentation simulation, in which the task is composed of the resources/services with the information flow, event flow, time-space consistency and collaborative cooperation.

THE VPEG SYSTEM

The prototyping system of VPEG developed by authors is illustrated in Figure 1, which includes:

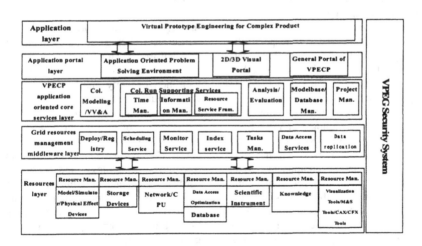

Figure 1 The architecture of VPEG

(1) Resource layer, which provides various VPECP resources for grid scheduling.

(2) Grid resource management middleware layer, which provides deployment/registry,

scheduling, monitor and index service for grid resources, and core management service for tasks and resource data.

(3) VPECP application oriented core services layer, which includes collaborative modeling/VV&A service, collaborative run supporting service, analysis/evaluation, modelbase/database management and project management.

(4) Application portal layer, which provides grid application portal for VPECP users.

(5) Application layer, which supports VPECP users with secure, collaborative and easy development, execution and evaluation of application systems in distributed virtual organization.

THE KEY TECHNOLOGIES OF VPEG

Some key technologies in resource layer

1) Project/Process/Product management technology for VPECP

The tool named COSIM-PM developed by authors takes the management and optimization for multi-constrained scheduling and resource planning as its core technologies, and realizes the overall lifecycle management of virtual prototype engineering through plan, control, tracking and optimization for personnel/group, scheduling, resource and cost respectively. Especially, COSIM-PM uses Petri nets based models to describe and simulate project scheduling, to assist scheduling manager to make decision [3].

2) The collaborative modeling, simulation and optimization technology for VPECP

In our research, the collaborative modeling and simulation technology system has been built from simulation component model specification, high level modeling specification and collaborative simulation runtime infrastructure specification [1]. A high level modeling language (HML) is developed for supporting hierarchical description of hybrid multidisciplinary system from structure and behavior views and integration with design environment

[4].

In order to get optimized design prototype according to function/behavior/performance, many key technologies in multidisciplinary design optimization technology for CPEVP are also studied [4].

3) VR/Visualization technology and virtual environment technology for CPEVP

There have raised emergent requirement for more natural and objective visualization technologies including flexible modeling and rendering technologies and integrated collaborative hierarchical architecture supported in CPEVP applications. The virtual environment developed by authors based on Image-based Rendering (IBR) technology [5] provides a well-defined three level modules as Central Visualization Server(CVS), Local Proxy Server(LPS) and Visualization Aid Environment(VAE), by which data and control for collaboration move through them followed the previous dataflow model. Referred to IBR-Driven dataflow model, the communication between any components within these three hierarchies can be remark as two usual categories: data and service code, control parameter.

The technology of grid resource management middleware GOS [6]

VPEG uses GOS as resource management middleware. In GOS, grid resource driver connects legacy resources to grid to hide their heterogeneity and dynamic features. Grid router realizes function of grid information management, and provides virtualization of grid resources and on-line scalability of grid system. GOS API constructs a unified, single system mapping, low level technology independent and hardware independent application interface and user application/development environment for top level grid management tools, grid programming environment and grid application.

VPECP application oriented core services technology

The VPECP application oriented core

services analyze and execute the tasks from application portal layer, and schedule the resources in resources layer via the grid resource management middleware.

1) The technology of Web enabled HLA/RTI

COSIM-RTI [7] is developed based on the technology of Web enabled HLA/RTI. It acts as the run time infrastructure for the simulation systems, which are deployed in the grid/WAN environment. It can support the integration of federates based on Web Service/SOAP, and simulation execution based on Web/Internet.

2) The technology of simulation models discovery based on semantics

At present, the discovery method provided by the grid resource management middleware is based on name-contrast and lacks the matching of the semantic context of the resources. To solve the problem, the ontology technology [8] is introduced and the semantic-based, universal and standard description ontology is defined to implement the semantic description for simulation models. Further more, the semantic matching algorithm based on the ontology inference is studied, and the simulation model discovery service based on semantics is developed [9].

3) The technology of dynamic simulation models composition

In VPEG, the simulation tasks are described using High Level Modeling Language provided by the problem-solving environments, and executed by the simulation engine service [10], which is the controller to implement composition and scheduling of the simulation systems.

The technology of Problem-Solving Environments

The VPEG Problem-Solving Environments (PSE) is an integrated system-level environment for multidisciplinary virtual prototype design and system level distributed simulation. It is composed of a set of problem-solving tools which can be extended.

Especially, the VPEG PSE provides a service-oriented High Level Modeling Language [4], which describes the static structure and dynamic behavior of complex system based on XML specification and meta-model technology. While the static structure is described using extended UML/OMDT/SOM, and dynamic behavior using XML/UML and finite state machine.

The technology of security mechanism and user management for VPEG [11]

Security mechanism of VPEG is based on GSI, which is accomplished by CA system (Gridshield) of GOS including providing certificate, user management compatible to Globus format, accessing control of resources, etc.

SOME TYPICAL CASES

Complex product argumentation based on VPEG

In the project for complex product argumentation, the number of simulation entities are more than 500, the number of federates are more than 30, and the number of distributed simulation nodes which can be scheduled are more than 10.

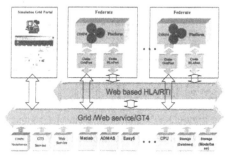

Figure 2 The argumentation simulation based on VPEG

The application system based on VPEG is illustrated in Figure 2. Before system running, users access the grid portals, and dynamically deploy model resources and running environment according to application requirements. During system running, the federates of "Red platforms", "Blue platforms" are dynamically constructed from the models resources and scheduled according to scheduling schema through GOS to execute the models. The federation is constructed dynamically and the FOM data communicate through HLA/RTI.

Collaborative design/simulation/evaluation for multidisciplinary virtual prototype based on VPEG

In the project, many design tools, such as PRO/E, PATRAN, NASTRAN, ICSL, ADAMS, MATLAB, etc., are collaboratively used to model, simulate and post-analyze the integrated virtual prototype system to design the mechanical structure of aerospace product, and to implement the simulation of kinematics and dynamics of controlled flexible system to fulfill synthetic optimization among related disciplinary domains of virtual prototype including system, control and structure domain. The system structure based on VPEG for virtual prototype system comprehensive simulation and visualization is shown in Figure 3.

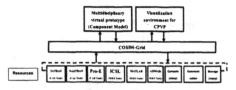

Figure 3 VP collaborative simulation and visualization system based on VPEG

FURTHER WORKS

Further works include to study deeply the full life-cycle management function of VPEG, to consummate key technologies of VPECP application oriented core service layer, and to increase VPEG application

types and scale, etc.

ACKNOWLEDGMENTS

Authors should like to express the sincere thanks to all colleagues for their help and valuable contribution.

REFERENCES

1. Bo Hu Li, Xudong Chai, Wenhai Zhu, et al, The Recent Research on Virtual Prototyping Engineering for Complex Product, The Proceedings of CSCWD2004.
2. I. Foster and C. Kesselman, Globus: A Metacomputing Infrastructure Toolkit, International Journal of Supercomputer Applications, 1997, 11-2, pp.115-128.
3. Guoqiang Shi, Bohu Li, Xudong Chai, Use of Petri Nets for Virtual Prototyping Engineering Scheduling, The Proceedings of ICSC2005, 2005, pp.13-17.
4. Peng Wang, Bohu Li, Xudong Chai, et al, Research on Collaborative Simulation Technology Based Multidiscipline Virtual Prototype Modeling and Optimization Design Method, The Proceedings of ICSC 2005, 2005, pp.347-351.
5. Runmin Yin, Changfeng Song, Research on IBR-Driven Distributed Collaborative Visualization System, Enformatika Journal, Volume 14, August 2006.
6. Zhiwei Xu, Wei Li, Li Zha, et al, Vega: A Computer Systems Approach to Grid Computing, Journal of Grid Computing, 2004.
7. Bo Hu Li, Xudong Chai, Baocun Hou, et al, Research and Application on CoSim (Collaborative Simulation) Grid, the Proceedings of SCSC 2006.
8. O'Leary D E, Using AI in Knowledge Management: Knowledge Bases and Ontologies, IEEE Intelligent Systems, 1996, pp.34-39.
9. Baocun Hou, Bo Hu Li, Xudong Chai, Model Resource Discovery Technology Based on Semantic for Simulation Grid, Accepted by Journal of Beijing University of Aeronautics and Astronautics. (in Chinese)
10. Di Yanqiang, Li Bo hu, Chai Xu dong, et al, Research on collaborative modeling & simulation platform for multi-disciplinary virtual prototype and its key technology, Computer Integrated Manufacturing Systems, 2005, 11-7, pp.901-908. (in Chinese)
11. GuanYing Bu, ZhiWei Xu, Access Control in Semantic Grid, Future Generation Computer Systems, 2004, 20-1, pp. 113-122.

Grid Computing Middleware for Microsoft Excel

Katsumi KONISHI * and Tohru NAKAZAWA**

* Department of Computer Science, Faculty of Informatics
Kogakuin University
1-4-2 Nishi-Shinjuku, Shinjuku-ku, Tokyo, 163-8677 Japan
(E-mail: konishi@kk-lab.jp)

** Dai Nippon Printing Co., Ltd.

ABSTRACT

This work provides a grid and parallel computing middleware, which enables Microsoft Excel users to make a parallel program on desktop grid computing environment. The proposed middleware uses no PC cluster and no special device, but needs only some personal computers with MS Excel. Most MS Excel VBA applications can be parallelized in a few steps with the middleware using Windows API developed in this work. This paper applies the proposed middleware to spreadsheet fluid dynamics (SFD), which is a kind of computational fluid dynamics and enables us to present analytical solutions in graphical forms via spreadsheet software. The results of numerical experiments show an efficiency of the proposed middleware for parallel computation in Microsoft Excel.

KEY WORDS: desktop grid computing, spreadsheet fluid dynamics, Microsoft Excel

1. INTRODUCTION

Microsoft Excel is one of the most popular spreadsheet software used in various fields. It is used not only for tabulate many kinds of information but also for complex calculation with VBA (Visual Basic for Application) macro and can be educational software for computer simulation in financial engineering, signal processing, control engineering and so on. Since users can make simulation programs using VBA macro in MS Excel easier than traditional programming languages like FORTRAN, C and C++ and since the instance check for VBA macro is possible, MS Excel programming with VBA macro is efficient for education and often be used for computer simulation in business such as financial simulation, stock market simulation and Monte Carlo simulation in finance.

One of the most interesting fields of a computer simulation using MS Excel is spreadsheet fluid dynamics (SFD). Spreadsheets enable us to present the analytical solutions in graphical forms easily and help us to calculate with cells. Therefore spreadsheet computing is easy to understand and to make programs for beginners and is suitable for education [1]. MS Excel users often wish to use high performance computing resources in order to speed up a long-running program without using MPI, but only with VBA macro. They do not want to use special devices and network such as PC cluster. This work provides a grid computing

309

middleware which enables them to make parallel program executed on multiple desktop PCs. The middleware uses no PC cluster and no special network device, but needs some personal desktop computers installed MS Excel. Most serial VBA macro programs can be parallelized in a few steps.

This paper is organized as follows. In Section 2, a grid middleware for MS Excel is introduced. Section 3 deals with spreadsheet fluid dynamics (SFD) and illustrates an SFD application with the proposed gird middleware. Section 4 shows numerical experiments of SFD by 1 – 16 desktop PCs.

2. Grid Computing Middleware for Microsoft Excel

The middleware proposed in this paper is developed based on the 'AD-POWERS', which is originally a grid middleware for MS Windows developed by Dai Nippon Printing Co., Ltd., and allows us to make master-worker style application with Visual C++ and Visual Basic. Fig. 1 illustrates how AD-POWERs works to implement a parallel computing. Using multicast, the master PC is able to acquire which PCs execute worker software and how many PCs are available for parallel computing. AD-POWERs implements parallel computing as follows:

Step 1 The master PC delivers a dynamic link library (DLL) file and data files to available worker PCs.
Step 2 Each worker software calls the dynamic link library, computes the data files, and creates a result file.
Step 3 The master PC collects the result files from all worker PCs.
Step 4 The master PC computes the result files.
Step 5 If a condition is satisfied, End. Else go to Step 1.

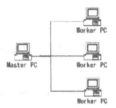

(a) A master PC finds worker PCs in a local area network automatically using multicast.

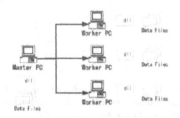

(b) A master PC delivers a DLL file and data files to each worker PC. Then Worker PCs compute the data files.

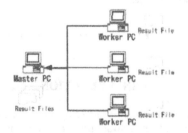

(c) A master PC collects results data from worker PCs and computes the result data files.

Figure 1. Process of parallel computing in AD-POWERs. It repeats (a)-(c) until a termination condition is satisfied.

When unexpected error occurs in a worker PC and no result returns to the master PC, the master PC re-delivers the DLL file and data files to another worker PC, and the worker PC recovers the stopped computing task. If there are more worker computers than the number of parallel tasks, recovery of the computation is achieved right after unexpected error stops a worker PC. Thus AD-POWERs supports fault tolerance.

We developed the grid middleware for MS Excel using AD-POWERs. A DLL file and MS Excel file (.xls file) with VBA macro are delivered from a master PC to each worker PC, and the DLL file calls MS excel. Then VBA macro is executed on MS Excel. In this work, we developed a new function 'quasi-shared memory' to enable worker PCs to communicate with each other. Quasi-shared memory is implemented using multicast in LAN. Each worker PC observes multicast and shares a part of its memory.

Several useful Windows APIs are available for VBA macro to make parallel programs and use quasi-shared memory.

3. Spreadsheet Fluid Dynamics via Excel Gird Computing

This section deals with a simple example of fluid dynamics - Laplace's equation as follows.

$$\nabla^2 \Psi = 0$$

The finite difference form of the above equation is obtained as

$$\Psi_{i,j} = \frac{1}{4}\left(\Psi_{i+1,j} + \Psi_{i-1,j} + \Psi_{i,j+1} + \Psi_{i,j-1}\right).$$

where $\Psi_{i,j}$ denotes the (i,j)-cell of a spreadsheet. It is easy to calculate the above equation in MS Excel with macro, but for VBA macro.

We made VBA macro for this simple example using the Winodws API provided by the proposed grid middleware for MS Excel. Fig. 2 shows an example of VBA macro, where the functions beginning with 'ADP_' are Windows API to utilize the proposed grid middleware.

```
If Init_count = 1 Then
    Init_count = 2
Else
    Call ADP_get_data
    ' get data from
      quasi-shared memory
End If

Call ADP_init_set(Node)

For i = 0 To 19
    Call Do_Marco
Next

Call ADP_set_result   'share result
Call ADP_End_Task

......

Sub Do_Marco()
    For j = Start_Y To End_Y
        For i = Start_X To End_X
            If Cells(j, i) = 99 Then
            Else
                Cells(j, i)=(Cells(j - 1, i) + _
                Cells(j + 1, i) + _
                Cells(j, i - 1) + _
                Cells(j, i + 1) _ ) / 4
            End If
        Next
    Next
End Sub
```

Figure 2. Example of VBA macro (partly extracted from worker's macro)

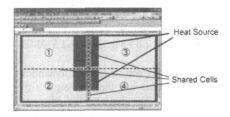

Figure 3. Screen shot of MS Excel's sheet (4 worker PCs).

Table 4. Results of fluid dynamics simulation.

		CPU time [s] Efficiency of parallelization[%]				
Num. of PCs sheets		1 1 × 1	2 2 × 1	4 2 × 2	8 4 × 2	16 8 × 2
Size of Sheet [cell]	40 × 50	64.0 100	43.3 148.8	29.0 220.7	36.3 177.8	52.0 123.1
	80 × 100	232.1 100	82.2 282.9	62.1 374.2	66.0 351.5	70.3 331.4
	120 × 150	611.2 100	179.0 341.3	121.0 504.9	108.2 565.7	100.1 611.0
	160 × 200	888.0 100	301.1 295.0	198.2 448.5	178.0 498.9	160.0 555.0
	200 × 250	1194.3 100	558.3 213.9	416.0 287.1	438.0 272.6	269.0 444.0

This VBA macro divides Excel's sheet into the same size $n \times m$ sheets and delivers them to worker PCs. Then it activates worker PCs to calculate their sheets. Worker PCs can share their cells on the boundary between adjoin sheets using quasi-shared memory. Fig. 3 shows a screen shot of Excel's for 4 worker PCs.

4. Numerical Experiments

Numerical experiments have been conducted to test efficiency of parallel computation in MS Excel. Laplace's equation mentioned in Section 3 was calculated by 1, 2, 4, 8 and 16 PCs in several conditions – the size of sheet is $40 \times 50, 80 \times 100, 120 \times 150, 160 \times 200$ and 200×250. The computation with 1 PC was carried out without the grid middleware. These experiments uses desktop PCs with same properties, 2.6 GHz CPU and 512MB memory.

Table 4 shows the results of fluid dynamics simulation. We can see that the larger size of sheet gives the better efficiency of parallelization. The proposed grid middleware takes time not only to translate files from a master PC to worker PCs, but also to activate MS Excel in each worker PC at the beginning of the computation. Therefore the parallel computing with MS Excel needs more cost than usual parallel computing.

The results show that the parallelization attains bad linearity on speedup ratio. The reason is due to a parallelizing algorithm. In these experiments, the original Excel's sheet was divided into the same size sheets, and they were delivered to worker PCs. It does not always take the same CPU time to compute each sheet even if they are the same size sheets and even if each worker PC has the same CPU and memory. Computation of fluid dynamics is so complicated that computational cost depends on the position of cells to compute. Since the initial value of each cell is 0, it takes a little computational cost to compute a sheet with cells most of which values 0. The algorithm, which parallelizes computation by dividing MS Excel's sheet according to complexity of computation on cells, brings speed up of computation in MS Excel though proposing such an algorithm is future work.

5. Conclusion

This work provides a gird middleware for Microsoft Excel, which allows us to make parallel programs on MS Excel. We can parallelize calculation in MS Excel using VBA macro and Windows API prepared by the proposed middleware.
This paper deals with spreadsheet fluid dynamics (SFD) and parallel computing of SFD. The results of numerical experiments show the efficiency of parallel computing of SFD on MS Excel.
The future work is to propose an adaptive algorithm which parallelizes computation by dividing Excel's sheet according to complexity of computation on cells and properties of worker PCs (CPU and Memory).

Acknowledgement

This research was supported in part by the exploratory software project of IPA (Information-Technology Promotion Agency, Japan).

REFERENCES

1. E. Morishita, H. Koyama, T. Okunuki, H. Asano, Y. Fujimaki, K. Nakamura and S. Tarao, "Spreadsheet Fluid Dynamics in Aerospace Engineering", Proc. Of 2nd International Conf. on Information Technology Based Higher Education and Training, 2001.
2. K. Konishi, T. Nakazawa and H. Miyachi, "Large-scale Visualization System on PC Grid", The 33rd Visualization Symposium, 2005 (in Japanese)
3. T. Tohyama, Y. Yamada and K. Konishi, "A Resource Management System for Data-Intensive Application in Desktop Grid Environments", The IASTED International Conference on Parallel and Distributed Computing and Systems (PDCS), 2006 (to appear)
4. K. Nadiminti, Y.-F. Chiu, N. Teoh, A. Luther, S. Venugopal, and R. Buyya. "ExcelGrid: A .NET Plug-in for Outsourcing Excel Spreadsheet Workload to Enterprise and Global Grids," In Proceedings of the 12th International Conference on Advanced Computing and Communication (ADCOM), 2004

A Resource Management System for Volume Visualization in Desktop Grid Environments

Toshiaki Toyama* , Yoshito Yamada** , and Katsumi Konishi* †

*Department of Computer Science
Kogakuin University
1-24-2 Nishi-shinjuku, Shinjuku-ku, Tokyo, 163-8677, Japan
†E-mail: konishi@cpd.kogakuin.ac.jp
**Department of Information Science and Engineering
Tokyo Institute of Technology
2-12-1 Ookayama, Meguro-ku, Tokyo, 152-8550, JAPAN

ABSTRACT

A desktop grid computing using idle PCs is popular as low-cost platforms for high-throughput applications, however they need high-cost data transfer from file servers to calculating nodes when they deal with very large amount of data. This high cost derives from cheap I/O of worker PCs and file systems of desktop grid computing. This work deals with a desktop grid computing and proposes a resource management system for volume visualization. The resource management system proposed in this work resolves problems with high-cost data transfer and helps us to use desktop grid computing for data-intensive applications. The resource management system provides efficient scheduling considering to data file location to make intelligent reuse of data and consists of three parts of techniques: resource management, multiple data replication, and worker selection. The experimental results show that the proposed system can achieve good performance for data-intensive applications compared with the traditional system.

KEY WORDS: desktop grid computing, resource management, data-intensive applications, volume visualization, parallel visualization

1 Introduction

Volume visualization is one of the simulation techniques utilized to facilitate understanding of complex behaviors and structures. However, although volume visualizing applications must process very large amounts of data, Visualization systems have limited the computation performance and required the use of expensive workstations or PC clusters with high throughput network.

Desktop grids using the existing PCs have attracted attention as a platform which provides high performance computing power without making up of special computers. Dealing with volume visualizing applications under desktop grid environments, there are three issues of data transfer: the data-intensive issue, the poor disk I/O of a PC, and the characteristics of the applications. These issues make the performance significantly decrease.

This paper proposes a resource management system for volume visualizing applications in local area networks using three techniques: resource management, multiple data replication, and worker selection. The resource management system manages worker PC's resource information such as storing data files, the frequency of the CPU clock, hard disk capacity etc. It also replicates multiple data files of worker PCs via P2P (peer-to-peer) data transfer and makes copies of data redundantly to increase the fault tolerance of the desktop grid environment involving inherent volatility. When the job is submitted, the resource management system assigns tasks to worker PCs by Dual Rank Algorithm (DRA) which task scheduling algorithm considering data locations. To execute data-intensive applications in desktop grid environments, computation tasks should be assigned to the worker PC which stores the exact data file to process. Therefore, DRA plays an important role in the resource management system. This paper demonstrates the benefits of reuse of data files. The resource management system can achieve good throughput compared with traditional system. This paper is organized as follows. Section 2 describes parallel volume visualization, and Section 3 introduces grid middleware AD-POWERs, Section 4 deals with the resource management system. Section 5 shows experimental evaluations.

2 Parallel Volume Visualization

Volume visualization is a rendering technique for visualizing voxel data typically describing physical phenomena in a spatial domain. A straightforward way to parallelize volume visualization is to separate the data set into subsets by object-space and time space partitioning and a subvolume is distributed to multiple PCs. This technique offers two benefits. First, we can execute visualization data that do not normally fit into physical memory or swap. Second, we can execute visualizations with a smaller memory footprint resulting in higher cache hits and little or no swapping disk [3].

Some visualizing applications will afford researchers the opportunity to visualize interactively a volume data. The researchers run visualizations using same volume data by different parameters. A conventional system transfers volume data whenever jobs are submitted. Therefore, the throughput is drastically reduced.

3 Desktop Grid Middleware

This work adopts AD-POWERs [4] as desktop grid middleware. It provides master-worker style parallel computation environment over Win32. Master PC manages all data files and communications and assigns tasks to worker PCs. Worker PC performs a task while the screen saver mode is active, and a worker PC stops the computation when the screen saver mode is turned off. Therefore, the desktop grid environment has the volatility of the resources.

Executing data-intensive applications in this type of computing environment lead to two problems of data transfer. First is simultaneous access to the nodes which store data such as NFS and NAS. Second is poor disk I/Os of PCs. Desktop grid uses desktop PCs without special devices. Therefore, whenever worker PCs transfer large amounts of data, the transfer cost becomes high [1]. To resolve the two problems, this paper proposes the method of data transfers between worker PCs via P2P.

4 Resource Management System

Although the cooperation systems between data replication and job scheduling have been studied, most of them do not offer efficient job executions for data-intensive applications. In Condor project [5], DAGMan which is higher level planners schedule computational jobs of Condor and replication jobs of Stork. However, these systems are not able to perform adaptive scheduling according to changes of the computational resources, because Condor and Stork perform scheduling separately.

Resource management system proposed in this paper can achieve efficient executions for data-intensive applications, and consists of three components: resource management, multiple data replication, and worker selection. The resource management is management of worker PC's information such as storing data, CPU, memory capacity, hard disk capacity etc.

4.1 Multiple Data Replications

The multiple data replications is performed before the submission of computation jobs for the jobs execution without data transfers. The desktop grid environments have inherent volatility. Therefore, data transfer between worker PCs via P2P is performed redundantly.

To achieve efficient replication, the resource management system creates a host table and a file table (shown in Table 1, 2). The Host table evaluates the number of data files which each host stores, while the file table evaluates scarcity of each data file.

Table 1: Host table.

Host Name									
$\min_{i \in F_l} N_i$	∞	3	2	2	2	2	1	1	0
N_l	0	1	1	2	3	4	1	3	8

Table 2: File table.

File Name	B	A	C	D	I	G	H	F	E
NP_i	0	1	1	2	2	2	2	2	3
$\min_{j \in W_i} N_j$	0	3	1	3	3	2	2	1	1

315

With two tables, the computational node which stores many data files can transfer a scarce data file to another node which stores a few data files. We assume that one or multiple file servers which store data files connect to the network.

To provide the replica scheduling algorithm, we define some sets. Let F a set of all data files. Let W a set of worker PCs. Let W_i a set of worker PCs which store a data file i. Let F_j a set of data files which a worker PC j stores. Let $\tilde{N}_i$ the number of worker PCs which store data file i. Let $\tilde{N}_j$ the number of data files which worker PC j stores. Let $\hat{N}_l$ the number of data files which host l stores. Let S a set of file servers. A host is a worker PC or a file server, that is. It denotes a set of hosts and is defined as $H \equiv W \cup S$. In Table 1, if the host have no data file, that is, $F_l = \quad$, the minimum value becomes $\min_i {}_{F_l} \tilde{N}_i \simeq \infty$. Finally, we define NP_i as a variable used in replica scheduling algorithm. A initial value of NP_i equals $\tilde{N}_i$. NP_i is incremented by one when a pair of replication of data file i is determined in scheduling algorithm. The following steps are the procedures to determine pairs of replications.

Replica Scheduling Algorithm

Step 1. Sort file table and host table
In file table, data files are sorted by the ascending order of NP_i . If NP_i are equivalent, these data files are sorted by the descending order of $\min_j {}_{W_i} \tilde{N}_j$ in the group of equivalent NP_i . If $\min_j {}_{W_i} \tilde{N}_j$ are equivalent, these data files are sorted by the registered order of data files in the group of equivalent $\min_j {}_{W_i} \tilde{N}_j$.

In host table, hosts are sorted by the descending order of $\min_i {}_{F_l} \tilde{N}_i$. If $\min_i {}_{F_l} \tilde{N}_i$ are equivalent, these hosts are sorted by the ascending order of $\hat{N}_l$ in the group of equivalent $\min_i {}_{F_l} \tilde{N}_i$. If $\hat{N}_l$ are equivalent, these hosts are sorted by the registered order of hosts in the group of equivalent $\hat{N}_l$.

Step 2. Select a transferred data file
Select a data file i which belong to the most left row of the file table. If moves back from Step 3 or Step 4, select data file which is next to right data file currently selected. If any data files don't

exist next to the data file, the procedure is terminated.

Step 3. Select a host H_{send} which sends a data file
Select a host H_{send} which stores data file i , first appears in the host table from right to left and have not reserved yet. If all hosts which stores data file i are already reserved, move back to Step 2 and select a transfer data file again. If all hosts are already reserved or only one worker PC is not reserved, the procedure is terminated.

Step 4. Select a host $H_{receive}$ which recieves a file
Select a host $H_{receive}$ which does not store data file i , first appears in the host table from left to right and have not reserved nor have shortage of available disk. If all hosts already store data file i , move back to Step 2 and select transfer data file again.

Step 5. Reserve a pair of H_{send} and $H_{receive}$
Reserve H_{send} and $H_{receive}$ for transferring data file i . NP_i is incremented by one. move back to Step 1.

After the resource management system determines multiple pairs of hosts, these hosts synchronously transfer a data file. This replication process is performed repeatedly until the number of each data file which worker PCs store corresponds to a given value by user. The replication procedure based on Gossip-Based algorithm [6].

4.2 Worker Selection

The resource management system can execute computation job without file transfers by using redundantly replicated data files. However, redundant file transfers result in that multiple worker PCs store same data file. And the number of worker PCs varies during job executions. Therefore, the resource management system needs a special algorithm which efficiently assigns tasks to worker PCs that store data files. This paper proposes Dual Rank Algorithm using a file rank list and a worker PC rank list. The file rank list evaluates scarcity of each data file, and the worker PC rank list evaluates the number of data files which each worker PC stores. Note that one data file corresponds to one task. Therefore the number of divided data corresponds to the number of tasks. The procedure of DRA is following.

Dual Rank Algorithm

Step 1. Create file rank list

Calculates FR_i (File Redundancy) of each data file i of non-assigned tasks. FR_i is defined as $FR_i = \tilde{N}_i / \sum_j w_j$. Data files are sorted by the ascending order of FR_i and are added to the file rank list. However, when $\tilde{N}_i$ equal 0, the data files i are deleted from the file rank list. Then we introduce FWR_i (Files-Worker PCs Rate) . If some of FR_i are equivalent to each other for the data file i , FR_i is prioritized in the file rank list such that FWR_i has a smaller value. FWR_i is defined as

$$FWR_i = \frac{\sum_j w_i \tilde{N}_j}{FWT}, \qquad (1)$$

where $FWT = \sum_i {}_F \sum_j w_i \tilde{N}_j$.

Step 2. Create worker PC rank list

Calculate WA_j (Worker PC Ability) of each worker PC j of non-assigned tasks. WA_j is defined as $WA_j = \tilde{N}_j / \sum_i {}_F i$. Worker PCs are sorted by the ascending order of WA_j and are added to the worker PC rank list. However when $\tilde{N}_j$ equal 0, the worker PCs j are added to the end of the worker PC rank list. Then we introduce WFR_j (Worker PCs-Files Rate) . If some of WA_j are equivalent to each other for the worker PC j , WA_j is prioritized in the worker PC rank list such that WFR_j has a smaller value. WFR_j is defined as

$$WFR_j = \frac{\sum_i {}_{F_j} \tilde{N}_i}{WFT}, \qquad (2)$$

where $WFT = \sum_j w \sum_i {}_{F_j} \tilde{N}_i$.

Step 3. Assign tasks

Assign a task to a worker PC which belongs to the top of the worker PC rank list. If the worker PC has two or more data files, it assigns a task which corresponds to a data file which belong to the top of the file rank list in the group of data files that the worker PC stores. If a worker PC does not have any data files, assign a task and download a corresponding data file from NAS to the worker PC. The download file should

be the fewest data files in the grid environment. Deletes the data file and the worker PC from the both lists, and update them. Repeat Step 3 until assigning tasks to all worker PCs.

Step 4. Get results

When a worker PC finishes the assigned task or new worker PC participates, update both the lists, and then go back to Step 3. Note that the worker PC finishing a task is treated as well as newcomer worker PC. If all tasks are completed, DRA is terminated.

5 Experiments

This work uses a desktop grid environment using 33 PCs of CPD center of Kogakuin university and a common NAS which has 1Tb HDD using Ultra ATA 133.Architectures of master PC and worker PC are identical. These PCs using Win XP Pro SP2 have 512Mb memory, Pentium4 2.6Ghz CPU, and 40Gb HDD$5400rpm/ATA100$. Network bridge between switches are connected 4Gbps and each switches are connected 21 PCs and 12 PCs respectively via 1000BASE/T. Note that all data files are stored on a NAS connected to a switch.

Two experiments are conducted with encoding application (Windows Media Encoder) consisting of 64 tasks. Input file is AVI file of size 1 GBytes and output file is WMV file of size 1.4MBytes.

5.1 Scenarios

The first set of experiment is to evaluate DRA. Each worker PC already has 1-10 data files. Parts of the data files are stored on worker PCs redundantly. The number of worker PCs is fixed at 8 PCs / 16 PCs / 32 PCs. Under this computational environment, we apply three techniques as following. Ex1-1 is that all data files are downloaded from NAS. Ex1-2 is that apply DRA on the conditions that both of the rank lists are sorted at random. Ex1-3 is that apply DRA.

Fig.1 shows the results of Experiment 1. We can see that it costs constant time in Ex1-1 in spite of varying the number of the worker PCs because the execution time depends on the performance of NAS. In Ex1-2, although the data files stored on local disks are utilized, the algorithm of Ex1-2 does not evaluate scarcity of data files and the number of data files which each worker PC stores. Therefore, the more worker PCs participated in the job, the more the number of data files which

317

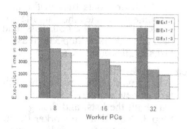

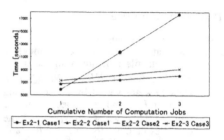

Figure 1: The result of experiment 1.

Figure 2: Traditional system vs. proposed system.

worker PCs already stored increased. The result of Ex1-3 shows DRA executes any jobs faster than the algorithm using random list (Ex1-2).

The second set of experiment is carried in order to evaluate the resource management system. The experiment is performed by submitting three jobs that input parameters varied each job, and consists of Ex2-1 and Ex2-2. In Ex2-1, all data files are downloaded from NAS to each worker PC, which encodes the data files (AVI file) to WMV files. Each worker PC always participates in three jobs. In Ex2-2, data files are replicated with three redundancies before jobs are submitted. Then, three jobs are submitted continuously. The number of worker PCs is varying as following. Case1 is that 32 worker PCs always participate in a replication job and three computation jobs. Case2 is that when the replication job is submitted under 16 worker PCs participations, worker PCs with no data files participate every 20 minutes through the replication job and three computation jobs executions. Case3 is that 32 worker PCs always participate in a replication job and three computation jobs on the condition that all data files which 16 worker PCs store are deleted after the replications completed.

Fig.2 shows the results of Experiment 2.Note that the Ex2-2 time of first job completed includes execution time of a replication job. When the first computation job is completed, Case 1 of Ex2-1 is the fastest execution time compared with Ex2-2, because Ex2-2 performs 3 multiple replications of each data file in all cases. However after second computation job completed, all cases of Ex2-2 accomplish better throughput. This means that the more jobs are submitted, the higher the throughput is.

6 Conclusions

This paper has proposed a resource management system for data-intensive applications that performs multiple replications before submitting computation jobs. When computation jobs are submitted, proposed resource management system performs efficient scheduling considering data file locations by Dual Rank Algorithm. In experiments, we confirm the usefulness of the proposed system.

References

[1] Katsumi Konishi, Tohru Nakazawa, Hideo Miyachi, *Large-scale Visualization System on PC Grid*, Visualization Symposium, 2005 (in Japanese).

[2] John Bent, Douglas Thain, Andrea C. Arpaci-Dusseau, Remzi H. Arpaci-Dusseau and Miron Livny, *Explicit Control in a Batch-Aware Distributed File System*, Proceedings of the First USENIX Symposium on Networked Systems Design and Implementation (NSDI '04), San Francisco, CA.

[3] James Ahrens, Kristi Brislawn, Ken Martin, Berk Geveci and Michael Papka, *Large-Scale Data Visualization Using Parallel Data Streaming*, IEEE Computer graphics and Applications, Vol.21, No.4, pp.34-41, 2001.

[4] AD-POWERs, http://www.ad-powers.jp/.

[5] Condor project, http://www.cs.wisc.edu/condor/.

[6] T. utt, F. Schintke, and A. Reinefeld, *Efficient synchronization of replicated data in distributed systems*, Proc. ICCS '03, 2003.

A Collaborative Virtual Simulation System Based on HLA for Emergency Rescue Training

Xin.Chen*, Huadong Ma*

*College of Computer Science Technology
Beijing University of Posts and Telecommunications
Beijing China
(E-mail: skybirdcx@hotmail.com)

ABSTRACT

ERT is a collaborative virtual simulation system supporting the emergency rescue training.The teams which are composed of 3-6 rescuers can be collaboratively trained under the supporting of ERT. ERT is implemented based on HLA. This paper introduces the problems facing during the development of ERT, such as shared objects, ownership management, efficient network communication, area of interest management, supporting for heterogeneous VR hardware systems. Furthermore, this paper introduces the benchmarking test, such as benchmarking scale of federation, benchmarking update latency, benchmarking time advancement, benchmarking federate real load, in order to make sure whether the performance of RTI meets to the requirements of ERT.

KEY WORDS : Distributed Interactive Simulation, Collaborative Virtual Simulation, High Level Architecture(HLA)

Introduction

Recent terrorist incidents, increasing a nstantly changing global environment are eating an ever-growing need for improved meland security measures. Government encies and forces need be better trained to ish the tasks of emergency rescue of foreseen incidents such as terrorist threats, ological threats, and natural disasters arthquakes or massively infectious diseases). rtual reality technology offer enormous ining potential with immersive trainees in a mputer generated world. They provide a cost fective environment to expose groups or dividual employees to a variety of hazardous critical experiences in a controlled manner.

With the virtual reality technology, we ilt an advanced training system called ERT. is system initially focuses on the emergency cue training for earthquakes. But it can be sily extended to be used in other emergency rescues, such as emergency rescues for mine, emergency rescues for city transportation.

ERT is responsible for training the emergency rescue commanders, the operational teams consisted of 3-6 persons. A 3D scenario creator can be used to assign a specific training scenario to the trainees by instructors. Trainees take on the role of the characters in the training scenario and control their actions and ultimately the scenario outcomes. All of the actions are recorded in the database system and can be replayed at anytime. The outcome of each trainee is evaluated by an expert system. Each trainee is assigned a credit based on the evaluation result of the outcome. The training missions are set up by the emergence rescue experts from the different fields, such as earthquake, mine, firefighting and so on. The missions will be used as the criteria for evaluating the training results of each trainee. The interface of ERT is presented in Figure 1.

Figure 1 The ERT system Interface

As a typical collaborative virtual simulation system (CVS), ERT allows multiple geographically distant rescuers to communicate with each other and interact with virtual objects in a shared virtual world.

When a training mission is assigned, the instructor will create a training scenario by using the 3D scenario creator. The scenario is used as the input of ERT. During the run of ERT, all trainees enter the same environments using the same tools to finish a common mission (shown as figure 1). They see with each other in a first person vision. And all changes of trainee state and environments state will keep the synchronization in the virtual spaces.

The challenges of ERT system

ERT system faces many challenges such as virtual reality interaction technique, physics engine technique and so on. But during the realization of ERT system, we found the most challenge was the middleware technique supporting collaborative virtual simulation. The middleware includes DIS protocol, Living Worlds (LW), Open Community (OC), High Level Architecture (HLA), Java Shared Data Toolkit (JSDT) and so on.. The problems presented as the follows:

● Shared Objects

A shared object is defined as an element in the virtual environment viewable by two or more participants in the session. The core problem of ERT is how to keep the consistency of the shared objects among all the trainees. The state changes about a given shared object must then be sent to all hosts who know about that object so that all participants can get an accurate representation about it. In ERT system,

all the ruins and tools will present as the share objects. The states of those objects not onl include the vision state but also the physica state such as weight, center of gravity and so o When the states of those objects are change all the trainees will receive the notifications c those changes.

● Ownership Management

An easy way to control manipulation of a object is to give the ownership of that object t the user who is interacting with it. Onc ownership is gained, that user may manipula the object based on its defined interactio methods. Before anyone else can change th object's state, control must be released by th owner and transferred to the second user. I ERT system, each trainee has the privilege t move the virtual ruins, use the virtual tool, when those actions happen, the system mus change the state ownership of those ruins an tools, and solve the conflict problem of tw trainee try to operation the same object.

● Area of Interest Management

Area-of-interest management (AIM) is technique for limiting the amount c information that one user receives during collaborative session. The aim of AIM is tha the user's host computer only has to proces information for objects within a well-define proximity with the ultimate goal bein minimization of hosts receiving specifi messages[2]. In the ERT system, each traine has Area of Interest that is the scope of traine who can see, hear and feel. How to define th Area of Interest and how to translate the da only the trainee can seeing, hearing and feelin are the key problems of ERT system.

● World State Management

World state management is defined a keeping a persistent record of the updates mac to the shared objects of a virtual world. The ke to the world state management is the persiste data. The record keeping implementation dependent upon how much information nee to be transmitted to a new user joining an acti collaborative session. The aim of world sta management is making sure that new use have a consistent, up-to-date representation the virtual world. In ERT, a new trainee or ne observer can join the simulation at any mome

320

system must ensure the newer can seeing, hearing and feeling the same with others.

- **Efficient Network Communication**

For the purposes of shared VR, the goal of such communication should maximize consistency among the shared objects (that may be frequently updated by a site) at all the nodes in a collaborative session while minimizing the network traffics[3]. In ERT, there are thousands of ruins and tools, which are distributed to the tens of computer, so the real-time performances and supporting large scale performances are the key points to keep the consistency among the shared objects.

- **Support for Heterogeneous VR Hardware Systems**

In CVS system, there are many VR hardware systems. Now the VR community has access to a wide variety of tools for doing VR work such as HMD, large-screen projection systems. Technological developments frequently improve, extend, and increase the availability of these tools. As a result, any two given VR hardware systems often use different interaction techniques or different display methods. ERT must support the various visualization and interaction methods by the middleware.

The Architecture of ERT system based on HLA

In order to solve the problems mentioned above, the ERT system adopt the architecture based on HLA, The architecture of ERT system is shown in figure 2. The ERT system includes two primary units: team training system and commander training system. Currently, the team training system supports simultaneously two teams. Each team is composed of 3 trainees. The commander training system supports one commander at once. Each trainee wears a 5DTTM HMD display. The CyberGlove is used to capture the motion of the trainees' fingers. The MotionStarTM tracks the motion of the trainees' bodies. Each trainee is equipped with sensors. The motion tracking unit with 12 sensors can track the main parts of the body. In order to avoid the electromagnetic interferences, is typically best to have not any metal at least - 30 feet away from the transmitters.

Therefore a minimal ceiling height of about 25 feet is ideal. In order to assure that the system can achieve the real-time responses to the trainees' actions, we give each team a suite of MotionStar system. That says each team is equipped with one transmitter and 36 sensors. Each team is located in one room which minimum dimension of 40' x 40' or greater is best. The two rooms are separated from 70-80 feet in order to avoid the interferences between the two transmitters.

All the ERT subsystem is connect by the RTI as a federate. In system, there are some federate as following:

- Commander training federate: the commander training federate will subscibe the state of all the ruins, tools and trainee of the team to construct the scene seen by the commander, and publish the commands of the commander.
- Team training display federate: the commander training federate will subscibe the state of all the ruin objects, tool objects and trainee object of the team to construct the scene seen by the team trainee, publish the hand motion data required by the CyberGlove.

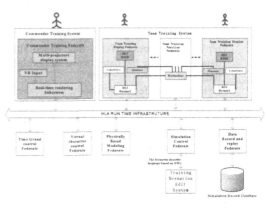

Figure 2 The Architecture of ERT

- Team training position federate: the team training position federate publishes the position data of each team trainee object captured by the MotionStarTM .
- Physics based modeling federate: the physics based modeling federate take

charge of changing the physics model of each entity objects such as the ruins and tools such as aerodynamic drag, collision of rigid bodies, kinetics and so on, and publishing the physical computing result.

- Virtual character control federate: the virtual character is generated by the computer such as the virtual crowds, the virtual wounded persons. The motion and aptitude reaction of the virtual character is controlled by the computer, the virtual character control federate will subscibe the interesting information to the virtual character and publish the reaction computed by the multi-agent technology.
- Simulation Control Federate: the simulation control federate has two functions, one is examining the whole state of system, such as who has joined to the federation, the time of system and so on. The other is control the whole simulation system, such as start up all the federate, load the scenarios describe file, pause and reload the federation run and so on. The realization of the simulation control federate is based on the MOM.
- Data Record and Replay Federate: the data record and replay federate collects the data of all the object states in real-time and restores in the database. The system can replay the process of training based the data captured by the data record and replay federate.

Besides these federate, another important subsystem is the training scenarios creator. The training scenario creator is a system which is to put forward the requirements in the whole training system. It is in the way of three-dimension visualization to support the users to set all kinds of training contents, including the scales of virtual scenes, the sorts and sizes of ruins, the places and quantity of victims, the tasks and goals of the training and so on. When the trainers need add new training tasks according to the new situations, they only need modify the training scenario but not to modify other function modules in the ERT system. So the flexibility and expansibility of the system are implemented.

The function of RTI in ERT

The HLA interface specification partitions the exchanges that take place between federate and federation into six management areas of the FedExec life cycle (federation management declaration management, object management ownership management, time management data distribution management). The remaining figures offer a light overview of how to use the management areas to resolve the challenges faced by the collaborative virtual environments in ERT[5][6][7].

- Federation Managementh

How to divide the objects in the ERT system to the right federate is one of importance problems in the collaborative virtual space. In the ERT system, the whole ruin training scene is a federation. What trainee entering the ruin training scene mall are considered as federates joining the federation When they leave the ruin train scene, the related federates resign from the federation because the RTI support the federates joining and resign from the federation dynamically.

- Declaration Management (DM) and Object Management (OM)

Before federates in a federation can see each other and start to exchange information they must tell the federation the data content they can provide to others and tht data content they need receive from others. These requirements are handled through declaration management and object management.

In ERT system, all avatars trainee declare their positions so that they can see each other Their position data are updated when they are moving, so other federates can obtain the new position value and update the trainee' real-time rendering subsystem respectively, refer to Figure 9. With the same mechanism, avatar can also declare their other behaviors so that they can interact with each other, such as sound interaction, message interaction.

- Ownership Management

In the ERT system, the trainee avatars will use many kinds of tools to operate the ruin This kind of interaction operation is realized by the ownership management. When some trainee avatars want to use the tool, the ownership of the tool object will be transfer the trainee federate. Now, the trainee avatar n move the tool or change the state.

Time Management

HLA accommodates a variety of time anagement policies. In some situations, it is propriate to constrain the progress of one derate based on the progress of another one. fact, any federate may be designated a gulating federate. Regulating federates gulate the progress in time of federates that e designated as constrained. In general, a derate may be "regulating," "constrained," egulating and constrained," or "neither gulating nor constrained."

There is a clock federate In ERT. The sponsibility of the clock federate is to vance the federation time following to the al-world time. Advance the federation time llowing to the real-world time. Any other derates can depend on federation time to date their status or actions respectively. So e clock federate is regulating federate and hers are constrained federate.

Data Distribution Management

In ERT, the trainee avatars are interested in e ruins in the environment that they can see. ey are interested in the ruins states, even ore, they are interested in what the other inee avatars are doing in the same ruins. But finitely, they don't want HLA to send their mputers all events and status of the whole vironment besides their vision or hearing. viously, any personal computer cannot ndle that. More importantly, customers are t interested in what happens in other ruins. us the data distribution management service very important and necessary.

The performance of RTI in ERT

There are many special requirements to the rformances of RTI in the ERT system. We alyze the requirements and designs an proach to test the performances of RTI. We plore five benchmarinf test, such as nchmarking scale of federation, nchmarking update latency, benchmarking date throughput, benchmarking time vancement, benchmarking federate real load. is paper only discuss the conclusion, the nchmarking method and process will discuss other papers in detail[10][11].

Benchmarking Scale of Federation

The ERT is an open system and can expand the scale by add more and more the trainee, so the ERT system must include the large scale of federates. How the RTI can support these objects? Can the large scale of federates meet the ERT system's real-time requirements? We benchmark the scale of federation. The result is show as figure 3. The RTI is the DMSO RTI. When the number of federate is less than 20, the update latency time is less than 20 millisecond. So the refresh ratio is the 40-50 frame /sec and meets the real-time requirements. But when the scale of federate is more than 20, the RTI can not meet the requirements of ERT system.

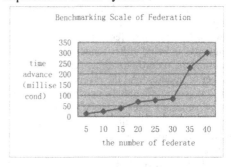

Figure 3 Benchmarking Scale of Federation

● Benchmarking Update Latency

Benchmarking update latency is designed to measure the average one-way latency of an update between two federates. The timer is started immediately before the sending federate calls the function of UpdateAttributeValues(). The receiving federate reflects the update, and sends an update back to the sending federate. The timer is then stopped immediately after the sending federate reflects the second update. The round-trip time (RTT) is divided by 2 to calculate average-one way latency. The result is shown in figure 4, The average RTI update latency will be 1-2 millisecond when the attribute size is 4096 bytes. The results meet to the requirement of ERT.

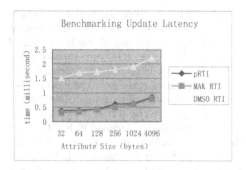

Figure 4 Benchmarking Update Latency

- Benchmarking Update Throughput

Benchmarking Update Throughput is designed to measure update throughput between two or more federates. Federates are designated as being either senders or receivers. The senders record the time sended a fixed number of updates, and the receivers record the time it takes to reflect those updates. This series can be repeated over a specified number of cycles, and the resulting two metrics are updates/sec and reflects/sec for senders and receivers, respectively. In addition the size of the update and several other characteristics, we don't explore are available for testing. The result is show as figure 5 and figure 6, the average send throughput will arrive 2000 Updates/Sec and the average send throughput will arrive 1500 updates/Sec, when the attribute size is 1024 and the federation include 8 federates.

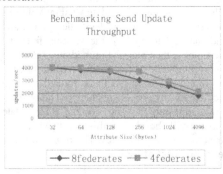

Figure 5 Benchmarking Send Update
Throughput

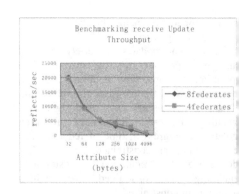

Figure 6 Benchmarking Receive Update
Throughput

- Benchmarking Time Advancement

Benchmarking Time Advancement designed to measure the time needed 1 advancethe time a specified number of unit Multiple cycles are then averaged to produce resulting grants/sec. Each test consisted of 3 cycles, where a cycle involved measuring th time to advance the time 1000 units. A seri of tests was run for an increasing number of federates. The benchmark also provides th ability to specify a federate lookahead, but w did not specifically use this feature. The defau lookahead is one unit of simulation time. Th result is shown in figure 7. RTI-NG performe similarly regardless of message bundling ar for all federation sizes RTI-NG averaged 18-2 grants/sec. But some new RTIs such as pR and MAK RTI use the new synchrono manner, and can arrive the 1000 grants/sec.

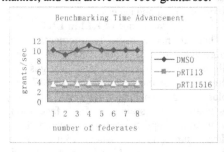

Figure 7 Benchmarking Time Advancement

- Benchmarking Federate Real Load

The benchmarking federate real load adopt ᴇ virtual person in the virtual environment as ᴀckground, and research how the RTI ᴎfluents the performance the whole ERT ᴧstem.The test contrast two group data, one is ᴀ the case of run system in one computer, the ᴛher is in the case of run system on the RTI. ᴛhe result is show in figure 8. When there are ᴧ-20 persons in the virtual environment, the ᴛI communicate latency is a majority of ᴛency. The refresh ratio of one computer is 60, ᴛherwise the RTI is 39. When there are 40-50 ᴇrsons in the virtual environment, the virtual ᴇrson computer latency is a majority of ᴛency. The refresh ratio of one computer is 18, ᴛherwise the RTI is 20.

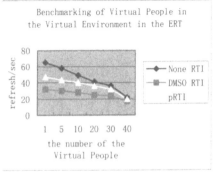

Benchmarking of Virtual People in
the Virtual Environment in the ERT

gure 8 Benchmarking of Virtual People in the
Virtual Environment in the ERT

The Shortage of HLA for ERT-VR
As a new DIS standard that was inspired ᴇm all old ones, HLA has powerful features to ᴘport a very wide range of DIS applications, ᴛ there are still two limitations [12][13].
The Dynamic Extend of Federation Object Model
HLA demands FOM for each federation. ᴑM definition is always required to build a ᴀeration. All exchangeable data must be ᴄlared in FOM. All federates in a federation ᴀ only utilize the attributes and parameters ᴛined statically by the FOM. FOM causes ᴍe limitation for ERT. ERT has the potential ᴑuirements for "Openess" which means that a ᴎv featured federate should be able to join in ᴇr the federation has started. Some experts ᴀ looking for alternatives[29]. But we have

not found a solution that enables new federates dynamically joining a federation, without predefinition in FOM.
● Lack of Scalability
RTI-NG reaches its performance ceiling when seven ~ eight federates run on the same machine. Adding a machine to a federation may have a greater negative impact on execution time than adding a federate. We have not found the statistical data of RTI's capability of supporting objects, but its previous version RTI1.3v5 can support less than 100 entities with real-time response requirements.
● Lack of Resource Management
RTI uses a two-threaded model and a coarse-grained locking mechanism, which is not efficient enough for resource management.
The conclusion and future work
The ERT system is a distributed, collaborative, immersive, man-in-loop environment supporting the emergency rescue training. By our researches, the HLA is a appropriate middleware supporting the ERT. Firstly, the function of RTI can resolve the challenge of shared virtual Environments in ERT such as shared objects, ownership management, area of interest management, world state management and so on. Secondly, the real time performance of the RTI can meet to the requirements of ERT in the small scale. But in the large scale such as more than 30 federates, the real time performance can not meet the requirements. At the future, we will research the real-time RTI supporting the collaborative virtual simulation.

REFERENCES

1. S. Singhal and M. Zyda, Networked Virtual Environments–Design and Implementation. http://www.npsnet.org/~zyda/NVEBook/Book.html
2. Greenhalgh, C., Benford, S., "Boundaries, Awareness, and Interaction in Collaborative Virtual Environments." Proceedings of the IEEE Sixth InternationalWorkshop on Enabling Technologies: Infrastructure for Collaborative Enterprises (WET-ICE), pp. 193–198. IEEE Computer Society, Cambridge, MA, June 1997.
3. Singhal, S., Zyda, M., Networked Virtual Environments. Addison-Wesley, New York, NY, 1999.
4. Stone G F, McGinnis M L. Building scenarios in the next generation of simulations [J]. Systems, Man, and Cybernetics, 1998 IEEE International Conference on,

1998, 4: 3652-3657.
5. Sydac Homepage. www.Sydac.com
6. X. Shen, R. Hage and N.D.Georganas, "Agent-aided Collaborative Virtual Environments over HLA/RTI", Proc. IEEE/ACM Third International Workshop on Distributed Interactive Simulation and Real Time Applications (D I S - R T ' 99),Greenbelt MD, Oct. 1999
7. J.C.Oliveira, X.Shen and N.D.Georganas, Collaborative Virtual Environment for Industrial Training and e-Commerce, Proc. Workshop on Application of Virtual Reality Technologies for Future Telecommunication Systems, IEEE Globecom'2000 Conference, Nov.-Dec.2000, San Francisco.
8. Approved Draft 1516.1-2000 IEEE Standard for Modeling and Simulation (M&S) High Level Architecture (HLA) - Federate Interface Specification. http://standards.ieee.org/catalog/simint.html
9. Approved Draft 1516.2-2000 IEEE Standard for Modeling and Simulation (M&S) HighLevel Architecture (HLA) - Object Model Template (OM Specification
http://standards.ieee.org/catalog/simint.html
10. Knight, P., et al. Independent Throughput an Latency Benchmarking for the Evaluation of R Implementations, in Proceedings of the Fa Simulation Interoperability Workshop, 2001. Pap 01F-SIW-033.
11. McLean, T. and R. Fujimoto, Repeatability Real-Time Distributed Simulation Executions, Proceedings of the 14th Workshop on Parallel an Distributed Simulation, 2000.
12. H, ZHAO, N.D.Georganas, HLA Real-Tim Extension, Simulation Interoperability Workshop, Fa 2001.
13. H, ZHAO, N.D.Georganas, Enabling Technologi for Real-Time Distributed Simulation, Simulatic Interoperability Workshop, Fall, 2001.

A Tetrahedron Matching Method Detecting for
Similarities between Scalar Volumes

Koji SAKAI*, Yasuhiro WATASHIBA**, Tomoki MINAMI* and Koji KOYAMADA*

* Graduate School of Engineering, Department of Electrical Engineering, Kyoto University
Yoshidanihonmatsu-cyo, Sakyo-ku, Kyoto, 606-8501 Japan
** Graduate School of Informatics, Kyoto University
1-Yoshida Honmachi, Sakyo-ku, Kyoto, 606-8501 Japan
(E-mail: sakai@mbox.kudpc.kyoto-u.ac.jp)

ABSTRACT

The traditional method for similarity calculations employing CPGs is unable to adequately express features of the data and does not have any structure definitions. Furthermore, this method is affected by data resolution and arrangement. To avoid this problem, a new definition of a CPG resulting in a complete graph is proposed. In this paper, we propose a similarity calculation method using this new type of CPG, which is also not affected by data arrangement and resolution. We employ a normalization method using Principal Component Analysis in order to avoid the data resolution and orientation effects. In order to evaluate its effectiveness, we evaluate the influence of data resolution and arrangement on our CPG-based method.

KEY WORDS: Critical Point Graph, tetrahedron, matching, similarity, scalar volume

1. INTRODUCTION

To obtain new knowledge from enormous numerical data sets, we need a suitable fast search system. It is desirable that the system (i) can extract appropriate features of the given data and then construct an index based on the extracted features, and (ii) can then search the data set using the constructed index. During the searching step, the system has to perform (iii) calculate similarities among indexes. We believe that an ideal system would allow a user to easily carry out steps (i) to (iii). In this paper, we propose a new fully automatic system to measure similarities between data sets by using features of the data. Our target is the scalar volume data set. To describe features of the data, we use a critical point graph (CPG), which is constructed in terms of the critical points

and integral curves of the gradient field of the given scalar data.

We will discuss the method of measuring similarity using the CPG in section 2. To evaluate our method, we examine the construction of the CPG as a similarity measure with an artificially created volume data set in section 3. In section 4, we will discuss the results from section 3. Finally, we summarize our method giving a brief description of possible future work.

2. The Tetrahedron Matching Algorithm

The CPG method [1] is affected by a lack of critical points. Differences in the number of CPs among CPGs will cause differences in the centres of gravity, rotation parameters, and scaling factors. These differences also imply that this method cannot be applied to calculate the similarity between a CPG and part of itself; it will always estimate a low value for this type of similarity. To solve this problem we propose a tetrahedron matching (TM) method. We construct a tetrahedron around CPs and use it for registration between two CPGs [2]. In these steps, we define the names of two CPGs "Reference" and "Test". Reference contains fewer CPs than Test. We assume different numbers of CPs for the two CPGs.

2.1 Selection of T_{ref} from Reference

We select a tetrahedron T_{ref} from Reference by using the connection of CPG with integral curves (ICs). Because an IC starts from a saddle point, we select the first point of four to be a saddle point. We call this saddle point "root". Subsequently, we select three other CPs joined to root by ICs and construct a tetrahedron. In this case we exclude CPs on boundary (BCPs). Figure 1 depicts the selection of a tetrahedron from a CPG. All combinations of three CPs excluding root in T_{ref} are attempted in CPG. If there are less than 3 CPs connected to root, another CP will be selected as root.

2.2 Selection T_{test} from Test

We select a tetrahedron T_{test} from Test in the same way as we selected T_{ref}. In the next step, we estimate the extent of the resemblance between T_{ref} and T_{test}. The root of each tetrahedron is matched. The other three CPs are matched between T_{ref} and T_{test} by using the type of the CPs (maximum, minimum , saddle). To estimate the resemblance between T_{ref} and T_{test} we

Figure 1 Selection of a tetrahedron from a CPG

calculate the ratio of the edge length of tetrahedrons.

$$r_i = \frac{lr_i}{lt_i} \quad \{i = 0,...,5\} \tag{1}$$

where i is a discrimination sign of a corresponding edge between T_{ref} and T_{test}. lr_i and lt_i denote the lengths of the ith edge of T_{ref} and T_{test}, respectively. When there is a high degree of similarity between T_{ref} and T_{test}, r_i will be approximately 1. On the other hand, if similarity is relatively low r_i will be distant from 1. We calculate c_{ij} to estimate the equivalence between T_{ref} and T_{test} based on another edges included in T_{ref} and T_{test}.

$$c_{ij} = \frac{r_j}{r_i} \quad \{i, j = 0,...,5\} \tag{2}$$

When c_{ij} satisfies equation (13) we define the resemblance between T_{ref} and T_{test} and use it for registration between Reference and Test.

$$0.95 < c_{ij} < 1.05 \quad \{i, j = 0,...,5\} \tag{3}$$

2.3 Registration and the similarity measure

We register Reference and Test by using the corresponding T_{ref} and T_{test}, calculating the similarity measure through the following process (i) to (iv).

(i) Translation of the CPG based on a root coordinate to the origin

(ii) Scaling normalization of CPG based on T_{ref} and T_{test}

We obtain the nearest point v_r to root in T_{ref}, and calculate the ratio r of the corresponding point v_t to v_r in T_{test}.

$$r = \frac{|\vec{v}_r|}{|\vec{v}_t|} \tag{4}$$

To achieve scaling normalization we multiply all CP coordinates and IC coordinates in both Reference and Test by the value r.

Figure 2 The basis scalar volume data

Table 1 Volume data sets

Name	Attribute	Resolution
A	Scalar volume data (basis)	25×25×25
B	90° rotation around X-axis	25×25×25
C	90° rotation around Y-axis	25×25×25
D	90° rotation around Z-axis	25×25×25
E, F	a part of data (A)	13×19×19
G	mirror data of data (A)	25×25×25
H	data (A) minus const. value	25×25×25

(iii) Rotation of the CPG based on T_{ref} and T_{test}

We place T_{ref} and T_{test} in the same coordinate system by using the root of each tetrahedron as a base point of rotation. Firstly, we obtain a normalized vector from root to the centre of gravity of T_{ref} as "nc_r". Secondly, we rotate nc_r to the position $[0\ 0\ 1]^T$ in data coordinates and thereby obtain the rotation matrix R. By multiplying all coordinates of CPs and constituents of ICs by R, we achieve rotation of both Reference and Test.

(iv) The similarity measure

We calculate the similarity measure by comparing the coordinates of CPs and ICs between two CPGs. We use subdivided regions where CPs or ICs exist. If there are many matching equivalent subdivided regions between the two CPGs, we obtain the information that the "two CPGs are similar". If there are not so many, we can decide that "the two CPGs are not similar". In equation (10), we define the similarity measure S between CPG_A and CPG_B by

$$S = \frac{N_{match}}{N_A + N_B - N_{match}} \quad (5)$$

where N_A and N_B indicate the numbers of sub-divided regions where CPs, BCP, or ICs exit. N_{match} denotes the number of subdivided regions which match between CPG_A and GPG_B.

3. EXPERIMENT

3.1 Computational Environment and Data

Our computation environment was as follows;CPU : Pentium M 1.1 GHz, Memory : 760 MB, OS : Windows XP. We used scalar volume data for evaluation of our method. Table 1 shows scalar volume data and its derivatives. Figure 2 shows the basis scalar volume data (Data (A)), which is provided as one of attached data to AVS/Express®.

3.2 Method

We measured the similarity between all data from (A) to (F) in round-robin fashion. We used the value 32 as the partitioning number for the enclosed rectangular parallelepipeds.

4. RESULTS AND DISCUSSIONS

Figures 3 and 4 show the similarity measurement results between all data from (A) to (H) using CPG and TM methods, respectively. Tables 3 and 4 show the computation time [ms] required for CPG and TM methods. These computation times are averaged over 10 computations.

4.1 Influence of data rotation on the similarity measurements

We could verify from Figures 2 and 3 that the similarity measurement is not affected by data rotation. This can be confirmed from the similarity measurement results between all data from Data (A) to (D) where both CPG and TM methods are unaffected by data rotations.

329

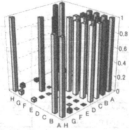

Figure 3 Similarity measurement results between all data from Data (A) to (H) when using CPG method

4.2 Influence of data translation on the similarity measurements

We could verify from Figures 2 and 3 that the similarity measurement is not affected by data translation. This can be confirmed from the similarity measurement results between Data (A) and (H) where both CPG and TM methods are unaffected by data translations.

4.3 Similarity between the complete data and a part of this data

We obtained low similarity values when comparing the entire Data (A) with small parts of Data (A), Data (F) and (G), using CPG method (Figure 3). This is because CPG method requires a higher number of CPs between two data for data matching. On the other hand, we obtained sufficient similarity values when measuring the similarity between Data (A) and (F) using TM method (Figure 4). However, the similarity between Data (A) and (G) using TM method was not measured. TM method needs at least one tetrahedron which includes a "root" saddle point. Figure 5 shows the CPGs extracted from Data (F)

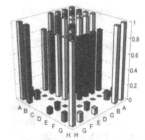

Figure 4 Similarity measurement results between all data from Data (A) to (H) when using TM method

and (G).

The "root" saddle point requires "three" connecting CPs. Data (F) possesses this kind of "root" saddle point, however Data (G) does not possess it. The TM method can only successfully measure the similarity when involved CPGs have "root" saddle points.

4.4 Influence of data translation on the similarity measurements

We used Data (A) and (H); Data (H) being a mirror image of Data (A) regarding their internal structure. The CPGs extracted from Data (A) and (H) remain a mirror image. Because of this reason, when using CPG method the similarity measurement result is not expected to be zero (dissimilar). On the other hand, TM method extracts similar tetrahedrons from Data (A) and (H). However, because TM method does not have a function which can decipher "mirror" image, the similarity measurement result will not reach one (totally similar).

4.5 Comparison of computation time

Table 3 shows the computation time of similarity measurement between all data

Table 3 Computation time when using CPG method

Name	A	B	C	D	E	F
A	3.7	2.9	2.6	3.5	3.3	3.7
B	2.9	3.8	3.4	4	3.6	3.4
C	2.6	3.4	3.6	3.6	2.8	3
D	3.5	4	3.6	4.2	3	2.9
E	3.3	3.6	2.8	3	2.5	2.7
F	3.7	3.4	3	2.9	2.7	2

Table 4 Computation time when using TM method

Name	A	B	C	D	E	F
A	18.5	47	14.1	14.7	48.3	0.1
B	47	15	64	59.9	48.5	0.1
C	14.1	64	17.4	14.2	46	0.1
D	14.7	59.9	14.2	15.6	48.5	0.1
E	48.3	48.5	46	48.5	8.2	0.1
F	0.1	0.1	0.1	0.1	0.1	0.1

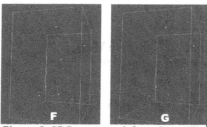

Figure 5 CPGs extracted from Data (F) and Data (G)

from Data (A) to (F) using CPG method. Table 4 shows the computation time of similarity measurement between all data from Data (A) to (F) using TM method. In the case of comparing Data (G) with the others, the computation time becomes very small and the similarity value becomes zero. This is because Data(G) does not possess any "root" saddle point and also possesses only a few CPs, therefore the computation for similarity measurement complete rapidly.

The computation time required for measuring the similarity between almost identical data is also relatively short. This is because TM method works in two major steps: Step 1 works by finding similar tetrahedrons, and Step 2 executes the tetrahedron-based registration and similarity measurement calculation. Although we used a similarity value of 0.99 as being the computation termination criteria, Step 2 was relatively short when comparing almost identical data. Table 5 shows the required computation times for Step1 and 2 when comparing Data (A) with (A) and Data (A) with (B).

Table 5 Computation time for Step 1 and 2

Data	Step1	Step2
A-A	2.0	13.0
A-B	2.0	38.0

5. SAMARRY

We proposed CPG based scalar volume matching and similarity measure. Our proposal method realized the registration by using CP, which is difficult problem for full matching method. CP based matching and similarity measure method can match up and calculate similarity measure between two scalar volume data, even if they are rotated, magnified (reduced), and translated each other. Our proposal method can also discriminate two scalar volume, their relationship that of mirror symmetry. Furthermore, CPG based matching and similarity measure method with employing TM method is able to possible matching and calculating between a scalar data and a part of it. Nevertheless, TM method requires at least one tetrahedron, which includes root saddle point. If a subject does not include this tetrahedron, TM method is inapplicable to this kind of scalar volume data.

In this paper, we made fundamental consideration about a matching and similarity measure method based on CPG for scalar volume data set. The fine details of searching, matching, and similarity measure techniques for scalar volume data exploring system will be our future works.

REFERENCES

1. Watashiba, Y., Sakai, K., Koyamada, K., Kanazawa, M.: Visualization of Similar Situation between Volume Datasets by Using Critical Point Graph and Character Recognition Technique, The Journal of the Society for Art and Science, Vol.5, No.1, pp.11-17
2. Sakai, K., Minami, T., Koyamada, K.: Tetrahedron matching method for detecting scalar volume similarity, Journal of the Visualization Society of JAPAN, Vol.26, Suppl.No.1 (2006), pp.25-28. (in Japanese)

Visualization of Tapping Sound on Concrete Wall using Ambiguous Phase Differences

Ryuichi SHIMOYAMA* and Ken YAMAZAKI*

* Department of Electrical and Electronic Engineering, College of Industrial Technology
Nihon University
1-2-1 Izumicho, Narashino, Chiba, 275-8575 Japan
(E-mail: shimor@cit.nihon-u.ac.jp)

ABSTRACT

The tapping sound sources were visualized from the ambiguous phase differences between the sound pressure signals measured with three microphones, when the concrete surface was tapped repeatedly in the reverberant room. Multiple source directions are identified from one phase difference value due to "phase ambiguity" at high frequencies, in which the sound wavelength is shorter than the microphone interval. By solving the phase ambiguity confusion, the colored circular source image represented the sound source position more clearly at higher frequencies. The relative broadband sound radiated from the area on its surface including the tapping position. The source area of tapping sound changed corresponding to the tapping position.

KEY WORDS: Tapping sound, Concrete strut, Visualization, Broadband, Phase ambiguity

INTRODUCTION

The tapping sound is sometimes used for evaluating the sound insulation of a construction, and for detecting the inner defects nondestructively [1]. The main frequency components included in the tapping sound signal have been investigated in the past. The tapping sound source distribution in space may give us more information for such evaluation. Two-dimensional microphone array system was conventionally used for visualizing the sound pressure distribution at a frequency [2]. However, it is not suitable to visualize the broadband sound, because it is necessary to obtain a lot of images over full of measuring frequency. Kamiakito et al. have shown that the point source distribution can express the broadband sound source position based on the ray trace model, in which each point source represented one sound source direction at a frequency [3]. The microphone interval was usually set shorter than the sound wavelength, because the multiple source directions were identified from one phase difference value due to "phase ambiguity" at high frequencies, in which the wavelength was shorter than the microphone interval. The similar problem due to "phase ambiguity" was solved in time domain in the midbrain mechanism of the barn owl for auditory localization [4]. Shimoyama et al. have proposed a new ray trace model in which the phase ambiguity confusion is solved in frequency domain for identifying the broadband sound sources at higher frequencies, even when the sound wavelength is shorter than the microphone interval [5].

In the present paper, the tapping sound sources are visualized using the ambiguous phase differences with three microphones, when the concrete strut is tapped repeatedly in the reverberant room. The advantage in the present algorithm is referred, comparing it with the conventional on the sound source image.

MODEL AND ALGORITHM

Model

Two microphones are located at the positions A and B as shown in Fig.1. When one sound source radiates broadband sound at position P, the path difference Δd between AP and BP corresponds to the phase difference $\Delta \phi$,

$$\Delta \phi = \frac{\Delta d}{c} f \times 360$$
(1)

where c is speed of sound, f is frequency. When we make use of the phase of wave at a high frequency, "phase ambiguity" leads to some difficulties for identifying the source angle. "phase ambiguity" is expressed in Eq. (2),

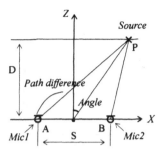

Figure 1   Ray trace model

$$\Delta \phi \to \Delta \phi + 360m$$
(2)

where m is integer. The phase difference in Eq. (2) is substituted to Eq. (1).

$$\Delta d = \frac{c(\Delta \phi + 360m)}{360 f}$$
(3)

Eq. (3) shows that multiple path differences can be defined from one phase difference value at a frequency, corresponding to integer value m. The angle is also calculated ambiguously from the obtained path difference, by using principles of plane geometry. The angle to one equivalent center is estimated from the sound wave fronts under the hypothesis that the sound propagates straightly without diffraction and reflection.

Algorithm

Two pairs of microphones are located horizontally and vertically with a common one. Fig.2 shows the algorithm in which

333

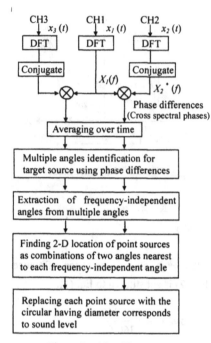

CH3   CH1   CH2
$\downarrow x_3(t)$ $\downarrow x_1(t)$ $\downarrow x_2(t)$

| DFT | | DFT | | DFT |

| Conjugate | | | | Conjugate |

$X_1(f)$

$\otimes$ $\otimes$

$X_2^*(f)$

Phase differences
(Cross spectral phases)

| Averaging over time |

| Multiple angles identification for target source using phase differences |

| Extraction of frequency-independent angles from multiple angles |

| Finding 2-D location of point sources as combinations of two angles nearest to each frequency-independent angle |

| Replacing each point source with the circular having diameter corresponds to sound level |

Figure 2   Algorithm

the point source location (θ, ω) is identified independently in the same following manner. The cross-spectrum of sound signals is averaged over time. Multiple path differences are calculated from a phase difference value measured at a frequency, corresponding to m (m=±1, ±2,...) shown in Eq. (3). The source angles calculated from multiple path differences are categorized as true and false angles. The true angle is frequency-independent, because the fixed broadband source location does not depend on frequency. One point source is located at the combination of two angles nearest to each frequency-independent

angle at arbitrary frequency. By replacing a point source with a circular colored source which color and diameter correspond to frequency, sound level respectively, the sound source image can be obtained as the distribution of circular sources.

EXPERIMENT AND RESULTS

The surface of the concrete strut (78cm in width) was repeatedly tapped by a small hammer in a reverberant room. Three microphones were set at approximately 1.2m distance from the surface and 1m in height. The microphone interval was 20cm. The frame period was set 500ms in DFT procedure. The sound pressure was averaged of ten measurements. Two different positions were tapped independently: position C was located just in front of the microphones, position D was approximately at an angle of elevation +16 degrees (ω) to position C. The frequency spectra on the angle of elevation identified from the measured phase difference is shown in Fig.3, tapping at position D. Multiple angles were identified at a higher frequency than approximately 1.2kHz. The frequency-independent angle was extracted as +12.6° on angle of elevation with a difference of 3° (position D: +16°), by applying Hough Transformation [6] to Fig.3. Processing data in the same manner horizontally, the frequency-independent

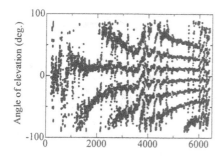

Figure 3 The frequency spectra on identified angle of elevation when position D was tapped (+16 degrees)

position was identified as [+6.9°, +12.6°]. The broadband circular source image was obtained in Fig.4 (a), as combinations of two angles nearest to this position at an arbitrary frequency. Fig.4 (b) shows other sound image when the point C is tapped. The converged sound source area in Fig.4(a) was slightly higher than that in Fig.4(b). This result indicates that the tapping sound is radiated from the area on the concrete surface including the tapping position. However, we don't know about the source area exactly in this case. Let's check the source image of a location-known sound source. One two-way loudspeaker was set 5m far in front of the microphones. The broadband noise was radiated from it. The sound pressure signal multiplied by Hanning Window was overlapped 75%. Fig.5(a), (b) show the sound source images in two different frequency ranges. Each circular source position can be identified unambiguously in Fig.5(a), because all of the sound wavelengths are longer than the

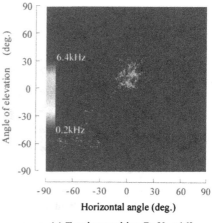

(a) Tapping position D: [0, +16]

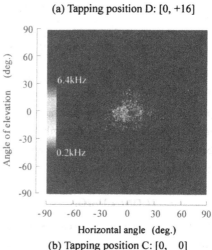

(b) Tapping position C: [0, 0]

Figure 4 Tapping sound source images when two different positions were tapped.

microphone interval. The circular sources scattered widely. We can not find the loudspeaker position clearly in this image. Fig.5(b) shows the case in which the wavelength is shorter than the microphone interval. A lot of circular sources converged on the true loudspeaker position especially at high frequencies. Larger phase difference value than 360 degrees

335

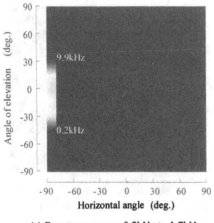

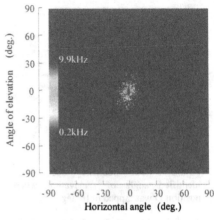

(a) Frequency range: 0.2kHz to 1.7kHz

(b) Frequency range: 1.8kHz to 9.9kHz

Figure 5 Sound source images in different frequency ranges when broadband noise was radiated from one two-way loudspeaker located 5m far.

can be utilized by solving "phase ambiguity" at high frequencies in the present algorithm. Setting the microphone interval wider than the wavelength leads a better resolution in the sound source image in the arbitrary frequency range.

CONCLUSION

The tapping sound sources were visualized using the ambiguous phase differences, when the concrete strut was repeatedly in the reverberant room. The advantage in the present algorithm was referred. As the results, first, relative broadband sound was radiated from the area on concrete surface including the tapping point. Second, the source area of tapping sound changed corresponding to the tapping position. Third, the colored circular source image represented clearly the sound source position, by solving the phase ambiguity at

high frequencies. One of next targets will be real-time 2-D imaging on various wave fields as same as acoustic field.

REFERENCES

1. Shi, W., Johansson, C. and Sundback, U., An investigation of the characteristics of impact sound sources for impact sound insulation measurement, Applied Acoustics, 1997, 51-1, pp.85-108.
2. Franagan, J. L., Berkley, D. A., Elko, W., West, J. E. and Sondi, M. M., Autodirective microphone systems, ACUSTICA, 1991, 73, pp.58-71.
3. Kamiakito, N., Nogami, H., Tominaga, D., Yamashita, Y., Zaima, T., Owaki, M., Sugiyama, T., Wada, H., Development of noise source identification system with multi-microphone sound signal process enhanced by visual image process – A study on decrease of reflection influence, J. Archit. Plann. Environ. Eng., 2003, 564, pp.1-7.
4. Konishi, M., Study of localization by owls and its relevance to humans, Compa. Biochem. & Physio., 2000, A, pp.459-469.
5. Shimoyama, R. and Yamazaki, K., Multiple acoustic source localization using ambiguous phase differences under reverberative conditions, Acoust. Sci. & Tech., 2004, 25-6, pp.446-456.
6. Dura, R. E., Hart, P. E., Pattern classification and scene analysis, Wiley, NewYork, 1973

Image Enhancing Technique for High-quality Visual Simulation of Fetal Ultrasound Volumes

Min-Jeong KIM*, Myoung-Hee KIM*,**,***

* Department of Computer Science & Engineering
Ewha Womans University
11-1 Daehyun-dong, Seodaemun-gu, Seoul 120-750, Korea
(E-mail: kimmj@ewhain.net)
** Center for Computer Graphics and Virtual Reality
Ewha Womans University
11-1 Daehyundong, Seodaemungu, Seoul Seoul 120-750, Korea
(E-mail: mhkim@ewha.ac.kr)

ABSTRACT

3D ultrasound (US) is a unique medical imaging modality for observing the growth and structural abnormalities of the fetus. But because of its low quality and contrast as well as need for fast processing, it is necessary to enhance and visualize 3D US effectively and rapidly by reducing speckle noise and artifacts. Previous methods have limited speed, quality, or are only applicable to 2D. We propose a new 3D enhancing technique for fetal US volume data which classifies the volume according to local coherence. The method applies nonlinear coherence enhancing diffusion filter to the fetus region determined automatically while fast and simple isotropic filter is applied to the rest. Our volume rendering results show that our enhancement technique can visualize 3D US fetus images more effectively than previous techniques, runs more quickly.

KEY WORDS: Image Enhancement, Diffusion based Filtering, Volume Rendering, Ultrasound Image

INTRODUCTION

Ultrasound (US) imaging is a very useful real-time medical imaging modality for detecting abnormalities in fetuses, because it needs no radioactivity or contrast media. Its drawback is low quality, with images compromised by speckle noise and artifacts.

There are ongoing efforts to improve visualization quality of the US image by changing rendering processes such as opacity transfer function directly and by adapting image enhancement techniques such as filtering before volume rendering. Especially, many kinds of filtering technique have been proposed to enhance ultrasound images by reducing the amount of speckle noise or enhancing the contrast. Mean and Gaussian filtering are easily implemented and extended to 3D, and execute rapidly. So they are still commonly used as preprocessing tools for real-time volume rendering of 3D US data obtained from fetuses. However, these simple filtering techniques tend to blur detailed structures. Recently, methods of enhancing US images based on diffusion theory [1]

*** Corresponding author.

337

have been introduced. Coherence enhancing diffusion (CED) filtering, developed by Weickert [2], enhances the contrast at the borders of regions and reduces the amount of speckle noise; but it works slowly in 3D. Nonlinear coherence enhancing diffusion (NCED) was proposed by Abd-Elmoniem [3] to reduce the execution time of CED, which it does by a nonlinear approach which applies different filtering to different regions of an image. An anisotropic filter, which runs slowly, is only applied to regions of high local coherence, while a rapid isotropic filter is applied to other regions. But NCED is still restricted to 2D.

In this paper, we present an image enhancing process based on 3D nonlinear filtering which is aimed at making volume rendering of fetal US images more effective. First, we classify the US volume into fetus region and others from a consideration of the typical structure of fetus images. Our filtering method can be performed relatively fast because we apply the NCED filter only to the fetus region, and use a simpler filter elsewhere. Our enhancement method can improve the visual quality of the volume rendered fetal US images while generating them more quickly.

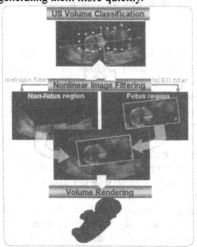

Fig. 1. The proposed enhancement process for fetal US image

AUTOMATIC IMAGE REGION CLASSIFICATION

In this section, we show how to classify the US volume into the fetus and other regions to apply NCED filter to the fetus region and apply isotropic filter to the others.

First, we extract the approximate region of fetus initially considering the anatomical structure of fetus images. Generally, the fetus region is surrounded by amniotic fluid with very low intensity values. So, we can estimate the boundary points of the approximate fetus region on the amniotic fluid region by searching the points with the lowest intensity value on several directions from the boundary of the image. To avoid local minima problem, a point on the boundary of the approximate region should be replaced by the point with the highest local coherence on the same scan line.

To determine the bounds on the VOI (Volume Of Interest) containing the fetus region, we apply principal component analysis (PCA), to the approximate fetus region to obtain its principal directions.

The principal directions are defined as the eigenvectors of the spatial covariance matrix of the voxels. The covariance matrix can be defined as Eq. (1) and the principal component analysis of the covariance matrix can represented as Eq. (2).

$$Cov = \begin{bmatrix} cov(x,x) & cov(x,y) \\ cov(y,x) & cov(y,y) \end{bmatrix} \quad (1)$$

$$Cov' = \begin{bmatrix} cov'(x,x) & 0 \\ 0 & cov'(y,y) \end{bmatrix} \quad (2)$$

Here, we can obtain the major and minor direction which is perpendicular to each other on the approximate fetus region. Then we determine an upper and lower bound on the VOI using projection curve, which is obtained by calculating the average intensity on each scan line in the major or minor direction.

The projection curve pc is calculated as Eq.

(3) on lines parallel to the principal directions m where I_{ij} is the image intensity with column i and row j, H and W are the height and width of the image.

$$pc = \frac{1}{n}\sum I_{xy}, \quad y = m \times (x - i) + j, \qquad (3)$$

if $0 \le x \le W - 1$, $0 \le y \le H - 1$ and $i = j$.

The upper bound of VOI is taken as the point on the projection curve with the highest curvature among the points above a certain threshold, while the lower bound is the point with the highest curvature among the points below that threshold. This method can prevent incorrect results for images with lean fetus region which may be occurred using scanning only horizontally or vertically in the previous work [4].

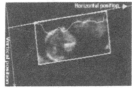

Fig. 2. Extraction of VOI using projection curve considering PCA.

NONLINEAR DIFFUSION FILTERING FOR FAST NOISE REDUCTION AND COHERENCE ENHANCEMENT

We applied NCED filter only to the fetus region with high local coherence. And we used mean or Gaussian filtering as isotropic filter to the outside region of the fetus region and to the fetus region with low local coherence. In this section, we describe CED filter and its 3D use in enhancing fetal US images.

3D CED Filtering

In order to implement 3D CED filter, it is necessary to define the 3D diffusion tensor and to extend the concept of local coherence by reformulating the structure

tensor in previous work [2, 3]. First, a 3D multiscale structure tensor based on 3D eigenvalue decomposition is defined as the following:

$$J_\rho(I) = \begin{pmatrix} j_{xx} & j_{xy} & j_{xz} \\ j_{xy} & j_{yy} & j_{yz} \\ j_{xz} & j_{yz} & j_{zz} \end{pmatrix} = \begin{pmatrix} K_\rho * I_x^2 & K_\rho * I_x I_y & K_\rho * I_x I_z \\ K_\rho * I_x I_y & K_\rho * I_y^2 & K_\rho * I_y I_z \\ K_\rho * I_x I_z & K_\rho * I_y I_z & K_\rho * I_z^2 \end{pmatrix} \quad (5)$$

The eigenvalues of the 3D structure matrix can be calculated by solving the following cubic equations:

$$x^3 + ax^2 + bx + c = 0,$$

where $a = -(j_{xx} + j_{yy} + j_{zz})$,

$$b = j_{xx}j_{yy} + j_{xx}j_{zz} + j_{yy}j_{zz} - j_{yz}^2 - j_{xy}^2 - j_{xz}^2, \qquad (6)$$

$$c = j_{xx}j_{xy}^2 + j_{yy}j_{xz}^2 + j_{zz}j_{yy} - 2j_{xy}j_{xz}j_{yz} - j_{xx}j_{yy}j_{zz}$$

The three eigenvalues μ_1, μ_2 and μ_3 are

$$\mu_1 = -\frac{a}{3} + 2\sqrt{\frac{p}{3}}\cos(\frac{A}{3}) \; ; \quad \mu_2 = -\frac{a}{3} + 2\sqrt{\frac{p}{3}}\cos(\frac{A-\pi}{3}) \; ;$$

$$\mu_3 = -\frac{a}{3} + 2\sqrt{\frac{p}{3}}\cos(\frac{A+\pi}{3}),$$

where $A = a\cos(-\frac{q}{2} \times \sqrt{\left(\frac{p}{3}\right)^3})$, $p = \left|\frac{3b-a^2}{3}\right|$, $q = c + \frac{2a^3}{3^3} - \frac{ab}{3}$.

$$(7)$$

The irregularity $\mu_1 \gg \mu_2 \approx \mu_3$ or $\mu_1 \approx \mu_2 \gg \mu_3$ hold in the anisotropic region and $\mu_1 \approx \mu_2 \approx \mu_3 \approx 0$ holds elsewhere. The diffusion tensor and its elements can also be represented as:

$$\frac{\partial I(x,y,z,t)}{\partial t} = div\,[D\nabla I].$$

$$d_{xx} = \frac{1}{2}\left(c_1 + c_4 + \frac{(c_4 - c_1)(j_{xx} - j_{yy})}{\alpha_1}\right);$$

$$d_{xy} = \left(\frac{(c_2 - c_1)j_{xy}}{\alpha_1}\right);$$

$$d_{yy} = \frac{1}{2}\left(c_1 + c_4 - \frac{(c_1 - c_4)(j_{xx} - j_{yy})}{\alpha_1}\right);$$

$$d_{xz} = \left(\frac{(c_3 - c_1)j_{xz}}{\alpha_2}\right);$$

$$d_{zz} = \frac{1}{2}\left(c_4 + c_3 - \frac{(c_4 - c_3)(j_{yy} - j_{zz})}{\alpha_3}\right);$$

$$d_{yz} = \left(\frac{(c_3 - c_2)j_{yz}}{\alpha_3}\right),$$

where $\alpha_1 = \sqrt{(j_{xx} - j_{yy})^2 + 4j_{xy}^2}$, $\alpha_2 = \sqrt{(j_{xx} - j_{zz})^2 + 4j_{xz}^2}$,

$$\alpha_3 = \sqrt{(j_{yy} - j_{zz})^2 + 4j_{yz}^2}. \tag{8}$$

And the diffusion speeds c_1, c_2, c_3 and c_4 can be determined considering 2D case as in [2, 3].

VISUALIZATION OF FETAL ULTRASOUND IMAGE

Ray casting is the most commonly used image-order technique which determines the value of each pixel in the image by sending a ray through the pixel into the scene according to the current viewpoint. The two main steps of ray casting are determining the values encountered along the ray, and then processing these values according to a ray function [5, 6].

We applied Levoy's volume rendering method [6] to the filtered images which is well-known volume rendering technique even for ultrasound images as mentioned in [5]. The improvement in [6], the magnitude of the local gradient vector as well as opacity are utilized to perform the classification process. The classifier is as the following [5]:

$$opacity = a \cdot \begin{cases} 1 & : g(u,v,w) = S \\ 1 - \frac{1}{r} \cdot \frac{|g(u,v,w) - S|}{|\nabla g(u,v,w)|} & : |\nabla g(u,v,w)| > 0 \\ 0 & : otherwise \end{cases} \tag{9}$$

EXPERIMENTAL RESULTS

We implemented our method using Pentium IV PC with 3.4GHZ CPU and 2GB RAM. The Enhancing effect using 3D NCED in comparison with 2D method is shown in Fig.4. The blurred patterns in 2D method are improved using 3D filter. Results obtained using mean and NCED filters, and NCED with VOI, are shown in Fig. 5. We conclude from these results that our 3D NCED filter with VOI can enhance the image contrast in the same say as the 3D NCED filter, while blurring the other regions like a mean filter. The results inside the VOI obtained by NCED and NCED with VOI are of similar quality, while the mean filter gives low contrast results, as shown in Fig. 5. Fig. 6 is shown the volume rendering results of the lower part of the fetus body from our filter and mean filter which is commonly used in 3D fetal US applications. The execution times of NCED and NCED with VOI using fetal US data with the size of 200×95×107 voxels is 163.21 and 12.71 seconds respectively. It shows that our proposed NCED with VOI filter is faster by above 90 % in comparison with the 3D NCED. The reduced volume size using VOI decreases the execution time in geometrical progression not linearly by eliminating many 3D convolution calculations.

Fig. 4. Enhancement by 3D NCED filter: (left) result of 2D filter (right) result of 3D filter.

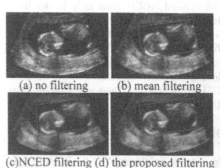

(a) no filtering   (b) mean filtering

(c)NCED filtering (d) the proposed filtering

Fig. 5. Comparison of results from different filters (box on each figure : VOI).

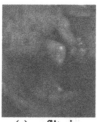

(a) no filtering

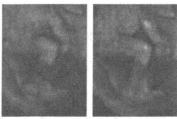

(b) mean filtering (c) the proposed filtering
Fig. 6. Comparison of volume rendering
results from different filters

CONCLUSIONS & FUTURE WORKS

We have developed improved nonlinear coherence-enhancing diffusion filtering and applied to volume rendering for 3D fetal US images. Our method can enhance the US image contrast and reduce speckle noise, and deals properly with 3D US data. Our experimental results show clear improvements in visual quality and speed, compared to previous techniques. We expect it will be utilized to diagnose fetus malformations more efficiently.

In the future, we plan to extend our filtering technique by applying region based approach using scale-space hierarchy or clustering methods. We also need to develop a new diffusion tensor to make further improvements in the contrast of US images.

ACKNOWLEDGEMENTS

This work is financially supported by the Ministry of Education and Human Resources Development, the Ministry of Commerce, Industry and Energy and the Ministry of Labor through the fostering project of the Lab of Excellency and by the KISTEP under the Real Time Molecular Imaging program. We would like to thank Medison Co. Ltd. for providing ultrasound image datasets for our experiments.

REFERENCES

1. P. Perona, J. Malik, Scale Space and Edge Detection using Anisotropic Diffusion, IEEE Transactions on Pattern Analysis and Machine Intelligence, 1990, **12**, pp.629-639.
2. J. Weickert, "Coherence-Enhancing Diffusion Filtering", International Journal of Computer Vision, 1999, **31**, 111-127.
3. Khaled Z. Abd-Elmoniem, Abou-Bakr M. Youssef, et al., "Real-time Speckle Reduction and Coherence Enhancement in Ultrasound Imaging via Nonlinear Anisotropic Diffusion", IEEE Trans. on Biomedical Engineering, 49, 2002, No. 9, 997-1014.
4. Tien Dung Nguyen, Sang Hyun Kim, and Nam Chul Kim, "An Automatic Body ROI Determination for 3D Visualization of a Fetal Ultrasound Volume", Lecture Notes in Artificial Intelligence, **3682**, KES 2005, 145-153.
5. Georgios Sakas, Stefan Walter, "Extracting Surfaces from Fuzzy 3D-Ultrasound Data", International Conference on Computer Graphics and Interactive Techniques, 1995, 465-474.
6. Levoy, M., "Display of Surfaces from Volume Data", IEEE Computer Graphics & Applications, **8**, 1988, No. 3, 29-37.

An Interactive Virtual Operating Room

Myoung-Hee KIM*,**, Jiyoung PARK*, Seon-Min RHEE* and Seong-Won PARK*

* Dept. of Computer Science & Engineering
Ewha Womans University
11-1 Daehyundong, Seodaemungu, Seoul, Korea
(E-mail: mhkim@ewha.ac.kr)
** Center for Computer Graphics and Virtual Reality
Ewha Womans University
11-1 Daehyundong, Seodaemungu, Seoul, Korea

ABSTRACT

We have implemented a virtual operating room in a CAVE^{TM}-like display system. By making interaction between a user and virtual objects more realistic it provides a better virtual space for medical education than existing monitor or table environments. 3D models of key organs and bone can be visualized, together with an anatomical chart that gives the name and structure of each body part, and user can interact with these virtual objects using a wand. The interaction is implemented with VRML sensor nodes and JavaScript. Realization of the virtual operating room involves planning and design, object modeling, model integration, interaction design and implementation, and system optimization. The resulting environment can help medical students to experience realistic operating room conditions cheaply and safely, and can also be used for designing and evaluating new operating rooms.

KEY WORDS: virtual reality, visual simulation, spatially immersive display, interaction

INTRODUCTION

A large-scale immersive display system like the CAVE^{TM} [1] provides a more effective way of simulating real situations and places than a monitor, a head-mounted display (HMD), or a virtual workbench. The broad field of view, the stereoscopic effect, and the ability to manipulate 3D models and simulations in a volumetric space enhances the feeling of immersion. The experience can also be shared to improve communication and to allow collaboration between research teams.

Many medical simulations have used large-scale immersive display environments. In a CAVE^{TM}-like system, Webb [2] implemented a large 3D model of a human eye that can be manipulated and examined by trainee doctors under the guidance of a medical expert. A group at the University of Hull created a simulation for planning radiation treatments [3] using the Fakespace PowerWall. Zhang [4] used a CAVE^{TM}-like system to visualize DT-MRI datasets, and Low [5] combined an HMD and a projector-based display for surgical training. In the Virtual Reality-Enhanced Medical Readiness Trainer (MRT) project [6], several technologies, including human patient simulators, immersive virtual reality CAVE systems, and virtual video conferencing were integrated for the training of emergency room staff.

We present a virtual operating room for

medical education using a CAVE™-like system. It allows interaction between a user and objects within the room which include a 3D model of key organs and bones, and an anatomical chart which gives the name and describes the structure of each body part. Another use of this virtual operating room is to design and evaluate plans for real operating rooms. To illustrate this possibility, we have added functions such as a holographic heart model.

HARDWARE SYSTEM OVERVIEW

We used a four-sided CAVE™-like system with front, left, right and bottom screens as our experimental environment. Figure 1 is an overview of the system hardware, which includes a master and four slave computers, each of which generates the image for one screen. The system includes wireless implementations of an Intersense IS-900 tracking system and a MiniTrax head tracker, which is attached to active shutter glasses. When viewed through the shutter glasses, displayed objects appear to be three-dimensional and, by sensing the viewpoint of the primary user, the system provides realistic motion parallax. The user can interact with virtual objects using a

wireless wand with five buttons and a center click joystick as an interface. Seven emitters are located on the top and rear of the screens to control the shutter glasses.

DESIGN AND IMPLEMENTATION

The construction of the virtual operating room involved five stages, as shown in Figure 2: planning and design, object modeling, model integration, interaction design and implementation, and system optimization.

We started by constructing a scenario and identifying the virtual objects which would be needed in the virtual operating room. To do this, we visited a real operating room in a hospital and interviewed doctors. Many medical facilities and surgical tools were observed and photographed using a digital camera. Initial interaction design and object arrangement were also included in this first stage.

Virtual objects were then generated using the 3DS Max modeler. Appropriate textures taken from the photographs and modified using 2D image editors from Adobe Photoshop and Illustrator were mapped on to each model.

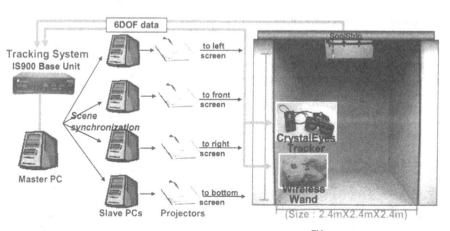

Figure 1 Hardware overview of the 4-sided CAVE™-like system.

A virtual world could then be constructed by converting all the object models to VRML and importing them into CosmoWorld. We limited the number of polygons created so as to maintain the response of the system as the user navigates the space. The light sources are also positioned in the virtual space.

We design the user interaction in detail and implement it using VRML sensor nodes and JavaScript.

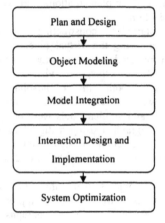

Figure 2 Design and implementation process.

The objects and their arrangement were then modified to maximize their visual effectiveness. This final stage included further reductions to the number of polygons, as well as tuning the lights and texture. These adjustments are necessary because visualization on the large-scale immersive display is qualitatively different from the images seen during development in a monitor-based environment.

Object Modeling

3DS Max and CosmoWorld were used to model objects in the operating room, including the operating table and sheet, and the display for medical images, as well as the models of organs and bones.

To reduce the number of polygons we removed surfaces which are known to be always occluded. Texture mapping makes objects more realistic without increasing the polygon count. But these optimizations cannot always achieve an acceptable combination of economy and realism. We therefore imported complicated sub-models separately and connected them to the main VRML file using the VRML *Inline* facility, which reduces the system load.

Interaction Design and Implementation

VRML and JavaScript are used to implement interactions, including switching devices on and off and changing information modes. VRML provides various types of node for generating, animating, and interacting with a virtual world. There are three types of sensor nodes to support interaction: *environmental sensors, pointing-device sensors* and *drag sensors*.

First, we use *ProximitySensor* and *TimeSensor*, which are environmental sensors. *ProximitySensor* detects where the user's position and then takes appropriate actions. One simple application is an automatic door to the operating room. *TimeSensor* activates an event at a predefined time. We used it to activate the 2D anatomical chart when the body model appears on the operating table. *TouchSensor* is a pointing-device sensor which can be connected to virtual objects and activated when the user points to them using a pointer such as a mouse or wand. TouchSensor detects when the user touches the display of CT, MRI and X-ray data with the pointing device. The last three sensors we use are *CylinderSensor, SphereSensor* and *PlaneSensor*. These are drag sensors which support the movement of objects connected to them. The three sensors have different ranges and modes of dragging. For example, an object connected to PlaneSensor can only be moved two-dimensionally. We used JavaScript to implement functions which are not supported by VRML sensor nodes. JavaScript can control nodes and objects, and it supports conditional and mathematical expressions. One use of JavaScript is the switching of device mode. A switching action by the pointing device is detected by TouchSensor and the mode of the corresponding device is then changed by a JavaScript routine.

The interactions that can take place in the virtual operating room are of three main types. Firstly, by interacting with the operating table, the user can make a sheet and a human body model appear. The mode of the 2D anatomical chart then can be selected to provide labeled images of organs. Secondly, the user can switch on a special device which projects a hologram of a heart model and animates it. At the same time, a large screen is activated which shows 2D images of a real cardiac operation. The third type of interaction activates a display to provide visual information such as MRI, CT and X-ray images.

EXPERIMENTAL RESULTS

We experimented with the virtual operating room, allowing a user to navigate the space and to interact with virtual objects.

Figure 3 shows the virtual operating room. Two different human body models can be located on the operating table as shown in Figure 4. Figure 5 depicts the display which can show CT, MRI and X-ray images, together with associated information. A hologram of a moving left ventricle is shown in Figure 6 and Figure 7 shows a 2D anatomical chart. By pressing buttons and moving the joystick on the wireless wand, the user can select different medical devices and switch them on and off. Changing the mode of virtual objects and navigating the space are very intuitive.

Figure 3 The virtual operating room.

(a)

(b)

Figure 4 The human body model; (a) skin and (b) bone.

Figure 5 Display to show CT, MRI and X-ray images.

Figure 6 Hologram of a moving left
ventricle.

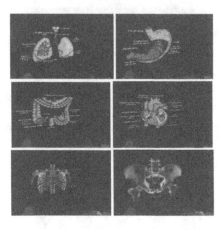

Figure 7 2D anatomical chart.

CONCLUSIONS

We have presented a virtual operating room that allows medical students to experience a real operating room by full immersion, and will also help in the design and validation of new operating rooms. Realistic visualization and stereoscopic effects enhance the feeling of presence, and a user can interact with virtual objects by means of a wireless wand. The system can simulate medical procedures which are costly and dangerous in the real world. In future work, we plan to allow the virtual operating room to be shared across multiple VR displays in a networked collaborative environment, and this will require changes to the interface and interaction methods.

ACKNOWLEDGMENT

This work was supported by the Korean Ministry of Information and Communication under the Information Technology Research Center (ITRC) Program.

REFERENCES

1. Cruz-Neira, C., Sandlin, D.J. and DeFanti, T.A., Virtual reality: the design and implementation of the CAVE. Proceedings of the SIGGRAPH 1993 Computer Graphics Conference, 1993, 135–142.
2. Webb, G. and Sharkey, P., Virtual reality and interactive 3D as effective tools for medical training, Proceedings of the Medicine Meets Virtual Reality Conference (MMVR2003), 2003.
3. Immersive visualization for medical research, http://www.fakespace.com/medical-research.htm (accessed July 2006).
4. Zhang, S., Demiralp, C., Keefe, D. F., DaSilva, M., Laidlaw, D. H., Greenberg, B. D., Basser, P. J., Pierpaoli, C., Chiocca, E. A. and T.S. Deisboeck, An immersive virtual environment for DT-MRI volume visualization applications: a case study, Proceedings of the IEEE Visualization Conference, 2001.
5. Low, K. L., Ilie, A., Welch, G. and Lastra, A., Combining head-mounted and projector-based displays for surgical training, Proceedings of the IEEE Virtual Reality Conference (VR03), 2003.
6. The Virtual Reality-Enhanced Medical Readiness Trainer (MRT) Project, http://www-vrl.umich.edu/mrt/index.html (accessed July 2006).

Astrophysical Simulations with Reconfigurable Hardware Accelerator

Naohito Nakasato and Tsuyoshi Hamada

Ebisuzaki Computational Astrophysics Labolatory,
The Institute of Physical and Chemical Research (RIKEN),
Hirosawa 2-1, Wako, Saitama, Japan, 3510198
(E-mail: nakasato@riken.jp)

ABSTRACT

We will present a novel approach to accelerate astrophysical hydrodynamical simulations. In astrophysical many-body simulations, GRAPE (GRAvity piPE) system has been widely used by many researchers. However, in the GRAPE systems, its function is completely fixed because specially developed LSI is used as a computing engine. Instead of using such LSI, we are developing a special purpose computing system using Field Programmable Gate Array (FPGA) chips as the computing engine. Together with our developed programming system, we have implemented computing pipelines for the Smoothed Particle Hydrodynamics (SPH) method on our PROGRAPE system. The SPH pipelines running on PROGRAPE-3 board have the peak speed of 40 GFLOPS and in a realistic setup, the SPH calculation using PROGRAPE-3 board is 4-11 times faster than the calculation without the board.

KEY WORDS: reconfiguable device, high performance computing, hydrodynamics

Introduction

Astronomical stellar objects such as star clusters and galaxies mainly consists of three components: 10^6 to 10^{10} stars with various mass, gaseous component and dark matter component. Stars were born from dense and low temperature gaseous component hence to simulate the formation of those stellar objects, one have to follow its evolution from early universe. For astrophyicsits working on formation of stellar objects, Smoothed Particles Hydrodynamics (SPH) method [1, 2] is the scheme of choice to solve hydrodynamical process in the course of the formation of stellar objects. In a sophisticated numerical code for modeling formation of galaxies, two most computationally expensive parts are (1) the calculation of gravity between material (stars, gaseous component and even dark matter component) and (2) the calculation of hydrodynamics.

The first part can be computed with a fast and approximated method such as tree or multi-pole methods, or with a help of special-purpose computer GRAPE; researchers in astronomy have invented and developed GRAPE (GRAvity piPE)[3] to significantly speed up the calculation of gravity between particles. In GRAPE, calculation of gravity interaction expressed as

$$f_i = -\sum_{j=1}^{N} m_j \frac{r_i - r_j}{(|r_i - r_j|^2 + \epsilon^2)^{3/2}}, \quad (1)$$

is implemented as fully pipelined logic on a LSI (a.k.a. GRAPE chip). Here r_i and m_i are the position and mass of i-th particle, and ϵ is the softening parameter to prevent divergence.

The second neck in simulation codes modeling formation of galaxies is the calculation of SPH method. In SPH method, fluid is expressed as bunch of particles and hydrodynamical interaction such as pressure gradient force is calculated with a following summation between particles;

$$f_i = \sum m_j \left(\frac{P_i}{\rho_i^2} + \frac{P_j}{\rho_j^2} + \Pi_{ij} \right) \nabla W(r_i - r_j; h_{ij}),$$
$$(2)$$

where ρ_i, P_i are density and pressure for i-th particle, respectively, and h_{ij} is the average smoothing length between i-th particle and j-th particle, and $W(r; h)$ is the kernel function for weighting physical quantities. Furthermore, Π_{ij} is an artificial viscosity term to preserve better numerical stability. Kernel function $W(r; h)$ has a parameter, smoothing length h, that represents the size of the averaging kennel. In its abstract from, gravity interaction and SPH interaction have a similar structure. However, hydrodynamical interaction is short-range, and summation for i-th particle in equation (2) is done over neighbor particles whose distance from i-th particle is less than $2h$. Accordingly, calculation cost of SPH interaction is $O(nN)$ instead of $O(N^2)$, where n is an average number of neighbor particles.

In principle, one could develop a special-purpose hardware (a.k.a SPH chip) similar to GRAPE to accelerate the SPH interactions. However, apparently SPH interaction is much more complex than gravity in-

teraction. This fact prevent us from implementing hardware computing accelerator like GRAPE. Here, in this paper, we present a novel approach to realize computing accelerator for SPH method. A key technique is to use FPGA (Field-Programmable Gate Array) chip instead of developing SPH chip. We call the concept of using a programmable FPGA chip as the pipeline processor for astrophysical simulations as PROGRAPE (PROgrammable GRAPE) that has been introduced by [4]. In the present paper, we report current status of our project that constructs a new generation of FPGA-based GRAPE-like hardware and tries to implement SPH pipeline on the hardware. We mainly concentrate to report about implementation of SPH pipelines on PROGRAPE-3 and its performance obtained so far.

Overview of PROGRAPE and its programming methodology

The physical structure of PROGRAPE is exactly same to GRAPE as present in Figure 1 except we have FPGA chips instead of ASIC on the board on a PROGRAPE board. Also, its logical structure is very similar to GRAPE system such that the host sends data to the board and receives the results from the board but the results are computed on computing pipeline on FPGA chips and one could arbitrary change inside of a computing pipeline. So far, we have developed four generations of PROGRAPE systems; PROGRAPE-3 and PROGRAPE-4 are most recent ones. A main difference between two recent system is that PROGRAPE-3 has four Virtex-II Pro 70 (XC2VP70-5FF1517) while PROGRAPE-4 has four Spartan-3 5000 (XC3S5000-5FG900).

To implement more general computing pipeline rather than the simple Newtonian gravity, we have developed a software (Pro-

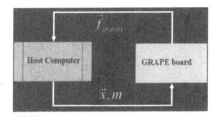

Figure 1: Schematic view of a GRAPE system. It consist of two parts: a host computer and GRAPE board. The GRAPE board is connected with the host computer through PCI interface on the host. The host computer sends position and mass (r_i and m_i) of particles and receiving the forces f_i for particles. Most time consuming part of the simulations is implemented as specially developed ASIC on the GRAPE board.

cessors Generator for Reconfigurable system; PGR) to implement computing pipeline on FPGA (for details see Hamada and Nakasato [5]). Here, a general computing pipeline is expressed as a following equation;

$$f_i = \sum_{j=1}^{N} G(X_i, X_j), \qquad (3)$$

where X_i is a vector contains information related to an element, f_i is the resulted *force* on the element, and G is a function which describes the interaction between i-th and j-th elements. To give a specific example, in the case of gravity interaction, $X_i = (x_i, m_i)$ and G is given as equation (1).
In PGR, a user have to specify how data are transfered and how data are computed with PGR Description Language (PGDL) instead of implementing a computing pipeline with VHDL or any other hardware description languages. For this purpose, we have developed a parameterized FP operations library in both VHDL and C language. This FP operations library is a building block of the computing pipeline. With PGDL, one

can specify how data should be computed, in other words, one can specify a function G using FP operations with arbitrary precision. An example of PGDL is presented in Figure 2. PGR analyze the PGDL source code, extract the data flow and eventually generate VHDL source codes that consist following three main parts; (1) top level VHDL codes that mainly create input/output function on local bus of the board, (2) pipeline definition itself, memory components and a controller of the pipeline, and (3) parameterized FP operation library. Then, we synthesize and place&route the generated VHDL codes with EDA tools supplied by the device vendor and obtain a configuration file for a specific FPGA chip. This automated process greatly reduce the complexity of implementing a numerical scheme on reconfigurable device.

SPH Implementation and its performance

A first important application of PGR software is to implement SPH method on PROGRAPE-3 and PROGRAPE-4 and to use the boards to accelerate the speed of astrophysical SPH simulations. As already noted, the formulation of SPH method is much more complicated compared to Newton gravity (equation (1)) although the structure of equations are so similar and all formulae in SPH method can be expressed with equation (3).
We have implemented a computing pipeline for SPH method. with FP operations $n = 17$ where n is the size of the fraction for variables including a hidden-bit. For the size of exponent, we use 8 bit. In PGDL, a main body of a source code that defines SPH computing pipeline is about 230 lines. A total number of arithmetic operations is 97 including 90 FP operations. For most of operations, we have used floating point num-

```
pg_float_sub(pxi,pxj,dx,NFLOAT,NFRACTION);           // dx = xi - xj
pg_float_sub(pyi,pyj,dy,NFLOAT,NFRACTION);           // dy = yi - yj
pg_float_mult(dx,dx,dx2,NFLOAT,NFRACTION);           // dx2 = dx*dx
pg_float_mult(dy,dy,dy2,NFLOAT,NFRACTION);           // dy2 = dy*dy
pg_float_unsigned_add(dx2,dy2,r2,NFLOAT,NFRACTION);  // r2 = dx2 + dy2
pg_float_sqrt(r2,r1,NFLOAT,NFRACTION);               // r1 = sqrt(r2)
```

Figure 2: A example of PGDL. Here, we compute distance between two points in a plane. Each line corresponds to one FP operation except first two lines. "NFLOAT" and "NFRACTION" specify the size of total bit-length and the size of the fraction of the variables and FP operations. Strings after "//" are regarded as comment and here it represents the corresponding calculation expressed with C-like notation.

ber operations. Only exceptions are the accumulation part of the pipeline where we use fixed point operations, After processing with PGR, a total number of lines of the generated VHDL source codes for the SPH pipeline is more than 8000 lines. Those generated VHDL source codes are synthesized using a CAD software provided by the vendor company of the FPGA chips into the configuration file for FPGA.

So far, we can successfully implemented the pipeline with $N_{operations} = 97$ with clock speed of 100 MHz on PROGRAPE-3. The peak speed of the computing pipeline is $\sim 10 \times 10^9$ operations per second per one chip and hence the peak speed of PROGRAPE-3 board with SPH pipeline is $\sim 40 \times 10^9$ operations per second while the peak speed of FPU on Opteron from AMD running at 2.4 GHz is 4.8×10^9 operations per second (4.8 GFLOPS). In terms of number of operation per second, the computing pipelines running on PROGRAPE-3 is ~ 8 times faster than FPU on a desktop PC.

Finally, we present the results for a test application using PROGRAPE. The test application is a standard test of SPH codes, so-called "Cold Collapse Test" [6]. This test has been used by many authors to see basic abilities of their SPH simulation code for astrophysical problem involving self gravity. In this problem, we follow the evolution of collapse of a gas sphere with the density pro-

file expressed as follows;

$$\rho(r) = \frac{M}{2}\frac{1}{R^2}\frac{1}{r}, \qquad (4)$$

where M is the total mass of the sphere and R is the radius of the sphere. We set total internal energy of the sphere is $E_{thermal} = 0.05M/R$ where $M = R = 1$ in the present work. With this setup, total potential energy of the sphere is much larger than total internal energy of the sphere. Accordingly, the sphere quickly collapse and shock is produced due to the collapse. We compare results with following two cases; (1) calculation with double precision operations and (2) calculation using PROGRAPE. In both case, initial particle distribution is exactly same. We find no significant deviation between two results. This means that SPH calculation on PROGRAPE with $n = 17$ is accurate enough to follow shock wave produced by collapse of cold gas sphere.

The speed performance of this test is much encouraging for us as shown in table 1. In this table, we compare the averaged time (in sec) for one step with four different cases; (1) all calculation with double precision operations on HOST (shown in 2nd column), (2) SPH calculation on PROGRAPE and gravity calculation with the tree method on HOST (3rd column), (3) SPH calculation on PROGRAPE and gravity calculation on PROGRAPE with the direct summation scheme (4th column), and (4) SPH calcula-

SPH Gravity	HOST HOST	PROGRAPE HOST(tree)	PROGRAPE PROGRAPE(direct)	PROGRAPE PROGRAPE(tree)
$N = 25,000$	2.30	1.39 (**1.6**)	0.54 (**4.3**)	0.49 (**4.7**)
$N = 50,000$	6.63	3.35 (**2.0**)	1.30 (**5.1**)	0.97 (**6.8**)
$N = 100,000$	17.8	7.96 (**2.2**)	3.47 (**5.1**)	1.95 (**9.1**)
$N = 500,000$	107	45.7 (**2.3**)	51.9 (**2.1**)	9.62 (**11.1**)

Table 1: In this table, we show the required time (in sec) for one step with 4 different cases; (1) all calculation with double precision operations on HOST (shown in 2nd column), (2) SPH calculation on PROGRAPE and gravity calculation with the tree method on HOST (3rd column), (3) SPH calculation on PROGRAPE and gravity calculation on PROGRAPE with the direct summation scheme (4th column), and (4) SPH calculation on PROGRAPE and gravity calculation on PROGRAPE with the tree method (5th column). The numbers inside parenthesis in the 3rd to 5th column show speedup factor compared to the results in 2nd column.

tion on PROGRAPE and gravity calculation on PROGRAPE with the tree method (5th column). The 1st column shows the number of particles used in those performance tests. The numbers inside parenthesis in the 3rd to 5th column show speedup factor compared to the results in 2nd column. The performance results with PROGRAPE is at least 4 times faster and in some case 11 times faster than the calculation on HOST.

Conclusion

In this paper, we describe a way to realize acceleration of SPH method with the reconfigurable hardware accelerator PROGRAPE. With combination of PROGRAPE and PGR software, it turns out that implementation of SPH pipeline on reconfigurable hardware is possible and and we have obtained 4-11 times better performance than conventional CPU. This clearly shows for the first time that using considerable computing power offered by a hardware we can accelerate the speed of SPH simulations of a simple astrophysical phenomena. Our results open new and extensive possibility of hardware acceleration of complicated and computing intensive applications using PROGRAPE or similar approach.

REFERENCES

[1] L. Lucy. A numerical approach to the testing of the fission hypothesis. AJ, 82:1013–1024, 1977.

[2] G. Gingold and J. J. Monaghan. Smoothed particle hydrodynamics - theory and application to non-spherical stars. MNRAS, 181:375–389, 1977.

[3] D. Sugimoto, Y. Chikada, J. Makino, T. Ito, T. Ebisuzaki, and M Umemura. A Special-Purpose Computer for Gravitational Many-Body Problems. Nature, 345:33–35, 1990.

[4] T. Hamada, T. Fukushige, A. Kawai, and J. Makino. Progrape-1: A programmable, multi-purpose computer for many-body simulations. PASJ, 52:943–954, 2000.

[5] T. Hamada and N Nakasato. Pgr: A software package for reconfiguable supercomputing. In Proceedings of FPL 2005, pages 366–373, 2005.

[6] A. E. Evrard. Beyond N-body - 3D cosmological gas dynamics. MNRAS, 235:911–934, December 1988.

Some Simulation Techniques for Surface Analysis

Umpei NAGASHIMA*, Tohru SASAKI** and Masaru TSUKADA***

* Research Institute for Computational Sciences
National Institute of Advanced Industrial Science and Technology
1-1-1 Umezono, Tsukuba, Ibaraki, 305-8568, Japan
** A Priori Microsystems, Inc
1102, 4-51-1 Nakasaiwai-cho, Saiwai-ku, Kawasaki, Kanagawa, 212-0012, Japan
*** Department of Nano-science and Nano-engineering,
Graduate School of Science and Engineering Waseda University,
513 Waseda Tsurumaki-cho, Shinjuku-ku, Tokyo 162-0041, Japan

ABSTRACT

STM (Scanning Tunneling Microscopy) is a kind of Scanning Probing Microscopy such as AFM, KFM etc, and they are powerful tools for surface analysis. Especially STM can observe the surface electronic structure of sample. But it does not directly observe atoms on the surface. Therefore it is important that STM images are compared with simulation images.

In view of this situation, we are developing STM simulator, which calculates the tunnel current in Tip-Surface system on each pixel point with given bias voltage.

The STM simulator is implemented with LCAO scheme, and we have another plan with Plane Wave basis scheme as CP (Car-Parrinello) method. In the latter case, large scale 3D-FFT calculation is necessary. Then we have made a prototype of reconfigurable hardware acceleration engine.

We introduce the outline of STM simulator and a 3D-FFT accelerator for CP method in this paper.

KEY WORDS: STM, MO, LCAO, Car-Parrinelo, 3D-FFT

NOMENCLATURE

STM/STS / Spectroscopy	:	Scanning Tunneling Microscopy
SPM	:	Scanning Probing Microscopy
AO	:	Atomic Orbital
MO	:	Molecular Orbital
LCAO	:	Linear Combination of AOs
DV-Xα	:	Discrete Variational Xα method
LDA	:	Local Density Apploximation
LUMO	:	Lowest Un-occupied MO
HOMO	:	Highest Occupied MO
Ef	:	Fermi Level
CP	:	Car-Parrinello Method
QMD	:	Quantum Molecular Dynamics
FFT	:	Fast Fourier Transformation

INTRODUCTION

STM is a kind of SPM. With very small tip (needle) scanning in the area near the surface of sample, SPM can detect various kinds of surface properties.

Figure 1 shows the concept of STM instrument. STM detects tunnel current in tip-surface system with given bias voltage, and then we can obtain the information about geometrical and electronic structure of sample surface. [1]

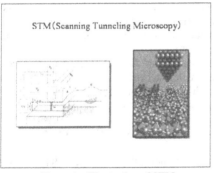

Figure 1 Illustration of STM

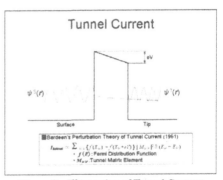

Figure 2 Illustration of Tunnel Current

Because STM does not directly observe atoms on the surface, it is very significant to compare the STM images with the results of computer simulation. In view of this situation, we are developing STM simulator.

THEORETICAL APPROACH

Figure 2 is an image illustration of tunnel current. The intensity of tunnel current depends on the interaction between the wave function in surface and that of tip.

The Outline of STM Simulation

■ Bardeen's Perturbation Theory of Tunnel Current (rewrite)

$$I_{tunnel} \propto \int^{E_F} dE \, [f(E) - f(E+eV)] \, A(R, E, E+eV)$$

- $f(E)$: Fermi distribution function
- $A(R, E, E') = \iint_\Omega d\mathbf{r} d\mathbf{r}' \, V^T(\mathbf{r}) V^T(\mathbf{r}') G^T(\mathbf{r}',\mathbf{r}, E') \, G^S(\mathbf{r}+R, \mathbf{r}'+R; E)$
- $G(\mathbf{r}, \mathbf{r}'; E) = \sum_\mu \psi^*_\mu(\mathbf{r}) \psi_\mu(\mathbf{r}') \, \delta(E-E_\mu)$

- -

● $A(R, E, E') = \sum_{ii'pp'jj'qq'} C^S_{ipi'p'}(E) \, C^T_{jqj'q'}(E+eV) \, J_{ipjq}(R) \, J_{i'p'j'q'}(R)$
- $G_{ipi'p'}(E) = \sum_\mu C_{\mu,ip} C^*_{\mu,jq} \{ (\pi/\triangle)/[(E-E_\mu)^2+\triangle^2] \}$
- $J_{ipjq}(R) = \int_\Omega d\mathbf{r} \, \chi^*_p(\mathbf{r}-R-R_i) \, V^T(\mathbf{r}) \, \chi_p(\mathbf{r}-R_j)$

- -

S: Surface i...atom index, p...orbital index
T: Tip   j...atom index, q...orbital index
J: Tunnel Matrix Element, χ : atomic oribital
ψ : moleculer orbital, V: potential, R: Vector from Surface to Tip
C: LCAO-Coefficient Matrix

Figure 3 Formulation of Tunnel Current in Tip-Surface System

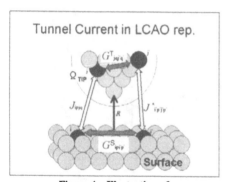

Figure 4   Illustration of

Tunnel Current Calculation in STM

Tunnel current can be estimated with Bardeen's perturbation theory. Tsukada et al. rewrote the theory using Green function for tip-surface system.[2]

Figure 3 and Figure 4 show the theoretical concept of tunnel current calculation in the tip-surface system based on LCAO scheme. Here we use LCAO-DVXα method for the first principle calculation of electronic states of tip and surface.

OBJECT STRUCTURE

Figure 5 shows static data structure of STM simulator in the form of class diagram.

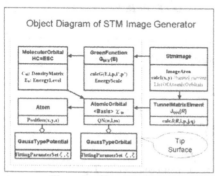

Figure 5   Class Diagram

G (Green function imaginary part) is generated from molecular orbital information such as energy levels of MO and LCAO

coefficient matrix, and J (tunnel matrix element) from atomic orbital information including position and local potential of each atom.

A Molecular Orbital consists of some atomic orbitals in LCAO scheme. Therefore each molecular orbital object has a link list of atomic orbital objects in the program.

SIMULATION SYSTEM

Figure 6 shows the overview of STM simulator. Calculation processes for tip and surface are separately executed from the stage of LCAO-DVXα calculation to the stage of Green function generation.

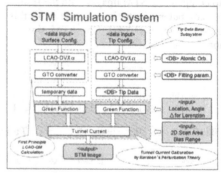

Figure 6   System Overview

Radial wave function which is the DVXα outputs are converted to a combination of Gauss type functions in order to make 3D spacial integrals simplified in tunnel matrix element calculation the same as other MO calculation. Tip data are often reused in simulation, the same as one tip is used so many times in experiment. Then we think that data base subsystem for tip data will be necessary in STM simulator.

SIMULATION EXAMPLES

We show a simulation example. Here the simulation sample is porphyrin molecule shown in Figure 7(a) with tungsten crystalline tip shown in (b).

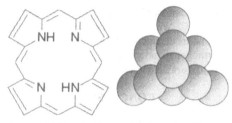

Figure 7 (a) Porphyrin   (b) Tungsten Tip

Simulation condition is shown as following.
Bias Voltage: -1.5V
Distance: 5 A.U.($\fallingdotseq 2.646 \text{Å}$)
Figure 8 and Figure 9 show the simulation results, Figure 8 shows LUMO image, and Figure 9 shows STM image.

Figure 8   Simulation Result of LUMO

of Porphyrin Molecule

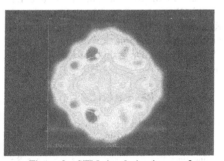

Figure 9   STM simulation image of

Tungsten Tip - Porphyrin Molecule System

Because bias voltage is negative value, Fermi level of the tip is higher than that of the surface. Therefore electrons move from tip to surface (i.e. Tunnel current flows

from surface to tip).
Comparing (a) and (b), we know STM image loose the symmetry which the geometrical structure of porphyrin molecule or its LUMO has. We think that the reason is the effect of anisotropic structure of 5d orbitals in the atom at the vertex of tungsten tip.
In the case of tungsten-porphyrin system, the simulation time in generating one STM image except execution time DVXα is about 10-30 minutes in the current version of STM simulator, using a middle class note PC. And we can get a LDOS image in about 10 seconds.

CAR-PARRINELLO METHOD

The STM simulator which we are developing is base on LCAO method for first principle electron state calculation of tip and surface. But calculation method using plane wave bases is effective for large scale sample models which have periodical boundary condition. In this case, we can use CP (Car-Parrinello) method. [3]
Plane wave method needs to execute 3D-FFT. So we tried to develop a hardware 3D-FFT accelerator for CP method. [4]

Figure 10 shows the reconfigurable accelerator board with 4 FPGA chips. The FPGA device has 3,000,000 equivalent logic gates. The 3D-FFT logic has a special function for large stride memory access to 3D array. We call it "pseudo burst transaction" shown in Figure 11. Then it can access to all directions XYZ in the same cost.

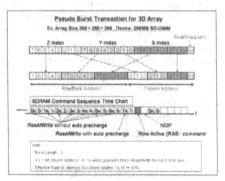

Figure 11   Pseudo Burst Transaction for Large Scale 3D-Array Access

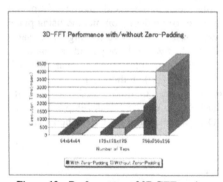

Figure 12   Performance of 3D-FFT engine

Figure 12 shows performance of the reconfigurable 3D-FFT accelerator.

   Chip: 500 MFLOPS
   Board: 2 GFLOPS

When 10,000,000 equivalent logic gage device is used, we estimate as following.

   Chip: 3 GFLOPS
   Board: 12 GFLOPS

This value in 10,000,000 gate device is about 10 times in performance against the fastest software routines on PC@3GHz, about 50 times in power-performance.

In large scale CP calculation with more than 2000 atoms, vector orthogonalization becomes another heavy load hot spot not only 3D-FFT. We think it is one of the best solutions to dispatch 3D-FFT logic and vector orthogonalization logic alternately on reconfigurable devices.

CONCLUSIONS

Simulation results show the followings,
a) Atom positions are often different from peek positions of tunnel current.
b) Tunnel current is seriously influenced by the electronic structure of the tip.

So we can conclude computer simulation is very important.

In the case of crystalline sample with periodical boundary condition, CP method is effective for electron state calculation. We have a plan to use reconfigurable 3D-FFT accelerator for CP method.

ACKNOWLEDGEMENTS

This work is supported in part by JST project "General Purpose Scanning Tunneling Probing Microscopy Simulators". And we thank the project members, Prof. Naruo Sasaki of Seikei University, Prof. Satoshi Watanabe of Tokyo University, Dr. Katsunori Tagami of Waseda University, and Dr. Naoki Watanabe of Mizuho Information & Research Institute, Inc. and express special gratitude to Dr. Tomoaki Nishino of Tokyo University and Dr. Isshiki of Kao Corporation.

REFERENCES

1. http://www.almaden.ibm.com/vis/stm/
2. Tsukada, M., Kobayashi, K., Isshiki, N., and Kageshima, H.: First-principles theory of scanning tunneling microscopy, Surface Science Reports, North-Holland, Netherlands, 1991, pp.267-304
3. Car, R. and Parrinello, M., *Phys. Rev. Lett.*, 55, 1985,pp.2471-2474
4. Sasaki, T., Betsuyaku, K., Higuchi, T., and Nagashima, U.: Reconfigurable 3D-FFT processor for Car-Parrinello Calculation, J.Comput. Chem. Jpn., 4, 2005, pp.147-154

A Communication Method for Molecular Orbital Calculations on a Compact Embedded Cluster

Kiyoshi Hayakawa*, Tohru Sasaki**,Hiroaki Umeda***, and Umpei Nagashima***

* Department of Electrical Engineering and Computer Science ,
Osaka Prefectural College of Technology
26-12 Saiwai, Neyagawa, Osaka 572-8572, JAPAN
(E-mail: hayakawa@ecs.osaka-pct.ac.jp)
** A-Priori Microsystems, Inc
4-51-1 Nakasaiwai, Saiwai, Kawasaki, Kanagawa, 212-0012, JAPAN
*** Research Institute for Computational Sciences,
National Institute of Advanced Industrial Science and Technology,
Tsukuba Central 2, Umezono 1-1-1, Tsukuba, Ibaraki, 305-8568, JAPAN

ABSTRACT

In molecular orbital calculations, one of the high performance applications, execution time of Fock matrix construction is approximately 99% of all execution time. We propose a communication method for a parallel Fock matrix construction program on a compact embedded cluster (called EMDC: Embedded Middle Density Cluster). The parallel Fock matrix construction program was developed on EHPC project, and EMDC has been developing for low power and small space. Network architecture (tree-base network) of EMDC conforms to parallel Fock matrix construction program. In order to communicate among the system, we developed a communication library for tree-base network. In evaluations, EMDC system achieved high parallelization efficiency (13.2 speed-up ratios at 14 nodes).

KEY WORDS: Molecular Orbital Calculations, Cluster Computing, Communication Library, Fock Matrix Construction

NOMENCLATURE

level : Level of Virtual tree topology.
r_pid : Relative processor ID.
Wtotal : Total elapsed time of the calculations.
Wfock : Total elapsed time of Fock matrix constructions for 13 SCF cycles.
PEtotal : Parallel efficiency of total calculations.
PEfock : Parallel efficiency of Fock matrix constructions

INTRODUCTION

Recent advances in microprocessor technology have made PC clusters the most effective solution to problems encountered in high performance computing. The PC clusters are capable of executing many parallel programs efficiently.

The PC clusters have become much faster, but they have also grown much larger space and much more power. The PC clusters require larger and more fans to cool down the CPU. Therefore, the PC clusters using low-power processor have been developed[1][2].

High-Density cluster systems, which aim to reduce power consumption and implementation space, have been proposed. By using low power processors, many processors are implemented into a chassis (involve one power unit). *Green Destiny*[1], One of the Low power and High Density Clusters, is contained entirely within a single 19-inch wide 42U rack.

Toward a same aim as *Green Destiny*, we are developing a compact cluster called EMDC[3]. It is built using PCs(21 nodes) for node-processor. Three nodes (center, right, and left node) packed into one chassis each. The chassis is half of 3U rack-mount. This is equivalent to six nodes/3U-chassis. Thus, EMDC is classified as Middle Density cluster.

In a chassis on High (or Middle) Density cluster, the mother boards are able to connect each other with a tightly coupled network, such as bus. On the other hand, among the chassis, the chassis are able to connect each other with a loosely coupled network, such as Ethernet. Network architecture of EMDC consists of 2 networks, Inner, and Outer network. It is able to construct tree network topology.

EHPC project[4], meanwhile, has proposed a platform of computer system which executes high performance applications, such as molecular orbital calculations. The computer system achieved extremely high parallelization efficiency for molecular orbital calculations[5]. A network topology of the platform is tree network. Thus, tree network topology matches up well with molecular orbital calculations. EMDC allows network to construct tree network topology.

This paper describes a communication library and shows the evaluation of the molecular orbital calculations of EMDC system. In order to compute the molecular orbital calculations on EMDC system, we ported the parallel Fock matrix construction program developed by EHPC project to EMDC system. In the process of the porting, we need the communication library on EMDC system.

EMDC SYSTEM

Figure 1 shows EMDC system. It was built using PC boards (PICMG, Pentium III 600 MHz, 256Mbyte memory, 21 nodes) for the node processor, Outer/Inner Chassis Network for the network, and a host computer for the control-node processor. The host computer consists of Pentium 4 (3.0GHz, Hyper Threading), and 1 G byte memory (dual channel).Three nodes packed into one chassis each (called center node, right node and left node).

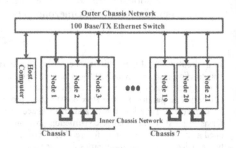

Figure 1 EMDC system archtecture

Organization of the network
The network of EMDC consists of two networks, Inner Chassis network and Outer Chassis Network. Inner Chassis network is characterized by low latency network. In this paper, the proposed communication method uses Ethernet instead of Inner Chassis network. Outer Chassis Network, on the other hand, is characterized by high throughput network relatively.

Virtual Tree Communication
Network Frame work: Inner/Outer chassis network fit for tree network topology. Since each node in a chassis is able to communicate frequently by Inner chassis network, we assume that the chassis has three links on Outer chassis network. The chassis,

therefore, is able to construct tree topology network.
In order to construct tree topology, the chassis (called "Blade Chassis" in this paper) of EMDC is arranged like Figure 3. Connection between level n and level $(n+1)$ employs Outer Chassis Network and level $(n+1)$ and level $(n+2)$ employs Inner Chassis Network.

used for communications between the nodes of level 0 and level 1(i.e. for Outer Chassis Network). L-com is used for communications between the nodes of level 1 and level 2(i.e. for Inner Chassis Network). HL-com is restricted to 1-up or 1-low communication. A communication function of HL-com issued by a level 0 node can't communicate any level 2 nodes directly. Communications between the node of level 0 and the node of level 2 was completed via a level 1 node.

Figure 2 Photo of EMDC

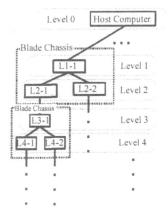

Figure 3 Network framework

The deeper level we specify, the longer latency it takes on the network. Thus, we organize three levels tree topology to compute molecular orbital calculations (see Figure 4). The center nodes of the blade chassis are connected with 1-up level node (or host computer), and the right and left nodes are connected with 1-low level. Thus, the host computer defines as level 0, and center nodes connected with host computer define as level 1. The right and left nodes connected with level 1 node define as level 2.

Communication Library: We developed a communication library (called HL-com) on EMDC. HL-com consists of 2 communication library, H-com and L-com. H-com is

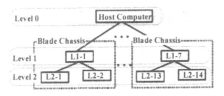

Figure 4 Tree network on EMDC

In order to handle collective communications (such as broadcast, barrier etc) between the nodes of level 0 and level 2 in the applications, we developed a new library using H-com and L-com.
Atomic operations of H (or L)-com library is specified as follows:

*H(or L)_operation(*p_buf, buf_count, dst);*

Where, *p_buf is a pointer of a communication buffer, buf_count is the number of the communication buffer and dst is a destination node number on the communication. An assignment method of the destination node number employs relative number. Both H-com and L-com handle the common relative number. An upper node number defines "0". Lower node numbers define "1", "2",..,"k" (k denotes the num. of lower nodes). For example, when a node of level 1 sends a node of level 0, destination node number is "0". When the node of level 1 sends a left node of level 2, destination node number is "1" (see Figure 5).

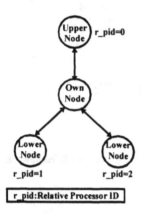

Figure 5 An example of destination node numbering

Level 1 node behaves as network server and level 0 and 2 nodes as network clients. The communications between nodes employ TCP socket communication.

Execution Model: We compute molecular orbital calculations by GAMESS[6]. The host computer executes GAMESS except for 2 electron integrals, and makes EMDC nodes compute 2 electron integrals to construct Fock matrix. The program executing on the compute nodes was developed by EHPC project. We ported it to EMDC system.

The node of level 0 broadcasts a command and data (or broadcasts a request and gathers data) issued from GAMESS to all nodes of level 1. The nodes of level 1 are bridge nodes between level 0 and level 2. The nodes of level 2 compute 2 electron integrals.

PERFORMANCE EVALUATION

In order to evaluate EMDC system, we made EMDC compute molecular orbital calculations for α-helix (Glycine)$_5$ using HF/6-31G(d,p) basis set (including 400 basis functions).

In the calculations, task division method was TASK_IJKL, task distribution method was SLB(static load balance) [5].

Table 1 shows the total elapsed time of α-helix (Glycine)$_5$ compared total elapsed time of calculation (Wtotal) with total elapsed time of Fock matrix constructions for 13 SCF cycles (Wfock). EMDC system achieved 13.2 speed-up ratios at 14 nodes in Wfock.

Table 1 Elasped time of α-helix (Glycine)$_5$

Num. of	Execution Time(sec)	
Node	Wtotal	Wfock
1	76946.7	76925.4
2	38986.4	38964.3
4	19640.8	19610.6
6	13193.1	13145.2
8	9979.5	9919.4
10	8030.2	7957.0
12	6746.4	6660.1
14	5836.5	5737.7

Figure 6 shows parallelization efficiency of the molecular orbital calculations of α-helix (Glycine)$_5$. EMDC system achieved high parallelization efficiency.

Ideally, parallelization efficiency of PEfock is near 100%, but 95.7% at 14 nodes. The

360

reason is not only communication overhead but also difference of task grain (i.e. unbalance of task load). In order to make load balance equal, a dynamic load balance method has been proposed[5]. We must propose dynamic load balance methods matching up EMDC system. One of the methods is a hierarchical task distribution. That is, a group of tasks is distributed to a chassis, and each task in the group is executed equally in the chassis. Since each node is able to commute frequency by using inner chassis network, it is easy to control the load balance dynamically.

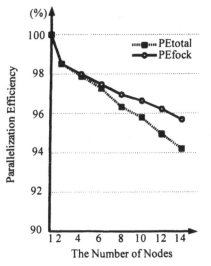

Figure 6 Parallelization Efficiency of α-helix (Glycine)₅ Calculations.

CONCLUSIONS

We implemented a communication library, and the parallel Fock matrix construction program works normally on EMDC system. EMDC system achieved high parallelization efficiency and scalability. Since EMDC system consists of 21 nodes, in terms of whole of the system, it is difficult to say that the method achieves high efficient parallelization. We will improve

the method to add nodes of level 1 in the calculations.
In the performance evaluation, we gave results of static load balance. We will improve the communication library to compute dynamic load balance. Since we plan a project that Pentium M nodes are added in EMDC system, we will propose load balance methods that are able to handle different CPUs.

ACKNOWLEDGEMENTS

This work is supported in part by Grant No. 18500044(Study of low power compact cluster) from Japan Society for the Promotion of Science. Hiroaki Umeda and Umpei Nagashima are participating in CREST basic research programs of Japan Science and Technology Agency.

REFERENCES

1. M.Warren, E.Weigle, and W.Feng, "High-Density Computing : A 240-Node Beowulf in One Cube Meter ",Super Computing , 2002, CD-ROM.
2. IBM and Lawrence Livermore National Laboratory, "An Overview of the Blue Gene/L Supercomputer", Super Computing, 2002, CD-ROM.
3. Kiyoshi Hayakawa, Satoshi Sekiguchi, "Design and Implementation of a Synchronization and Communication Controller for Cluster Computing Systems," Proc. 4th Intel. Conf. High Performance Computing in Asia-Pacific Region, 2000, vol. I, pp76-81.
4. Tohru SASAKI and Kazuaki MURAKAMI, "A Platform System of Special Purpose Computers for Various Kinds of Chemical Simulations", Journal of Computer Chemistry, Japan, Vol.4, No.4, 2005, pp139-145.
5. Hiroaki UMEDA, Yuichi INADOMI, Hiroaki HONDA and Umpei NAGASHIMA, "Parallel Fock Matrix Construction Algorithm for Molecular Orbital Calculation Specific Computer", Journal of Computer Chemistry, Japan, Vol.4, No.4, 2005, pp179-187.
6. M. W. Schmidt, K. K. Baldridge, J. A. Boatz, S. T. Elbert, M. S. Gordon, J. H. Jensen, S. Koseki, N. Matsunaga, K. A. Nguyen, S. Su, T. L. Windus, M. Dupuis, J. A. Montgomery, " General atomic and molecular electronic structure system", Journal of Computational Chemistry Vol. 14, Issue 11 , 1993, pp.1347-1363.

Three Quads: An Interconnection Network
for Interactive Simulations

Tomoyuki YOSHIMURA*, Keita SAITO** , Hajime SHIMADA*, Shinobu MIWA*,
Yasuhiko NAKASHIMA***, Shin-ichiro MORI** and Shinji TOMITA*

* Department of Communications and Computer Engineering,
Graduate School of Informatics, Kyoto University
Yoshida-hon-machi, Sakyo-Ku, Kyoto, 606-8501 Japan
(E-mail: revolver@lab3.kuis.kyoto-u.ac.jp)

** Department of Information Science, Graduate School of Engineering, University of Fukui
Bunkyo 3-9-1, Fukui, 910-8507 Japan

*** Department of Information Systems, Graduate School of Information Science,
Nara Institute of Science and Technology
8916-5 Takayama, Ikoma, Nara, 630-0192 Japan

ABSTRACT

In this paper, we have proposed an interconnection network for Medium Scale Commodity Cluster. This network h
originally designed for the Visualization Subsystem of the Sensable Simulation System (Scube) which the authors ha
been developing. Scube is a 64-nodes PC-based cluster system in which a commodity GPU as the visualizati
accelerator is configured with each node. There is no dedicated special purpose networks for the numerical simulati
and visualization, however, the high cost-performance inter-connection network which we call Three Quads
originally designed for Scube. All the hardware components for this network is essentially the small-scale a
commodity hardware designed for Giga-bit Ethernet. The network configuration and its characteristics are discussed
this paper.

KEY WORDS: Parallel Processing, Cluster Computing, Interconnection Network, Interactive Simulation

Introduction

Beyond the reality chase in gaming industries, it is a time to investigate the interactiveness, while maintaining the accuracy or the truth, of the simulation in medical and/or engineering industries.

We have also been doing a research on Real-Time Sensable Simulation Systems[1]. As a part of this research, we have developed a commodity cluster system Scube primarily intended for interactive simulations.

In this paper we propose the architecture of an interconnection network specially designed for interactive simulation systems.

Overview of the Scube

The Scube[2,3] is 64-node PC cluster system which configured with Graphics Processing Unit (GPU) each node. The visualization task as well as t simulation task is executed simultaneously on each no while the display of the final result of the visualizati task and the steering of the simulation are done throu the host PC as a client terminal of the simulation serv The simultaneous execution of simulation a visualization become possible by assigning a simulati task and a visualization task to CPU and GP respectively.

Figure 1 shows the overview of Scube and Tabl

ows the hardware specification of the Scube Node
C.

Since both simulation and visualization tasks
emselves are executed in parallel using 64 nodes, the
terconnection network of Scube must have a
pability to deal with the bandwidth requirements from
th tasks. For this purpose, we have proposed a new
terconnection network which we call *Three Quads*.

Figure 1 Sensable Simulation System (Scube)

ble 1 Hardware Specification of the Scube Node PC .

U	Pentium 4 3.4MHz
	Linux 2.6.9
emory	1.0GB
otherboard	ASUSTeK P5AD2-E Premium
x Card	GeForce6800GT PCI-Express
x Memory	256MB
twork	Gigabit Ethernet x 3

Three Quads

ree Quads is an interconnection network specially
igned for medium-scale PC cluster system for
ractive simulations.
r this purpose, it is mandatory to efficiently
lement the following communication patterns: the
imensional near-neighbor communication which is
essary for the scientific computations[5,6] that
ctly map the 3D simulation space onto processor
ce, and three dimensional reduction type
munication which is necessary for both simulation
  visualization, the real-time 3D image
position[8] in particular.
  addition to such architectural requirements, we
erely consider the hardware cost to implement the
work. It is because we thought this kind of
ractive simulation system should be owned by

relatively small organization, like a laboratory in a
university, since otherwise it is difficult to benefit from
the interactiveness of the system.

So that, in the development of the network for Scube,
we have targeted to the medium scale commodity
cluster system, and restrict the use of fairly expensive
giant switch. Thus, Three Quads can be implemented
only with inexpensive small-scale gigabit ethernet
switches. However, the redundancy in its sub-networks
and appropriate scheduling of communications utilizing
the unique feature of Three Quads make it possible to
realize the co-existence of different kinds of
communications for simulation and visualization.

In the rest of this section, we explain the detailed
feature of Three Quads as an interconnection network
for parallel processing systems.

Topology (Hardware Configuration)
Let's assume that each node of Scube is logically
arranged along the three axes, Z,Y, and X, as in Figure 2
left-side and is labeled with a 3D coordinates (Nz, Ny,
Nx)[1] according to the position of the node in Z,Y, X
axes. In case of 64 nodes system, $0 \leq Nx, Ny, Nz \leq 3$.

The hardware component of Three Quads is three
groups of switches (SW-X, SW-Y, and SW-Y) where
each group of switches consists of several small-scale
off-the-shelf Giga-bit Ethernet Switches(GbE SW, for
short) which are independent with each other (Figure 2).

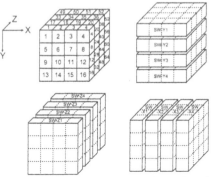

Figure 2. Node assignment to switches in Three
Quads.(In case of 64 nodes).

All the nodes labeled with (*,*, i) is connected to a
switch labeled with SW-Xi as in Figure 3. Since the
maximum of Nx is 3 in 64node Scube, the SW-X is
composed of 4 GbE SWs each of which has 16 GbE
ports. Similarly, all the nodes labeled with (*, j, *) is

---

[1] We use two type of notation to indicate the location
of a node, binary 2n digits notation $(a_{3n},a_{3n-1},...,a_2,a_1)$
and 3D coordinates notation (A_3,A_2,A_1), alternatively in
the following discussion.

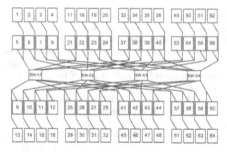

Figure 3 Sub-network for X-axis.

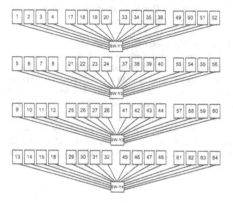

Figure 4 Sub-network for Y-axis.

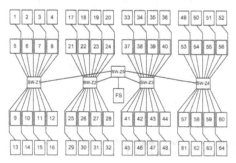

Figure 5 Sub-network for Z-axis.

connected to a switch labeled with SW-Yj as in Figure 4 and all the nodes labeled with (k,*,*) is connected to a switch labeled with SW-Zk as in Figure 5. Thus, Three Quads for 64node Scube can be physically constructed with 12 16-port GbE SWs. Here, we have to mention that for the purpose of maintenance and control of node PCs, only the GbE SWs belong to SW-Z group have an additional port for up-link through which each node

can communicate with Host computer and a file ser
(FS). In the following sections, however, we ignore th
up-link for the simplicity of discussion.

In Three Quads, *Three* stands for the existence of thr
independent sub-networks, while *Quads* stands for t
fact that the coverage of each GbE is the nodes inside
rectangular area in one of the X-Y, Y-Z, or Z-X planes.

Three Quads can be thought as a 2D extension
base-m 3-cube[7] and in this case Three Quad can
represented as base-m^2 3-cube.

Diameter of Three Quads

In this section, we show the diameter of Three Quad 2. For the simplicity of discussion, we assume that nodes are equally arranged in each axis. Then, node and B in Scube can be represented as $(a_{3n},a_{3n-1},...,a_2,a$ and $(b_{3n},b_{3n-1},...,b_4,b_3,b_2,b_1)$, or (A_3,A_2,A_1) a (B_3,B_2,B_1).

Now, we can consider a node C such that one digit C's 3D coordinate is the same as the corresponding dig of A's 3D coordinate, and the other digits of C's 3 coordinates are the same as the corresponding digits B's 3D coordinates, like (A_3,B_2,B_1).

Since a node C in Three Quads can direct communicate with nodes where at least one digit their 3D coordinates is the same as the correspondi digit of node C's 3D coordinates. Then, in Three Quad node A can directly communicate with node C and no C can directly communicate with node B. Thus, nodes and B can communicate with each other via node C the relay node.

Here, we have to mention that we made no assumpti on the selection of nodes A and B, therefore, we c conclude that any two nodes in Three Quads c communicate in 2 hops, or the diameter of Three Qua is 2. Nevertheless to say, neighboring nodes c communicate with each other in one hop.

There are only three candidates for node C if v follow the assumption in the above explanatio However, there are indeed many other candidates node C if we consider the selection of node C wi binary notation of the node. For example, in case of n $(a6,a5,a4,b3,b2,b1)$, $(a6,a5,b4,a3,b2,b1)$ a $(a6,a5,*,*,b2,b1)$ are a part of such candidates.

Fault tolerance

In this section, we are going to demonstrate that Thr Quads tolerant a single point failure of the switch in context of network diameter, that is 2 hops.

As we have discussed before, communicatio between any two nodes can be done in 2 hops vi certain relay node C and there are many candidates the relay node.

Therefore, in case of a single point failure on switch between nodes A and C (or, B and C), we c alternate the relay node C to C' which is one of the ot candidates for the relay node.

Figure 6 illustrates another example of alternative routing paths between nodes N_1 and N_{64}. In this example, alternate routing path is chosen in somewhat different way as in the above explanation. Indeed, in case of the failure at SW-Z1, the following example does not change the relay node, instead it changes the routing path such that the routing path uses SW-Y1. In those ways, Three Quads can sustain the single point failure of the switch and can keep its diameter as

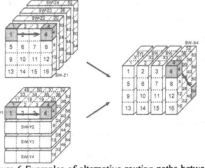

gure 6 Examples of alternative routing paths between nodes N_1 and N_{64}

mbeddability

Embeddability of other networks is one of the most important features of the network architecture for parallel processing system. In case of 64 nodes system, the Scube, the following network topologies can be embedded into Three Quads.

1/2/3D Torus[4]
Simple Tree, FAT Tree
Hypercube(Binary 6-Cube)
Base-m n-cube(Base-4 3Cube)[5,6,7]

These are the well-known network topologies used in high performance computing systems, like ueGene/L[4], PACS-CS[5,6], Prodigy[7]. Many other network topologies may be embedded into Three Quads, well. Due to the page limitation, we only show how 2D Torus network is embedded into Three Quads. ase refer [3] for detailed description on how these ologies are embedded into Three Quads.

First of all, let's consider the 2D expansion of the switches in SW-Z group as in Figure 7. In this figure, horizontal rings between SW-Z1 and SW-Z2 (or, /-Z3 and SW-Z4) can be implemented with the itches in SW-Y group, while the vertical rings ween SW-Z1 and SW-Z3 (or, SW-Z2 and SW-Z4) be implemented with the switches in SW-X group. this manner, horizontal and vertical rings in 2D torus work can be embedded into Three Quads. In this ation, the switches in SW-Z group are left unused. if a user requires the 2D torus network to solve his ulation program, then the visualization program can

use the SW-Z switches freely without disturbing the communications for the simulation program.

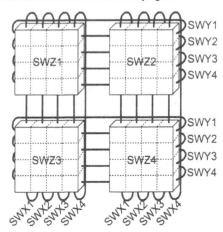

Figure 7 Embedding of 2D torus onto Three Quads

Matrix Transpose on Three Quads

The matrix transpose operation which is frequently used in scientific computations generally requires all-to-all communication which incurs severe network congestion and thus declines the overall network throughput.

In this section, we would like to demonstrate how the matrix transpose operations can be executed efficiently on Three Quads without any congestion.

Now we assume that each node of 64-node Scube initially owns a matrix of size N by N which is a sub-matrix of M whose size is 8N by 8N. Again, let's consider the 2D expansion of the switches as in Figure7 and 8. Here we also assume that the node at the i-th column and j-th row in these figures is assigned a sub-matrix M_{ij} of matrix M. We also introduce another sub-matrices A,B,C and D of size 4N by 4N and represent M as Eq. (1) with these sub-matrices.

$$M = \begin{pmatrix} A & B \\ C & D \end{pmatrix} \qquad (1)$$

And A, B, C and D are further divided into sub-matrices $a_{ij}, b_{ij}, c_{ij}, d_{ij} (0 <= i, j <= 3)$.

Now, the transpose of this matrix M can be done in the following two steps.

First Step: This step computes A^t, B^t, C^t, D^t. In this step, the communications required to compute the transpose of each sub-matrices can be done inside a single switch in one-of SW-Z switches according to the poison of

365

A,B,C and D. Thus no network congestion is observed in this step. Now we get new matrix M' as in Eq.(2).

$$M' = \begin{pmatrix} A' & B' \\ C' & D' \end{pmatrix} \quad (2)$$

Second Step: This step swaps the position of B^t and C^t. Nothing should be done on A^t and D^t. Here, let's compare the 3D coordinates of two nodes containing c^t_{ij} and b^t_{ij}. Now we can find that two digits of the 3D coordinates of these two nodes are the same. Thus, these nodes can directly communicate through a single switch in SW-X or SW-Y group. Therefore, no network congestion is observed even in this step.

Further optimizations, like blocking and communication pipelining, of this algorithm make it possible to fuse these two steps into one step because the sub-networks used in these two steps are different and all the communications required in this algorithm are congestion free.

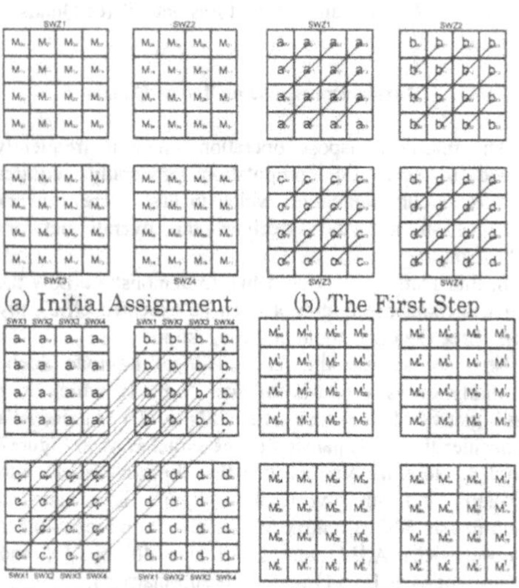

(a) Initial Assignment.   (b) The First Step

(c) The Second Step   (d) The Final State

Figure 8 Matrix Transpose on Three Quads

CONCLUSIONS

In this paper, we have proposed an interconnection network Threee Quads for interactive simulations. In order to satisfy the requirements for simultaneous execution of simulation and visualization tasks, Three Quads has various features like embeddability of various network topologies including 3D torus and 3D tree and fault tolerancy by utilizing the various

redundancies exist in Three Quads.

In this paper, we also demonstrate the congestion fre matrix transpose algorithm on Three Quads.

REFERENCES

1. Tomita, S., Real-Time Sensable Simulation System Abstracts of Grant-in-Aid for Scientific Research (S Japan Society for the Promotion of Science, 200 pp.10-11.
2. Yoshimura, T., et al,, Development of Large Sca Visualization Cluster with Commodity GPU, Proc. the 33rd Symp. on Visualization (Journal of t Visualization Society of Japan), 200 25-Suppl-1,pp.277-280.
3. Yoshimura, T., et al., Three Quads :A Versati Interconnection Network for Medium Sca Commodity Cluster, IPSJ SIG Technical Repo 2006, 2006-ARC-167, pp.79-84.
4. The Blue Gene/L Team, An overview of Blue Gene Supercomputer, Proc. Supercomputing, 200 http://www.sc-2002.org/paperpdfs/pap.pap207.pdf
5. Boku, T., et al., PACS-CS: A massively parallel cluster computational sciences, IPSJ SIG Technical Report, 200 2005-HPC-103, pp.133-138.
6. Sumimoto, S., et al., A Design of High Performan Communication Facility Using Ethernet for the PACS-C system, IPSJ SIG Technical Report, 2005-HPC-1C pp.139-144.
7. Suzuoka, S. et al., An Evaluation of the Interconnecti Network of Parallel AI Machine Prodigy, Trans. IEIC 1988, J71-D-8, pp.1496-1501.
8. Ogata, M, et al., An Evaluation of Communicatio Cost for Simultaneous Processing with Simulati and Visualization using an Image Compositi Device, Proc. High Performance Computi Symposium, 2006, pp.63-72.
9. Kadota, H., et al., Parallel Computer ADENART – Architecture and Application-, Proc. of ACM In Conf. on Supercomputing, 1991, pp.1-8.
10. Amano, H., Parallel Computer, Shokodo, Toky 1996.
11. Tomita, S., Parallel Computer Engineering, Shoko Tokyo, 1996. pp.17-72.

ACKNOWLEDGEMENTS

A part of this research is done by Grant-in-Aid Scientific Research(S) #16100001, Japan Society for t Promotion of Science.

Interactive Manipulation and Stress Visualization with Multi-finger Haptic Device

Yoshihiro KURODA*, Makoto HIRAI**, Megumi NAKAO***,
Tomohiro KURODA**** and Hiroyuki YOSHIHARA****

* Graduate School of Medicine, Kyoto University
54 Shogoin Kawahara-cho, Sakyo-ku, Kyoto, 606-8507 Japan
(E-mail: ykuroda@kuhp.kyoto-u.ac.jp)
** Production Systems Research Laboratory, Kobe Steel, Ltd.
1-5-5, Takatsukadai, Nishi-ku, Kobe, Hyoto, 651-2271 Japan
***Graduate School of Information Science, Nara Institute of Science and Technology
8916-5, Takayama-cho, Ikoma, Nara, 630-0192 Japan
****Department of Medical Informatics, Kyoto University Hospital
54 Shogoin Kawahara-cho, Sakyo-ku, Kyoto, 606-8507 Japan

ABSTRACT

In conventional medical education, residents train their skills via clinical experiences (OJT). However, training opportunity is decreasing due to the increasing respect of patient's rights. Virtual reality simulator allows a flexible and repeatable interaction with living organs without spoiling them. Therefore, for training of surgical manipulations, In this study, we propose an organ exclusion training simulator with multi-finger haptic device and stress visualization. The method was applied to a medical application of exclusion which is an important manipulation to make workspace or enlarge surgical view in surgery. The system equips FEM-based soft tissue deformation and CyberForce haptic device. Real-time simulation was achieved with a prototype system and training trial has been conducted. The results suggested the effectiveness of the system and stress visualization for exclusion training.

KEY WORDS: Multi-finger Interaction, Stress visualization, Force Feedback, Surgical Simulation

INTRODUCTION

In conventional surgical training, surgeons cannot avoid training their skills with real patients, because training with rubber models and animals is not realistic enough. So far, many virtual reality training simulators have been developed. However, no training simulator of organ exclusion, which is a surgical manipulation of pushing aside organ to enlarge workspace or to make a hidden object visible as shown in Fig.1, has been developed. Improper manipulation causes fatal damage of soft tissue. The system should support interactive manipulation with multiple fingers.

Figure 1 Liver exclusion. A vessel behind a liver is visible by exclusion with fingers.

367

Although visualization of stress distribution was found in suturing simulation [1], the training effect with multi-finger manipulation has not been studied.

This paper proposes an exclusion training virtual reality environment with multi-finger haptic display and interactive visualization of stress distribution.

METHODS

The simulation of soft tissue deformation has been studied in Bioengineering. However, interactive simulation system with haptic display requires high update rate of reaction force (more than 300 Hz or higher [2]) and fast calculation of the simulation. Thus, in general, some optimization methods are applied for real-time simulation. In the study of surgical simulation, finite element method (FEM) has been recognized as one of the most accurate methods. The real-time simulation of non-linear elastic deformation is hard with CPU power of a current personal computer. Thus, FEM with linear elasticity is employed in the system. Hirota proposed a method of real-time calculation of reaction force with finite element model [3]. Forces on the finger contact node are calculated as the following equations.

$$f = Ku$$

(1)

$$\begin{pmatrix} * \\ u_i \\ u_j \\ * \end{pmatrix} = \begin{pmatrix} * & \cdots & \cdots & * \\ \vdots & L_{ii} & L_{ij} & \vdots \\ \vdots & L_{ji} & L_{jj} & \vdots \\ * & \cdots & \cdots & * \end{pmatrix} \begin{pmatrix} * \\ f_i \\ f_j \\ * \end{pmatrix}$$

(2)

where $L = K^{-1}$

(3)

$$\begin{pmatrix} f_i \\ f_j \end{pmatrix} = \begin{pmatrix} L_{ii} & L_{ij} \\ L_{ji} & L_{jj} \end{pmatrix}^{-1} \begin{pmatrix} u_i \\ u_j \end{pmatrix}$$

(4)

Most traditional haptic device supporting multi-finger interaction is glove-type haptic device such as CyberForce^{TM}[4] as shown in Figure 2.

Figure 2 Multi-finger haptic device CyberForce. Forces can be displayed to each finger and a wrist.

Due to the restriction of freedom of a fingertip movement, amount of reaction force is projected to the tangential direction of a finger and the force is output to a fingertip. On the other hand, with this device, no force is conveyed to a wrist, because the device is attached on the back of the finger and the output forces on the fingertip are canceled in the fingers. Thus, a sum of finger forces is output to the wrist as shown in Equation 3.

$$f_{fingertip} = f_i \cos\theta$$
$$f_{wrist} = \sum_i^5 f_i \qquad (i = 1,2,3,4,5)$$

(5)

As shown in Figure 3, the system consists of PC (Intel Xeon 2.6GHz x 2, 1GB memory, RADEON9600 256MB graphic board), display and CyberForce system (CyberForce, CyberGrasp, CyberGlove).

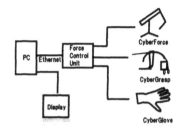

Figure 3 System configuration.

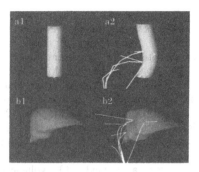

Figure 4 Exclusion simulator of soft tissue model. (a1, 2) vessel exclusion (b1, 2) liver exclusion.

RESULTS

Real-time simulation is essential for virtual reality system with interactive manipulation. Table 1 shows calculation time for reaction force and deformation of the model (820-noded object). Although time for deformation depends on the component nodes of the simulated objects, time for reaction force depends on the number of contact fingers and is independent of the component nodes of the simulated objects.

Table 1 Calculation time for reaction force and deformation with number of contact fingers

Number of contact fingers	1	2	3	4	5
Reaction force	0.20	0.63	2.36	8.18	29.7
Deformation	1.32	1.95	4.41	12.29	32.36

Figure 4 shows a simulation example of multi-finger haptic interaction with soft tissue models. Figure 5 shows results of stress visualization with a vessel. Figure 6 shows stress concentration in the case, where an object has several parts of different stiffness and stress concentration around the boundary. The object is modeled as a lung, which has a harder part in the bronchus and Pulmonary-artery.

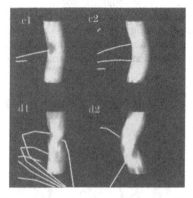

Figure 5 Stress distribution caused by different finger numbers (c1,2) and by different finger manipulation (d1,2).

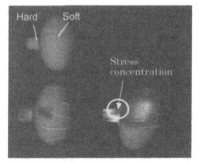

Figure 6 Stress concentration occurred in a simplified lung situation

369

The effectiveness of a developed prototype system for exclusion training was examined by training trial. Figure 7 shows two environments of the experiment (object A and B). Object A has 0.3 MPa Young Modulus (0.4 Poisson's ratio) in the whole body, and object B has 0.1 MPa in the soft region and 1.0MPa Young Modulus (0.4 Poisson's ratio) in the hard region in Fig.6. A task was to push aside a target object until a hidden line behind the object is kept visible for a second. 13 volunteers performed 30minutes training in each day for 5days. Stress visualization is provided to group1 (7 persons) and not to group2 (6 persons). A subject was told that he/she tried performing a task with less max stress value. 3 minutes training and a test without stress visualization was performed in each day.

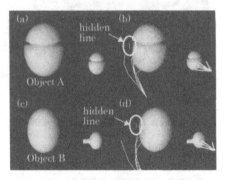

Figure 7 Two environments of training trial. Left side is a front view and right side is a side view in each figure. To make a hidden line behind the object visible is a goal in the task.

Figure 8 and 9 shows results of the experiment. The result of training trial with object A showed that a learning effect is higher than without displaying stress distribution especially during first two days. The result with object B showed that max stress went down in both groups with an exception of the second day, which has higher stress than in first day. This might be why the place of stress concentration in the object B was clear if stress was visible.

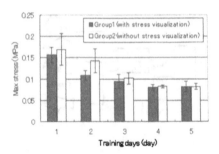

Figure 8 Result of exclusion training with object A.

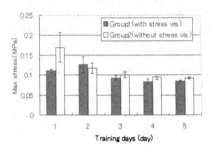

Figure 9 Result of exclusion training with object B.

CONCLUSION

This paper proposed an organ exclusion training simulator with multi-finger haptic device with stress visualization. The results of the experiments suggested that the system was effective for exclusion training and stress visualization was effective for the training.

ACKNOWLEDGEMENT

This research was partly supported by Grant-in-Aid for Scientific Research (S) (16100001) from JSPS, Grant-in-Aid (H18-Medicine-General-032) from the Ministry of Health, Labour and Welfare, Japan, Grant-in-Aid for Young Scientists (A) (18680043) and Exploratory Research (18659148) from The Ministry of Education, Culture, Sports, Science and Technology, Japan, and Kurata Fund, Japan.

REFERENCES

1. Berkley, J. et al., "Real-Time Finite Element Modeling for Surgery Simulation: An Application to Virtual Suturing", IEEE Trans. on Visualization and Computer Graphics, 2004, 10(3), pp.1-12
2. Burdea, G. et al.., "Virtual Reality Technology", Wiley Interscience, 2003.
3. Hirota, K. et al., "Haptic Representation of Elastic Objects", MIT Presence, 2001, 10(5), pp.525-536
4. Immersion, www.immersion.com

Speculative FEM Simulation System
for Invasive Surgical Operation with Haptic Interaction

Naoto KUME*, Yoshihiro KURODA**, Megumi NAKAO***, Tomohiro KURODA**,
Keisuke NAGASE**, Hiroyuki YOSHIHARA** and Masaru KOMORI****

* Department of Social Informatics, Graduate School of Informatics,
Kyoto University
54 Shogoin Kawahara-cho, Sakyo-ku, Kyoto. 606-8507, Japan
(E-mail: kume@kuhp.kyoto-u.ac.jp)
** Department of Medical Informatics, Kyoto University Hospital
54 Shogoin Kawahara-cho, Sakyo-ku, Kyoto. 606-8507, Japan
*** Graduate School of Information Science, Nara Institute of Science and Technology
8916－5 Takayama-cho, Ikoma-shi, Nara, 630-0192, Japan
**** Department of Medicine, Shiga University of Medical Science
Seta Tsukiwa-cho, Otsu-shi, Shiga, 520-2192, Japan

ABSTRACT

Conventional virtual reality surgical simulators are provided for non-invasive operation because of the calculation resource limitation of personal computer. For development of advanced simulator, simulation of invasive operation such as incision and ablation is required. Besides, for interactive haptic simulation, the rupture model should be adopted based on physics. Therefore, achievement of huge scale rupture simulation system with interactivity is desired. This study aims to provide real-time rupture simulator with physics-based haptic interaction. The proposed system adopts speculative calculation of stiffness matrix for concealing of calculation delay on FEM rupture model. The system assumes implementation on PC cluster adopting simulation cache for hiding calculation delay. This paper provides a report of hit ratio performance of speculation.

KEY WORDS: Surgical simulator, haptics, speculation, FEM

SURGICAL SIMULATION

In a field of education of medicine, medical residents or premedical students do not have a chance to train surgical skills enough before clinical practice. Especially, conventional training environment such as cadavers, animals, and plastic models never support flexible training scenarios. Conventional training systems are not only incapable of simulating several surgical operations but also their maintenance is expensive. In other circumstances, enhancement of computer science technology facilitates implementation of virtual reality (VR) simulators. Consequently, VR-based surgical simulators are expected to realize effective surgical training environment that provides easy implementation of several cases and inexpensive maintenance. Above all, VR systems achieve environments for repetitive training with low cost.

372

So far, several surgical simulators have been provided for training of each fundamental surgical skill. Currently, the efficiency of haptic feedback in training is indicated [1]. Some soft tissue models employed by haptic simulators are based on physics. Because of the difficulty of rupture modeling, conventional surgical simulators that support haptic feedback were provided only non-invasive operations such as palpation and exclusion. Apparently, because the failure in rupture manipulation could be fatal to patients, training of invasive operation is important. Simulation on personal computer is difficult for simulating invasive operation such as incision and ablation because of the computational complexity of physics-based model. For development of an advanced surgical simulator, training simulator for invasive operation with hapitc feedback is desired. Therefore, real-time simulation system for haptic interaction with physics-based soft tissue model is required. Until now, this study developed a soft tissue rupture model that based on linear finite element method. Because of the computational complexity, the physics-based approach to simulate ruptures with haptic feedback was not able to achieve interactivity. This paper proposes a distributed system that employs an application level speculative calculation method for acceleration of haptic interaction by hiding the calculation delay of stiffness matrix construction. The soft tissue rupture model that determines ruptured element by shear stress distribution is employed on the system.

SOFT TISSUE RUPTURE MODEL

The proposed soft tissue rupture model was implemented on a personal computer [2]. The model based on FEM with tetrahedral mesh calculates shear stress distribution while the model deforms. When stress of an element amounts to rupture parameter, the model determines that the element is fractured. The Young's modulus of the element is set to approximately zero. Then stiffness matrix is recalculated on fracture loop in Figure 1. Result of tension test simulation with a two-layered board model that had different stiffness a value on each layer, the model expressed specific three pattern of fracture by different tension direction. The first one is near by the manipulation point, the second is near by the fixed region that is a counterpart to the manipulation point, and the third is border of the two layers. After a fracture of an element, shear stress distribution is varied. Until the model down to a stable state that does not include stress concentration, calculation in the fracture loop is to be continued. Figure 1 illustrates time sequence of soft tissue deformation and fracture loop. Duration of every step was measured. Requirement of real-time simulation achievement is under 4 $msec$ for haptic feedback and under 33 $msec$ for visualization [3]. Measured two objects consisted of 586 and 1594 vertices, respectively. During deformation loop, the system can calculate visualization of soft tissue deformation with force feedback in real-time. On the other hand, when the model determines fracture at step (5) in Figure 1, the model should reconstruct stiffness matrix that takes time in seconds order.

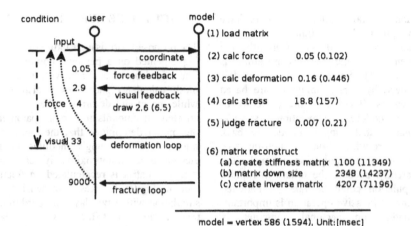

model = vertex 586 (1594), Unit:[msec]

Figure 1 Performance of the pervious proposed soft tissue deformation and fracture model.

SPECULATIVE PREPARATION OF STIFFNESS MATRIX

This study aims to provide haptic interaction system with the previous proposed soft tissue model. And the distributed system consists of client-server architecture. The system processes physics-based computation on server-side. And, client-side simulation treats user interface with haptic devices and visualization. Figure 2 shows design of the proposed distributed system. The server-side system speculatively calculates the inverse matrix reconstructed in step (c) of (6) in Figure 1 to prepare before user manipulation that causes determination of fracture. Then, the server-side system replies to the client-side requests by the prepared matrix loading. The number of fracture patterns by shear stress distribution is increased proportionally by increasing n as the number of tetrahedra elements. Therefore, reduction of speculative pattern tree is required. In this paper, because the soft tissue rupture model is designed for using in surgical situation, the fracture of elements can be restricted to surface elements. The speculative pattern

tree decides an operation priority from following conditions; position of manipulation, direction of tension and depth of destruction progressing. When the direction of tension is steady, candidates of rupture element can be predicted with maximum shear stress. Specific stress distribution variation caused by changing direction is limited to three patterns based on empirical knowledge in conventional tension test simulation. For hiding calculation delay at the first time, matrix reconstruction is started before user's manipulation by appropriate prediction of manipulation point that user should touch to manipulate appropriately. 36 processing units on distributed system are needed at least in a condition of tension test as same as personal computer based conventional simulation. The simulation assumes depth of the fracture progressing as 4, pattern of different direction of manipulation as 3, and pattern of different manipulation point as 3. Additionally, successive calculation of the destruction loop until the model settles down stable state could be condensed to one time of the destruction loop. *Selector* node in Figure 2 manages speculation branch for distributing rupture element number to proper processing

unit to order the next prepared matrix.
The client-side simulation should be designed under consideration with connection delay. Therefore, the client is needed to adopt matrix cache for interpolation of speculation miss hit. The client-side system caches temporal force matrix that is generated at the first step of

matrix reconstruction. When speculation missed, the client system calls cached force matrix to continue force feedback. From stand point of users, deformation is to be continued when speculation missed.

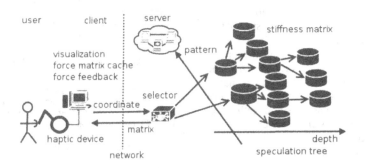

Figure 2 Distributed system for haptic VR.
Client server model is employed for speculative calculation with branch reduction by depth and pattern.

ESTIMATION

Detail of the proposed distributed system architecture is illustrated in Figure 3. Following FEM model was used for estimation of computational complexity; slab model, the number of vertices is 586, the number of tetrahedra is 1785, and stiffness matrix size is 1758 by 1758. Every value of each step was measured on standard personal computer (Intel Pentium4 2.8GHz, memory 2GB, 100base-T Ethernet, peer to peer environment). The proposed client-server architecture is consists of four parts of communication. Coordinate of user manipulation is sent to server front-end through client. If client back-end has cached force matrix, client front-end represents force feedback in about 0.1 msec. Server front-end that works as the selector controls speculation branch by communicating matrix number to back-end. If requested

matrix has been constructed already, the selector loads the matrix to calculate force and deformation. It takes about 4000 msec to reconstruct matrix at server back-end. Next 18.8 msec after reconstruction, server back-end calculates stress distribution by predicted manipulation pattern that is ordered from the selector. The best response time between client requests to server responses is about 5 msec. And also, client-side visualization can be estimated to perform in 8 msec in the best case. The worst situation is that the requested matrix is not prepared. It takes 4000 msec for back-end response. The hit ratio of speculative operation k is defined as $(z\ p\ d)$ $/n$. In assumption that z as number of processing unit is 64, p as pattern of direction is 3, d as depth of continuous rupture progressing is 5, and n as number of tetrahedral elements is 1500, the hit ratio k is approximately 0.64. In addition, in that assumption, an average time of response to users is about 1200 *msec*. To avoid haptic freezing caused by miss hit, client front-end should employ a force matrix cache system.

CONCLUSION

This study aims to provide surgical simulator with haptic interaction that is simulated by physics-based modeling. To achieve real-time simulation of soft tissue fracture, proposed distributed system employs application level speculative calculation on client-server architecture. In this paper, performance of conventional soft tissue rupture model was parsed. The speculative operation of stiffness matrix reconstruction was indicated to achieve real-time simulation as a result of estimation of the proposed system's performance. In the next step, the proposed system will be implemented on 64 nodes PC cluster.

REFERENCES

1. M. Nakao, et.al., Evaluation and User Study of Haptic Simulator for Learning Palpation in Cardiovascular Surgery, International Conference of Artificial Reality and Tele-Existence (ICAT), (2003) pp. 203-208.
2. N. Kume, et.al., Ablation simulator based on soft tissue destruction model, The First International Conference on Complex Medical Engineering, (2005) pp. 283-286.
3. M. Komori, et.al., User haptic characteristics measurement for design of medical VR applications, Proc. of Computer Assisted Radiology and Surgery (CARS), (2000) pp. 17-22.
4. K. Hirota, et.al., Physically-Based Simulation of Object Manipulation, Proc. of the ASME (Dynamic Systems and Control Division - 2000), DSC-Vol.69-2 (2000) pp. 1167-1174.

ACKNOWLEDGEMENT

This research was partly supported by Grant-in-Aid for JSPS Fellows and Grant-in-Aid for Scientific Research(S) (16100001) from the Japan Society for the Promotion of Science, supported by Grant-in-Aid (H18-Medicine-General-032) from the Ministry of Health, Labour and Welfare, Japan, and supported by Grant-in-Aid for Young Scientists (A) (17680008) and Exploratory Research (18659148) from The Ministry of Education, Culture, Sports, Science and Technology, Japan.

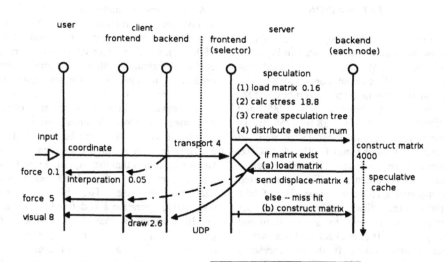

model – vertex 586, , Unit: msec

Figure 3 Estimation of expected performance of haptic and visual interaction on proposed client server system.

Physics-based Manipulation of Volumetric Images for Preoperative Surgical Simulation

Megumi NAKAO*, Tomotaka MATSUYUKI*, Tomohiro KURODA**, Kotaro MINATO*

* Graduate School of Information Science, Nara Institute of Science and Technology
8916-5 Takayama Ikoma, Nara, 630-0192 Japan
(E-mail: meg@is.naist.jp)
** Dept. of Medical Informatics, Kyoto University Hospital
54 Kawahara Shougoin, Sakyo, Kyoto, 606-8507 Japan

ABSTRACT

Volume visualization software allows medical stuffs to extract meaningful information in patient specific surgical planning and diagnosis. In recent days, in order to discuss surgical strategy and to share the plan, their interest is not only visualizing 3D anatomical structure but simulating surgical procedures directly on the volumetrically rendered image. This study aims to establish interactive volume surgical simulation that allows surgeons to rehearse surgical procedure on patient's volumetric CT/MRI images. Physical phenomena between surgical instruments and organs like tumor resection and pinching/pushing manipulation are simulated with a FEM-based deformable model. We also consider interactive performance on standard PCs. This presentation reports details of the methods, the prototype surgical simulation system and some experimental results simulating surgical procedure in minimally invasive surgery.

KEY WORDS: Volume Manipulation, User Interface, Physics-Based Deformation, Surgical Simulation

INTRODUCTION

Volumetrically rendered images (called volumetric images in this paper) of patient 3D CT/MRI dataset are widely used in diagnosis and preoperative surgical planning. While the volumetric images are efficient to grasp 3D shape of organs and positional relationship of tumors, most current viewers can not simulate surgical process or surgical procedure like cutting, resection and pinching manipulation etc.

So far, some studies proposed basic techniques for volume edit [1-3] and physics-based deformation [4-5] on volumetric images. These methods are effective to represent volume cut or deformation interactively. However, sophisticated and practical simulation models are necessary to reproduce physical phenomena like pinching and ablation between surgical instruments and organs (see Fig. 1). Also, in order to support surgical planning by surgeons themselves, it is essential to provide user-friendly and intuitive interaction environment where surgeons can rehearse surgical procedure regarding volumetric images as virtual organs.

Considering these features, development of practical interface and volume representation is required for enabling intuitive interaction with volumetric images on the simulation system.

This study aims to establish an advanced preoperative rehearsal system where surgeons try surgical procedure on patient's volumetric CT/MRI images. In this paper, we propose a volume manipulation framework based on real-time volume visualization and physics-based simulation technique. Unlike foregoing studies, the framework enables 6DOF surface constraint based manipulation of volumetric organ images. As the manipulator operated by a user is not a point but has 3D shape, realistic physical phenomena like pinching/grasping manipulation can be simulated. We also consider the system achieves interactive performance (over 30Hz refresh rate) on standard PCs, which is essential for interactively rehearsing surgical procedure. This paper describes details of the proposed methods, the prototype volume manipulation system and reports some experimental results.

Fig. 1 Pinching manipulation with forceps in thoracoscopic surgery

PHYSICS-BASED MANIPULATION FOR PREOPERATIVE REHEARSAL

The developed framework supports user's interactive manipulation on volumetrically rendered images reconstructed from patient CT/MRI dataset. We describe such manipulation consistently as volume interaction between manipulators and organ objects (see Fig. 2). The geometry has a grid topology (e.g. tetrahedral mesh) generally used in finite element (FE) analysis and handles one elastic /rigid object like an organ, tissue and surgical instrument. The geometry of organs, for example, is created through general modeling process: volume segmentation, surface definition and grid generation.

Our framework deals with physics-based manipulation of tetrahedral grids while representing interaction results as volume deformation in real time. Note that updating large number of voxels is time consuming process and becomes serious drawback to interactive performance. The proposed algorithms do not update any voxels but visualize physical phenomena on the geometry by interpolating internal voxels using 3D texture mapping techniques.

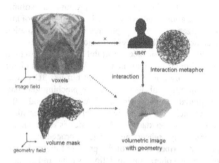

Fig. 2 Basic concept of our volume interaction framework

SURFACE CONSTRAINT AND DEFORMATION

In order to simulate surface constraints by surgical instruments, we developed a volume manipulation model which enhances applicability compared to conventional point-object interaction models. In this case, it is valid to assume organs are soft object and surgical tools are rigid. Fig. 3 briefly illustrates this interaction model and a deformation example. When intersection between the organ object and the manipulator is detected, the intersected area is regarded as grasped and displacement is applied to the vertices of the organ model.

More specific description is needed for the interaction between the organ object and the manipulator. Because we focus on surgical manipulation with forceps, the manipulator was currently modeled as simple two surfaces facing each other and a center point like in Figure 4. The virtual forceps is controlled through a 6DOF input device. The displacement d for each displaced vertex is obtained by the following equation.

$$\vec{d} = \vec{n} \cdot (q - p_0) \times \vec{n} \qquad (1)$$

where n is the normal vector of the surface of the virtual forceps, q is the initial position of the displaced vertex and p_0 is a vertex on the surface.

If the position of the vertices is geometrically transformed while satisfying displacement by the virtual forceps surfaces, additional manipulation like both pinching and rotation is performed.

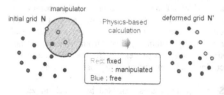

Fig. 3 Surface constraint based manipulation

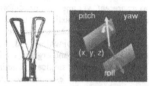

Fig. 4 A real forceps illustration and a basic virtual forceps model

Using the given displacement as boundary condition, we calculate physics-based deformation based on linear finite element formulation. Although non-linear representation is valid for accurate simulation, we currently focus on interactive performance for smooth animation.

$$f = Ku, \quad L = K^{-1} \qquad (2)$$

We divided the vertices into two groups: contacted vertices and other free vertices. Contacted vertices are directly displaced by the user's manipulation. Equation (2) expands $u = Lf$ by using the initial letters of categorized vertices to represent the coefficients of the matrices.

$$\begin{pmatrix} u_o \\ u_c \end{pmatrix} = \begin{pmatrix} L_{oo} & L_{oc} \\ L_{co} & L_{cc} \end{pmatrix} \begin{pmatrix} f_o \\ f_c \end{pmatrix} \qquad (3)$$

where u_c is displacement of the contacted vertex manipulated through the haptic device. Considering that f_o is constant zero, the relationship between u_c, and f_c is described as

$$f_c = L_{cc}^{-1} u_c \qquad (4)$$

f_c is external pressure on the contacted vertex. Applying f_c to Equation (3) provides the displacement u_o on other free vertices.

$$u_o = L_{oc} f_c = L_{oc} L_{cc}^{-1} u_c \qquad (5)$$

Note that we can obtain the inverse stiffness matrix L by pre-computation because it is specifically defined by Young's modulus and Poisson's ratio of the elastic object. We re-calculate L_{cc} and L_{oc} for all free vertices when manipulated vertices are updated. Although the order of the calculation cost is $O(m^3)$ (m: the number of manipulated vertices), m is not large in representing pinching area. Moreover, since this approach does not need inverse matrix calculation during manipulation, real-time computation is possible.

VOLUME VISUALIZATION

Slice-based volume rendering of tetrahedral grid and 3D texturing techniques volumetrically visualize deformation results in real time [6]. In this case, if a set of vertices of the geometry N is updated into N' by physics-based simulation, our process creates base polygons using new coordinates N', and a set of previous coordinates N is used for their texture

coordinates. Since voxel values in each tetrahedral element are correctly mapped on newly generated base polygons through this process, deformed volumetric image is visualized.

In addition to visualize model deformation with image voxels, we focus on coloring volumetric images. We utilize this representation for visualizing selected volume area by the virtual forceps. Also, volumetrically colored elements are effective to visualize internal stress simulated by the proposed FEM model.

Based on the same concept of interactive volume visualization of deformable geometry, we do not update any image voxels. For overlaying color on each element in real-time, we developed the following algorithms.

(1) Slicing tetrahedral grid and obtain the cross sections consisting triangle and square polygons. The cross sections are called based polygons in this paper.
(2) The color of vertices of base polygons is calculated from vertices color of tetrahedral element by simple linear interpolation.
(3) The color is set to the base polygons before texturing voxels.

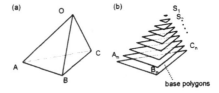

Fig. 5 Real-time color overlay per vertex for tetrahedral slice-based volume rendering

RESULTS

Overall methods were implemented on a standard PC (CPU: Pentium4 3.2GHz, Memory: 2048MB, GPU: nVidia Quadro FX3400) and a prototype volume manipulation system was developed. The PHANToM Omni was implemented into our system as 6DOF input and force feedback device. To confirm applicability and performance of our approach, we tried to simulate pinching manipulation on volumetric lung and liver models.

The lung geometry was semi-automatically created from 256x256x256 16bit CT dataset. Amira 3.1 (Mercury Inc.) was utilized to extract lung region and tetrahedral grid generation. The geometry consisted of 344 vertices and 1188 elements. The Young's Modulus 0.5 MPa and Poisson's ratio 0.4 were set as based on surgeons' empirical knowledge. Fig. 6 shows simulation results. The volumetric image is grasped by the manipulator and interactively manipulated. The green vertices represent grasped area and slice-based volume rendering process interpolates voxels between displaced vertices and visualizes volume deformation. We confirmed overall algorithms are processed within 30 msec and smooth force feedback can be also achieved.

Fig. 7 demonstrates surface constraint based deformation of a liver model with volumetric color representation. The intersection between the organ and the manipulator is visualized as green area on the volumetric image (Fig. 7-b). Fig. 7-d visualizes Mises stress value using overlaying red color on the

model. This graphical representation is processed in real time and therefore interactive surgical simulation is performed.

CONCLUSION

As a first stage for developing advanced preoperative rehearsal system where surgeons try surgical procedure on patient's volumetric CT/MRI images, we proposed interactive volume manipulation and visualization methods. The results partly confirm the achieved quality and performance. As future direction, we plan clinical examination for validation of the FEM-based modeling and improvement of methods.

ACKNOELEDGEMENTS

This research is supported by Grant-in-Aid for Scientific Research (S) (16100001) and Young Scientists (A) (16680024) from The Ministry of Education, Culture, Sports, Science and Technology, Japan.

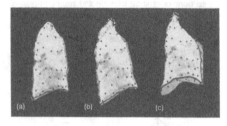

Fig. 6 Pinching manipulation and lung volume deformation results

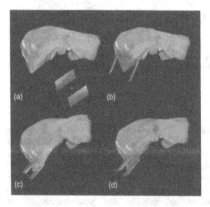

Fig. 7 Interactive surface constraint based manipulation and visualization: (a) liver volume model and manipulator, (b) real-time visualization of the volume area selected by the manipulator, (c) volume deformation and (d) volumetric color representation of the simulated Mises stress

REFERENCES

1. B. Pflesser, R. Leuwer, U. Tiede, K.H. Hohne, "Planning and rehearsal of surgical interventions in the volume model", Stud. Health Tech. Inform. Vol. 70, pp. 259-264, 2000.
2. D. Weiskopf, K. Engel and T. Ertl: "Interactive Clipping Techniques for Texture-Based Volume Visualization and Volume Shading", IEEE Trans. on Visualization and Computer Graphics, Vol. 9, No. 3, pp. 298-312, 2003.
3. M. Agus, A. Giachetti, E. Gobbetti, G. Zanetti and A. Zorcolo: "Adaptive techniques for real-time haptic and visual simulation of bone dissection", Proc. of IEEE VR, pp.102-109, 2003.
4. C. Rezk-Salama, M. Scheuering, G. Soza and G. Greiner: "Fast Volumetric Deformation on General Purpose Hardware", Proc. The ACM SIGGRAPH / EUROGRAPHICS workshop on Graphics hardware, pp. 17-24, 2001.
5. Y. Masutani, Y. Inoue, K. Ishii, N. Kumai, F. Kimura and I. Sakuma, "Development of surgical simulator based on FEM and deformable volume-rendering", Proc. SPIE Vol. 5367, p. 500-507, 2004
6. M. Nakao, T. Kuroda, T. Sato, T. Kuroda and K. Minato, "Volume Interaction Framework for Preoperative Surgical Simulation on Volumetric Images", Computer Assisted Radiology and Surgery (CARS2006), pp. 156-158, 2006.

Development of A VizGrid Volume Communications Environment

Motoi OKUDA *, ***, Yukihiro KARUBE *** , Ryuichi MATSUKURA *** ,
Masahiro WATANABE** and Teruo MATSUZAWA *

* School of Information Science,
Japan Advanced Institute of Science and Technology
1-1 Asahidai, Nomi, Ishikawa 923-1292 Japan
(E-mail: o-motoi@jaist.ac.jp)
** Center for Information Science
Japan Advanced Institute of Science and Technology
1-1 Asahidai, Nomi, Ishikawa 923-1292 Japan
*** Computational Science and Engineering Solution Center
Fujitsu Limited
9-3, Nakase 1-chome, Mihama-ku, Chiba City, Chiba 261-8588, Japan

ABSTRACT

As the number of interdisciplinary collaborations between remotely located researchers increases, a communication environment with high reality becomes essential as a collaboration support tool. In the VizGrid project, we have proposed a concept called Volume Communication as a new collaboration support tool, to provide a highly realistic remote conference system. In the Volume Communication concept we set up a virtual collaboration room and allocate three-dimensional (3D) video images of researchers at remote locations, 3D simulation results, and measured data. In this paper we report on the voxel communication environment which realizes the volume communication concept by handling all data as a voxel data format, and evaluate experimental results of the functionality and performance of this experimental system.

KEY WORDS: Remote Conference System, VizGrid Project, Volume Communication,
Remote Collaboration

INTRODUCTION

As interdisciplinary collaboration between remotely located researchers increases, a communication environment with high reality becomes essential as a collaboration support tool [1]. In other words, we need a environment in which researchers in a number of remote locations can communicate as if they are talking in the same meeting room, sitting around a table and sharing 3D visualized data. To realize a highly realistic remote conference system (RCS), there must be real-time representation of the motion, eye contact, and gaze awareness between researchers, a positional relationship between researchers and the ability to share data [2][3]. 3D information about the shared data, such as cross section data, is also essential. Several research and development projects are ongoing, such as the Virtual Rooms Video Conference Service (VRVS) [4], The Office of the Future [5], TELEPORT [6], and I3DVC (Immersive 3D Video conferencing) [2]. However, these approaches are based on 2D video images, which insufficiently represent reality, and they also have less consideration for shared data. A method which constructs a virtual conference room

(VCS) in a computer system is another approach to realizing a high-reality RCS [7].

In our method, 3D video images of participants and shared data are allocated in the VCR, and the VCR is visualized from each participant's point of view. We call this type of RCS a "virtual conference room system" (VCRS). Since the VCRS handles all data as 3D images, we can achieve a natural representation of 3D objects (both human images and shared data images), share location relationship of 3D objects between remotely located sites, and connect a number of sites. In the VizGrid project, the authors are conducting research and development of VCRS by treating all 3D objects data as voxel representations [8].

We have developed a "volume communication" environment (VCE) which can generate, transmit, allocate, visualize, and operate 3D voxel objects and realize high reality RCS. Since VCRS handles all data as 3D voxel data, we now need a high performance computer for processing and visualizing these data. Aiming for a wide use of RCS, we are targeting development of a PC based VCRS. In this paper we report on the architecture of the VCE and experimentally evaluate its functionality and performance.

VOLUME COMMUNICATION ENVIRONMENT

Distributed processing among sites

There are two system configuration types for VCR, concentrated processing (CP) and distributed processing (DP). For VCE we adopt the DP method, which defines the control node that controls and distributes all system data such as the location of each object, each participant's viewpoint, and visualization parameters. Object voxel data are transmitted among the sites and visualized at each site from that site participant's viewpoint. In the CP method, 3D human images and shared data are gathered from each site at a central visualization node. At the visualization node, VCR visual images from each site participant's viewpoint are generated and distributed to corresponding sites.

Compared with the CP method the DP method can reduce visualization throughput time to 1/(No. of nodes) and can reduce communication costs if the data size of human images is adequately less than the data size of visual images. But system control of the DP method is more complex than the CP method, and the DP method needs to synchronize image data and audio data. Figure 1 shows the system configuration and operation flow of the VCE.

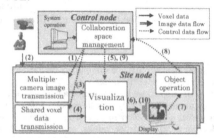

Figure 1 The VCE system configuration and operation flow

First a conference control process, which is allocated in the control node, directs a multiple-camera image transmission process and a shared data transmission process in each node to start voxel data import and transmission ((1), (2), (3), (4)). Each voxel of the objects is transmitted to a visualization process allocated in each site and the VCR is visualized in a stereo vision image according to visualization parameters such as object locations and view point from control node ((5), (6)). Object operations by each site participant such as rotation, or scaling up and down, are sent to the control node and reflected to all sites for visualization ((7),(8),(9),(10))

Voxel data type and its transmission
Two voxel types are used in the VCE. One is a full voxel data type which represents voxel data as continuous color information data in a voxel space. Other is a surface voxel data type which represents only the object surface as a pair of position and color information. The surface voxel data type can reduce data size when objects do not have inner information, such as human 3D image voxel data. The transmitting of voxel data is done by a communication library which implements a voxel communication protocol [9]. This protocol uses SIP (Session Initiation Protocol) for connection control and transmits still data by a TCP and video data by an RTP (Real-time Transport Protocol). For synchronization of voxel and audio data, we installed a synchronization node in the network [10].

Object allocation and visualization
The VCRS can allocate any number of objects at any position in any assignment. A system administrator first sets these object voxel location parameters according to the conference control process and these parameters are reflected to the visualization process. The VCE applies a distributed visualization method by object to speed up visualization time. In this method, stereo vision images of each object are generated in each of the PCs configured in a PC cluster. Then these images are transmitted to another PC which overlays the object image and displays it on a stereo vision display.

Figure 2 shows the distributed visualization method process flow in each node. The image generation process generates perspective images of each object by volume rendering for the full voxel data and by polygon rendering for the surface voxel data. Each object image is transmitted to the image overlay process and superimposed by an order of distance from the viewpoint. Since the image overlay process repeats its process automatically,

and as each object is visualized independently from any other object, the visualization of a human 3D image will not be dragged down by the other object visualization process.

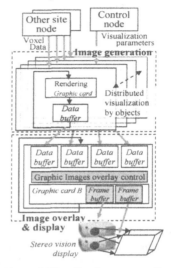

Figure 2 Visualization process flow

EXPERIMENT BY THE EXPERIMENTAL VCE

Environment for experiment
We developed the experimental VCE to verify the techniques adopted. In the experiment we used a 3D human voxel image configured by 128^3 and 256^3 voxels. If we represent a human face with a 256^3 voxel image, one voxel corresponds to about 1 mm real length. Assuming a medical application, CT and MRI images with 256^3 resolution and computer graphic (CG) images of simulated results with 128^3 and 256^3 resolution were used as shared data.

Figure 3 shows the PC system and network configuration of the experimental system. The multiple-camera image transmission process was assigned in a PC with a Pentium4 3.8 GHz CPU and other processes were assigned in PCs with

383

Pentium4 2.4 GHz CPUs. Assuming a conference between three sites, with two shared objects, the image generation process was performed on a PC cluster configured with 4 PCs. The experimental system used a 1Gbps network.

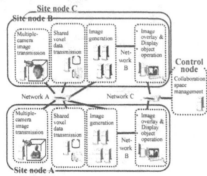

Figure 3 Configuration of the experimental system

Experimental results

By adopting the surface voxel data format, we achieved a average 99.3% data size reduction ratio for 20 sample human 3D images. The average data size of a 256^3 voxel space human 3D image is 240KB.

Table 1 Visualization performance of the experimental VCE

Data type	Voxel Data type	Rendering method	Voxel space size	Frame rate (fps)	
				2D display	Stereo vision display
3D human video image[1]	Surface voxel data	Polygon rendering	128^3	6.1	2.0
			256^3	6.2	2.0
CG image [2]	Full voxel data	Volume rendering	128^3	2.8	1.6
			256^3	1.8	0.44

1 : Average of 20 image data
2 : Average of 5 times measurement

For visualization performance, we measured a visualization speed (fps: frame per second) of 128^3 and 256^3 voxel space size human 3D images and 128^3 and 256^3 voxel space size 3D CG images. Table 1 shows examples of the visualization performance of the experimental VCE.

A 2.2% increase of visualization time for an average of 15 cases was measured when human 3D images and 3D CG images were visualized concurrently. Figure 4 shows an example of object allocation in the VCR and its visualization. Two 3D medical images are located in the VCR and two participant human 3D images are located behind the medical images. The participant on the right points to the medical image with his hand and the participant on the left gazes at it.

256^3 3D human Voxel video image

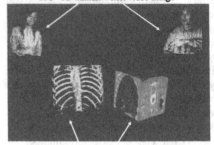

256^3 Medical image voxel data

Figure 4 Example of objects allocation in the VCR and its visualization

DISCUSSION AND CONCLUSION

Discussion

By using our VCRS method for RCS, the VCE can realize the simultaneous allocation and visualization of 3D human images and 3D shared data. As shown in Figure 4, each participant can see the other site participants and share data as if they were in a same conference room. We believe that using a 256^3 voxel space size will enable participants to follow each other's gaze and recognize what the other participants are doing. Adopting site distributed processing and an object distributed visualization method enables the VCE to realize the visualization performance shown in Table 1, and each object is visualized independently. In our experiment, the VCE achieved 2D display visualization performance of about 6 fps for the 3D human images and 1.8-2.8 fps for 3D CG images of computer simulation results. Since the 3D human image data size is reduced to about 240KB by the surface voxel data format, and display image size is about 3MB, the communication costs of the DP method is lower than that of the CP method.

To achieve higher reality for more natural communication between remotely located researchers, we need to speed up visualization performance (video frame rate). Since a normal meeting scene will not have rapid human movement, we assume that the minimum required video frame rate for RCS is about 15 fps (half of the usual TV video rate). According to a detailed investigation of the measured data, a major bottleneck for speed-up is the time needed to transmit display image data between the image generation process and the image overlay process. By using a higher speed network and more efficient communication methods, we think it is possible to achieve our target video frame rate.

Conclusion

The VizGrid project is aiming to develop a VCRS type RCS that can handle all 3D object data as voxel representations. We developed a VCE which generates, transmits, allocates, visualizes, and operates 3D voxel objects and created a high reality RCS. Through the evaluation of the experimental VCE system, we verified that the site-distributed processing and object-distributed visualization methods are effective for high speed visualization in the VCRS. As future work, we will speed up the network and adopt more efficient communication protocols, to achieve a higher video frame rate for 3D human images. We also will perform a detail evaluation of the obtained VCR to assess its realism.

ACKNOWLEDGEMENTS

As a part of the e-Science project of the IT program, the VizGrid project is funded by the Ministry of Education, Culture, Sport and Science in Japan. In addition, the authors would like to thank all of the members of the VizGrid project.

REFERENCES

1. L. Rowe and R. Jain, ACM SIGMM retreat report, ACM TOMCCAP, Vol. 1, No. 1, pp. 3-13, Feb. 2005.
2. O. Schreer and P. Kauff, An Immersive 3D Video-Conferencing System Using Shared Virtual Team User Environments, Proc. of CVE'02, pp. 105-112, Bonn, Germany, October 2002.
3. A. Kendon, Some Functions of gaze direction in social interaction, Acta Psychological, 26, pp. 22-63 (1967).
4. http://www.vrvs.org/About/index.html
5. Ramesh Raskar, Greg Welch, Matt Cutts, Adam Lake, Lev Stesin and Henry Fuchs, The Office of the Future: A Unified Approach to Image-Based Modeling and Spatially Immersive Displays, ACM SIGGRAPH 1998.
6. S.J. Gibbs et al, TELEPORT-Towards Immersive Copresence, Multimedia Systems, No.7, pp. 214-221, Springer-Verlag, 1999
7. Tetuo Ogi, Toshio Yamada, Yuji Kurita, Yoichi Hattori, Michitaka Hirose, Usage of Video Avatar Technology for Immersive Communication, First International Workshop on Language Understanding and Agents for Real World Interaction, 2003
8. M. Okuda, H. Morishige, Y. Karube, M.Yamada, H.Shitara, VizGrid: Development of teleimmersive collaboration environment, Proceedings of the Third International Conference on Parallel and Distributed Computing, Applications and Technologies, pp. 94-99, 2002.
9. R. Matsukura, K. Koyamada, Y. Tan, Y. Karube, M. Moriya, VizGrid: Collaborative Visualization Grid Environment for Natural Interaction between Remote Researchers, FUJITSU Scientific and Technical Journal, Vol. 40, No. 2, pp. 205-216, 2004
10. Takeshi Tsuchiya, Takahiro Komine, Yasuo Tan, A Network Node for Synchronizing Multiple Streaming Data Based on Timestamp Information, Proceedings of The International Sympsium on Towards Peta-Bit Ultra-Networks(PBit), PP.96-102 A&I Ltd., ISBN4990033035, 2003

Realistic Simulation of Internet

Toshiyuki Miyachi[†‡$]   Junya Nakata[†‡$]   Razvan Beuran[‡$]   Ken-ichi Chinen[†‡$]
Kenji Masui[§‡$]   Satoshi Uda[§‡$]   Yasuo Tan[†‡$]   Yoichi Shinoda[§‡$]

[†]School of Information Science / [§]Center for Information Science
[‡]Internet Research Center, Japan Advanced Institute of Science and Technology
[$]Hokuriku Research Center
National Institute of Information and Communications Technology

ABSTRACT

The Internet is a complex collection of various nodes which run independently. The hardware and software of nodes are quite diverse and these elements make the complexity of the Internet. It is difficult to model these behaviors, so we proposed and implemented StarBED, a large-scale testbed using general PCs and switches. Thus we created an environment for experiment using realistic nodes and software. We also designed and implemented SpringOS, which is a supporting software for making experiments on StarBED. Using SpringOS, users can make experiments on StarBED easily. In this paper, we describe the design of StarBED, and how to make an experiment on the StarBED using SpringOS. Moreover, we describe the design of StarBED2, StarBED2 is a testbed for ubiquitous and sensor networks based on StarBED.

KEY WORDS: Experiment, Verification, Network Testbed

INTRODUCTION

Current Internet has grown as one of the infrastructures for human life. Therefore, running and evaluating newly developed distributed software directly on the current Internet is no longer an option, because they may severely impact the existing crucial services. So, today, the changes and additions to services on the Internet must be tested for certain level of correctness before they are actually deployed, just like with any other social infrastructures, such as electricity, telephone, gas and water.

In order to develop and evaluate the technologies for the Internet, we need a realistic simulated environment of Internet. The best way of realizing this test process is to make an exact copy of the current Internet including people's activities and make changes to this copy, which is next to impossible.

We built StarBED, a facility which has many PCs only for making experiments. We have tried to simulate the Internet using StarBED. In this paper, we describe our approach to simulate realistic Internet.

Our approach achieves a realistic simulation of Internet through the following: (i) use of real nodes in a large scale setup; (ii) flexibility of the test environment; (iii) a powerful management system; (iv) extension capabilities for ubiquitous networks.

REALISM OF INTERNET

In this section, we describe the nature of the Internet and our approach.

The difficulty of simulating the Internet

Fundamental nature of the Internet is a complex collection of autonomously operated networks with so many services running simultaneously. The nodes which belong to these networks are also various, and they use the same protocols to communicate with each other, however, assessing their behavior in detail is difficult including bugs. The complexity of the Internet comes from the

Table 1: PC nodes in StarBED

Client group	Number of nodes	CPU Type	CPU Clock	Memory	Disk Type	Network Interface GbE	Network Interface FE	Network Interface ATM
A	208	Pentium3	1GHz	512MB	ATA	1	0	0
B	64	Pentium3	1GHz	512MB	ATA	0	1	1
C	32	Pentium3	1GHz	512MB	SCSI	0	4	1
D	144	Pentium3	1GHz	512MB	ATA	0	1	0
E	64	Pentium3	1GHz	512MB	ATA	0	1	0
F	168	Pentium4	3GHz	2GB	SATA	4	0	0

variety of elements that form the Internet. Understanding the behavior of these elements independently is not so difficult, however, expecting and modelling behaviors of the network which consists of many of these elements are difficult.

The scale of the Internet is now quite large, which is a reason of the difficulty of the Internet simulation. The result of experiments sometimes varies according to the scale of the environment, however, we often don't know where is the point of changing the result.

Existing Approach

Software simulation is the most popular approach to evaluate networks, ns-2[1] and SSFnet[2] is the well known examples of such simulators. users can make assumed environment for their target using software simulation. The environment is suitable for evaluating the ideas and steps of their target. However, we often cannot use implementations of target technologies directly on the Internet. Since they often require simulator-specific implementations which are different from those which will actually be running on the Internet. The implementations for simulators may differ from those for the Internet. The behaviors of the implementation for software simulators may also be different from those for the Internet, and it is difficult to model the new technologies for software simulation.

Our approach

Our motivation is to make a realistic environment for experiment, and evaluate real software/hardware implementations for the Internet. Therefore, we consider to build the realistic simulation environment using only the realistic elements or implementations on the Internet. Our

approach is to build an environment using many actual nodes like generic PC which is used on the real Internet. We can run real software implementations on these nodes. We assume that many nodes are located on the same site, and all these resources are physically accessible. So we can get all of information about the experiment traffic since all switches that connect experiment nodes are located on the same site. In order to build an Internet-like environment, we need a variety of equipments and installations, which make such kinds of projects quite difficult to achieve. To solve the difficulty of building experiment topologies, the network will be built beforehand based on fixed hardware connections and using virtual networks, customized topology will also be built. These connectivity and switch configuration will be used to produce a target network topology. The experiment can be driven on the virtual environment, thereby we don't have to change the physical topology. We also decided to make our environment as a multi-user system. Nodes are assigned by the administrator to the users.

A simulation environment behaves very similar to real network because of directly using real nodes of real networks. However, it is very difficult to build a large simulation environment by this approach, since it requires huge money and costs such as human resource, time and physical space. To minimize these costs, we are developing a supporting software which helps user to make experiment. A user should write a configuration file, and the experiment will execute following the file. Moreover it will improve the accuracy of experimental results. It can execute user's scenarios according to the description correctly.

We design and implement StarBED and SpringOS. StarBED is a general purpose network testbed based on many actual nodes and SpringOS is the supporting software for experiments on the StarBED. StarBED was built in 2002 as National Institute of Information and Communications Technology(NICT) Hokuriku IT Open Laboratory, and it is renewed as NICT Hokuriku Research Center with updating the facilities in April 2006.

STARBED AND SPRINGOS

In this section, we describe StarBED and SpringOS. More details on the design of StarBED are described on the StarBED Project website [3] and the design and the behavior of SpringOS are described in [4][5].

Construction of StarBED

At the core of the StarBED, there is an array consisting of about 700 nodes, which are actually standard PCs, with redundant connectivity into a large switch cluster. Table 1 shows the specifications of PC nodes of StarBED, the PC nodes are separated to 6 groups according to the specifications.

We can use a popular end-user operating system such as Windows on these nodes, or software router system based on Unix operating system, or even a special piece of software that turns nodes into delay lines. There are additional but empty positions in the core, where users of the simulator can plug in their own devices to form an appropriate target network. These devices may be the products under test, commercial routers, measurement equipments, and so on. Surrounding the core, there is a dedicated management network that controls and monitors the nodes and switch activities. Nodes can be loaded with appropriate software, controlled and monitored using the management network, without affecting a running simulation. The switch cluster has backdoor connection that can be used to monitor network activities or to create connections to link the core to external world. Figure 1 shows the concept topology of StarBED. By separating the network for management from that for experiment, traffic of management and experiment don't affect each other. Moreover, users can use their desired IP addresses for their experiments. If there

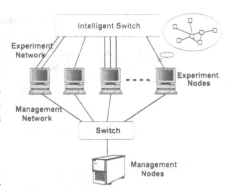

Figure 1: Concept Topology of StarBED

is no fixed network for management, they should set up the IP address via console. This is not a feasible approach when using many nodes.

Making Experiments on StarBED

We implement SpringOS which helps to make experiments on StarBED, and enhance StarBED functionalities. SpringOS is not single module program, it consists of many modules which has special functions. In this subsection, we describe the behavior of SpringOS on StarBED, in order to make experiments.

First, we describe the core technologies for controlling facilities on StarBED.

Power management of nodes

In order to power on PC nodes, we use Wake on LAN based on the magic packet[6] technology. To power off and reboot the nodes, we adopt SNMP. Therefore a SNMP client should run on every node. Nodes of group F support IPMI[7]. Using IPMI, we can control nodes' power state in detail, and we will support IPMI to power management.

Switching boot methods of nodes

Nodes for experiments load OS using the bootloader provided by PXE[8]. The bootloader specifies whether the node starts as diskless system or boots from a partition of local disk. The bootloader configurations are specified by the DHCP server. Before booting up leased nodes, the user

```
1) Design the experiment, including
   topologies, using OS, applications and
   etc.
              ↓
2) Introduce software to nodes and config-
   ure it
              ↓
3) Configure switches to make target topol-
   ogy
              ↓
4) Drive user's scenarios by executing
   commands on each node
              ↓
5) Analyze logs of experiments
```

Figure 2: General step of making experiments on StarBED

may setup the PXE so that the node boots from a specified partition and using Wake on LAN to boot up nodes.

Building target topologies

We design StarBED to reduce the costs in building target experiment. Therefore, the target topology of the experiment is configured virtually without changing physical topologies. We can set the desired topology for the experiments using VLAN and ATM VP/VC.

We describe next the main procedures of StarBED and SpringOS. The general step of making experiments is showed with Figure 2. SpringOS helps steps 2)-4), we describe the behavior for that. SpringOS loads the user's configuration file including node definition, target topologies and scenarios for experiment. It executes the steps automatically according to the user's description. Many experiments have been executed on StarBED.

Introduce software to nodes

Almost all of the time, we have the same OS and applications installed on nodes having the same role in the experiment. Therefore, disk images could be created for every role and installed in the node collection having the same role at the same time. In many cases we only need a few disk images to setup all the experiment nodes. Moreover, the setup of IP addresses of each network interface is done according to the configuration file.

When a user needs to boot up nodes it is as a diskless system. The user should prepare the disk images, kernel images and bootloader for their system, and switch the bootloader.

Build the target topology

SpringOS configure the VLAN setting on switches on network for experiment automatically.

Drive user's scenarios

We adopt server-client model to drive user's scenarios. In this paper, we call the server as scenario master, and client as scenario slave. The usual method is to distribute the scenario before the experiment starts by scenario master, and generally each scenario slave on nodes execute the scenario independently. When an experiment node has to synchronize, it connects to the scenario master to mediate with other experiment nodes. When a node should synchronize with other nodes, the scenario master controls the nodes with message passing. The details of the scenario driving of SpringOS, especially concerning synchronization of nodes, are described in [5].

STARBED2

Today various kind of ubiquitous networks including sensor networks and home networks are researched more and more actively, or are already in use. As the ubiquitous networks have been connected to the Internet and introduced to our life, their influence on our life grows.

In order to simulate ubiquitous networks, a testbed has to have some specific properties which are sometimes different from those of the ordinary network simulators. First of all, it is required to support simulation of a great number of heterogeneous nodes connected to each other with various kind of network media. Moreover, it is also needed to have functionalities to simulate surrounding environments since the behavior of applications executed in ubiquitous network system, especially in sensor networks, depends on the information obtained from the surrounding environments. In addition, to have ability to run simulation in real-time is really useful when the simulation is done in a real/virtual mixed environment, that is when simulated nodes cooperate with real nodes during the simulation.

To implement a testbed which has the functionalities mentioned above is not easy because simulating an ubiquitous network system in real-time is a highly computational-power-consuming task, not only because of the huge number of nodes each network has, but also because of the complexity of the behavior of surrounding environments as well as themselves.

Our approach to implement StarBED2, a ubiquitous network simulator, is to utilize StarBED as its basis. By doing so, StarBED2 can have ability to emulate ubiquitous network system in which thousands of heterogeneous network nodes exist, and accomplishes such a heavy task efficiently.

The major aim of StarBED2 is to create an emulation environment in which various kind of nodes, networks, and environments can be emulated under real-time constraint cooperatively with real nodes so that it can be widely used for prototyping, evaluation and testing of ubiquitous networks at any point of the development phase.

CONCLUSION

Currently the evaluation of new software and hardware for the Internet is very important. However, it is difficult to make realistic environments dedicated to experiments.

Simulating the Internet is difficult because it is very complex and large. In order to realize the complexity, we created a testbed built with network equipment and computers used in real environments. With this approach, users can use realistic hardware and software on it. On the testbed, they can introduce many kinds of applications for the Internet on their target environment, and these many kinds of applications will build the desired complexity. Our approach to build a large-scale environment for experiments is building a cluster composed of many general computers, and preparing supporting software which control the testbed.

We designed and implemented StarBED which is a cluster composed of 680 PCs dedicated to experiments, and SpringOS which is a supporting software for making experiments on StarBED. Using StarBED and SpringOS, we can make a larger topology than other methods, and the re-sult of the experiments is more realistic. Using SpringOS on StarBED, the steps of experiment are executed automatically. Users should prepare only the description of their experiment.

In order to enable ubiquitous experiments, now we design StarBED2, by enhancing StarBED for realizing a large-scale ubiquitous network emulator. It enables emulation of ubiquitous networks with thousands of heterogeneous nodes.

REFERENCES

[1] The VINT Project. *The ns Manual.* April 2002. http://www.isi.edu/nsnam/ns/ns-documentation.html.

[2] *SSFnet network simulator.* http://www.ssfnet.org.

[3] The StarBED Project. http://www.starbed.org/.

[4] Toshiyuki Miyachi, Ken-ichi Chinen and Yoichi Shinoda. Automatic configuration and execution of internet experiments on an actual node-based testbed. In *International Conference on Testbeds and Research Infrastructures for the Development of Networks and Communities(Tridentcom)*, February 2005.

[5] Ken-ichi Chinen, Toshiyuki Miyachi and Yoichi Shinoda. A rendezvous in network experiment — case study of kuroyuri. In *International Conference on Testbeds and Research Infrastructures for the Development of Networks and Communities(Tridentcom)*, March 2006.

[6] Advanced Micro Devices, Inc. *Magic Packet Technology*, November 1995.

[7] Intel Corporation. *IPMI v2.0 specifications Document Revision 1.0*, February 2004.

[8] Intel Corporation. *Preboot Execution Environment (PXE) Specifiction Version 2.1*, sep 1990.

Visualization of the Blood Flow and the Stress Distribution with the Diagnostic Support System for Circulatory Disease in the Volume Communications Environment

Masahiro Watanabe*, Motoi Okuda**, Teruo Matsuzawa***

* Center for Information Science, Japan Advanced Institute Science and Technology
**Japan Advanced Institute Science and Technology and Fujitsu Limited
*** Center for Information Science, Japan Advanced Institute Science and Technology
*m-wata@jaist.ac.jp, **o-motoi@jaist.ac.jp, *** matuzawa@jaist.ac.jp

ABSTRACT

We have constructed a diagnosis support system for circulatory disease based on a volume communications environment. This system can communicate 3D data of the object under discussion and create visuals with high sensibility. It can display three-dimensional data taken from medical treatment images, and also handle the simulation results of flow in a blood vessel with circulatory disease. With this system in the Volume Communications Environment, it became easy to discuss objects that were difficult to explain, like the simulation results. Moreover, it is easy to understand the shape of the object being discussed from the display of three dimensional spaces in the Virtual Reality system. Patient's disease part constructed from CT images was able to be displayed in three dimensions by using this environment. In addition, the output from the general-purpose visualization software can be displayed in the collaboration space. In this paper we describe the effectiveness of visualization in the Volume Communications Environment.

KEY WORDS: Volume Communication, Virtual Reality, Computational Fluid Mechanics, Computational Structure Mechanics

INTRODUCTION

We are developing a volume communication environment, which is a teleimmersive collaboration environment on a grid infrastructure [1] [2] [3].

As interdisciplinary collaborative research has become more common, the demand for high quality collaboration support environments has intensified. In addition, the fact that researchers and experimental facilities are now dispersed globally also has increased the need for remote collaboration capabilities. One of the three great challenges in the multimedia field is construction of a high presence remote collaboration environment [5]. The

AccessGRID Project has developed a multicast communication videoconferencing environment that uses a grid [4]. Many participants can confer with this system. However, it is difficult to obtain a high presence because the participants are displayed on a large scale screen in two dimensions. Thus, present tele-immersive systems are largely implemented with conventional video, which results in a very different experience from that of a face-to-face meeting.

On the other side, the development of Tele-immersive Applications that use Virtual Reality, like CAVE, is advanced, and the interface for understanding the discussion object is being prepared [7][8]. With these approaches the discussion object and the participant are communicated as the same data, and we begin to obtain a high-presence collaboration environment. In this method, the participant is displayed as avatar. It is easy to understand complex shapes in the data for discussion. However, it is thought that other sources information in the discussion, such as eye contact, may not be so easily understood.

In addition, the research that constructs the interface, like sharing of 3D space, has been done [8] [9]. The participant is also transmitted as data in these systems, and it is displayed as 3D data in which the participants mutually obtain a high presence. In addition, the object of the discussion is transmitted in the system [9], and pointing is possible.

For real collaboration, researchers should be able to not only communicate in real time, but also to share related information as if they were sitting side by side. We propose a volume communication environment which handles 3D image data for real time communication and information sharing.

Visualization data for the medical treatment on the volume communications environment has been examined so far [10]. In the previous study, it was confirmed the CT data was to display it minutely. However, the flow in the blood vessel was not able to be displayed.

To confirm the effectiveness our system, we executed by a diagnostic support system for circulatory disease based on the volume communication environment [11]. The simulation result recreates a patient's blood vessel geometry constructed from a MRI/CT images, and should present the result to the doctor (Clinician) immediately. Therefore, we share 3D data and simulated data on the system and the system has a visualization system in which the viewpoint can freely change. In this paper, we describe the current prototype system and effectiveness of visualization for medical data.

THE VOLUME COMMUNICATION ENVIRONMENT

Figure 1 presents a schematic view of the prototype of a volume communication environment. This environment has four components: volume data generation, synchronized multi volume data transmission, volume data allocation in virtual collaboration space and volume data visualization. Handling data for medical treatment describe as follow. The data utilized today by medical equipment for CTs and MRIs is known as volume data; this data has depth and is three-dimensional. To unite formats for rendering, a part of simulation data is converted into voxel data. This voxel data is used to display the velocity distribution and the pressure distribution by the section. Data of unstructured grid (shape data, simulation data) is converted into the voxel data by the interpolating calculation. Resolution of all data is 256×256×256. We use a firstly algorism to convert the voxel data. The participant of the discussion can freely change the parameter for visualizing.

On the other hand, the output from visualization system is treated as polygon data on the volume communications environment. General purpose visualization software used to experiment is AVS/Express 6.2. The flow by streamline and particle flow can be displayed by inputting the simulation data to the visualization software. The participant of the discussion can freely change the parameter for visualizing.

We used two stereo cameras of two eyes to generate the human data in real time. It takes the data of the left side and the right of the face with two cameras and three dimension data is generated.

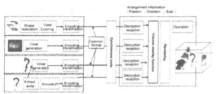

Fig.1 Schematic View of Volume Communication Prototype System

The stereo camera-generated image resolution of the system is 128 x 128 x 128 and the frame ratio is from 4 to 5 frames per second.

Various information such as the image, the voice, the simulation data, and the 3D data reconstructed from MRI/CT images, a pointer and the control data is done streaming by RTP (Real-time Transport Protocol). And the synchronization between the stream data is done by the Synchronous node [16].

We allocate these volume data in a 512 x 512 x 512 resolution virtual collaboration space. We used the volume communication environment for the visualization and collaboration systems. In this study, Portable Virtual Reality system with two projectors was used for the final display of the system.

RESULTS

Figure 2 showed the display image of the system. Three points were set in this case, and two cameras in a site were used. The participant who exists left and right in remote place was displayed. And, the voxel data constructed from CT images and the simulation data for the medical treatment were displayed at the center. Figure 2(a), (b), (c) ware a display of CT data. In these displays, the color map is changed, and the state of the display for the data has been changed. Figure 2(d) showed the particle

flow in the shape of blood vessel with a disease (Aortic Dissection). The particles moved along the aortic arch as animation. The result of the simulation was obtained in by the method in previous study [14] [15].

The flame rate for the participant is 4.0 [fps]. The frame rate for the data is from 0.5 [fps] to 1.0 about the resolution 256×256×256 and the polygon data from the visualization data.

Each participant could output the operation panel by right-clicking in the mouse on the screen displays. The rotation, the movement, and the expansion, the changing in the color map (Fig2 (a)∼(c)) and the putting a mark in the object could be done by the mouse operation. The importance of the display of data for the medical treatment by the change of color map is described by Pealman [17]. In our system, the output was obtained by Virtual Reality system, the participant was able to obtain the distance feeling of data for the medical treatment.

Moreover, after selecting the pointing switch, the participant could mark it on the each data. The system is possible to indicate the part of object exactly on virtual space.

In the simulation results for medical treatment, we could see the flow in the blood vessel with the disease and the distribution of the target physical quantity. The transportation and making the polygon data visible became possible, because it input the output of the commercial software for visualization to this environment. As a result, the flow and stress distribution (Pressure or Wall Shear Stress) could be displayed more in detail.

In normal 2D visualization, the possibility of misunderstanding always exists. Moreover, it should be understood that a participant's glance sees one angle of the object.

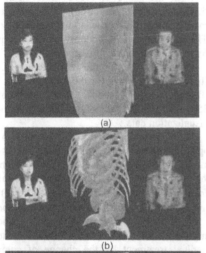

(a)

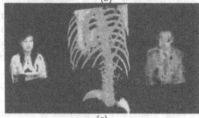

(b)

(c)

(d)

Fig. 2 Display the 3D data: The color map was changed to the data. (a) Surface of body, (b) Bone and Blood Vessel, (c) Bone (d) Particle flow by Simulation about Aortic Dissection (Color of Particle of Velocity Magnitude)

In Fig.2, for example, the participant on the left side was looking at a right simulation result. The other participant, who was looking at the screen, could immediately comprehend that aspect.

SUMMARY

We constructed the volume communications environment that was able to input the volume data and the polygon data. In addition, we confirmed the effectiveness of visualization for medical data. Especially, the output of commercial software for visualizing was able to be input to the volume communications environment. On the system, the participant of the discussion easily understands the part of 3D data that the speaker is watching.

In addition, we verify the new system that has function of sharing viewpoint because the person expression of a high resolution is possible, and the pointing function.

ACKNOWLEDGEMENTS

We wish to express our gratitude for the opportunity to participate in the VizGrid project. This work is supported by the IT-Program of Research Revolution 2002 (RR2002) from MEXT (Ministry of Education, Culture, Sports, Science and Technology of Japan)

REFERENCES

1. VizGrid Project Web Page, http://www.vizgrid.org
2. T. Matsuzawa , " VizGrid: Achievement of real experimental environment on super computer network" , The Institute of Systems, Control and Information Engineers (Japanese), Vol. 47, No. 2, pp. 65-70, 2003.
3. M. Okuda, H. Morishige, Y. Karube, M.Yamada, H.Shitara, " VizGrid: Development of teleimmersive collaboration environment", Proceedings of the Third International Conference on Parallel and Distributed Computing, Applications and Technologies, pp. 94-99, 2002.
4. AccessGrid Project, http://www.accessgrid.org/

5. ACM SIGMM Retreat Report on Future Directions in Multimedia Research, L. A. ROWE, R. JAIN, ACM Transactions on Multimedia Computing, Communications and Applications, Vol. 1, No. 1, 2005.

6. R.Raskar, G.Welch, M. Cutts, A Lake, L. Stesin and H. Fuchs, "The Office of the Future : A Unified Approach to Image-Based Modeling and Spatially Immersive Displays", ACM SIGGRAPH , 1998.

7. J. Leigh, A.E. Johnson, T.A. DeFanti, M. Brown, "A Review of Tele-Immersive Applications in the CAVE Research Network", Proc. IEEE Virtual Reality, 1999.

8. J. Mortensen, V. Vinayagamoorthy, M. Slater, A. Steed, "Collaboration in Tele-Immersive environments", ACM International Conference Proceeding Series;Proceedings of the workshop on Virtual environments 2002, Vol. 23, pp93-101, 2002.

9. H. Towles, Wei-Chao Chen, R. Yang, Sang-Uok Kum, H. Fuchs, N. Kelshikar, J. Mulligan, K. Daniilidis, L. Holden, B. Zeleznik, A. Sadagic, J. Lanier, "3D Tele-Collaboration Over Internet2," International Workshop on Immersive Telepresence (ITP2002), Juan Les Pins, 2002.

10. M. Watanabe, T. Matsuzawa,"Visual Data Mining for Medical Treatment on Volume Communications Environment", Proceeding of The 33th Visualization Symposium, 2005 (in Japanese)

11. M. Okuda, M. Watanabe, T. Matsuzawa, "Construction of a diagnostic support system for circulatory disease", Proceedings of the 5th IEEE International Symposium on Cluster Computing and the Grid 2005(CCGrid), 2005.

12. Y. Yasuhara, N. Kukimoto, N. Sakamoto, Y. Ebara, K. Koyamada, "3D Data Transmitting and Displaying System with an Omni-directional Display for Group Learning" The Third International Conference on Creating, Connecting and Collaborating through Computing(C5 2005), pp.171-174, 2005

13. M. Billinghurst, H. Kato,"Collaborative Augmented Reality", Communication of the ACM, Vol.45, No.7, p64-70, 2002.

14. M. Watanabe, T. Matsuzawa, "Numerical flow simulation in an aneurysm shape reconstructed with images for medical treatment", Japan Society for Simulation Technology, Vol.23, No.1, p 14-21, 2004 (in Japanese).

15. M. Watanabe, T. Matsuzawa,"Computational Simulation of Flow in A Dissecting Aortic Aneurysm Reconstructed From CT Images", Proceedings of ISCT: 5th International Symposium on Computational Technologies for Fluid/Thermal/Chemical Systems with Industrial Applications, ASME, 2004

16. R. Matsukura, K. Koyamada, Y. Tan, Y. Karube M. Moriya, VizGrid: Collaborative Visualization Grid Environment for Natural Interaction between Remote Researchers, FUJITSU Sci. Tech. J., 40,2,pp 205-216, 2004.

17. J. D. Pearlman, "Visualization in Medicine: Multidimensional Object Presenttion Methods for Computer Displays and Volume Holography", Proceeding of the 1995 Biomedical Visualization (BioMedViz '95), ISBN 0-8186-7198-X/95, 1995.

Study on Remote Collaborative System for Face-to-face Communication

Mitsugu MIYAZAKI*, Norihisa SEGAWA*, Yasuo EBARA**,
Koji KOYAMADA***, Yoshihiko ABE* and Jun SAWAMOTO*

*Graduate School of Software and Information Science
Iwate Prefectural University
152-89, Sugo, Takizawa-mura, Iwate, 020-0173 Japan
(E-mail: g231c034@edu.soft.iwate-pu.ac.jp)
**Academic Center for Computing and Media Studies
Kyoto University
Yoshida-honmachi, Sakyo-ku, Kyoto, 606-8501 Japan
***Center of the Promotion of Excellence in Higher Education
Kyoto University
Yoshida-Nihonmatsu-cho, Sakyo-ku, Kyoto, 606-8501 Japan

ABSTRACT

In this paper, we study on face-to-face communication technology in remote collaborative environment by the volume communication technology. We proposed a system that can determine whether or not local user's face is turned for user in remote site by estimation of the face direction with video image captured from camera. The advantage of our system is a simple, and special hardware is not necessary in order to realize user-friendly system and reduction of user's task. We apply OpenCV as facial recognition technology in our system. From experimental results, we showed that the regions of both eyes are detected, when the user is turning to the front, and the single eye is detected when user is turning to other direction.

KEY WORDS: Remote collaboration, face direction estimation, videoconference.

INTRODUCTION

The simulation technology is expected as a solution for complicated and sophisticated problems in cross-sectional study. As example of the cross-sectional study, prediction of global cycle and environmental changes, support for next-generation manufacturing, realization of efficient drug discovery process, and realization of tailor-made medicine that finds personalized medical agents and treatments are given. In addition, the demands for high-accuracy and high-resolution for the simulation technology have risen, and it need to process large-scale data. Furthermore, the remote collaboration technique via network is considered important by the spread of the Internet technology, and remote collaborative environments that relational experts can discuss by

396

sharing large-scale data in remote places are required. In this research, we study on the construction of the remote collaborative environment that based on volume communication technology. The volume communication is to exchange various information by numerical data (volume data) which calculated with large-scale simulation. Moreover, the remote collaborative visualization means to combine with video-conference system and visualization technique.

In this paper, we study on face-to-face communication technology in remote collaborative environment by the volume communication technology. The face-to-face communication technology in our proposed system has a feature that it can determine whether or not local user's face is turned toward remote user by estimating the face direction with camera images at three or more sites via network. Another users would feel that attentions are given to themselves, by informing results of decision to remote site.

RELATED WORKS

In remote collaboration, we consider that eye-to-eye contact during face-to-face communication is important to understand each other. However, the direction of eyes in video image is fixed by the relation of speaker's eyes to camera and is recognized regardless of the listener's position in conventional video-conference systems. In our research, we study remote collaborative system to realize tele-awareness by the estimation of face direction. As a research on the estimation of face direction, Min et al. worked the method measured from a triangle which connected with facial characteristic points[6]. Moreover, Ben et al. proposed the face re-orientation in video conferencing by approximating normal distributed depth[9]. In this paper, we apply OpenCV as facial recognition technology, and try to estimate

the face horizontal direction.

SYSTEM ARCHITECTURE

We constructed remote collaborative system consists of three hardware elements, two USB cameras, a PC, and a LCD display. The advantage of our system is a simple, and special hardware is not necessary in order to realize user-friendly system and reduction of user's task. The outline of our system is shown as Figure 1.

Algorithm for estimation of face direction

In this section, we describe a method to determine of face direction. A determination algorithm of face direction is as follows (see Figure 2).

1. Extract user's face region by using facial recognition technology from video image captured from USB camera.

2. Capture both eyes region from the face region.

3. Measure the width of each eye from deformation of both eyes region.

4. Estimate the face direction (left, center, and right)from the width of each eye.

We apply OpenCV as facial recognition technology in our system. OpenCV is implemented a pattern recognition by Haar-like feature[2][3]. Haar-like feature is defined as the value that are obtained by color value difference between two contiguous rectangle area[1][4][5].
Model of the eye region is shown as Figure 3. As reference model of user's eyes, we use some available models by Urtho[7] or Project EyeFinder in Technische Universitat Munchen[8] to capture eyes from detected faces.

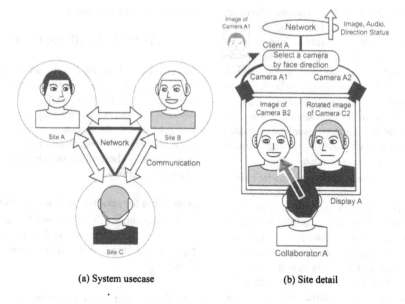

(a) System usecase   (b) Site detail

Figure 1: Outline of our proposed system

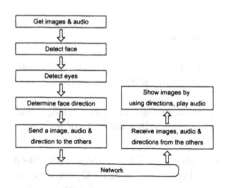

Figure 2: The flow of processing

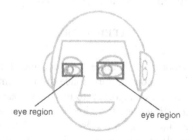

Figure 3: Capturing of both eyes region

In this paper, we try to estimate for horizontal direction. We estimate face horizontal direction by comparing the width of both eyes region.

Transmission of video image

In our system, data of three kinds, video image, audio and estimation results of face direction are transmitted and received between each site (See Figures 1 and 2). In addition, it is necessary to select a video image should transmit from two camera images, because two cameras are used in each site. The video image is determined by estimation result of

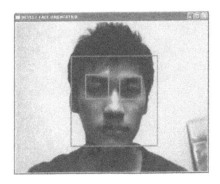

Figure 4: An example of captuing result (case of user is turning front)

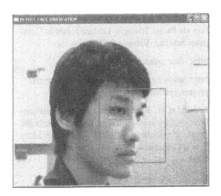

Figure 5: Another example of captuing result (case of user is turning to other direction)

face direction in each site, and is transmit an image of camera, which is turned the front for camera. However, if the image of frontal face is displayed directly, users in remote site may feel to watch oneself. Therefore, we use estimation results of face direction in order to display suitable video image on the display of each site. Example of Estimation results of face direction are shown in Figures 4 and 5. From these results, when the user is turning to the front, the regions of both eyes are detected. Moreover, the single eye is detected when user is turning to other direction.

CONCLUSION AND FUTURE WORK

In this paper, we studied on face-to-face communication technology to realize remote collaborative environment by the volume communication technology. we proposed a system that can determine whether or not local user's face is turned for user in remote site by estimation of the face direction with video image captured from camera. As quantitative evaluation of the system performance, we will consider to measure the accuracy on estimation of face direction and its processing time.

ACKNOWLEDGEMENTS

This research is supported by VizGrid project which is funded by the Ministry of Education, Culture, Sports, Science and Technology of Japan.

REFERENCES

1. C. P. Papageorgiou, et al., A General Framework for Object Detection, Sixth International Conference on Computer Vision (ICCV'98), 1998.

2. G. Bradski, et al., Learning-Based Computer Vision with Intel's Open Source Computer Vision Library, Intel Technology Journal, 2005.

3. P. Viola, et al., Rapid Object Detection using a Boosted Cascade of Simple Features, IEEE Conference on Computer Vision and Pattern Recognition, Kuaui, Hawaii, 2001.

4. R. Lienhart, et al., An extended set of haar-like features for rapid object detection, IEEE International Conference on Image Processing, NewYork, USA, 2002.

5. R. Lienhart, et al., Empirical Analysis of Detection Cascades of Boosted Classifiers for Rapid Object Detection, 25th German Pattern Recognition Symposium (DAGM '03), Magdeburg, Germany, 2003.

6. Min Gyo Chung, et al., Estimating Face Direction via Facial Triangle, Lecture Notes in Computer Science, Volume 3070, 2004.

7. http://face.urtho.net/

8. http://www9.cs.tum.edu/people/wimmerm/se/project.eyefinder/

9. B. Yip, et al., Face reorientation in video conferencing by approximating normal distributed depth, Proceedings of SPIE – Volume 5308, Visual Communications and Image Processing, 2004.

Framework for Simulation Analysis of Information and Communication Technology Systems

Hiroshi YAMADA*, Takehiro KAWATA*, and Akira KAWAGUCHI**

* NTT Service Integration Laboratories, Communication Traffic Project
3-9-11 Midori-Cho, Musashino-Shi, Tokyo 180-8585, Japan
(E-mail: yamada.hiroshi, kawata.takehiro@lab.ntt.co.jp)
** Core Networks Business Headquarters, Systems Verification Unit
NTT Advanced Technology Corporation
1-19-3 Nakacho, Musashino-Shi, Tokyo 180-0006, Japan
(E-mail: akira.kawaguchi@ntt-at.co.jp)

ABSTRACT

Managing complex ICT systems is a challenge for the service provider. We have been constructing a simulation environment to resolve the performance issues. We describe our framework for simulation analysis of ICT systems. In our framework, we consider three layers: network, application, and business processes. We consider two types of simulation modeling. One type deals with the complicated problem of one layer. The other type considers the mutual influences of the three layers. In order to deal with complexity, the simulation tool needs hierarchical-object-oriented modeling. We use OPNET, which has many standard protocol models and enables us to develop and expand protocol models. We show some case studies in which we resolved performance problems using this simulation environment.

KEY WORDS: ICT system, Performance evaluation, Protocol, Modeling, OPNET

NOMENCLATURE

ACK: acknowledgment
AS: autonomous system
BGP: border gateway protocol
EAI: enterprise application integration
ICT: information and communication technology
LAN: local area network
MAC: media access control
MPLS: multiprotocol label switching
SOA: service oriented architecture
UML: unified modeling language
VoIP: voice over IP
VPN: virtual private network

INTRODUCTION

ICT systems consist of several components: the network, computers, and applications. The network has become larger and more complex. Multiple routing protocols and traffic control technologies are implemented on the network. Applications use various communication protocols: synchronous or asynchronous communication. Web service technologies enable several applications to work together. Some application servers exchange messages with different application servers according to the business logic, which is defined by the business process execution language. The complexity of the interactions among components affects the performance. Most users require the end-to-end performance to satisfy an

401

appropriate service level. Therefore, there is a challenge for the service provider to manage such complex ICT systems.

In this paper, we describe our framework for simulation analysis of ICT systems and show some case studies in which we resolved performance problems using this simulation environment. To deal with the above complexity, we use the commercial hierarchical-object-oriented simulation-modeling tool, OPNET [1]. In OPNET, we can develop network, node, and process models. In the process modeling, we create a state transition diagram and program, which describes the protocol behavior in the C program language. We can add newly developed, expanded, or customized protocol models to the standard protocol library.

FRAMEWORK

We consider that the ICT system consists of the following three layers: network, applications (AP), and business processes (BP) [2]. We conduct BP profiling, AP traffic profiling, and network simulation (Figure 1). There are two types of simulation modeling. One is a simulation modeling that deals with the complicated problem of one layer. The other is a simulation modeling considering the mutual influences of these three layers (network, AP, and BP).

To analyze the behavior of a new protocol or expanding functions of an existing communication protocol, the first type of model is developed. Because of a space limitation, we cannot describe the details of the modeling and numerical results. However, in the next section, we briefly show examples of expansions of BGP and wireless MAC protocols. In the second type of simulation modeling, our developed business-process-driven simulation techniques are implemented. Through BP and AP traffic profiling, we create two simulation models: the BP simulation model and network simulation model. We briefly explain the modeling concepts of the later model.

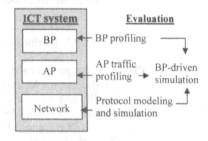

Figure 1. Framework overview

INTER-AS VPN

This is an example of simulation modeling for expanding the standard BGP protocol model to evaluate the network performance of the inter-AS VPN. Most VPN providers need to provide connectivity across different AS boundaries like in an inter-AS VPN because of the geography. There are several methods to make an inter-AS VPN [3]. To evaluate end-to-end network performance, we expanded the OPNET standard models of BGP and MPLS [4]. The expanded model enables the BGP protocol to change the next hop attribute in the AS border router appropriately and enables the MPLS to forward the VPN packet to the provider edge router appropriately. The snapshot of the state transition diagram of the BGP in OPNET is shown in Figure 2. To achieve the above expansion, the program code in the *Update_Message* state that describes the protocol procedure when the update message is received is modified. We can make various network models where the expanded protocol is implemented in all routers and evaluate the link utilization and end-to-end delay between each customer edge router for several scenarios of communication traffic volume.

402

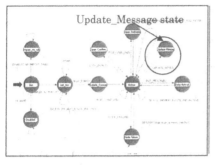

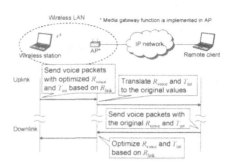

Figure 2. State transition diagram of BGP

TRAFFIC CONTROL OF 802.11

IEEE 802.11 wireless LAN supports the Link Adaptation (LA) function to improve throughput under fluctuating wireless link conditions, which allows a wireless transmitter to select an appropriate transmission rate (R_{link}) on a frame basis according to wireless link conditions. However, if a lower R_{link} is selected, packet delays and losses will increase due to insufficient bandwidth availability and, as a result, the quality of real-time applications will deteriorate. To resolve such a problem, we proposed an adaptive multi-rate VoIP (MRV) control scheme [5]. MRV is based on cross-layer optimization [6], which violates the layering principles by allowing interdependencies and joint design of protocols crossing different layers. If R_{link} is low, the offered traffic in the wireless link should be decreased. In MRV, a voice encoder in a wireless station changes the encoding rate (R_{voice}) and packetization interval (T_{int}) in the application layer depending on information about R_{link} from the physical layer to optimize the amount of traffic. We also introduced a media gateway implemented at an access point (AP), which translates R_{voice} and T_{int} between the original values and the optimized values, so the voice applications at remote clients do not need to be changed. The procedure of MRV is shown in Figure 3.

Figure 3. The procedure of MRV

First, we developed a simulation model for LA. We used an ACK-based principle for LA. The transmitter reduces R_{link} when a certain number of expected ACKs have been missed because of insufficient wireless channel quality, and it increases R_{link} when a certain number of ACKs are received successfully. Then, we implemented the MRV algorithm.

Using this model, we analyzed the performance of MRV in IEEE 802.11b when eight wireless stations are connected to an AP and using voice applications. The simulation model we used is shown in Figure 4. We defined $R_{voice,r}$ and $T_{int,r}$ as the adjusted voice encoding rate and packetization interval, respectively, when $R_{link} = r$. The 90th percentile of end-to-end delay including codec delay and the average packet loss ratio on the downlink are shown in Table 1. We consider the G.711 codec ($R_{voice} = 64$ (kb/s), $T_{int} = 20$ (ms)) and MRV ($R_{voice,1} = 16$, $R_{voice,2} = 32$, $R_{voice,5.5} = R_{voice,11} = 64$, $T_{int,1} = T_{int,2} = T_{int,5.5} = 40$, $T_{int,11} = 20$). The signal-to-noise ratio in the wireless LAN area fluctuates at exponentially distributed intervals with an average of 1 sec and its value is normally distributed with an average of 10 dB and a variance of 15 dB. As shown in the table, MRV significantly reduces end-to-end delay and packet loss ratio of voice packets.

Table 1. Simulation results

	90th percentile of end-to-end delay (ms)	Average packet loss ratio
MRV	115.6	0.011
G.711	377.9	0.066

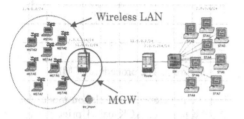

Figure 4. Simulation model

BUSINESS-PROCESS-DRIVEN SIMULATION

Recently, most enterprises have adopted EAI and SOA. Microsoft Biztalk is an example of a commercial EAI product [7]. The broker server in EAI products orchestrates several APs according to the designed BP. The BP is modeled by a UML or modeling tool of a workflow diagram. When a request is received by the broker, the orchestration program generates the workflow entity. This entity moves through workflow phases according to the designed BP. The orchestration program calls an appropriate AP when the entity enters an activity phase of the BP. System managers are required to reconfigure the BP in the broker server when the business environment changes. They are also required to maintain the performance of the response time of the overall orchestrated application. In software performance engineering, simulation modeling considering the mutual influences of BP and AP has been studied [8], [9].

We developed a generic business-process-driven simulation method using OPNET [10], [11]. BP and AP communications on the network are simulated in parallel. There are two approaches. One approach is that the BP model is added to the network simulation model as a BP node model on OPNET. The correspondence between the UML diagram and the OPNET BP node model is shown in Figure 5. The communication flow between both simulations is shown in Figure 6. When the workflow entity is generated in the broker server, the BP starts. When the entity arrives at the Proc module in the BP node model, the Proc module sends a simulation interruption to a predefined application process. Then, the predefined application is invoked, and it generates and forwards messages in OPNET network model. In simulation modeling, communicating between the BP and network simulation process to determine when and which simulation event in the BP or in the network application process should be executed is necessary.

The other approach is the co-simulation method. OPNET has an API that can connect to an external program, which is called esys API. Through the esys API, the simulation program can access the external program and send parameters to it. Using this, we can simulate the BP and the network application process on different computers. Instead of the simulation interruption of the first method shown in Figure 6, the actual messages, which include the necessary information to execute both simulation processes appropriately, are exchanged between both simulations via the middleware program according to the sequence shown in Figure 6. This program determines which simulation event should be processed as the next event.

Using these techniques, we can evaluate several performance measures: the overall response time of the orchestrated application, the total received requests in the server, or server utilization. We can proactively detect the bottleneck point of the system when the BP is changed. The above method is still at the desk examination level, and we need to perform more case studies.

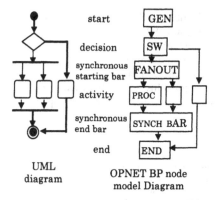

Figure 5. UML and OPNET BP Diagram

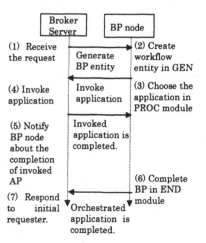

Figure 6. Communication between broker server and BP node

CONCLUSION

We described our framework for simulation

analysis of ICT systems and showed three case studies using this environment. The simulation analysis should be embedded in the service and system management workflow efficiently. Making the network, application communication, and BP models automatically from the configuration data is necessary.

REFERENCES

1. OPNET, http://www.opnet.com.
2. H. Yamada and T. Yada, Information Technology System Architecture Planning Platform (ITAP), NTT Review, 2001, 13-5, pp. 78-84.
3. I. Pepelnjak, J. Guichard, and J. Apcar, MPLS and VPN Architectures Volume II, Cisco Press, Indianapolis, 2005.
4. H. Yamada, End-to-End Performance Design Framework of MPLS Virtual Private Network Services Across Autonomous System Boundaries, to appear in Proceedings of NETWORKS2006, 2006, New Delhi, India, November 6-9.
5. T. Kawata and H. Yamada, Adaptive multi-rate VoIP for IEEE 802.11 wireless networks with link adaptation function, to appear in Proceedings of GLOBECOM2006, 2006, San Francisco, November 27- December 1.
6. S. Shakkotai, T. S. Rappaport, and P. C. Karlsson, Cross-layer design for wireless networks, IEEE Commun. Mag., pp. 74–80, Oct. 2003.
7. S. Mohr and S. Woodgate, Professional BisTalk, Wrox Press, Birmingham, 2001.
8. A. Korthaus and S. Kuhlins, BOOSTER process – a software development process model integrating business object technology and UML, Lecture Notes in Computer Science 1618, Springer-Velag, Berlin, 1998.
9. R. Pooly and P. King, The unified modeling language and performance engineering, Proceedings on Software, 1999, 146-1, pp. 2 - 10.
10. H. Yamada and A. Kawaguchi, Performance evaluation of workflow-driven network system using OPNET co-simulation method, Proceedings of OPNETWORK2005, 2005, Washington DC., August 22-27.
11. A. Kawaguchi and H. Yamada, Methodology of performance evaluation of integrated service systems with timeout control scheme, Proceedings of the 8th APNOMS, 2005, Okinawa, Japan, pp. 235-246, September 27-30.

Simulation Study of Hop-Based Burst-Cluster Transmission for Delay-Sensitive Traffic in Optical Burst Switching Networks

Takuji TACHIBANA*, Shoji KASAHARA** and Hiroaki HARAI***

* Graduate School of Information Science, Nara Institute of Science and Technology
8916-5 Takayama, Ikoma, Nara, 630-0192 Japan
(E-mail: takuji-t@is.naist.jp)
** Graduate School of Informatics, Kyoto University
Yoshida-honmachi, Kyoto, Kyoto, 606-8503 Japan
*** New Generation Network Research Center, National Institute of Information and
Communications Technology, 4-2-1 Nukui-kita, Koganei, Tokyo, 184-8795 Japan

ABSTRACT

In order to improve the fairness of the burst loss probability in terms of the number of hops, we propose the hop-based burst cluster transmission. In this method, bursts with different numbers of hops are assembled simultaneously, and a hop-based burst cluster is generated so that the bursts in the cluster are arranged in order from the smallest number of hops to the largest one. Then the hop-based burst cluster is transmitted along with multiple control packets. We also clearly specify how this method accommodates delay-sensitive traffic. We evaluate by Monte Carlo simulation the performance of the proposed method for delay-sensitive traffic in a uni-directional ring network. Numerical examples show that the proposed method not only improves the fairness of the burst loss probability but also decreases the overall burst loss probability significantly. Moreover, it is shown that the proposed method can provide acceptable delays for all delay-sensitive traffic.

KEY WORDS: Optical burst switching, Fairness in terms of the number of hops, Hop-based burst cluster transmission, Monte Carlo simulation, Delay-sensitive traffic

INTRODUCTION

In optical burst switching (OBS) networks, the burst loss probability increases as the burst traverses OBS nodes. Therefore, several schemes have been proposed in order to solve the unfairness in the literature. However, these methods increase the overall burst loss probability and degrade the performance of the OBS network.

In this paper, in order not only to improve the fairness of the burst loss probability in terms of the number of hops but also to decrease the overall burst loss probability, we propose the hop-based burst cluster transmission. The proposed hop-based burst cluster transmission is the enhanced version of the burst-cluster transmission for providing service differentiation [1].

In the proposed method, bursts with different numbers of hops are assembled simultaneously based on the burst assembly algorithm. With the assembled bursts, a hop-based burst cluster is generated so that the bursts in the cluster are arranged in order from the smallest number of hops to the largest one. Then the hop-based burst cluster is transmitted along with multiple

406

control packets according to the transmission scheduling. We also clearly specify how this method accommodates delay-sensitive traffic.

We evaluate the performance of the hop-based burst cluster transmission for delay-sensitive traffic in a uni-directional ring network by Monte Carlo simulation. In numerical examples, we compare the performance of the proposed method with the existing method, and we show that the proposed method succeeds in improving the fairness of the burst loss probability, as well as decreasing the overall burst loss probability.

The rest of the paper is organized as follows. We explain the hop-based burst cluster transmission, and then we explain the application of this method for delay-sensitive traffic. Simulation results are shown and finally, conclusions are presented.

HOP-BASED BURST-CLUSTER TRANSMISSION

In this section, we explain our proposed hop-based burst cluster transmission.

Burst assembly algorithm

Now, we focus on an ingress edge node which has N-1 egress nodes and L ($L \le N$-1) output ports. Let $l(i)$ denote the ith output link ($i=1,\cdots,L$) and $N(i)$ ($1 \le N(i) \le N$-1) the number of egress nodes where bursts are transmitted with $l(i)$. Moreover, let H denote the maximum number of hops.

The ingress node has L burstifiers corresponding to the L output links, and the burstifier for $l(i)$ has $N(i)$ queues corresponding to the $N(i)$ egress nodes (see Figure 1).

We consider the burst assembly performed at the burstifier for $l(i)$. Let B_{total} denote the total size of IP packets stored in all the $N(i)$ queues. We define B_{min} as the

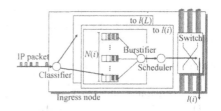

Figure 1 Edge-node configuration

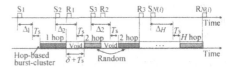

Figure 2 Hop-based burst cluster

minimum size of a burst and BC_{max} as the threshold of B_{total}.

The burstifier has a timer which starts when an IP packet arrives at the burstifier in idle state, that is, there are no IP packets in any queue in the burstifier. Let T denote the timer value and T_{max} the timeout value of T. According to the timer/burst-length based algorithm, $N(i)$ bursts are assembled simultaneously from the $N(i)$ queues when T becomes T_{max} or B_{total} becomes BC_{max}. If the size of a burst is smaller than B_{min}, the burst is assembled with padding.

With the $N(i)$ assembled bursts, a hop-based burst cluster is generated as shown in Figure 2. In this burst cluster, the $N(i)$ bursts are arranged in order from the smallest number of hops to the largest one. When the number of bursts with the same number of hops is larger than one, the transmission order of the bursts is determined at random.

In addition, there is a void between two successive bursts, and this void is given by the sum of the processing time of a control packet δ and the switching time T_s. This prevents a burst from contending with the following burst when the two bursts are switched to different output ports at any switch. Then the hop-based burst cluster is forwarded to the scheduler.

Burst transmission scheduling

In order to transmit the hop-based burst cluster containing the $N(i)$ bursts, $N(i)$ SETUP messages and $N(i)$ RELEASE messages are used. According to the burst transmission scheduling, the scheduler determines when the $N(i)$ SETUP messages, the hop-based burst cluster, and the $N(i)$ RELEASE messages are sent into the OBS network.

Figure 2 shows how the control packets and burst cluster are transmitted from the scheduler. In this figure, S_m and R_m ($1 \le m \le N(i)$) denote the SETUP message and the RELEASE message for the mth burst in the cluster, respectively.

There are two principal ideas for the burst transmission scheduling: one is that bursts whose number of hops is small are transmitted before bursts whose number of hops is large (Principal 1), and the other is that the RELEASE message of a burst is transmitted after the transmission of the SETUP message of the next burst (Principal 2).

Processing mechanism of control packets at each node

In order to transmit the hop-based burst cluster, the SETUP and RELEASE messages are processed at each node as follows. Consider that a call reference value V_m ($1 \le m \le N(i)$) is allocated to S_m and R_m for the mth burst. We assume that S_m has information about the call reference values V_1 to V_m.

In the following, we denote the output link for the mth burst at a node as l_m. In terms of the SETUP message, when S_m arrives at the node, S_m checks the resource status on l_m. If the resource with a call reference value V_n ($n<m$) has been configured by the SETUP message S_n, which is sent ahead in the same cluster, S_m updates V_n to V_m and is sent to the next node.

If the resource with V_n ($n<m$) has not been configured and there is an available resource on l_m, S_m configures the resource on l_m and sets the call reference value of the resource to V_m. Then S_m is sent to the next node. Therefore, a burst in the rear part of a cluster can be transmitted with the resource which has been configured for a burst in the forward part. According to Principal 1, it is expected that bursts whose number of hops is large can be transmitted to the next node with a small loss probability.

On the other hand, in terms of the RELEASE message, R_m checks the resource status on l_m when it arrives at the node. If there is the configured resource with V_m, R_m releases the configured resource. If there exists no configured resource with V_m, R_m is transmitted to the next node. According to the Principal 2, it is expected that multiple bursts in the same cluster can be transmitted consecutively without the release of the configured resource.

Figure 3 shows an example of the hop-based burst-cluster transmission. In this figure, the burst-cluster consists of two bursts B1 and B2 whose egress nodes are nodes N1 and N2, respectively. Moreover, let V_1 and V_2 be the call reference value for S_1 (R_1) and S_2 (R_2). In this example, note that the number of configuration procedures

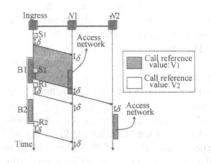

Figure 3 Impact of hop-based burst cluster transmission

408

by S_1 and that by S_2 are the same and equal to one, regardless of the number of hops. As a result, it is expected that the burst loss probability for B2 is almost the same as that for B1.

APPLICATION FOR DELAY-SENSITIVE TRAFFIC

In this subsection, we consider the application of the hop-based burst-cluster to delay-sensitive traffic. We define the transmission delay of an IP packet as a time interval from the arrival time of the IP packet at its ingress node to the epoch at which the burst including the IP packet arrives at its egress node.

Here, we focus on a delay-sensitive IP packet whose number of hops is i. This packet is contained in the jth burst ($j \geq i$) in a cluster. Figure 4 shows event sequence for the jth burst on its ingress and egress nodes. Note that τ, the time interval between the start time of the timer and the starting time of the first control packet S1, is equal to the generation time of a hop-based burst cluster T_{gen}.

Now we consider the worst case for the transmission delay of the IP packet with i-hops, where the IP packet arrives at the burstifier in idle state. From Figure 4, transmission delay of the IP packet comprises of the generation time T_{gen}, the initial burst delay of the first burst $\Delta1=2\delta$, the switching time T_s, the propagation delay with i hops P_i, and the transmission time from the first burst to the tagged jth burst $B_j/C+(\delta+T_s)(j-1)$ where B_j denotes the size from the first burst to the jth burst and C the transmission speed of a wavelength. Because T_{gen} and B_j depend on T_{max} and BC_{max}, when the acceptable maximum delay of the IP packet in the OBS network is D_j, T_{max} and BC_{max} should satisfy $T_{max}+\Delta1+T_s+P_i+BC_{max}/C+(\delta+T_s)(j-1) \leq D_j$. If bursts for every hop are delay-sensitive, BC_{max} is set to the minimum value among those obtained for all j's ($1 \leq j \leq H$).

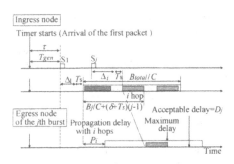

Figure 4 Transmission scheduling for delay-sensitive traffic

SIMULATION RESULTS

We evaluate the performance of the proposed method for a uni-directional ring network by Monte Carlo simulation. In this network, the number of nodes is ten and the distance between adjacent nodes is 200 km. Each link consists of an optical fiber with eight wavelengths and the transmission speed of a wavelength is 10 Gbps. We assume that the processing time of a control message is $\delta=1.0$ μs and that each node has a full-range wavelength conversion capability. The switching time T_s at each node is set to 1.0 ms

We assume that IP packets arrive at the network according to a Poisson process with rate 200,000 [packets/ms] and that the pair of ingress and egress nodes of an arriving packet is distributed uniformly. The size of an IP packet is fixed equal to 1,250 bytes. All IP packets are delay-sensitive, and those maximum acceptable delays are 100 ms. In order to satisfy those maximum delays, the timeout value T_{max} is set to 10 ms and BC_{max} is given by the previous equation. The minimum size of a burst B_{min} is set to 64 Kbytes. We assume that the time interval between two consecutive burst-cluster transmissions is exponentially distributed with rate 0.002 [clusters/ms].

In this scenario, we calculate the loss

probability of the burst whose number of hops is j (j=1,$\cdots$,9), $P_{loss}^{(j)}$, and the overall burst loss probability P_{loss}. Moreover, we calculate the coefficient of variation for burst loss probability CV_{loss} in terms of the number of hops. We also calculate the maximum transmission delay of burst with each number of hops.

For performance comparison, we also evaluate the performance of the conventional method by simulation. Here, all IP packets are also delay-sensitive.

Figure 5 shows the burst loss probability $P_{loss}^{(j)}$ against the number of hops. From this figure, we find that the discrepancies among the burst loss probabilities are significantly small in the proposed method. Therefore, the proposed method can improve the fairness.

Table 1 shows the overall burst loss probability P_{loss} of each method. We find from Table 1 that the overall burst loss probability for the proposed method is much smaller than that for the conventional method. This is because the hop-based burst cluster transmission reduces the overhead of wavelength reservation time.

Figure 6 shows the observed maximum transmission delay of burst with each number of hops. From this figure, we find that the observed maximum transmission delay is smaller than the acceptable transmission delay regardless of the number of hops. Therefore, the hop-based burst cluster transmission can accommodate

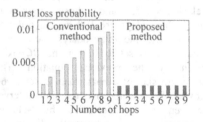

Figure 5 $P_{loss}^{(j)}$ vs. number of hops

Table 1 P_{loss} of each method

	Overall burst loss probability
Conventional	0.005672
Proposed method	0.001400

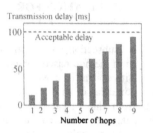

Figure 6 Maximum transmission delay for each number of hops

delay-sensitive traffic regardless of the number of hops.

CONCLUSIONS

In this paper, we proposed the hop-based burst cluster transmission and evaluated its performance for delay-sensitive traffic by Monte Carlo simulation. Simulation results showed that the proposed method can not only improve the fairness but also decrease the overall burst loss probability. Moreover, we found that the proposed method can accommodate delay-sensitive traffic.

REFERENCES

1. Zhou, B., Bassiouni, M., and Li, Guifang., Improving Fairness in Optical-Burst-Switching Network, The Journal of Optical Networking, 2004, **3**-4, pp.214-228.
2. Ueda, M., Tachibana, T., and Kasahara, S., Last-Hop Preemptive Scheme Based on the Number of Hops for Optical Burst Switching Networks, The Journal of Optical Networking, 2005, **4**-10, pp.648-660.
3. Tachibana, T., and Kasahara, S., Burst-Cluster Transmission: Service Differentiation Mechanism for Immediate Reservation in Optical Burst Switching Networks, IEEE Communications Magazine, 2006, **44**-5, pp.46-55.

On Spreading of Computer Viruses in Mobile Ad Hoc Networks

Jong-Pil PARK†   Keisuke NAKANO†   Akihiro KAMAKURA†

Yu KAKIZAKI†   Masakazu SENGOKU†   Shoji SHINODA‡

†Department of Information Engineering, Niigata University

2-8050, Ikarashi, Niigata 950-2181, Japan.

‡Department of Electrical, Electronic and Communication Engineering

Chuo University, Tokyo 112-8551, Japan.

(Email: jpark@net.ie.niigata-u.ac.jp, {nakano, sengoku}@ie.niigata-u.ac.jp

shinoda@elect.chuo-u.ac.jp)

ABSTRACT

While spreading of a computer virus in wired computer networks has been analyzed for different network topologies, a computer virus which spreads via a wireless link in an ad hoc manner has been found. Hence, it is important to investigate spreading of computer viruses over mobile ad hoc networks. In mobile ad hoc networks, spreading of viruses is affected by various factors such as the communication range, the velocity of a node, and the maximum number of hops. Furthermore, as opposed to wired networks, different mobility patterns cause various spreading patterns in ad hoc networks. In this paper, we investigate effects of topology of routes along which mobile nodes move on spreading of viruses as well as those of the above basic factors.

KEYWORDS: Computer virus, Ad hoc network, Mobility pattern, Network of routes

INTRODUCTION

Spreading of computer viruses in wired computer networks has been analyzed for different network topologies [1], [2]. As a result of the analyses, it has been shown that computer viruses spread in a scale-free network, which is a model of the Internet, differently from in a random network due to existence of hub nodes. While these researches mainly pay attention to fixed networks, a computer virus which infects mobile devices in an ad hoc manner has been found. The virus called Cabir spreads via Bluetooth link [3], and this fact means that computer viruses may spread over a mobile ad hoc network.

A mobile ad hoc network is a wireless network consisting of mobile devices connected by wireless links. In this network, relaying capability of each node enables a mobile node to communicate with another mobile node via a wireless multi-hop path. Then, the size of communication range is a factor affecting the spreading of viruses. While the number of hops is sometimes limited to one when mobile devices have no routing function, such a limitation of the number of hops also affects the virus spreading.

In [4], spread of worms over a vehicle ad hoc network on a road has been analyzed. In [5], information diffusion over a single hop ad hoc network has been analyzed with an assumption that a service area includes a pipe, along which mobile nodes tend to gather. As discussed in these articles, it is obvious that the epidemic spreading over an ad hoc network is affected by mobility, and it is important to investigate effects of mobility on the spreading; however, effects of topology of mobility patterns on epidemic spreading is not well understood. The topology of mobility pattern means topology of routes along which persons with mobile devices move or routes between workplaces of mobile robots. The topology of mobility pattern is a factor which never appears in wired networks.

In this paper, we define some mobility patterns, and investigate how computer viruses spread over mobile ad hoc networks differently due to topology of mobility patterns by comparing various mobility patterns. We also discuss how spreading of computer viruses in an ad hoc network is affected by the above basic factors such as communication range, velocity, infection models and the number of hops.

DEFINITIONS AND ASSUMPTIONS

We consider a square service area with a side $L = 300$m. Assume that 1000 terminals are randomly distributed in the service area. Let r be the maximum radio transmitting range of a terminal. We assume that the number of hops is limited, and examine a single hop ad hoc network like Bluetooth networks and an ad hoc network with more hops.

Let v be the velocity of a node. We consider the following three basic mobility models:

1. Static (ST): All nodes are fixed.
2. Random Walk (RW): All nodes move according to a two dimensional random walk model like Fig. 1 (a).
3. Random Way Point (RWP) [6]: In this model, a node randomly decides its desti-

nation in the service area, and moves toward the destination. After arriving at the destination, it decides a new destination and moves toward the new destination. Fig. 1 (b) is an example, where D_1, D_2, D_3 are destinations.

In the pure RWP, start points and destination points are randomly decided, and mobile nodes move independently from each other; however, in actual situations, we usually move along streets. Also, operational robots move between fixed workplaces. In such cases, there are some fixed starting points and destination points. By connecting starting points and destination points, we have a kind of a network consisting of routes, and it is expected that the topology of this network affects viruses spreading. Then, we consider the following models as well:

4. Street Network: This model is a modified version of RWP. In this model, start points and destinations are given in advance. Hence, each mobile node seems to move along streets between the given points. We consider five patterns in Fig. 1 (c) to (g). These patterns are denoted by SN1 to SN5, respectively. They include nine points. In SN1, there is a route between every pair of the points. While there are eight routes in SN2 to SN5, routes are randomly placed in SN2 and SN3. On the other hand, in SN4 and SN5, there is a central point and routes are connected to the central point. SN4 and SN5 are different in the place of the central point. SN6 in Fig. 1 (h) is a lattice street network.

We compare spreading of viruses in ad hoc networks with that in a wired network which is generated by an algorithm proposed in [1], which generates a scale-free network. We denote this model by SF. In SF, there are a small number of hub nodes and a large number of nodes with small degree, and it is said that viruses spread more quickly than in a random network like a

412

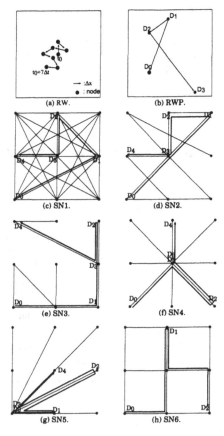

(a) RW. (b) RWP.

(c) SN1. (d) SN2.

(e) SN3. (f) SN4.

(g) SN5. (h) SN6.

Fig. 1: Mobility Models.

static ad hoc networks.

To simulate virus spreading, we use the following models for infection [7].

1. SI model: This model includes two states. A mobile node in S state is healthy but susceptible, and a node in I state is infected and infects the virus with other nodes in S. There are three state transitions with state transition probabilities $P_{SS}(t)$, $P_{SI}(t)$ and $P_{II}(t)$ as shown in Fig. 2(a).

2. SIR model: This model is the same as SI model except it has R state and the state transition probabilities $P_{IR}(t)$ and $P_{RR}(t)$. A mobile node in R state means a node of which virus is removed.

In the SI model and the SIR model, a node in I state tries to send a virus to its neighbors every 0.1 second. This trial succeeds with probability P_{inf}. In this paper, $P_{inf}=0.01$. In the case of n hop systems, the virus is transmitted to all n hop neighbors. In the SIR model, a trial to remove a virus from a node in I state is done every 0.1 second, and it succeeds with probability $P_{IR}(t)$. Assume that two events do not happen at the same time.

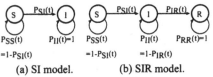

(a) SI model. (b) SIR model.

Fig. 2: Infection Models.

Define that $R_I(t)$ is the ratio of the number of infected nodes to the total number of nodes at time t, and $R_I(t) = \frac{N_I(t)}{N_N}$, where $N_I(t)$ is the number of infected nodes at time t, and N_N is the number of nodes in a service area.

RESULTS AND DISCUSSIONS

With the above assumptions, we analyze how a computer virus spreads in a mobile ad hoc network by computer simulation. We show $R_I(t)$ at intervals of 5 seconds. It is assumed that

$$N_I(t) = \begin{cases} 0 & t < T_{infection} \\ 1 & t = T_{infection} \end{cases} \qquad (1)$$

and $T_{infection} = 450$ seconds to observe epidemic spreading in a steady state of the distribution of nodes. It is assumed that $r = 10.71$m or 16.93m. Although the network tends to be connected for $r = 16.93$m, it is not connected for $r = 10.71$m. Let h be the maximum number of hops in the system.

Figure 3 shows $R_I(t)$s of ST and RWP with $v = 1$m/sec, where $r = 10.71$m and 16.93m are examined, $h = 1$ and the SI model is used. For ST, although $R_I(t)$

413

rapidly increases for $r = 16.93$m, it does not increase so much for $r = 10.71$m because connectivity is low due to the short communication range. As opposed to this result, for RWP, $R_I(t)$ increases even if $r = 10.71$m. From these results, we can confirm that mobility helps spreading of viruses in an ad hoc network.

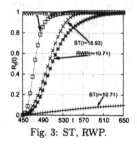

Fig. 3: ST, RWP.

Figures 4 and 5 show $R_I(t)$ for the SI model and the SIR model for ST and RWP with $v = 1$m/sec, respectively. In these figures, $P_{IR}(t) = 0.01$, 0.005 and 0.0025 in the SIR model, $r = 16.93$m and $h = 1$. In the SI model, $R_I(t)$ monotonously increases. On the other hand, in the SIR model, $R_I(t)$ increases gradually and decreases from some moment because infected nodes are recovered. Then, we can confirm that introducing the R state to the system is effective on keeping $R_I(t)$ low. In the following, we pay attention to how fast viruses spread in the system and use the SI model.

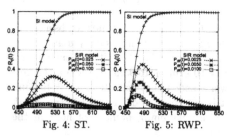

Fig. 4: ST. Fig. 5: RWP.

Figures 6 and 7 compare $R_I(t)$s of ST, SF, RW and RWP for various velocities. In the simulation, the mean degree of a node is set to be the same at $t = 0$, $r = 16.93$m

and $h = 1$. $R_I(t)$ of SF is larger than ST because of existence of hub nodes; however, $R_I(t)$ of RWP approaches that of SF as velocity increases. On the other hand, $R_I(t)$ of RW is not close to that of SF even if velocity is large. From these results, we can see that dynamic mobility such as RWP causes rapid spreading of viruses like SF.

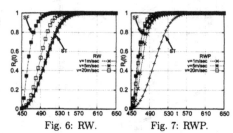

Fig. 6: RW. Fig. 7: RWP.

Figures 8 and 9 show effects of h on the viruses spreading, where $r = 16.93$m and $v = 1$m/sec. $R_I(t)$ of RWP is larger than that of RW in the case of single hop; however, as the number of hops increases, their difference becomes smaller.

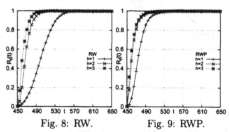

Fig. 8: RW. Fig. 9: RWP.

In the following, we compare $R_I(t)$ for the mobility models represented in Fig. 1. At first, we consider mobility patterns SN1, SN2 and SN3. In these patterns, there are 9 points which can be start points and destination points. In SN1, there are 36 roads between the 9 points, and a mobile node at one of the points can randomly choose one of the 8 adjacent points as a destination. In SN2 and SN3, there are only 8 roads, and a mobile node has less candidates for destinations than SN1. Figure 10 shows $R_I(t)$ for SN1, SN2 and SN3, where $r = 16.93$m, $h = 1$ and $v = 1$m/sec. Figure 11 shows the same graph for $v = 5$m/sec. These figures show that $R_I(t)$ depends on the topology of the network of routes, and the restrictions on the number of routes does not always increase $R_I(t)$ even if density of nodes increases because of the restriction. $R_I(t)$ depends on the topology of the network of routes. If the velocity is large, the effect of topology is small.

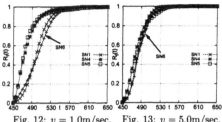

Fig. 12: $v = 1.0$m/sec. Fig. 13: $v = 5.0$m/sec.

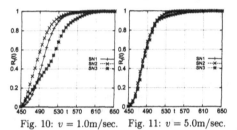

Fig. 10: $v = 1.0$m/sec. Fig. 11: $v = 5.0$m/sec.

Next, we consider some special topologies SN4, SN5 and SN6. In the network of SN4, mobile nodes always move from or to the central point, and it is expected that mobile nodes gather at this point. Such a special point does not always exist at the center of the service area like SN5. Figures 12 and 13 show $R_I(t)$ of the topologies SN4, SN5 and SN6 together with that of SN1, where $r = 16.93$m, $h = 1$ and $v = 1$m/sec or 5m/sec. The mobility patterns SN4, SN5 and SN6 are included in SN1, and the mobility pattern SN6 is a lattice network, which is a typical model of a street network. Both of mobility models SN4 and SN5 include a central point, but locations of the points are different. From Figs. 12 and 13, we can confirm that star and tree topologies like SN4 and SN5 make $R_I(t)$ the largest, and the location of the central point does not affect $R_I(t)$. $R_I(t)$ in a lattice network is less than in the mobility model SN1.

CONCLUSIONS

In this paper, we discussed spreading of computer viruses over ad hoc networks. We showed effects of some basic factors such as the communication range, velocity, infections models and the maximum number of hops. We evaluated spreading of viruses for various mobility patterns and showed that it is affected by topology of mobility patterns. In the case that mobile nodes move along star and tree structures, computer viruses spread quickly over ad hoc networks.

REFERENCE

[1] A. -L. Barabási, "LINKED: The New Science of Networks," *Perseus Books Group*, 2002.

[2] R. Pastor-Satorras et al., "Epidemic Spreading in Scale-Free Networks," *Phy. Rev. Let.*, Vol. 86, No. 14, 2 April 2001.

[3] N. Leavitt, "Mobile Phones: The Next Frontier for Hackers?," *Computer*, April 2005.

[4] S. A. Khayam and H. Radha, "Analyzing the Spread of Active Worms over VANET," *ACM Mobicom International Workshop on VANET*, October, 2004.

[5] J. Kurhinen and J. Vuori, "Information Diffusion in a Single-Hop Mobile Peer-to-Peer Network," *ISCC, 10th IEEE Symposium on Computers and Communications*, 137-142, 2005.

[6] C. Bettstetter, H. Hartenstein, and X. Perez-Costa, "Stochastic Properties of the Random Waypoint Mobility Model," *Wireless Networks*, Vol.10, NO. 5, 555-567, 2004.

[7] W. O. Kermack et al., "A Contribution to the Mathematical Theory of Epidemics," *Proc. Roy. Soc.*, A 115, 700-721, 1927.

415

Algorithm Construction of Pedestrian Detection
Based on Image Processing by using Infrared Camera

Yue ZHAO and Osamu ONO

Department of Electric and Electronic Engineering, Meiji University,
Kanagawa, JAPAN 243-8571
{ce55034, ono}@isc.meiji.ac.jp

ABSTRACT

The purpose of this study is to construct an algorithm to detect pedestrian based on image processing methods by using an in-vehicle far infrared camera. By using the infrared camera, the radiation is detected and turned into an image. Hotter objects will be showed up in different shades than cooler objects, enabling us to acquire significant targets. Therefore, our algorithm can help drivers detect pedestrian on the roadway at night, especially in where out of the range of light.

As detection methods, we pick out the heat objects by basing on the relation between the gray-level value of pixel and the threshold which is according to the image depths of the maximum and the minimum. And then we color the area of heat object red, green or blue, and color the rest black. We can recognize plural objects in an image through labeling method and judge whether they are pedestrians by analyzing chain code and characteristics of shape. Based on the detection methods described above, the experiments were carried out in real environment. For safer system, we are going to consider the detection methods and carry out more extensive tests in different conditions.

KEY WORDS: Infrared, Pedestrian Detection, Image Processing

INTRODUCTION

If we analyze the numbers of deaths and injuries in traffic accident, we can see that there are many accidents caused by night driving. For example, 80,714 pedestrians were injured and 2,104 were killed in 2005 in Japan. In particular, the deaths occurred at night were more than during the day, since human vision is weaker at night.

With these premises, the development of systems that are capable of reducing the number or the severity of traffic accident involving pedestrians is welcomed, especially night driver assistance system.

In our study, we use images obtained from far infrared camera to detect pedestrians. In addition to giving the driver an enhanced view of the road ahead at night, we construct an algorithm to provide cautions that inform the driver of the presence of pedestrians who are either on the road ahead or want to cross the vehicle's path.

CHARACTERIZATION OF INFRARED IMAGE

Infrared image is used to simplify pedestrian detection in this study. The radiation is detected and turned into an image, hotter objects showing up in different shades than cooler objects, enabling us to acquire significant targets. Therefore, pedestrian belonging to the upper range in the gray-level scale will enable us to separate from the surroundings sufficiently. However, there are many other warm objects, such as lights, traffic signals, motorcycles and automobiles, which have a similar behavior to pedestrian. This problem makes the image more complex and pedestrian detection more difficult.

DETECTION METHODS

In this paper, we present an algorithm for detecting pedestrian using infrared images. It is based on the following methods.

4-color Image Reorganization

It is extremely essential to distinguish between the objects of interest and the rest in image analysis. As the process of this method, thresholding is performed for every pixel. A parameter called *border* is calculated and applied to the original image $a[m,n]$ as follows:

$$border = \frac{max + min}{2}$$

In this expression, the max is the maximum gray-level value of the pixels in the image $a[m,n]$ and the min is the minimum one. After thresholding process, the image will be colored red, green, blue, and black, based on the concept that infrared heat-emitting objects in infrared image belonging to the upper range in the gray-level scale. The output is an image where objects are on red, green and blue and background is on black, due to its gray-level value. The red area is higher than the green and the green area is higher than the blue in temperature. The standard is established and the coefficients of the following expressions were experimentally determined.
Red area:
The area where heat is radiated from object;

If $a[m,n]>(border - max)*0.6 - border$.
Blue area:
The area where only a little heat can be detected;
If $a[m,n]<(border - max)*0.25 - border$.
Green area:
The area is between the red and the blue.

Except the area that is colored above, the rest is taken as the background of the image and is colored black. These four colors will be used as temperature distribution to provide more confident information, helping us to achieve accurate result.

Image Complement

Just 4-color image reorganization process is inadequate to detect object exactly. Because, for example, the upper half and the lower half of the body are separated by some hollows of background color when the temperature of the abdominal region cannot be detected. Therefore, it is necessary to complete 4-color image. Image complement is performed by following steps:
1. To search pixel that was colored red, green or blue.
2. To detect the edge of the pixels searched in step1, based on Prewitt edge detection.
3. If the gray-level value of the pixel within the edge detected in step2 is not too low, to fill up the pixel to complete the shape of the object.
The results are shown in Fig.1.

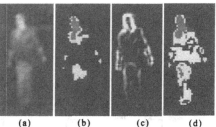

(a)   (b)   (c)   (d)
Fig.1 Detection results: (a) original infrared image, (b) result of 4-color image reorganization, (c) result of edge detection, (d) result of image complement.

417

Labeling

Labeling is the process of assigning a unique value to the pixels belonging to the same connected region. Labeling using the 8-neighborhood is adopted in this study.

The result of labeling, all pixels in a heat-emitting object sharing similar value, is imperative for pedestrian analysis when there are plural pedestrians in an image.

Chain Code

Several techniques exist to represent the region or object by describing its contour. In this study, we use chain code to realize contour representation. The codes associated with eight possible directions are the chain codes. With x as the current contour pixel position, the codes are generally defined as:

5	6	7
4	x	0
3	2	1

Even codes {0,2,4,6} correspond to horizontal or vertical directions; odd codes {1,3,5,7} correspond to diagonal directions. Each code can be considered as the angular direction, in multiples of 45 degrees. We must move to go from one contour pixel to the next to find out its chain code. Then we can get a complete description of the contour by using the absolute coordinates of the contour pixels and the chain codes. It is illustrated in Fig.2.

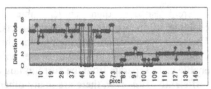

Fig.2 Example of diagramed chain codes

Diagramed chain codes signifying shape characteristic, are used to analyze its contour.

ALGORITHM DESCRIPTION

The algorithm, whose block diagram is shown in Fig.3, is divided into the following parts:
· distinguishing between the objects of interest and the rest, based on 4-color image reorganization.
· reducing false detection, based on image complement.
· simplifying the detection of respective pedestrian, based on labeling.
· obtaining the characteristic of contour, based on chain code.

And furthermore, elimination processes are performed to remove the object which has non-pedestrian characteristic. Elimination I is based on the size, the center of gravity and temperature distribution. Elimination II is based on the length and the complication of the contour.

DISCUSSION OF RESULTS

As the fundamental road situation assumed, it is in the night pedestrian exists

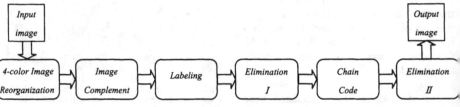

Fig.3 Block diagram of the algorithm

on the road ahead and cannot be seen easily. Especially the area where is without sufficient lighting.

The purposes of our algorithm are to provide cautions to driver and to increase the safety of the pedestrians. The two main tasks are as follows:

1. The distance range of detection is aimed at between 50 and 80M.

2. The infrared heat-emitting object without any specific characteristic of human is to be removed. In other words, this algorithm is designed to detect only pedestrian.

The original images and the results in different situations are shown in Fig.4 and Fig.5.

· case1: few heat-emitting objects exist, excluding pedestrian.

· case2: many heat-emitting objects (automobile, etc.) exist, excluding pedestrian.

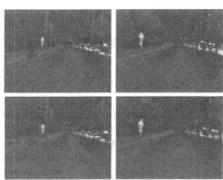
Fig.5 Result of pedestrian detection in case2

The results show that this algorithm is able to detect one or more, faraway or close pedestrians, even in a complex background. The algorithm developed proves to be effective in different situations. We will carry out more extensive tests in different conditions.

REFERENCES

1. F.Takeda, Algorithm Construction of Pedestrians Detection Based On Image Processing, Meiji University, Japan, 2006
2. M. Bertozzi, A. Broggi, P. Grisleri, T. Graf and M. Meinecke, Pedestrian Detection for Driver Assistance Using Multiresolution Infrared Vision, IEEE TRANSACTIONS ON VEHICULAR TECHNOLOGY, VOL. 53, NO. 6, NOVEMBER 2004, pp.1666-1678.
3. Emmanuel Goubet, Joseph Katz, and Fatih Porikli, Pedestrian Tracking Using Thermal Infrared Imaging, Mitsubishi Electric Research Laboratories, Cambridge, USA

Fig.4 Result of pedestrian detection in case1

Color Based Tracking Vision for the Intelligent Space

Kazuyuki MORIOKA*, Takeshi SASAKI** and Hideki HASHIMOTO**

* Department of Electrical Engineering, School of Science and Technology
Meiji University
1-1-1 Higashimita, Tama-ku, Kawasaki, Kanagawa, 214-8517 Japan
(E-mail: morioka@isc.meiji.ac.jp)
** Institute of Industrial Science
University of Tokyo
4-6-1 Komaba, Meguro-ku, Tokyo, 153-8505 Japan

ABSTRACT

We proposed the intelligent space as the human-robot coexistent system. The intelligent space is the space where many intelligent devices, such as computers and sensors like the color CCD cameras, are distributed. The Intelligent Space requires functions of identifying and tracking the multiple objects seamlessly in order to realize appropriate services to users under the multi-camera environments. In this paper, color based tracking vision modules of the intelligent space are described. MeanShift method is applied for tracking of the objects. Object tracking performance depends on the configuration of the color histograms because this method calculates the object movement between frames based on the color histogram models of objects. This paper investigates how the quantization level of the color histogram affects the tracking performance using the Meanshift method. Then, color based tracking vision system is developed and the tracking results are shown.

KEY WORDS: Image processing, Color histogram, Tracking, Intelligent Environment

INTRODUCTION

Robot systems for supporting human life are desired recently. For that purpose, the robots need to recognize a human living environment that changes dynamically. However, it is difficult to achieve it only with the sensors carried in a stand-alone robot. Then, the research field on the intelligent environments based on the sensor network has been expanding [1][2]. The intelligent environments generally utilize many intelligent devices, such as computers and sensors in order to improve the performance of the robots. We proposed the intelligent space (iSpace) [3] as the human-robot coexistent system with the networked vision sensors. Vision sensor network offers promising prospects as the

infrastructure for the robots in order to coexist with human in the environment such as house, factory, hospital and so on. The intelligent space is designed to achieve a human-centered service by accelerating the physical and psychological interaction

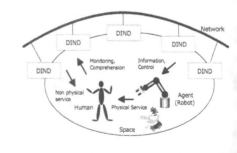

Figure 1 Intelligent Space

420

between humans and robots. Color CCD camera based vision modules are exploited as the intelligent devices of the iSpace. These vision modules include processing and networking parts in addition to sensing images. We call these modules DINDs (Distributed Intelligent Network Devices). A concept of the iSpace is shown in Fig.1. Location information of the objects in the space is required for improving the recognition performance of the robots. It is the most important for the sensing system in the intelligent space to track the objects and to get the location of them by processing of the images acquired in the DINDs. This paper focuses on color based tracking with DINDs. Hybrid tracking based on mean shift algorithm [4] is proposed for tracking of the objects. Object tracking performance depends on the configuration of the color histograms because this algorithm calculates the object movement between frames based on the color histogram models of objects. This paper investigates how the quantization level of the color histogram affects the tracking performance using the mean shift method.

VISION SYSTEM IN ISPACE

DIND
Figure.2 shows the configuration of DINDs in the intelligent space. The role of each DIND is separated into two parts. Object ID assignment, tracking, and position estimation are basic functions of each DIND. Each DIND need the basic function independently of condition of other cameras, because of keeping the robustness and the flexibility of the system. On the other hand, cooperation between many cameras is also needed for achievement of the advanced function of the intelligent space. Up to now, control of mobile robots supporting human [5] and guiding robots beyond the monitoring area of one camera [6] were

proposed and developed as the advanced application of the intelligent space. The target objects of tracking in the sensing basis based on DINDs includes many kinds of objects such as human, robots and the other mechanical objects. Then, it is impossible to teach the models of all objects to all DINDs in advance. The ability of modeling the object for seamless tracking without prior information is required for each DIND.

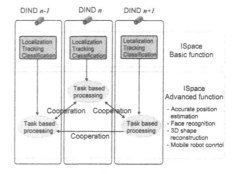

Figure 2 DIND Configuration

Color Histogram Based Object Model
Object tracker in the DIND exploits color histograms which represent the target feature. The object representation based on the color histogram is relatively stable against deformation and occlusion. New moving object regions are extracted after the dilation, erosion, and clustering to the binary image separated from captured image by comparison with the background image. The small object region is removed as the noise. Color histogram of bounding box including each object region is treated as the object model. Object model is denoted by Q and its component q_u ($u=1,...,m$) is computed as

$$q_u = C \sum_{i=1}^{n} k(\|\mathbf{x}_i^*\|) \delta[b(\mathbf{x}_i^*) - u] \qquad (1)$$

$$C = \{\sum_{i=1}^{n} k(\|\mathbf{x}_i^*\|^2)\}^{-1} \qquad (2)$$

where, x_i^* ($i=1,\cdots,n$) is the pixel locations of the object model centered at 0. k is the kernel function. Details are described in the next section. The function b associates to the pixel at location x_i^* the index $b(x_i^*)$ of its bin in the quantized feature space. n is the number of pixels in the object region. The feature space is configured by HSV color space. Fig.3 shows the example of the color model in the case of using HS color space. δ is the Kronecker delta function.

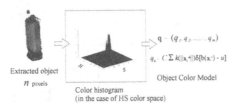

Extracted object
n pixels

Color histogram
(in the case of HS color space)

$q = (q_1, q_2 \cdots q_m)$

$q_u = C \sum k(\|x_i^*\|)\delta[b(x_i^*) - u]$

Object Color Model

Figure 3 Object Color Model

COLOR BASED TRACKING

Overview of Tracking Algorithm
Recently, the tracking system based on mean shift algorithm is reported that it is suitable for the color region tracking [4]. In this algorithm, weighted mean shift is used for multiple color region tracking. Weight is computed as follows based on the color information of the object regions and background image. In the research field of motion-based object tracking, one of the challenging tasks is how to deal well with the rapid movement of the object. An integrated method mean shift and Kalman filter has been proposed in the previous studies. It has proven to be efficient and relatively robust to the rapid movement of the object. In addition, this method has been compensated the weakness of mean shift tracker with kalman filter. However, in case that the movement of a target is changed suddenly by collision with obstacles such a human, floor, and so on, the tracker loses the target object and there are few chances

to recover. By adding changes to this algorithm, we were able to deal with the above problem. The dissimilarity of histograms between the model and the candidate region is expressed by a metric based on the Bhattacharyya distance. This measure has shown the benefit to achieve stable and efficient tracking in our research. In order to localize the target object, the mean shift procedure and the Kalman filter is used. In our research, we added feedback loop after the mean shift procedure. Tracking experiments in which our method coped with the sudden change of the object movement are presented.

MeanShift Tracking
In the model based object tracking using color, decline in reliability of the target color information derived from the background is inevitable. A kernel tracking has been introduced in order to reduce adulteration of the background color. In this method, the target region is assigned higher weights to the center pixels against the peripheral pixels. Thus, the reliability of color information of the target is increased. In our research, we exploit the triangle kernel to achieve the robust tracking toward the rapid moving object. Triangle kernel is given by

$$k(x) = \begin{cases} 1-x & |x| < 1 \\ 0 & otherwise \end{cases} \qquad (3)$$

where x is coordinates in the target area centered at 0. Bhattacharyya distance is recommended for real time object tracking which attaches importance to efficiency and stability. Bhattacharyya distance is given as

$$d(Q,P) = \sqrt{1 - \sum_{u=1}^{m} \sqrt{p_u q_u}} \qquad (4)$$

Component q_u of target model Q is represented by Eq.(1). Component p_u of target candidate P is represented by Eq.(5).

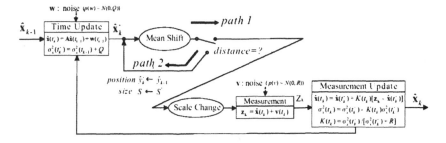

Figure 4 Hybrid Tracking Algorithm

$$p_u = C_h \sum_{i=1}^{n_h} k(\|x_i\|) \delta[b(x_i) - u] \qquad (5)$$

$$C_h = \{\sum_{i=1}^{n_h} k(\left\|\frac{y - x_i}{h}\right\|^2)\}^{-1} \qquad (6)$$

where x_i denote the pixel locations of the target candidate centered at y. h is the $\max\|y - x_i\|$. y is the weighted mean coordinate based on the similarity of color between object model and object candidate. y is used as the center of the target candidate.

$$y = \frac{\sum_{i=1}^{n_h} x_i w_i}{\sum_{i=1}^{n_h} w_i} \qquad (7)$$

$$w_i = \sum_{u=1}^{m} \sqrt{\frac{q_u}{p_u}} \delta[b(x_i) - u] \qquad (8)$$

Hybrid Tracking

A new approach toward target localization is shown in Fig.5. In conventional algorithm using mean shift and Kalman filter, the target location is decided through the "path1" on the Fig.5. To handle the sudden change of the movement, we added feedback loop "path2" after the mean shift process. In this algorithm, regular target localization process goes through "path1". In case that unexpected change of the movement happened and the tracker lost the object, this estimation depends on the Bhattacharyya distance, the second

localization procedure starts from the position of the target in the previous frame and with the size of the region is temporarily expanded through "path2". The magnification ratio is application dependent. We use an area less than twice the target area and adopt scalar value of the velocity vector of the target object. The means shift tracker has the weakness. That is unable to cope with rapid movement of object because the object is not included in the predicted area with Kalman filter. On the other hand, the mean shift tracker shows stability and efficiency in case that the target region overlaps with the target object. The function of "path2" is to operate the mean shift. The greatest advantage of our hybrid algorithm is that continuation of the object tracking is possible efficiently, without applying load to a system. Tracking

Figure 5 Tracking Results

423

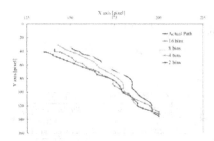 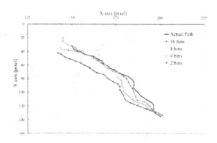

Figure 6 Tracking Performance

results are shown in Fig.5. In this experiment, each axis of the HSV color space is divided to 32 bins.

Tracking Performance

Color number of the model histogram changes the performance in the mean shift tracking. In this subsection, tracking performance using HS color histogram is described. Object model based on the histogram of 32 bins was used for the tracking experiment in Fig.5. Tracking based on simplified object models shorten the image processing time in every frame. Fig.6 shows the example of this change depending on the color number of the histogram during tracking with mean shift tracker. Horizontal axis and vertical axis indicate the X and Y coordinate of the image respectively. The target object was tracked from bottom right to top left of the image. When the tracking performance is evaluated by the distance from the actual path to the tracked path, this result shows that the tracking performance decreases in cased that the number of H bins are too big or too small. On the other hand, the tracking performance doesn't change largely according to the number of S bins. The configuration of the HS histogram has an effect on the tracking performance in this way.

CONCLUSION

In this paper, color based tracking method in the intelligent space was described. Hybrid tracking algorithm based on mean shift tracking and color histogram was proposed. Experimental results showed that the proposed method was efficient for multiple objects tracking under the occlusion. The tracking performance according to the variance of the color histograms was also described. As a future work, representation method of objects that are close to achromatic color will have to be investigated.

REFERENCES

1. Rodney A.Brooks, The Intelligent Room Project, Proceedings of the Second International Cognitive Technology Conference (CT'97), Aizu, Japan, August 1997.
2. T. Sato, T. Harada, T. Mori, Environment-Type Robot System "Robotic Room" Featured by Behavior Media, Behaviour Contents, and Behavior Adaptation, IEEE/ASME Trans. on Mechatronics, Vol.9, No.3, 2004, pp.529-534.
3. J.-H. Lee, H. Hashimoto, Intelligent Space - concept and contents, Advanced Robotics, Vol.16, No.3, 2002, pp.265-280.
4. D. Comaniciu, V. Ramesh, P. Meer, Kernel-Based Object Tracking, IEEE Transactions on Pattern Analysis and Machine Intelligence, Vol.25, No.5, 2003, pp.564-577.
5. K. Morioka, J.-H. Lee, H. Hashimoto, Human-Following Mobile Robot in a Distributed Intelligent Sensor Network, IEEE Trans. on Industrial Electronics, Vol.51, No.1, 2004, pp.229-237.
6. J.-H. Lee, K. Morioka, N. Ando, H. Hashimoto, Cooperation of Distributed Intelligent Sensors in Intelligent Environment, IEEE/ASME Trans. on Mechatronics, Vol.9, No.3, 2004, pp.535-543.

A Study on Less Computational Load of ALE
for Estimating Sinusoidal Noise

Toshihiro MIYAWAKI*, Naoto SASAOKA*, Yoshio ITOH* and Kensaku FUJII**

* Department of Electrical and Electronic Engineering, Faculty of Engineering
Tottori University
4-101 Koyama-minami, Tottori, 680-8552 Japan
(E-mail: sasaoka@ele.tottori-u.ac.jp)
** Graduate School of Engineering
University of Hyogo
2167 Shosha, Himeji, 671-2201 Japan

ABSTRACT

A noise reduction system based on adaptive line enhancer (ALE) and noise estimation filter has been proposed to reduce both wideband and sinusoidal noise in noisy speech. However, the noise reduction system cannot avoid increasing computation load. ALE for estimating the sinusoidal noise especially uses large numbers of taps in order to increase the estimation accuracy of the sinusoidal noise. In this paper, the ALE with less computation load is proposed. The tap coefficients of the ALE have a peak for each pitch period of sinusoidal noise. The proposed method decreases the number of taps by making use of a characteristic of the ALE.

KEY WORDS: Noise reduction, Wideband noise, Sinusoidal noise, ALE, Less computational load

INTRODUCTION

A large variety of noise reduction systems have been proposed to reduce the background noise in noisy speech. Spectral Subtraction method is well-known as the noise reduction system which uses only one microphone [1]. However, musical tones are caused by residual error. In addition the processing delay occurs due to frame processing. Furthermore, the SS requires prior estimation of a noise spectrum. In order to solve these problems, we have proposed the noise reconstruction system (NRS) based on linear predictor (LP) and system identification [2]. However, since both the sinusoidal noise and speech are represented by a sinusoidal signal with a fundamental frequency and harmonics, it cannot be reduced by the NRS. In real environments, the background noise includes not only wideband noise but also sinusoidal noise. Therefore, it is important to reduce both the wideband noise and the sinusoidal noise.

We have already proposed the noise reduction system to reduce wideband and sinusoidal noise [3]. The system uses two ALEs and noise estimation filter (NEF). The noise reduction system reduces the wideband and sinusoidal noise well. However, the system cannot avoid increasing the computation load because the system uses several adaptive filters. Especially, ALE for estimating the sinusoidal noise uses large numbers of taps in order to increase the estimation accuracy of sinusoidal noise.

In this paper, the noise reduction system with less computation load is proposed. The tap coefficients of the ALE have the peak for each pitch period of sinusoidal noise. Therefore, in the proposed system, only the tap coefficients reacting to the pitch period are updated. Thus, the number of taps decreases.

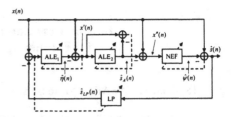

Figure 1 Noise reduction system with feedback path

NOISE REDUCTION SYSTEM BASED ON ALE AND NOISE ESTIMATION FILTER

Principle of Noise Reduction System
The noise reduction system based on ALE and NEF [3] is shown in Fig.1. The input signal is given as follows:

$$x(n) = s(n) + \psi(n) \tag{1}$$

where $\psi(n)=\xi(n)+\eta(n)$ represents the background noise. $\xi(n)$ and $\eta(n)$ are wideband and sinusoidal noise respectively.

The sinusoidal noise is reduced by ALE_1. ALE_1 estimates the sinusoidal noise in noisy speech. Then, the signal occupied by the speech and wideband noise is obtained by subtracting the estimated sinusoidal noise from $x(n)$. The principle of sinusoidal noise estimation is explained in next sub-section. The wideband noise is reduced by ALE_2 after obtaining $x'(n)$. Assuming that the signal delayed by the pitch period of speech is included in the tap inputs of ALE_2, the ALE_2 can estimate only the speech $s(n)$ [3]. In addition, NEF which is an adaptive filter is used to improve the noise reduction ability and the quality of enhanced speech. The signal occupied by the background noise $x''(n)$ is obtained by subtracting $\hat{s}_A(n)$ from the noisy speech. In the NEF, $x''(n)$, $\psi(n)$ and $s(n)$ are assumed to be an input signal, a

desired signal and a disturbance respectively. The enhanced speech is obtained by subtracting the estimated background noise $\hat{\psi}(n)$ from $x(n)$. In the ALE_1, the estimation accuracy of sinusoidal noise is degraded due to the speech components included in an input signal of ALE_1. We introduce a feedback path to the noise reduction system in order to solve the problem. The feedback path with a LP decreases the speech component included in an input of ALE_1.

Sinusoidal noise estimation using ALE
Let the sinusoidal noise be the stationary periodic signal, for example, ventilating fan noise. On the other hand, the speech signal is the non-stationary signal during the long time interval. The output of ALE_1 is given by

$$\hat{\eta}(n) = \sum_{k=1}^{L} h'_k(n) \cdot x(n - d_1 - k) \tag{2}$$

where $h'_k(n)$ and d_1 are k-th tap coefficient and decorrelation parameter, respectively. Assuming that there is enough delay d_1 to fade out the autocorrelation of speech, the ALE_1 can estimate only the sinusoidal noise. The stationary period of speech is known to be 20ms [4], that is 160 samples by the signal sampled by 8kHz. Thus d_1 needs to be set to more than 160 at least.

LESS COMPUTATIONAL LOAD

The noise reduction system based on ALEs and NEF uses several adaptive filters. Therefore, increasing computation load is unavoidable. Especially, ALE_1 needs large numbers of taps for improving the estimation accuracy of sinusoidal noise. In this paper, ALE_1 with less computational load is proposed in order to solve the problem.

Figure 2 shows the tap coefficient of ALE_1 at the time the noise reduction system is carried out. The number of taps and d_1 were set to 400 and 160 respectively. The speech superposed on wideband and sinusoidal noise was used as input signal. The sinusoidal noise is represented as follows:

$$\eta(n) = \sum_{k=1}^{10} \cos(2\pi k f_0 nT + 2\pi r(k)) \quad (3)$$

where f_0 is pitch frequency of sinusoidal noise, which is set to 125 Hz and pitch period is 64 samples in the case of signal sampled by 8 kHz. T and $r(k)$ ($0 \le r(k) < 1$) represent a sampling period and a uniform random number respectively. From Fig. 2, it is verified that the tap coefficients has the peak for each pitch period of sinusoidal noise. In the proposed system, on the assumption that the pitch period of the sinusoidal noise is known, only the tap coefficients reacting to the pitch period are updated. Thus, the number of updated tap coefficients is decreased and ALE_1 with less computation load is realized.

The computation load of the noise reduction system is evaluated. Parameter shown in Table 1 is used to evaluate the computation load. The adaptive algorithms for updating tap coefficients are least mean square (LMS) algorithm and normalized LMS (NLMS) algorithm [5]. The algorithms are given as follows:
(LMS algorithm)

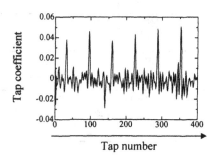

Figure 2 Tap coefficients of ALE_1

$$\mathbf{h}(n+1) = \mathbf{h}(n) + \mu \mathbf{u}(n)e(n) \quad (4)$$

(NLMS algorithm)

$$\mathbf{h}(n+1) = \mathbf{h}(n) + \mu \frac{\mathbf{u}(n)e(n)}{\|\mathbf{u}(n)\|^2} \quad (5)$$

where $\mathbf{h}(n)$, $\mathbf{u}(n)$, $e(n)$ and μ are tap coefficient vector, tap input vector, an error signal and a step size respectively. In addition, the number of multiplications, additions and divisions per sample of adaptive filter, which uses M tap coefficients, is shown as follows:
(LMS algorithm)
  Multiplication; $2M+1$
  Addition; $2M-1$
(NLMS algorithm)
  Multiplication; $3M+1$
  Addition; $3M-1$
  Division; 1
Table 2 shows the number of multiplications, divisions and additions. Comparing ALE_1 of the proposed system with that of the conventional system, the number of multiplications and additions decreases by about 95%. Additionally, the number of multiplications and additions decreases by about 60% in a total system. It is verified that the computation load decreases by the proposed system.

Table 1 Parameter

ALE$_1$ (NLMS)	Decorrelation parameter d_1	160
	Number of tap coefficients L	400
	Step Size	0.001
ALE$_2$ (LMS)	Decorrelation parameter d_2	19
	Number of tap coefficients M	83
	Step Size	0.3
NEF (NLMS)	Number of tap coefficients K	128
	Step Size	0.001
LP (LMS)	Number of tap coefficients S	90
	Step Size	0.1

Table 2 Computation load

Conventional System

	Multiplication	Division	Addition
ALE$_1$ (NLMS)	1201	1	1198
ALE$_2$ (LMS)	167	0	165
NRF (NLMS)	385	1	382
LP (LMS)	181	0	179
Total	1934	2	1928

Proposed System

	Multiplication	Division	Addition
ALE$_1$ (NLMS)	55	1	52
ALE$_2$ (LMS)	167	0	165
NRF (NLMS)	385	1	382
LP (LMS)	181	0	179
Total	788	2	778

SIMULATION RESULTS

The performance of the proposed noise reduction system was evaluated. All sound data prepared in simulations were sampled by 8kHz in 16bit resolution. The speech signal spoken by a female talker was used. As the stationary background noise, the wideband noise and the sinusoidal noise were used. The sinusoidal noise represented as Eq. (3) was used. In this simulation, the power ratio of wideband noise to sinusoidal noise was set to 0 dB. The signal to noise ratio (SNR) and QS were used to evaluate the noise reduction ability and quality of enhanced speech respectively. In addition, $E_{SN}(n)$ is used to evaluate the estimation accuracy of sinusoidal noise. The SNR$_{IN}$ and SNR$_{OUT}$ represent the input and output SNR respectively. These indices are defined as follows:

$$SNR_{IN} = 10\log_{10}\frac{\sum_{j=1}^{N}s^2(j)}{\sum_{j=1}^{N}\psi^2(j)} \quad (6)$$

$$SNR_{out} = 10\log_{10}\frac{\sum_{j=1}^{N}y_s^2(j)}{\sum_{j=1}^{N}y_\psi^2(j)} \quad (7)$$

$$QS = 10\log_{10}\frac{\sum_{j=1}^{N}s^2(j)}{\sum_{j=1}^{N}\{s(j)-y_s(j)\}^2} \quad (8)$$

$$E_{SN}(n) = 10\log_{10}\frac{\sum_{j=0}^{127}\eta^2(n-j)}{\sum_{j=0}^{127}e_\eta^2(n-j)} \quad (9)$$

where N is the number of samples. $y_s(j)$ and $y_\psi(j)$ are components of speech and noise in the output $y(j)$ respectively. $e_\eta(n) = \eta(n)-\hat{\eta}(n)$ represents the estimation error of sinusoidal noise in ALE$_1$.

Figure 3 shows the estimation accuracy of sinusoidal noise. From the simulation results, $E_{SN}(n)$ is not degraded by the proposed system. Figure 4 and 5 show the results of noise reduction. Compared Fig. 4(d) with Fig. 4(c), the SNR and QS do not decrease in a 0dB environment. From Fig. 5, SNR$_{OUT}$ and QS are not degraded at each SNR$_{IN}$. It is verified that the ALE$_1$ with less computation load does not decrease the noise reduction ability.

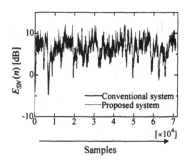

Figure 3 Estimation accuracy of sinusoidal noise

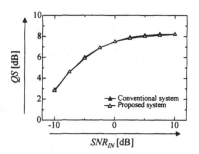

Figure 6 QS performance

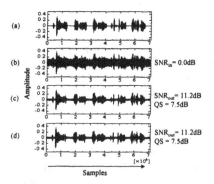

Figure 4 Waveforms of noise reduction. (a)Clean speech. (b)Noisy speech. (c)Enhanced speech by conventional system. (d)Enhanced speech by proposed system

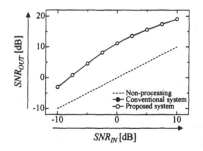

Figure 5 SNR_OUT performance.

CONCLUTIONS

The ALE with the less computation load is proposed. It makes use of the convergence characteristic. From the simulation results, we have verified that the estimation accuracy of sinusoidal noise is not degraded by the proposed system. In future work, we will research the noise reduction ability for actual background noise.

REFERENCES

1. S. F. Boll, "Suppression of acoustic noise in speech using spectral subtraction," IEEE Trans. Acoust., Speech, Signal Processing, vol. ASSP-27, no.2, pp.113-120, April 1979.
2. A. Kawamura, K. Fujii, Y. Itoh and Y. Fukui, "A new noise reduction method using estimated noise spectrum," IEICE Trans. Fundamentals, vol.E85-A, no.4, pp.784-789, April 2002.
3. N. Sasaoka, K. Sumi, Y. Itoh and K. Fujii, "A new noise reduction system based on ALE and noise reconstruction filter," Proc. of 2005 IEEE Int. Symp. Circuits Syst., pp.272-275, May 2005.
4. L.R. Rabiner, R.W. Schafer, Digital Processing of Speech Signals, Prentice-Hall, New Jersey, 1978.
5. S. Haykin, Introduction to adaptive filters, Macmillan publishing, New York, 1984.

Evaluation of Adaptive Modulation and Coding Applied on a 400 Mbps OFDM Wireless Communication System

Notuaki OTSUKI, Singo YOSHIZAWA and Yoshikazu MIYANAGA

Graduate School of Information Science and Technology, Hokkaido University
Kita-14 Nishi-9, Kita-ku, Sapporo, Hokkaido,060–0814 Japan
(E-mail : noppi@csm.ist.hokudai.ac.jp)

ABSTRACT

This paper presents a high throughput wireless system which is able to reach up to 400 Mbps using OFDM with adaptive modulation and coding (AMC). Our objective is to increase an actual throughput in the OFDM wireless system under various environments. We apply an adaptive modulation technique to each subcarriers to keep required BER performance for realizing high-quality communications. Convolutional coding is added to the adaptive modulation scheme to obtain higher PER performance under small CNR environments. In the computer simulation, we evaluate PER performance and demonstrate the efficiency of the AMC in a throughput analysis.

KEY WORDS:OFDM, Adaptive modulation

Introduction

As a demand of high data rate transmissions through radio channels has been growing recent years, lots of wide band OFDM (Orthogonal Frequency Division Multiplexing) wireless communication technologies are proposed. OFDM is well known especially in the field of wireless LAN communication systems. The OFDM technique divides a channel into some subchannels which have so narrow frequency bandwidth that each of them can be regarded as a flat fading channel independently. In spite of it, modulation schemes are all same. The system has to choose a lower modulation scheme so as to fulfill required performance under the bad conditions in each sub-channel.

Adaptive modulation and coding (AMC) is applied to solve the above issue [3]. In OFDM systems using the AMC, the subcarriers with the good channel condition can employ a higher modulation scheme and realize high throughput performance as a result. The AMC is also paid much attention as a module of cognitive radio systems. The cognitive radio systems can compose a optimized radio system by itself making any of parameters and modules reasonable for channel condition [4]. We apply the AMC to a 300 Mbps OFDM wireless LAN system [2] and evaluate the throughput performance on the PHY layer.

1 300 Mbps OFDM system

This section introduces the OFDM system in an 80 MHz bandwidth on which we consider the AMC. This OFDM system is based on a packet communication extending the IEEE802.11a standard. Figure 1 shows the structure of a OFDM packet frame format. Their parameters are listed on Table 1. The short preamble is used to synchronize the received signals. Each of

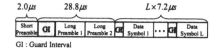

2.0μs   **28.8μs**   **L×7.2μs**

GI : Guard Interval

Figure 1: Packet frame format

Table 1: Parameters of OFDM system

Parameter	Value
F_b : Bandwidth	80 MHz
K : FFT point	512
N_s : Number of data subcarrier	480
N_p : Number of pilot subcarrier	20
T_{short} : Short Preamble duration	2.0 μs
T_{long} : Long Preamble duration	14.4 μs
T_{sym} : Symbol duration	7.2 μs
T_{gi} : Guard Interval duration	0.8 μs
T_{fft} : FFT/IFFT window duration	6.4 μs
N_b : Coded bits per subcarrier	2,4,6
R : Coding rate	1/2, 3/4

two long preambles inserted just before the data symbols has the same data sequence to estimate a noise power and a channel frequency response used for equalizing the multipath fading affection. According to the IEEE802.11a standard [1], the transmit rate is given by:

$$D = \frac{N_b \cdot N_s \cdot R}{T_{sym}} . \qquad (1)$$

When it adopts the mode 4 shown in Table 2, the parameters of $R = 3/4$ and $N_b = 6$ are substituted to the above equation and a 300-Mbps data rate is worked out.

2 Adaptive Modulation and Coding

The principle of AMC, which uses a channel state information (CSI) and a noise power, is presented in this section.

Table 2: Transmit Mode

Mode	Transmit Rate	N_b	R	Modulation
1	66.6 Mbps	2	1/2	QPSK
2	133.3 Mbps	4	1/2	16QAM
3	200 Mbps	6	1/2	64QAM
4	300 Mbps	6	3/4	64QAM

We consider a half duplex transmission system assuming wireless LANs. On the assumption of a quasi-Gaussian channel, the channel is not changing so rapidly that we can consider the channel at the transmitting time as the channel at the receiving time right before transmitting. Hence the OFDM transceiver can get the CSI and the noise power before transmitting and execute the AMC.

2.1 Estimation of CSI

The AMC optimizes the modulation of each subcarriers according to each CNR of subcarriers at the transmitter so that BER fulfills required performance. The CSI and the noise power are used for estimation of CNRs. When the modulated signals $\mathbf{X}$ is transmitted, We can express the received signals $\mathbf{Y}$ in frequency domain as following:

$$Y_i = H_i \cdot X_i + N_i , \qquad (2)$$

where H and N are the transfer function and AWGN respectively. The suffix i shows i-th sub-channel. The CSI of H_i can be easily estimated with the conventional method:

$$\bar{H}_i = \frac{Y_i}{X_i} \qquad (3)$$

$$= H_i + \frac{N_i}{X_i} \qquad (4)$$

since the known data of $\mathbf{X}$ is obtained from the long preamble at the receiver side. The ideal $\mathbf{H}$ can be taken if a noise free condition is considered.

2.2 Estimation of CNR

From the fact that the transfer function over a packet is constant and the patterns of two long preambles are identical, the noise power can be obtained by the following equation:

$$\sigma^2 = \frac{1}{2M} \sum_{i=0}^{N} \| P_{1,i} - P_{2,i} \|^2 , \qquad (5)$$

where $P_{1,i}$ and $P_{2,i}$ are the signals at i-th subcarrier of the first and the second long

431

preamble respectively. The CNR of each subcarrier is calculated as following on the assumption that the power of AWGN is uniformly distributed over the whole frequency band:

$$CNR_i = |\bar{H}_i|^2 \cdot \frac{\mathbf{P_s}}{\sigma^2} , \qquad (6)$$

where $\mathbf{P_s}$ is the power of the transmitted signal in frequency domain. Since the power of the transmitted signal is uniformed to 1 at the modulator, Eq.(6) is expressed as:

$$CNR_i = \frac{|\bar{H}_i|^2}{\sigma^2} . \qquad (7)$$

2.3 Assignment of Modulation Scheme to each subcarrier

We can theoretically know the BER performance of digital modulated transmissions under the AWGN condition with the following formulas. The modulation scheme of each subcarrier is decided on the basis of these equations so that theoretical BER with estimated CNR_i can be better than required BER on as high order modulation as possible:

$$Prob(CNR) =$$

$$
\begin{cases}
\frac{1}{2} \cdot erfc\left(\sqrt{CNR}\right) & \text{BPSK} \\[2mm]
\frac{1}{2} \cdot erfc\left(\sqrt{\frac{CNR}{2}}\right) & \text{QPSK} \\[2mm]
\frac{3}{8} \cdot erfc\left(\sqrt{\frac{CNR}{10}}\right) - \frac{9}{64} \cdot erfc^2\left(\sqrt{\frac{CNR}{10}}\right) & \\
& \text{16QAM} \\[2mm]
\frac{7}{24} \cdot erfc\left(\sqrt{\frac{CNR}{42}}\right) - \frac{49}{384} \cdot erfc^2\left(\sqrt{\frac{CNR}{42}}\right) & \\
& \text{64QAM}
\end{cases}
$$

$$(8)$$

Figure 2 shows how to decide the modulation scheme. In this case, we take $BER = 10^{-3}$ for example which is generally considered as the criterion to be fulfilled. The system chooses the modulation among NONE, BPSK, QPSK, 16QAM and 64QAM which the estimated CNR of the subcarrier inhabits. NONE means that the subcarrier has no data.

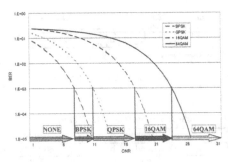

Figure 2: Theoritical BER performance against CNR

Table 3: the principle of adjusting CBPS

C	pattern of degraded modulation
1	QPSK ⇒ BPSK
	BPSK ⇒ NONE
2	64QAM ⇒ 16QAM
	16QAM ⇒ QPSK
	(QPSK ⇒ BPSK)×2
	(QPSK ⇒ BPSK) + (BPSK ⇒ NONE)
	(BPSK ⇒ NONE)×2
3	(64QAM ⇒ 16QAM) + (QPSK ⇒ BPSK)
	(64QAM ⇒ 16QAM) + (BPSK ⇒ NONE)
	(16QAM ⇒ QPSK) + (QPSK ⇒ BPSK)
	(16QAM ⇒ QPSK) + (BPSK ⇒ NONE)
	(QPSK ⇒ BPSK)×3
	(QPSK ⇒ BPSK)×2 + (BPSK ⇒ NONE)
	(QPSK ⇒ BPSK) + (BPSK ⇒ NONE)×2
	(BPSK ⇒ NONE)×3

2.4 Adjustment of CBPS for FEC

Coded bits per symbol (CBPS) has to be adjusted so that a forward error correcting (FEC) code can be applied to the system. In the other words, we have to make CBPS multiples of four when we consider coding rate $R = 3/4$.

We adjust CBPS by degrading couple of subcarriers' modulation schemes. All the patterns to be degraded are listed in TABLE 3 where C is the value of mod(CBPS,4). (64QAM ⇒ 16QAM) means that a 64QAM modulation subcarrier is degraded into a 16QAM modulation subcarrier. 2 is subtracted from CBPS by the degradation since a 16 QAM modulation subcarrier can carry 4 bits while a 64QAM modulation subcarrier can 6 bits. 2 is subtracted from CBPS by the

3 Evaluation of performance

In this section, the computer simulation verifies the system performance. Since We aim at a high throughput total system, the system should be evaluated in throughput performance. We prepare a throughput value, Th, with the following equation extending the way to calculate the theoretical data rate of the IEEE802.11a:

$$Th = \frac{\sum_{k=1}^{n}(1 - \text{subPER}_k) \cdot DBPS_k}{n \cdot T_{sym}},$$
(10)

Table 4: Simulation parameters

Modulation	fixed, adaptive
FEC	Convolutional coding Soft Viterbi decoding
BER criterion	10^{-3}, 10^{-5}
No. Symbols in a packet	8
Channel environment	HIPERLAN/2 { MODEL:A (RMS delay=50ns) MODEL:C (RMS delay=150ns) 8 path rayleigh fading (Doppler freq=50Hz) AWGN
No. transmitted packets	5000

degradation of (16QAM ⇒ QPSK) in the same way. The degradations of (QPSK ⇒ BPSK) and (BPSK ⇒ NONE) make 1 subtracted from CBPS since a QPSK modulation subcarrier and a BPSK modulation subcarrier can carry 2 bits and 1 bit respectively.

In the case of C=3 for example, 3 must be subtracted from CBPS. The best way to subtract 3 from CBPS is degradeing a 64QAM modulation subcarrier and a QPSK modulation subcarrier into a 16QAM modulation subcarrier and a BPSK modulation subcarrier respectively according to TABLE 3. If a 64QAM modulation subcarrier changes into a 16QAM modulation subcarrier, the BER performance of remaining 4 bits of the degraded subcarrier gets extremely higher. If two BPSK modulation subcarriers change into two NONE modulation subcarriers, BER performance of the other subcarriers does not get higher. Therefore the combination of as high order modulation as possible should be chosen from the options to be degraded. The higher order modulation the combination is, the more priority it has. Besides, the subcarriers that have the lowest CNR among the chosen modulation subcarriers should be degraded. Eventually we can obtain adjusted CBPS and data bits per symbol (DBPS) to be transmitted by the following equation:

$$DBPS_k = \text{adjusted}CBPS_k \times R.$$
(9)

where n is the number of transmitted packets and subPER$_k$ equals 1 if k-th packet has at least one error bit, otherwise subPER$_k$ equals 0. Table 4 shows the conditions used in the simulations. Channel model A is used for simulations of a typical office environment and channel model C for a large open space (indoor and outdoor) environment. We assume that the transmitter and receiver know overall modulation schemes completely during a packet transmittion. Figure 3 and 4 show the throughput performance in the channel model A and C respectively. The modulation scheme and coding rate of the types from 1 to 9 are corresponding to Table 5. In both channel A and C, all of the adaptive modulated transmission except for type 6 perform better than the fixed modulated transmissions until 35 dB. The type 6 and 8, which are adaptive modulated transmission without coding, go up to approximate 400 Mbps in the channel model A as the channel's noise condition becomes better. The reason why the type 5, 6 and 8 go up to 400 Mbps in the channel model A is that they are not coded for error correcting. On the contrary, the type 6 and 8 in channel model C drop down on very low transmission level after CNR of 35 dB. That is because inter symbol interference (ISI) occurs in the model C which causes a longer excess delay than a guard interval. The process of demodulation gets affected more by ISI as the transmitter

433

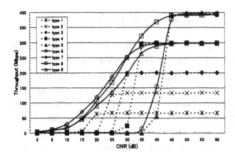

Figure 3: Throughput performance in the channel MODEL A

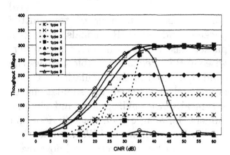

Figure 4: Throughput performance in the channel MODEL C

adopts higher order modulations. However the adaptive modulation with coding keeps good performance even in the channel model C. It shows that convolutional coding and soft decision Viterbi decoding work well even in a severe condition.

4 Conclusion

This paper presented the effectiveness of the AMC applied to an OFDM wireless LAN system which can attain 400 bps throughput in a certain channel. The computer simulation results showed that the AMC applied to a high data rate OFDM system is efficient in various environments. The adaptive modulated OFDM with the criterion of BER=10^{-3} and FEC (R=3/4) is the best totally. However, the throughput performance of adaptive modulated OFDM with the criterion of BER=10^{-5}

Table 5: the types of modulation and coding rate

line	modulation	coding rate
type 1	QPSK-fixed	1/2
type 2	16QAM-fixed	1/2
type 3	64QAM-fixed	1/2
type 4	64QAM-fixed	3/4
type 5	64QAM-fixed	no coding
type 6	adaptive (BER=10^{-3})	no coding
type 7	adaptive (BER=10^{-3})	3/4
type 8	adaptive (BER=10^{-5})	no coding
type 9	adaptive (BER=10^{-5})	3/4

and no FEC does not differ from adaptive modulated OFDM with the criterion of BER=10^{-3} and FEC (R=3/4) so much. This maximum throughput is higher after CNR of 35 dB in the channel where a maximum excess delay is not over guard interval. From this fact, the adaptive modulated OFDM with the criterion of BER=10^{-5} and no FEC may be preferred in term of achievable maximum throughput and reducing the hardware complexity.

Acknowledgments

This work is supported in parts by Semiconductor Technology Academic Research Center (STARC) in Japan, Project J-17.

References

[1] IEEE Std. 802.11a-1999, "Wireless LAN medium access control (MAC) and physical layer (PHY) specifications : high-speed physical layer in 5GHz band," 1999 Edition.

[2] Shigo Yoshizawa, Yoshikazu Miyanaga, et.al, "300-Mbps OFDM Transceiver for Wireless Communication with an 80-MHz Bandwidth," Intelligent Signal Processing and Communication Systems(ISPACS), 2005, Proceedings of 2005 International Symposium, pp.213-216, Dec.2005

[3] Hideo Kobayashi, Tadayuki Fukuhara, Hao Yuan, "Single Carrier OFDM Technique with Adaptive Modulation Method," IEICE Trans A Vol.J86-A No.12 pp.1329-1339, Dec.2003

[4] Simon Haykin,Life Fellow,IEEE "Cognitive Radio: Brain-Empowered Wireless Communications," IEEE Journal on selected areas in communications, Vol.23, No.2, Feb.2005

Deblocking of Motion JPEG using a Nonlinear Digital Filter and Frame Shift

Kentarou HAZEYAMA and Kaoru ARAKAWA

Department of Computer Science
Meiji University
1-1-1, Higashimita, Tama-ku, Kawasaki 214-8571 Japan
(E-mail: ce66732@isc.meiji.ac.jp, karakawa@cs.meiji.ac.jp)

ABSTRACT

A method to reduce blocking artifacts caused by Motion JPEG is proposed using a nonlinear digital filter and frame shift. Motion JPEG is widely used for video compression for its simple realization. But the compression rate is not high enough, thus when the compression is too much, blocking artifacts become outstanding. Authors proposed before a nonlinear digital filter, named as time and spatial ε-filter, to reduce such artifacts motion-compensated inter-frame predictive DCT coding for video. This filter is effective for the predictive coding, but is not effective enough for Motion JPEG, because the artifacts appear at the same position in different frames. In this paper, a method to reduce the artifacts using the time and spatial ε-filter combined with frame shifting is proposed. This method can effectively reduce the artifacts by shifting their position in continuous frames. Computer simulations show its high performance.

KEY WORDS: Motion JPEG, deblocking, frame shift, a nonlinear digital filter

INTRODUCTION

In the area of video data compression, DCT coding with motion-compensated inter-frame prediction has been the main technique, utilized in the standard methods, such as MPEG-1,2,4, because of its high compression rate. On the other hand, Motion JPEG, which performs JPEG compression for each frame as a still image, is also widely used in PC video capture and digital cameras, because it is realized with simple encoder and decoder. This method is also useful to extract an arbitrary frame from a video as a still picture. However, compression rate of Motion JPEG is not so high as that using inter-frame predictive coding, because the former does not utilize the information of adjacent frames as the latter. When the compression rate is set high, blocking artifacts caused by DCT coding remarkably appear.

Authors proposed before a time and special ε-filter for deblocking, that is to reduce such artifacts by data compression, for motion-compensated inter-frame predictive coding. The time and special ε-filter is a nonlinear digital filter which can be realized with a simple hardware structure, thus is suitable for real time processing of video with a small-scale hardware. This filter can reduce such artifacts enough, while keeping the edges of images sharp. When this filter is applied to Motion JPEG for deblocking, the artifacts cannot be fully reduced because they appear almost in the same style at the same position in different frames: the time-domain filtering becomes meaningless in this case.

In this paper, a new method to reduce the artifacts for Motion JPEG is proposed by combining the time and special ε-filter and frame shift. Frame shift is introduced here in order to change the position of the artifacts in adjacent frames. Since the positions are different, the artifacts come to be easily smoothed by the time and spatial ε-filter. Moreover, this method is kept quite simple, not requiring much calculation.

In this paper, first, the principle of the time and special ε-filter is described. Then, the time and spatial ε-filter with frame shift is proposed and its performance is explained. Finally, computer simulations show the high performance of the proposed system.

PRINCIPLE OF TIME AND SPATIAL ε-FILTER

Basic principle of ε-filter

The input-output relationship of the ε-filter is represented as

$$y(n) = x(n) + \sum_{i=-N}^{N} a_i F(x(n+i) - x(n)) \qquad (1)$$

where $x(n)$ and $y(n)$ are the input and output signal at time n respectively. $x(n)$ is supposed to be the sum of an original signal and small-amplitude random noise. a_i is the filter coefficient of a linear non-recursive low-pass filter, satisfying the following condition to keep the DC level unchanged.

$$\sum_{i=-N}^{N} a_i = 1 \qquad (2)$$

F is a nonlinear function which takes a form as Fig.1, bounded within a certain value ε as follows.

$$|F(p)| \leq \varepsilon ; \quad -\infty \leq p \leq \infty \qquad (3)$$

When $|p| \leq \varepsilon$, $F(p)=p$ and this filter works as a linear nonrecursive low-pass filter. Thus, if the amplitude of the added noise is less than $\varepsilon/2$, this filter can smooth the noisy input signal in the part where the original signal does not change much. On the other hand, in the part where the original signal largely changes, this filter preserves the changes in the original signal, since the difference between the input and the output of this filter is limited to a certain value ε' as follows.

$$|y(n)-x(n)| = \left| \sum_{i=-N}^{N} a_i F(x(n+i) - x(n)) \right|$$

$$\leq \sum_{i=-N}^{N} |a_i| \varepsilon \equiv \varepsilon' \qquad (4)$$

Thus, this filter smoothes out small-amplitude random noises, while preserving large-amplitude changes in the original signal, even if these changes contain high-frequency abrupt components. This filter is named as an ε-filter.

The ε-filter can effectively reduce small-amplitude random noise on images including artifacts caused by data compression, because it smoothes out such noises while keeping the edges in images sharp. In this case, two-dimensional ε-filter as follows is used for each pixel (n,m).

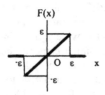

Fig.1 The nonlinear function F.

$$y(n,m) = x(n,m) + \sum_{i=-N}^{N}\sum_{j=-N}^{N} a_{i,j} F\big(x(n+i,m+j) - x(n,m)\big)$$

$$(5)$$

In comparison with other edge preserving type filters, the filter structure and the algorithm of the ε-filter are quite simple, which means that this filter is suitable for hardware implementation.

Time and spatial ε-filter

Time and spatial ε-filter is realized by combination of the intra-frame ε-filter and one-dimensional ε-filter in time domain as shown in Fig.3. Here, x(n,m,k) denotes the input image signal at the (n,m)pixel in the k-th frame. The frames are first processed by intra-frame ε-filter and then processed by time-domain ε-filter at each pixel. The output signal at the (n,m) pixel in the k-th frame y(n,m,k) is expressed as follows.

$$y(n,m,k)$$

$$= z(n,m,k) + \sum_{l=-L}^{L} b_l F_2\big(z(n,m,k-l) - z(n,m,k)\big)$$

$$(6)$$

$$z(n,m,k)$$

$$= x(n,m,k) + \sum_{i=-N}^{N}\sum_{j=-M}^{M} a_{i,j} F_1\big(x(n-i,m-j,k) - x(n,m,k)\big)$$

$$(7)$$

Here, eq(6) corresponds to two-dimensional intra-frame ε-filter as eq(5), and eq(7) to one-dimensional ε-filter as eq(1), where b_l denotes the filter

coefficients of one-dimensional linear low-pass filter. Since the magnitude and the shape of the nonlinear functions can be different in the intra-frame and the time-domain filtering, they are differently defined as F_1 and F_2 here.

In the time and spatial ε-filter, the difference between the input and the output is also limited within a certain value.

Thus, small-amplitude random noise can be reduced while keeping the abrupt changes both in time and spatial domain unchanged in the same way as the ε-filter.

TIME AND SPATIAL ε-FILTER WITH FRAME SHIFT

The ε-filtering in time domain is powerful to reduce small-amplitude random fluctuation on the time axis. When it is applied to reduce the blocking artifact of Motion JPEG, it cannot reduce the artifact sufficiently, because the blocking artifacts appear almost in the same style in adjacent frames in the same position, not making random fluctuation on time axis. The artifacts appear as a small-amplitude low-frequency noise on the time axis. Thus, the time domain ε-filter can be more powerful for deblocking of Motion JPEG video, if the boundary of DCT window is changed depending on frames. In this case, since the artifacts appear in different positions, they make small-amplitude

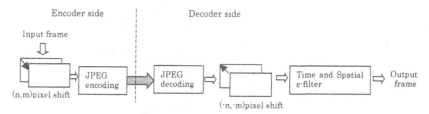

Fig.2 Schematic diagram of time and spatial e-filter with frame shift.

random fluctuation on the time axis. Fig. 2 shows the schematic diagram of the proposed method.

First, shifting the frame to be encoded by (n,m) pixels. Suppose that 8x8 DCT coding is applied, n and m take numbers from 0 to 7. Moreover, we suppose that the number n and m are different depending on frames and are known for each frame on the decoder side. A simple way to do so is to change (n,m) cyclically form (0,0) to (7,7) in 8 patterns. After shifting, the frame is encoded by JPEG. Here, the overflowing part of the frame is discarded. Finally, the code words are transmitted to the decoder side.

On the decoder side, each encoded frame is decoded and then the frame shift is recovered. For instance, if the frame was first shifted by (n,m) pixels, the decoded frame is shifted by (-n,-m) pixels. Finally, the video data is correctly reconstructed, while the position of the boundary of DCT window is changed in each frame. Such video data is suitable for time domain ε-filtering, because the blocking artifacts make random fluctuation on the time axis. Spatial ε-filtering is also useful to reduce the artifacts, thus the decoded video is proposed to processed with the time and spatial ε-filter.

In this method, boundary part of the frame is lost due to the shifting, but most of the important video objects are not placed in the boundary part, it is not a problem to discard it.

COMPUTER SIMULATIONS

Color video sequence "Susie" is used as the input. The frame size if 640x480 pixels. 8x8 DCT coding is used in Motion JPEG. Examples of the results of actual video processing are shown in Fig.3. Here, the value ε is changed in three ways depending on the location of the pixel to be processing in DCT window. The value ε is set at a large value at the corner of the 8x8 window, a moderate one on the boundary of the window besides the corners, and a small one inside the window, because the blocking artifact is large on boundary part of the window, especially at the corner, and small in the inside.

We can see that the proposed method can smooth the cheek of the face sufficiently, while keeping the roughness of the hair clear, compared with others. Here, the value ε and the window size are set experimentally, but they can be set automatically depending on the compression rate, since the amplitude of the blocking artifacts depend on the compression rate.

CONCLUSIONS

Time and spatial e-filter with frame shift is proposed for deblocking of Motion JPEG video. This method is quite simple for realization and the performance is high enough. Realization of this system by hardware for real-time processing of video is for further research.

REFERENCES

1. M. Yuen, and H.R. Wu, " A survey of hybrid MC/DPCM/DCT video coding distortions", Signal Processing, 70, pp.247-278, 1998.
2. H. Harashima, K. Odajima (currently K. Arakawa), Y. Shishikui, H. Miyakawa, "□-separating nonlinear digital filter and its applications", Trans. IEICE vol.J-66-A, no.4, pp.297-304, April 1982 (in Japanese).
3. S. Aihara, and K. Arakawa, "Motion compensated ε-filter for improving image quality of video", Proc. IEEE ISPACS2002, Nov. 2002.
4. B.Ramamurthi and A. Gersho, "Nonlinear space variant postprocessing of block coded images", IEEE Trans. Acoust., Speech & Signal Process., vol.34, no.5, pp.1258-1268, Oct.,1986.
5. S.D.Kim, J.Y.Yi, II.M.Kim, and J.B.Ra, "A deblocking filter with two separate modes in block-based video coding", IEEE Trans. Circuit & System for Video Technology, vol.9, no.1, pp.156-160, Feb.1999.
6. Watabe, Y. Arakawa, and K. Arakawa, "Nonlinear filters for multimedia applications", Proc. IEEE ICIP'99, 27AO3.6, pp.174-179, Oct.1999.

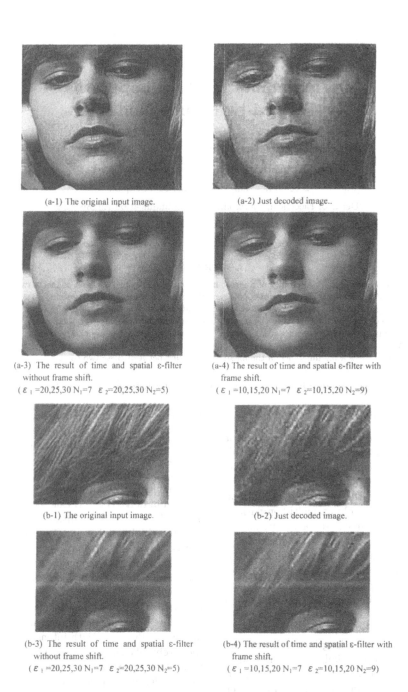

(a-1) The original input image.

(a-2) Just decoded image..

(a-3) The result of time and spatial ε-filter without frame shift.
(ε_1 =20,25,30 N_1=7 ε_2=20,25,30 N_2=5)

(a-4) The result of time and spatial ε-filter with frame shift.
(ε_1 =10,15,20 N_1=7 ε_2=10,15,20 N_2=9)

(b-1) The original input image.

(b-2) Just decoded image.

(b-3) The result of time and spatial ε-filter without frame shift.
(ε_1 =20,25,30 N_1=7 ε_2=20,25,30 N_2=5)

(b-4) The result of time and spatial ε-filter with frame shift.
(ε_1 =10,15,20 N_1=7 ε_2=10,15,20 N_2=9)

Fig.3 Results of processing actual video data. (a-4)and (b-4) are the results of the proposed method.

On Reliability of Multi-hop Paths Formed by Mobile Nodes

Keisuke NAKANO[†], Masakazu SENGOKU[†] and Shoji SHINODA[‡]

†Dept. of Information Engineering, Niigata University

2-8050, Ikarashi, Niigata 950-2181, Japan.

‡Dept. of Electrical, Electronic and Communication Engineering

Chuo University, Tokyo 112-8551, Japan.

(Email: {nakano, sengoku}@ie.niigata-u.ac.jp, shinoda@elect.chuo-u.ac.jp)

ABSTRACT

In this paper, we analyze reliability of a street mobile multi-hop network which connects two fixed nodes considering effects of change of topology with time. As a measure of reliability, we use the mean waiting time from the moment when a source node fails to transmit data to a destination due to absence of the multi-hop path to the moment when a multi-hop path appears between them. We theoretically compute the mean waiting time in a case where the fixed nodes can be connected by a two hop path and in another case where they need at least a three hop path to be connected, and show that there is a big difference in the mean waiting time between these two cases.

KEYWORDS: Multi-hop network, Connectivity, Reconnection, Mobility

INTRODUCTION

In a mobile multi-hop network, a source node is connected to a destination node through a multi-hop path consisting of mobile nodes [1]. Mobility of nodes changes topology of the network with time, and it sometimes splits a multi-hop path connecting a source S and a destination D although S and D may be connected again. In some cases, such a dynamic behavior causes a problem that S and D have no multi-hop path during a long time period. To well understand this problem, we analyze how long S and D have to wait for appearance of a multi-hop path. Define that T_{wait} is the length of an interval from the time when S fails to send data to D in the absence of multi-hop path to the time when a multi-hop path appears between S and D. While there may be several mea-sures for connectivity which reflect effects of mobility [2], the waiting time defined above has not been analyzed in detail.

In this paper, we theoretically compute $E(T_{wait})$, where $E(\cdot)$ is the mean of $\cdot$, in a street multi-hop network under the following assumptions: S and D exist on a street in Fig. 1, where x is the distance between S and D. Mobile relay nodes move along a street towards S or D at a constant velocity v. Mobile nodes moving toward S and D are represented by black nodes and white nodes, respectively, as depicted in Fig. 1. At the initial moment, black nodes and white nodes are distributed according to Poisson Processes with intensity $\frac{\lambda}{2}$, respectively. We suppose a situation where S and D are difficult to be connected due to a low density of nodes because the wait-ing time is reasonably short in the case of high connectivity. Two nodes can be directly linked if distance between them is not longer than r, which is a positive constant. We pay attention to the following two cases: In Case 1, $x \leq 2r$ and a two hop path can connect S and D. In Case 2, $x = 2r + \Delta x$ and S and D need at least three hops to be connected. We theoretically compute $E(T_{wait})$ in Case 1 and Case 2, and show that there is a big difference in $E(T_{wait})$ between the two cases.

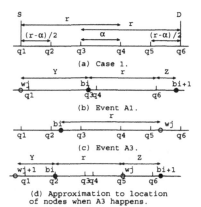

(a) Case 1.

(b) Event A1.

(c) Event A3.

(d) Approximation to location of nodes when A3 happens.

Fig. 2: Case 1.

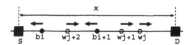

Fig. 1: Fixed nodes S and D, and mobile nodes.

CASE 1

To compute $E(T_{wait})$, we consider T_{off}, which is the length of a time interval during which there is no multi-hop path between S and D at all, which was firstly defined in [3]. The time interval is called an OFF period in this paper. Assume that the length of an OFF period is independent from those of other OFF periods. Then, we can compute $E(T_{wait})$ as $\frac{E(T_{off}^2)}{2E(T_{off})}$ [4]. To compute $E(T_{off})$ and $E(T_{off}^2)$, we consider the following three events: Suppose that an OFF period begins. Define that A_1 is an event that the OFF period begins due to absence of a direct link to D, A_2 is an event that it begins due to absence to a direct link to S, and A_3 is an event that it begins due to absence of a link between mobile nodes between S and D. A_1 and A_3 are depicted in Fig. 2, where q_1 and q_6 are the coordinates of S and D, respectively, $q_3 = q_6 - r$, $q_4 = q_1 + r$, $\alpha = q_4 - q_3$, $q_2 = q_1 + \frac{r-\alpha}{2}$ and $q_5 = q_6 - \frac{r-\alpha}{2}$.

At first, suppose that a black node b_i is at q_3 and there is no node between q_3 and q_6 as shown in Fig. 2 (b). Then, A_1 happens only after this situation, and the OFF period ends when w_j arrives at q_3, b_{i+1} arrives at q_4 or distance between w_j

and b_{i+1} becomes equal to r. From the assumptions, Y and Z are exponential random variables with mean of $\frac{2}{\lambda}$. Then,

$$
\begin{aligned}
E(T_{off}|A_1) &= E(T_{off}|A_2) = \frac{1}{2v}E(Y|Y \leq Z) \\
&+ \frac{1}{2v}E\left\{ Z + \min\left(\frac{Y-Z}{2}, r-\alpha\right) | Y > Z \right\} \\
&= \frac{1}{v}\left\{ \frac{1}{\lambda} + \frac{1}{2\lambda}(1 - e^{-\lambda(r-\alpha)}) \right\}. \quad (1)
\end{aligned}
$$

$$
\begin{aligned}
E(T_{off}^2|A_1) &= E(T_{off}^2|A_2) \\
&= \frac{1}{2v^2}E(Y^2|Y \leq Z) + \frac{1}{2v^2}E(Z^2|Z \leq Y) \\
&+ \frac{1}{2v^2}E\left(\min\left(\frac{Y-Z}{2}, r-\alpha\right)^2 \right) \\
&+ \frac{1}{v^2}E(Z|Z \leq Y)E\left(\min\left(\frac{Y-Z}{2}, r-\alpha\right) \right) \\
&= \frac{2}{\lambda^2 v^2} + \frac{2(1 - e^{-\lambda(r-\alpha)})}{\lambda^2 v^2} - \frac{(r-\alpha)e^{-\lambda(r-\alpha)}}{\lambda v^2} \\
&\quad (2)
\end{aligned}
$$

Next, suppose that the distance between b_i and w_j is equal to r, and there is no node between them as depicted in Fig. 2 (c). A_3 happens only after such a situation. Assume that b_i is at q_2 and w_j is at q_5 as represented in Fig. 2 (d) for simplicity. The OFF period ends when w_{j+1} arrives at q_3, b_{i+1} arrives at q_4 or distance between w_{j+1} and b_{i+1} becomes equal to r. Then,

$E(T_{off}|A_3)$

$$= \frac{1}{v}E\left\{Z + \min\left(\frac{r-\alpha}{2}, \frac{Y-Z}{2}\right)\Big| Z \le Y\right\}$$

$$= \frac{1}{v}\left\{\frac{1}{\lambda} + \frac{1}{\lambda}(1 - e^{-\frac{\lambda(r-\alpha)}{2}})\right\}. \tag{3}$$

$$E(T_{off}^2|A_3) = \frac{1}{v^2}E(Z^2|Z \le Y) + \frac{2}{v^2}E(Z|Z \le Y)$$

$$\times \quad E\left(\min\left(\frac{r-\alpha}{2}, \frac{Y-Z}{2}\right)\Big| Z \le Y\right)$$

$$+ \frac{1}{v^2}E\left(\min\left(\frac{r-\alpha}{2}, \frac{Y-Z}{2}\right)^2 \Big| Z \le Y\right)$$

$$= \frac{2}{\lambda^2 v^2} + \frac{4(1 - e^{-\frac{\lambda(r-\alpha)}{2}})}{\lambda^2 v^2} - \frac{(r-\alpha)e^{-\frac{\lambda(r-\alpha)}{2}}}{\lambda v^2} \tag{4}$$

Also, $E(T_{off}) = \sum_{i=1}^{3} E(T_{off}|A_i)P(A_i)$, and $E(T_{off}^2) = \sum_{i=1}^{3} E(T_{off}^2|A_i)P(A_i)$, where $P(A_1) = P(A_2) = \frac{1}{2+\lambda(r-\alpha)}$ and $P(A_3) = \frac{\lambda(r-\alpha)}{2+\lambda(r-\alpha)}$. Then, $E(T_{wait})$ is computed as $\frac{E(T_{off}^2)}{2E(T_{off})}$.

CASE 2

In Case 2, $x = 2r + \Delta x$ and S and D need at least three hops to be connected. Assume that $\Delta x \approx 0$ but a two hop path cannot connect S and D for simplifying analysis. We call links in a three hop path Link 1, Link 2 and Link 3, respectively, as represented in Figure 3 (a), where $q_1 = 0$ and $q_6 = 2r + \Delta x$, which are the coordinates of S and D, respectively, $q_2 = \frac{r+\Delta x}{2}$, $q_3 = r$, $q_4 = r + \Delta x$, and $q_5 = q_6 - \frac{r+\Delta x}{2}$. When an OFF period begins in Case 2, let A_i be an event that the OFF period begins due to absence of Link i, where $i = 1, 2$ and 3.

Suppose that b_i is at q_4 and there is no node between q_4 and q_6. There must be at least a node between $q_1 + \Delta x$ and q_3 so that S and D are connected. Right after this situation, S and D become disconnected and A_1 happens. Suppose that there is at least a node between $q_1 + \Delta x$ and q_3. Let B_1 be an event that one of these nodes between $q_1 + \Delta x$ and q_3 is white like Figure 3 (b). Let B_2 be an event that all of these nodes are black like Figure 3 (c).

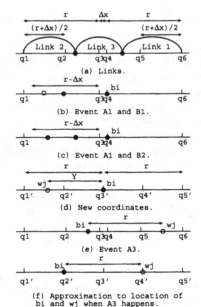

(a) Links.

(b) Event A1 and B1.

(c) Event A1 and B2.

(d) New coordinates.

(e) Event A3.

(f) Approximation to location of b_i and w_j when A3 happens.

Fig. 3: Case 2.

Let us consider $E(T_{off}|A_1, B_1)$. We use new coordinates $q_1', ..., q_5'$ as represented in Fig. 3 (d) based on the assumption that $\Delta x \approx 0$. In this figure, q_3 and q_4 are replaced by the same point q_3', and q_1, q_2, q_5 and q_6 are rewritten as q_1', q_2', q_4' and q_5', respectively. Then, b_i is at q_3'. Let w_j be the white node which is nearest to q_3' in the white nodes on the left of q_3'. Let Y be the distance between q_3' and w_j. When w_j arrives at q_3', the distance between b_i and w_j is not longer than r, and b_i is between q_1' and q_3'. Hence, the OFF period ends when w_j arrives at q_3'. We neglect an event that the distance between w_j and b_{i+1} becomes equal to r before w_j reaches q_3' because we consider a low density of nodes. Then,

$$E(T_{off}|A_1, B_1) = \frac{E(Y|Y \le r)}{v}$$

$$= \frac{1}{v}\left\{\frac{2}{\lambda} - \frac{re^{-\frac{\lambda r}{2}}}{1 - e^{-\frac{\lambda r}{2}}}\right\}. \tag{5}$$

$$E(T_{off}^2|A_1,B_1) = \frac{8}{\lambda^2} - \frac{4r}{\lambda(e^{\frac{\lambda r}{2}} - 1)} - \frac{r^2}{e^{\frac{\lambda r}{2}} - 1}.$$ (6)

Next, let us consider $E(T_{off}|A_1,B_2)$. As shown in Fig. 4 (a), b_i is again supposed to be at q_3' just before A_1 and B_2 happen, and the white node nearest to q_1' is denoted by w_j. Then, b_{i+1}, b_{i+2}, ... are on the right of q_5', and w_j, w_{j+1}, ... are on the left of q_1'. We plot the distance from q_5' to b_{i+m} at this moment on a line for $m \geq 1$, where q_5' corresponds to the origin. We also plot the distance from q_1' to w_{j+n} at the same moment on the same line for $n \geq 0$, where q_1' corresponds to the origin. The result is in Fig. 4 (b). Denote the nodes on the line in Fig. 4 (b) by bw_0, bw_1, ... Let Z_0 and Z_k be the distance from the origin to bw_0 and that between bw_{k-1} and bw_k, respectively.

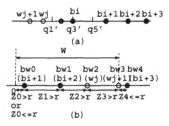

(a)

(b)

Fig. 4: A situation where A_1 and B_2 happen.

Suppose that $Z_{k+1} \leq r$. If both of bw_k and bw_{k+1} are black nodes or white nodes, S and D becomes connected when bw_k arrives at q_3' because a connected three hop path is constructed by bw_k and bw_{k+1}. Even if bw_k and bw_{k+1} are different in colors, these nodes can connect S and D because distance between bw_k and bw_{k+1} becomes equal to r before bw_k leaves q_3'. If $Z_{k+1} > r$, distance between bw_k and bw_{k+1} is always longer than r while one of the nodes is between q_1' and q_3' and another is between q_3' and q_5', and, as a result, these nodes cannot connect S and D. Define that $W = \sum_{k=0}^{K} Z_k$ given that $Z_1 > r$, $Z_2 > r$, ..., $Z_K > r$, $Z_{K+1} \leq r$ as depicted in Fig.

4 (b). Then, $T_{off} = \frac{W+r}{v}$ if both of bw_K and bw_{K+1} are with the same color, and $T_{off} = \frac{W + \frac{r+Z_{K+1}}{2}}{v}$ otherwise. Hence,

$$E(T_{off}|A_1,B_2) = \frac{1}{2v}E(W+r)$$
$$+ \frac{1}{2v}E\left(W + \frac{r+Z_{K+1}}{2}|Z_{K+1} \leq r\right)$$
$$= \frac{5}{4\lambda v} + \frac{3r}{4v} + \frac{3r}{4v(e^{\lambda r}-1)} + \frac{1}{\lambda v(e^{\lambda r}-1)}$$ (7)

because $E(Z_{K+1}|Z_{K+1} \leq r) = \frac{1}{\lambda} - \frac{r}{e^{\lambda r}-1}$, and

$E(W)$
$$= \frac{1}{\lambda} + \sum_{K=1}^{\infty} K\left(r + \frac{1}{\lambda}\right)e^{-K\lambda r}(1 - e^{-\lambda r})$$
$$= \frac{1}{\lambda} + \frac{\left(r + \frac{1}{\lambda}\right)e^{-\lambda r}}{1 - e^{-\lambda r}}.$$ (8)

Also,

$$E(T_{off}^2|A_1,B_2) = \frac{1}{2v^2}E\{(W+r)^2\}$$
$$+ \frac{1}{2v^2}E\{(W + \frac{r+Z_{K+1}}{2})^2|Z_{K+1} \leq r\}$$
$$= \frac{E\{W^2\}}{v^2} + \frac{3rE\{W\}}{2v^2} + \frac{5r^2}{8v^2}$$
$$+ \frac{E\{W\}E\{Z_{K+1}|Z_{K+1} \leq r\}}{2v^2}$$
$$+ \frac{rE\{Z_{K+1}|Z_{K+1} \leq r\}}{4v^2}$$
$$+ \frac{E\{Z_{K+1}^2|Z_{K+1} \leq r\}}{8v^2},$$ (9)

$$E(W^2) = \frac{2}{\lambda^2} + \frac{\left(r + \frac{2}{\lambda}\right)^2}{e^{\lambda r} - 1} + \frac{2\left(r + \frac{1}{\lambda}\right)^2}{(e^{\lambda r} - 1)^2},$$ (10)

$$E(Z_{K+1}^2|Z_{K+1} \leq r) = \frac{2}{\lambda^2} - \frac{2r}{\lambda(e^{\lambda r} - 1)} - \frac{r^2}{e^{\lambda r} - 1}.$$ (11)

$$P(B_1) = \frac{1 - e^{-\frac{\lambda r}{2}}}{1 - e^{-\lambda r}}, P(B_2) = \frac{e^{-\frac{\lambda r}{2}}\left(1 - e^{-\frac{\lambda r}{2}}\right)}{1 - e^{-\lambda r}}$$ (12)

Then, with the above equations, we can compute $E(T_{off}|A_1)$ and $E(T_{off}^2|A_1)$.

We assume that b_i and w_j are at q_2' and q_4', respectively, just before A_3 happens as depicted in Fig. 3 (f) for simplifying analysis. Then, with a small modification that bw_0, bw_1, ... are plotted based on the distances from q_2' and q_4', we can also compute $E(T_{off}|A_3)$ and $E(T_{off}^2|A_3)$ in the same manner as $E(T_{off}|A_1,B_2)$ and $E(T_{off}^2|A_1,B_2)$.

$$E(T_{off}|A_3) = \frac{1}{2v}E\left(W + \frac{r}{2}\right)$$
$$+ \frac{1}{2v}E\left(W + \frac{Z_{K+1}}{2}|Z_{K+1} \leq r\right). \quad (13)$$

$$E(T_{off}^2|A_3) = \frac{1}{2v^2}E\{(W + \frac{r}{2})^2\}$$
$$+ \frac{1}{2v^2}E\{(W + \frac{Z_{K+1}}{2})^2|Z_{K+1} \leq r\}, \quad (14)$$

where $E(W)$, $E(W^2)$, $E(Z_{K+1}|Z_{K+1} \leq r)$ and $E(Z_{K+1}^2|Z_{K+1} \leq r)$ are the same as the above equations. We compute $P(A_1) = P(A_2)$ as $\frac{1-e^{-\lambda r}}{2(1-e^{-\lambda r})+\lambda r}$ and $P(A_3)$ as $\frac{\lambda r}{2(1-e^{-\lambda r})+\lambda r}$. Then, we can compute $E(T_{off})$, $E(T_{off}^2)$, and $E(T_{wait})$.

NUMERICAL RESULTS

The numerical results of the above equations are shown in Fig. 5 with computer simulation results, where $r = 10$ m and $v = 1$ m/seconds. In the computer simulations, the system is observed at intervals of $\Delta t = 0.05$. This figure shows that the numerical results agree well with the computer simulation results although our analyses include some approximations.

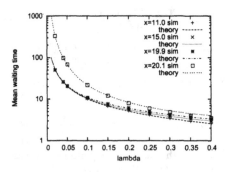

Fig. 5: Numerical results.

From Figure 5, we can observe what happens at the boundary of Case 1 and Case 2. Even though the difference in x between Case 1 ($x = 19.9$ m) and Case 2 ($x = 20.1$ m) is small, $E(T_{wait})$ rapidly increases at the boundary between these cases. As can be seen from the analysis

of $E(T_{wait})$, in Case 1, S and D can be connected every time a mobile node enters the region between q_3 and q_4 in Fig. 2 and $E(T_{wait})$ does not depend on $E(W)$ as opposed to Case 2, where $E(T_{wait})$ depends on $E(W)$ and successive overlaps of gaps make $E(W)$ large for a small λ. Such properties cause the above difference.

CONCLUSIONS

In this paper, we have considered connectivity between two fixed nodes in a street mobile multi-hop network. We have theoretically computed $E(T_{wait})$ in Case 1 and Case 2, and have shown that $E(T_{wait})$ for Case 1 is quite different from that in Case 2 even though there is a small difference in x. Although we have analyzed $E(T_{wait})$ just for $x \leq 2r + \Delta x$, as reported in [5], $E(T_{wait})$ for $x > 2r + \Delta x$ is close to each other if it is represented as a function of the probability that S and D are instantaneously disconnected, which can be computed by the theory of random clumping [6]. Then, from the equations to compute $E(T_{wait})$ for $x = 2r + \Delta x$ and the probability that S and D are instantaneously connected, it is possible to estimate $E(T_{wait})$ even for $x > 2r + \Delta x$.

REFERENCE

[1] C.E. Perkins, Ad Hoc Networking, Addison-Wesley, 2001.

[2] P. Santi, "Topology control in wireless ad hoc and sensor networks," ACM Computing Surveys, June 2005.

[3] K. Nakano et al., "On connectivity and mobility in mobile multi-hop wireless networks," Proc. IEEE VTC2003-Spring, Apr. 2003.

[4] L. Kleinrock, Queueing Systems Volume 1: Theory, John Wiley & Sons, 1975.

[5] K. Nakano et al., "On waiting time for path reconstruction in mobile multi-hop networks," Proc. NOLTA2006, Sept. 2006.

[6] P. Hall, Introduction to the Theory of Coverage Processes, John Wiley & Sons, 1988.

On an Assignment Problem for Wireless LAN and the Voronoi Diagram

Hiroshi Tamura[†], Masakazu Sengoku[††] and Shoji Shinoda[‡]

†Niigata Institute of Technology
1719, Fujihashi, Kashiwazaki, Niigata 945-1195,Japan
Email: tamura@iee.niit.ac.jp
††Faculty of Engineering, Niigata University
8050, Ikarashi-2nocho, Niigata 950-2181, Japan
‡Faculty of Science and Engineering, Chuo University,
1-13-27, Kasuga, Bunkyo-ku, Tokyo 112-8551, Japan

ABSTRACT

In wireless LAN, like IEEE802.11x, the number of accessible terminal is limited for each access point. Therefore, it is necessary to assign each terminal to the access points under the limitation. It is well-known that this problem can be solved in polynomial time by solving a maximum flow problem in graph theory.

However, there is a weak point in the above solution. If a terminal newly tries to access an access point, many terminals may change the access points. Therefore, this solution is not realistic. It is important to minimize the number of terminals that change the access points. In this paper, we propose a polynomial algorithm to solve the problem.

KEY WORDS: Wireless LAN, Assignment algorithm, Multihop network, Graph theory, Voronoi diagram

1. Introduction

In wireless LAN, like IEEE802.11x, the number of accessible terminal is limited for each access point(AP). Therefore, it is necessary to assign each terminal to the access points under the limitation. For example, in Fig.1(a), the circle that includes an access point b is called the area of b. The area of b means that all terminals in the circle can communicate to b. Let the number of accessible terminals for each access point be three. In this case, we assign each terminal to the access points like Fig.1(b). In a simple case, we can apply the theory of flow networks in graphs to this problem. This problem can be solved in polynomial time by solving a maximum flow problem in graph theory[1]. First, we construct a flow network N as follows. The vertex set of N is $\{b1,...,bh, v1,...,vk, s, t\}$ where bi represents an access point, vi represents a terminal, s is a source and t is a sink. A vertex pair (x,y) is an edge in N if and only if

i) x=s and y=bi or
ii) x=vi and y=t or
iii) x=bi, y=vj and vj is in the area of bi.

In case of i), the edge weight is the number of accessible terminals for bi, and in all other cases, an edge weight is one. Here, we calculate the maximum flow from s to t. In case of Fig.1(a), the flow network N is Fig.2(a). In Fig.2(a), we omit edge weights in case of 1. The maximum flow from s to t is Fig.2(b). Each bold edge means that the flow value of the edge is the maximum. We assign each terminal vj to the end access point bi of the bold edge being incident to vj (see Fig.1(b)).

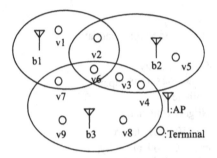

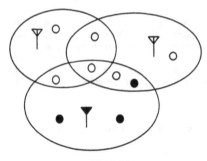

Fig.1(a)

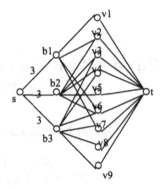

Fig2(a)

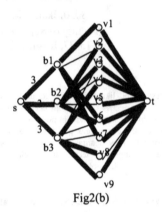

Fig2(b)

Fig.1(b)

However, there is a weak point in this solution. If a terminal newly tries to access an access point, many terminals may change the access points. Therefore, this solution is not realistic. It is important to minimize the number of terminals that change the access points. In this paper, we propose a polynomial algorithm to solve the problem. We apply "Optimal Cardinality -Constrained Territory Map [2]" to this problem. The territory map is known as the Voronoi diagram[3] that is special kind of decomposition of an area in computational geometry. And in this case, the number of elements in each territory is limited.

2. Formulation with graphs

We formulate this problem using graph theoretical terms as follows. We apply the formulation in Optimal Cardinality-Constrained Territory Map to this problem.

Let G be a directed graph. Each vertex v represents an access point. A directed edge (u,v) means that there is a terminal x in areas of u and v, and x communicates to the access point u at this time.

Next, we set vertex weights of G. The weight of vertex v represents the number of terminals that communicate to v, and f(v) represents the maximum number of terminals that can communicate to v.

446

For example, in case of Fig.3 and f(v)=5 for each access point v, the directed graph is in Fig.4.

In this formulation, we obtain the following theorem.

[Theorem]
We assume that a terminal x newly tries to communicate to an access point A and x is in the area of A. The terminal x can communicate to A if and only if in the constructed directed graph G, there is a directed path from A to B, where the vertex weight of B is less than f(B).

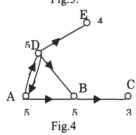

Fig.3.

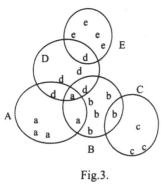

Fig.4

In Fig.4, a terminal x in area of A is newly tries to communicate to A, there is a directed path from A to C, where the vertex weight of C is less than 5. Therefore, x can communicate to A in Fig.5 after changing access points of terminals.

Therefore, we have to find paths from a vertex v to vertices u, where the vertex weight of u is less than f(u). If the distance from v to u0 is the minimum, the distance means the minimum number of terminals that change the access points. Namely, we can obtain a solution by solving a single-source shortest-paths problem [4] in polynomial time.

Since the distance from A to C is 2 in Fig.4, the number of terminals that change the access points is 2 in Fig.5, where the underlined terminals changed the access points.

3. Formulation with hyper graphs

The formulation with graphs does not express all information in a wireless LAN about this assignment problem.

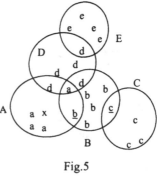

Fig.5

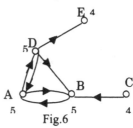

Fig.6

The directed graph corresponded to Fig.5 is Fig.6. Compared with Fig.4, the direction of edge (B,C) is converse, and there is a new edge between A and B in Fig.6.

In the above case, the position of a2 turned into B from A in Fig.7. If the position of a1 instead of a2, turned into B from A, the directed graph is in Fig.8.

447

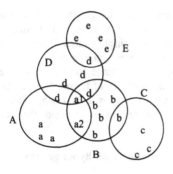

Fig.7

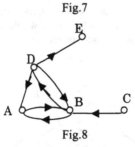

Fig.8

Fig.8 is different from Fig.6. Namely, this formulation does not express all information of this situation. Therefore, we have to change the access point of terminals using Fig.3 and Fig.4.

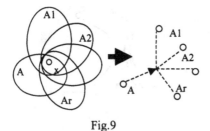

Fig.9

Here, we propose another formulation. We construct a directed hyper graph instead of a graph. If a terminal x is in areas of A, A1, A2,...,Ar and x communicates to A, we set a directed hyper edge from A to A1,...,Ar (see Fig.9). For example, In case of Fig.3, the hyper graph is Fig.10. Dotted lines represent a hyper edge.

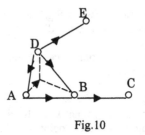

Fig.10

The hyper graph corresponded to Fig.6 is Fig.11.

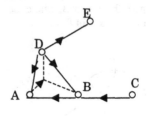

Fig.11

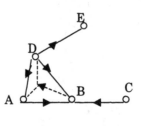

Fig.12

The hyper graph corresponded to Fig.8 is Fig.12.

In this formulation, if a new terminal x is in areas A, A1, A2,..., Ar and x tries to communicate to A, we add a directed hyper edge from A1 to A2,...,Ar, to the hyper graph H, like Fig.9. If x is only in the area of A, we do not add an edge. Then we find a directed path from A to B in H, where the vertex weight is less than f(B), we reverse directions of all edges on the directed path and increase one of the vertex weights of A and B. Update of the hyper graph H is completed at this time. In this formulation,

448

necessary operation is only on the hyper graph H. Namely, this formulation represents all information of a wireless LAN about this assignment problem.

4. Multihop wireless LAN

In this section, we consider multihop wireless LAN. In this case, each terminal relays data and sends it to an access point. So, we can share wireless access resources effectively. We show an example.

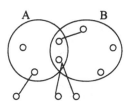

Fig.13

In Fig.13, each edge means the end terminals of the edge can relay data. In case of f(A)=f(B)=5, we can assign terminals to Access Point A and B like Fig.14.

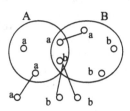

Fig.14

We can solve this problem with mathematical programming. However, this is not an efficient solution because the number of expressions is enormous by simple modeling. It is a future problem to solve this problem with network programming or some effective algorithm.

5. Conclusion

In this paper, we formulate an assignment problem of wireless LANs using hyper graphs. This formulation represents all information of a wireless LAN about this assignment problem.

We will find assignment algorithms solving the problem and evaluate the algorithms with computer simulations. On practical use side, each terminal chooses access point distributedly. It is a future problem to take in these practical studies[5] for this modeling.

References

[1] M.Sengoku, H.Tamura and S.Shinoda, " Roles of Computational Geometry and Graph Theory in Cellular Mobile Communications," Proc. 1996 IEEE/IEICE International Workshop on Multi-Dimensional Mobile Communications (MDMC'96), pp.372-375, July 1996.
[2] T. Morizumi, S. Tsukiyama, S. Shinoda, M. Sengoku and I. Shirakawa: "An Optimal Cardinality-Constrained Territory Map on a Network," Proc. IEEE International Symposium on Circuits and Systems (ISCAS'88), vol. 2 of 3, pp. 1541-1544, June 1988.
[3] F.P. Preparata and M.I. Shamos: Computational Geometry: An Introduction, Springer-Verlag, New York, NY, 1985.
[4] T.H.Cormen, C.E.Leiserson and R.L.Rivest: Introduction to Algorithms, MIT Press and McGraw-Hill, 1990.
[5] Y. Fukuda, A.Fujiwara, M.Tsuru and Y.Oie: " Analysis of access point selection strategy in wireless LAN," Proc. IEEE VTC2005-fall, CD-ROM(6-E-5), Sept, 2005.

449

Low Overhead Deterministic Cluster Heads Selection in Wireless Sensor Networks

Mohammad Rajiullah[*], Shigeru Shimamoto[**]
Graduate School of Global Information and Telecommunication Studies
Waseda University
1011 Okuboyama, Nishi-Tomida, Honjo-shi, Saitama 367-0035, Japan
*rajiullah_shammi@suou.waseda.jp, **shima@waseda.jp

ABSTRACT

Wireless sensor networks are expected to be one of the main building blocks for the future ubiquitous world. These sheer numbers of sensor network present a unique challenge to design data communication protocol for the unattended autonomous wireless sensor networks. In this paper, we propose a new communication protocol for the periodic data collection in wireless sensor network. This is a cluster based protocol where cluster heads collect data from the other cluster members and send the fused data to the base station. This protocol uses the scheduled rotation of cluster heads to evenly distribute the energy consumption load among all the sensors in the network field with the minimum association of the base station at the beginning of the protocol. This protocol outperforms existing protocol in terms of network lifetime and simplicity of the protocol.

KEY WORDS: Cluster head, sensor network, energy, life time.

INTRODUCTION

Wireless sensor networks consist of large number of tiny sensing devices where each device has the recent advancement of micro-electromechanical system (MEMS) technology, including sensors, actuators and RF communication components. Sensor networks are used in large scale environmental monitoring, battle field surveillance, location tracking, industrial plant monitoring, medical monitoring and security management [1, 2]. The goal is to enable the scattering of thousands of these nodes in areas that are difficult to access by using conventional method [1].

Sensor nodes are typically battery-powered and replacing and recharging batteries are often not possible. So reducing energy consumption is an important design consideration for sensor networks. Also data aggregation can eliminate data redundancy, reduce communication overload and thus save energy [3]. Sensor network protocol may vary according to the specific nature of the application [5]. A common sensor networking application is gathering sensed data at a distant base station (BS) [4]. Here we consider periodical data collection problem from a sensor field to a remote BS in energy efficient manner. In our proposed protocol the fixed BS is located far from the sensor field. All sensor nodes are homogeneous, energy constrained and started with uniform energy. The nodes are equipped with the power control abilities to vary their transmitter power and each sensor also possesses the ability to transmit to any other node or directly to BS. And all the sensors are immobile.

Here in this paper, we propose an improved energy efficient cluster oriented communication protocol for wireless sensor network. This proposed protocol uses non randomness in the cluster head selection and unlike LEACH [4], it never faces the situation of no cluster head or one cluster head in the whole sensor field [7]. And unlike LEACH the cluster head rotation is based on their remaining energy level which decreases the unnecessary cluster head rotation at every round, simplifies the protocol implementation and decreases the overhead as well.

RELATED WORK

As we are networking with a lot of low power nodes together, conventional technique like direct transmission must be avoided. On the other hand multi hop transmission like Minimum Transmission Energy (MTE) routing causes equally undesirable effect. In this case, nodes closest to the BS will incur more energy loss as these nodes are engaged for the routing of large data message to the BS [4].

Different communication protocol has been proposed to solve such kind of problem. Clustering the whole network is an effective solution in this respect. A cluster based network can be partitioned in to disjoint clusters. Then in each cluster, one particular node is assigned as the local head and other member nodes of the cluster work as the followers of that cluster head thus implementing a virtual backbone of the network. Then the cluster head collects all the sensed data from the follower and sends the same to the BS.

Heinzelman et al. proposed the cluster based LEACH (Low-Energy Adaptive Clustering Hierarchy) [4] protocol is an elegant solution to this data collection

problem. It utilizes randomized rotation of cluster heads to form self organized clusters. The operation of LEACH is divided in to rounds. In each round a new set of cluster heads (CH) are chosen randomly to evenly distribute the energy consumption of the CHs. LEACH achieves a factor of eight improvement compared to direct approach, before the first node dies. Each round consists of set up phase followed by steady state phase. During the set up phase nodes decided on their own to be a CH or not by evaluating a certain probability without negotiating with other nodes. After the selection procedure of CHs, clusters are organized. During the steady state phase all cluster member nodes (CM) sense data and transmit to the CHs according to the predefined TDMA schedule by the CHs. Here all the CM nodes turn off their radio unless they are transmitting data. CH head node aggregates the received data and sends the fused data to the remote BS. Among the class of distributed, dynamic and randomized protocol, LEACH has the highest dominance due to its effectiveness in providing load balancing, scalability and energy efficient solution. However it has some limitation. Authors at [7] showed that due to the random CH selecting strategy, the number of CHs resulted by LEACH and other protocol in its class is not guaranteed to be equal to the expected optimal value. They used a bi dimensional Markov chain model and showed that the number of CHs produced by LEACH is a random variable and for this the number of CH does not concentrate in a small range around the target value. They also showed that in the worst case when no CH is selected, the clustering structure will be broken down and when one CH serves the whole network; its energy would drain rapidly. The authors at [6] showed that the probability of the worst case is high when the desired value of CHs is small.

Therefore, the variability in the number of CHs adversely affects the energy efficiency, fairness among nodes and the system life time. Also it uses cluster formation in every round which increases the overhead of the protocol. Lastly in the CH selection procedure any node select itself as the CH does not ensure that its residual energy sustain for the whole round.

LOW OVERHEAD DETERMINISTIC CLUSTER HEADS SELECTION PROTOCOL

In the proposed protocol, we consider the same MAC protocol used in LEACH [4]. We assumed that the BS knows all the location of all the nodes in the network. Then the BS selects four nodes from the four corners in the quadrangular sensor field as CH. Then the newly assigned CHs broadcast a cluster head advertise message to all the sensor nodes. Depending on the received signal strength, sensor nodes decide to which CH they want to belong. And for more than one CH at the same distance, one CH is randomly chosen. All nodes inform their decision back to the CH. Then the clusters are formed. These are the primary clusters of the protocol. CH nodes then create a schedule containing both the primary CH id and the serial information in which order they will elect themselves as CH in the network lifetime. Then the CH nodes broadcast this message to all the CM nodes.

After the primary cluster setup phase the proposed protocol is divided into rounds. And the protocol starts with the same CH node and the respected clusters selected in the primary cluster set up phase. In the proposed protocol all the CH always remember the amount of energy (*used_Energy*) it used in the last round. So, at the beginning of each round the CH

nodes compare its residual energy (*res_Energy*) with the *used_Energy*. And the round can be started if all the CH nodes have sufficient energy. So, clusters are not formed in every round. Now the problem is to find the difference of *res_Energy* and the *used_Energy* in the last round, up to which any CH node can continue with the same clusters.

$$res\_Energy \rangle diff \times used\_Energy \qquad (1)$$

So, if the *diff* value is large then the number of cluster formation will be increased in the network life time and the minimum *diff* value will cause the quick die of the CH nodes for longer continuation as high energy dissipating nodes. We conclude that the value of *diff* must be set as it lengthens the time at which the first node dies yet minimize the number of cluster formation process.

So, when the CH ensures that it has sufficient energy to continue the present round in Eq. (1), it uses the same cluster for present round. On the other hand if the CH does not find sufficient energy for serving the present round, it broadcasts a *cluster_head_release* message with its cluster head number and primary CH id. This is received by all the nodes. In this stage of the protocol, all the CH in the sensor field again performs cluster formation process even if any of them has sufficient energy for the present round. So, the next scheduled node checks the CH number in the received message and match with the primary CH id it belonged to. Now if all the information are matched it declares itself as the CH for the next round broadcasting an advertise message to all the nodes. In the same way as used in primary cluster formation phase new clusters are formed. As the schedule for becoming CH continues in a round fashion until all of its sensor node dies, any node can get its turn multiple times in its life time and from the next schedule it is allowed to act as CH only if it has more res_Energy than the used_Energy at the beginning of new round. Again if it does not have much energy or if the node is dead then after certain timeout period, the next schedule node examines its energy for becoming CH and so on.

So after the cluster formation process sensor nodes start data collection. So, when the new clusters are formed the CH makes one schedule for the data transmission with the number of nodes that would like to be included in the cluster. Like LEACH this is a TDMA schedule describes when any of the CM can transmit data to the CH. This schedule is broadcasted to all the CM nodes. So, when all the CM nodes get their TDMA schedule, they start data transmission. And they follow the same schedule in every round until new clusters are formed. Also like LEACH all the CM nodes keep their radio off while they are not transmitting data. It minimizes energy dissipation. When all the data has been received, CH sends the composite data to the BS. After a certain time, the next round begins with each CH node determining whether it should continue the next round or not as described previously.

PERFORMANCE EVALUATION AND DISCUSSION

We mainly compared our proposed protocol with LEACH. We used the same radio model introduced in [4]. In LEACH it is assumed that the radio dissipates, $E_{amp}=100pJ/bit/m^2$ through the medium which is consumed in the transmitter amplifier for a descent Signal to Noise ratio (SNR). Also in addition radio requires $E_{elec}=50nJ/bit$ to run the transmitter or receiver circuitry and the radio is symmetric. Like LEACH in our

experiment we also assume that all sensors are sensing the environment at a fixed rate and thus always have data to send to the base station. Moreover the energy cost for data fusion is considered as $5nJ/bit/message$. In our simulation, we considered 100 sensor nodes randomly deployed in a place of 100 meter X 100 meter. The base station is located in (50 meter, 200 meter). All the sensors started initially with the 0.5J of energy. We kept our network life time is for 2000 rounds. Every CM node sends 2000 bits of message to the CH and CH also sends 2000 bits of aggregated data to the remote BS. We ran the experiment with diff value 10 and 80.

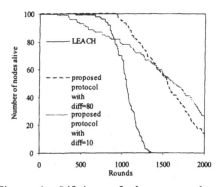

Figure 1: Lifetime of the proposed protocol

Figure 1 shows that our proposed protocol gives longer network lifetime then LEACH. Small diff value (e.g. diff =10), we get fewer cluster formation but the continuation of the same CH for long time causes its quick die. And we can lengthen the die of the first sensor node with large diff value (e.g. diff =80). We ran similar experiments with different initial energy given to the sensor nodes and in every case the proposed protocol outperforms LEACH. Every time we varied the diff value for the best performance according to the different initial energy given to the sensor nodes. The data from the experiment are shown in the table 1.

Table 1: Lifetime using different amounts of initial energy to the sensor nodes.

Energy (J/node)	Protocol	Round 1st node dies	Round 60% nodes die
0.25	Proposed protocol with $diff$=40	460	832
	LEACH	318	543
0.50	Proposed protocol with $diff$=80	927	1656
	LEACH	418	1083
0.75	Proposed protocol with $diff$=120	1382	*
	LEACH	782	1663

* more than 70% nodes are alive in 2000 rounds.

In the proposed protocol during some round, all the scheduled CHs may not be enough separated due to their position in the primary cluster but it is ensured that all the CHs will never be in one end of the field which is common in LEACH and causes intra cluster long distance transmission. Also assuming that the base station is aware of all the location information about the sensor nodes can be difficult to realize in the large dense sensor field. But this difficulty can be eliminated by using node identity, node degree property (the number of its neighbors within a pre-specified transmission range) etc for any node to contend for being CH for the primary cluster formation. The ultimate improvement of the proposed protocol from LEACH is that, it reduces energy consumption by nonrandom CH selection process and eliminating cluster formation process at every round.

CONCLUSION

In this paper, we propose an improved solution for data collection in energy constrained wireless sensor network. This protocol uses prescheduled cluster head selection in the network life time with the minimum association of the base station at the beginning of the protocol. Our future work will focus on the more energy aware cluster head scheduling process and the determination of the optimum number of primary cluster in any size of wireless sensor network.

REFERENCES

1. Estrin, D.Girod, L.Pottie, G.Srivastava, M. " Instrumenting the world with wireless sensor networks," Proc. of the International Conference on Acoustics, Speech and Signal Processing (ICASSP 2001), Salt lake, Utah, May 2001.
2. R. Szewczyk, J. Polastre, A. Mainwaring, and D. Culler, "Lessons from a sensor network expedition," Proc. of the 1st European workshop on Wireless Sensor Networks (EWSN'04), Berlin, Jan 2004, pp. 1-16.
3. B. Krishnamachari et al., "The impact of data aggregation in wireless sensor networks," Proc. of the 22nd International Conference on Distributed Computing Systems Workshops (ICDCSW'02).
4. Wendi Rabinder Heinzelman, Anantha Chandrakasan and Haribalakrishnan, "Energy efficient communication protocol for wireless microsensor networks," Proc. of the Hawaii International Conference on System Science, Maui, Hawaii, January 2000.
5. Jamal N. Al-karaki and Ahmed E. Kamal, "Routing Techniques in Wireless Sensor Networks: A Survey," IEEE Wireless Communications, vol. 11, no. 6, Dec 2004.
6. Ying Wang and Mudi Xiong, " Monte Carlo Simulation of LEACH Protocol for Wireless Sensor Networks" Proc. of the 6th International Conference on Parallel and Distributed Computing, Applications and Technologies, PDCAT 2005.
7. Q. Wang, G. Takahara, and H. Hassanein, "Stochastic Modeling of Distributed, Dynamic, randomized Clustering Protocols in Wireless Sensor Networks," Proc. of the 2004 International Conference on Parallel Processing Workshops (ICPPW'04).

Author Index